Ages in Chaos

Volume IV:
The Dark Age of Greece

Immanuel Velikovsky

Edited by Lewis M. Greenberg

With Contributions by Edwin M. Schorr, Jan Sammer and Lewis M. Greenberg

Special Acknowledgement to Julian West

Recommended order of reading of the series *Ages in Chaos:*

- *From the Exodus to King Akhnaton* (Vol. I)
- *The Assyrian Conquest* (not yet published)
- *Ramses II and His Time* (Vol. II)
- *The Dark Age of Greece* (Vol. IV)
- *Peoples of the Sea* (Vol. III)

Annotations by Jan Sammer are marked by * at the beginning of the sentence or paragraph.

Notes by the publisher are marked by { }.

Copyright © 2023 by Rafael H Sharón

All rights reserved. No part of this book may be reproduced or transmitted in any form or by any means, electronic or mechanical, including photocopying, recording, or by any information storage and retrieval system, without permission in writing from the copyright owner, except by reviewers who may quote brief passages to be printed in a magazine or newspaper.

Published by   Paradigma Ltd.
                      Internet: www.paradigma-publishing.com
                      e-mail: info@paradigma-publishing.com

ISBN 978-1-906833-19-0 (Softcover edition)
       978-1-906833-59-6 (Hardcover edition)
       978-1-906833-79-4 (eBook)

Contents

Preamble (by Lewis M. Greenberg) 11
Chronologies in Doubt 12
A Handful of Torr's Critiques 14
Select Bibliography 18

A Technical Note (by Jan Sammer) 21

Preface (by David Flusser) 23

The Reconstruction of Ancient History (by I. Velikovsky) 25
Egyptian History 25
Astronomical Dating 26
Hebrew History 27
The Revised Chronology 28
The Greek Past 30

Chapter 1   The Homeric Question 35
The Setting of the Stage 35
Why no Literary Relics from Five Centuries? 39
Troy in the Dark Ages 41
The Dark Age in Asia Minor 42
The Homeric Question 43
The Allies of Priam 46
Aeneas 52
Olympic Games in the *Iliad* 53

Chapter 2 Mute Witnesses 55

Troy and Gordion 55
The Lion Gate of Mycenae 57
Olympia 61
"The Scandal of Enkomi" 66
Tiryns 75
Mute Witnesses 79
A Votive Cretan Cave 80
Etruria 83
Sicily 84
Mycenae and Scythia 86

Chapter 3 Words Set in Clay 89

Pylos 89
Linear B Deciphered 90
The Greek Pantheon 94
Mycenaean City Names in the *Iliad* 96
The Mycenaean Dialect 98
Cadmus 99

Chapter 4 A Gap Closed 103

Seismology and Chronology 103
Celestial Events in the *Iliad* 105
Changes in Land and Sea 109
A Gap Closed 112
Competing for a Greater Antiquity 118
Summing Up 121

Further Relevant References and Expositions 127
(by Lewis M. Greenberg)

Supplement I Applying the Revised Chronology 165
(by Edwin M. Schorr)

Foreword 167

Chapter 1 Mycenae 169

The Entrance to the Citadel 169
The Grave Circles 173
Shaft Grave Art: Modern Problems 178
Later Use of the Grave Circles 191
The Warrior Vase 196
A Chariot Vase 201
Other LH III Figural Pottery 203
Bronze Tripods 212
A Terracotta Figurine and a Terracotta Head 218
The Religious Center of Mycenae 224
Dark Age Burials 229
The Northeast Extension 234
Ivory Carvings 237
Mycenaean Jewelry 240
The Palace 246
The Design of the Palace 253

Chapter 2 Further Evidence 263

Tiryns 263
Troy 272
Pylos 279
Ugarit 282
Alalakh 285
Résumé 287

Supplement II New Light on the Dark Age of Greece . 289
(by Jan Sammer)

The Tombs at the Argive Heraion 291
The Identification of Troy 296
The Archaeology of Hissarlik 299
Blegen at Pylos 304
The Trojans and their Allies 310
The Western Colonies 317
The Date of Carthage's Founding 322
Tarshish 324
The Dark Age Spanned 329

Supplement III Additional Light on the Dark Age of Greece (by Lewis M. Greenberg) 335

The Lion Gate at Mycenae Redux 337

Introduction 337
Of Potsherds and Pharaohs 338
The Tomb of Ahiram 342
Will the Real Shishak Please Stand Up? 345
Chronological and Historical Considerations 349
Aesthetic Considerations 353
Additional Considerations and Questions 361
Conclusion 364

Ramesses II and Greek Archaic Sculpture 367

Introduction 367
Egypt and Greece 367
Conclusion 374

You Can't Have Amnesia if There's Nothing to Forget .. 377

	7
Memories of Yesteryear	381
Lefkandi	383
Thera	387
Hercules	397
Carthage, Rome, Dido, And Aeneas	399
The Ara Pacis Augustae: New Perspectives	409
Epilogue (by Lewis M. Greenberg)	445
Index	467
Bibliography	479
Illustration Credits	511
Around the Subject	515

For

Immanuel Velikovsky
Scholar, Mentor, Friend

and for

Rafael H. Sharón
Who commissioned and supported the publication of this book

Preamble

This book, *The Dark Age of Greece*, and its contents have had a lengthy gestation period. It was first conceived in 1940 and developed in the early 1940s as part of the *Ages in Chaos* series. In 1945 its author Immanuel Velikovsky published a pamphlet in a concise format stipulating his various chronological revisions of ancient history that were to come in future book form. It was presented as 284 theses under the title **THESES FOR THE RECONSTRUCTION OF ANCIENT HISTORY**. Those dealing with the Dark Age numbered 103-112. The most relevant was number 107: "No 'Dark Age' of six centuries [later changed to five] duration intervened in Greece between the Mycenaean Age and the Ionian Age of the seventh century."

Velikovsky continued to work on the manuscript for the Dark Age throughout the following decades both alone and with the aid of research assistants right up to the time of his death in 1979. In 1981 the present editor was invited by Velikovsky's widow, Elisheva, to come to Princeton, read the manuscript, and give an opinion regarding its publication possibility. I happily accepted the invitation, went to Princeton, and spent two days reading the manuscript very carefully. I gave the green light for it to be immediately published with only minimal changes. Unfortunately, other manuscripts took priority. *Mankind in Amnesia* (1982) and *Stargazers and Gravediggers* (1983) were published next. But then sadly Elisheva passed away during the Summer of 1983 and my publication recommendation was cast into limbo.

Forty more years have now come and gone; however, under the auspices of Dr. Rafael Sharon, Velikovsky's grandson, who approved and supported the publication of this book, its appearance has finally come to fruition and takes its rightful place among others in this series. The original text appears intact as it existed back in 1981, but key updating has been made via the addition of more recent appropriate referential material as well as substantive supportive appendices.

Before proceeding further to the full text, it is essential that the scholarly opinion of a number of scholars – Historians, Egyptologists, Classicists – be quoted here pertaining to the credibility and reliability of Egyptian and early Greek chronology as well as how the former affected the latter. The *raison d'être* for this book will then become obvious.

Since the Greeks had no reliable internal chronology of their own prior to the later 8th century BC (some would drop the date down to 664 BC), it was the Egyptian chronology – considered the absolute chronological standard by the late nineteenth century AD – that dominated and controlled centuries' worth of the historical and cultural dating for the entire eastern Mediterranean world. Classicists and Orientalists alike both yielded to Egypt even though it contradicted their own observations, conclusions, and expertise.

Chronologies in Doubt

Our journey begins in the late nineteenth century AD. It was then that the first absolute dates were being applied to early Greek (Aegean) art and culture resulting in the assumption that one was now dealing with the Mycenaean Age of the early and mid second millennium BC. This was based upon the fact that the material remains of Greece at this time acquired their dates from Egyptian Dynastic links and a date for the Trojan War (a "red herring") which were assumed to be fundamentally sound. What has not been sufficiently scrutinized is the fact that the chronological linkage was done at a time (the 1880s) when Egyptology itself was in its infancy; its own absolute dates were fluid and being seriously questioned, challenged, and debated.

An English Egyptologist, W. M. Flinders Petrie, was among the first if not *the* first to establish the methodological dating system that still primarily prevails to the present day – a stratigraphical approach. Buried objects when uncovered could be dated by both the layered depths of burial and the supposedly "known" dates of other objects buried with them.

Nevertheless, this dating method did not go unchallenged. As far back as 1890, Cecil Torr, a British antiquarian and author took on Petrie in a series of published acrimonious debates (reprinted in 1988 as an addition to Torr's own book *Memphis and Mycenae*).

Torr disputed Petrie's approach to stratigraphical dating and objected to the fact that Egypt was the singular control and major determinant for early Greek archaeological material. It should be noted here that Petrie initially dated the beginning of Egypt's First Dynasty 2000 years earlier than the currently accepted one. This is not intended as a criticism of Petrie whose seminal work was outstanding at times, but merely meant to highlight the difficulty in establishing just one problematic absolute date during the days of early Egyptology – a date that is still unsettled as of this writing. Torr's position and attitude were certainly valid for its day; and even with the addition of new scientific ways to date or relate archaeological material – C14, astronomical observations, calendrical records, thermoluminescence, and dendrochronology – problems still remain up to present times as we shall see *infra*.

In 1896 when Torr published his own chronology for Ancient Egypt and its relationship to early Greece in *Memphis and Mycenae* it was critically reviewed by John L. Myres, a British archaeologist and academic. Following that review Torr engaged in a published heated exchange with Myres over a two year period (1896-1897). Viewed as an interloper, Torr proved to be a knowledgeable and formidable opponent who gave as good as he got. As the story goes, Torr wore his opponents down by raising numerous argumentative cogent points. Despite spending more than half a decade defending his position Torr and his chronology were rejected, yet his insights remain worthwhile.

Consider this concluding observation made by Torr at the end of his main text:

> "... Greek coins and gems of about 700 to 600 resemble the Mycenaean gems so closely that any judge of art would be prepared to place the Mycenaean age immediately before 700."

The totality of the wide ranging contents of this current book by Velikovsky who seemingly did not know of Torr should *en passant* partly vindicate Torr in addition to shedding eye opening light on the Greek Dark Age. At the same time, a partial listing of Torr's erudite critique of the foundation of Egyptian and early Greek chronology (see *infra*) lends additional credence and support for Velikovsky's far more comprehensive and, one is almost tempted to say, holistic approach to the subject at hand. Torr's pioneering efforts are laudatory, but are confined primarily to a period in Egypt that embraces Dynasties XII through XXVI, the Egyptian calendar, and Egypt's connection with Greece. Velikovsky, on the other hand, dealt with *multiple centuries and civilizations* as he attempted to *reconstruct* more than 1500 years of ancient history. He also had the task of evicting as well as rebuilding.

A Handful of Torr's Critiques

1) Torr examined and questioned the reliability of particular stratigraphical evidence for dating purposes.
2) He exposed the inherent weakness in the codified acceptance of Manetho's dynastic structuring of Egyptian chronology.
3) He referred to the problem of volcanic pumiceous tufa deposits specifically citing the eruption and potential effect of Thera on stratigraphy and chronology.
4) He noted a basic flaw in Sothic dating that cannot be completely dismissed even today. As an aside, Torr never mentioned Venus.

The similarity between what Torr found fault with and the comments made by respected late 20th century and early 21st century scholars and authorities presented below should prove to be quite jolting.

*****

"... without a secure chronology for Egypt, the history of the early Aegean, the Levant, even of the Mesopotamian cultures, begins to fall apart.

"The accepted chronology of Egypt is derived from an amalgam of otherwise quite disparate sources."

M. Rice: *Egypt's Making* (1991)

"What is proudly advertised as Egyptian history is merely a collection of rags and tatters." One example indicative of the problem: "To abandon 1786 B.C. as the year when Dynasty XII ended would be to cast adrift from our only firm anchor, a course that would have serious consequences for the history, not of Egypt alone, but of the entire Middle East."

A. Gardiner: *Egypt of the Pharaohs* (1964)

"[Regarding Greek history,] before the eighth century ... no traditional date deserves credence in itself, and belief even in traditional events is largely a matter of faith."

C. G. Starr: *The Origins of Greek Civilization* (1961)

"Although the relative chronology of Egypt's history is secure [sic], the absolute dates are not and remain a subject of much research and debate." [Manetho's king lists have several major flaws and the different excerpts of his work make it impossible to build a secure timeline.]

"Chronological information from the other king lists is too fragmentary to provide reliable figures. So the absolute chronology needs to be reconstructed with other sources."

"There are thus multiple [dating] systems in use in various publications appearing today; each one has its defenders but none is absolutely certain." One such method, recorded astronomical observations, which a number of scholars used to take "as firm anchors for dating periods [are now] more skeptical of their value."

M. Van De Mieroop: *A History of Ancient Egypt* (2nd ed., 2021)

"The system of dynasties devised [by Manetho] in the third century BC is not without its problems – for example, the Seventh Dynasty is now recognized as being wholly spurious, while several dynasties are known to have ruled concurrently in different parts of Egypt ...

"Hence, our modern understanding of Egyptian history regards Manetho's Twenty-second, Twenty-third, and Twenty-fourth dynasties as at least partially overlapping ... while the Ninth and Tenth dynasties seem to represent only one ruling family, not two."

T. Wilkinson: *The Rise and Fall of Ancient Egypt* (2010)

In the PREFACE to *The Oxford Encyclopedia of Ancient Egypt* (2001), Editor In Chief Donald B. Redford had this to say:

"In selecting an absolute chronology, the editors entered a world of uncertainty and acrimonious debate. At one time, the prospect appeared bright that a critical evaluation of king lists and offering lists, coupled with the results of accelerated radiocarbon testing, would solve the problem once and for all; such hopes are now apparently illusory. The late John Wilson, introducing a lecture on the Amarna Age, once declared: 'I have before me all the current chronologies suggested for this period, and I don't believe any of them.'

"While the same could be said today with equal skepticism, it would ill serve the pedagogic and synthetic overview purposes of the present work to allow each contributor to decide on his or her own schema. An editorial decision has therefore been made to select one of the current chronological schemes circulating in the scholarly world, modifying it appropriately where new evidence has become available ..."

In a recent multi-authored book – *A Companion to Greek Art* (2018) – Nicki Waugh of Edinburgh University contributed a section on Greek chronology in one of the opening chapters. Covering nearly seven full pages, it was clear, detailed, and touched all the appropriate bases.

For all that, consider what Waugh had to say on key specific points: "Modern attempts to provide a chronology of ancient material culture have utilized scientific methods to provide absolute dates ..., but these have *serious limitations for classical archaeology*."

Regarding C14 in particular: "While the use of accelerator mass spectrometry (AMS) has decreased the amount of sample required, calibration with dendrochronology has highlighted that levels of carbon-14 in the atmosphere are not always constant, which affects the accuracy of any calculations. This difficulty is particularly true for samples *before 1000 BC*. Even with calibration of the timescale, the curve of decay can be so limited that it is not possible to distinguish between 400 calendar years, as is the case for the period from 800 to 400 BC..." [And perhaps even 1200 to 800 BC.]

Additional comments by Waugh on stratigraphy are also enlightening. Interpretation of strata "may be complicated by disturbance of the strata." This could be due to intrusions by animals, humans, and natural forces; i.e., floods, earthquakes, or volcanism. Finally, the date that an item was deposited in a strata *does not guarantee a correct date for the object itself*. [*Cf.* to similar comments made by Torr back in the 1890s.]

Related to what was just presented is a remark made by C. D. Fortenberry on Helladic chronology in *The Dictionary of Art*, Vol 14 (1998):

> "Although the chronological periods of the [Helladic] system are divided into discrete units, there was some overlap from one phase to the next: the inhabitants of one site might *retain older pottery types for many years while another site changed to new styles*. This 'regionalism' was particularly common during the Neolithic and EH periods, and at the end of the LH period [the end of the Mycenaean Age]." [Again *cf.* to similar comments made by Torr. NB: Emphasis was added to all of the above.]

In the first volume of the newly published *Oxford History of the Ancient Near East* (2021; four more projected to follow), the editors made the following request to all contributors:

"[Since] The absolute and relative chronology of the third millennium BC is still not securely anchored ... [and] Because the chronology is so uncertain, we have asked our authors to use a *bare minimum of absolute dates*. When such information is mentioned [it] should certainly not be understood as the passionate endorsement of a specific chronology ..."

A discussion of the absolute chronology and its reconstruction for the first half of the second millennium BC was then promised for Volume 2. [Emphasis above added.]

When discussing foundation dates for some Western Phoenician colony-cities, B.H. Warmington in his book *Carthage: A History* (1969) said the following:

Various authors dated these colonies to a time period immediately after the Trojan War in the early 12th century BC. These dates "look legendary. One of the difficulties is that even for their own history the Greeks had no very certain chronological knowledge for the period before the middle of the eighth century, and had to reckon by inexact methods such as generations to calculate early dates." When it came to non-Greek peoples, the Greeks had "little grasp ... of early Oriental history ... consequently, caution has to be used in dealing with dates for non-Greek history which the Greeks fitted into their own chronological system, with the added possibility of error in their use of foreign traditions."

There are those authors who, while recognizing the manifold problems currently existing in the complex restructuring of Egyptian chronology, appear nonetheless to be content to follow the conventional pathway. Despite the "existential" threat to the entire chronological edifice there is no dramatic change to the way the history, art history, or cultural history of Egypt is presented. Here are two references whose perusal should make the point:

1) *The Oxford History of Ancient Egypt* (2002), edited by Ian Shaw with fifteen chapters and multiple authorship. Shaw was responsible for two of the chapters, the first – Introduction: Chronologies and Cultural Change in Egypt – contained an excellent summary overview of Egyptian chronology and the structural weaknesses it still faces. Yet when it came to dealing with the suggestion by a "small number of scholars that the period of 400 years occupied by the Third Intermediate Period (and numerous other, roughly contemporaneous,

'dark ages' elsewhere in the Near East and the Mediterranean) may have been artificially inflated by the historians," Shaw descended into hyperbolic vagary in dismissing that suggestion. He claimed that it had been refuted by Egyptologists, Assyriologists, and Aegeanists (all anonymous), and then ultimately fell back on the very scientific methods whose weaknesses he had just exposed to once again support the strength of the conventional chronology.

Regarding the comments made by Shaw in the paragraph above, let me help him with an educated guess. I believe that he was referring to the book titled *Centuries of Darkness* (1991) written by fellow British scholar Peter James along with four of his fellow British colleagues. The book also contains an excellent foreword by Colin Renfrew. Though I have my own criticisms of that book, Shaw's generic and anemic response to what was proposed in *Centuries* was most disappointing and it deserved a far more detailed discussion.

2) One final book with a purely conventional approach also needs to be mentioned here – *An Introduction to the Archaeology of ANCIENT EGYPT* (2008) by Kathryn A. Bard. Laden with information and illustrations in a large format and small font with 400 pages, it is a fine and comprehensive introduction to the subject. Alas, Bard gives us only four text pages for a rather tepid discussion of Egyptian chronology of which two only deal with an historical outline of pharaonic Egypt. One sentence near the end of her chronological presentation does bear notice: "Analyses of the king lists along with dated monuments and documents have helped Egyptologists devise chronologies in years BC, but no exact dates before the 26th Dynasty are agreed on by all scholars, hence the variations in published chronologies of pharaonic Egypt."

Select Bibliography

I. Velikovsky: »Astronomy and Chronology«, *Pensée* IV (Spring-Summer, 1973)

I. Velikovsky: »Astronomy and Chronology«, *Peoples of the Sea* (NY, 1977)

L. E. Rose: *Sun, Moon, and Sothis* (Deerfield Beach, 1999)

R. D. Long: »A Re-examination of the Sothic Chronology of Egypt«, *Kronos* II:4 (Summer-1977); reprinted with permission from *Orientalia*, Vol. 43 (Nova Series – 1974)

L. M. Greenberg: »Astronomy and Chronology: An Assessment«, *Kronos* II:4, *op.cit.*

»On Sothic Dating: A Special Supplement«, *Kronos* VI:1 (Fall-1980), Greenberg, Parker, Rose, Mage, Sammer, Velikovsky, Dayton, Gammon and James

P. James, et al.: *Centuries of Darkness* (London, 1991)

D. Courville: *The Exodus Problem and its Ramifications*, V.2 (Loma Linda, 1971), *inter alia*

Civilizations of the Ancient Near East, Volumes One & Two, Editor in Chief J. M. Sasson (NY, 1995); F. H. Cryer: »Chronology: Issues and Problems«, pp. 651-664

The Oxford Handbook of the Bronze Age Aegean, ed. by E. H. Cline (Oxford, 2010), S. W. Manning: »Chronology and Terminology«, pp. 11-28

The Oxford History of the Ancient Near East, V. II, ed. by K. Radner et al. (F. Hoflmayer: »Establishing a Chronology of the Middle Bronze Age«) (NY, 2022), pp. 1-46

The Oxford History of the Ancient Near East, V. III, ed. by K. Radner et al. (NY, 2022), »Chronology«, pp. 16-18

M. Duncker: *History of Greece ...* (V.1, London, 1883-86), pp. 122-141. Despite its age an excellent examination of how the Greeks derived their chronology.

Lewis M. Greenberg, Professor Emeritus – Ancient & Oriental Art History and Culture (MCAD)

A Technical Note

I have been asked ... to briefly explain the present condition of Velikovsky's unpublished manuscript entitled *The Dark Age of Greece*. Velikovsky worked on the manuscript of *The Dark Age of Greece* fairly intensively during the last years of his life, drawing in part on the library research of Edwin Schorr, a graduate student at the University of Cincinnati, whom he employed for this pupose in Princeton for several summers in a row in the mid-seventies. Readers of *Pensée* know Schorr under his nom de plume Israel M. Isaacson, which he used to protect himself from the wrath of his professors at Cincinnati. At the time that I began to work for Velikovsky in 1976, the manuscript was still "work in progress." While Velikovsky was writing and rewriting the main text, my task was to annotate the material, drawing in part on the voluminous notes and photocopies of articles prepared by Schorr and partly on my own research. In addition, Velikovsky and I co-authored certain sections; others, written solely by me, were to have been included in a supplement to the book. Subsequent to 1980, pursuant to Elisheva Velikovsky's wishes, I moved some of these contributions from the main text into footnotes and removed the rest from the manuscript altogether. Several of them were published in *Kronos* VIII.2 in 1983. Another planned supplement to *The Dark Age of Greece* was to have been Edwin Schorr's work on Mycenae »Applying the Revised Chronology«. This detailed study on the archeology of Mycenae was commissioned by Velikovsky and written specifically for this purpose. Although incomplete, it is an impressive work of scholarship that deserves publication.

Jan Sammer

Preface

The task of my few words is to ask prominent scholars to reconsider their opinions about the dark age of Greece in the light of Velikovsky's present book. My personal difficulty is mainly caused by the fact that a short preface cannot be a scholarly treatise and therefore it is impossible to ask here all the questions which arise when Velikovsky's theory is applied to our special problem. And as I am not an archaeologist, but a Greek scholar, I am not able to control how far Velikovsky is right in questions of stratigraphy. Here I depend on his quotations of archaeological reports and it is not possible for me to decide how far his selection of passages from these reports is subjective. My difficulty is that now I have to accept the view that the period of Geometric style overlaps, at least partially, the Mycenaean and Minoan period. This is new for me, but I admit that it is not impossible that two different artistic approaches can exist at the same time.

But the most important problem in connection with the present book is how far this theory is dictated by the whole of Velikovsky's chronological system and how far his results in the present study are valid independently from it. Velikovsky puts the "true time of the events recounted in the *Iliad* in the second half of the eighth century and the beginning of the seventh. ... The time in which the drama of the *Iliad* was set was -687; yet the poet condensed the events of more than one year into the tenth year of the Trojan siege, the time of the *Iliad*'s action." Velikovsky came to this date because he identified the description of the battle between the gods in the *Iliad* with a cosmic catastrophe. His date for the conquest of Troy is unusually late. As Homer had to live after the events he describes, the space of the time between Homer and the classical Greek literature seems to me personally to be too short. But the main question is about the interrelation between Velikovsky's chronological system and the single historical facts. Or in other words: Does this system solve the concrete difficulties in our approach to ancient history? The present book tries to solve such a serious problem, namely, does the so-called dark age of Greece really exist? Is the supposed span between Mycenae and classical Greece too long? Are we not in this case victim of a false

Egyptian chronology, which was invented by Egyptian patriots in order to show that the Greeks were in comparison with the Egyptians mere children? Was the history of Egypt in reality much shorter than it is supposed today? If this could be shown, then the problem of the dark age of Greece would disappear. Only open-minded specialists can reject or accept Velikovsky's solutions. One thing is clear: The new book treats a real problem. It was not its author who created it. The whole complex of questions was re-opened by the decipherment of the Linear B script, when it was definitely shown that the Mycenaeans were Greeks, speaking a language which was an older stage of the linguistic substrate of the *Iliad* and *Odyssey*. It is a merit of the new book that it offers an original solution for a real problem. Will there be a sufficient number of good specialists who are prepared to wrestle with the proposed solution?

Prof. David Flusser
Hebrew University

The Reconstruction of Ancient History

The history of the ancient East is an interwoven nexus, embracing Egypt, Israel, Syria and Mesopotamia, known also as the Biblical lands. The interconnections extend to Asia Minor, to Mycenaean Greece, and to the Mediterranean islands – Cyprus, Crete, and the Aegean archipelago. The histories of many of these nations are, for most of their existence, devoid of absolute dates and depend on interrelations with other nations.

The chronologies of the Mycenaean civilization in Greece and of the Minoan civilization on Crete are built upon contacts with Egypt, for Egypt's chronology is considered reliable. In turn, the widespread Mycenaean and Minoan contacts and influences found in the archaeological sites of many countries are distributed on the scale of time by detailed study of Mycenaean and Minoan pottery and its development. This pottery is found in countries as far apart as Italy and the Danubian region.

Egyptian History

Although Egypt's chronology is used to determine the dates of other cultures, Egypt had no written account of its history, and the earliest surviving effort to put its past into a narrative is from the pen of Herodotus of the mid-fifth century before the present era, regarded by modern historians as largely unreliable.[1]

Though various king-lists from earlier times have been preserved, it is the list of Manetho, an Egyptian priest of Hellenistic times (third pre-Christian century), that served the historiographers as the basis for making a narrative out of the Egyptian past. The names read on monuments were equated, often by trial and error, with Manethonian dynasties and kings. The mathematics of history, it was agreed, could not be entrusted to Manetho, and is largely borrowed from the sixteenth-century European chronographers, notably Joseph Scaliger,

---

[1] *Cf. Ion Ghica: *Istoriile lui Erodot*, vol. II (Bucuresti, 1912).

and his sixteenth- and seventeenth-century emulators Seth Calvisius and others,[1] who dated in the same tables also various mythological motifs, such as the scandals among the Olympian gods or Heracles' heroic exploits.

With the reading of the Egyptian hieroglyphs achieved in the nineteenth century, some selected dates of Scaliger were used by Lepsius (1810 – 84) to date the monuments and thus the reigns of the kings of Egypt whose names were on the monuments. Lepsius was, for instance, of the view that Ramses II was the pharaoh of the Exodus – and thus Biblical history, too, was drawn into a comprehensive scheme on which other histories could find their first foothold. Such was also the case with "Hittite" history because of a peace treaty of Ramses II with one of the Hittite kings (Hattusilis). Manethonian mathematics, or the number of years allotted to dynasties and kings, was soon disregarded.

Astronomical Dating[2]

Even before Young and Champollion first read the hieroglyphic texts in the 1820s, Biot and others decided that astronomical calendric calculations could be used to ascertain the dates of the Egyptian dynasties. It was known that the Egyptian civil year consisted of 365 days, approximately a quarter of a day short of the true sidereal year. Thus the calendric dates of the Egyptians would gradually have fallen out of their proper place in relation to the seasons, and made a complete circle in $365 \times 4 = 1460$ years.

With the decipherment of the multitudinous Egyptian texts, a few references to a star *spdt* were found, and were interpreted as recording the heliacal[3] rising of the southern fixed star Sirius – and if from monuments it could also be learned in which months and on what day the star rose heliacally, events could be dated within the 1460-year-long "Sothic cycle". This made it possible to build a chronology of Egypt around the few dates so fixed – and much work was spent in such an effort. With this as a basis, refinement could be achieved in various

---

[1] They wrote long before the Egyptian hieroglyphics were deciphered.
[2] See my essay, »Astronomy and Chronology«,"Supplement to *Peoples of the Sea*, (New York, London, 1977); first published in Pensée IVR IV (1973).
[3] By heliacal rising is meant the first appearance of a star after invisibility due to conjunction with the sun.

ways, most notably by trying to ascertain the length of the years of a king, usually relying on the highest year of his reign found recorded on monuments. Each king counted the years from his coronation – Egypt had no continuous timetable. However, in Egyptian texts no reference to calculating by Sothic observations was ever found.

Archaeological work in Egypt showed that besides the so-called pre-dynastic times, from which the data are incomplete, the historical past was twice interrupted for centuries when the land fell into neglect. The First Intermediate Period intervened between the epochs that received the names of the Old and Middle Kingdoms; the Second Intermediate Period between the Middle and New Kingdoms; the New Kingdom consists of the Manethonian dynasties Eighteen, Nineteen and Twenty – what follows is called the Late Kingdom.

Hebrew History

Hebrew history has a narrative that consists of the book of Genesis – the history of the world in which catastrophic events (the Deluge, the overturning of the Tower of Babel, the destruction of Sodom and Gomorrah) come to the fore, the latest of these coinciding with the beginning of the age of the Patriarchs which ends with the migration of the fourth generation to Egypt because of drought in Canaan. This part of the history is considered largely legendary. Following a sojourn in Egypt, the Exodus – the subject of the other four books of the Pentateuch – inaugurates the historical period. The historical events until the Exile to Babylon are further narrated in the books of Joshua, Judges, Kings, Chronicles, and Prophets and the post-Babylonian period in the books Nehemiah, Ezra, and of the later prophets. Many non-Scriptural books with varying degrees of historical veracity add and take over where the Old Testament ceases its narrative.

It was agreed since the days of Josephus Flavius, the Jewish historian of the days of Emperor Vespasian, that the Exodus of the Israelites from Egypt took place after the Second Intermediate period, during the Egyptian New Kingdom, whether at its very beginning or several generations later. However, they disagree among themselves, some placing the Exodus under Thutmose III of the Eighteenth Dynasty, others under Amenhotep III or his heir Akhnaton of the same dynasty (the time of the el-Amarna correspondence), some placing it under Ramses II or Merneptah of the Nineteenth Dynasty ("Israel Stele"), and some as late as the Twentieth Dynasty (after Ramses III repelled the invasion of the Peoples of the Sea, supposedly in the first quarter of the twelfth century). So many various dates for the Exodus – a point that connects the Hebrew and the Egyptian histories – could be contemplated because these two histories as they are usually taught are remarkably out of contact for the entire length of the New Kingdom, and equally so for the rest of their histories, down to the time of Alexander of Macedon.

The Revised Chronology

My approach to the problem of the synchronization of ancient histories took the following form. Upon realizing that the Exodus was preceded and accompanied by natural disturbances described as plagues of darkness, of earthquake, of vermin, accompanied by hurricanes and followed by a disruption of the sea, by volcanic phenomena in the desert and then by the prolonged "Shadow of Death" of the years of wandering, I looked for similar descriptions in Egyptian literary relics and found them in a papyrus ascribed to a certain Ipuwer, an eyewitness and survivor of the events. Additional data I found in an inscription carved on a stone shrine found at el-Arish on the Egyptian-Palestinian frontier. Taking the latest possible date for the events described in the papyrus Ipuwer, namely, the collapse of the Middle Kingdom in Egypt on the eve of its being overrun by the Hyksos, the date was still centuries earlier than the earliest considered dates for the Exodus on the Egyptian time-scale.

If the parallels in texts elucidated by me are not a matter of coincidence, then the test would be in whether it would be possible, in leveling the two histories by synchronizing the end of the Middle Kingdom and the Exodus, to trace contemporaneity also in subsequent generations, not yet deciding whether the Egyptian history would need extirpation of "ghost centuries" or the Israelite history extension by the insertion of "lost centuries".

The next clue in my work of reconstruction was in equating the Asiatic Hyksos (called Amu by the Egyptians) that overran Egypt, prostrated as it was by the natural disaster described in the Ipuwer Papyrus, with the Amalekites that the Israelites met on their flight from Egypt. The autochthonous Arab sources, as preserved by medieval Moslem historians, refer to a several-centuries-prolonged occupation of Egypt by the Amalekites, evicted from the Hedjaz by plagues of earthquakes and vermin, while tidal waves swept other tribes from their lands.

I could establish that the period of the Judges, when the population was oppressed by the Amalekites and Midianites, was the time of the Second Intermediate Period in Egypt and that Saul, who captured the capital of the Amalekites (el-Arish being the ancient Hyksos capital Avaris) put an end to the Amalekite-Hyksos domination from Mesopotamia to Egypt. In Egypt the Eighteenth Dynasty came into existence, thus inaugurating the New Kingdom. Was it ca. -1030, the time the Biblical scholars would assign to Saul's capture of the Amalekite fortress, or ca. -1580, the time the Egyptologists would place the fall of Avaris?

King David fought the remnants of the Amalekites; his marshal Joab invaded Arabia, while Amenhotep I ruled in Egypt; Solomon accordingly had to be a contemporary of Thutmose I and of Hatshepsut; I could establish that this queen came to Jerusalem and had reliefs depicting her journey to the Divine Land carved on the walls of her temple at Deir el-Bahari. In Hebrew history and legend she lives as the Queen of Sheba who visited Solomon.

The next generation saw Thutmose III invade Judea, sack the palace and temple of Jerusalem, and impose a tribute on the now-divided country. The furnishings of the Temple, carried away by Thutmose, were depicted by him on a temple wall in Karnak. These depictions match the Biblical record of some of the Temple furnishings.

Amenhotep II was identified with the king whom an ancient epic poem portrayed as leading an enormous army against the city of Ugarit, only to be pursued to the Sinai Desert. He was further shown to be the alter ego of the Scriptural Zerah, whose enterprise started similarly and ended identically.

The last three chapters of the first volume of *Ages in Chaos* deal with the el-Amarna correspondence; if the reconstruction is correct then the time in Judah must be that of King Jehoshaphat and in Israel of King Ahab. It so happened that the books of Kings and Chronicles are especially rich in many details of the events that took place under these kings, and the numerous letters on the clay tablets of the el-Amarna archive present a perfect ground for comparison as to persons, places, names, and events. Scores of identifications and parallels are brought forth. Did Jehoshaphat and his generals and Ahab and his adversaries in Damascus exchange letters with Amenhotep III and his heir Akhnaton across the centuries?

At first we left the problem open, which of the two histories would require re-adjustment – is the Israelite history in need of finding lost centuries, or does the Egyptian history require excision of ghost centuries? Soon it became a matter of certainty that of the two timetables, the Egyptian and the Israelite, the former is out of step with historical reality by over five centuries.

A chronology with centuries that never occurred made necessary the introduction of "Dark Ages" between the Mycenaean and the Hellenic periods in Greece. Thus the shortening of Egyptian history by the elimination of phantom centuries must have as a consequence the shortening of Mycenaean-Greek history by the same length of time.

The Greek Past

The theme pursued in this volume is the basic design of Greek history – the passage of the Mycenaean civilization and the intervening Dark Age of five centuries duration before the Hellenic or historical age starts ca. 700 years before the present era. This structure of the Greek past is subjected to a reexamination as to the historicity of the Dark Age.

Greek antiquity is conventionally divided into three periods – Helladic, Hellenic, and Hellenistic. The Helladic period in its later subdivision comprises the Mycenaean civilization. It ends not long after the conquest of Troy, regularly put about -1200. Its last generation is dubbed "the Heroic Age". At this point five centuries of dark ages are inserted into Greek history. The Hellenic period embraces the Ionian and classical ages, and stretches from ca. -700 to the conquest of the East by Alexander of Macedon. With his march toward the Nile, the Euphrates, and the Indus (-331 to -327), the culture of Greece was spread through the Orient and was itself modified by oriental elements; this was the beginning of the Hellenistic Age. Mycenae can be regarded as the cultural center of the Late Helladic period; Athens of the Hellenic; and Alexandria of the Hellenistic. In this scheme, as just said, the five centuries of the Dark Age are inserted between the Helladic and the Hellenic or, in other nomenclature, following the Mycenaean and preceding the Ionian ages.

The Mycenaean Age in Greece and the contemporary and partly preceding Minoan Age on Crete have no chronologies of their own and depend on correlations with Egypt. Objects inscribed with the names of Amenhotep II, Amenhotep III and Queen Tiy of the Eighteenth Dynasty, found at Mycenae, were like a calendar leaf. Then excavations at el-Amarna in Egypt established the presence of Mycenaean ware in Akhnaton's short-lived city. Such quantities of Mycenaean ware came to light in the course of the excavations that a street in el-Amarna was dubbed "Greek Street". Since Akhnaton's capital existed for only about a decade and a half, a very precise dating for the Mycenaean ware could be evinced, thus providing a link between Mycenaean history and the established Egyptian chronology. It was therefore concluded that the Mycenaean civilization was at its apogee in the days of Amenhotep III and Akhnaton of the Eighteenth Egyptian Dynasty.

The first and most important consequence was a radical recasting of Greek history. Since Akhnaton's conventional date was the fourteenth and thirteenth centuries before the present era, Mycenaean ware was also ascribed to the same period. By the end of the twelfth century before the present era, the Mycenaean civilization would have run its course. The Greek or Hellenic time does not start until about -700. The years in between are without history on Greek soil. There existed tenacious memories of the time of the tyrants who ruled in the late eighth and seventh centuries, but beyond that, there was complete darkness.

Thus by the 1890s the Hellenists were coerced by the evidence presented by the Egyptologists to introduce five centuries of darkness between the end of the Mycenaean Age and the beginning of the Hellenic. As we shall read on a later page, there was some consternation on the part of classical scholars when first the fact dawned on them that between the Mycenaean age and the historical Greek time there was a span, more in the nature of a lacuna, of several centuries' duration. In the end they accepted the Egyptian plan as being valid for Greece – still without having investigated the evidence on which the claim of the Egyptologists was founded.[1]

In *Ages in Chaos* we have seen that, with the fall of the Middle Kingdom and the Exodus synchronized, events in the histories of the peoples of the ancient world coincide all along the centuries.

For a space of over one thousand years records of Egyptian history have been compared with the records of the Hebrews, Assyrians, Chaldeans, and finally with those of the Greeks, with a resulting correspondence which denotes synchronism.

In Volume I of *Ages in Chaos* it was shown in great detail why Akhnaton of the Eighteenth Dynasty must be placed in the latter part of the ninth century. If Akhnaton flourished in -840 and not in -1380, the ceramics from Mycenae found in the palace of Akhnaton are younger by five or six hundred years than they are presumed to be, and the Late Mycenaean period would accordingly move forward by about half a thousand years on the scale of time.

Yet independently of the results attained in *Ages in Chaos*, the problem of blank centuries, usually termed "dark ages", increasingly claims the attention of archaeologists and historians. Although the enigma of "dark centuries" reappears in many countries of the ancient East, in no place did it create such discomfort as in Hellenic history. There it is an inveterate problem that dominates the so-called Homeric question: The historical period in Greece, the Hellenic Age, is ushered in by the sudden and bright light of a literary creation – the Homeric epics, of perfect form, of exquisite rhythm, of a grandeur unsurpassed in world literature, a sudden sunrise with no predawn light in a previously profoundly dark world, with the sun starting its day at zenith – from almost five hundred years that divide the end of the Mycenaean Age from the Hellenic Age, not a single inscription or written word survived.

Against this set-up the Homeric Question grew to ever greater proportions. In the light of – or better to say – in the darkness of the Homeric problem, we will try to orient ourselves by scanning some early chapters of Greek archaeology, and having done this, we should

---
[1] See my »Astronomy and Chronology«, cited above.

return to the problem of the deciphered Linear B script. Two timetables are applied simultaneously to the past of Greece, one built on the evidence of Greece itself, the other on relations with Egypt; thus instead of any new discovery reducing the question to smaller confines, every subsequent discovery enlarged the confines and decreased the chances of finding a solution.

Chapter 1

The Homeric Question

The Setting of the Stage

A traveller afoot, steadily on the road, marching from Athens westward, crosses the Corinthian Isthmus and, by continuing to the south, may arrive at Mycenae before the sunset of the second day. He follows the rocky road uphill and reaches the fortification wall of the ancient citadel. Rampant stone lions in relief crown the gate of Mycenae. Inside the gate, immediately to the right, he is shown the shaft graves of the ancient kings. The place is deserted; no village occupies the site. Resting at the gate, the traveller has before him the Argive plain, the scene of some of the most celebrated events of the human past.

Before the historical age of Greece started, called also the Ionian or Hellenic Age, Greece had another civilization. It centered at Mycenae; it spread over Greece and over the Helladic islands; vestiges of it were found in many places of the ancient world. It was closely contemporaneous with the last phase of another civilization, the so-called Minoan, centered on the island of Crete to the south. These two great cultures left cities and palaces, ruined and deserted, and rich relics – pottery of exquisite forms, and gold and jewels – but no history known to modern man. Yet of Mycenae and of her heroes such a treasure of legend is preserved in Greek lore that some of the heroes of that kingdom in the Argive plain and their contemporaries are more familiar to us than leaders of other races and other times much more recent. Agamemnon, Menelaus, Nestor, Achilles, and Odysseus are better remembered and more widely known than most of the military leaders of the great wars of our own century. Heroes of other times and nations are too often not known at all.

> Their names were ... Ask oblivion!
> "They had no poet, and they died."[1]

---
[1] Don Marquis, quoting Pope.

This is said not just of heroes but of whole civilizations.

Agamemnon and Menelaus were sons of Atreus, king of Mycenae; and legends were told about Atreus and Thyestes, brothers who quarreled over the throne, and about the sign in favor of Atreus that was seen in the sun retracing its course. These legends lived in Greek lore. Another cycle of legends centered on Thebes in Boeotia, and on the Argonaut expedition to Colchis on the Caucasian coast of the Black Sea, which preceded the Trojan War by several decades.

The world of these legends, cruel and heroic and treacherous, occupied the fantasy of the Greeks; and Greek tragic poets of the fifth century, Aeschylus, Sophocles, and Euripides, had an inexhaustible store of themes to draw upon.

There is hardly any problem in the entire history of literature that occupies the minds of scholars as much as the origin of the Homeric epics – the *Iliad* and the *Odyssey* – especially the question as to the time of their origin.

The *Iliad* tells of the events of the final stage of the siege of Troy by the host of the Achaeans under Agamemnon, king of Mycenae. The *Odyssey* tells of the long wanderings of Odysseus, one of the heroes of that siege, on his circuitous way home.

Tradition has it that Homer was a blind bard who lived and wandered on the Aegean coast of Asia Minor. Among the cities and islands that claimed to have been his birthplace were Smyrna, Chios, Colophon, Salamis, Rhodes, Argos, and Athens. Beyond this the tradition is very meager as to the personality of the poet and the events of his life. Several apocryphal writings pretending to tell something of him were composed in Greece, but had nothing to commend them. When did he live and create? In his great epics he described the Mycenaean world which supposedly ended almost five centuries before him; he shows a very great knowledge of that time – yet he knew the world of the seventh century, too.

There are those who argue that the author of the *Iliad* and *Odyssey* was not one man but a group of bards, or a succession of wandering poets, each of whom added of his inspiration to the epics; and sometimes it is also argued that there was no historical siege of Troy and that the story of the war is but the poet's creation. The *Odyssey* appears to be just a story of fancy. However, a war expedition in which many leaders, kings of cities in Greece, took part, and the capture of a fortress named Ilion or Troy, ruled by King Priam, could not be easily relegated, all and sundry, to the domain of fancy. Many Greek and Latin authors referred to it, though their source was invariably Homer. Among the early authors Aeschylus, Sophocles and Euripides wrote cycles of tragedies dealing with the personalities of the Homeric epics and with their families, and many other poets followed in the path of the ancient bard. Virgil's *Aeneid*, telling the story of the peregrinations of Aeneas, one of the defenders of Troy, is famed as emulation of Homer's *Odyssey*.

Through the classical period of Greece, through the Hellenistic age that followed, through the age of the Roman Empire, then through the Middle Ages, the Trojan War was the main event of the past, competing in this with the exploits of Alexander of Macedon, for whom Achilles of the *Iliad* served as the model. But in the nineteenth century, in the "age of reasonableness" that followed the "age of reason", the view prevailed that the Trojan War was part of the imagery of a poet and Troy itself had never existed.

However in the 1870s the skeptics were confounded by Heinrich Schliemann, an adventurer with rich imagination, who as a cabin boy went on a merchant ship bound for America that suffered shipwreck.[1] He was a clerk in Holland, an importer in St. Petersburg, a man not to miss the California goldrush. Having grown rich through the years of adventures, Schliemann went to Hissarlik, a low hill near the Dardanelles, on the Aegean shore of Turkey, after proclaiming that he would find Troy there. Schliemann's advance public announcement as to his intent to discover Troy was met partly with disbelief and sarcasm, but mostly with indifference. He dug, destroyed much valuable material and disturbed some of the archaeological sequence; but he discovered beneath the mound of Hissarlik the remains of seven cities, one beneath the other.[2]

He identified the second city from the bottom as the Troy of which Homer sang: it was a fortress, strong and rich in treasures, seemingly destroyed in a violent earthquake.[3]

---

[1] Of this shipwreck Schliemann wrote to his sisters in Hanover an exciting account of miraculous escape from death. In his later autobiography he exposes his letter-report as more fantasy than truth.

[2] In *Troy and Its Remains* (London, 1875) Schliemann distinguished four cities; in *Ilios, The City and Country of the Trojans* (London, 1880) he recognized seven.

[3] This is the view of C. F. A. Schaeffer, argued in his *Stratigraphie comparée et chronologie de l'Asie occidentale (IIIe et IIe millenaires)* (Oxford University Press, 1948), p. 225. C. Blegen ascribed the destruction to a human foe.

Later scholars identified King Priam's city as the sixth from the bottom, still later as Troy VIIa.

In 1876 Schliemann, now crowned with success, went to the Argive plain in Greece, to Mycenae, to locate the tomb of Agamemnon, "king of men", the leader of the Achaeans at the siege of Troy. Soon he cabled to King George of the Hellenes that he had opened the grave of his predecessor among the five large shaft tombs which he discovered hewn in rock, with the skeletons of their occupants, with gold crowns and gold masks and much jewelry, gold vessels with oriental designs, and pottery. All kinds of voices were now heard. One scholar announced that the find and its treasures date from the Byzantine age (first millennium A.D); but in time the royal graves came to be accepted for what they were – of an era preceding the historical period in Greece – however not of Agamemnon and his house who supposedly lived in the thirteenth or early twelfth century, but of an age several centuries earlier. How was this figured out? In the buildings and tombs of Mycenae cartouches of Amenhotep II, Amenhotep III, and Queen Tiy, wife of Amenhotep III and mother of Akhnaton were found,[1] and in Akhnaton's short-lived city Akhetaton, deposits of typical Mycenaean pottery were unearthed. The age of these pharaohs in the conventional timetable belongs to the first half of the fourteenth century. Schliemann was wrong again in his identification, but right in the main: Here were for all to see rich relics of the Mycenaean civilization.

Schliemann made further diggings at Tiryns, in the Argive plain, and next intended to dig on Crete, but he did not come to terms with the owners of the land, for which he made a bargain offer.

At the beginning of [the 20th] century Arthur Evans, having obtained a concession, dug at Knossos on Crete and brought to light the Minoan civilization – palaces and frescoes and paved courts, a silent world of bygone days. The Minoan civilization could be traced to various stages separated by definite interruptions – Early Minoan, Middle Minoan, and Late Minoan – and it was the Late Minoan age that ran parallel with the Mycenaean age. If anything, the Minoan civilization appeared as the dominant of the two. It was Evans' excavations o~ Crete that established the contemporaneity of Mycenaean ware with that of the Late Minoan period. On Crete Evans also found tablet

---

[1] J. D. S. Pendlebury: *Aegyptiaca* (Cambridge, 1930), pp. 53-57.

with incised signs of two scripts, called by him Linear A and Linear B. Later tablets with the Linear B script were found in large numbers at Pylos and at other ruined cities on the Greek mainland, and still later they were deciphered. But we are ahead of our story.

Why no Literary Relics from Five Centuries?

The Dark Ages left no literary remains, not even a single word on a sherd or a few characters on a clay tablet.

M. Bowra in his book *Homer and His Forerunners* puts the problem in straight terms:

> There is no evidence whatsoever that the Mycenaean script continued anywhere in Greece after c. 1200. There is no trace of writing of any kind in the sub-Mycenaean and Protogeometric periods, or indeed before the middle of the eighth century, when the new and totally different Greek alphabet makes its first appearance. Now, this is surely not an accident. A single scratched letter from this period would be enough to show that writing survived; but not one has been found. This is undeniably a most remarkable phenomenon, for which it is hard to find either a parallel or an explanation. A society seems suddenly to have become illiterate, and to have remained so for centuries. How and why this happened we do not know...[1]

Bowra expresses his wonder at "this astounding state of affairs." It "undermines any hope that the transmission of heroic poetry was maintained by a succession of written texts from the time of the Trojan War."

On the one hand, "the Homeric poems contain material which is older than 1200." On the other hand, Bowra states his conviction that we can be "reasonably confident that Homer worked in the latter part of the eighth century, since this suits both the latest datable elements in his details and his general outlook." Is this not an impasse – the poet separated from his subject by almost five centuries, with an intimate knowledge of a vanished civilization and no art of writing in between?

Alan J. B. Wace challenged this view, and in his preface to Ventris' and Chadwick's *Documents in Mycenaean Greek* (1956) wrote that

---

[1] Sir Maurice Bowra: *Homer and His Forerunners* (Edinburgh, 1955) pp. 1-2.

future discoveries and study would "undoubtedly make clear" whether the Dark Age was really dark:

> The orthodox view of classical archaeologists is that there was a 'Dark Age' when all culture in Greece declined to barbarism, at the close of the Bronze Age and in the early period of the ensuing Iron Age. Even now, when it is admitted that the Greeks of the Late Bronze Age could read and write the Linear B Script, it is still believed by some that in the transition time, the Age of Bronze to that of Iron, the Greeks forgot how to read and write until about the eighth century when they adapted the Phoenician alphabet. It is incredible that a people as intelligent as the Greeks should have forgotten how to read and write once they had learned how to do so.[1]

Then where are the documents, what is the testimony?

"... Letters or literary texts may well have been on wooden tablets or some form of parchment or even papyrus; some fortunate discovery will possibly one day reveal them to us." A quarter century since this was written nothing has been found that would substantiate this hope, as nothing was found in the preceding eighty years of excavation in Greece. In the quoted passage the words "it is still believed by some that ... the Greeks forgot how to read and write" refers to almost every classicist who agrees that the Dark Age left no written record because none was written.[2]

"There is no scrap of evidence," writes Denys L. Page in *History and the Homeric Iliad*, "and no reason whatever to assume that the art of writing was practiced in Greece between the end of the Mycenaean era and the eighth century B.C. ..."[3]

And one hundred pages later: "... The Iliad preserves facts about the Trojans which could not have been known to anybody after the fall of Troy VIIa."[4]

---

[1] P. xxviii; cf. J. Chadwick: »The Linear Scripts« in *The Cambridge Ancient History*, vol. II, ch. XIII (1971) p. 26; V. R. d'A. Desborough: *The Greek Dark Ages* (London, 1972) p. 321.
[2] The contention that during the Dark Ages the Greeks wrote only on perishables does not carry weight. In Mycenaean times, and again from the eighth century on, the Greeks left writing on imperishable materials, such as baked clay or stone, as well as on perishable ones, such as papyrus or wood. The view that all writing during the Dark Ages was on perishable materials, none of which was found, is thus rather difficult to uphold. In *The Local Scripts of Archaic Greece* (Oxford, 1961) p. 17, L. H. Jeffrey convincingly disputes the "perishables" theory.
[3] (Berkeley, Ca., 1959) p. 122.
[4] *Ibid.*, p. 221.

Then back to the question one hundred pages earlier: "How did the truth survive through the Dark Ages into the Iliad?"[1]

Troy in the Dark Ages

The Dark Age enveloped Greece; it enveloped Troy too,

> for the site is barren of deposits which might be referred to the period c. 1100-700 B.C. Not one sherd of proto-geometric pottery is known to have been found at Troy – not by Schliemann, or by Doerpfeld, or by Blegen himself. We are now in effect asking what happened at Troy during the Dark Ages of Greece, from the [beginning of] the 11th to the [end of the] 8th century B.C.: And this is the answer which we must accept – that there is nothing at Troy to fill the huge lacuna. For 2000 years men had left traces of their living there; some chapters in the story were brief and obscure, but there was never yet a chapter left wholly blank. Now at last there is silence, profound and prolonged for 400 years.[2]

This observation of Denys Page, Professor of Greek at the University of Cambridge, is in the nature of amazement: Out of a mound covering a ruined place, an archaeologist expects to extract stray objects that accumulated there in the space of centuries. In Troy there is "silence profound and prolonged" as if time itself had stopped.

But the same author stresses that "the *Iliad* preserves facts about the Trojans which could not have been known to anybody after the fall of Troy VIIa."[3]

Thus not only did Homer know of the kingdom and people of Mycenae that were buried for centuries of the Dark Ages, but he knew also of the kingdom and people of Troy who, too, were dead, buried, and forgotten in the darkness of the Dark Ages.

The site of Troy was reoccupied late in the seventh century; but from the fall of Troy, now put by archaeologists ca. -1260, until Homer's

---

[1] *Ibid.*, p. 120. Rhys Carpenter is among those who argue that an oral tradition stretching over centuries was not capable of preserving a detailed picture of Mycenaean Greece (*Folk Tale, Fiction and Saga in the Homeric Epics*); yet Denys Page and many other scholars state unequivocally that an accurate picture was somehow preserved.

[2] D. Page: »The Historical Sack of Troy«, *Antiquity*, Vol. XXXIII (1959), p. 31.

[3] *Ibid.*, p. 221.

time, there was nothing on the surface of the mound that could disclose to the poet the many intricate details which he webbed into his epics.

It is realized that Homer knew the scene of the Aegean coast of Asia Minor of the eighth and seventh centuries; therefore, it was argued, he could not have lived in the days of the Trojan War (or shortly thereafter) in the 12th century. A poet having composed the poems in the twelfth century would not be able to introduce into them innumerable references to the Iron Age in Greece and the post-Phrygian Age in Asia Minor of the seventh century.

Was the site of Troy alone in Asia Minor an archaeological void for five hundred years, following that city's destruction at the end of the Mycenaean Age?

The Dark Age in Asia Minor

Like Greece and the Aegean, Asia Minor has no history for a period of close to five centuries. Certain scholars disagree with this verdict, but it comes from the pen of one of the foremost authorities on archaeology and art of Asia Minor, Professor Ekrem Akurgal of the University of Ankara:[1]

> ... Today [1961], despite all industrious archaeological exploration of the last decades, the period from 1200 to 750 for most parts of the Anatolian region lies still in complete darkness. The old nations of Asia Minor, like the Lycians and the Carians, the names of which are mentioned in the documents of the second half of the second millennium, are archaeologically, i.e., with their material heritage, first noticeable about 700 or later ... Hence the cultural remains of the time between 1200 and 750 in central Anatolia, especially on the plateau, seem to be quite irretrievably lost for us.

The huge land of Asia Minor for almost five centuries is historically and archaeologically void. The cause of the interruption in the flow of history about -1200 is assumed to lie in some military conquest; but the Phrygians, who are supposed to have been these conquerors, did

---

[1] Akurgal: *Die Kunst Anatoliens von Homer bis Alexander* (Berlin, 1961), pp. 5-7; cf. his *Phrygische Kunst* (Ankara, 1955), p. 112.

not themselves leave any sign of their occupation of the country from before -750.

Thus the explanation that the end of the Anatolian civilization about -1200 was due to the incursion of the Phrygians is not supported by archaeological finds. According to Akurgal, the repeatedly undertaken efforts to close the hiatus by relics of Phrygian art "cannot be harmonized with the results of archaeological study. None of the Phrygian finds and none of the oriental ones found with them can be dated earlier than the eighth century." "Such results compel us to exclude from the study of Asia Minor between 1200 and 750 any Phrygian presence and heritage."

If there is no sign of Phrygian occupation for the period, are there possibly some vestiges of occupation by other peoples?

"It is startling," writes Akurgal, "that until now in Central Anatolia not only no Phrygian, but altogether no cultural remains of any people, came to light that could be dated in time between 1200 and 750." Nothing was left by any possible survivors of previous occupants, namely by Hittites, and nothing by any people or tribe that could have supplanted them. Also on the rim of Asia Minor the darkness of the Dark Age is complete: "In the south of the peninsula, in Mersin, Tarsus and Karatepe, in recent years important archaeological work was done ... here, too, the early Iron Age, i.e., the period between 1200 and 750, is enwrapped in darkness."[1]

Even after only a few decades of settlement a town should leave discernible relics for archaeologists; usually under such circumstances potsherds or a few beads, or a clay figurine, are found. Ash and kitchen refuse are ubiquitous finds wherever there was human habitation. But that on an area over 250,000 square miles in extent there should, as Akurgal claims, be found nothing, not even tombs, from a period counted not just by decades but by centuries, actually a period of almost five hundred years, is hardly less than miraculous.

The Homeric Question

The idea of a wide gap separating the Mycenaean Age from the historical age of Greece has gained almost universal acceptance since

---
[1] *Ibid.*, p.7.

it was first advanced more than a century ago. Because no literary documents and almost no signs of culture could be found for that long period, it came to be known as the Dark Age.

Hellenists and historians in general use the term Dark Age for the twelfth, eleventh, tenth, ninth, and most of the eighth centuries, or the period that lies between the Mycenaean and Archaic ages, the latter being the opening of the Ionian period that in due course developed into the Classical period. The time from about -1200 to -750 is the Dark Age in continental Greece, on the Aegean islands and shores, and in the interior of Asia Minor. The reader may think that the term is bequeathed to us from ancient times, from Greek historians or philosophers of the classical period. The fact, however, is that no Greek historian, philosopher, or poet used the term Dark Age or dark centuries or any substitute for such a concept; nor did Roman writers, much occupied with the Greek past, have a concept of a Dark Age for the period following the Trojan War and preceding the historical age in Greece. The term, and the concept as well, are a creation of modern scholarship in Hellenic studies for the period from which we have neither history, nor literary remains.

If, as most scholars now believe, Homer lived and created at the end of the eighth or the beginning of the seventh century, and if the Trojan War took place just before the beginning of the Dark Age, he could hardly have omitted to refer in some direct or only indirect way to the more than four centuries of the Dark Age that separated him from the epic events he described. Why did no poet – and Greece had many – ever mention a lengthy Dark Age, if only in passing? Neither Herodotus, nor Thucydides,[1] nor Xenophon – the Greek historians – had anything to say about a four or five centuries' span that separated the Greek history from the Mycenaean. Greece had also many outstanding philosophers; then how are we to explain that a period – not covering just a few decades, but more than four centuries – is passed over in silence by Greek poets, philosophers and historians alike? Should not Aristotle or, much later, Diodorus of Sicily or Pausanias in their

---

[1] *A passage from the first book of Thucydides' *Peloponnesian Wars* (I.17) which tells of a period of political chaos and economic deprivation after the fall of Troy, is sometimes cited as a reference to the Dark Ages. That the end of the Mycenaean Age was followed by several decades of migrations and poverty is a fact that is discussed at some length below (section »A Gap Closed«). But Thucydides' words cannot be construed as referring to a period of time longer than a century.

voluminous writings have devoted as much as a single passage to the Dark Age – if there was one? Neither the Roman writers, nor the chronographers of the Renaissance, applied themselves to the illumination of the Dark centuries, and it is only since the last decades of the nineteenth century that the term Dark Age in Greek history has been used.

Despite being separated by five centuries from the Mycenaean civilization of which he sings, Homer displays a surprising knowledge of details no longer existent in the Greek world of his day:

> We know from the archaeological evidence that Homer attempts to archaeologize, even to take us into the Mycenaean Age ... yet in Homer's day there was no science of archaeology, no written history to assist the historical novelist. Where then did he get these details from the past?

So writes one author in the preface to his translation of the *Iliad*.[1]

As an example of such knowledge, the author cites Homer's description of Nestor's cup with doves on its handles, a description that fits a vessel actually disinterred in the Mycenaean strata which according to the conventionally written history were deposited some five centuries before Homer began to compose his epics.

The technique of metal inlay of the shield of Achilles – described by Homer in the *Iliad* – was practiced in Greece in the Bronze Age and "disappeared before its close, and apparently never returned there." The boar's tusk helmet described by Homer was reconstituted by Reichel from slivers of tusk found in many Bronze Age graves. "It is difficult to imagine Homer transmitting a description of an object which we could not visualize ... For four centuries at least no one could possibly have seen a boar's tusk helmet ..."

On the other hand in Homer are found descriptions of objects "which cannot have found a place there before the 7th century." One such object is the clasp which fastened the cloak of Odysseus when on his way to Troy. "It points to the second decade of the 7th century as the time of the composition of the *Odyssey* (unless it is an interpolation, the dates of which could not be much earlier or later than the first half of the 7th century)."

If the Mycenaean Age closed with the twelfth century and Homer composed at the end of the eighth, four and a half centuries constitute a hiatus, and separate the poet from the objects he describes.

---

[1] E. V. Rieu: *The Iliad* (London, 1953).

The blending of elements testifying to the Mycenaean Age together with elements the age of which could not precede the seventh and certainly not the eighth century is a characteristic feature of the *Iliad*. Some scholars have expended enormous efforts in trying to separate passages of the epics and ascribe their authorship to different generations of poets, from contemporaries of the events to the final editor of the poems in the seventh century. But all these efforts were spent unprofitably, and their authors at the end of their labors usually declared their perplexity. The following evaluation is from the pen of M. P. Nilsson:

> To sum up. There is considerable evidence in Homer which without any doubt refers to the Mycenaean Age... The Homeric poems contain elements from widely differing ages. The most bewildering fact is, however, that the Mycenaean elements are not distributed according to the age of the strata in the poems.

Nilsson continued:

> The Mycenaean and the orientalizing elements differ in age by more than half a millennium. They are inextricably blended. How is it credible that the former elements were preserved through the centuries and incorporated in poems whose composition may be about half a millennium later?[1]

The Allies of Priam

I must admit that not so long ago I tended to consider the Trojan War as a legend, with more mythology in it than history: Neither in its cause nor in its conduct did this conflict seem to reflect historical events. The cause of the war, according to tradition, was a seduction or abduction of the spouse of one of the Helladic chiefs; and this, we are told, raised the leaders of all Hellas to undertake a mobilization and campaign to the coast of Asia and to endure hardships for ten years, leaving their own spouses to be ravished or besieged by suitors in the meantime. And if Hissarlik is the site of Troy, there is the additional incongruity of a great war effort the goal of which was to capture a fortress occupying not much more than two acres of land (Troy VIIa) – so Carl Blegen, the last excavator of the site. And what of the par-

---

[1] M. P. Nilsson: *Homer and Mycenae* (1933), pp. 158-59.

ticipation of Ares, Athene, Zeus, and other divinities? The emphasis is on the courage and proficiency of a few single heroes who trace their descent, and in some cases even their parenthood, to various deities and other mythological figures (Thetis in the case of Achilles).

With the end of the siege of ten years' duration and the fall of Troy, the navy of the Achaeans – of which the second book of the *Iliad* gives a record enumerating the number of ships that carried the warriors from each of the cities[1] – is as if no more existent. Victory and triumph are followed by only a few wretched returns home. Nothing is heard of the return to Greece of the Achaeans, victorious in war, as an organized force. We hear of single warriors, like Agamemnon, the leader of the expedition, returning only to find violent death waiting for him in his own town and house or, like Odysseus, spending another ten years striving to reach home by a round-about way. Those of the heroes who succeed in returning find their wives, some faithful, some unfaithful, some in cohort with their scheming lovers and having to be avenged by their children – but little is said of the continuing royal houses, whether of Agamemnon in Mycenae, or of Menelaus in Sparta, or of Odysseus in Ithaca, or of Nestor in Pylos.

Then in a matter of hardly half a generation a curtain descends on Achaean Greece, which presumably for close to five hundred years presents only a picture of void enveloped in primeval darkness. Nothing is known of the subsequent history of these city states, the personal tragedies having ended in family blood-baths. It is as if in the theater the curtain descended for the last time, the lights are extinguished, the hall hurriedly locked, and then five hundred years of impenetrable darkness. Yet a success of the protracted expedition, if undertaken, as some scholars have theorized, to protect the marine route through the Hellespont, across the Black Sea, and to the Caucasian coast, should have made the Hellenes, having forged their national unity in war, exploit the success by expansion of overseas trade and traffic.

The curtain of darkness descends also on Troy – and the void endures there almost as long as in Greece, though it is presumed that some wretched inhabitants settled in hovels, but not before centuries passed. Of the defenders of Troy, from among those who survived the siege, we read also very little – as if they evaporated into thin air – with the exception of Aeneas and his household; and he, like Odysseus, spends a decade or so in wanderings, before reaching Italy.

---

[1] See below, section »Mycenaean City Names in the *Iliad*«.

Strangely, in that substantial portion of the enormous literature on the Trojan War and Troy that I consulted, I scarcely ever found a discussion of the nationality of the people of Troy.[1]

In the *Iliad* they are regularly referred to as "the people of Priam," their king, but this is not an ethnic designation.

Thus while it is known that the besiegers of Troy were Achaeans, also called Danaans, and it is generally accepted that they were Mycenaean Greeks – actually the last generation of them, sometimes designated as the Heroic Generation – the question of which race were the people of Priam was left unanswered by Homer. But at least let us look at Priam's allies. Here some clear indications come to the fore; and if we are still not helped in our pursuit – which nation did the Achaeans fight at Troy? – at least we see a ray of hope that, by knowing the allies we may be guided to the proper time. By knowing the correct century of the events we may obtain an insight into the interplay of nations and races and perhaps come to realize the true reason for the conflict that summoned the Achaean host to the Troad, the region surrounding Troy.

Phrygians are named as allies of Priam;[2] also Ethiopians are counted among his allies. The identification of both these nations carries indications as to the century to which the most famous war of ancient times needs to be ascribed.

Of the Phrygians it is told that their origin stems from Thrace, north of Macedonia, west of the Hellespont. The time of their migration to Asia Minor is not known. No Phrygian antiquities from before the first half of the eighth century have been found,[3] and the opinion is expressed that Homer's reference to the Phrygians is an anachronism. It seems that in one of the earliest waves of the eighth century migrations the Phrygians moved from Thrace over the Hellespont to Asia Minor.

Tradition has it that the first king in their new domicile was Gordias, and the story of his selecting the site for his capital Gordion is a well known legend.[4]

---

[1] Cf. Strabo: *Geography* XII.8.7.
[2] Actually, repeated reference to Phrygians as Priam's allies leaves the question open whether Priam's people were not Phrygians themselves.
[3] Ekrem Akurgal writes that their "first archaeological traces appear in the middle of the eighth century." *Ancient Civilizations and Ruins of Turkey,* (Istanbul, 1970), p. 14.
[4] Arrian: *The Anabasis of Alexander,* II.3; Justin, XI.7; G. and A. Körte: *Gordion* (Berlin, 1904) pp. 12ff.; R. Graves: *The Greek Myths* (London, 1955), no. 83.

The son of Gordias, Midas, is even more than his father an object of legendary motifs – whatever he touched turned to gold, he had the ears of an ass – yet he was a historical figure as well who, according to the chronicle of Hieronymus, reigned from -742 to -696.[1]

Soon the Phrygians came into conflict with the Assyrians who opposed the penetration of newcomers into central Asia Minor; and Sargon II (-726 to -705), the conqueror of Samaria and of the Israelite tribes, moved westward to stop the penetration of the Phrygians.[2] Altogether the Phrygian kingdom in Asia Minor had a short duration.[3] Already the Körte brothers, the early excavators of Gordion, noted that of the royal mounds (kurgans) only three could be dated before the Cimmerian invasion of the early seventh century which put an end to the Phrygian kingdom, and probably the number of royal successions did not exceed this number.[4] Little is known of its history besides the fact that ca. -687 Gordion was overrun by the Cimmerians.

The Cimmerians came from the north, traversing the coastal routes of the Caucasus; their original homeland is often thought to have been the Crimea in southern Russia. They occupied Gordion, displacing the Phrygians westward, toward the Lydian kingdom and the Aegean

---

[1] *Eusebius Werke*, ed. R. Helm (Leipzig, 1913), vol. VII, pp. 89, 92.
Modern historians usually calculate the date of Midas' death as -676. It was under Midas that the Phrygian kingdom reached the peak of its power, as archaeology also attests. See R. S. Young: »Gordion: Preliminary Report, 1953« in *American Journal of Archaeology* 59 (1955), p. 16.

[2] *According to Assyrian records, Sargon's campaign against Midas and the Phrygians, which took place in -715, was the result of Midas' conspiring with the king of Carchemish against Assyria. See M. J. Mellink: »Mita, Mushki, and the Phrygians«, *Anadolu Arastirmalari* (Istanbul, 1955). E. Akurgal: *Die Kunst Anatoliens*, p. 70; P. Naster: *L'Asie mineure et l'Assyrie* (Louvain, 1938), p. 37. Sargon's expedition was, however, not altogether successful in pacifying the region, and continuing disturbances brought Sargon several more times to the defense of his northwestern frontier; he finally met his death there in battle in -705.

[3] R. S. Young, the excavator of Gordion, estimated a period of "a half century" or more for the flourishing of Phrygian culture at the site – »The Nomadic Impact« in *Dark Ages and Nomads*, p. 54. No Phrygian presence can be recognized in the archaeology until the middle of the eighth century – and soon after the start of the seventh, about the year 676 BC, the Phrygian kingdom was destroyed in the catastrophic Cimmerian invasion. This is also when Midas met his end (by suicide, according to Eusebius, (*Chron*. p. 92) and Strabo *Geography* I. 3. 21), and his capital Gordion was burned to the ground. The Cimmerian destruction level was found in 1956; see Young: »Gordion 1956: Preliminary Report« in *American Journal of Archaeology* 61 (1957) p. 320. Cf. also idem: »The Nomadic Impact: Gordion« pp. 54f.

[4] *Gustav and Adolf Körte: *Gordion* (Berlin, 1904). Young: »The Excavations at Yassihuyuk-Gordion, 1950« in *Archaeology* 3 (1950) pp. 196-199. The non-royal tumuli were much more numerous. A royal tomb, perhaps of Gordias, was excavated in 1957 – Young: »The Royal Tomb at Gordion«, *Archaeology* 10 (1957) pp. 217-219.

coast. While the displaced Phrygians may have continued to live for a time in the western confines of Asia Minor, the year -687 saw the end of their kingdom.

It appears that the Cimmerians did not tarry for any length of time in Phrygia; like the Scythians, a nomadic race from the steppes of Russia, who soon followed them on the coastal roads of the Caucasus, they were but transient conquerors. The time they came from their native land, -687 or soon thereafter,[1] makes it quite certain that they were put on their migration by the natural events of that year – described at some length in *Worlds in Collision*:[2] by the world-wide upheavals, earthquakes, frightening apparitions in the sky, as well as by the changes in climate that made many accustomed pursuits and agricultural practices obsolete. -687 (or possibly -701) was also the year that Sennacherib met his famous debacle as described in the books of Isaiah, II Kings, and II Chronicles, while threatening Jerusalem with capture and its population with eviction and exile.

Phrygians as allies of Priam, in the hinterland of the Troad, in conflict with the Cimmerians, themselves pursued by the Scythians, would limit the period of the Trojan War to the years between -720 and -687.

After the passing of the Cimmerians, Phrygia was exposed to the occupation and influence of neighboring states, in particular to that of the Lydian Kingdom to the west, with its capital at Sardis. Lydia was ruled by Gyges, a great king who played a conspicuous role in the politics of the Near East. He was on friendly terms with Assurbanipal, grandson of Sennacherib, king of Assyria; then, feeling the threat of the growing Assyrian empire, he supported Egypt's rise to independence: He sent Ionian and Carian detachments to Psammetichus, king of Egypt, which enabled that country to free itself from the supremacy of Assyria.

The Homeric epics were created on the Asia shore of Asia Minor; it is most probable that Homer was a contemporary of Gyges, king of Lydia.[3]

This view was also offered and supported with arguments by Emile Mireaux; moreover, Mireaux ascribed also the very events of the poems to the time of Gyges.[4]

---

[1] In the *Odyssey* (XI.14) there is reference to the land of the Cimmerians; and if Homer knew of the presence of the Cimmerians in Asia Minor, then the scene is not earlier than -687.
[2] Herodotus, Bk. IV.
[3] The dates of Gyges' reign are given as -687 to -652 by H. Gelzer and as -690 to -657 by H. Winckler.
[4] E. Mireaux: *Les poèmes homériques et l'histoire grecque* (Paris, 1948-49).

The allies of Priam also included Ethiopians under Memnon;[1] the Ethiopian allies of Priam must date in all probability to the period when the Ethiopians were one of the most honored nations, highly regarded for their military prowess. What is called here Ethiopians were actually Sudanese: In Egyptian history the Ethiopian Dynasty and their most glorious period is dated from ca. -712 to -663, when Assurbanipal pursued Tirhaka to Thebes, occupied it, and expelled the Ethiopian from Egypt proper. The tradition concerning Memnon, the Ethiopian warrior who came to the help of Troy, would reasonably limit the time of the conflict also to the end of the eighth and the beginning of the seventh century.[2] The possibility of an Ethiopian landing at Troy in the days of the Ethiopian pharaoh Tirhaka need not be dismissed because of the remoteness of the place: As just said, close to the middle of the seventh century, and possibly at an earlier date, Gyges, the king of Sardis, sent in the reverse direction Carian and Ionian mercenaries to assist the Egyptian king Psammetichus in throwing off the Assyrian hegemony.

Thus it seems that if the participants in the Trojan War all belong to the eighth-seventh century, Homer, who is thought to have lived at the end of the eighth century or the beginning of the seventh, must have been either a contemporary of the siege of Troy, or separated from it by one generation only.

A correct historical placement of the Trojan War may contain a clue to its real cause: We can surmise that the Helladic city-states, alarmed by rumors of hordes of Cimmerians, preceded by dispossessed Phrygians, pushing towards the Hellespont, united under the leadership of Agamemnon and moved across the Aegean sea to preclude the invasion of their land, should the migrating Cimmerians or displaced Phrygians attempt to cross the straits into mainland Greece. Troy was located in the vicinity of the Hellespont, crossed by armies in ancient times, by Alexander, by Darius I, and by other conquerors before them.

While the Greek expedition may have had some limited success, its forces were wrecked and dispersed in the natural upheavals that accompanied the fall of Troy.

---

[1] *In the *Odyssey* (III.111-2) Nestor recalls the death of his son Antilochos who died by the spear of "the glorious son of shining Dawn," (*Odyssey* IV.185-202) which is the epithet reserved for Memnon. Later in the *Odyssey* the Ethiopian warrior is mentioned by name as "great Memnon." (*Odyssey* XI. 522)

[2] Those called here Ethiopians actually were the inhabitants of what is today Sudan. Cf. Mireaux: *Les poèmes homériques et l'histoire grecque*, vol. I, ch. iv.

Aeneas

Following the fall of Troy Aeneas, son of Anchises, a Trojan hero second only to Hector, fled the fortress; he lost his wife in the escape, himself carrying his aged father on his back and leading his young son by the hand. This is the way Virgil, in the first century before our era, imagined the beginning of Aeneas' travels; but already before Virgil, the fate of Aeneas was the subject of poetic tradition. Virgil's creation is regarded as the greatest of Roman epics; Virgil, however, studied the subject drawing on Greek authors.

Upon visiting Thrace and the islands of the Aegean Sea, and following a sojourn on Crete, Aeneas and his little band of companions landed at Carthage; there Queen Dido fell in love with him; his refusal to make Carthage his home and Dido his wife caused her, upon his departure, to take her own life.

Aeneas' further wanderings brought him finally to Latium in Italy, the land of the Latini. According to the Roman legendary tradition, he became the progenitor of the Romans through his son Ascanios, the first king to reign in the new capital of Latium, Alba Longa, of which Rome was a dependent city; or, in another version, through Numitos in direct descent from Ascanios. But a more popular tradition had Aeneas himself as the founder of Rome; the Greek historian Timaios (ca. -346 to ca. -250) followed this tradition. A still better known legend has Romulus for the founder of Rome; sometimes Romulus is made a descendant of Aeneas and Ascanios.

Rome was founded, according to Varro, in -753.[1]

As to Carthage, the generally accepted view is that it was founded in the second half of the ninth century; Timaios placed its foundation in the year -814. Timaios was the first to fix the chronology of the Olympiads.[2]

Philistos, a Greek author, born in -435, placed Carthage's foundation "a man's life length" before the Trojan War; but Philistos' dating of the Trojan War is unknown. Philistos' date for the foundation of Carthage, sixty or seventy years before the fall of Troy, is thought to be in conflict with Timaios' date because the Trojan War would

---

[1] Fabius Pictor gave -747 as the date of Rome's founding.
[2] He was a native of Sicily, the history of which he wrote from the earliest times to -264; of that history, regarded as authoritative in antiquity, only single passages survived in authors who quoted him; Carthage is across the straits from Sicily.

need to be placed in the middle of the eighth century, shortly before the foundation of Rome. But is there a conflict between the founding dates of Carthage in Timaios and in Philistos?

A refugee from Troy in the first half of the twelfth century could not find Carthage, a city built almost three centuries later by colonists from Phoenicia; and he could not be associated with the founding of Rome either directly or by one of his descendants of several generations, the gap between -1183, the conventional year of Troy's fall, and -753, the traditional date of Rome's foundation, being more than four centuries wide.

Olympic Games in the *Iliad*

The recording of events in ancient Greece was by the years of the Olympiads, four years apart, the first year of the first Olympiad having been -776. An important contest at the Olympiads was among charioteers, each driving a four-horse team. Olympia was located in the district of Elis in the western part of the Peloponnesian peninsula.

Tradition has it that the Olympic games were initiated by Pelops, an immigrant from Phrygia in Asia Minor. Another account ascribes the founding of the festival to Heracles, as a celebration of his conquest of Elis.[1] In *Worlds in Collision* the identity of Heracles with the planet Mars was brought out from the statements of several ancient authors:[2] While the founding of the games was attributed to Heracles, or Mars, the festival also honored Athene, or the planet Venus. This is shown by the fact that the early games were held at eight-year intervals,[3] typical for Venus festivals, since eight terrestrial years equal five synodical years of Venus. Later they were celebrated every four years, or two and a half synodical periods of Venus.

The eighth century was a time when the planet Mars was prominent among the heavenly bodies and caused much destruction on earth. Nestor, the future king of Pylos, was but a young man at the time of

---

[1] Pindar: *Olympian Odes*, X 43ff; Hyginus: *Fabula* 273.
[2] *Eratosthenis catasterismorum reliquiae*, ed. C. Robert, 1878: "Tertia est stella Martis quam alii Herculis dixerunt." Cf. Macrobius: *Saturnalia* iii. 12. 5-6, reporting the opinion of Varro.
[3] W. R. Ridington: *The Minoan-Mycenean Background of Greek Athletics* (Philadelphia, 1935), pp. 82-83.

the rampage of Heracles-Mars through the western Peloponnese – he himself saw all his elder brothers killed by the god and his native Pylos burned to the ground[1] – but by the tenth year of the siege of Troy, Homer tells, "two generations of mortal men had [already] perished: those who had grown up with him and they who had been born to these in sacred Pylos, and he was king in the third age."[2] This information permits the rough guess that some fifty to sixty years passed between the founding of the Olympic Games in Nestor's youth and the Trojan War.

In the *Iliad* the aging Nestor recalls that soon after the rebuilding of Pylos his father Neleus sent from Pylos a team of four horses with a chariot to race for a tripod for a competition to be held at Elis. But the fine steeds were detained by the Elean king and their driver was sent home to Pylos empty-handed.[3]

> ... For in Elis a great debt was his [Neleus'] due: a four-horse team of racing horses and their chariot that would have contended in the games and raced to win the tripod.

That this passage from the *Iliad* is a reference to the Olympic Games was understood already in antiquity, as we gather from a discussion of it by the geographer Strabo.[4] This means that Homer knew of the Olympic games and had Nestor refer to them as an event that began to be celebrated several decades before the drama that is the subject of the *Iliad*. However, it is beyond dispute that the beginning of time reckoning by Olympiads was in the eighth century, more precisely in -776. The fact that these games are mentioned as taking place when Neleus, the father of Nestor, was a young man gives some indication of the time in which the Trojan War was fought.

---

[1] Homer: *Iliad* XI. 688-692; Pausanias II.2.2; III.26.6 and V.3.1; Apollodorus II.7.3.; Diodorus Siculus IV.68.
[2] Homer: *Iliad*, transl. by R. Lattimore (1951), Book. I, 250-252.
[3] Homer: *Iliad* XI. 698-701.
[4] Strabo: *Geography* VIII.3.30; Pausanias V.8.2

Chapter 2

Mute Witnesses

Troy and Gordion

When Schliemann dug through the strata of Hissarlik's hill, he discovered, on the second level from the virgin ground beneath, great walls of a fortress, and in the same level some treasures, all of which he attributed to Priam's Troy. His view was invalidated, and properly so, because a correlation with Egypt made it appear too early for Troy. The second level, Troy II, was shown to have been in existence during the Old Kingdom of Egypt, and thus long before the traditional date for Troy's fall. The end of Troy VI, identified by Wilhelm Dörpfeld as the Ilion of the siege, was found to have been contemporaneous with the mid-Eighteenth Dynasty of the Egyptian New Kingdom, and was therefore also too early for the Trojan War.

Carl Blegen identified forty-six layers of occupation of the mound of Hissarlik, the Troy of the excavators, but divided them between the nine strata of occupation classified by Dörpfeld. Troy VI was a well-built fortress; Blegen specified eight separate levels of occupation in this stratum alone. It ended in a violent earthquake. Blegen, however, looked for a fortress that fell not due to an earthquake, but in a siege and assault; thus he identified the Troy sung by Homer as Troy VIIa.

The sixth city of Troy is conventionally placed in the fourteenth-thirteenth centuries before the present era, a dating which ultimately depends on Egyptian chronology. Here an observation by Rodney Young, the excavator of the Phrygian capital Gordion,[1] needs to be cited:

> In their batter as well as their masonry construction the walls of the Phrygian Gate at Gordion find their closest parallel in the wall of the sixth city at Troy.

---

[1] Gordion, the capital of Phrygia, was excavated by the Körte brothers at the beginning of this century. In 1950 Rodney Young led there a team and then returned for many seasons sponsored by the University of Pennsylvania Museum. The date of the Phrygian remains found at Gordion was ascribed to the late eighth and early seventh centuries before the present era.

But a gulf of time separates these two constructions in the conventional timetable.

> Though separated in time by five hundred years or thereabouts, the two fortifications may well represent a common tradition of construction in north-western Anatolia; if so, intermediate examples have yet to be found.[1]

Still today no intermediate examples have been found. As to the date of the Phrygian Gate and wall of Gordion, Young wrote:

> The Phrygian Kingdom was ... at the apex of its power toward the end of the eighth century, when it apparently extended as far to the southeast as the Taurus and was in contact with Assyria. This period of power was apparently the time of the adornment and fortification of its capital city.

This points to the eighth century for the erection of the city wall and gate.[2] Eighth-century Gordion is similar to thirteenth-century Troy, yet intermediate examples of the peculiar way of building the gate and the wall beg to be found.[3]

---

[1] R. Young: »Gordion 1953«, *American Journal of Archaeology*, (1954). *The post-Hittite and pre-Phrygian levels at Gordion have not provided the much looked-for intermediate examples.

[2] *The Phrygian Gate of Gordion was uncovered in 1953 by a team from the University of Pennsylvania led by Rodney Young. It was in the form of a large double gateway with a central courtyard. Since it belonged to the Phrygian period, its date, like that of most of the Phrygian constructions at Gordion, was put sometime in the eighth century.

[3] *Whereas the Trojans had a long tradition of building in stone, the Phrygian gateway appears suddenly, without any other close antecedents; nevertheless, it displays technical skills that speak of a long period of development. This apparent contradiction is also noted by Young (»The Nomadic Impact: Gordion«, p. 52): "... The planning of the [Phrygian] gateway and the execution of its masonry imply a familiarity with contemporary military architecture and long practice in handling stone for masonry. The masonry, in fact, with its sloping batter and its more or less regular coursing recalls neither the cyclopean Hittite masonry of the Anatolian plateau in earlier times, nor the commonly prevalent contemporary construction of crude brick. The closest parallel is the masonry of the walls of Troy VI, admittedly very much earlier. If any links exist to fill this time-gap, they must lie in west Anatolia rather than on the plateau." According to the revised chronology, the Trojan fortifications were standing and in use as late as the ninth century; the Phrygian fortifications at Gordion, dating from the late eighth, could well have been part of the same tradition of building in stone.

The Lion Gate of Mycenae

The Lion Gate of Mycenae was the entrance to the city. Atop the gate, two lions rampant are carved in stone relief. Similar bas-reliefs of two lions rampant facing each other are found in a number of places in Phrygia in Asia Minor.[1]

Fig. 1: The Lion Gate of Mycenae

Fig. 2: Arslantas, Rock-cut Phrygian tomb

---

[1] Cf. especially the relief on the "Lion Tomb" at Arslan Tash near Afyonkarahisar (Fig. 2)

"The resemblance in idea is complete," wrote W. M. Ramsay in 1888.[1] He considered the scheme "so peculiarly characteristic of Phrygia, that we can hardly admit it to have been borrowed from any other country." He found himself "driven to the conclusion that the Mycenaean artists either are Phrygians or learned the idea from the Phrygians."[2] "It is not allowable to separate them [the Phrygian and Mycenaean monuments] in time by several centuries."[3]

"The Phrygian monuments," in Ramsay's view, belong to the ninth and eighth centuries.[4]

"... The end of the Phrygian kingdom is a fixed date, about 675 B.C.,"[5] when the invasion of Asia Minor by the Cimmerians put an end to the Phrygian culture and art. Ramsay went on:

> I do not think it is allowable to place the Mycenaean gateway earlier than the ninth, and it is more likely to belong to the eighth century.
>
> The view to which I find myself forced is as follows. There was in the eighth century lively intercourse between Argos and Asia Minor: in this intercourse the Argives learned ... to fortify their city in the Phrygian style with lions over the gate. Historically there is certainly good reason to assign at least part of the fortifications of Mycenae to the time when the Argive kings [the tyrants of the eighth century] were the greatest power in Greece [here follow the names of several authorities among the historians who hold the same view].[6]
>
> On the other hand, the almost universal opinion of archaeologists rejects this hypothesis. ...

---

[1] Ramsay: »A Study of Phrygian Art«, *Journal of Hellenic Studies* IX (1888), p. 369. *Ramsay: »Studies in Asia Minor«, *Journal of Hellenic Studies* III (1882), p. 19 – but see G. Mylonas: *Mycenae and the Mycenaean Age* (Princeton, 1966), p. 173.]

[2] Ramsay: »A Study of Phrygian Art«, pp. 369-370. *Earlier representations of two rampant lions facing each other are known from Crete; however, it is for the carving technique on stone on a monumental scale that Mycenae seems to be indebted to Phrygia. For a link to Assyria, see L. M. Greenberg: »The Lion Gate at Mycenae«, *Pensée* IVR III, p. 26.

[3] *Ibid.*, p. 70.

[4] {Footnote by Edwin Schorr} Emilie Haspels in *Highlands of Phrygia* (Princeton, 1971) dates the Phrygian reliefs at Arslan Tash to "the last third of the eighth century B.C., the period of the 'Phrygian City' of Gordion" (vol. I, p. 135; cf. vol. II, pl. 131-32). E. Akurgal, however, puts the same reliefs in the early sixth century, deriving them from Ionian, and ultimately Egyptian models – *Die Kunst Anatoliens von Homer bis Alexander* (Berlin, 1961) pp. 86-90, 95.

[5] Ramsay: »A Study of Phrygian Art«, p. 351.

[6] U. v. Wilamowitz-Moellendorf: »Oropos und die Graer«, *Hermes* XXI (1886), p. 111, n. 1, and idem: *Isyllos von Epidauros* (Berlin, 1886), p. n.1; B. Niese: *Die Entwicklung der homerischen Poesie* (Berlin, 1882), p. 213, n. 1. A. S. Murray and S. Reinach are also among those cited by Ramsay as concurring with his opinion (p. 370, n. 3).

Oriental influences found in the remains of Mycenae are "precisely what we should expect in a kingdom like the Argos of the eighth century," when this kingdom had intercourse with Asia Minor, Phoenicia and Egypt. "I wish however to express no opinion here about the date of the Mycenaean tombs and about Mycenaean pottery, but only to argue that the fortifications of the Lion Gate belong to the period 800-700 B.C."[1]

I quote this opinion of Ramsay with the special intention of showing how this viewpoint was invalidated.

The Egyptologist Flinders Petrie made the following reply:

> [A] matter which demands notice is Professor Ramsay's conclusion that the lion gateway is of as late a date as the eighth century B.C. This results from assuming it to be derived from Phrygian lion groups, on the ground of not knowing of any other prototype. As however we now have a wooden lion, in exactly the same attitude, dated to 1450 in Egypt ... it seems that the Phrygian designs are not the only source of this motive for Mykenae.[2]

In Egypt of the latter part of the Eighteenth Dynasty a single instance of a rampant lion (not two rampant lions facing each other as at Mycenae and in Phrygia) made Petrie claim Egypt as a possible place of origin of this image rather than Phrygia. He had discovered heaps of Mycenaean ware in Egypt of the time of Akhnaton. He could not but conclude that these heaps coming from Mycenae must be dated to the fourteenth century.[3]

Equally impressive was the discovery at Mycenae of a number of objects of Eighteenth-Dynasty date, such as objects bearing the cartouches of Amenhotep II, Amenhotep III, and Queen Tiy.[4]

---

[1] Ramsay: »A Study of Phrygian Art«, pp. 370-71.

[2] Sir W. M. Flinders Petrie: »Notes on the Antiquities of Mykenae«, *Journal of Hellenic Studies* XII (1891), pp. 202-03. *Petrie also attempted to fix the dates of many of the finds from the Mycenaean tombs by comparing them with objects from Egypt whose antiquity he considered to be well-established.

[3] Cf. J. D. S. Pendlebury: *Aegyptiaca* (Cambridge, 1930), pp. 111ff. *V. Hankey and P. Warren: »The Absolute Chronology of the Aegean Late Bronze Age«, *Bulletin of the Institute of Classical Studies* (University of London) XXI (1974), pp. 142-152.

[4] Cf. Pendlebury: *Aegyptiaca*, pp. 53-57; Hankey and Warren: »The Absolute Chronology of the Aegean Late Bronze Age«.

Therefore Petrie decidedly opposed Ramsay in his estimate of eighth century for the Lion Gate and the fortification wall of Mycenae.[1]

Here is a case where evidence from Anatolia pointed to the eighth century;[2] but the Egyptologist demanded of the classical scholar that he disregard this evidence in favor of the time scale of Egypt.

The debate between Ramsay and Petrie took place before Evans' archaeological work on Crete; there rampant lions were found engraved on Late Minoan gems,[3] conveying the idea that Mycenae must have borrowed the image from there, from a period well preceding the Phrygian models.[4] Yet one should not lose sight of the fact that Crete's chronology was also built upon relations with Egypt. In the section »The Scandal of Enkomi« we shall read how Evans objected to the chronological implications of Cypriote archaeology by stressing relations between the Egyptian and the Minoan (Cretan) chronologies on the one hand, and Minoan and Cypriote on the other. In *Ages in Chaos* it was shown in great detail why the end of the Eighteenth Dynasty of Egypt must be placed in the latter part of the ninth century. Thus even if Crete was the original source of the motif, Mycenae and Phrygia both deriving it thence, the dependence of Cretan chronology on that of Egypt constitutes the crux of the problem.[5]

---

[1] Boardman notes that monumental sculpture of this kind is unknown in Greece from the time the Lion Gate of Mycenae was built until the eighth century: "More than five hundred years were to pass before Greek sculptors could [again] command an idiom that would satisfy these aspirations in sculpture and architecture." *Greek Art* (New York, 1964), p. 22. *A few other 500-year enigmas appear at Mycenae. See below, Supplement I, »Applying the Revised Chronology«, by Edwin Schorr.

[2] {Footnote by Edwin Schorr} In *The Sea People* Sandars points out the stylistic similarity between the Lion Gate of Mycenae and the Lion Gate of Boghazkoi.

[3] *Some of these gems were known even before Evans' digs – see for instance the intaglio in G. Perrot and C. Chipiez: *History of Art in Primitive Greece* II (London, 1894), pp. 214 and 246, depicting two rampant lions facing each other in a way similar to that on the Lion Gate. Cf. also the gems shown in *Corpus der minoischen und mykenischen Siegel*, ed. F. Matz and H. Bisantz (Berlin, 1964) nos. 46, 144, 145, 172.

[4] *N. Platon, (»Cretan-Mycenaean Art«, *Encyclopaedia of World Art* IV (New York, 1958), p. 109) thought that "the technique of the execution [of the Lion Gate] is clearly inspired by Cretan sculpture." But the Cretan sculptures, unlike those in Phrygia, are miniatures, and Platon needs to assume "the effective translation of a miniature theme into a major sculptural creation" (R. Higgins: *Minoan-Mycenaean Art* (New York, 1967), p. 92). Sandars in *The Sea Peoples* points out the similarity of the monumental carving style of the Lion Gate of Boghazkoi in central Anatolia to the Lion Gate of Mycenae.

[5] *The discovery of Late Helladic IIIB pottery in strata excavated underneath the gate is used to establish the date of its construction. But this pottery, too, is dated on the basis of relations with Egypt.

Let us keep in mind that in the 1880s and 1890s classical scholars of the stature of W. M. Ramsay (1851 – 1939) questioned the inclusion of the Dark Ages of several hundred years' duration between the Mycenaean past and the Ionic age in Greece. And let us not overlook what was the supposedly crushing argument for wedging more than half a millennium into the history of ancient Greece.

Olympia

The scholarly world without any further deliberation decided not to bring the Mycenaean Age down to the first millennium, but this decision did not eliminate the disturbing facts. At the same time another one-man battle was being carried on at the other end of the front. Greek antiquities, commonly regarded as belonging to the eighth and seventh centuries, were declared by a dissenting authority to date from the second millennium, to have been contemporaneous with the Mycenaean Age, and even to have partly preceded it.

According to the accepted view the Mycenaean ware came to an end in the second millennium, and the Dorian invasion subsequently brought a "primitive" art, a pottery with incised designs; later a pattern of painted geometric designs developed, reaching its full expression by the late eighth century. Thereafter new motifs were brought into Greek art – griffins, sphinxes and other oriental figures; this is the period of the orientalization of the art of Greece in the seventh century.

This scheme was accepted; and today, with only slight variations, it is the credo of archaeological art.

According to Dörpfeld in the second millennium two or three different cultures met in Greece.[1]

Dörpfeld insisted that the geometric ware ascribed to the first millennium was actually contemporaneous with, and even antecedent to, the Mycenaean art of the second millennium, and that the "primitive" pottery was also of the second millennium.

The archaeological evidence for the contemporaneity of the geomet-

---

[1] W. Dörpfeld: *Homers Odyssee, die Wiederherstellung des ursprünglichen Epos* (Munich, 1925), vol. I, pp. 304ff.

ric and Mycenaean ware and of all other products of these two cultures, and even of the partial precedence of the geometric ware, was the basic issue for Dörpfeld, who spent a lifetime digging in Greece. Observing that the Mycenaean Age is contemporaneous with the period of the Eighteenth dynasty, and that the geometric ware is contemporaneous with the Mycenaean ware, he referred the geometric ware also to the second millennium.[1]

This aroused much wrath.

A. Furtwängler, who during the excavations of Olympia in the western Peloponnesus, under the direction of Curtius, was the first to attach importance to bits of pottery, and who spent over a quarter of a century classifying small finds, bronzes, ceramics and other products of art, and devised the system of their development, disagreed on all points.

Dörpfeld chose to prove his thesis on the excavations of Olympia, on which he and Furtwängler had both worked since the eighties of the last century. In those early days Curtius, one of the excavators of Olympia, was strongly impressed by proofs of the great antiquity of the bronzes and pottery discovered under the Heraion (temple of Hera) at Olympia; he was inclined to date the temple in the twelfth or thirteenth century and the bronzes and pottery found beneath it to a still earlier period, and this view is reflected in the monumental volumes containing the report of the excavation.[2]

At that time Furtwängler was also inclined to disregard the chronological value of occasional younger objects found there.[3]

New excavations under the Heraion were undertaken by Dörpfeld for the special purpose of establishing that the finds, as well as the original Heraion, date from the second millennium.[4] But the excavat-

---

[1] "This geometrical style is very old; it existed before and next to the Mycenaean art, nor was it replaced by it." W. Dörpfeld: *Alt-Olympia* (Berlin, 1935) vol. I, p. 12.

[2] *Olympia, Die Ergebnisse der von dem deutschen Reich veranstalteten Ausgrabungen*, ed., E. Curtius and F. Adler, 10 vols. (Berlin, 1890-97).

[3] A. Furtwängler: »Das Alter des Heraion und das Alter des Heiligtums von Olympia«, *Sitzungsberichte der Philosophisch-Philologischen Klasse der Königlich Bayerischen Akademie der Wissenschaften*, 1906, reprinted in *Kleine Schriften* (Munich, 1912).

[4] *Dörpfeld distinguished three consecutive temples – the existing Heraion, built at the beginning of the ninth century, the original temple which, on the evidence of Pausanias (V.16.1) he dated to -1096, and an intermediate structure, which in his view was never completed. Today scholars find no basis for positing this intermediate temple and, furthermore, on the basis of the geometric pottery found beneath the first temple, discount the "erroneous tradition" (H. E. Searls and W. B. Dinsmoor: »The Date of the Olympia Heraeum«, *American*

ed bronzes and pottery strengthened each side still more in its convictions. Each of the two scholars brought a mass of material to prove his own point – Dörpfeld, that the geometric ware, which he had himself found together with the Mycenaean at such sites as Troy and Tiryns[1] was contemporaneous with the Mycenaean ware and therefore belongs to the second millennium; Furtwängler, that the geometric ware is a product of the first millennium, and especially of the ninth to eighth centuries, and is therefore separated from the Mycenaean by "einer ungeheueren Kluft" (a tremendous chasm).[2]

Who but an ignoramus, argued Furtwängler, would place in the second millennium the geometric vases found in the necropolis near the Dipylon Gate at Athens?[3] Were there not found, he asked, in this same necropolis porcelain lions of Egyptian manufacture dating from

---

Journal of Archaeology 49 (1945) p. 73) of Pausanias which originally led Dörpfeld to his early dating of it. The Elean tradition recorded by Pausanias has the Olympia Heraion built "about eight years after Oxylus came to the throne of Elis." (V.16.1) Elsewhere (V.3.6) he puts Oxylus two generations after the Trojan War. The tradition is "erroneous" only if the Trojan War is placed in the thirteenth or early twelfth centuries. If it was in fact fought in the late eighth, the tradition then would accord well with the findings of the archaeologists who place the first temple ca. -650 (A. Mallwitz: *Olympia und seine Bauten* (Munich, 1972) pp. 85-88; H.-V. Herrmann: *Olympia, Heiligtum und Wettkampfstätte* (Munich, 1972) pp. 93-94; E. Kunze: »Zur Geschichte und zu den Denkmälern Olympias« in *100 Jahre deutsche Ausgrabung in Olympia* (Munich, 1972) p. 11).

[1] See below, section »A Palace and a Temple at Tiryns«. Only small quantities of Mycenaean ware were found at Olympia, and none beneath the Heraion.

[2] *Quite early on, Furtwängler had become convinced that none of the bronzes found at Olympia could be dated before the eighth century (»Bronzefunde aus Olympia«, *Abhandlungen Berl. Akad.*, 1879, IV; *Kleine Schriften*, Munich, 1912, I, pp. 339-421). In 1880 more bronzes were discovered in the black stratum beneath the floor of the Heraion (*Olympia*, vol. IV), and they seemingly confirmed a late eighth century date; this meant that the temple had to be somewhat more recent. Furtwängler later admitted that the evidence of several small finds, indicating a much more recent date of construction of the temple, had been rejected by him at the time because it diverged too radically from accepted views. In 1906 he published his influential study of the objects newly dug up from beneath the floor of the Heraion (»Das Alter des Heraion und das Alter des Heiligtums von Olympia«, *Sitzungsberichte der philosophisch-philologischen Klasse der koeniglich bayerischen Akademie der Wissenschaften*) in which he concluded that the Heraion and the pottery associated with it belong in the latter part of the seventh century.

[3] *The Dipylon period, so named after the funeral vessels first discovered near the Dipylon Gate at Athens by the Greek Archaeological Society in 1873-74, was dated originally to the tenth or ninth centuries BC According to Schliemann, Dipylon ware was at one time "commonly held to be the most ancient pottery in Greece ... When it was recognized that the Mycenaean pottery was of a higher antiquity, it was also found that the Dipylon graves must belong to a later time ..." *Tiryns* (London, 1886) p. 87. Of course, Mycenaean pottery was "recognized" as being "of a higher antiquity" largely because of synchronisms with Egypt.

the Twenty-sixth, the Saitic, Dynasty of Psammetichus and Necho?[1]

Were not also a great number of iron tools found beneath the Heraion in Olympia? The Mycenaean Age is the Late Bronze Age; the Geometric Age that of iron. It is true, claimed Furtwängler, that a few iron objects have been found in the Mycenaean tombs – but they only show that iron was very precious at the time these tombs were built.

Both sides linked the question of the date of the origin of the Homeric epic to the question at hand. Most scholars claimed that the epics originated in the eighth century. But, according to the dissident Dörpfeld, they originated five or six centuries earlier, in the Mycenaean Age, which is also the Geometric Age.

The dispute was waged with "ungehörigen persönlichen Beleidigungen" (outrageous personal slander);[2] and a quarter century after one of the disputants (Furtwängler) was resting in his grave, the other (Dörpfeld), then an octogenarian, filled two volumes with arguments. They vilified each other on their deathbeds, and their pupils participated in the quarrel. In the end the followers of Dörpfeld, the dissident scholar, deserted him and went over to the camp of his detractors.

But by that time he had already been completely discredited, and his obstinacy made him a target for further attacks by the younger generation of scholars properly trained in the science of archaeology, who are able at a glance to tell the exact age and provenance of a sherd. They have no doubt whatsoever that the Mycenaean Age came to a close ca. -1100 and that the real Geometric Age belongs to the ninth and eighth centuries, and for a long time now the issue has not been open to dispute.

But this does not mean that the facts ceased to perplex. According to E. A. Gardner, "fragments of geometrical vases ... have been found on various sites in Greece together with late examples of Mycenaean pottery."[3]

When then did the Mycenaean Age end, ca. -1100 or ca. -700?

---

[1] "The two porcelain lions were found in tombs excavated in 1891 near the Dipylon Gate, together with "vases of characteristic Dipylon ware," according to E. A. Gardner: *Ancient Athens* (London, 1902) p. 157. However, cf. *Ramses II and his Time* (1978) in which monuments now attributed to the Twenty-sixth Dynasty are redated for the most part to the subsequent period of Persian domination.

[2] Dörpfeld: *Alt-Olympia*, vol. I, p. 12.

[3] E. A. Gardner: *Ancient Athens* (New York, 1902) pp. 157-58.

In this dispute between the two scholars, both were guided by the chronology of the Egyptologists, according to which the Eighteenth Dynasty ended in the fourteenth century, the Nineteenth came to a close before ca. -1200, and the Twenty-sixth Dynasty belongs to the seventh and early part of the sixth centuries. In their application of these undisputed facts to the past of Greece, both disputant scholars agreed that the Mycenaean Age belongs to the second millennium.

The Geometric Age did not follow the Mycenaean Age, but was of the same time or even earlier, argued one scholar (Dörpfeld), and was he wrong? The Geometric Age belongs to the first millennium, argued the other scholar (Furtwängler), and was he wrong? Wrong was their common borrowing of dates for the Mycenaean Age from the Egyptologists.

In view of the fact that later generations of archaeologists followed Furtwängler and not Dörpfeld, it is worthwhile to reproduce the assessment of the latter as an archaeologist by one who knew him and his work, herself a great figure in classical studies built on Mycenaean and Classical archaeology, H. L. Lorimer, author of *Homer and the Monuments* (1950). In her Preface to that book Lorimer writes:

> I wish to record the debt which in common with all Homeric archaeologists I owe to a great figure, forgotten to-day in some quarters and in others the object of an ill-informed contempt. To Wilhelm Dörpfeld, the co-adjutor of Schliemann in his later years and long associated with the German Aracheological Institute in Athens, scholars owe not only the basic elucidation of the sites of Tiryns and Troy which ensured their further fruitful exploration, but the establishment of rigidly scientific standards in the business of excavation, an innovation which has preserved for us untold treasures all over the Aegean area. That in later years he became the exponent of many wild theories is true but irrelevant and does not diminish our debt. In his own realm his work, as those testify who have had access to the daily records of his digs, was as nearly impeccable as anything human can be ...

This is an evaluation of Dörpfeld as an archaeologist from the hand of a scholar who did not follow the lonely scholar on his "wild theories." The archaeological work that brought him to his theories regarding the sequence of pottery styles was impeccable; and his theories were wild mainly because he did not make the final step and free Greek archaeology and chronology from the erroneous Egyptian timetable. The contemporaneity of the Mycenaean and early Geometric wares, if true, contains the clue to the removal of the last argument for the preservation of the Dark Ages between the Mycenaean and Greek periods of history.

"The Scandal of Enkomi"

The lengthening of Egyptian history by phantom centuries must have as a consequence the lengthening of Mycenaen-Greek history by the same length of time. On Cyprus, Aegean culture came into contact with the cultures of the Orient, particularly with that of Egypt, and unavoidably embarrassing situations were in store for archaeology.

In 1896 the British Museum conducted excavations at the village of Enkomi, the site of an ancient capital of Cyprus, not far from Famagusta, with A. S. Murray in charge.[1]

A necropolis was cleared, and many sepulchral chambers investigated.

> In general there was not apparent in the tombs we opened any wide differences of epoch. For all we could say, the whole burying-ground may have been the work of a century.
> From first to last there was no question that this whole burying-ground belonged to what is called the Mycenaean Age, the characteristics of which are already abundantly known from the tombs of Mycenae ... and many other places in the Greek islands and in Egypt.

However the pottery, porcelain, gems, glass, ivory, bronze, and gold found in the tombs all presented one and the same difficulty. From the Egyptological point of view many objects belong to the time of Amenhotep III and Akhnaton, supposedly of the fifteenth to the fourteenth centuries. From the Assyrian, Phoenician, and Greek viewpoint the same objects belong to the period of the ninth to the eighth or seventh centuries. Since the objects are representative of Mycenaean culture, the excavator questioned the true time of the Mycenaean Age. But as the Mycenaean Age is linked to the Egyptian chronology he found himself at an impasse.

---

[1] Murray: »Excavations at Enkomi«, in A. S. Murray, A. H. Smith, H. B. Walters: *Excavations in Cyprus* (London: British Museum, 1900).

We shall follow him in his efforts to come out of the labyrinth. He submitted a vase, typical of the tombs of Enkomi, to a thorough examination. The dark outlines of the figures on the vase are accompanied by white dotted lines, making the contours of men and animals appear to be perforated. This feature is very characteristic.

> The same peculiarity of white dotted lines is found also on a vase from Caere [in Etruria], signed by the potter Aristonothos which, it is argued, cannot be older than the seventh century B.C. The same method of dotted lines is to be seen again on a pinax [plate] from Cameiros [on Rhodes] in the [British] Museum, representing the combat of Menelaos and Hector over the body of Euphorbos, with their names inscribed. That vase also is assigned to the seventh century B.C. Is it possible that the Mycenae and Enkomi vases are seven or eight centuries older?

Analyzing the workmanship and design of sphinxes or grifins with human forelegs on the vase, the archaeologist stressed

> its relationship, on the one hand, to the fragmentary vase of Tell el-Amarna (see Petrie: Tell el-Amarna, Plate 27) and a fragment of fresco from Tiryns (Perrot and Chipiez, VI, 545), and on the other hand to the pattern which occurs on a terracotta sarcophagus from Clazomenae, [in Ionia] now in Berlin, a work of the early sixth century B.C.

The connection between the Mycenaean and Aristonothos vases caused "a remarkable divergence of opinion, even among those who defend systematically the high antiquity of Mycenaean art."

The problem of pottery which belongs to two different ages is repeated in ivory. The ivories of the Enkomi tombs are very similar to those found by Layard in the palace of Nimroud, the ancient capital of Assyria. There is, for example, a carving of a man slaying a griffin,

> the man being remarkable for the helmet with chin strap which he wears. It is a subject which appears frequently on the metal bowls of the Phoenicians, and is found in two instances among the ivories discovered by Layard in the palace at Nimroud. The date of the palace is given as 850-700 B.C.

An oblong box for the game of draughts, found in Enkomi, "must date from a period when the art of Assyria was approaching its decline," five or six centuries after the reputed end of the Mycenaean age.

Among the Nimroud ivories (850-700 B.C.) is a fragmentary relief of a chariot in pursuit of a lion to the left, with a dog running alongside the horses as at Enkomi, the harness of the horses being also similar.

The style of the sculpture (of Nimroud) "is more archaic than on the Enkomi casket." But how could this be if the objects found in Enkomi date no later than the 12th Century? Comparing the two objects, I. J. Winter wrote:

> A hunting scene depicted on a rectangular panel from an ivory gaming board of 'Cypro-Mycenaean' style found at Enkomi, with its blanketed horses and chariot with six-spoked wheel, so closely resembles a similar hunting scene on one of the pyxides from Nimroud that only details such as the hairdo of one of the chariot followers or the flying gallop of the animals mark the Enkomi piece as a work of the second millennium B.C., separated by some four centuries from the Nimroud pyxis.[1]

A bronze of Enkomi repeats a theme of the Nimroud ivories, representing a woman at a window.

> The conception is so singular, and the similarity of our bronze to the ivory so striking, that there can hardly be much difference of date between the two – somewhere about 850-700 B.C.
>
> Another surprise among our bronzes is a pair of greaves... It is contended by Reichel[2] that metal greaves are unknown in Homer. He is satisfied that they were the invention of a later age (about 700 B.C.).

Bronze fibulae, too, were found in the Enkomi tombs, as well as a large tripod "with spiral patterns resembling one in Athens, which is assigned to the Dipylon period," and a pair of scales of a balance like the one figured on the Arkesilaos vase. But such finds are separated by a wide span of time from the twelfth century.

The silver vases of the Enkomi tombs "are obviously Mycenaean in shape." "On the other hand," there were found two similar silver rings, one with hieroglyphics and the other engraved on the bezel

> with a design of a distinctly Assyrian character – a man dressed in a lion's skin standing before a seated king, to whom he offers an oblation. Two figures in this costume may be seen on an Assyrian sculpture from Nimroud of the time of Assurnazirpal (884-860), and there is no doubt that this fantastic idea spread rapidly westward.

---

[1] *Iraq* 38 Issue 1 [1976] pp. 9-10
[2] W. Reichel: *Homerische Waffen* 2nd ed. (Vienna, 1901), p. 59.

Next are the objects of gold. Gold pins were found in a tomb of Enkomi. "One of them, ornamented with six discs, is identical in shape with the pin which fastens the chiton [tunic] on the shoulders of the Fates on the François vase in Florence (sixth century B.C.)." A pendant "covered with diagonal patterns consisting of minute globules of gold soldered down on the surface of the pendant" was made by "precisely the same process of soldering down minute globules of gold and arranging them in the same patterns" that "abounds in a series of gold ornaments in the British Museum which were found at Cameiros in Rhodes" and which were dated to the seventh or eighth century.

Among the pottery of "the ordinary Mycenaean and pre-Mycenaean type" gems were found. A scarab "bears the cartouche of Thi [Tiy], the queen of Amenophis [Amenhotep] III, and must therefore be placed in the same rank as those other cartouches of her husband, found at Ialysos [on Rhodes] and Mycenae, which hitherto have played so conspicuous a part in determining the Mycenaean antiquities as being in some instances of that date (fifteenth century)."[1]

As for the porcelain, it "may fairly be ranked" with the series of Phoenician silver and bronze bowls from Nimroud of about the eighth century. A porcelain head of a woman from Enkomi "seems to be Greek, not only in her features, but also in the way in which her hair is gathered up at the back in a net, just as on the sixth century vases of this shape." Greek vases of this shape "differ, of course, in being of a more advanced artistic style, and in having a handle. But it may fairly be questioned whether these differences can represent any very long period of time."

Murray surveyed the glass:

> In several tombs, but particularly in one, we found vases of variegated glass, differing but slightly in shape and fabric from the fine series of glass vases obtained from the tombs of Cameiros, and dating from the seventh and sixth centuries, or even later in some cases. It happens, however, that these slight differences of shape and fabric bring our Enkomi glass vases into direct comparison with certain specimens found by Professor Flinders Petrie at Gurob in Egypt, and now in the British Museum. If

---

[1] Since the beginning of the present century, the conventional date of the reign of Amenhotep III has been reduced to the end of the fifteenth and the first quarter of the fourteenth century.

Professor Petrie is right in assigning his vases to about 1400 B.C.,[1] our Enkomi specimens must follow suit. It appears that he had found certain fragmentary specimens of this particular glass ware beside a porcelain necklace, to which belonged an amulet stamped with the name of Tut-ankhamen, that is to say, about 1400 B.C.

Murray comes to the conclusion that "Phoenicians manufactured the glass ware of Gurob and Enkomi at one and the same time." Consequently

> the question is, what was that time? For the present we must either accept Professor Petrie's date (about 1400 B.C.) based on scanty observations collected from the poor remains of a foreign settlement in Egypt, or fall back on the ordinary method of comparing the glass vessels of Gurob with those from Greek tombs of the seventh century B.C. or later, and then allowing a reasonable interval of time for the slight changes of shape or fabric which may have intervened. In matters of chronology it is no new thing for the Egyptians to instruct the Greeks, as we know from the pages of Herodotus.

With this last remark the excavator at Enkomi came close to the real problem, but he shrank from it. He did not dare to revise Egyptian chronology; all he asked was that the age of the Mycenaean period be reduced. How to do this he did not know. He quoted an author (Helbig) who thought that all Mycenaean culture was really Phoenician culture, the development of which remained at a standstill for seven centuries.

> In 1896 there was found in a tomb at Thebes in Egypt a bronze patera [a shallow vessel] which in shape and decoration has so much in common with the bronze Phoenician bowls from Nimroud that we feel some surprise on being told that the coffins with which it was found belong unmistakably to the time of Amenophis [Amenhotep] III or the first years of Amenophis IV [Akhnaton]. It is admitted that this new patera had been a foreign import into Egypt. Equally the relationship between it and the bronze Phoenician bowls is undeniable, so that again we are confronted with Helbig's theory of a lapse of seven centuries during which little artistic progress or decline had been effected.[2]

---

[1] Sir W. M. Flinders Petrie: *Illahun, Kahun and Gurob* (London, 1891) Plate 17. Compare also Plate 18 with two identical glass vases which are assigned to Rameses II. Murray: »Excavations at Enkomi«, in Murray, Smith and Walters: *Excavations in Cyprus*, p. 23, note. Since the above evaluation of the time of Tutankhamen by Petrie, the conventional date of this king, son-in-law of Akhnaton, has been reduced to ca. -1350.

[2] Murray: »Excavations at Enkomi«, *loc. cit.*

It was necessary to assume a state of hibernation of almost seven hundred years.

The endeavor of the excavator of Enkomi was directed toward bringing the Mycenaean Age closer in time by five or six hundred years, so that there would be no chasm between the Mycenaean Age and the Greek Age. As curator of Greek and Roman antiquities of the British Museum, he constantly had before him the numerous connections and relations between Mycenaean and Greek art, which could not be explained if an interval of many centuries lay between them. He tried to disconnect the link between Mycenaean and Egyptian archaeologies and chronologies, but he felt that this was an unsolvable problem.

The proposal to reduce the time of the Mycenaean Age was rejected by the scholarly world.

Arthur J. Evans, at the time having just embarked on a long series of excavations at Knossos on Crete, came out against Murray's work, "so full of suggested chronological deductions and – if its authors [i.e., A. S. Murray and his collaborators] will pardon the expression – archaeological insinuations, all pointing in the same direction," namely, "a chronology which brings the pure Mycenaean style down to the Age of the Tyrants" of the eighth century, and makes it "the immediate predecessor of the Ionian Greek art of the seventh century B.C."[1]

Evans had to admit that "nothing is clearer than that Ionian art in many respects represents the continuity of Mycenaean tradition," but he built his argument on the manifold connections of Mycenaean art with Egypt of the Eighteenth Dynasty. Are not the flasks of the Enkomi tomb almost as numerous in Egyptian tombs of the Eighteenth Dynasty? A fine gold collar or pectoral inlaid with glass paste, found in Enkomi, has gold pendants in nine different patterns, eight of which are well known designs of the time of Akhnaton (Amenhotep IV), "but are not found a century later." The metal ring of Enkomi, with cartouches of the heretic Akhnaton, is especially important because "he was not a pharaoh whose cartouches were imitated at later periods," and so on.

One of the silver vases of Enkomi, Evans wrote, "is of great interest as representing the type of the famous gold cup of the Vapheio tomb.[2]

---

[1] Evans: »Mycenaean Cyprus as Illustrated in the British Museum Excavations«, *Journal of the Royal Anthropological Institute* XXX (1900) pp. 199ff.

[2] Two gold cups with designs representing men hunting bulls were found in a beehive tomb at Vapheio in the neighborhood of Sparta.

These cups, as their marvellous repousse designs sufficiently declare, belong to the most perfect period of Mycenaean art." This should establish that the theory of the latency of Mycenaean art for six or seven centuries after its flowering in the second millennium cannot help to solve the problem of Enkomi; the Enkomi finds date from the apogee of the Mycenaean Age.

Evans insisted that the material supplied by the Cypriote graves "takes us back at every point to a period contemporary with that of the mature art of the class as seen in the Aegean area," and this despite his own admission that a number of objects from Enkomi point to a later age, like the porcelain figures "which present the most remarkable resemblance, as Dr. Murray justly pointed out, to some Greek painted vases of the sixth century B.C." Nevertheless, he concluded with regret that "views so subversive" should come from so high an authority in classical studies.

Two scholars clashed because one of them saw the close connection between Mycenaean art and the Greek art of the seventh century, and the other saw the very same Mycenaean objects disinterred in the Egypt of Akhnaton, dated to the fourteenth century.

The Mycenaean Age has no timetable of its own independent of that of Egypt. I have referred to this question in the chapter dealing with Ras Shamra in *Ages in Chaos*.

If Evans had had some evidence, independent of Egypt, on which to calculate the ages of the Minoan and Mycenaean cultures, we would have needed to take into account all Minoan and Mycenaean chronological material, as we did with the Egyptian. But there is none.[1]

"The chronological scheme depends ultimately upon Egyptian datings of Aegean pottery," wrote H. R. Hall,[2] who served as curator of Egyptian and Assyrian antiquities at the British Museum.

> Using this Egyptian evidence as his guide, and checking the results of excavation with its aid, Sir Arthur Evans finds that the Bronze Age pottery and with it the general culture of Crete divides itself into three main chronological periods: Early, Middle, and Late, each of which again is divided into three sub-periods."[3]

---

[1] The ancient Greek calculations of such past events as the time of Minos, of Heracles, of the Return of the Heracleidae, of the date of the Trojan War and other past events also depend on Egypt.
[2] H. R. Hall: *Aegean Archaeology* (London, 1915), p. 2.
[3] *Ibid.*, p. 3.

The Mycenaean Age started at the same time as the Late Minoan Age.

Dr. Murray's case was lost. He had built its defense on two points, one strong, the other weak. His strong point was this: he analyzed and made clear the close interrelation between Mycenaean culture and the early Greek culture of the seventh century. His weak point was his anxiety to disregard the connection between Mycenaean culture and the Egyptian world of the end of the Eighteenth Dynasty. But in el-Amarna of Akhnaton scattered heaps of Mycenaean ware were found.

It was asked: Which fact should be given greater weight by an unbiased judge: the close relation between Mycenaean and Greek cultures or the fact that Mycenaean ware was found in the city of el-Amarna (Akhet-Aton), which was built and destroyed in the fourteenth century?

The verdict in the matter of the age of Mycenae was unanimous: Its period of greatest influence is dated between the fifteenth and the twelfth centuries.

> This [Mycenaean] ware did not appear in large quantities in Egypt until about 1375 B.C., and little of it was received in the coastal countries after the middle of the thirteenth century. Therefore, whenever a piece of it is found in place in an ancient city, it dates the context between about 1375 [the first year of Akhnaton according to the presently accepted chronology[1] and 1225 B.C.[2]

The verdict with regard to Enkomi was, in the words of Hall, as follows:

> Excavations of the British Museum at Enkomi and Hala Sultan Tekke (near Larnaka on Cyprus) have brought to light tombs filled with objects of Minoan or Mycenean art, now mostly in the British Museum, most of which cannot be later in date than the fourteenth and thirteenth centuries B.C. The Egyptian objects found in them are demonstrably of this date, and not later, being all of the late Eighteenth and Nineteenth Dynasties. Rings of Akhenaten [Akhnaton] and a scarab of Teie [Tiy, mother of Akhnaton] have been found here as at Mycenae, and fine Egyptian necklaces of gold also, which, from their style, one would adjudge to the Eighteenth or Nineteenth Dynasty. Probably, too, the greater part of the

---

[1] As was noted above, since the time of the Murray-Evans controversy the age of Akhnaton and of Tutankhamen has been reduced by a few decades. This point needs to be kept constantly in mind when one is examining the older scholarly literature on these subjects.

[2] G. E. Wright: »Epic of Conquest«, *Biblical Archaeologist* III No. 3 (1940).

treasure of gold-work found in the tombs and now in the British Museum is of this early date. The golden tiaras and bands certainly seem to connect with those of the Myceanean shaft-graves. But at the same time there are many objects of later date, such as a bronze tripod ... which are demonstrably of the Dipylon period, and cannot be earlier than the tenth or ninth century.[1]

Thus, in effect the excavator of Enkomi is accused of having been unable to distinguish burials of different ages in a grave.[2]

He denied that the graves of Enkomi had been re-used.

Somewhere I came upon the expression, "the scandal of Enkomi." I ask: Was the excavator to be blamed for something that was not his fault? The allegation that possibly objects dating from two different epochs were mixed up in Murray's archaeological heaps does not meet his main arguments. His elaborated statements dealt with simultaneous relationships of single objects with Egypt of the fourteenth century and Assyria and Greece of the ninth and eighth centuries.

We learn from this case the fact which both sides admitted: The Greek culture of the seventh century has many interrelations with Mycenaean culture. The resulting chronological gap, as we have seen in Chapter I, had to be taken as a Dark Age.

"Cyprus no less than Greece itself passed through a long and tedious Dark Age." "Cyprus withdrew into herself, and life during this transitional age was dull and poverty-stricken, unenterprising and dim," and after the Mycenaean Age came to its close elsewhere, "in Cyprus it was perpetuated."[3]

A generation after the excavations at Enkomi in 1896, other excavators opened more graves there and passed the following judgment:

The burials in the graves belong to the second or Bronze Age, its

---

[1] Hall: *Aegean Archaeology*, pp. 23-24. {Annotation by Edwin Schorr:} The tripod mentioned by Hall is dated to the twelfth century by H. W. Catling (*Cypriote Bronzework in the Mycenaean World* (Oxford, 1964) pp. 154-55). It was compared to a tripod found in a grave on the Pnyx in Athens, variously dated, but now assigned by the associated pottery to the eighth century BC. By analogy to the Enkomi stand and other contemporary examples, Catling judged the Pnyx tripod to be a twelfth-century heirloom. Adding to the controversy, C. Rolley (»Les trépieds à cuve cluée«, *Fouilles des Delphes* 5.3, (Paris, 1977) pp. 126-29), who accepts the Egyptian-based date, now challenges Catling's assessment of the Pnyx tripod, assigning both it and a very similar example recently discovered in a contemporary grave on the island of Thera to the eighth century..

[2] See also H. R. Hall: *The Oldest Civilization in Greece* (London, 1901), p. 16, and Evans in *The Journal of the Royal Anthropological Institute*, XXX (1900), p. 201, note 2.

[3] S. Casson: *Ancient Cyprus* (London, 1937), pp. 64, 70.

Late or third period, the second part (out of three) of this third period, more precisely to the subdivisions A (9 graves), B (10 graves) and C (8 graves) also a few belong to Late Bronze IA and IB. Thus the graves on the acropolis are "all intermingled with each other in a seemingly arbitrary way."[1]

What does this mean? It means that simple and great questions are eclipsed by nomenclatures.

In recent years French and French-British campaigns at Enkomi[2] have failed to solve the problems left by the British Museum excavations of 1896. The finds are still evaluated by Egyptian chronology.

Tiryns

The same problem that caused the difference of opinions at Enkomi and at the Heraion of Olympia arose at other excavated sites. To demonstrate this on another case of Greek archaeology, I chose Tiryns, south-east of Mycenae. Tiryns was excavated by Schliemann and Dörpfeld in 1884-85. Along with Mycenae, it was an important center of Mycenaean culture. On the acropolis, foundations of a palace were discovered. Together with Mycenaean ware, and mixed with it,[3] geometric ware of the eighth century and archaic ware of the sixth century were found, among them many little flasks in which libations had been brought to the sacred place.[4]

According to Schliemann, Tiryns was destroyed simultaneously with Mycenae and the palace was burned down. But his collaborator Dörpfeld, who agreed with him as to the time the palace had been built, disagreed as to when it was destroyed, and their opinions differed by six hundred years.[5]

---

[1] E. Gjerstad and others: *The Swedish Cyprus Expedition*, 1927-1931 (Stockholm, 1934), I. 575.

[2] Claude F. A. Schaeffer: »Nouvelles découvertes à Enkomi (Chypre)«, in *Comptes rendus, Académie des Inscriptions et Belles Lettres*, Paris, 1949; *Revue archéologique*, XXVII (1947), 129ff; *American Journal of Archaeology*, LII (1948), 165ff.

[3] {Annotation by Edwin Schorr:} The late eighth-century pottery was found immediately above, or mixed with, Late Helladic IIIB/C wares on the citadel, in the lower town, on the plain and in a wall chamber: see W. Rudolph: »Tiryns 1968« in *Tiryns* ed. U. Jantzen (Mainz, 1971) p. 93.

[4] H. Schliemann: *Tiryns* (London, 1886).

[5] See A. Frickenhaus: *Tiryns* vol. I: *Die Hera von Tiryns* (Athens, 1912), p. 34.

From Greek literature it is known that in early Greek times, in the eighth or seventh century and until the first part of the fifth century, there was a temple of Hera in Tiryns which was deserted when the Argives vanquished the city in -460. In later times Tiryns was occasionally visited by travelers coming to pay homage to the sacred place of bygone days.[1]

When the excavation of Tiryns was resumed in 1905 by a team headed by A. Frickenhaus and continued in the following years, special attention was paid to the question of the time in which the Mycenaean palace there was destroyed.

On the site of the palace and, in part, on its original foundations a smaller edifice was built, identified as the temple of Hera of Greek times. The excavators felt that many facts point to the conclusion that the Greek temple was built over the Mycenaean palace very shortly after the palace was destroyed by fire.[2] The altar of the temple was an adaptation of the Mycenaean palace altar;[3] the plan of the Mycenaean palace was familiar to the builders of the temple; the floor of the palace served as the floor of the temple.[4]

However, the Greek temple was built in the seventh century.[5]

After deliberating on the evidence, the excavators refused to accept the end of the Mycenaean Age in the second millennium as the time of the destruction of the palace, and decided that the palace had survived until the seventh century. In their opinion the Mycenaean pottery was the refuse of an early stage of the palace; the terracotta figures and flasks of archaic (seventh-century) type were offerings of the pilgrims

---

[1] Pausanias was one of those pilgrims in the year 170 of the present era.

[2] *Frickenhaus: *Tiryns*, pp. 31-40, K. Müller: *Tiryns III Die Architektur der Burg und des Palastes* (Augsburg, 1930), pp. 214ff, Per Alin: *Das Ende der mykenischen Fundstätten auf dem griechischen Festland* (Lund, 1962), p. 32. But see G. Mylonas: *Mycenae and the Mycenaean Age* (Princeton, 1966), pp. 48-52, who argues that the temple was built five centuries after the burning of the megaron. Cf. W. Voigtländer: *Tiryns* (Athens, 1972) p. 8; U. Jantzen: *Führer durch Tiryns* (Athens, 1975) p. 333; H. Plommer in *Journal of Hellenic Studies* 97 (1977), pp. 81-82; J. W. Wright in *American Journal of Archaeology* 84 (1980), p. 242.

[3] Alin: *Das Ende der mykenischen Fundstätten*, p. 33; Jantzen: *Führer durch Tiryns*, p. 33; Frickenhaus: *Tiryns* I pp. 5f.; Müller. *Tiryns III*, pp. 137ff.

[4] *Frickenhaus: *Tiryns* I; However, M. P. Nilsson: *The Minoan-Mycenaean Religion and Its Survival in Greek Religion* (Lund, 1927) pp. 475-77 thought the floor of the later structure may have been at a higher level, a conclusion which has recently been argued by Mylonas: *Mycenae and the Mycenaean Age*, p. 51.

[5] Frickenhaus placed it in the middle of the seventh century (*Tiryns* I, pp. 31ff.)

to the Greek temple of Hera. A continuity of culture from Mycenaean to Greek times was claimed; even the worship of Hera, they felt, must have been inherited.[1]

Frickenhaus and his team realized that their explanation required some unusual assumptions: for instance, that the inhabitants of the palace did not undertake any alteration for the entire period of more than half a millennium,[2] and that in one part of the palace the refuse of centuries was preserved, while in another part life went on.[3]

But the excavators knew no other explanation, because it was clear to them that "the fire of the palace was followed immediately by the erection of the temple."[4]

A decade later, when the temple of Hera was found to be very similar in plan to a Mycenaean building excavated at Korakou, near Corinth, "grave doubts" were expressed about the correctness of the above interpretations of the excavators of Tiryns, who had been "involved in a number of difficulties, both architectural and chronological."[5]

The critic (C. W. Blegen) agreed that the temple had been built immediately after the palace was destroyed, but he could not agree that the temple was a building of the seventh century.

> How is it possible, if a Greek temple was established at the Mycenaean level in the megaron [the throne room] and if the open court before the megaron was used at its Mycenaean level from the seventh century B.C. onward, – how is it then possible that this same area was later covered over with almost purely Mycenaean debris?[6]

He therefore concluded that "the later building within the megaron at Tiryns is not a Greek temple" but "a reconstruction carried out toward the end of the Mycenaean Period after the destruction of the palace by fire." He also denied the significance of the capital of a Doric column found during the excavation of the temple.

---

[1] Frickenhaus: *Tiryns* I, 31.
[2] *Ibid.*, p. 35.
[3] *Ibid.*, p. 36.
[4] *Ibid.*, p. 38. But see Notes for the contrary view of Mylonas and others.
[5] C. W. Blegen: *Korakou, a Prehistoric Settlement near Corinth* (American School of Classical Studies at Athens, Boston, 1921), p. 130.
[6] **Ibid.*, p. 132. At the same time, Blegen noted, "the debris and potsherds which we should expect from the seventh century and subsequently during the period when the temple was in use, have almost completely vanished." Cf. Mylonas: *Mycenae and the Mycenaean Age*, p. 49.

Although Blegen's arguments seemed to carry weight when he denied that the Myceaean palace had survived the Mycenaean Age by almost five centuries, they appeared without force when he asserted that the building erected on the foundations of the palace was not a Greek temple.[1] Blegen's view was also questioned by an eminent classicist, M. P. Nilsson.[2]

Because it is as inconceivable that the Greek temple was built in the thirteenth century as it is that the Mycenaean palace stood until the seventh century without alterations, its floor not even showing signs of wear,[3] Nilsson confessed his inability to draw a conclusion:

> The time of the reconstruction being uncertain, the question whether or not the building is the temple of Hera remains unanswerable.[4]

In a book on the architecture of the palace of Tiryns, another excavator of that city, K. Müller, arrived at the conclusion that the difference of opinions is irreconcilable, but he shared the view of the scholars who ascribe the palace fire to about -750 and consider the edifice a Greek temple.[5]

---

[1] *Mylonas: *Mycenae and the Mycenaean Age*, p. 52 and Jantzen: *Führer durch Tiryns*, p. 33 reaffirm Frickenhaus' conclusion that the later building is a Greek temple. Per Alin: *Das Ende der mykenischen Fundstätten*, p. 32 supports Blegen's view.

[2] *The Minoan-Mycenaean Religion and Its Survival in Greek Religion*.

[3] *Rodenwaldt, quoted by K. Müller in *Tiryns III*. However, see above, footnote 213 about the floor level. Rodenwaldt himself agreed with Blegen in placing the destruction of what he considered a rebuilt megaron in Mycenaean time: *Tiryns II*, p. 235, n.2. Cf. idem: »Zur der monumentalen Architektur in Griechenland«, *Athenische Mitteilungen* 44 (1919), pp. 179-180; »Mykenische Studien I« in *Jahrbuch des deutschen archäologischen Instituts* 34 (1919) p. 95 and n.2. But cf. above, n. 6 about the floor level.

[4] *Nevertheless, Nilsson inclined more to the view of Frickenhaus that the later building was indeed a Greek temple, and not a smaller megaron of Mycenaean time; he stressed the evidence for the cult of Hera: "the thousands of votive terracottas of a standing and seated goddess and others cannot be so lightly pushed aside as is done by Mr. Blegen"; and he argued that "we know from votive deposits that there was a temple on the acropolis of Tiryns, if the building itself is not accepted as satisfactory evidence... Under these circumstances the doubt concerning the identity seems unreasonable." Additional sacred objects were found by Müller in 1926 (*Tiryns III*, pp. 214ff.) in a refuse pit; they were assigned dates from the mid-eighth to the mid-seventh centuries. An attempt to explain them in the light of Blegen's theory was made by Alin: *Das Ende der mykenischen Fundstätten* p. 32.

[5] *Müller: *Tiryns III*, pp. 207ff. Time did not help to reconcile the divergent views. H. Lorimer, writing in 1950 (*Homer and the Monuments*, p. 435) admitted that at "Tiryns the circumstances are obscure" yet opted for Frickenhaus' and Müller's conclusion. "It appears certain," she wrote, "that ... the megaron remained intact and uninhabited until it perished in a conflagration probably ca. 750. It is difficult to conceive what purpose it could have served through the long post-Mycenaean period if not that of continuing to house the ancient cult." But it was against exactly such a possibility that Blegen had brought arguments a quarter of

Most of the archaeologists agreed on the continuity of the culture and cult of both buildings,[1] but each of the attempts to bridge the chasm of almost five hundred years met with insurmountable difficulties. The answer would not be difficult if the Mycenaean Age were not displaced by this interval of time, pushed back into history, before its proper place.

Mute Witnesses

The divergence of almost five hundred years in the archaeological age evaluations repeats itself with respect to many sites of the Greek past. Because two timetables are applied simultaneously to the past of Greece – one built on the evidences of Greece itself, the other on the evidences of relations with Egypt – a clash of opinions in matters of age appraisal is almost inevitable.

The theory that "a period covering the seventh century and extending, perhaps, into the eighth century, was the time in which pottery and other antiquities of the Mycenae class were produced for the home market of Greece and possibly in Greece itself" (Murray)[2] was pronounced an "archaeological insinuation" (Evans).[3]

The other attempt at synchronizing the geometric with the Mycenaean ware by ascribing them to the second millennium (Dörpfeld) was called "the naivete of complete ignorance" (Furtwängler).[4]

The separation of the Mycenaean Age from the Greek Age by five hundred years of Dark Age was paid for with an ever-growing mass of conflicting facts. Already in the shaft tombs of Mycenae some of the finds bore conflicting and unreconcilable evidence:

---

a century earlier. In the same year W. B. Dinsmoor published *The Architecture of Ancient Greece* (New York, 1950), in which he advocated Blegen's solution (p. 21 and n.1). More recently Per Alin (see above, n. 14) brought additional arguments in support of Blegen.

[1] {Annotation by Edwin Schorr:} However, G. Mylonas had argued that the later Greek temple was built long after the destruction of the Mycenaean megaron by new settlers who followed the plan of the by then five-hundred-years-old ruins. This view is also followed by U. Jantzen in his *Führer durch Tiryns* (Athens, 1975), who nevertheless sees a continuation of the religious cult from Mycenaean into archaic times (p. 33).

[2] A. S. Murray: *Handbook of Greek Archaeology* (New York, 1892), p. 57.

[3] Evans: *Journal of the Royal Anthropological Institute* 30 (1900), p. 200.

[4] Furtwängler: *Kleine Schriften*, vol. I, p. 456.

Nor ... is the evidence of Greek excavation always as simple and convincing as it looks. It has been usual to regard all the contents of the acropolis-graves at Mycenae as dating more or less to the same period. But some of the objects from these graves can be shown, if we are not to throw aside all that we have learned of the development of early Greek art, to be of far later date than others.[1]

The same author admitted that the graves in Greece were as a rule not re-used. This makes the presence of objects of two different epochs in the Mycenaean graves in Greece very enigmatic.[2]

The epochs, as usual, are separated by close to five hundred years.[3]

A Votive Cretan Cave

On Crete a long interval is thought to separate the last period of the Minoan civilization from the late Geometric period in art and history, which belong in the eighth century; six hundred years of Dark Age if Evans is right that the Minoan civilization came to its end in -1400, and four hundred years if Leonard Palmer is right in claiming that it endured to almost -1200. But if, as we maintain, the Minoan civilization continued until the eighth century or even until the later part of it, then, of course, the Minoan ware in its latest style must be found contemporary with the geometric ware and the same perplexing relations would be discovered on Crete as were discovered in continental Greece.

The Dictaean Cave on Crete supplied the Cretan Collection in Oxford's Ashmolean Museum with many objects; the cave was a votive place in the Late Minoan III age and an abundance of bronze figures was stored there. J. Boardman published a study of the Cretan Collection and tried to classify the finds by their style and affiliation.[4]

---

[1] H. R. Hall: *The Oldest Civilization of Greece* (London, 1901), p. 16.
[2] {Annotation by Edwin Schorr:} Hall later retracted his opinion for the shaft graves of Mycenae, but the same 500-year enigma has since been found in other Late Helladic tombs throughout the Aegean. See J. N. Coldstream's article on hero cults in *Journal of Hellenic Studies* (1976).
[3] For many more 500-year enigmas, see, Israel M. Isaacson: »Applying the Revised Chronology«, *Pensée* IVR, no. 4 (Fall 1974), 5-20; cf. Suppl. I of the present book.
[4] *The Cretan Collection in Oxford* (Oxford University Press, 1961).

Of bronze figurines of men from the votive cave he wrote: "These Cretan figures have been dated, apparently by style, to Late Minoan III. They must be related in some way to the well-known Geometric type of mainland Greece which exhibits the same characteristics."[1]

Of the bronze figures of women from the same cave, the author says: "Although no such figures of women have been recovered from Late Minoan III deposits [elsewhere], it is likely that the cruder specimens from the cave are of this date, although Pendlebury[2] thought some might be Geometric."[3]

The bronze male and female figurines divided the experts, with the Minoan and the Geometric ages contesting for them. Would the animal figures from the same assemblage make the decision easier?

> Again there is as yet no reason to believe that bronze animal votives were being made uninterruptedly from Minoan to Geometric times. It should then be possible to distinguish the early from the late, but it is not easy.[4]

Next came knives with human heads at the end of the handles. "The style of the head is exceptionally fine. ... Its superficial resemblance to a group of Cretan Geometric bronzes is noteworthy, and although the shape of the blade and solid handle point to the latest Bronze Age, there is much in the style to be explained." The layers in which it was found "suggest a Middle Minoan III – Late Minoan I context" and this "considerably complicates the problem to which no solution is offered here."[5]

A "cut-out plaque from the cave ... is of a woman with a full skirt. The dress and pose, with elbows high, seem Minoan, but the decoration of the small bosses is more Geometric in spirit."[6]

Thus bronze figurines, rings and plaques perplex the art expert when he tries to determine the period from which they date, and the difference frequently amounts to more than half a millennium. Will not then the pottery – vases and dishes, the hallmark of their age – throw some light on the problem?

---

[1] *Ibid.*, p. 7.
[2] J. D. S. Pendlebury: *The Archaeology of Ancient Crete: An Introduction* (London, 1939) p. 332.
[3] Boardman: *The Cretan Collection*, p. 8.
[4] *Ibid.*, p. 9.
[5] *Ibid.*, p. 20.
[6] *Ibid.*, p. 43.

For the storage jars with reliefs, (pithoi) from the Dictaean Cave, two authorities[1] "imply a Geometric date." But two other authorities[2] "have them Minoan."[3]

Then what is the verdict of the fifth expert, familiar with the opinions of the other four?

> It is tempting to see in these pieces the immediate predecessors of the finely moulded and impressed pithoi of seventh-century Crete, but for these the independent inspiration of mainland Greece or the islands can be adduced, and the cave fragments are best regarded as purely Minoan in date.[4]

The very same features tend to confuse the experts. Some Cretan vases have a very characteristic decoration on them and it could be expected that this would help solve the problem of the age, but it does not.

> There are several Cretan examples of heads or masks being used to decorate the necks of vases. ... The example from Knossos was published by Evans as Minoan, and the signs on the cheeks thought to be signs in a linear script. The technique and the decoration tell against this. The patterns are purely Geometric. ... The outline of the features is common in Cretan Geometric.[5]

In other cases the confusion is still greater when a decision is to be made between the Minoan (or Mycenaean) of the second millennium, the Geometric of the eighth century and the Archaic (of the seventh-sixth centuries).

The case of the votive Dictaean Cave and its contents was selected here to illustrate how the problem stands on Crete. The verdict drawn by the art expert quoted on these pages did not clarify the issue by its recourse to our ignorance of what transpired during the Dark Age:

> After the collapse or overthrow of the major Bronze Age civilizations of the Aegean world in the twelfth century B.C. Crete, with the rest of Greece, entered upon a Dark Age which the still inadequate archaeological record can illuminate but little and the literary record not at all.[6]

---

[1] F. Courby: *Les Vases grecques à relief* (Paris, 1922) pp. 42f. and Pendlebury: *The Archaeology of Crete*, p. 334.
[2] J. Schäfer: *Studien zu den griechischen Reliefpithoi des 8.-6. Jahrhunderts v. Chr. aus Kreta, Rhodos, Tenos und Boiotien* (1957); Mustili: *Annuario della R. Scuola Archeologica di Atene XV-XVI* (1932-33) p. 144, n.5.
[3] Boardman: *The Cretan Collection*, p. 57.
[4] *Ibid., loc. cit.*
[5] *Ibid.*, p. 103.
[6] *Ibid.*, p. 129.

Etruria

The Etruscans are thought to have arrived in northern Italy sometime before the end of the eighth century before the present era. In Etruria, between the rivers Arno and Tiber, are found vaulted structures erected by the Etruscans: they are of the type known as "false vaulting." O. W. von Vacano in his *Etruscans in the Ancient World* (1960) comments with wondering:

> ...The Mycenaean corridor design and tholos [circular domed tomb] structures are related to the vaulted buildings which make their appearance in the orientalizing period in Etruria – and here it is even more difficult to solve, even though the connection itself is undisputed.[1]

The Etruscan vaulted chambers impress one by their similarity to Mycenaean architecture. Other Etruscan structures of the seventh-sixth centuries also show such similarity.

> The remains of the city walls of Populonia, Vetulonia and Rusellae, consisting of huge stone blocks which have a 'Mycenaean' look, do not date further back than the end of the sixth century B.C.: their gateways may well have had arches rounded like the entrance doors to the Grotta Campana, on the outskirts of Veii, which dates from the second half of the seventh century B.C., and is one of the earliest painted chamber-tombs of Etruria.[2]

---

[1] Von Vacano: *The Etruscans in the Ancient World*, p. 81. *After the monuments of Mycenae and Tiryns received, on the basis of Egyptian chronology, dates in the second millennium, some scholars attempted to age the Etruscan tombs by five hundred years to make them contemporary with their Mycenaean conterparts: so "striking" was the similarity, so "evident" the relation of the two architectural styles, that if the Mycenaean tombs belong in the second millennium, one expert argued, the ones found in Etruria "are probably not of inferior antiquity." (G. Dennis: *The Cities and Cemeteries of Etruria* (London, 1878), vol. I, p. 265, n.2; cf. p. 368, n. 6.) But what of the contents of the tombs, which invariably consisted of Etruscan products of the eighth century and later? The surmise that this situation reflected "a reappropriation of a very ancient sepulchre" (Dennis: op. cit., p. 154) was unanimously rejected by experts (e.g., A. Mosso: *The Dawn of Mediterranean Civilization* (New York, 1911), p. 393). There was no reason to suppose that the tombs had been built by anyone but the people who used them; and these people first arrived on the scene in the middle of the eighth century. The relation of these eighth-century tombs to the five-hundred-years-earlier structures of Mycenean Greece has remained a puzzle. *The Dawn of Mediterranean Civilization* (New York, 1911) pp. 392-93; A. N. Modona: *A Guide to Etruscan Antiquities* (Florence, 1954), p. 92; S. von Cles-Reden: *The Buried People: A Study of the Etruscan World*, transl. by C. M. Woodhouse (New York, 1955), p. 180; A. Boethius and J. B. Ward-Perkins: *Etruscan and Roman Architecture* (Baltimore, 1970) p. 78 and pl. 47. The oldest is the Grotta Regolini Galassi, dated to ca. 650 BC.

[2] *Ibid.*, p. 82; cf. Cles-Reden: *The Buried People*, p. 122. *Numerous other Etruscan cul-

A dilemma no less serious is posed by a vase fashioned by a Greek master who signed it with his name, Aristonothos; between -675 and -650 he studied in Athens, then migrated to Syracuse (Sicily) and later to Etruria (Tuscany). The vase was found at Cerveteri, in southern Etruria. "There is an obvious link between the design of the Aristonothos crater and another earthenware vessel, scarcely less often discussed and more than five hundred years older, the vase known from the principal figure decorating it as 'the Warrior Vase of Mycenae.'"[1]

It becomes ever clearer that the end of the Mycenaean Age, put at ca. -1200, is placed so not by a true verdict.

Sicily

In Mycenean times Sicily had a prosperous civilization that carried on a busy commerce with the Helladic city-state of mainland Greece and the Minoan empire of Crete. This civilization disappears from view about the same time that the chief Mycenean centers were destroyed, and five centuries of darkness are said to descend on the island.[2] Not till the beginning of the seventh century is the gloom dispelled by the arrival of the first Greek colonists.

---

tural traits reflect Mycenaean models, something that would be not unexpected if, as the revised timetable postulates, the two cultures were contemporary, yet most difficult to account for if, as the conventional scheme requires, five hundred years of darkness intervened.
(a) Columns. The types of columns used in Etruscan buildings derive from columns of Knossos and Mycenae, and have nothing in common with the Doric columns of seventh and sixth-century Greece.(S. von Cles-Reden: *The Buried People: A Study of the Etruscan World*, transl. by C. M. Woodhouse (New York, 1955), p. 35.) But it is presumed that no Mycenaean or Minoan structures were left standing in Etruscan times. Where, then, did the Etruscans find the models for their wooden columns?
(b) Frescoes. The famous Etruscan frescoes, such as those that decorate the tombs near Veii, display an "obvious reminiscence of Crete" – however not of Crete of the Dark Ages, but rather of Minoan Crete (von Cles-Reden: op. cit., p. 143). But had not the Cretan palaces with their frescoes been destroyed many centuries earlier?
(c) Burials. The sepulchral slabs used in some Etruscan tombs, especially those bearing reliefs of men and animals, resemble those found by Schliemann at Mycenae (Dennis: op. cit., p. lxix, n. 9). Also Etruscan burial customs appear to be derived from Mycenaean models (S. von Cles-Reden: op. cit., p. 150.)

[1] Von Vacano: *The Etruscans in the Ancient World*, p. 81. See I. M. Isaacson: »Applying the Revised Chronology«, *Pensée* IX (1974), pp. 5ff; cf. Suppl. I of the present book.
[2] L.B. Brea: *Sicily Before the Greeks* (New York, 1966), p. 130

The earliest of the Greek settlements was at Gela on the southern coast, founded by migrants from Crete and Rhodes at a date fixed by the ancient chronographers as -689. Tradition also claimed that Gela's founder was Antiphemos, one of the Greek heroes returning from Troy: and Virgil has Aeneas, the Trojan hero, sail along the southern coast of the island and admire flourishing Gela and two other Greek settlements which by all accounts did not come into existence till the beginning of the seventh century.[1] Besides furnishing further proof of our dating of the Trojan War, these traditions are especially important in linking the Greek colonization of Sicily with the close of the Mycenean age, and help explain the many survivals of Mycenean culture in the Greek colonies of seventh century Sicily.

A little to the north of Agrigento, somewhat west of Gela on Sicily's southern coast, are found tholos tombs of the Mycenean type.[2] Inside of one of the tombs were found gold bowls and seal rings manufactured in a style that derives from Mycenean gold work.[3] Yet neither the tombs nor the objects found inside them can be dated before the end of the eighth century. It is a puzzle how "splendid gold rings" with incised animal figures, so reminiscent of Mycenean objects and having nothing in common with contemporary Greek prototypes could have been manufactured by Greek colonists in the seventh century if "a real Dark Age"[4] of five hundred years' duration did in fact separate them from the latest phase of the Mycenean civilization. In Sicily the time between the end of the Mycenean age and the beginning of Greek colonization is an absolute void, with a total lack of archaeological remains: even the Protogeometric and Geometric pottery which elsewhere is claimed to span the Dark Age, is absent; only late Geometric ware appears with the arrival of the Greeks.[5] The decorative motifs used by the Greek colonists are once more under strong Mycenean influence; a detailed comparison of the motifs in use in the seventh cen-

---

[1] *The Aeneid* Book III, lines 671-673
[2] P. Griffo and L. von Matt: *Gela: The Ancient Greeks in Sicily* (Greenwich, Connecticut, 1968), p. 47; Brea: *Sicily Before the Greeks* p. 174.
[3] Brea: *Sicily Before the Greeks* p. 175; cf. G. Karl Galinsky: *Aeneas, Sicily and Rome* (Princeton, 1969), p. 86; E. Langlotz: *Ancient Greek Sculpture of South Italy and Sicily* (New York, 1965), p. 15.
[4] Brea: *Sicily Before the Greeks* p. 130.
[5] T. J. Dunbabin: »Minos and Daidalos in Sicily«, *Papers of the British School at Rome*, vol. XVI. New Series, vol. III (1948), p. 9.

tury with those on Mycenean ware caused much amazement among art historians, but not even a suggestion of how the motifs could have been transmitted through the Dark Ages.[1] Moreover, Minoan influences were identified in the shape and decoration of pottery discovered at Gela, presenting the same problems.

All the evidence we have examined argues against a long gap between the Mycenean age in Sicily and the arrival of the Greek colonists in the seventh century. Then why is it necessary for historians to postulate a five hundred year long Dark Age between the two epochs? Of the sherds found on the island some were fragments of "exactly the same pottery as that found in Egypt in the ruins of Tell el Amarna, the capital of Pharaoh Amenophis IV (Akhnaton) (1372 – 1355 B.C.)."[2] It was the erroneous timetable of Egypt which caused the historians to remove the Mycenean civilization of Sicily into the second millennium, severing its links to its Hellenic successor.

Mycenae and Scythia

"According to the account which the Scythians themselves give," reported the fifth-century Greek historian Herodotus, "they are the youngest of all nations."[3] It was the great disturbances and movements of people of the eighth and seventh centuries before the present era that brought these nomadic tribes from the depths of Asia to the doorstep of the civilized nations of the ancients East – Assyria, Egypt and Greece. Formerly the Scythians dwelt east of the Araxus[4] – their first settlements in southern Russia date to the end of the eighth century, about the time also that the Assyrians clashed with them in the vicinity of Lake Urmia.[5] In the course of the decades that followed the Scythians attained the peak of their power, menacing Egypt and helping to bring about the downfall of Assyria. Later the powerful Chaldean and Persian empires succeeded to confine them to the steppes north of the Caucasus.

---

[1] Galinsky: *Aeneas, Sicily and Rome*, p. 83
[2] Langlotz: *Ancient Greek Sculpture of South Italy and Sicily*, p. 15.
[3] Herodotus: *The Histories*, Bk. IV, ch. 5.
[4] The Araxus may be either the Oxus, which flows through today's Afghanistan, or the Volga.
[5] In the reign of Sargon II (-722 to -705). T. T. Rice: *The Scythians* (London, 1975), p. 44.

The appearance of the Scythians on the scene of the ancient East coincides in the revised scheme with the final years of the Mycenaean civilization; the accepted timetable, however, needs to place their arrival fully five centuries after the last of the Mycenaean citadels had been abandoned.

The tombs of the Scythian kings in the Crimea were built in a way "surprisingly reminiscent of Mycenaean constructions,"[1] the burial chamber consisting of "enormous blocks of dressed stone set to overlap each other so as to meet in the center in an impressive vault."[2] To explain the use by the Scythians of the corbelled vault of the type common in the Mycenaean period, it was suggested that there must have been a continuing tradition going back to Mycenaean times, despite the lack of even a single exemplar between the twelfth and seventh centuries. "I have no doubt," wrote the historian Rostovzeff, "although we possess no examples, that the corbelled vault was continuously employed in Thrace, and in Greece and in Asia Minor as well, from the Mycenaean period onwards..."[3] We, on the contrary, must begin to have doubts about a scheme which needs to postulate a five hundred year tradition of work in stone for which not a thread of evidence exists. Stone constructions of the type, had they existed, would have survived.

Gregory Borovka in his *Scythian Art* writes of "the striking circumstance that the Scytho-Siberian animal style exhibits an inexplicable but far-reaching affinity with the Minoan-Mycenaean. Nearly all its motives recur in Minoan-Mycenaean art."[4]

Solomon Reinach, long ago, called attention to certain striking resemblances between Scythian and Minoan-Mycenaean art.[5] For in-

---

[1] E. g., Altan Oba ("The Golden Barrow") and Tsarskij Kurgan ("Royal Barrow"). See Rice: *The Scythians*; E. H. Minns (*Scythian and Greeks* (Cambridge, 1913), p. 194) also considered the plan of the tombs to be of Mycenaean derivation.

[2] Rice: *The Scythians*, p. 96.

[3] M. Rostovzeff: *Iranians and Greeks in South Russia* (Oxford, 1922) p. 78. Similar "Mycenaean type" constructions of the Scythians were found in Bulgaria (at Lozengrad), and in Asia Minor (Pontus. Caria and Lycia) – *Ibid.*, p. 77. R. Durn in *Jahrhefte der k. Arch. Instituts zu Wien*, X (1907), p. 230.

[4] *Scythian Art* (London 1928), p. 53.

[5] S. Reinach: »La représentation du galop dans l'art ancient et moderne« in *Revue archéologique*, 3e série, tome XXXVIII (1901) fig. 144 bis "Lion au galop sur une rondelle en bois mycénienne." p. 38: "Il a déjà été question d'une rondelle de bois mycénienne, découverte en Egypte, sur laquelle est figuré un lion bondissant, l'arrière-train soulevé avec une telle violence que les rattes de derrière vinnent toucher le front (fig. 58). Nous reproduisons ici cette figure (fig. 144 bis) pour la rapprocher d'une plaque d'or sibérienne représentant un

stance, the design of animal bodies in "'flying gallop' in which the animal is represented as stretched out with its forelegs extended in a line with the body and its hind legs thrown back accordingly, is at once characteristic of Minoan-Mycenaean art and foreign to that of all other ancient and modern peoples; it recurs only in Scythia, Siberia and the Far East."

Another example of great similarity in style is in "the Siberian gold and bronze plaques depicting scenes of fighting animals." Borovka supplies his description with illustrations. "How often are the animals depicted with the body so twisted that the forequarters are turned downwards, while the hind quarters are turned upwards? Can the agonized writhings of a wounded beast or fury of his assailant be more simply rendered?"[1]

> Other motives of the [Scythian] animal style, too, reappear in Minoan and Mycenaean art. We may cite the animals with hanging legs and those which are curled almost into a circle. Conversely, the standard motif of the Minoan-Mycenaean lion, often represented in the Aegean with reverted head, reappears again in Scythian and Siberian art.

The similarity first observed by Reinach and elaborated upon by Borovka is very unusual. But what appeared to them most surprising was the fact that two such similar art styles should be separated not only by a vast geographical distance, but also by an enormous gulf in time.

> How are we to explain this far-reaching kinship in aim between the two artistic schools? It remains, on the face of it, a riddle. Immediate relations between Minoan-Mycenaean and Scytho-Siberian civilizations are unthinkable; the two are too widely separated in space and time. An interval of some 500 years separates them ... Still, the kinship between the two provinces of art remains striking and typical of both of them.[2]

---

cheval attaqué par un tigre. Cheval et tigre offrent également ce singulier motif des membres postérieurs rejetés vers le dos et l'enclosure (fig. 114)."

[1] Borovka: *Scythian Art*, pp. 53-54.
[2] Borovka: *Scythian Art*, p. 54 Similar observations were made by Minns (*Scythian and Greeks*, p. 260), who termed a Scythian depiction of a deer with its head turned around "a Mycenaean survival." He also compared an ibex on a casket from Enkomi, Cyprus to similar Scythian depictions.

Chapter 3

Words Set in Clay

Pylos

Pylos in Messenia, on the western coast of the Peloponnese, was the capital of Nestor, the elderly statesman in the league headed by Agamemnon, king of Mycenae, against Priam, king of Troy, and his allies.[1] In 1939 Carl Blegen came to Messenia to search the countryside for signs of the ancient city of Pylos with Nestor's famous palace, celebrated by Homer. Blegen selected for his first dig a prominent hilltop, a short distance from the sea, which seemed to him eminently suitable to be the site of a royal palace; and in fact, as soon as he began to lift the earth from his first trench, extensive structures began to appear, and much pottery of Mycenaean time. He soon arrived at the conclusion that the palace was Nestor's: the building he excavated had been occupied, in his estimate, in the second part of the thirteenth century before the present era – the preferred time for the Trojan War.[2]

Already early during the work of excavation Blegen unearthed scores of tablets written in the Linear B script, and soon there were hundreds of them. Linear B had been first discovered on Crete by Sir Arthur Evans, who found tablets with incised signs of two scripts, which he termed Linear A and Linear B. The profusion of tablets found in Pylos made the archaeologists question whether the script was Minoan or had its origin on the mainland of Greece; and when subsequently more tablets inscribed with these characters were found in other sites of the Greek mainland – at Mycenae and at Thebes – the name Mycenaean became rather regularly applied to the script.

For over a decade after their discovery the tablets were neither published nor read;[3] but when read – and the story will be told on subse-

---

[1] *Iliad* XI. 689. *Odyssey* III.3f.
[2] C. W. Blegen and M. Rawson: *The Palace of Nestor at Pylos in Western Messenia* (Princeton, 1966) vol. I, pt. 1, pp. 3ff.
[3] They were published in 1951 (*The Pylos Tablets: A Preliminary Transcription*) and the decipherment was completed by 1953. See below, section »Linear B Deciphered«.

quent pages – they were found to contain no literary text: they were regularly archive notes, dealing with taxation or conscription, or human and animal census or storage inventory. Nevertheless, interesting parallels could be drawn with the Homeric epics: Pylos is mentioned at the head of nine other towns that profess allegiance to it – both in Homer and on the tablets;[1] again, a seven-town coastal strip mentioned in the *Iliad* finds a parallel in a strip of seven coastal settlements referred to on one of the tablets. And to Blegen's great satisfaction Pylos was found repeatedly mentioned on the tablets retrieved from the palace he identified as Nestor's.[2]

Nestor's name, however, was not found.

The tablets, originally not fired but only dried, would have disintegrated long ago, were it not for the fire that destroyed the palace and baked the tablets. A great conflagration raged over the structure; it came rather suddenly, since most furniture, pottery, the contents of the storage rooms and archives were not removed: but humans all fled.[3]

Blegen placed the destruction not long after the Trojan War, at the close of the Mycenaean Age.[4]

However, no signs of warfare, siege, re-occupation by people of another culture or occupation in general were found.[5]

The palace presented Blegen and his collaborators with problems not unlike those that were to occupy him later at Troy. In the report of the excavations Blegen wrote: "In some places ... in the upper black layer ... were found, along with the usual Mycenaean pottery, a few glazed sherds of Late Geometric Style, as in so many other parts of the site, where similar deposits were encountered."[6]

Linear B Deciphered

For a long time the Linear B script did not disclose its secret to those who worked on its solution. Nor was the decipherment facilitated by the manner in which Sir Arthur Evans published the texts of the Lin-

---

[1] *Iliad* II. 591-94; Blegen and Rawson: *The Palace of Nestor*, vol. I, pt. 1, p. 419.
[2] *The Palace of Nestor*, loc. cit.
[3] *Ibid.*, p. 424.
[4] *Ibid.*, p. 422.
[5] *Ibid.*, p. 422.
[6] *The Palace of Nestor*, p. 300.

ear B tablets – not all at once, but seriatim. When Blegen discovered the Linear B tablets on the Greek mainland in the ruins of the ancient palace in Pylos, they were ascribed to the Heroic Age of Troy, the final stage of the Mycenaean Age that ended abruptly.

Yet even after the Linear B tablets were found on the mainland of Greece their language was not thought to be Greek. The reason for that was, first of all, in the accepted chronological scale: the Ionian age, according to conventional chronology, was separated from the Mycenaean Age by five hundred years. Greek writing appears for the first time in the eighth century. Efforts to read the tablets made by classical philologists were unsuccessful, and whatever clue was tried out, the result was negative.

One of the most important and far-reaching theses of the reconstructin of ancient history is in the conclusion that the so-called Dark Ages of the Greek and Anatolian histories are but artifacts of the historians, and never took place. The Mycenaean Age ended in the eighth century and was followed by the Ionic times, with no centuries intervening, the break in culture being but the consequence of natural upheavals of the eighth century and of the subsequent migrations of peoples. Consequently the Ionic culture must show great affinity with the Mycenaean heritage; and therefore I have claimed that the Linear B script would prove to be Greek; but this was not a view that had many supporters.

In 1950 the eminent authority on Homeric Greece, Helen L. Lorimer, in her treatise *Homer and the Monuments* wrote of this script and of the efforts to read it: "The result is wholly unfavorable to any hope entertained that the language of the inscriptions might be Greek."

Nevertheless, on the occasion of addressing the Forum of the Graduate College of Princeton University on October 4, 1953, I formulated my expectations:

> I expect new evidence from the Minoan Scripts and the so-called Hittite pictographs. Texts in the Minoan (Linear B) script were found years ago on Crete and in Mycenae and in several other places on the Greek mainland. I believe that when the Minoan writings unearthed in Mycenae are deciphered they will be found to be Greek. I also claim that these texts are of a later date than generally believed. "No 'Dark Age' of six centuries' duration intervened in Greece between the Mycenaean Age and the Ionian Age of the seventh century."

The address was printed as a supplement to *Earth in Upheaval*, but the last passage in the address was quoted from my *Theses for the Reconstruction of Ancient History*, published eight years earlier, in 1945.[1]

When speaking to the Princeton Forum in October 1953 I did not know that a young English architect was by then on the verge of publishing the solution to the riddle of the Linear B script. Only six months passed since my addressing the Graduate Forum, and the April 9, 1954 front page news of *The New York Times* made known the exciting performance of decoding Linear B by Michael Ventris. The ancient script "that for the last half century and longer has baffled archaeologists and linguists has been decoded finally – by an amateur." Ventris, an architect and "leisure-time scholar of pre-classic scripts", served as a cryptographer during World War II. The script that had been tried without avail in a variety of languages – Hittite, Sumerian and Basque among others – was found by Ventris to be Greek.[2]

Ventris as a boy attended a lecture by Sir Arthur Evans on the Minoan tablets with unread scripts and, like Schliemann who since boyhood was determined to find Troy and the tomb of Agamemnon, was intrigued to decipher the script of which he heard Evans speak. Thus the greatest discoveries in the world of classical studies were made by non-specialists, a merchant and an architect.

But Ventris was not immediately on the right path. In 1949 he had sent out a questionnaire on Linear B to leading authorities on Aegean questions; he privately distributed the replies in 1950 as *The Languages of the Minoan and Mycenaean Civilizations* (known as the "Mid-Century Report"). None of his queried correspondents came upon the right trail.

In 1962 Leonard R. Palmer testified as to the stand the Hellenic scholars and Ventris himself had taken prior to the achievement; in his book *Mycenaeans and Minoans*, Palmer wrote: "Evans ventured no guess at the possible affinities of the Minoan language. That it was Greek never entered his head." Also Blegen, who was the first to find the tablets on Greek soil, "was 'almost certain' that the language of his

---

[1] In this publication, distributed only to a limited number of large libraries in Europe and America, I stated, without any elaboration, the findings to which I had come in the work of reconstruction of ancient history, thus outlining the projected *Ages in Chaos* and its sequel volumes.

[2] Cf. J. Chadwick: *The Decipherment of Linear B* (Cambridge, 1958).

tablets was 'Minoan' ... Nor did the possibility that the Linear B tablets concealed the Greek language occur to Michael Ventris." He "guessed that the language was related to Etruscan ... This wrong diagnosis was maintained by Ventris right up to the final stages of his decipherment."

> It figures in the so-called 'Mid-Century Report,' which records what could be deduced by the most eminent living authorities from the archaeological and other evidence available at the time preceding the decipherment of the script. The remarkable fact stands out that not one of the scholars concerned suggested that the language could be Greek.

But a few years more and Ventris found the true solution. Even then loud voices of skepticism and opposition made themselves heard.[1]

But the method being perfected disclosed more and more Greek words and names which could not result from a mistaken decipherment. The entire field of early Greek civilization experienced the greatest shock since the discovery of Troy. To the even greater surprise of the scholarly world the names of the deities of the Greek pantheon, supposedly "created" by Homer and Hesiod, were found on the deciphered Linear B tablets.

The reading of these tablets in the Greek language raised the question: How could a literate people in the fourteenth century become illiterate for almost five centuries, to regain literacy in the eighth century? Thus the problem already answered in *Ages in Chaos* was brought into relief, and a heretical idea crept into the minds of a few scholars: is there some mistake in the accepted timetable? In the last century a Dark Age of five centuries' duration between the Mycenaean and the Ionian ages was forced upon the scholars of the Greek past by students of Egyptology, and in three quarters of a century this notion, first bitterly opposed, became as bitterly defended by the new generation of classical scholars, only to be confronted with the riddle of the Mycenaean tablets written in Greek more than five hundred years before the oldest known Greek inscription in alphabetic characters adapted from the Hebrew-Phoenician script.

Ventris died young, in an auto accident, soon after his triumph. One of the most tantalizing riddles of classical archaeology was solved, but not without creating some puzzling situations. The Homeric Question, instead of being solved, grew now to astonishing, one would like to say, Homeric, proportions.

---

[1] E.g., that of Prof. Beattie in *Journal of Hellenic Studies* 76 (1956), pp. 1ff.

The Greek Pantheon

When the texts in Linear B were read the so-called Homeric problem did not approach a solution but, contrariwise, grew more urgent, more enigmatic, more perplexing.

Since antiquity it had been believed that "Homer and Hesiod were the first to compose Theogonies, and give the gods their epithets..."[1] Therefore reading the names of Greek gods and goddesses on the Linear B tables from Knossos on Crete and Pylos on the mainland was something of a shock to classical scholars.[2] Hera, Artemis and Hermes were worshipped in Pylos. Zeus and Poseidon were worshipped in Pylos and Knossos. Athene was deified in Knossos; Dionysus' name was found on a Pylos tablet.[3]

With Greek gods and goddesses spelled by their names on the tablets, it was conducive to recognize Apollo in a figure on a vase, singing among the Muses, or Poseidon in a figure depicted driving a chariot over the sea, or Zeus with Europa in the depiction of a bull carrying a woman. The Minotaur and centaurs were recognized as likely Mycenaean images.[4]

Not less unexpected were the names of Achaean heroes known from the Homeric epics when found on the Pylos and Knossos tablets, and a "wealth of Trojan names," too. Ajax (called by his patronymic "Telamonian") and his brother, Telamonian Teucer, have namesakes in Homer; "and between them they killed two Trojans with tablet names Pyrasos and Ophelestas, and a third Simoeisios, whose father's name, Anthemos, occurs at Knossos." Hector's name and Priam's name, and that of Tros, are found in Pylos. Achilles' name is found both at Knossos and at Pylos, and Kastor's at Knossos.[5]

---

[1] Herodotus II.53

[2] *M. Ventris and J. Chadwick wondered that the tablets "unexpectedly reveal the worship of gods and goddesses known from classical sources" – *Documents in Mycenaean Greek* (Cambridge University Press, 1956), p. 275

[3] *M. Ventris and J. Chadwick: *Documents in Mycenaean Greek*, second ed. (Cambridge University Press, 1973), pp. 279, 286-288. Cf. G. Mylonas: *Mycenae and the Mycenaean Age* (Princeton, 1966), pp. 159-160; F. R. Adrados: »Les Institutions religieuses mycéniennes« — III »Les dieux et leur culte« in *Minos* XI (1972), pp 183-192; A. Heubeck: *Aus der Welt der frühgriechischen Lineartafeln* (Göttingen, 1966), pp. 96-106.

[4] These and the following examples are from T. B. L. Webster: *From Mycenae to Homer* (London, 1958)

[5] *Ibid.*, p. 101; *D. H. F. Gray: »Mycenaean Names in Homer«, *Journal of Hellenic Studies* 78 (1958), pp. 43-48; D. Page: *History and the Homeric Iliad* (University of California Press, 1959), pp. 197-199.

In Homer Laodokos's father is Antenor and on a Pylos tablet Laodokos holds land in a village or suburb where Antenor is mayor. In Homer Laodokos is from Pylos, where the tablet with his name was found.

Aigyptos of the *Odyssey* has a namesake on a Knossos tablet; admittedly, there was no contact with Egypt during the Dark Ages and until the seventh century, and how could a bard of one of those centuries, if the epos was not yet completed in the Mycenaean Age, come upon calling a hero after the river Nile, asked T. B. Webster. The name Neritos is met in both, the *Iliad* and the *Odyssey*, and it was thought to be a misnomer for some Greek term, corrupted in the later versions of the epics to look as a private name, but the name was found on a table as that of a sheep owner. "Unfortunately the establishment of Neritos as a good Mycenaean name does not help the difficult geographical problem of Ithaca's location."

The campaign of the *Seven against Thebes* and the sack of the city by the Epigoni are alluded to by Homer. "Mycenaean names in the story are Amphiaros (Knossos), Adrastos, Eteocles, Polyphontes (Pylos)." One of the sons of Eteocles in Pylos was called Alektryon, a name known from the *Iliad* (XVII.602). In Pylos a man was called Theseus and men at Knossos bore the names Selenos and Iakchos known from the *Odyssey*. The name Aeneas is read on a tablet from Mycenae. Phegeus' name, found in the *Iliad* (V.10f) is found also on a tablet from Mycenae. The Trojan Pedasos (*Iliad* VI.21) had a namesake at Knossos.

Not less amazing are the attributes and adjectives accompanying the names as used by Homer and found on the tablets. "The evidence of the tablets" is "that such formulae as Telamonian Ajax were Mycenaean titles."[1] Nestor of Homer "has Mycenaean titles";[2] Agamemnon's title "wanax" is "certainly Mycenaean";[3] "king of men" is a title most probably "remembered from Mycenaean poetry" half a millennium before Homer.[4]

> The epithet hippiocharmes (chariot-fighter), which is applied to Troilos in the Iliad and to Amythaon (a name found on the Pylos tablets) in the Odyssey, has been recognized as derived from the Mycenaean word for chariot.[5]

---

[1] Webster: *From Mycenae to Homer*, p. 286
[2] Ibid., p. 218.
[3] Ibid., p. 121; *Page: *History and the Homeric Iliad*, pp. 188 and 209, n. 48.
[4] Webster: *From Mycenae to Homer*, p. 107.
[5] Ibid., p. 103; *Page: *History and the Homeric Iliad*, pp. 190 and 209, n. 55.

If five hundred years separate Homer from the tablets, is it not a cause for wonder that the poet should know these names and titles and use them for his epics?

Mycenaean City Names in the *Iliad*

Most notable among the passages in the *Iliad* traceable to Mycenaean times is the so-called *Catalogue of Cities and Ships*.[1]

It is an enumeration, in the second book of the *Iliad*, of the contributions in ships made by various cities and towns of the Achaeans or Greeks of the Heroic Age to the expedition against Troy. There are scores of localities in the list and many of them, actually about half, did not survive into the modern Ionian Age; then how could the Greek poet, separated from the Mycenaean Age by dark centuries, have had such an extensive and detailed knowledge of these localities?

Archaeological research has already identified the ruins of quite a few sites which had not been rebuilt and were not known in the classical period of Greece; and it is safe to assume that future digging will reveal more of the cities of this list. By assuming that the oral delivery from one generation to another can account for the survival of the epics, it is also necessary to assume that a long list of localities, many of them small, many of them no more extant, was capable of surviving by means of such oral tradition. But would generations of bards carry over centuries of the Dark Ages the multitudinous names of towns and villages of which nothing was extant for century upon century? It is conceivable that a few names of ancient palace cities would defy time and survive in the memory of bards. But to assume that almost a hundred names of localities that were but abandoned mounds in the time when the *Iliad* was put to writing survived in that manner implies nothing short of a miracle. In the view of Denys Page, "There is no escape from this conclusion: the names in the Catalogue afford proof positive and unrefuted that the Catalogue offers a truthful, though se-

---

[1] See R. Hope Simpson and J. F. Lazenby: *The Catalogue of the Ships in Homer's Iliad* (Oxford University Press, 1970). *Several scholars claim the Catalogue to be a compilation of the late eighth or early seventh centuries. See Rhys Carpenter: *Folk Tale, Fiction, and Saga in the Homeric Epics* (Berkeley, 1946). J. Chadwick held a similar view. Here again is the five-hundred year controversy.

lective, description of Mycenaean Greece."[1] At the same time, "there is no scrap of evidence, and no reason whatsoever to assume, that the art of writing was practiced in Greece between the end of the Mycenaean era and the eighth century B.C."[2]

Yet "it is inconceivable that such a list should have been first compiled during or after the Dark Ages."[3] But is it a solution that bards transmitted all those names?[4]

And where did the bards sing? Was not the land without palaces and with hardly any houses of occupation?

Denys Page continues on the subject with growing wonderment: "Descriptive epithets are attached to some fifty of the place names. ... Many of the epithets are distinctive, not generally applicable. One place is a meadowland, another is rocky; one place is rich in vineyards, another is famous for its sheep; one place is rugged, another has many flowers; one place is on a riverbank, another on the seashore." "Let us ask," Page continues, "how could an Ionian poet living in the 10th or 9th or 8th century B.C. know how to describe so many places – some of them very obscure places – all over Greece? How could he know that there were many doves at Messe (if anyone could still find the place); and vineyards at Hine (if it had not yet been swallowed up by the lake); that Aegylips was rugged, Olosson white, Enispe windy, Ptellos a meadowland, Helos on the coast?"[5]

And is it thinkable that the bards came to Greece from the Aegean coast of Asia Minor towards the end of the Dark Ages? But Asia Minor together with its Ionian coast was also immersed in a Dark Age;

---

[1] Page: op. cit. *A. R. Burn: *Minoans, Philistines and Greeks: B.C. 1400-900* (London, 1930), p. 10: "The Catalogue ... has all the appearance of being a genuine document dating from before the Dorian invasion and the Ionian migration. ...".

[2] Page: op. cit., p. 123.

[3] Page: *History and the Homeric Iliad*, p. 122. Cf.G. S. Kirk: *The Language and Background of Homer* (Cambridge, 1964), p. 175. *Kirk writes: "... Much of the substance of the Catalogue of Achaean contingents in the second book of the Iliad, which gives a complex and largely accurate survey of the Mycenaean geography, disrupted by the Dorian invasion, can hardly have been completed more than a generation or so later than the final upheaval..." But cf. Chadwick (*Minos* (1975), pp. 56-58).

[4] Cf. Rhys Carpenter: *Folk Tale, Fiction, and Saga in the Homeric Epics* (Berkeley, Ca, 1946).

[5] Page: *History and the Homeric Iliad*, p. 123. *Carpenter (*Folk Tale, Fiction, and Saga in the Homeric Epics*, pp. 178-79) denies the possibility of such accurate transmissions and argues instead that the Catalogue points "to the situation in early archaic classical times when Pheidon had extended his rule over Argos, when a league of towns was forming in Boeotia. ..." His view that Homer wrote about recent events does not in fact contradict the assertions by Page and others that the Catalogue refers to Mycenaean times. Cf. also Chadwick in *Minos* (1975) pp. 56-58.

nor was there recovered a palace in which a bard upon return from Greece could sing of those Mycenaean cities, towns and hamlets – so impoverished was the Greek region of Asia Minor during the Dark Ages, with the highland of Anatolia being quite empty of any human habitation.[1]

The problem of the Mycenaean heritage in the Homeric poetry is staggering and remains unresolved through hundreds of volumes dealing with it; it is the despair of anyone endeavoring to solve it within the framework of the accepted chronological timetable.

The Mycenaean Dialect

When Mycenaean Linear B was deciphered by Michael Ventris, it was thought to be an archaic form of Greek, preceding Homer by almost five centuries. A name was proposed for it – "Old Achaean." However, a closer examination of Mycenaean resulted in a startling conclusion expressed by A. Tovar:

> But contrary to what we expect from Greek documents of the fourteenth and thirteenth centuries B.C., the Mycenaean dialect is not seen to be closer to proto-Greek than are Homer or Thucydides. If sometimes Mycenaean shows very primitive features, it also sometimes appears more advanced than the dialects of the first millennium.[2]

John Chadwick, who collaborated with Ventris in the decipherment of Linear B, writes:

> Since 1952 important new work has modified the general view and this has entailed a shift of emphasis, and the abandonment of the name proposed for this dialect, 'Old Achaean.'[3]

The Mycenaean Linear B dialect was found to be best preserved in the southern (Arcado-Cyprian) group, and to be distinct from the Ionian-Attic dialect; the theory that Mycenaean was the mother tongue of all Greek dialects conflicts with the fact expressed in these words:

---

[1] See above, section »The Dark Age in Asia Minor«.
[2] A. Tovar: »On the Position of the Linear B Dialect«, *Mycenaean Studies*, ed. by E.L. Bennet, Jr. (University of Wisconsin Press, 1964).
[3] J. Chadwick: *Decipherment*, p. 78.

But Mycenaean presents many dialectal phenomena of quite recent aspect and is in some traits as far from 'common [early] Greek' as the dialects known a millennium later.[1]

Against the view of E. Risch that Mycenaean was the proto-language of all Greek dialects, Tovar writes: "The weak point in Risch's argument is that it ignores the fact that against the innovations which appear in Mycenaean (and Arcado-Cyprian), Ionic shows many old forms." E. Benveniste, too, expressed his criticism of the view of Mycenaean as proto-Greek, or "Old Achaean":

> It must be admitted that according to the hypothesis maintained by Risch during this period [the 450 years between the last Mycenaean texts and the first literary testimony in eighth-century Greek] a remarkable conservation of Mycenaean was upheld in its Arcado-Cypriote dialect and a profound evolution of Mycenaean in its Ionian dialect took place. Is it not more plausible to assume that in the epoch of our tablets the Ionian (not represented in the tablets) already substantially differed?[2]

Four hundred and fifty years passed between the last Mycenaean texts and the first literary testimony. Is not the confusion discussed here a result of this erroneous premise? If the true figure is something like sixty years and not five hundred, all perplexities disappear.

Cadmus

The classical Greek alphabet, its order of letters, and their form, were borrowed from the Hebrew-Phoenician alphabet; alpha, beta, gamma, delta, are but Grecized aleph, beth, gimel, daleth of the Hebrew language.[3]

In early times Greek was also written from right to left, as Hebrew is still written today.

Cadmus, the legendary hero who came to Greece from Phoenicia and founded Thebes in Boeotia, is credited with the introduction of the Hebrew or "Phoenician" alphabet to the Greek language; in its

---

[1] Tovar, p. 146.
[2] E. Benveniste in *Etudes myceniennes* (Paris, 1956) p. 263.
[3] *Aleph* means "ox" in Hebrew; *beth* means "house" etc. The corresponding letter names have no meaning in Greek.

Hellenized early form the alphabet is called Cadmeian. As Herodotus tells the story,

> The Phoenicians who came with Cadmus ... introduced into Greece, after their settlement in the country, a number of accomplishments, of which the most important was writing, an art till then, I think, unknown to the Greeks. At first they used the same characters as all the other Phoenicians, but as time went on, and they changed their language, they also changed the shape of their letters. At that period most of the Greeks in the neighborhood were Ionians; they were taught these letters by the Phoenicians and adopted them, with a few alterations, for their own use, continuing to refer to them as the Phoenician characters – as was only right, as the Phoenicians had introduced them.[1]

However, Cadmus, the founder of Thebes, preceded by several generations the Trojan War; on this the Greek tradition is unanimous. Tradition also has it that the Cadmeian alphabet originally consisted of sixteen letters and that four additional characters were introduced later, about the time of the Trojan War.[2]

The Theban cycle of legends deals with the time preceding the Trojan War. Thebes in Boeotia was outside of the Mycenaean dominion. No contingent from Thebes participated with the other Greek cities in the Trojan War for, according to tradition, Thebes as a city had been reduced shortly before the new war started. With the conventional date of the Trojan War in the beginning of the twelfth century, Cadmus needed to be placed in the fourteenth: His dynasty comprised several generations of rulers before the Epigoni conquered and ruined the Boeotian Thebes; some of the Epigoni later participated in the siege of Troy.

This order of events in the semi-historical, semi-legendary Greek past conflicts with the fact that the Cadmeian alphabet has not been found in Greece before about the middle of the eighth century. Furthermore, because of certain characteristics in their form, the earliest Cadmeian letters bear the best resemblance to the Hebrew-Phoenician letters of the ninth century – as exemplified by the Mesha stele.[3]

---

[1] Herodotus: *The Histories* V. 58 (transl. by A. de Selincourt, 1954).

[2] {Annotation by Edwin Schorr:} There were three traditions, each of which placed him at a different period – three, six or nine generations before the Trojan War. See R. B. Edwards: *Kadmos, the Phoenician* (Amsterdam, 1979), pp. 165f.

[3] King Mesha of Moab was a contemporary of King Ahab of Samaria. See *Ages in Chaos*, vol. I, Sections »Mesha's Rebellion« and »The "Great Indignation"«.

But in Greece no inscription in Cadmeian letters was found that could be attributed to even so early a time as the ninth century. Therefore among the classical epigraphists a protracted debate was waged between those who claimed a date in the ninth century as the time the Cadmeian alphabet was introduced into Greece and those who claimed the seventh century.[1] Yet independently of the question whether the Cadmeian letters originated in the ninth or in the seventh century, it is generally agreed that the fourteenth century is out of the question;[2] but even should we follow the proponents of the earlier date – that of the mid-ninth century –, we still would be at pains to harmonize dates so far apart as the ninth and fourteenth centuries, the date assigned to Cadmus. If the tradition about Cadmus, the originator of the Greek alphabet, has any historical value,[3] and if Cadmus lived in the ninth century, his descendants, participants in the Trojan War, could not have flourished about -1200.

---

[1] At that time the Cadmeian alphabet had not been found in Greece before the seventh century. However, since this debate between Carpenter and Ullman, an inscription of the middle of the eighth century has come to light, the earliest known inscription in Greek employing the Cadmeian letters.

[2] Cf. the debate between Rhys Carpenter (»The Antiquity of the Greek Alphabet«, *American Journal of Archaeology* 37 (1933) pp. 8-29) and B. Ullman (»How Old is the Greek Alphabet?« in *American Journal of Archaeology* 38 (1934) pp. 359-381). Cf. P. Kyle McCarter Jr.: *The Antiquity of the Greek Alphabet and Early Phoenician Scripts* (Ann Arbor, 1975). *Cf. also Carpenter's reply: »The Greek Alphabet Again« in the same journal, vol. 42 (1938) pp. 58-69. While Carpenter defended a date ca. -700 for the adoption of the alphabet by the Greeks, Ullman argued for "the eleventh or twelfth century or even earlier as the time for the introduction of the alphabet into Greece." A. Mentz (»Die Urgeschichte des Alphabets«, *Rheinisches Museum für Philologie* 85 (1936) pp. 347-366) judged Ullman's proposed dates to be too low and suggested ca. -1400 as the date for the adoption of the alphabet, based on the Cadmus tradition. W. Dörpfeld (*Alt-Olympia* II (Berlin, 1935) pp. 401-409), V. Bérard (*Les Phéniciens et l'Odyssée* (Paris, 1927-28) held similar views. Cf. also Livio C. Stecchini: »The Origin of the Alphabet«, *The American Behavioral Scientist* IV.6 (February, 1961), pp. 2-7.

[3] *M. C. Astour has suggested (*Hellenosemitica* (Leiden, 1967) p. 168) that Linear B, the administrative script of the Myceneans and Minoans, was what the later Greeks remembered as *phoinikeia grammata*, or "Phoenician letters," introduced by Cadmus. There appears to be little justification for such a view since the Linear B script had, as far as is known, no connection to Phoenicia, whereas the Greek alphabet was directly adapted from the ninth-eighth century Hebrew-Phoenician script. Herodotus' statement on the subject could not be less ambiguous. In the same book, Astour vigorously defends Cadmus' Phoenician origin (pp. 147ff.) Cf. J. Rason: »La Cadmée, Knossos et le linéaire B«, *Revue archéologique* (1977) p. 79.

Chapter 4

A Gap Closed

Seismology and Chronology

Independently of my effort to construe a synchronical history starting with the common event that overwhelmed and vexed all nations of the globe – the great catastrophe that ended the Middle Kingdom – a similar effort was made by Claude F. A. Schaeffer, Professor at College de France. The reader of *Ages in Chaos* is familiar with his work of excavating Ras-Shamra (Ugarit) from the chapter carrying this title. He observed in Ras-Shamra on the Syrian coast obvious signs of great destruction that pointed to violent earthquakes, tidal waves, and other signs of a natural disaster. At the occasion of his visit to Troy, excavated by C. Blegen, Schaeffer became aware that Troy was destroyed by the elements – and repeatedly so – at the same times when Ras-Shamra was destroyed.

The distance from the Dardanelles, near which the mound of Troy lies, to Ras-Shamra is about six hundred miles on a straight line. In modern annals of seismology no earthquake is known to have affected so wide an area. Schaeffer investigated the excavated places in Asia Minor, and the archaeologists' reports, and in every place found the same picture. He turned his attention to Persia, farther to the East – and the very same signs of catastrophes were evident in each and every excavated place. Then he turned his attention to the Caucasus – and there, too, the similarity of the causes and effects was undeniable. In his own excavations on Cyprus he could once more establish the very same series of interventions by the frenzied elements of nature. He was so impressed by what he found that during the next few years he put into writing a voluminous work, *Stratigraphie comparée et chronologie de l'Asie occidentale (IIIe et IIe millennaires),* published by Oxford University Press in 1948. In over six hundred pages supplemented by many tables, he presented his thesis.

Several times during the third and second millennia before the present era the ancient East was disturbed by stupendous catastrophes; he also found evidence that in the fourth, as well as in the first millennium, the ancient East went through great natural paroxysms, but their description Schaeffer reserved for future publications. In the published work covering the third and second millennia, Schaeffer discerned five or six great upheavals. The greatest of these took place at the very end of the Early Bronze, or the Old Kingdom in Egypt. At each of these occurrences, life was suddenly disturbed and the flow of history interrupted. Schaeffer also indicated that his acquaintance with European archaeology made him feel certain that Europe, too, was involved in those catastrophes; if so, they must have been more than continental – actually global in dimension.

Thus Schaeffer, like myself, came to the conviction that the ancient world was disturbed by repeated upheavals. We even arrived at the same number of disturbances, a common realization of their grandiose nature, and the same relative dating of these events. However, we came to the same conclusions travelling by entirely different routes. In this there was a considerable assurance of our having closely approached the historical truth.

A reader unequipped to follow Schaeffer through his large and technical volume may well let the last chapter (*Résumé et Conclusion*) impress him by its questions and answers. In concluding his book Schaeffer epitomized: "Our inquiry has demonstrated that these repeated crises which opened and closed the principal periods ... were caused not by the action of man. Far from it – because, compared with the vastness of these all-embracing crises and their profound effects, the exploits of conquerors and all combinations of state politics would appear only very insignificant. The philosophy of the history of antiquity of the East appears to us singularly deformed" – namely, by describing the past of nations and civilizations as the history of dynasties, rather than as a history of great ages, and by ignoring the role physical causes played in their sequence.

As to the chronology – in his printed work Schaeffer follows with certain reservations the accepted timetable. In correspondence, however, he envisaged the possibility of shortening the Egyptian history, but not to the extent claimed in *Ages in Chaos*. Then how can we be in agreement as to the times of the catastrophes?

The answer lies in the fact that both of us relate these catastrophes to the termination of the (identical) great periods in history. In other words, we are in agreement as to the relative chronology, not the absolute one.

At the end of his long discourse, Schaeffer also made clear his stand even before he became aware of my work. He wrote: "The value of absolute dates adopted by us depends, understandably, to an extent on the degree of precision obtained in the field of study of the historic documents that can be used for chronology and that derive from those collected in Egypt, Palestine, Asia Minor, Mesopotamia, and Persia."

Thus the absolute dates used in his work are dependent on chronology that in its turn depends on historical documents. But he adds: "On the other hand, thanks to the improvement of archaeological methods, today we no longer depend so completely on epigraphic documentation for an absolute chronology."

I regard myself very fortunate that the task of presenting the archaeological evidence from the lands of the Middle and Near East was performed by a scholar of great stature, Claude F. A. Schaeffer. The almost superhuman enterprise of unraveling the manifold ramifications of the recent tribulations of this planet was not committed all to one scholar.

Celestial Events in the *Iliad*

The eighth century, starting with -776, was together with the beginning of the seventh a period of great natural upheavals. Populations migrated, partly to Asia Minor, and other populations descended from the north. The siege of Troy might therefore have been an effort of the Greeks to plant a foothold on the coast of Asia Minor. The true time of the events recounted in the *Iliad* was the second half of the eighth and the beginning of the seventh centuries before the present era.

In *Worlds in Collision* an effort was made to recognize in the description of theomachy and of the natural phenomena that accompanied the battle of the gods, the events that took place in the sky and on earth between -747 and -687.[1]

---

[1] See *Worlds in Collision*, section »When Was the Iliad Created?«

The Trojan War was waged to the accompaniment of blows exchanged by the planetary gods – Earth (Hera), Moon (Aphrodite), Venus (Athene), Mars (Ares) and Jupiter (Zeus).

These celestial phenomena could not have taken place in the sky over Troy alone: The entire world had to witness the events, if they were not mere creations of the bard. That they were not can be deduced from the fact that these very events, witnessed in all parts of the world, are also described in sacred epics from Finland (*Kalevala*), Lapland and Iceland (*Edda*), from Mexico, Peru, India, the South Sea Islands, China and Japan, and, of course, by the poets and dramatists, annalists and astronomers, of the Near and Far East. It would require repeating close to two hundred pages of *Worlds in Collision*, actually the entire part II (Mars) of that book, should we desire here to evidence and illuminate this in some detail.

Perturbations in the celestial sphere, or Theomachy, in which Mars endangered the Earth at nearly regular intervals during this century, preoccupied the minds of men and repeatedly intervened in human history. Pestilence also broke out, and many references in the cuneiform literature ascribe its cause to Nergal (Mars). Earthquakes, overflooding, change of climate, evidenced by Klimasturz, did not spare a single land. These changes moved entire nations to migrations. Calendars were repeatedly thrown out of order and reformed – and the reader will find abundant material in the second part of *Worlds in Collision* and also in *Earth in Upheaval*, where no human testimony, but only the testimony of nature was presented; and this material could be multiplied by any dedicated researcher.

It appears, however, that in the *Iliad* Homer telescoped into a few weeks events that took place in the space of several decades. At least some of the events may be placed in a chronological order with the help of ancient Israelite sources: Namely, on the day when King Ahaz was interred the motion of the Earth was disturbed so that the Sun set before its appointed time;[1] at the time of the destruction of Sennacherib's army in the days of Hezekiah, son of Ahaz, another disturbance occurred with the contrary effect: the Sun appeared to return several degrees to the east before proceeding on its regular westward path. It is asserted in the rabbinical literature that the second disturbance rectified the effects of the first – and this is also the meaning of the

---

[1] *Tractate Sanhedrin* 96a; *Pirkei Rabbi Elieser* 52. Cf. L. Ginzberg: *The Legends of the Jews* (Philadelphia, 1929) vol. VI, p. 367, n. 81.

sentence in Isaiah 38:8: "So the sun returned ten degrees by which degrees it was gone down."[1]

In Greek legendary tradition the first event took place in the days of the two brothers, Atreus and Thyestes, contesting the throne of Mycenae – when, according to Seneca, the Sun set earlier than usual.[2]

Yet a certain compression or amalgamating of two events, separated in time, must have taken place, for another version of the story tells of a reversal of the sun's motion. This version is recorded by Apollodorus and several other authors.[3]

The event described as the reversal of motion of the sun took place, as illuminated *Worlds in Collision*, on March 23rd, -687.[4]

The fixing of the event to the early spring of -687 is made on the strength of the information from Hebrew sources that the event took place on the night of Passover, during the second campaign of Sennacherib against Judah, the ninth campaign of his reign. The exact date for the last of this series of catastrophes[5] is provided by the records of the astronomical observations of the Chinese, where we learn that in the year -687, on the 23rd of March, "during the night the fixed stars did not appear, though the sky was clear. In the middle of the night stars fell like rain."[6]

This date is also confirmed by Roman sources – Romulus found his end during a celestial-terrestrial catastrophe connected with the planet Mars:

> Both the poles shook, and Atlas lifted the burden of the sky ... The sun vanished and rising clouds obscured the heaven ... the sky was riven by shooting flames. The people fled and the king [Romulus] upon his father's [Mars'] steeds soared to the stars.[7]

---

[1] Cf. II Kings 20:9ff.; Hippolytus on Isaiah, and sources cited above, fn. 1.

[2] Seneca: *Thyestes*: "Not yet does Vesper, twilight's messenger, summon the fires of night ... the ploughman with oxen yet unwearied stands amazed at his supper hour's quick coming." *Cf. Plato: *The Statesman* 269a.

[3] Apollodorus, Bk. II, ch. xii; cf. scholium to the Iliad II.106; Euripides: *Electra* 699-730; *Orestes* 996-1012; Plato: *The Statesman* 268e.

[4] See *Worlds in Collision*, section »March 23rd«. *See also *Iliad* II 413ff., where an expected delay in the setting of the Sun during the siege of Troy is mentioned.

[5] The other dates are -747, and -701; -776 is also connected with celestial events between Venus and Mars that did not, however, directly affect the Earth. See *Worlds in Collision*, section »The Year -747«.

[6] E. Biot: *Catalogue général des étoiles filantes et des autres météors observés en Chine après le VIIe siècle avant J.C.* (Paris, 1846). The statement is based on old Chinese sources ascribed to Confucius. "The night was bright" adds the Tso Chuen commentary (J. Legge: *The Chinese Classics* vol. 15, p. 80).

[7] Ovid: *Fasti*, transl. by J. Frazer, Vol. II, lines 489ff.

Romulus was a contemporary of Hezekiah;[1] and the 23rd of March was the most important day in the Roman cult of Mars.[2]

We must not forget that the Romans and the Greeks worshipped their gods in the planets, not as gods of the planets. Invocations to the gods, such as the Homeric Hymn to Ares (Mars) are addressed directly to the planet as an astral power.[3]

The siege of Troy under Agamemnon followed by less than one generation the natural disturbances of the days of his father Atreus, when this king of Mycenae competed with his brother Thyestes for the crown of the realm and the Sun was disrupted in its motion.

Atreus and Thyestes, being contemporaries of Ahaz and Hezekiah, and Agamemnon, son of Atreus, a contemporary of the latter king of Jerusalem, it seems that the time in which the drama of the *Iliad* was set was the second half of the eighth century, and not later than -687;[4] yet the poet condensed the events separated by decades into the tenth year of the Trojan siege, the time of the *Iliad*'s action.[5]

Thus we come to realize that it was a rather late time; clearly Homer could not have lived before the events he described; and therefore Homer's time cannot be any earlier than the end of the eighth century. But more probably he wrote several decades after the Trojan War, when the events of the war had become enveloped in a veil due to a certain remoteness in time, and obtained a halo of heroic, god-like exploits. The *Odyssey*, describing the wanderings of Odysseus after the Trojan War, requires, too, a distancing between the poet and the Trojan War, on the assumption that both Homeric poems were the product of one author. If not of one, then we must assume that two poets of unique genius lived close in time to one another.

Placed in its true time, the Trojan War may obtain some historical plausibility; and, as we have seen, its mythological parts also serve,

---

[1] Augustine: *The City of God*, Bk. XVIII, Chap. 27.

[2] W. W. Fowler: »Mars« in *Encyclopaedia Britannica*, 14th ed.

[3] W. H. Roscher: *Ausführliches Lexikon der griechischen und römischen Mythologie*, s.v. »Ares«.

[4] If to harmonize the involved chronological problems the debacle of Sennacherib's army needs to be placed fifteen years earlier (not in -687 but in -701), and the first invasion in -715, and the beginning of Hezekiah's reign in -729, then I would need to change the date for the last global catastrophe from -687 to -701 or -702. *See also *Worlds in Collision*, section »When Was the Iliad Created?«: "... The time of the birth of the Iliad must be lowered to -747 at least, and probably to an even later date."

[5] At least two conjunctions between Venus and Mars are described in the *Iliad*, in the Fifth and Twenty-first Books. See *Worlds in Collision*, section »When Was the Iliad Created?«.

instead of obfuscation, to the elucidation of some complex chronological problems. With theomachy displayed on the celestial screen, the story in the *Iliad* gains, rather than loses, its historical validity.

Changes in Land and Sea

The celestial phenomena that pervade the narrative of the *Iliad* and even dominate it in books five, twenty and twenty-one, were accompanied also by terrestrial changes – Earth, called Hera, participated in the strife among the gods. In the *Iliad* these terrestrial disturbances are narrated too: Earthquakes shook the Trojan plain amid the battle of the celestial gods.

> Then terribly thundered the father of the gods and men from on high; and beneath did Poseidon cause the vast earth to quake and the steep crests of the mountains. All the roots of many-fountained Ida were shaken and all her peaks, and the city of the Trojans, and the ships of the Achaeans. And seized with fear in the world below was Aidoneus, lord of the shades ... Lest above him the earth be cloven by Poseidon, the Shaker of the Earth, and his abode be made plain to view for mortals and immortals ... So great was the din that arose when the gods clashed in strife.[1]

Strabo of the first century before the present era and Pliny of the first century of this era were well aware of the physical changes that the area of western Asia Minor and of the Aegean islands did undergo. Some of these changes are ascribed to the time of the Trojan War or the time closely preceding or following it; but others may refer to earlier upheavals.[2]

Strabo cited Democles "who recalls certain great earthquakes some of which long ago took place about Lydia and Ionia as far north as the Troad, and by their action not only were villages swallowed up, but Mount Sipylus was shattered – in the reign of Tantalus. And lakes arose from swamps, and a tidal wave submerged the Troad."[3]

---

[1] *The Iliad*, transl. by A. T. Murray (1925), Bk. XX.56-67.
[2] *For geological and archaeological evidence, see I. Velikovsky: *Earth in Upheaval* (New York, 1955). Cf. Claude F. A. Schaeffer: *Stratigraphie Comparée* (Cambridge, 1949). See also above, »Seismology and Chronology«.
[3] Strabo: *Geography*, transl. by H. L. Jones (1949), I. 3. 17; *Tantalus' reign is traditionally

Pliny described the changes in land and sea distribution. "Land is sometimes formed ... rising suddenly out of the sea. Delos and Rhodes, islands which have now been long famous, are recorded to have risen up in this way. More lately there have been some smaller islands formed," and he names them: Anapha, Nea, Halone, Thera, Therasia,[1] Hiera, and Thia, the last of which appeared in his own time.[2]

Pindar said that "the isle of Rhodes was not yet to be seen in the open main, but was hidden in the briny depths of the sea"; then it was born in the darkness – the sun was absent. When the sun finally lighted the earth again, a plot of land was seen "rising from the bottom of the foaming main."[3]

Under the heading *Lands Which Have Been Separated by the Sea* Pliny mentions: "The sea has torn Sicily from Italy,[4] Cyprus from Syria, Euboea from Boeotia," and other similar instances.

Under the heading *Islands Which Have Been United to the Main Land* Pliny mentions Antissa which was added to Lesbos, Zephyrium to Halicarnassus, and the like in other places.

> *Lands Which Have Been Totally Changed Into Seas:* The sea has totally carried off certain lands, and first of all, if we are to believe Plato, for an immense space where the Atlantic Ocean is now extended. More lately we see what has been produced by our inland sea; Acarnania has been overwhelmed by the Ambracian Gulf, Achaia by the Corinthian, Europe and Asia by the Propontis and Pontus. And besides these, the sea has rent asunder Leucas, Antirrhium, the Hellespont and the two Bospori.[5]

Pliny tells about *Cities Which Have Been Absorbed by the Sea*:

---

placed two generations before Atreus and Thyestes i.e., three generations before Agamemnon. Strabo goes on to tell of many other changes that occurred in the region of the Mediterranean, among them the opening up of the strait at the Pillars of Heracles, or Gibraltar.

[1] *The story of Thera and Therasia is told at greater length by Strabo: "For midway between Thera and Therasia fires broke forth from the sea and continued for four days, so that the whole sea boiled and blazed, and the fires cast up an island which was gradually elevated as though by levers and consisted of burning masses – an island with a stretch of twelve stadia in circumference. After the cessation of the eruption, the Rhodians, at the time of their marine supremacy, were first to venture upon the scene. ..." – *Geography* I.3.16. On the great volcanic eruption on Thera in Late Minoan times, cf. the bibliography collected by S. Hiller: »Die Explosion des Vulkans von Thera«, *Gymnasium* 82 (1975), pp. 32-74.

[2] Pliny: *Natural History*, transl. by J. Bostock and H.T. Riley (London, 1853), II.89.

[3] Pindar: »Seventh Olympian Ode«, transl. by J. E. Sandys (*Loeb Classical Library*, 1919).

[4] *Diodorus Siculus IV. 85: "Some say that great earthquakes occurred, which broke through the neck of the land and formed the straits [of Messina], the sea parting the mainland from the island." Cf. also Ovid: *Metamorphoses* XV, 290-91; Seneca: *Quaestiones Naturales* VI. 29.

[5] Pliny: *Natural History* II. 94.

Pyrrha and Antissa, Elice and Bura [on the Gulf of Corinth][1] from the island of Cea the sea suddenly tore off 30,000 paces "with many persons on them." In like manner it carried off Eleusina in Boeotia, and half of the city of Tyndaris in Sicily.

> And not to speak of bays and gulfs, the earth feeds on itself: It has devoured the very high mountain of Cybotus with the town of the Curites; also Sipylus in Magnesia, and formerly in the same place, a very celebrated city, which was called Tantalis.[2]

These descriptions by Pliny have corroborating references in other classical authors.[3]

Minor changes they were not: The Bosporus tearing Asia apart from Europe, like the breaking of the Mediterranean into the Ocean at Gibraltar were major changes. Smaller changes where single cities were engulfed or isles born could have been the after-effects of the cataclysms, which for hundreds of years still agitated the distorted strata of the earth; even today they have not completely subsided. Some of these changes occurred earlier and some later, but for the most part they occurred in historical times; the memory of them survived, and the same testimony comes from all quarters of the globe.

In the effort to regard the fantastic events in the sky as pure invention or flights of poetic imagination, the terrestrial changes described by Homer were also kept out of the discussion. Actually, Carl Blegen rejected Wilhelm Dörpfeld's identification of Troy VI with the Troy of the siege because he found that the walls and structures of Troy VI had been destroyed by an earthquake apparently oblivious of the fact that the *Iliad* contains a description of an earthquake at the final stage of the siege.[4]

Thus Blegen became besieged by contradictions, derived from misinterpreting the *Iliad* and from following an erroneous chronology as well. To the confusion of the Furtwängler-Dörpfeld debate,[5] a misreading of the *Iliad* brought more confusion, and made the tragedy complete.

---

[1] Cf. Strabo: *Geography* I.3.18; Pausanias II.25; Aristotle: *Meteorologica* I.6, II.8; Diodorus XV.49; Seneca: *Quaestiones Naturales* VI.23,26; VII.5,16.
[2] Pliny: *Natural History* II. 93.
[3] Cf. in addition to the works cited above Lucretius: *De Rerum Natura* Bk. VI *passim*, Ovid: *Metamorphoses* Bk. XV.
[4] C. W. Blegen et al.: *Troy, Settlements VIIa, VIIb and VIII*, vol. IV (Princeton, 1958).
[5] See above, section »Olympia«.

A Gap Closed

A chronology with centuries that never occurred made necessary the introduction of "Dark Ages" between the years -1100 and -750 in many areas of the ancient world; these upper and lower figures are already pulled together on the chronological timetable, and still some 400 years are unaccounted for – thus it is spoken of the "mysterious spell of Dark Ages."[1]

But when the hinges of history are fastened at correct levels the ghost centuries vanish and the chasm is shown to be imaginary.

Yet it cannot be denied that there was some interruption between the Late Bronze and Early Iron Ages in Greece and elsewhere; no smooth and evolutionary transition took place from the Mycenaean to the Ionian Age. There were great migrations in the eighth century and in the first part of the seventh. What kind of interruption, then, occurred in the entire ancient East?

In his book *Discontinuity in Greek Civilization* (1966) Rhys Carpenter stands before observations made by a number of investigators in the archaeology of Greece and the Helladic islands and, after reviewing the evidence on the mainland in its various regions and on the islands, one by one, he comes to the conclusion:

> Despite the fact that there is no indication that the late Myceneans were driven out by any human intervention, they abandoned the south Aegean islands even as they deserted the central Peloponnese. For some reason and for some cause over which they had no control they found life in Greece and in the southern Aegean so unendurable that they could not remain."[2]

And Carpenter asks: "What caused them to evacuate their towns and villages?" From here on he gropes in the dark and asks, was it a pestilence or a famine, was it a change of climate? and he continues:

> In the seventh book of his *History* Herodotus recounts that Crete was so beset by famine and pestilence after the Trojan War that it became virtually uninhabited until its resettlement by later inhabitants. Could Herodotus by any chance have had access to a true tradition?[3]

---

[1] M. J. Mellink: »Archaeology in Asia Minor«, *Journal of American Archaeology* vol 63, no. 1 (January, 1959).

[2] R. Carpenter: *The Discontinuity in Greek Civilization* (Cambridge University Press, 1966), p. 58.

[3] *Ibid.*, p. 59; Herodotus VII. 171.

There is a rather vague reference to the Dorian wandering: The Dorians migrated from Thrace and, moving presumably along the Adriatic coast, crossed into the Peloponnese and occupied Sparta, becoming the progenitors of this severe and puritan tribe. In the absence of any other known cause for the cessation of the Mycenaean world, the Dorian invasion was considered as the most probable. But the Minoan civilization on Crete, which in the later stage showed much affinity with the Mycenaean, was also terminated; and the Dorian invasion was made to continue over the sea to Crete.

It was not the Dorians who dispossessed the original population of eastern and central Greece: "The Dorian Greeks," writes Carpenter, "seem to have moved into a depopulated land." (p. 16) "...The Dorians had nothing whatever to do with the collapse of Mycenaean civilization, since they did not enter the Peloponnese until long after the collapse had already taken place."[1] It was some natural event: "A 'time of trouble' was occasioned by climatic causes that brought persistent drought with its attendant famine to most mainland Greece; and it was this unbelievable condition of their native abode that forced the Mycenaeans to emigrate, ending their century-long prosperity." But was there any specific cause for the climatic change?

Carpenter surveys the available evidence: G. Welter, in a monograph on the island of Aegina, maintains that it became uninhabited after the Mycenaean Age. V. R. d'A. Desborough holds that the island of Melos had been abandoned by its Mycenaean inhabitants. Discussing the island of Kos, Desborough "was puzzled at finding 'no clue as to the cause of its final desertion' in Late Mycenaean times." There must have been some serious disaster, 'he decides...' It can hardly be supposed that there was a complete depopulation, and yet there is no clear evidence of continuity into the Protogeometric period.'"[2]

Carpenter stresses here, too, "a definite instance of interruption of cultural continuity."[3]

---

[1] P. 52. *V. R. d'A. Desborough emphasizes that the abandoned sites were not occupied by any other race: "Nowhere is there any evidence of settlement by new peoples." This fact "has very serious consequences for the traditional conception of the Dorian invasion." See *The Last Mycenaeans and Their Successors* (London, 1964), pp. 251-252. Cf. idem: »History and Archaeology in the Last Century of the Mycenaean Age«, *Incunabula Graeca* XXV.3 (1968), pp. 1076-77; E. Vermeule: »The Decline and End of Minoan and Mycenaean Culture« in *A Land Called Crete* (Northampton, Mass., 1967), p. 86; A. Andrewes: *The Greeks* (London, 1967), p. 33.

[2] Carpenter: *Discontinuity in Greek Civilization*, p. 58; Desborough: *The Last Mycenaeans and Their Successors*, pp. 157-58..

[3] Carpenter: *loc. cit.*

In his search for climatic changes and physical upheavals Carpenter comes to cite three cases, during the Libyan and Ethiopian dynasties in Egypt, when unseasonal and excessive flooding took place in Egypt: In the eighth century, under the Libyan king Osorkon II, the Nile rose, breaking all the dykes;[1] in the days of Shabaka, the Delta was repeatedly flooded and earth was heaped against the towns to protect them;[2] and in the sixth year of Taharka, "the land was like the sea."[3]

But how could these instances in Egypt of the eighth and early seventh centuries help to understand what happened in Greece at the end of the Mycenaean Age if this end occurred shortly after -1200?

Carpenter goes on:

> Even more spectacular, but somewhat insecure chronologically, is the inference from circumstantial evidence that the Hungarian plain, an immense tract of comparatively low-lying land in which a number of large rivers converge, must have become almost totally submerged early in the first millennium B.C. How else shall we explain the fact that the rich and active phase of the Hungarian Bronze Age known to archaeologists as Bronze IV and dated by Alberg as lasting from about 1000 to about 850 B.C. (the drought period in Greece!) met, in Alberg's words, 'an unexpected and sudden end... after which the country is without any discoverable sign of occupation and seems deserted'?[4]

The words in Carpenter's preface to his 1966 book reveal that were he to follow Plato, quoted by him, he would have been led to the realizations familiar to readers of *Worlds in Collision* and *Earth in Upheaval*. I quote from Plato's *Timaeus* in Carpenter's translation. The speaker is an Egyptian priest and the listener is Solon, one of the Seven Wise Men of antiquity.

> ... All this, though told in mythic guise, is true, inasmuch as a deviation of the celestial bodies moving past the earth does, at long intervals, cause destruction of earthly things through burning heat ...

---

[1] *Ibid.*, p. 72. *J. R. Breasted: *The Ancient Records of Egypt* (Chicago, 1906), IV, Sec. 743. Cf. J. Vandier: *La famine dans l'Egypte ancienne* (1936), p. 123. The date of this inundation, calculated by Carpenter, is -776, the very year assigned to the first Olympiad; however, the basis of this calculation is the accepted chronology of the Libyan Dynasty, which is questionable. The description of the inundation may actually refer to a later upheaval.

[2] Carpenter: *loc. cit.*; Herodotus (II. 137) describes the construction of massive earthworks during the reign of Sabacon (Shabaka); these were evidently flood control measures.

[3] Carpenter: *loc. cit.*; cf. the Coptos Stele of Taharka in V. Vikentiev: *La haute crue du Nil et l'averse de l'an 6 du roi Taharqa* (Cairo, 1930).

[4] Carpenter: *Discontinuity*, p. 74.

So this is the reason why among us here oldest traditions still prevail and whenever anything great or glorious or otherwise noteworthy occurs, it is written down and preserved in our temples; whereas among you and other nations that chance to be but recently endowed with the art of writing and civilized needs, at stated turn of years there has recurred like a plague brought down upon you a celestial current, leaving only an unlettered and uncivilized remnant; wherefore you have to begin all over again, like children, without knowledge of what has taken place in older times either in our land or in yours. ...[1]

As set forth at great length in *Worlds in Collision*, part II, the world in the eighth and seventh centuries before the present era was going through a series of natural catastrophes, with frightening apparitions in the sky, disturbances in the position and direction of the terrestrial axis, drastic changes in climate, and subsequent mass movements of populations. The Cimmerians descended from Russia into Asia Minor and engulfed the Phrygian kingdom. Dorians presumably reached Crete, Latins were pushed from their homeland into Italy by newly arrived tribes – these were only a few of the migrating hordes that then moved in many directions all around the globe. The Minoan civilization of Crete did not succumb to the Dorians; it succumbed to the ravages of nature, and if the Dorians reached the devastated island, it was only because in desperation they looked for any room to move into, and there was nobody able or willing to defend the island from invaders.

Digging on Crete Arthur Evans arrived at the conclusion that each of the various stages of civilization on the island had come to its end in enormous natural paroxysms until the last of the stages found its end in the overturned palaces and cities, not to be rebuilt again.[2]

The interruptions in the flow of Minoan civilization had baffled Evans until the day when he experienced an earthquake on Crete. Now he understood the nature of the agent of the destruction that he observed in the ruins of the palaces: the agent was not an enemy reaching the island; and from that moment Evans filled his volumes on Knossos (*The Palace of Minos*) with the evidence of seismic catastrophes that terminated the great ages of Minoan civilization.[3]

---

[1] Carpenter: *Discontinuity*, p. vii; the quoted passages are from *Timaeus* 22 C-D and 23 A-B; cf. *Worlds in Collision*, section »Phaethon«.

[2] Evans: *The Palace of Minos at Knossos* (1921-1935); cf. *Earth in Upheaval*, section »Crete«.

[3] *Earth in Upheaval*, section »Crete«.

Spyridon Marinatos detected a devastation ascribed by him to an overwhelming wave coming from the north and sweeping over the mountainous island and carrying also ashes of volcanic eruptions.[1] "A normal earthquake, however, is wholy insufficient to explain so great a disaster."[2]

That climate changed, and repeatedly so, between the eighth and seventh centuries is well documented, and since the works of the Scandinavian scientists A. Blytt, R. Sernander[3] and others, and also of H. Gams and R. Nordhagen[4] of Germany, no effort needs to be spent to prove the point anew. The change was global, as the work of Helmut de Terra in Mexico[5] and the inquiry of C. E. P. Brooks and F. E. Zeuner[6] amply document. Of the changes in nature many eloquent descriptions were left by their contemporaries, by Assyrian annalists and Hebrew prophets, and also in many other documents of the literate peoples of the world.

Migrations were the consequences of destruction of domiciles, subsequent plagues, and of changes in climate that made agricultural experience dependent on former climates inapplicable. The climate in Europe that changed in the eighth century to dry and warm changed soon again to wet and cold.[7] This double change is documented equal-

---

[1] Marinatos: »The Volcanic Destruction of Minoan Crete«, *Antiquity* XIII (1939), pp. 425ff. *For a review of the extensive literature, cf. Hiller: »Die Explosion des Vulkans von Thera«, *Gymnasium* 82 (1975), pp 32-74. L. Pomerance has suggested that the collapse of Thera and the resulting tsunami devastated not only Crete, but the entire East Mediterranean basin at the end of the Late Helladic IIIB ceramic phase – »The Final Collapse of Santorini (Thera)«, *Studies in Mediterranean Archaeology* vol. XXVI (Göteborg, 1970).

[2] Marinatos: »The Volcanic Destruction of Minoan Crete«, p. 429.

[3] R. Sernander: »Klimaverschlechterung, Postglaziale« in *Reallexikon der Vorgeschichte* ed. Max Ebert, VII (1926).

[4] »Postglaziale Klimaänderungen und Erdkrustenbewegungen in Mittel-Europa«, *Mitteilungen der geographischen Gesellschaft in München*, vol. XVI, no.2 (1923), pp. 13-348.

[5] *Man and Mammoth in Mexico* (London, 1957).

[6] Brooks: *Climate through the Ages* 2nd edition (New York, 1949); Zeuner: *The Pleistocene Period* (London, 1945).

[7] *Carpenter dated the change to a dry climate to before -1200; he posited "a northward shift of the Saharan drought zone into southern Europe," (p. 10) with the resulting famine causing the abandonment of large areas, no longer able to sustain the large populations characteristic of late Mycenaean times. The shift was reversed, in his view, in the eighth century, with the return of a wet climate. Carpenter's inability to explain the cause of these shifts has invalidated his thesis in the eyes of many of his colleagues – cf. H. E. Wright: »Climatic Change in Mycenaean Greece«, *Antiquity* 42 (1968), p. 126. For a recent review of the physical evidence for Carpenter's thesis, see R. A. Bryson, H, H. Lamb and D. L. Donley: »Drought and the Decline of Mycenae« in *Antiquity* 48 (1974), pp. 46-50. Cf. P. Betancourt: »The End of the

ly well in the New World (Helmut de Terra).[1]

The upheavals of nature continued through the major part of the eighth century and climaxed in the last great cosmic disturbance which I was able to date on March 23rd, -687.[2]

The Mycenaean age came to its end in the catastrophic events of the eighth and seventh centuries – thus there were no Dark Ages between the Mycenaean Age and the Greek or Ionian Age. Whether the catastrophic changes that accompanied and followed these upheavals were by themselves enough to cause the end of the Mycenaean Age, or whether the migrations and invasions contributed, the great Mycenaean age came to its close not before the eighth century was over. There were no dark ages in between.

Certain changes did take place between the end of the Mycenaean and the beginning of the Ionian ages – but they are better understood not by assuming four or five hundred intervening dark years, but by the very fact of dislocations created by catastrophes. Cities with their palaces crumbled; surviving populations migrated and were partly replaced by new settlers – in the case of Greece by the Dorian invaders, the returning Heraclid Greeks who at an earlier date had migrated northward.

These upheavals of nature were responsible for the break in continuity that is found in Greece, in Asia Minor and in many other places. There was a disruption in occupation of lands and a discontinuity in civilizations. But there were no Dark Ages and the four centuries inserted between the Mycenaean and Greek periods are unreal. Thus we have the explanation of the fact that so much in common is found in the late Mycenaean and early Greek ages, and also an explanation of the fact that no literary relics and scarcely any archaeological ones are found from the four or five centuries of the presumed Dark Ages, and yet that, on the other hand, there was some break in continuity.

Greek Bronze Age«, *Antiquity* 50 (1976), pp. 40-45. Cf. also J. Camp: »A Drought in the Late Eighth Century B.C.« in *Hesperia* 48 (1979). The shifts in the Earth's climatic zones, if real, would have been a direct consequence of shifts in the inclination of the terrestrial axis in the eighth and early seventh centuries, as documented in *Worlds in Collision* (esp. sections »Poles Uprooted« and »A Hemisphere Travels Southward«) and in *Earth in Upheaval*.

[1] *Man and Mammoth in Mexico*, p. 76.
[2] *Worlds in Collision*, section »March 23rd«.

Competing for a Greater Antiquity

The date of Trojan War is traditionally placed in the beginning of the twelfth century before the present era: This tradition goes back to Eratosthenes, a Greek scholar in the employ of Ptolemy III Euergetes in the third pre-Christian century. He calculated that the last year of the ten-year-long siege of Troy fell in the year that in the modern calendar corresponds to -1183.[1]

This date is still upheld today by many scholars – a very unusual case of adherence to a chronological computation made over twenty-two centuries ago, and dealing with an event presumably nine hundred years earlier.[2] In antiquity some other, differing calculations were made, too,[3] but that of Eratosthenes survived until our time as the conventional date of Troy's fall. Only in recent years has a trend showed itself among the Homeric scholars to remove the date in question by a few decades into the past[4] – into the thirteenth century: With the chronological scheme arranged according to the timetable of Egyptian history, certain advantages were seen in moving the Trojan War to greater antiquity than the inroad of the Peoples of the Sea into Egypt, computed to have taken place in -1174.[5] Eratosthenes, however, did not connect in any way the events that took place in the days of Ramses III with the Trojan expedition.

---

[1] Eusebius: *Chronicle* in Eusebius: *Werke* (Leipzig, 1913), vol. VII, p. 60. Cf. J. Forsdyke: *Greece Before Homer* (London, 1956) pp. 28ff.

[2] *A. R. Burn: *Minoans, Philistines, and Greeks: B.C. 1400-900* (London, 1930) pp. 52-54: "It cannot be too strongly emphasized that the traditional date of the Trojan War, 1194-84, adopted by Eratosthenes and more or less tentatively accepted in so many modern books, is absolutely worthless" being based on Eratosthenes' "wild overestimate of the average length of a generation." Cf. idem: »Dates in Early Greek History«, *Journal of Hellenic Studies* 55 (1935) pp. 130-146. Cf. also D. Page: *History and the Homeric Iliad* (University of California Press, 1959) p. 96, n. 159: "[the date] given by Eratosthenes is nothing but a guess proceeding from flimsy premises which could not possibly have led to a scientific calculation." Another writer adds: "sober historical judgement must discard the ancient chronological schemes in toto; they are nothing more than elaborate harmonizations of myths and legends which were known in later times and have no independent value whatever for historical purposes." (G. Starr: *The Origins of Greek civilization: 1100-650 B.C.* (New York, 1961) p. 67.

[3] Herodotus, for instance, put the Trojan War a little more than 800 years before his time, or ca. -1250. Appian dated it after the founding of Rome, traditionally put at -753 or -747.

[4] C. Blegen et al.: *Troy*, vol. IV (1958) pp. 10-13 and idem: »The Mycenaean Age. The Trojan War, the Dorian Invasion, and Other Problems«, *Lectures in Memory of Louise Taft Semple* (Princeton, 1967) p. 31. Cf. also G. Mylonas: *Mycenae and the Mycenaean Age* (Princeton, 1966) p. 215.

[5] See I. Velikovsky: *Peoples of the Sea* (Doubleday: New York, 1977).

Was there any special intent in Eratosthenes' effort to place the Trojan War more than nine centuries before his own time? If his motive was to prove that the Greeks were an ancient nation, then his reasoning should be viewed as tendentious. This is, in fact, the case.

When the Greeks under the leadership of Alexander of Macedon subjugated Mesopotamia and Egypt, and soon thereafter established there Greek dynasties of Seleucus and Ptolemy, and introduced the Greek language and Hellenistic civilization, the erudites in what was once Babylonia and equally so in Egypt felt an urge to prove to their conquerors that they, the conquered, belonged to cultures more exalted, because more ancient. Berosus, a Chaldean priest who flourished in Babylon in the first part of the third century, wrote his famed *Babyloniaca*, or, History of Babylonia and Chaldea, and in it he stretched the history of his land and nation to a gargantuan length. In order to do so he ascribed unnatural lengths of reign to earlier kings and also invented kings (his list largely disagrees with the cuneiform king-lists).[1]

Manetho – a Greek-writing Egyptian, and a contemporary of Berosus – composed under Ptolemy II Philadelphus the story of his nation, and a few passages from it are preserved by Josephus; his genealogies of kings and dynasties are preserved in the writings of the Fathers of the Church, Pamphilius, Eusebius, and Julius Africanus.[2]

The regnal years ascribed to single Manethonian dynasties (30 in number until shortly before the arrival of Alexander in Egypt) are excessively long: Kings are often invented – no monumental confirmation of the existence of many of them was ever found; complete dynasties were invented by him, too. Like Berosus, Manetho tried to impress the Greek masters with the fact that his nation was already ancient when the Greeks only began to emerge from their barbarous state.

Such an attitude toward the Greeks was already expressed almost three centuries earlier in the narrative of the priest of Sais to Solon as told in the *Timaeus* by Plato. Because of written records stored in their temples, the Egyptians were aware of the past of their land, "so this is why among us here oldest traditions still prevail, and whenever anything great or otherwise noteworthy occurs, it is written down and preserved in our temples, ... [but] you and other nations that chance

---

[1] P. Schnabel: »Die babylonische Chronologie in Berossos Babyloniaca«, *Mitteilungen, Vorderasiatisch-ägyptische Gesellschaft* (1908). See also F. Cornelius: *Berossus und die Altorientalische Chronologie*, KLIO 35 (1942) pp. 1ff.

[2] See the volume *Manetho* in the *Loeb Classical Library*.

to be but recently endowed with the art of writing and civilized needs, at stated turn of years there has recurred like a plague brought down upon you a celestial current, leaving only an unlettered and uncivilized remnant, wherefore you have to begin all over again like children, without knowledge of what has taken place in older times in our land or in yours..."[1]

The same pride in the antiquity of the nation is found also in the narrative of another priest of Sais, a hundred years later, who gave the following account to Herodotus: From their first king until Sethos, the king-priest who was about to meet Sennacherib in battle when the latter's host was destroyed by a natural cause, 341 generations passed. Calculating three generations to a century, Herodotus found that it would comprise 11,340 years[2] – quite a long time if we should consider that from the foundation of Rome to the present day not even a quarter of such time has passed.

When the Egyptians came under foreign domination they experienced an even greater need to impress their masters with the excellence of their culture and its duration, in order not to be counted as barbarians; they wished to provoke and sustain a feeling of admiration on the part of the subjugators. Such claims could produce in the Greeks a feeling of their own inadequacy and inferiority – they had, since their first contacts with the Egyptians, developed for them a feeling of respect bordering on awe, whereas to the Persians, despite the magnificence of their court and bearing, the Greeks applied the name "barbarians." With excessive claims as to national antiquity the orientals were combatting their own feelings of shortcomings as politically subordinate nations.[3]

Eratosthenes was a contemporary of Manetho and Berosus. Born in Cyrenaica, he was of Greek origin. In his calculations of the time of the Trojan War he was evidently guided by the same motive as Berossus and Manetho, namely, to show the antiquity of his nation; the date of -1183 for the end of the Trojan War served that purpose.[4]

---

[1] Transl. by Rhys Carpenter in *Discontinuity in Greek Civilization* (Cambridge University Press, 1966) p. vii.
[2] Herodotus II. 142.
[3] Isaac Newton (*The Chronologyes of Ancient Kingdoms Amended*, (London, 1728)) recognized this hidden intent of Berosus and Manetho and therefore refused to give them credence as chronographers. Cf. Frank Manuel: *Isaac Newton, Historian* (Harvard University Press, 1963).
[4] *Eratosthenes allegedly relied on the Spartan king-lists to establish his chronology; in part he may have been influenced also by Manetho. But since the date he gives is identical to that

The "Dark Age" inserted between the Mycenaean and Ionic ages originated in the old calculations performed by Eratosthenes as to the time of the Trojan War, and on the reliance of modern historians of Greece on Egyptian chronology and order of dynasties as offered by Manetho; both of them lived in Egypt in the Ptolemaic age in the third century before the present era. It is not excluded that Eratosthenes based himself on Manetho.[1]

However, neither Eratosthenes, nor before him Homer, nor any other Greek historian or philosopher ever referred to such a Dark Age;[2] it is a creation of modern historians. But they found support for its historical existence in the Egyptian chronology built on Manetho's list of dynasties – the Mycenaean Age was dated by the archaeologically documented contacts of Mycenaean sites with Egypt. Thus Eratosthenes found support in Manetho and Manetho in Eratosthenes.[3]

Summing Up

Having started on a journey that first took us to Mycenae, but then also to Tiryns, Olympia, Pylos and a number of other ancient sites on the mainland of Greece and the Peloponnesos, also on Crete, Cyprus, the Troad and the interior of Asia Minor, we found at all sites one and the same embarrassing problem: Close to five hundred years between conflicting evidences or discordant views. The list of archaeological sites discussed could be enlarged to encompass almost every excavated place in the area, with hardly any of them standing a chance of escaping the very same perplexing state of affairs.[4]

---

computed by Ctesias, it is acknowledged that it was Ctesias' writings which actually formed the basis of Eratosthenes' system. Since antiquity scholars have questioned the reliability of Ctesias. Cf. the opinion of Plutarch in his *Life of Artaxerxes*; also Forsdyke: *Greece Before Homer*, pp. 68-79.

[1] *Eratosthenes became librarian of the Library of Alexandria in -240, and must have had access to Manetho's writings.

[2] V. R. d'A. Desborough: *The Greek Dark Ages* (London, 1972) p. 321; A. M. Snodgrass,: *The Dark Age of Greece* (Edinburgh, 1971) pp. 1-21.

[3] *As early as the fifth century, writers like Hekataeus and Herodotus (II.145) put the Trojan War into the 14th –12th centuries – they, too, were misled by the Egyptians. See for example the above-mentioned story told to Herodotus by a priest of Sais.

[4] See the article of Israel M. Isaacson: »Applying the Revised Chronology«, *Pensée* Vol. IV, no. 4 (1974), pp. 5-20; cf. Suppl. I of the present book.

What I call here "the perplexing state of affairs" often took the form of a dispute – to which of the two ages, separated by nearly half a millennium, does a stratum, a building, or a tomb belong? The holders of conflicting views are usually at equal disadvantage in meeting archaeological facts that, with the conventional chronological scheme not questioned, point simultaneously to two widely separated ages. Was Tiryns' palace rebuilt in the Mycenaean or in the Ionic Age – in other words, in the Bronze Age or in the Iron Age? And if the first alternative is selected, how could it be that for almost five hundred years the building lay abandoned, unoccupied by any of the twenty intermediate generations, since they left nothing of their own, no relic whatsoever? The alternative situation is equally beset with perplexing evidence.

Are the Mycenaean lions, carved in the peculiar position of standing erect on their hind legs facing a pillar that divides them, contemporary with similar Phrygian monumental sculptures, and if not, how does one explain the many centuries' gap? How is it that the wall of the Phrygian Gate at Gordion is built like that of Troy VI, if some five hundred years separate them? In what way does one explain the affinity of Mycenaean art of the pre-twelfth century with the art of Scythia, the Danubian region, and Etruria of the eighth and seventh centuries? Was the great strife between Furtwängler and Dörpfeld ever resolved? Because two timetables are applied simultaneously to the past of Greece, a clash of opinions is almost inevitable.

How is it that Greece and the entire Aegean area of the Mycenaean Age suddenly became depopulated, with scarcely any traces of human activity surviving? And if such was the case, how is it that so many details of Mycenaean life, habits and armaments were well known to Homer who knew equally well the life, habits, and armaments of the eighth and seventh century, though a Dark Age of several centuries' duration intervened?

When the decipherment of the Mycenaean Linear B script, to the surprise of many Hellenist scholars proved the language to be Greek, the so-called Homeric problem did not approach a solution but, contrariwise, grew more urgent, more enigmatic, more perplexing. The historians were startled because the Minoan-Mycenaean inscriptions are ascribed by them at the latest to the twelfth century, and the earliest Greek texts were of the eighth century. How could a people that was already literate forfeit its literacy so completely for over four hundred years?

The very fact that none of the Greek philosophers, historians, geographers, statesmen or poets ever referred to a Dark Age preceding the Ionic Age and separating it from the Mycenaean Age, should have been enough to cast doubt on the soundness of the overall construction.

Wherever we turn – poetry, arms, architecture, arts – the same Nemesis disturbs the excavator, the explorer and the critic, and from all sides the very same problem in various forms mockingly stares in the face of all of them, whatever their persuasion.

Where lies the root of all this confusion, a root hidden from sight and discussion? The Mycenaean Age in Greece and in the Aegean, as well as the Minoan Age on Crete, do not have an absolute chronology of their own, and this is not disputed. As I have already stressed on several occasions on preceding pages, the dating depends on contacts with other countries that have an absolute chronology of their own, and Egypt was selected for that purpose.[1]

When a cartouche of Queen Tiy was found at Mycenae, that stratum was dated accordingly to ca. -1400. When in the short-lived city of Akhet-Aton, built by Akhnaton and abandoned in the same generation, Mycenaean ware was found in profusion, the ware was regarded as contemporary with Akhnaton, and was dated to the fourteenth century. We have already dwelt on the subject, but it needs repetition in the light of what was brought to discussion all through the foregoing chapters and sections. In an extended examination of the Egyptian chronology its structure was put on a scale and found wanting. Now it is clear that if there is a miscalculation in Egyptian datings, the error must have spread through more than one land and vitiated more than one nations's chronology.

The problem is once more thrown to Egypt. In *Ages in Chaos* we have seen that, with the fall of the Middle Kingdom and the Exodus synchronized, events in the histories of the peoples of the ancient world coincide all along the centuries.

For a space of over one thousand years records of Egyptian history have been compared with the records of the Hebrews, Assyrians, Chaldeans, and finally with those of the Greeks, with a resulting correspondence which denotes synchronism.

---

[1] "The Aegean prehistorians have no choice but to adapt themselves to the Egyptologists" – G. Cadogan: »Dating the Aegean Bronze Age Without Radiocarbon«, *Archaeometry* 20 (1978) p. 212.

In Volume I of *Ages in Chaos* it was shown in great detail why Akhnaton of the Eighteenth Dynasty must be placed in the latter part of the ninth century. If Akhnaton flourished in -840 and not in -1380, the ceramics from Mycenae found in the palace of Akhnaton are younger by five or six hundred years than they are presumed to be, and the Late Mycenaean period would accordingly move forward by about half a thousand years on the scale of time. If the ages of Amenhotep III, of Tiy and of Akhnaton, need to be reduced by about five hundred years, classical studies could take a deep breath.

Actually, when in the eighties of the nineteenth century, the Hellenists were coerced, upon the evidence presented by Egyptologists, to introduce those five dark centuries, they did it only after a period of protest and resistance. But now that three generations of historians have lived with those dark centuries as a historical reality, it is even more difficult to part with them. Nevertheless, sooner or later, they will have to part with the phantom centuries, and have the history of Greece and the development of its writing as a normal process without a four-hundred-year gap.

The conclusion at which we have arrived is this: Between the Mycenaean and the Ionian Ages there was no Dark Age, but one followed the other, with only a few decades intervening. The natural catastrophes of the eighth century and of the beginning of the seventh brought an end to the civilization that centered at Mycenae in Greece, to cities and citadels and kingdoms; even the profile of the Greek mainland changed and many islands submerged and others emerged. These changes moved entire nations to migrations in the hope that beyond the horizon fertile lands, not damaged by unchained forces of nature, awaited the conquerors. This explains the break in continuity – the change is not due to some intervening dark ages that left no vestige of themselves, but to the paroxysms of nature and the migrations.

Classical studies have been troubled by many unresolved situations, archaeological and cultural. The field has been plagued by the presence of the Dark Age – a presence only schematic, never in effect. It engendered and continues to engender an ever-growing scholarly literature. If it can be shown that the Egyptian timetable is off its hinges, the bondage of these studies and their dependence on Egypt may terminate.

The removal of the Dark Age from the historical sequence unshackles what was for centuries shackled and releases the scholarly endeavor from travelling on the same circular paths with no exit from the modern version of the Cretan Labyrinth. Moreover, it rehabilitates scholars accused of ignorance or negligence, their having been guilty only of not perceiving that the problems they dealt with were not problems at all, as soon as unreal centuries are stricken out.

Further Relevant References and Expositions

The following material by Lewis M. Greenberg is meant to update, supplement, and augment the various sections of this book written by Velikovsky. It also follows the sequence of those sections for the most part. The text of the book itself remains exactly as it was at the time of Velikovsky's death in 1979. Additional references and information contributed by his research assistants Schorr and Sammer prior to that date also remain intact and untouched.

"It is quite certain that human beings have an irresistible tendency to reconstruct their own past endlessly, to color it in ever-changing hues. No object, no human memory, is immutable, nor is it acquired once and for all. History is a category of the mind; it is living and cannot be objective. History is by its very nature a creator of myths."

> Pierre Grimal: Preface to *The Foundation of Rome Myth and History* by Alexandre Grandazzi (Ithaca, 1997), p. x; See Chapter 11, »The Paths of Memory«, pp. 177-211.

- *The Greek World*, ed. by Anton Powell (London, 1995), »Linear B as a source for social history«, pp. 7-26; »»The Greeks in the West and the Hellenization of Italy«, pp. 347-353; »Rome in the Greek World«, pp. 368-383.

- *The Phoenicians*, ed. by Sabatino Moscati (NY, 1997), »The Question of the Alphabet«, pp. 101-119; »Dido and Her Myth«, pp. 654-656.

- E. Sweeney: *Gods, Heroes and Tyrants – Greek Chronology in Chaos* (NY, 2009)

- C. Marek: *In the Land of a Thousand Gods* (A History of Asia Minor in the Ancient World) (Princeton, 2016). The historicity of the Trojan War is a complicated subject. The history of the question itself is problematic. "The ancient Greek writers were firmly convinced that the war for Troy actually occurred. They made various calculations and observations regarding when and where it took place. Their dates for the destruction of Troy fluctuate between 1300 and 1150 BCE (in our chronology). However, this is not a scientific chronology, but rather consists of convoluted extrapolations and learned speculations: so far as historical writing is concerned, for the Greeks the time before 700 was terra incognita, as Walter Burkert put it." (p. 92); aside from the chronological problem there is a serious lack of written records for the period under discussion herein. See Chapter 4 – »The Late Bronze and Iron Age«.

An inexplicable cultural rupture occurred in Central Anatolia around 1200 BC according to conventional chronology. Again, the words of Marek: "Whereas in the south and southeast many place-names have continued to exist down to the present day ... there was no comparable continuity in the middle of the [Anatolian] region. The external marks of civilization, such as the active use of writing and monumental architecture, largely disappear. Much the same happens in Greece. Since in the world of that time the written sources were completely drying up or greatly diminishing, historians speak of the Dark Age. However, the 'dark' periods were regionally variable in duration. In the east and southeast, the tradition remained partially intact. This holds without qualification for Egypt and Assyria. In the west, the tradition resumes between the eighth and the sixth centuries BCE, through the Greek literature that was then emerging. ... The Hittites were a land power [who politically dominated almost the whole of Asia Minor] and entered into conflict and exchange with the great neighboring cultures of the Middle East. It is no accident that the Hittite heritage long remained alive in this zone of contact – so that the name of this people even appears in the Bible – whereas in the west it disappeared and in the whole of the Greek and Latin literature of classical antiquity the Hittites are not mentioned at all. This people and its history were recovered only in the twentieth century." (pp. 94-96).

Before we proceed further with Marek, a key question must be asked and answered: Why did Egypt and Assyria remain "intact"? That's because each had its own internal chronology and did not depend upon an outside dating system to determine their respective chronologies as did the Greeks and Hittites. Re the latter and who they possibly really were, I. Velikovsky: *Ramses II and His Time* (London, 1978), Chapters IV, V, & VI. Back to Marek – see the section of his book titled »Alphabetic Script and Homer«, pp. 130-133.

- M. R. Bachvarova: *From Hittite to Homer* (Cambridge, 2016), Chapter 14,»Continuity of memory at Troy and in Anatolia«; Chapter 15, »The history of the Homeric tradition«.

- The words of Akurgal cited in Velikovsky's text regarding the demise of the Hittites in Asia Minor were repeated in the English translation of his earlier work. "In almost every Hittite site of the second millennium BC so far excavated, the Hittite cultural strata cease with a layer of conflagrations [cf. Hawkins infra]. It is, however, significant that the succeeding Phrygian culture showed no signs that might connect it in any way with foregoing Hittite civilization. ... None of present day city names of Central Anatolia ... can be traced back to a Hittite source. ... the almost total ignorance of the Greeks concerning the Hittites shows the cessation of Hittite tradition. ... Furthermore it is striking that up to date not only no Phrygian, but no cultural remains of any sort have been found which might belong to the period between 1200 and 800 BC. ... Although Henri Frankfort has asserted that in Syria too a dark period followed between 1200 and 850 BC, W. F. Albright convincingly explained soon afterwards that historical tradition suffered no break in Syria." – E. Akurgal: *The Art of the Hittites* (NY, 1962), pp. 124-125.

As it turned out, Albright was wrong in the way he "solved" the problem; and Akurgal was equally wrong for accepting the way Albright obtained his conclusion. Frankfort was also wrong because he could not recognize continuity between particular art forms. His conclusion: There was a "cultural Dark Age" – a phrase James, et al. employed in their book *Centuries of Darkness* (1991), p. 123 when discussing Frankfort's conclusion. Here's Frankfort's exact words: "... in a number of places, the attempts to fill the gap between 1200 and 850 BC with transitional works can be abandoned. The monuments never called for such attempts, which were made in accordance with a preconceived idea of continuity between north Syrian and imperial Hittite art." Interestingly, at Byblos, Frankfort faced the same problem. Both he and Albright could not find a way to lower the 1200 BC date for the collapse and destruction of the Hittite Empire nor even accurately account for the "how" of it. Both Frankfort and Albright faced the same dilemma, for each was following the traditional chronology. Albright was irreversibly locked into the accepted conventional chronology of Ancient Egypt and was the prime critic of *Ages in Chaos* when it first appeared. He was fundamentally incapable of accepting the reality of a Dark Age, but was correct in his conclusion. There was none. However, he filled it with imaginary "golden age" art and architecture. In the 8th edition (1993) of his book *Ancient Civilizations and Ruins of Turkey*, Akurgal reiterated his earlier position with a slight variation. He blamed the catastrophic end to the Hittites on the "merciless aggression" of various peoples who invaded and "destroyed the civilizations of Asia Minor with such cruelty and violence that a dark age resulted which lasted for two hundred years in western Anatolia and at least 400 years in the rest of the peninsula" (pp. 11-12). But the dating of that "immense human tidal wave" was dependent upon Egyptian dating from the time of Rameses III – whose date Velikovsky questioned in his book *Peoples of the Sea*.

Perhaps the destruction that Akurgal described was actually caused by the 8th century cosmic catastrophe involving Mars that Velikovsky described in *Worlds in Collision*, pp. 210ff. Following Velkovsky's revised down dating of the 18th Dynasty and the time of the Amarna Letters (ca. 870-840 BC) would also help to solve the Dark Age situation in Anatolia. Their presence in the Hittite archives would bring the beginning of the end of the Hittites in Anatolia down to ca. 850 BC with an acceptable gulf between the Hittites and their successors, the Phrygians. If I read James, et al. correctly, in the end because of peculiar stratigraphy at Gordion they opted for "cutting the chronology" (i.e. lowering the earlier dates and closing the gap to what can now "be seen as a short interim period" – pp. 139-141. The suggested new dates for Gordion and the Phrygians doesn't affect their conclusion. But it wasn't clear if they would abandon the 1200 BC date altogether.) For more on Gordion, see the Section »Troy and Gordion« by Velikovsky supra.

A final remark by J. G. Macqueen about Anatolia after the fall of the Hittite Empire is worthwhile quoting here. "Linguistic and archaeological research-work is gradually dispelling the gloom of the Dark Age which followed the invasion of the 'Sea Peoples' [sic], and revealing the movements that took place within Anatolia, and the new political units which were formed. A great deal of work remains to be done, but it seems increasingly clear that we cannot now postulate four hundred years of chaos and an almost complete return to nomadic conditions. Anatolia continued to play an important part in the life of the Aegean and the Middle East." – *THE HITTITES and their contemporaries in Asia Minor* (London, 1986), p. 154.

- E. Akurgal: »Asia Minor, Western«, PHRYGIA, *Encyclopedia of World Art I* (Rome, 1959), pp. 883-890. According to Akurgal the Phrygians were settled in the interioir of western Anatolia at the end of the second millennium BC. "Since the remains of Phrygian culture are found immediately above the burnt stratum that signals the end of the great Hittite empire, and since, according to Assyrian sources, the Muski [Phrygians] appeared on the Assyrian borders at the time of Tiglath-pileser I (1115 – 1093 B.C.) earlier scholars believed that the beginnings of Phrygian art could be placed as early as the 11th century B.C. However, more recent investigations have demonstrated that none of the material remains of the Phrygians can be dated earlier than the 8th century B.C."; also see S. Ferri: »Frigia, Arte«, *Encyclopedia Dell'Arte Antica* III (Rome,1960), pp. 739-741, especially the comprehensive Bibliography on p. 741.

The date of 1200 BC for the Late Hittite Empire was most likely dependent upon Egyptian chronology since the identical pottery styles employed at Troy and elsewhere in the pre-Classical period of Greece – already shown to be highly problematic by Schorr in Supplement I of this book – helped in part to determine the subsequent dates for the Hittites. Hittite documents have left no reliable internal evidence to build a chronology upon. Attempted synchronisms with Egypt and Assyria have been made, but are circumstantial at best and not trustworthy: "The Pharaoh Tutankhamun died in the year the Hittite king Suppiluliuma I conquered the Mitannian kingdom of Carchemish, which was some six years prior to Suppiluliuma's own death. The Amarna letters *may* [emphasis in original] provide a series of synchronisms (some of those suggested are very speculative) between events in Suppiluliuma's reign and the reigns of contemporary Near Eastern rulers – the kings of Mitanni, Babylon, and Assyria, and the rulers of Hittite, Egyptian, and Mitannian vassal states in Syria. The battle of Kadesh was fought between the Hittite king Muwattalli II and the pharaoh Ramesses II in the fifth year of the latter's reign." - T. Bryce: *The Kingdom of the Hittites* (New Edition) (NY, 2005), pp. 376-377. Bryce's comments and analysis of astronomical dating techniques on pp. 378-379 are devastating for those who still rely on Sothic dating. "In view of these uncertainties, most Egyptologists now make little use of astronomical data. ... Yet the internal evidence presents a further set of variables." (p. 379) However, Sothic dating has been the backbone of contemporary Egyptology for more than a century. Note well Bryce's remarks about Venus as well for chronological purposes on p. 378. I would once again draw the reader's attention to Velikovsky's SUPPLEMENT »Astronomy and Chronology« in *Peoples of the Sea* (NY, 1977), pp. 205-244.

- Thanks to advances in the scientific area regarding dendrochronological and radiocarbon systems, "The final destruction dates of Hittite, Arzawan (in post-Hittite western Anatolia), or Mycenaean centers as well as the occupation sequences of Phrygian, Lydian, Urartian, and Neo-Hittite sites are coming into better focus as the contexts of various cultural assemblages are dated independently using a combination of [the scientific methodology cited *supra*]." None of the new dating technology confirms the conventional dates for the Mycenaean Age. The site of Gordion, for one, has yielded dates of ca. 827-803 BC and 845-800 BC. The history of Gordion under the Phrygians requires a chronological revision with revised dates of 743-741 BC. – Jak Yakar: »Anatolian Chronology and Terminology«, *The Oxford Handbook of Ancient Anatolia*, Edited By S.R. Steadman & G. McMahon (NY, 2011), pp. 82-83.

In this same volume, in a different chapter, here are the remarks of Jürgen Seeher pertaining to the end of the Hittite Empire: "... our knowledge about the collapse of the empire and the end of the Late Bronze Age around 1200/1180 B.C.E. is based almost totally on textual evidence ...This means we know almost nothing about the reasons and the course of events that led to the disappearance of the Hittites from the central plateau. Some Empire period sites have yielded evidence of fiery destruction, which may or may not represent extensive conflagrations and which may or may not have to be assigned to a single period and a single reason." (p. 379); also see Chapter 34, K.W Harl: »The Greeks in Anatolia from the Migrations to Alexander the Great«, pp. 752-763. The Aftermath to the fall of the Hittites and their capital early in the 12th century BC is fascinating. Despite the passage of centuries many questions remain as to what exactly caused the fall and why particular areas such as the Near Eastern world in this period survived. The Sea Peoples are still brought into the picture which doesn't really help. Who were they? How did they come together from disparate places to be able to threaten even the Egyptian Empire? Who was really capable of organizing them? Were the Peleset really Philistines? Interestingly, to the last question, Bryce cited (ref.#90) Marc Van De Mieroop: *A History of Ancient Egypt* (2004, p. 192) who commented that "there is nothing to confirm the hypothesized identification." Yet in the 2nd edition of his book (2011), Van De Mieroop simply wrote that "Peleset, for example, became Philistines ..." (p. 251). What does one make of that?! (In *Peoples of the Sea*, Velikovsky identified the Peleset as Persians.)

When the Dark Age that permeated Ancient Asia Minor came to an end, various surprising continuities were noted by Bryce. While a variety of different people spread out along the area known as the Fertile Crescent and "significantly altered the political and cultural environment and

configuration of the region ... a Hittite veneer persisted. Tangible illustrations of this are provided by Hittite-type monuments and sculptures, and above all by the 'Hittite' hieroglyphic inscriptions of the region. ... the Bible makes reference to the local Syrian rulers as 'Kings of the Hittites'. Indeed in Assyrian records a number of the kings of the region continued to have names strongly reminiscent of those of the Late Bronze Age Hittite kings – ... Such names may reflect attempts by later local rulers to claim traditional links, justifiably or not, with the Great Kings of Hatti, and serve to indicate that *memories of these kings* [emphasis added] were kept alive at least into the early centuries of the first millennium. So too the hieroglyphic inscriptions of the neo-Hittite region helped perpetuate Late Bronze Age Hittite traditions, even though the cuneiform script disappeared entirely from both Anatolia and Syria. Because of the persistence of this Hittite veneer, the kingdoms which emerged in Syria out of the obscurity of the Dark Age are sometimes known as the neo-Hittite, or Syro-Hittite kingdoms." (T. Bryce, p. 351). Also see Bryce, Chapter 14 – »The Trojan War: Myth or Reality?«, pp. 357-371 – on p. 361, Bryce had this to say: "Disappointingly, we have yet to find any clear evidence of a tablet archive at Hisarlik itself." – a genuine conundrum. (cf. J. Crowe: *The Troy Deception*, 2011, *inter alia*.)
Compare to what was just quoted *supra* to the parallel situation in Greece where many names were supposedly carried across a 500 year Dark Age gap only to be mentioned by Homer and others. How were "memories" carried through a Dark Age of similar length in Anatolia?

- M.J. Mellink: »Phrygian«, *The Dictionary of Art* 24, ed. by Jane Turner (NY, 1996), pp. 689-691. In an almost casual way Mellink states that "The citadel of the former Hittite capital, Bogazkoy [Hattusa], was rebuilt by the Phrygians, and a cult relief of Kybele was placed in the outer east gate." (p. 690). After 400+ years what enticed the Phrygians to build there? It was obliterated by whatever catastrophe destroyed it. Did the Phrygians know the site they were building on was the former capital citadel of the Hittites – and if so, how? There would have been neither record nor evidence unless the site had only been destroyed a decade or so prior to their arrival. Moreover, I cannot find any reference that reveals how modern scholarship definitively knows that ca. 1200 BC marked the termination of Hattusa and the Hittite Empire. Other than the discovery of a small stele of Tudhaliya IV who is believed to have reigned ca. 1260 – 1230 BC, there are no contemporary written records despite their large numbers and varied subject matter nor any other artifacts whose discovery could be utilized for uncontested dating purposes for that particular period. The El-Amarna correspondence is unequivocally accepted and the Phrygians built on places now reduced by erosion to foundation levels. – J. D. Hawkins: »Bogazkoy«, *The Dictionary of Art* 4 (1996), pp. 229-231. Hawkins, D. F. Easton, and D. Collon have all subscribed to only a 200 year Dark Age in Anatolia (1200-1000 BC): »Anatolia, ancient«, *The Dictionary of Art* 1, pp. 820-840; »Hittite«, *The Dictionary of Art* 14, p. 591.

- *The Oxford Handbook of the Archaeology of the Levant c. 8000-332 BCE*, ed. by M. L. Steiner & A. E. Killebrew (Oxford, 2014), H. Klengel: »Anatolia (Hittites) and the Levant«, pp. 90-97.

- H. Frankfort: *The Art and Architecture of the Ancient Orient*, 4th ed. (New Haven, 1970).

- B. Newgrosh: *Chronology at the Crossroads* (2007).

- O. R. Gurney: *The Hittites* (Reprinted with revisions 1990; still worthwhile for Gurney's perspective and knowledge. He refrains from using the term Dark Age, but when discussing the rise of the Neo-Hittite Kingdoms Gurney has this to say: "Yet in the south-eastern provinces of the Hittite Empire Hittite culture had a *strange afterglow which lasted for no less than five centuries*. ... It seems that Syria must have been overrun by another people coming from one of the Hittite provinces, who had adopted the Hittite civilization..." (pp. 32-33 – emphasis added; and pp. 34-50). On pp. 178-179 Gurney reveals an unsolved contradiction that exists between Hittite anthropology and what we see in their art and archaeology. It has to do with Hittite skull typology that differs significantly from earlier to later times. I pointed this out back in 1974 in a published letter in the journal *Pensée* based upon the information provided by Gurney.

- S. Scully: *Homer and the Sacred City* (Cornell, 1994).

- A. Nicolson: *The Mighty Dead Why Homer Matters* (London, 2014), pp. xvii-xxii and *inter alia*.

- *TROY, City, Homer, Turkey* (Istanbul, 2012), International editors and contributors, over sized book with 9 chapters ranging from »The Story of Troy« to »Eternal Troy«. Excellent and informative overview.

- J. S. Burgess: *The Tradition of the Trojan War in Homer & the Epic Cycle* (Baltimore, 2001), Chapter TWO, pp. 47-131, especially noteworthy.

- S. Sheppard: *Troy Last War of the Heroic Age* (Oxford, 2014); Complete light survey of the entire Trojan War and beautifully illustrated.

- D. P. Thompson: *The Trojan War* (London, 2004). Deals with the literature and legends from the Bronze Age to the Present.

- L. Clarke: *The War at Troy* (NY, 2004). A captivating retelling of the Trojan War as if it were a work of Historical Fiction.

- M. Tanner: *The Last Descendant of AENEAS* (New Haven, 1993); A magisterial study of the influence of Aeneas on the mythic image of the Emperor and other rulers in Western European history. Does not deal with the story of Dido and Aeneas, but is an unforgettable read otherwise.

- A. M. Young: *Troy and Her Legend* (Pittsburgh, 1948). A history of Troy through the ages in the epic tradition, literature, the visual arts, and opera.

- C. G. Thomas & C. Conant: *The Trojan War* (London, 2005); A survey of Troy in different categories, the last of which is »Troy and the Twenty-first Century«.
Chapter 4, »The Force of Legend« (sub-titled »The Cup of Nestor«) recounts a discovery made in 1954. What is relevant here is a brief discussion of a cup that was uncovered in a burial site on the island of Pithecoussae (modern Ischia) just across from the Bay of Naples inscribed with the name "Nestor". The writing and the cup along with the burial were estimated to be ca. 735-720 BC. The writing was in *retrograde* which refers to the practice of writing from right to left "in the manner of the Phoenician and other West Semitic scripts from which the Greek alphabet was ultimately derived. ... this short inscription is quite an early example of Greek writing, which is generally thought to have been introduced to Greece by Phoenician traders in the early or middle eighth century" (pp. 68-69).
The authors consider this to be a "parody" of *Homer's Nestor*. Because the cup did not fit the description of Homer's Nestor, "It is possible, but unlikely, that the cup really did belong to Nestor – that is, that the cup's owner, the boy in the burial, was named Nestor. It was in fact *uncommon* for children to be named after characters from Greek myth and legend until the third or second century. Almost certainly this cup was dedicated in playful parody to Homer's Nestor ..." (p. 70, emphasis added), who they considered much too old to be able to lift the original or desire the love of the goddess Aphrodite.

Thus, the authors accept that this cup of Nestor may fit the accepted date for Homer but not for the Nestor of the epic who is called the "Gerenian horseman" in the *Iliad*. However, neither is it likely the cup of a boy named Nestor because that name would not have been applied to children for another 500 – 600 years.

The authors of these statements never dared to speculate if the object under discussion actually did belong to Homer's Nestor because that would have meant lowering the date of the Trojan War to the 8th century BC. See *infra* for more on Nestor and Etruria who lived through two generations of his warrior colleagues and was assuredly not always old. All too often the aged today in Western societies are looked upon as if they were born old. (See the sections on »Pylos« by Velikovsky, Schorr, and Sammer elsewhere in this book.)

- R. Castleden: *The Attack on Troy* (2006). Castleden's final words takes the entirety of the Trojan War in a different direction and gives one something to ponder whether you agree with his thought or not. "The Trojans lost and vanished. The Mycenaeans too lost and vanished. The victory of the Mycenaeans over the Trojans was the ultimate hollow victory, a multiple tragedy, and as such it became for ever after the archetype of the tragedy of war" (p. 144).

- A. Strong: *The Phoenicians in History and Legend* (2002). The introduction of the alphabet into Greece is a controversial matter. Once thought to be brought into Greece by a legendary Phoenician named Cadmus (Kadmus) sometime around the 13th century BC (conventional chronology) when he also founded the city of Thebes, that conclusion has now been challenged. While "the existence of Kadmus as a historical figure is still unproven ... Additional evidence now suggests that the letters may have come to Greece much later than previously stated, about 800 BC." (pp. 125-126). Cf. Velikovsky's section on »Cadmus«.

- *The Oxford Handbook of the Phoenician and Punic Mediterranean*, ed. by C. Lopez-Ruiz & B. R. Doak (NY, 2019). "Cadmus and his family appear in Greek myths as early as Homer, although it is only from the sixth or fifth century BCE that they are associated with Phoenicia in our surviving evidence." According to Herodotus, it was Cadmus who "brought the Greeks their Phoenician alphabet as well as the worship of Dionysus at the same time he came to found Thebes" (pp. 673 and 723).

- P. Cartledge: *Thebes* (London, 2020), see "Cadmus" in Index.

- When it comes to the subject of the Olympic games and others held at different sites in Greece, it is notable that the Greeks may have abandoned most of their lands for a period of 500 years and yet retained the names and attributes of their major gods and heroes. Zeus, Hera, Demeter, Apollo, Artemis, Pallas Athena, Kronos, and Hermes are all mentioned. According to legend, as already noted by Velikovsky, Heracles (Hercules) is credited with clearing the field for the first Olympic games. That would put Hercules definitely in the time of the 8th century, not the 13th.
For a scholarly recounting of the early years of Heracles, see R. Miles: *Carthage Must Be Destroyed* (already cited elsewhere in this book), Chapter 3 »The Realm of Heracles-Melqart«, pp. 96-111. See the Section on »Hercules« by Greenberg also elsewhere in this book.

- S. G. Miller: *Ancient Greek Athletics* (New Haven, 2004). See Index for divinity names. Equally important, Chapter 3, »The Origins of Greek Athletics« where athletic events from the time of the Bronze Age are cited in the *Iliad* and *Odyssey* (pp. 20-30). Accompanying illustrations enhance every athletic activity.

- L. Drees: *OLYMPIA Gods, Artists, and Athletes* (NY, 1967). Chapters Two, Three, and Four deal with the Olympian gods.

- D. Sansone: *Greek Athletics and the Genesis of Sport* (LA, 1988). The following remarks drew my attention: "The ancient Olympic Games were held with meticulous regularity every four years, at the time of the second full moon after the summer solstice." (p. 35); S. G. Miller: »The Date of Olympic Festivals«, *Mitteilungen des Deutschen Archäologischen Instituts: Athenische Abteilung* 90 (1975) pp. 215-231. Cf. to Velikovsky's commentary about the periodicity of Venus and the earlier Olympic Games. J. Swaddling: *The Ancient Olympic Games* (Austin, 1980). According to the poet Pindar, Hercules "instituted the first games in honour of Zeus" which is now considered standard "knowledge". That means that Hercules was in Olympia in the early 8th century. However, once again we read something that indicates contradictory dating in the early history of Greece. Some individuals have him in Italy in the 13th century meeting Evander and Aeneas while the dates for the other two also fluctuate. The traditional date for the establishment of the Olympic Games was 776 BC. But, as we shall see, even this date did not go unchallenged; and that is another important factor when utilizing the date for the Olympic Games as a starting point for recreating a chronology for Ancient Greece.

> The Olympic festival was celebrated once every four years in accordance with the Greek calendar, which was based on the lunar month. It was always timed so that the central day of the festival coincided with second or third full moon after the summer solstice. This may well indicate the assimilation at some stage of the Games with fertility rites which celebrated the harvesting. (p. 12)

The questions to be raised here are: If the start of the Olympic Games was employed as a means of establishing a chronology, where and how did a secure date of 776 BC come about in the first place for the Games? What Greek calendar was being referred to in the quote *supra*? Any association with a lunar month becomes meaningless for absolute dating purposes without an independent secure chronological marker. Cf. the problem faced and created by Sothic dating. *A Companion to Sport and Spectacle in Greek and Roman Antiquity*, Ed. P. Christesen & D. G. Kyle (Singapore, 2014); Kyle: »Greek Athletic Competitions: The Ancient Olympics and More«.

> The traditional foundation date of 776 for the ancient Olympics has been challenged since antiquity ... and archaeology now suggests that major contests at Olympia developed only around 700. Limited and local games probably arose slowly at Olympia, perhaps in response to gatherings of worshippers and as a supplement to an early religious festival. By the seventh century Olympia offered events in two broad categories: gymnic or 'naked' contests ... track and field and 'combat' (fighting) events and equestrian or hippic contests (hippikoi agones: horse and chariot races). (p. 23)

Horse and Chariot racing existed back in Trojan War times and were highlighted in the various sources just cited. Velikovsky alluded to them as just one significant event that helped to bridge the false gap created in Greek history. Despite the comprehensive coverage in *A Companion to Sport and Spectacle* ... which is to be admired, there appears to be circular reasoning when referring to particular victory dates and then converting them into conventional contemporary absolute dates. To use 776 BC as an Olympic starting date that is already questionable and retroject it back in time to another questionable date, the time of the Trojan War, in order to construct a viable and credible absolute chronology is already indicative of a built in problematic chronology.

- M. I. Finley, et al.: *A History of Sicily* (NY, 1987). In his own inimitable way, Finley immediately disposes of the legendary stories of Daedalus and Heracles with regard to any Sicilian connection and proceeds to cover more than 2700 years of Sicilian history in this excellent survey. At the outset, Finley states: "The Bronze Age objects so far found in Sicily are either imports from mainland Greece and the Aegean islands, or else local ware based on prototypes from these areas. Very few identifiably Cretan ('Minoan') artefacts are known. ... The capacity of the ancients for invention should not be underestimated." (p. 5).

No dates are provided for any of the objets d'art. However, Mycenaean vessels or their imitations have been found in southern Italy and Sicily which belong to LH IIIB and LH IIIC periods; (R. Leighton: *Sicily Before History* (Ithaca, 1999), pp. 170-180). Since their dates as we've seen so many times depend upon Egyptian chronology, there isn't anything really new here. Mycenaean ware is found in Sicily over the next few centuries. Then basically ceases. This does not mean that Sicily entered a "Dark Age". Only those cities in Greece whose dates depended upon Egyptian chronological correlations. Sicily continued to evolve in a very positive way (*Sicily from Aeneas to Augustus*, ed. by C. Smith and J. Serrati (Edinburgh, 2000), *infra*).

In the early 8th century BC we have a veritable "explosion" of newly founded Western Greek cities, more than half a dozen beginning with Naxos in 734 down to Akragas in 580. In the *Aeneid* (Book 5), Virgil has Aeneas return to Sicily to celebrate games at Segesta on the anniversary of his father's death. Segesta certainly did not exist in the 13th century BC; and the end of the Mycenaean Age only served to shift the focus onto Sicily for what was a relatively brief period of time. "Although we know little about their political organisation, Iron Age society was one of articulated social roles, probably based on factors such as age, gender, handicraft skills and physical prowess. The presence of warriors, weavers, potters, metalworkers and traders can at least be inferred. Moreover, this was a time of technological innovation and intensification of local production, particularly evident in metal-working.

> "The 'Dark Age' epithet which is applied to contemporary Greece would therefore be misleading for Sicily, although there are analogies with the Aegean, where profound social changes took place at about the same time. One reason for social change may be the decline of trade with the Aegean at the end of the Mycenaean period." (*Sicily Before History*, pp. 188-189).

A question: If Greece was just emerging from a 500 year Dark Age, how were so many of its cities capable of suddenly coalescing and able to cross half way across the Mediterranean to land successfully in Sicily and found cities there?

- Regarding the Scythians, Tamara Talbot Rice, cited by Velikovsky, is still one of the best sources (T. T. Rice: *The Scythians* (NY, 1961), »The Tombs«, pp. 92-123, 30-31); T. Taylor: »Scythian & Sarmatian Art«, *The Dictionary of Art*, 28 (1996), pp. 319-326 with superb Bibliography on the last page; D. S. Rayevsky: »Animal Style«, *The Dictionary of Art*, 2 (1996), pp. 100-102; Vladimir Blawatsky: »Greco-Bosporan and Scythian Art«, *Encyclopedia of World Art* VI (NY, 1962), pp. 846-858. Genuine Scythian animal-style art was discovered in Maeotian burial tumuli of Kelermes in the Kuban Basin. Rudimentary stone sculpture was placed atop the tumuli. "The sources of this tomb architecture can be traced to the Bronze Age." (p. 847) But that would require going back several centuries through a Dark Age period. "The magnificent monumental tomb structures – in particular, the crypts with corbeled roofs – [represent] a significant and distinctive aspect of Bosporan artistic development. ... Although the structures of these tombs are typically Greek, the question of their origin is very involved. Neither the corbeled beehive vaults that were widespread throughout the Aegean world nor the burial monuments of Asia Minor, of Thrace, or of Etruria provide a basis for establishing their origin. ... Among the tombs of the Bosporan region, ... the Golden Tumulus near Kerch occupies a unique place. ... it consists of a small dromos and circular chamber of beehive shape that finds a close analogy in the well-known tholoi of *Mycenae*." (pp. 852, 854, emphasis added).

However, there is a structural difference in the method of vaulting the dome. In the end, even a possible Thracian influence with a Mycenaean type vault that would be closer chronologically to Bosporan tombs of the 6th century BC is cast aside in favor of the Bosporan tombs themselves. Yet it is "the circular-chambered tombs of Thrace – in which, as in the Mycenaean tholoi, the section of the vault formed a smooth curve ..." that catches our attention. "The 'Thracian' type is considered to be antecedent to the Bosporan group [and] it seems unlikely that this type of burial chamber, so different from the others in the Bosporan region, was an indigenous form. Even granting a Thracian origin, the local influence of the building style of the Bosporan tombs with corbeled roofs is still undeniable. No definite date can be assigned to the Golden Tumulus; tentatively it can be placed in the last decade of the 4th century BC or perhaps a little later." (p. 854).

One can almost feel the struggle that Blawatsky faced when attempting to chronologically explain similar sophisticated architectural features whose analysis and historical perspective were constrained by an existing chronological framework. It wasn't geographical distance that was the problem; it was the chronological distance. If the Mycenaean Age actually ended ca. 750 BC as opposed to 1250 BC, as brilliantly archaeologically demonstrated by Schorr elsewhere in this book, the architectural aspects of the tholos type tombs in the Bosporan area make complete sense. (Also see B. Cunliffe: *The Scythians Nomad Warriors of the Steppe* (Oxford, 2019), pp. 9-16, for discussion and excellent photos of the burial mounds and corbel vaulting.)

- We must now turn to Thrace itself. But first, I wish to acknowledge historian Emmet Sweeney who personally directed me to Thrace when I first began work on this current project (Sweeney, pp. 69-83). Ancient Thrace was first mentioned in the *Iliad* of Homer and covered an area that extended along the Aegean coast to the southwest, covered what today would be southern Bulgaria in the north, European Turkey in the area surrounding Istanbul, and its eastern region extended next to the Black Sea. It would have had access to western Anatolia, Greece, and part of Central Asia. It is extremely difficult to think of Thrace as a united polity and attempts to establish a decent chronology outside of archaeological finds has proven to be problematic. Not until the 6th to 4th centuries BC does the picture become clearer. "Only a few inscriptions in the Thracian language have been found, all written in the Greek alphabet, and mostly just names. They left us no written records, and their history has to be pieced together from archaeological discoveries and short texts written by their enemies." (C. Webber: *The Gods of Battle*, Barnsley, 2011, p. xiii.).

"In the case of Thracian history there are grave doubts as to the equivalence between historical reality and its presentation. It is not possible to compare texts, archaeological finds, numismatic objects and mythological data without first chronologically grading them, because very often sources of one and the same calendar date provide information from different periods." (A. Fol & I. Marazov: *Thrace & The Thracians* (NY, 1977), pp. 9-13).

When it came to religion, the Thracians embraced the totality of divinities found in Greece, Rome, Iran, India, and Asia Minor. "The hero was no doubt the central figure in Thracian religion, the hope and faith of the people. Their hero was all-seeing and all-hearing [and] portrayed on thousands of votive reliefs. ... The Thracians were unable to give their god a distinctive name or image, as the Greeks had done for their Olympians. But *if we compare Thrace of the Classical period with*

Mycenaean Greece, we shall find many affinities. During Pericles' time, the Thracians were still hearing the clash of swords as the ancient heroes fought. Archaism was an inherent feature of Thracian religious thinking. This also meant that it has preserved the intensity of passion which characterized the Mycenaean age." (p. 34, emphasis added). "In their archaeology you see the same style of tombs, metal work, and pottery right across the area. The Thracians who lived near the Danube and further north had the same cultural motifs, although they may have used different weapons and armour (and clothing to some extent) from other Thracians. ... From before the Trojan War until the Roman conquest they were a tribal Homeric society, with *many similarities to that of Mycenae.* Thracians were still burying their kings in *beehive tombs* in the the third century." (Webber: *The Gods of Battle*, pp. xii-xiii – emphasis added.).

The term "Archaism" used above seems hardly appropriate to describe cultural items that had to travel across a hiatus of 500 years of an illiterate Dark Age where we then find Thracian inscriptions written in the Greek alphabet which didn't exist until ca. 800 BC. Could it be that the latter phase of Mycenaean Greece (ca. 750 BC – revised chronology) was actually a near contemporary with what is called the Thracian Classical period – the 7th - 6th centuries BC? (T. Taylor: »Thracian and Dacian Art«, *The Dictionary of Art* 30 (1996), pp. 767-772). Apparently, Thrace did not experience the same kind of "Dark Age" that enveloped Greece probably because, for Thrace, the vague and contradictory chronology of that period was not indebted to that of Egypt. "Certainly, there was no marked interruption in life between the second and first millennia BC: the Iron Age continued to use the tools of the Bronze Age, as it did some types of weapon and pottery. Some Bronze Age ornaments continued to be used during the first millennium BC. Nor did the plan of dwellings change; the fortification system was developed and the communication network extended to meet growing needs." (*Thrace & The Thracians*, p. 139). From the earliest times the ruler or rulers of Thracian society consisted of a military-political organization which had no specific title. The term *basileus* or king taken from Homer is not exactly applicable. "Its Roman equivalent, *rex*, was applied to anyone who wore the attributes of high office, no matter what its prerogatives. There is no Thracian equivalent. The Thracian would be *closer to Mycenaean Greece*, where the king had both military and priestly power, and was also the biggest landowner. He was surrounded by the notables of the family, who could rival him in every respect, except in the exercise of his priestly functions. The situation in Thrace was similar during the second millennium BC ..." (*Thrace & The Thracians*, p. 146 – emphasis added).

- Etruria and the Etruscans also offer a significant conundrum. What Velikovsky said about the arrival of the Etruscans in northern Italy can no longer be sustained (see *infra*). However, he was correct about their dating and the other information provided in the section titled »Etruria«. The origin of the Etruscans was already a heatedly debated topic back in antiquity. Herodotus believed that they came from Lydia in Asia Minor. But he threw the Etruscans back into a "mythical event occurring half a millennium earlier" in the words of Pallotino. Dionysius of Halicarnassus, who lived at the time of Augustus in Rome, claimed that they were an indigenous people. His conclusion was based upon significant linguistic and theological differences between the Etruscans and Lydians. A third alternative was put forth in the late 18th century by one Nicolas Freret. According to him and his followers the Etruscans came from the North as part of the Indo-European invaders who descended on the Italian peninsula from 2000 BC on. The latter proposal has been summarily dismissed (R. Bloch: *The Etruscans* (1960), pp. 19-64). In 1947, the preeminent scholar on the Etruscans – Massimo Pallottino – substantially settled the dispute by affirming that the Etruscans in Italy and specifically Etruria were the *conclusion* of a *formative* process that resulted in a distinct *ethnic formation*. (M. Pallottino: *L'Origine degli Etruschi* (Rome, 1947), pp. 113ff., my emphasis here.) That enabled Bloch in 1960 (p. 62) to declare:

> The Etruscans must derive from a mixture of ethnic elements of various origins, and it is out of this mixture that there emerged an *ethnos*, a nation with well-defined characteristics and physical traits. The Etruscans would thus again become what they never ceased to be – namely a purely Italic phenomenon. We can then dispense, without regrets, with the hypothesis of an alien migration, the origin of which would in any event have to be treated with caution.

Also in 1960, R. Bianchi Bandinelli, a foremost Italian authority on Roman and Etruscan art, discussed in detail the "formation of the Etruscan civilization" placing its beginnings around the 8th century BC. (R. Bianchi Bandinelli: *Enciclopedia Dell'Arte Antica* - III, »Etrusca, Arte« (Rome, 1960), pp. 466-468 with an additional 20+ pages of meaningful discussion and a massive Bibliography in tiny print on pp. 500-502.) Adding to the above, G. A. Mansuelli had this to say in his 1965 book

The Art of Etruria and Early Rome, pp. 16-17: "... Etruscan civilization takes on a physiognomy of its own by using the means of artistic expression offered by the orientalizing style, thereby showing affinity with a movement of Mediterranean-wide importance; but also shows that it is constructed as the fundamental principle of urban life, synchronous in this respect with the general phenomenon of colonizing currents which dotted the Euro-African coasts of the central and western Mediterranean with city units. It might therefore seem logical, following the 'oriental' theory, to see the 'origin' of the Etruscans as a part of this phenomenon. But the Etruscan cities, far from being coastal centers of the colonial, that is, Graeco-Phoenician type, seem to be offshoots of forces building up from the *interior*, ... Pallottino's interpretation of the 'ethnic formation' of the Etruscan nation ... is valuable in turning our attention in a fresh direction, towards an historical point of view, and as a determining factor to further developments. The problem shifts, in fact, as far as the chronological starting-point is concerned, from the beginning of the Iron Age II to the beginning of the First, and the Villanovan civilization, in all respects, is by it taken over and assimilated. Etrurian civilization, therefore, seems to us an *Italic phenomenon*, modified in its outward and visible forms – moral and artistic – by a complex of Mediterranean influences" (emphasis added).

The late renowned German Classical archaeologist Maja Sprenger wrote back in 1976 (shortly before her accidental death): "The weightiest argument for the Etruscans' eastern origin, now the most favored theory [no longer], is the Orientalizing phase of Etruscan art in the seventh century B.C., which scholars explain as the natural consequence of an emigrant eastern population. However, this does not explain why the Etruscan Orientalizing phase took so long to appear if, as Herodotus said, their migration from the East had occurred *as far back as the thirteenth century*. In linking the Etruscans with Asia Minor, much has been made of similarities in their grave mounds and in certain peculiarities of dress. A further indication would appear to be the inscription on a grave stele found on the island of Lemnos that has striking affinities with the Etruscan language. One theory to be taken with a grain of salt is the not infrequently proposed notion that the Etruscans were none other than the tribe of the Turscha who, along with other peoples, invaded Egypt at the time of the Pharaohs Merenptah ... and Rameses III ..." (also see Velikovsky's *Peoples of the Sea*).

Most important are Sprenger's additional remarks that appear right after those quoted above. "Present-day research concedes less importance to the ethnic character of the Etruscans. The chief interest of authorities such as Pallottino no longer lies in the problem of their origin, but in how the Etruscans became a unified population in the Italic area. Archaeologically the Etruscans are already identifiable in prehistoric times as exponents of the Villanova culture that arose around 900 B.C., even *if their first historical appearance was not until the seventh century*. The unity they then achieved probably came through the merging of different ethnic elements, the most important being the indigenous people of the Villanova culture and a migrating people from Asia Minor who arrived in central Italy in the *latter half of the eighth century*. The Etruscan development should be seen as a gradual process, of different streams of migrating newcomers joining native Villanovan settlements and fusing, in time, into a unified population." (M. Sprenger & C. Bartoloni: *The Etruscans Their History, Art, and Architecture* (NY, 1983), pp. 11-12 (emphasis added).)

"The consolidation of Etruria as a 'nation' during the Final Bronze and Early Iron Ages occurred through the steady coalescence of huge agglomerations known as proto-urban settlements, a phenomenon that had practically no parallels outside Etruria, and secondly outside Latin territories." (G. Colonna: »The Original Features of the Etruscan Peoples«, *The Etruscans*, Ed. M. Torelli (NY, 2000), p. 30.) "It is, in any case, indisputable that Etruscan culture emerged from the fusion of diverse elements in an environment – the area of central Italy that faced the Tyrrhenian Sea – that was particularly receptive. The oldest signs of this fusion can be found in the so-called Villanovan culture at the city of Villanova near Bologna, where the earliest archaeological evidence has been uncovered." (F. Borrelli & M. C. Targia: *The Etruscans Art, Architecture, and History* (LA, 2004), p. 6.) Also see, M. E. Moser: »The Origins of the Etruscans: New Evidence for an Old Question« in *Etruscan Italy*, Ed. J. F. Hall (1996), pp. 29-43 and »Introduction«, pp. 3-13; S. Haynes: *Etruscan Civilization A Cultural History* (LA, 2000), pp. 1-5, 47-55, 71-74.

Turning now to Massimo Pallottino himself, here are his own words regarding the origins of the Etruscans from the "revised and enlarged hardcover edition, based on the sixth Italian edition, published 1975, in the U.S." (*The Etruscans*). There are also later contributions by Pallottino in 1986 and 1989 to the subject at hand that apparently remain fundamentally the same as this one (see *The Etruscan World*, Ed. by J. M. Turfa (NY, 2013), pp. 29-34 and the Bibliographical references on p. 34). The importance of Pallotino's discourse is his powerful affirmation of the placement and establishment of the earliest Etruscans as a cohesive and recognizable entity solidly and squarely ca. 800 BC to the early 7th century BC. At the same time, it is necessary to emphasize once again the fact that any Mycenaean contact with Italy or Etruria is dated according to pottery finds (e.g., Mycenaean IIIA and B) whose dating is determined solely by an Egyptian chronological reference, the reliability of which has been questioned and found wanting many times in this book. This would result in a serious down dating in a revised chronology of any Mycenaean objects discovered in the vicinity of Etruria. (See Velikovsky's comments in the section titled »Etruria«; and for the weaknesses in ceramic chronology, once again the reader is referred to the various sections by Schorr in Suppl. I of this book.)

According to Pallottino, the Etruscans "formed a complex of eastern, continental and indigenous elements which must be isolated, weighed, and compared one with the other. ... for the time being we can state quite safely that the formative process of the Etruscans can only have taken place on the territory of Etruria itself; and we can witness the final stages of this process thanks to the rich archaeological documentation we possess for the period from the ninth to the seventh centuries. This point of view, which [I have] been expressing for some years, cannot be confused with an autochthonous theory except in so far as it stresses the conclusion of an historical process rather than its supposed starting-point." (p. 79). *E Pluribus Unum!*

Having ca. 800 BC as an absolute key marker for a definitive fusion date for the creation of the Etruscans as we know them makes the following comment by Pallottino especially noteworthy. On p. 247 of his 1975 book there is an *Additional Note to Chapter Two* (italicized heading as you see it here) that contains the following: "*The recent discovery of evidence for a Mycenaean presence in Etruria would appear to be relevant.*" (emphasis added). What that evidence is Pallottino never said. (But this possibility will be explored *infra*.) The one certain thing that can be said in lieu of Pallottino's laconic yet most significant revelation is that you cannot have a 13th century BC Mycenaean presence in 8th century BC Etruria unless there actually were Mycenaeans alive and well in the Etruria of the 8th century (or at the very end of the 9th century BC). Among other things, it would appear that Virgil got it right when he had the Trojan Aeneas slay the Rutulian Turnus as the final act of his *Aeneid* since Dionysius named him Tyrrhenus which means Etruscan.

An oft neglected contribution also by Pallottino on the Etruscans is his extensive and comprehensive contribution to the *Encyclopedia of World Art* V (NY, 1961), »Etrusco-Italic Art«, pp. 100-141, with a vast Bibliography and plates 24-55; Cited here as well is David H. Trump: *Central and Southern Italy Before Rome* (NY, 1965), pp. 177-180 and a Postscript (p. 183) where he stated that "In Apulia there is surviving cultural influence from Mycenaean Greece" during the Iron Age. Sadly, he never stated specifically what that influence was nor when it dated from. But earlier (p. 124), he did state that "the trading post at Taranto goes back only to the Late Helladic, Mycenaean IIIA" and then Mycenaean contacts stopped when "the Aegean world collapsed during IIIC, in the twelfth century." That date and others are all dependent upon Egyptian correlations with pottery fragments and make far more sense when down dated by 500 years. Apulia is an area of south-eastern Italy where Taranto (Tarentum), one of the earliest of the Greek colonies was established. But that didn't occur until the late eighth century (706 BC); (See N. Degrassi: »Taranto« in the *Enciclopedia Dell'Arte Antica* - VII (Rome, 1966), pp. 602-617.) Consider the following from A. G. Woodhead (*The Greeks in the West*, 1962, p. 23):

> At Taranto, the most likely candidate as a regular Mycenaean colony, the picture has been blurred by a remarkable stratification of finds from excavations conducted at the beginning of the [20th] century *which associated Mycenaean and Protocorinthian sherds in the same stratum.* This led T.J. Dunbabin to suggest that 'contact with the Aegean was *not broken for long, if at all*, between the Mycenaean imports of the late thirteenth century and the coming of the Greeks': but the pottery evidence may well have been confused at the time of discovery. The pattern here as elsewhere seems to be that on the collapse of Mycenaean power in Greece contacts were broken. Traces of Aegean influence remained in some architectural and ceramic usages and styles, but it was not until the late Geometric period in Greece that pottery of Greek manufacture began to find its way once more to the west. (Emphasis added.)

Despite the fact that stratigraphic finds indicated a chronological problem, Woodhead knew he couldn't move the date of Greek settlements or full colonies back in time; nor could he find a reason for justifiably moving the Mycenaean finds downward in time. Thus, any literary evidence or claims were dismissed outright and forced to yield to the archaeological evidence no matter what the contradictory outcome. The stories of the Argonauts, Arethusa, Heracles, Trojan and Greek Heroes, and the Cretans were all treated as fanciful fiction and fell by the wayside, unable to compete with archaeological dating methods and its silent partner – Ancient Egypt. Yet, for all that, in the matter of the events surrounding the story of Daedalus, the King of the Sicans (Sicily), and Minos the Cretan King, Woodhead wrote, almost wistfully (p. 30):

> Although it is correct to follow Dunbabin in being sceptical of any alleged visits of Greeks to Italy in the prehistoric [sic] period where literary sources alone provide the evidence, there is in this case just sufficient in the available archaeological material for one to fancy that, through the mists of romance and myth, something real and tangible is there to be grasped.

Indeed. One of the more fascinating subjects of early Greek history involves the establishment of Greek cities in the western Mediterranean, specifically Sicily and Southern Italy. Not just the activity, but the rapidity of Greek colonization in that part of the world and the abundant information about it, "which is better known than that of any other large area ..." Moreover, "Even though most of the mother cities responsible are known to have been strong, the speed and scale of the movement, once the region was opened to Greek colonization, are *striking*. It has been suggested that the Phoenicians taught the Greeks to colonize." But the latter has been refuted. (A. J. Graham: »The colonial expansion of Greece« *The Cambridge Ancient History* III, 2nd ed., part 3 (Cambridge, 2002), pp. 94-113, emphasis added). Could it be that the Greeks of the late 8th century BC, ca. 720, learned of this part of the Mediterranean from their Mycenaean forebears? And, if so, is there any evidence?

Let us examine some of that possible evidence. According to Strabo (264, 222), "The Pylians who sailed away from Troy with *Nestor* [see *supra*] are credited with the foundation of Metapontum on the Gulf of Taranto, and even of *Pisa* [ca. 720 BC?] *in distant Etruria*; Crimisa [or Krimisa] is said to have been founded by Philoctetes [ca. 720 BC], and the same [Trojan] hero is later associated with the foundation of the more famous colonies of Croton and Sybaris in the same area [between the toe and heal of the Italian peninsula] ..." (F. H. Stubbings: »The Recession of Mycenaean Civilization«, *The Cambridge Ancient History* II, 3rd ed., part 2 (Cambridge, 2000), p. 356 (emphasis added). Philoctetes became a Trojan hero who dispatched Paris with the bow and arrows he inherited from Hercules. Some years after the Trojan War he sailed westward to the Italian peninsula where he eventually was killed during a key battle between Croton and Sybaris – the latter two cities having been founded sometime between 720 and 710 BC. (See the appropriate entries in the *Encyclopedia Britannica* and *Wikipedia*.) Additional germane information here is the attribution of a particular remark made by Cato (Marcus Porcius, 234 – 149 BC), statesman, moralist, writer, and orator best known for his opposition to the very existence of Carthage. So much so that concluded every speech he gave in the Senate no matter what the subject by stating that "Carthage must be destroyed". Of greater import for us is Cato's explicit statement that Pisa was founded by the *Etruscans* and relegates the Greek presence to a vague area, with an equally vague population that he refers to as "talking Greek". While the fact of that statement has been questioned and Cato was known to be anti-Hellenic, nevertheless "he wrote a historical work of great importance, the unfinished *Origins*, in seven books, on which he worked between 168 and his death. It owed much to Hellenistic predecessors, but broke new ground and included the fruits of some real historical research; it covered Roman and Italian history from Aeneas and the times of the kings down to his own day. Of this work only fragments survive." (J. Hazel: *Who's Who in the Roman World* (NY, 2001), pp. 58-59.) And there we have it – Achaeans (or Mycenaeans as they are often called) associated with Italian cities of the late 8th century BC, though they arrive after the Trojan War has been concluded.

Stubbings did earlier mention Mycenaean exploits in Asia Minor, but when it comes to southern Italy and Sicily he treats the previously just discussed colonies there as if they were a short time continuation of earlier Mycenaean contacts; and is totally blind to the chronological contradiction of what he is discussing. Here is his exact language: "The coasts of southern Italy and Sicily were not of course unknown to the Mycenaeans before this date:" ... However, he fails to identify "this date", preferring to fall back on references to LH II and LH IIIb which one must assume follows a conventional dating scheme whose source is Egypt which is being challenged herein. He then goes on to say – "There is at present no trace of Mycenaeans in Campania or Etruria" (p. 357, but see *infra*). Then what about *Nestor* (re Pisa) and the others? You cannot assume that settlements are occurring "there in the disturbed twelfth century" when those settlements are not being founded until the very end of the 8th century BC. Piling one rationalization upon another does not help. Is there a difference between Mycenaeans of ca. 1200 BC and Achaeans of ca. 700 BC? It is the absolute dependence upon and, dare I say, devotion to the exclusivity of pottery chronology that allows the continuance of a "Dark Age" mentality to prevail.

Another interesting story involving possible contradictory chronology is found in Etruscan myths of origin. The Etruscans were known as notorious pirates who were especially dreaded by those early Greeks willing to sail the western seas. However, the "Tyrrhenians" were only a particular branch of the Etruscan *ethnos*. According to "Etruscan myths of origin, the archetype of Etruscan piracy is found in the figure of Tyrrhenus" who may or may not have been one and the same as one of the founders of the Etruscan League of twelve cities, along with his brother Tarchon. Tyrrhenus was also the brother of Liparus (the text is not clear on this as to whether or not we are still dealing with the same personage referred to before). "After forcing Liparus to abandon Campania, his brother [unclear again who is being referred to] planned 'Peloponnesum vastare' [rampaging the Peloponnesian peninsula], inducing *Agamemnon* to send Aeolus [King of the Winds] to the west to block his way out of the Straits." (A passage in Servius: *ad Aeneidem*, I, 52; quoted from Torelli: *op. cit.*, p. 34, emphasis added.) In any event, the reference to *Agamemnon* definitely gives one pause. The author, Giovanni Colonna, of the statement just quoted apparently assumed he was dealing with a late 13th or early 12th century incident, yet chose to ignore the "Etruscan connection" via Tyrrhenus which clearly indicates a much later date. This would not be an anachronism if one applied Velikovsky's revised chronology.

These days Agamemnon is most remembered when one visits the Museum of Mycenae (actually in Athens). There "in the penultimate room Homer's king of kings makes his belated appearance. ... Displayed in this room is a large plate with the name of Agamemnon scratched into it. Here is a potsherd found at the Grave Circle inscribed 'to the hero'..." Shelves abound with a variety of *objets d'art*, "just some of the countless offerings left at the city's two principal shrines. One shrine was sacred to the memory of Agamemnon; the other was dedicated to the deity in whose scorched and bloody footprints the hero was destined always to follow – Ares, the god of war. ... the cult of Agamemnon really begins here; not during the city's Late Bronze Age heyday, but a little *over 400 years later*, when the ruins of the citadel wall stood higher than anything human-made in the surrounding landscape, attesting to a way of life that had passed away completely." (C. Gere: *The Tomb of Agamemnon* (2006), pp. 25-27, emphasis added).

Greece at the start of the eighth century BC had entered the Iron Age while the hero cult swept across the Peloponnese thereby making Mycenae "an important center of this new religious movement. During the *five illiterate centuries* that had interposed their dark bulk between the Trojan War and the spread of the Homeric epics, Agamemnon's capital had enjoyed an unusual degree of continuity with its heroic past" (p. 30, emphasis added). In florid prose, Gere then goes on to describe an endless sequence of internecine warfare among the Greeks – a legacy of the Trojan War – who were finally forced to unite against the greater power of the menacing Persian Empire. For Gere, the many new cities that the Greeks established all across the northern rim of the Mediterranean take an almost invisible back seat to the one-sided described martial activity that seemed to be a magnified version of an unending deadly athletic contest. Indeed, the Greek contribution to art, literature, and philosophy is completely overlooked as if they didn't even exist. No stratigraphic or archaeological information is provided for the intervening half a millennium. Nevertheless, a cult of Agamemnon arises at the site of Mycenae after a lapse of almost 500 years set against a background of ruin. Gere even states that "the 'Cult of the Hero'... sprang up in the ruins of Mycenae in the eighth century BC ..." This makes no sense. Why the long wait for such a cult? (An identical question was asked by Schorr regarding the creation of shrines for Agamemnon, and Menelaus and Helen of Sparta 500 years *after* the Trojan War – *Pensée* IX, »Applying the Revised Chronology« (Fall 1974), pp. 9-10 and Suppl. I of the present book) And in the case of Mycenae, why establish a cult at a supposed abandoned locale and what were the resources to do so? And where is the evidence for a resuscitated Mycenae to combine forces with Tiryns and send a total of 400 troops to fight the vast Persian forces in the deciding battle at Plataea in 479 BC, after sending 80 troops to help detain the Persians in the earlier battle of Thermopylae in 480 BC? (Gere, pp. 34-35, referred to again *infra* in a later section.)

Another important question to be asked: What was the key influential source for Gere's colorful if not hyperbolic account of the cults, warfare, and violence that she claims permeated Greek culture and history? The answer? Homer's Iliad! Omnipresent "Wandering minstrels were arriving at the towns and villages, reciting, along with all the other myths of gods and heroes, two great tales set during and after the Trojan War. ... Throughout their whole turbulent history the Greeks engaged in perpetual war, a way of life that was imbued with religious significance by the unshakeable authority of the *Iliad*" (pp. 27, 31). Perhaps Gere was thinking of the *theomachy* that imbued the *Iliad* for the many wars that did exist in Greek history; that it gave the Greeks a pass to justifiably imitate what they believed to be the behavior of their celestial gods and conduct their own terrestrial warfare. However, it was hardly "perpetual" and certainly not exclusive to the Greeks. Consider Assyro-Babylonian history and its wars for one; or what was uttered during the Crusades and beyond – "God wills it!", "Holy Wars" – "Jihad"; the untold number of soldiers blessed by a divine representative prior to going off to war; the multitude of religious symbols and banners carried into the heat of battle, the endless universal wars of conquest and conversion through the millennia down to our own day with invocations to the astral gods and their symbols. Is all this and more just the legacy of the *Iliad*? I will leave all that to the reader to conjure with. (I would also suggest Velikovsky's book *Mankind in Amnesia* which is cited and quoted at the end of this section; additionally, see L. M. Greenberg & W. B. Sizemore: »Cosmology and Psychology« in *Kronos* I:1 (April, 1975), »Cataclysm«, pp. 35-36; Z. Rix: »The Great Fear« in *ibid.*, pp. 51-64 ; Greenberg & Sizemore: »From Microcosm to Macrocosm: The Fearful Symmetry of Catastrophism« in *Kronos* I:2 (June, 1975), pp. 3-16; J. V. Myers & L. M. Greenberg: »Theomachy in the Theater: On the Fringes of the Collective Amnesia«, *ibid.*, pp. 23-34.) The so-called "wandering minstrels" have already been dealt with elsewhere in this book; the subject of Homer has been extensively covered.

Despite any criticism I may have had, this book by Cathy Gere is a most enjoyable and instructive read, except when she crosses the boundaries between scholarly discourse and fanciful recreations. Written with a gifted style and vocabulary, the latter two-thirds of the book is devoted not only to more retelling of Mycenae's story, but covers the period from the late 1870s until 2003 when the Museum opened. That alone does make this book worthwhile as it involves a number of disciplines, with Mycenae and Greece serving as both subject and back drop. The last section titled »FURTHER READING«, covering seven pages, gives us a chapter by chapter Bibliography with commentary that is truly excellent. Relevant illustrations in black & white are strategically placed in the text and quite helpful. A couple of them will be referred to shortly when we deal with the subject of pre-Classical tomb architecture.

Regarding the latter subject, a photo of the entrance way to the socalled Treasury of Atreus (p. 44), one of the entrance to the Tomb of

Clytemnestra (p. 185), and an engraving of the interior of the former by Edward Dodwell (p. 52) – all in black & white – make an excellent comparison with the techniques of corbelling that we see in the tomb architecture ca. 600 to early 6th century BC of the Etruscans in the Crocefisso del Tufo necropolis in Orvieto, or the corbelling of Tomb B of Melone di Camucia at Cortona. (G. Barker and T. Rasmussen: *The Etruscans* – The Peoples of Europe series (Oxford, 1998), pp. 234-236.) There is even a 21st century imitation of Mycenaean corbelling in the facade of the "neo-Mycenaean National Bank" in the main square in Nauplion. (Gere, ill., p. 148). However, there is a momentous difference between being merely imitative or derivative as opposed to something that was directly influenced by a predecessor; and the latter is the case when it comes to Etruscan tomb architecture which supposedly followed a noteworthy architectural typology. Consider the scholarly words of Axel Boethius: "Archaic rectangular corbelled grave chambers seem to have been used mainly in the southern city-states of Etruria. Towards the north, we find instead corbelled domes. These beehive tombs (*tholoi*) have no doubt inherited structural traditions from the *Mycenaean Age* [from a chronological distance of 7 centuries?!] or from yet earlier primitive constructions both of the Mediterranean countries and of Asia Minor [see material on Scythia and Thrace *supra*]. In any case, the corbelled dome is another monumental type which appears fully developed in Italy. Among these beehive tombs the so-called Montagnola and La Mula at Quinto Fiorentino are the most prominent examples." (A. Boethius: *Etruscan and Early Roman Architecture* (NY, 1978), pp. 96-97 and ill. 96, emphasis added.); F. Prayon: »Tomb Architecture« in *The Etruscans*, Ed. M. Torelli (2001), pp. 335-343.

The legacy of Etruscan tumulus funerary architecture (and that of Mycenae) lived on in the guise of the Mausoleum of Augustus, the largest Roman tomb ever built based upon its diameter. Since early Roman temples were derived from Etruscan architecture it would not be surprising to find Etruscan influence in Roman tomb architecture as well. (See M. J. Johnson: »The Mausoleum of Augustus: Etruscan and Other Influences on Its Design« in *Etruscan Italy*, Ed. J. F. Hall (Provo, 1996), pp. 217-239; 3-13)

Regarding the Mausoleum of Augustus, it has been suggested by several scholars that Augustus may have been influenced by the design of the tomb of Alexander the Great which he saw when he was in Alexandria; or perhaps that of Cleopatra as well (as suggested in the Ara Pacis section *infra*). There would be good political and architectural reasons for this. However, there is insufficient evidence to prove or disprove this theory. According to Johnson, "Given the affinities with Roman and Etruscan tombs which [he outlined], it does not appear necessary to look beyond the confines of Italy in order to explain the origins of the design of the mausoleum of Augustus. The primary features of the design of the imperial tomb can all be found in other Roman and Etruscan funerary monuments ..." (p. 231).

There is still a key question posed by Johnson regarding Augustus's choice of a Tumulus designed funerary monument for himself and his dynastic family: Why? There were a number of architectural funerary types to choose from, yet Augustus chose the "simple tumulus type, known for centuries in funerary architecture in Italy." Was it because Augustus was specifically looking towards an Etruscan model for his tomb or "more likely that this design was chosen at least in part because it had become a traditional type in aristocratic Roman funerary architecture" as well as a type preferred by the upper classes of Etruria for status purpose?

In answer to his own question – "Why? – Johnson suggested yet "another source of inspiration for Augustus in choosing the tumulus type." The proposed "other source would be the so-called tomb of Aeneas at Lavinium, modern Practica di Mare. According to the legend, Aeneas disappeared following a battle near the Numicus River, and his body was never found. Dionysius of Halicarnassus records that 'the Latins built a hero-shrine to him ... It is a small mound, around which have been set out in regular rows trees that are well worth seeing'." (pp. 231-232). In the early 1970s excavations were done in the area of Lavinium and the remains of a small tumulus were discovered. A mound covered the tomb structure which was dated to the seventh century BC. In the fourth century BC, modifications changed the tomb to a *heroon*, or hero shrine.

> This tumulus has been identified by its excavator as the heroon of Aeneas described by Dionysius, though not all scholars are in agreement on this issue. ... [However,] the key point is that the account of Dionysius remains unchallenged: there was a heroon of Aeneas at Lavinium, and it took the form of a tumulus. Although it is unclear if the tumulus was thought to be the tomb proper of Aeneas or if there was no actual burial, as a heroon its form was that of a tomb, an architectural link commonly found in such buildings. It is also important to recognize that the cult of Aeneas was propagated in the time of Augustus, and it is impossible to believe that Augustus would have been unaware of its presence and prac-

tices at Lavinium. ... there are several important points of comparison between it and the mausoleum of Augustus. Both are located near rivers; both were surrounded by trees; and, most importantly, both are tumuli. There was also a similarity of function. Though the mound may not have contained the burial of Aeneas, it was built near the site of his disappearance or death and it was meant to honor the man and historians his deeds. As a heroon, it would have also been the site of the cultic worship of Aeneas. The mausoleum of Augustus held the urn of Augustus and therefore had the function of a tomb, but it also commemorated the man and his deeds. In this connection it is worth remembering that the tablets containing the Res Gestae were displayed near the entrance to the tomb. ... A writer of the early third century A.D., Cassius Dio, calls the mausoleum a 'heroon'. (p. 233).

The Pantheon in Rome may have also played a key role beyond the assumed, but unproven, belief that it was a temple. Instead, thanks to its orientation which from the outset was directed at the entrance way to the Mausoleum of Augustus and the structuring of the great domed interior, the Pantheon actually continues the principle of corbeling that is traceable back to Apulia in the sixteenth century BC and even further back to Sardinia, ca. 1800 BC. (These two dates may be questionable.) It could have also served as a kind of commemorative type quasi-mausoleum, a dynastic sanctuary with dynastic implications. (See *The Pantheon From Antiquity To The Present*, ed. by T. A. Marder & M. W. Jones (2015), pp. 4-7, 127-131.) I would even go so far as to suggest that the Church of the Holy Sepulchre and the Dome of the Rock in Jerusalem have an architectural relationship with the corbeled vaulted structures of the eastern and western Mediterranean.

Augustus made every effort to link his name and persona to that of Aeneas. He permitted Agrippa to place a statue of himself and one of Agrippa in the portico of the Pantheon while one of Aeneas may have been in the interior. In his Forum, Augustus placed a statue of Aeneas among others representing his ancestors; and the depiction of Aeneas on a panel of the Ara Pacis is carefully balanced by the image of Augustus on the same monument. For our purposes, the dating of the tumulus in Lavinium combined with the story of Aeneas and Dido, along with the information already presented *supra* concerning tholoi tombs in Etruria, Thrace, and Scythia in itself is a formidable argument against the legitimacy of the self-created "Dark Age" of Greece. Of course, there already has been considerable evidence brought forward *supra* casting doubt on any Dark Age – and there is even far more yet to come. (See the many Supplement Sections by Schorr, Sammer, and Greenberg *infra*.)

For now, we will conclude this referential and informational section with a final look at some other Etruscan material objects. In her book *The Etruscans* (1995 reprint), Agnes Carr Vaughan devoted an entire chapter to »Clothing and Toilet Accessories«. There, she began her discussion of what types of clothing could be worn by the different classes of the Etruscan populace. The information was gleaned from what was depicted in the fresco artistry that was found on the walls of their tombs. "Early frescoes and bas-reliefs show men wearing a kind of embroidered kilt, which left the upper part of the body bare, a costume frequently seen in Minoan-Mycenaean frescoes. Later on, probably under Greek influence, Etruscan men wore a kind of chiton, or short tunic, similar to what was worn by the Greeks of the same period ..." (p. 71). Since we are reading a description of clothing no doubt dating to the 8th century BC or later, how could Etruscan men see, much less copy, Minoan-Mycenaean dress from 500 years earlier that would have disappeared among the ruins of that civilization? Unless, of course, Cretan and Mycenaean travelers and traders were having contemporary contact with Etruria and there was no Dark Age.

Next, we have a description of Etruscan jewelry seen by Vaughan in the British Museum. "This collection, which dates from the seventh to the second century B.C., as do other collections in museums, brings forcibly home to us the luxury of those far-off days. Fastened to a wall are two large glass-covered cases: one contains Minoan-Mycenaean jewelry, the other Etruscan. Though centuries apart in time, the jewelry in both cases seems *closely related* in beauty, refinement, and craftsmanship." (p. 76, emphasis added). Other museums, Perugia, the Vatican, the Louvre, Boston Museum of Fine Arts, Florence, Rome, also display their Etruscan treasures. For what it's worth, the Met in New York "displays its Cretan and Etruscan jewelry in adjoining cases" (p. 77). Did the person in the Met who set this up sense something?

One last reference of particular relevance involving the Etruscans is a book titled *Mycenaeans in Early Latium* (Rome, 1980) which will be discussed in more detail in the section *infra* on Carthage, Rome, Dido, and Aeneas. For now it must be emphasized that any dates for Mycenaean contact with Italy in remote times is founded upon ceramic dating involving a variety of sherds; and those "are few and very fragmentary". Most are from a period marked as Mycenaean III A – Mycenaean III B whose dates, as stated many times, were obtained via

Egyptian contexts. In absolute dating the Mycenaean pottery that has been discovered there has been retrieved from several sites in Apulia and chronologically placed sometime between 1425 and 1200 BC. Those dates alone conflict with what we know of the dates for the existing settlements in Apulia and elsewhere in the Italian peninsula. The author, Lucia Vagnetti, of this Appendix (II) to the book even admits that "The present writer is aware of the discussion about the validity of this chronological scheme, especially about the division and chronology of the latest phases [Submycenaean and Mycenaean III C 1 periods] which is now in doubt and the whole problem needs a thorough study. However, this conventional chronology is sufficient to give an idea to the general reader" (p. 165). But it doesn't. The conventional chronology is confusing and the archaeological discovery of more sherds merely perpetuates the same problem – the source for the dating. A previous Appendix (I) titled »Mycenaeans and Etruscans« only adds to the confusion. With Etruscans firmly established as a coherent society in Etruria around the beginning of the 8th century BC or even later in Italy, you cannot have Mycenaeans or Arcadians or whatever name you choose, invoke the Trojan War, ambiguous script, and be satisfied with placing Evander or Aeneas in the 13th century BC. Nearly a third of the way into this Appendix, its author Emilio Peruzzi hopefully states: "Perhaps archaeology will eventually provide some proof of a Mycenaean presence in early Etruria" (p. 142). Perhaps it will, just NOT in the 13th century BC.

Last but not least, in the section titled »Celestial Events in the *Iliad*«, which is a brief reiteration of the »Mars« part of *Worlds in Collision* (pp. 207-297), Velikovsky revealed the role that the planetary gods played in the different battles that took place during the Trojan War. These conflicts among the Olympian gods known as theomachy occurred in the celestial sphere but were grafted onto the terrestrial melee that took place below. The main focus of all this was the specific part that the planet Mars assumed in the cosmic history of the inner solar system at that time which Velikovsky understood to be somewhere between 747 and 687 BC. These dates were gleaned from his research into the ancient literary legacy of the world's cultures. From China to India, to the Ancient Near East, Northern Europe, the Mediterranean world, and pre-Columbian America, Velikovsky combed the ancient sources and compiled sufficient evidence to present his dramatic and heterodox conclusions. Among those was the belief that Mars, on an errant orbit and not yet settled in its current one, interacted with Earth and the planet Venus – itself only recently settled into a circular orbit. This caused immense destruction globally and brought a disruption of varying duration or actual termination to several different societies. Anyone who knows the history of *Worlds in Collision* and the way it and its author were treated still finds it difficult to believe, even though 70 years have passed. (See Velikovsky's *Stargazers and Gravediggers*.) That's why the following book – *Homer's Secret Iliad: The Epic of the Night Skies Decoded*, published in 1999 – should raise eyebrows.

The following quotes from the Acknowledgements page and Prologue should be sufficient to give a clear picture of what this book is all about:

> The material on Homeric astronomy in the following pages is derived from the pioneering studies of Edna Leigh [nee Johnston] ... The aim of this book is to show that it is also the world's oldest substantial astronomical text, whose learning has been lost for two millennia or more. Embedded in its accounts of gods and mortals is an abundance of information about the planets, the constellations and hundreds of stars, from the brightest in the sky to those just visible to the naked eye. Homer's stories were the vehicle for preserving this knowledge and passing it down through the ages. ... This book seeks to show that the *Iliad* was created to preserve ancient knowledge of the heavens and is not only a poem about the Siege of Troy, but also a comprehensive record of the ancients' knowledge of the skies. ... The rediscovery of the *Iliad* as a repository of astronomical knowledge had an unlikely genesis, beginning in Kansas where Edna Johnston was born in 1916. ... 'Eventually I was able to identify the general subject matter of Homeric epic as astronomy,' she wrote in 1965. ... Edna's trailblazing work shows that even in today's high-technology world there is room for the *grand amateur* to make an outstanding contribution, particularly in the interdisciplinary borderlands between two subjects – in this case, between literature and the history of astronomy. ... 'When Homer wrote of the wine-dark seas, he wanted us to look at the heavens, not the oceans'. (pp. ix-8).

From this starting point the authors (Florence & Kenneth Wood – Edna's daughter & son-in-law) travail their way through ca. 300 pages of Homeric history, astronomical jargon, numerous figures, tables, charts, mathematical calculations, dates, appendices, short glossary of astronomical terms, notes, references, and sources. In the end we are left with a laudatory paean to Homer the scientist, knowledgeable in astronomy and geography. Who knew? Apparently Strabo for one. But after his death, Homer's "secret *Iliad*" remained hidden and was not revealed for another 2000 years. What are some of the many revelations that emerge from this book? And how does it relate to the oeuvre and theories of Velikovsky? First let us consider what the authors accept. They accept the chronology for the Mycenaean Age and bring no challenge to it; accept a Dark Age in Greece for some 500 years, and quote the words of Peter Green, an historian of Ancient Greek history relating to it:

> Before Homer and Hesiod, to put it bluntly, we lack the entire intellectual framework of Greek society, and the far-ranging archaeological discoveries made during the past 100 years should never obscure the central truth ... Unless we count the oldest layer ... in Homer and other accounts of the traditional myths, we have no literature whatsoever to illuminate either Crete or Mycenae. Oddly, this is not true of other Near East civilizations. (p. 43, P. Green: *A Concise History of Ancient Greece to the Close of the Classical Era* (London, 1973), p. 10).

No cosmic catastrophes are proposed and no terrestrial catastrophes as a result of the former. They reject the very idea that there was even a Trojan War involving any human combat. We know from archaeology that there were many Troys, though the accepted site for that city has been questioned by others as indicated elsewhere in this book. Of the many levels so far uncovered at the putative site for Troy, it is level VIIa that is assumed to be the one that influenced Homer to create his epic. Here is the succinct stance of *Homer's Secret Iliad*'s authors on the entire matter:

> That Troy burned is without a doubt, but who put the city to the torch? There is no convincing evidence that the Siege of Troy so graphically described in the *Iliad* ever happened. Nor is there any proof that Greek and Trojan leaders such as Achilles, Agamemnon, Hector and Paris, or any other characters in the *Iliad*, ever existed except in the imagination. A more likely explanation for the burning of Troy VIIa may be with a mysterious force of marauders known as the Sea Peoples ..." (p. 53).

The latter proposal has never been made to my knowledge. If anything, there are a few who have considered the possibility that a number of Achaeans participated in that group after their war on Troy had been concluded. That too has been rejected. Indeed, the identity of the Sea Peoples is still being debated to the present day. As for Troy, "Archaeological work continues ... at Troy, but nothing has been found to indicate that a great Greek army of many thousands of men laid siege for ten long years before razing it to the ground." (p. 55).

With those words, the authors of *Homer's Secret Iliad* spend the next five chapters of their book attempting to show that "the gods, Greek and Trojan warriors and other characters in Homer's epic represent planets, stars and constellations, and by their activities they preserve a remarkable volume of astronomical learning, encompassing everything that can be seen in the heavens by the naked eye. In purely astronomical terms, Homer's aim was to enable his audiences to identify the stars and constellations and to know their relative position in the sky. ... There is such a breadth and depth to the astronomical content of the *Iliad* that it is almost overwhelming." (pp. 56-57). Forget the word "almost". What is presented in this book is absolutely overwhelming. So much so that one must wonder how a society newly introduced to literacy could even begin to grasp the complexity of what is depicted and discussed. I leave it to others to judge. Suffice it to say, there is an enormous amount of material in this book. Its relevance to *this* book and Velikovsky's other published work must now be considered. For one, it is more than a matter of passing interest and even somewhat satisfying to read the theories of others, aside from Velikovsky's, pertaining to a celestial connection involving Homer and the *Iliad*, though the pathway for each is quite different (see *infra*). What is most disappointing, however, is the lack of any acknowledgement by the Woods of *Worlds in Collision* and its section on the *Iliad*.

Worlds in Collision is still in print after 70+ years and was already well-known by the late 1950s when the original intended author of *Homer's Secret Iliad* had "discovered how Homer used astronomical knowledge to guide ancient peoples in their travels the length and breadth of Greece and Asia Minor ..." (p. 5). As an aside, one may rightfully ask how all this guidance was to be conveyed to a diverse number of people newly recovering from a Dark Age which these authors do not deny. There were no books containing stellar guidelines for a general populace to absorb even if it was possible to fully understand what was in them which I sincerely doubt. And how did Homer manage to draw the complex charts that appear in a 20th century AD publication? Let's see a sampling of the proposed celestial identifications for those divinities and heroes who participated in the Trojan War and their planetary and stellar counterparts: Hera = the Moon (ordinarily Queen of the sky associated with the Earth); Aphrodite = Venus; Athene = Jupiter (Velikovsky identified her with the planet Venus while standard mythology has her born from the head of Zeus-Jupiter who is always associated with the planet Jupiter.) Is she now born from her own head with a gender change?; Ares = Mars; Poseidon = Saturn (How does Poseidon-Neptune god of the seas come to be associated with the planet Saturn? This goes against not only Greco-Roman religion, but any others when it comes to this ringed planet); Achilles = Sirius and Canis Major; Aeneas = Spica and Virgo; Agamemnon = Regulus and Leo; Hector = Orion and Rigel; Patroclus = Procyon and Canis Minor; Paris = Betelgeuse and Orion; Troy = Ursa Major.

Worlds in Collision had been available for 50 years when *Homer's Secret Iliad* was finally published. Particular individuals who knew of the latter book and its authors were approving and communicated as much to the Woods – Giorgio de Santillana, co-author of *Hamlet's Mill*, for one. Others who were cited by the authors of *Homer's Secret Iliad* appear to have expressed no negativity. Yet they were highly disapproving of *Worlds in Collision*, to put it mildly, and made up just part of a large contingent of individuals from different disciplines who vilified Velikovsky from the moment *Worlds in Collision* appeared on the scholarly scene. He was looked upon as an interloper in their fields of expertise. Why is it that these later authors of *Homer's Secret Iliad* escaped the wrath of the academic community even though they stepped firmly on the proverbial establishment toes of Literature, History, Geography, Cosmology, Astronomy, Archaeology, and Archaeo-Astronomy with what appears to be a number of far out theories? Very simply put – they weren't *threatening*!

Therefore, the reception to this book was quite different. Ironically, *Homer's Secret Iliad* indirectly validates Velikovsky's conclusion regarding the presence of celestial events in the *Iliad*. The authors of *Homer's Secret Iliad* could have put the following postscript to their book: "No sacred cows were harmed during the course of writing this book." A final irony has to do with the date when *Homer's Secret Iliad* was released – 1999. By that time when it came to Homer, the question could easily have been: Who cares? A curtain was rapidly descending upon the subject of Classical studies. And in that very same year the following book by Victor Davis Hanson and John Heath had only recently appeared: *Who Killed Homer?* – a sign of contemporary times and attitudes. Another book of interest that approaches the *Iliad* primarily from a martial standpoint is *The War That Killed Achilles – The True Story of Homer's Iliad and the Trojan War* by Caroline Alexander (2009). The last sentence of the Preface says it all: "This book is about what the *Iliad* is about; this book is about what the *Iliad* says of war." Velikovsky's approach to the *Iliad* actually echoes in a way both the book by Alexander and that of the Woods. Consider the following quote taken from Velikovsky's intended *magnum opus* published posthumously in 1982 – *Mankind in Amnesia*:

> Stoic philosophers taught the recurrent conflagrations of the world; the Pythagoreans were immersed in speculations of cosmic order and disorder; and before them, in Homer's *Iliad*, there are numerous scenes of *theomachy*, or war among the planetary gods. The entire Greek pantheon is but a pandemonium on Olympus; and Mount Olympus, in later times located in several vicinities of Greek lands, was originally but the vault of the sky. (p. 48).

"The gods and goddesses of war are prominent members of the pantheons of both Greece and Rome; in addition many other deities and heroes were by no means averse to belligerence and dabbled in conflict in one form or another. ... The battles fought by and between Titans, Giants, Amazons, between centaurs and Lapiths, and by heroes like Heracles were pivotal in the annals of Greek civilization. ... conflict in mythology and legend resonated loudly as *essential, even existentialist* symbols in Greek culture ... A myth expresses and confirms society's religious values and norms, it provides a *pattern of behavior to be imitated*, testifies to the efficacy of ritual with its practical ends and establishes the sanctity of cult. ... the fabric of Greek society was made out of war ..." (Paul Chrystal: *War in Greek Mythology* (Barnsley, 2020), pp. xi-1, 24 and *inter alia*, emphasis added. Also see his *War in Roman Mythology* (Barnsley, 2020).

The history of humankind is the history of warfare. What was it that could inculcate the very DNA of Homo sapiens for the desire, nay the need, to wage constant war on an ever looping redundancy even up to the present? Greek chronology begins with a war and competitive games mark its official beginning. The history of Dynastic Egypt had its beginnings after a final battle victory resulted in the Union of the Two Lands. – *In the Beginning* and *Worlds in Collision* anyone?

- And finally, two more references that may serve as an homage for what is contained in this book:

THE AGES OF HOMER
A Tribute To Emily Townsend Vermeule
Ed. by Jane B. Carter and Sarah P. Morris (Austin, 1995)
With 31 Chapters, each written by a different authority in the field

&

THE TROJAN WAR AS MILITARY HISTORY
by M. E. Kambouris (Phil., 2023)

Lewis M. Greenberg

Supplement I

Applying the Revised Chronology

(by Edwin M. Schorr)

Foreword

Edwin M. Schorr, formerly a graduate student of the ancient Eastern Mediterranean and Near East, and a doctoral candidate in Pre-classical Aegean archaeology, also served as a research assistant to Dr. Velikovsky for a number of years. He has previously published articles in the journals *Pensée* and *Kronos*.

In 1974 (under a nom de plume) he wrote an article in *Pensée*, showing instances of archaeological discoveries from Greece, Anatolia and North Syria which lend support to Velikovsky's revision of ancient history (I. Isaacson: »Applying the Revised Chronology«, *Pensée*, IVR IX [1974], pp. 5ff). This supplement is an updated portion of that article.

Chapter 1

Mycenae

The Entrance to the Citadel

Both literary accounts and archaeological discoveries indicate that the ancient city of Mycenae in the Peloponnese of Greece was the political and cultural center of the Late Bronze Age (or "Late Helladic [LH]") Greece. For this reason one calls that period, its culture and its material remains "Mycenaean". Since Mycenae is the type-site for LH Greece, its history and its relics will be of chief concern in this essay.

According to tradition, the city's founder was the legendary hero Perseus, and the later Greeks attributed its fortifications of tremendous stones to mythical giants, the one-eyed Cyclopes. It was for Eurystheus, a later king of Mycenae, that Heracles performed his twelve labors. One of the city's last heroic kings was Agamemnon, commander of the pan-Hellenic expedition against Troy. Upon his return from that long war, his queen and her paramour murdered him in the palace, for which crime his children, Orestes and Electra, took their terrible revenge.[1]

First excavated by Heinrich Schliemann in the 1870s, in one of the earliest systematic campaigns at a Late Helladic (LH) center, Mycenae is one of the most thoroughly excavated and studied places in the world. For over a century now, German, Greek and British prehistorians have revealed a wealth of archaeological information, as well as costly and beautiful artifacts. Work still continues there on a yearly basis.

Since the absolute dates for Mycenae and the entire East Mediterranean Late Bronze Age come directly from Egypt,[2] if Immanuel Velikovsky's revised chronology is valid, one should expect, that numer-

---

[1] Pausanias I:16. 3-5.
[2] A. Furumark: *The Chronology of Mycenaean Pottery* (Stockholm, 1941), especially pp. 110-115. More recently, see V. Hankey and P. Warren: »The Absolute Chronology of the Aegean Late Bronze Age«, *Bulletin of the Institute of Classical Studies* (Univ. of London) (henceforth BICS), 21 (1974), pp. 142-152.

ous 500 to 700-year problems trouble those who deal with Mycenae and the Mycenaean Age – which is the topic of the present essay.

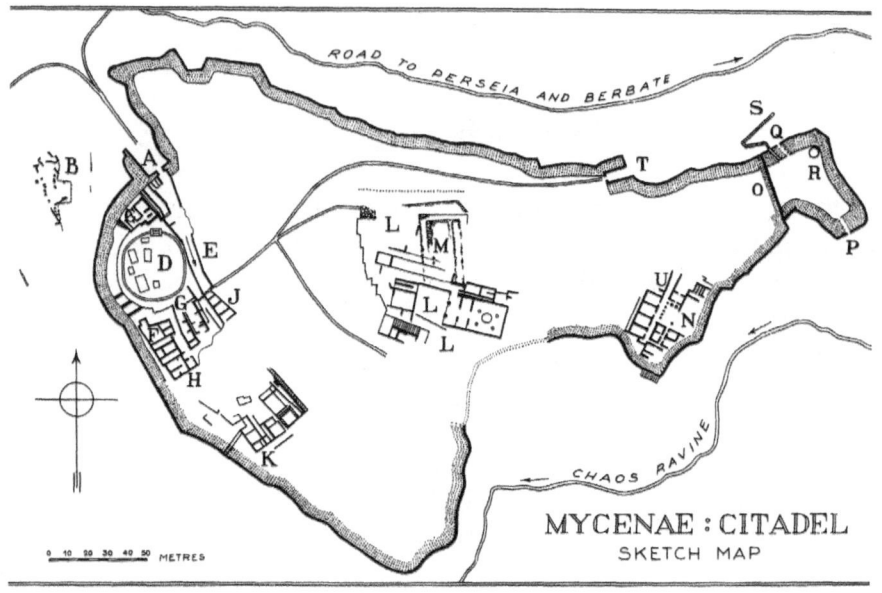

Fig.1: Ground Plan of Mycenae

In the present volume, Velikovsky treated the Lion Gate of Mycenae (Fig. 1, A), and brought out how, and why, late nineteenth-century art historians and excavators, who studied the stone carving and the gateway it surmounts, originally ascribed them to the eighth century BC; he also showed how adherents to Egyptian chronology pushed the date back by half a millennium to ca. 1250 BC. The debate over those 500 years, long ago resolved in favor of the Egyptian time scale, still presents problems for modern archaeologists. Thus, John Boardman, who does accept a thirteenth-century attribution for the gate, recently concluded that "more than five hundred years were to pass before Greek sculptors could [again] command an idiom which would satisfy these aspirations in sculpture and architecture."[1]

The Lion Gate was the main entrance-way of Mycenae. Between the Gate and the building known as the Granary (Fig. 1, C), A. J. B.

---

[1] J. Boardman: *Greek Art* (New York, 1964), p. 22.

Wace dug a test trench in 1920. The location was ideal for two reasons. First, being near the gate and along the main street into the city, the spot collected all tangible evidence of those who passed along the route.[1] Second, the area was a perfect sedimentation trap, enclosed by three walls, with the fourth side open to the steeply sloping ground of the citadel, so that it also collected the material that constantly rolled or washed down from above. Since that trench provides the best stratigraphical section of the site, and "is the main basis for trying to date the fall of Mycenae,"[2] the findings are of particular interest to us. Wace differentiated thirteen layers, which had collected between the fortification wall, the gate, and the Granary, all constructed in the middle of the Late Helladic (LH) III B period (ca. 1250 BC).[3] The bottom ten layers belonged exclusively to the period of construction until late in the pottery phase known as LH III C (set at 1250 – 1100/1050 BC), at most 150 – 200 years.[4] On the average, then, each of those layers represented ca. 15 – 20 years.

The eleventh layer from the bottom, in addition to "eleventh-century" LH III C pottery, contained a significant number of fragments of Orientalizing ware (i.e., seventh to sixth century BC). That layer, which, by the accepted scheme, must represent the passage of ca. 500 years, was only about 1/6 the total thickness of the ten layers beneath it, which represent only 150 to 200 years. It was, in fact, thinner than one of the earlier layers representing ca. 15 – 20 years.

---

[1] A. J. Evans (*The Palace of Minos* [London, 1935], IV, pp. 63-64 n. 1) was perhaps correct in viewing that narrow alley-way as a dumping ground, but it was better stratified than he believed.

[2] A. D. Lacy: *Greek Pottery in the Bronze Age* (London, 1967), p. 221.

[3] A. J. B. Wace: »The Lion Gate and Grave Circle Area«, *Annual of the British School at Athens* (henceforth *BSA*), 25 (1921-23), p. 18; G. Mylonas: *Mycenae and the Mycenaean Age* (Princeton, 1966), pp. 21, 33.

[4] Lacy, (1967), pp. 221-2. Although Furumark (1941, p. 115) assigned the end of the LH III C to ca. 1100, A. M. Snodgrass (*The Dark Age of Greece* [Edinburgh, 1971], pp. 134-5) had it end at 1125 BC in W. Attika, 1050 BC in the Argolid, and still later in the hinter regions. Realizing that he chose his Argolid dating in order to have continuous occupation there until the next pottery style (Protogeometric) arrived, he acknowledged that the duration might be too long, and that there might be a break (*ibid.*, pp. 57-124). V. Desborough (*The Last Mycenaeans and Their Successors* [Oxford, 1964], p. 75; *The Greek Dark Ages* [London, 1972], pp. 69, 79), did not grant Argolid LH III C the extra 50 years which Snodgrass postulated, though he later conceded that Wace's eleventh layer possibly extended into the early eleventh century (»Late Burials from Mycenae«, *BSA*, 68 [1973], p. 100). For our purposes, current scholarly disagreements on chronology are of interest, but compared to the 500-700-year problems treated in this volume, 50-year differences seem rather inconsequential.

It is very important to note that the eleventh layer contained no pottery dated to 1050 – 700 BC. If people continued to inhabit, enter, and leave Mycenae between the eleventh century and the seventh, one would expect some evidence of that fact to appear in that trench near the gate, yet none does. Even if the site was abandoned for centuries, one would still expect a layer of "wash," consisting of ashes and dissolved mud brick from ruined structures on the citadel to lie above the eleventh-century pottery and below that of the seventh,[1] but there was none. Neither was there a seventh-century layer distinguishable from the eleventh-century one, as if centuries of debris and/or wash had been removed before the seventh-century pottery was deposited. One thin layer contained pottery of two styles customarily separated by hundreds of years, yet the trench showed no evidence that those centuries actually transpired.[2]

In the 1920s, Wace considered the eleventh layer, its seventh-century pottery, to be "the last true Mycenaean stratum," (i.e., it followed immediately after the tenth layer, and began to form in the twelfth century).[3] Some thirty years later, however, disturbed by the 400-year-later material, he changed his mind, and reduced the age of the entire layer, proposing that its LH III C contents were deposited centuries after they were made.[4] That solution, however, still runs into the same problem as before – unless removed (for no apparent reason), the evidence of centuries' duration, either as pottery or as wash, should still appear somewhere in the section – if not within the eleventh layer, then beneath it and the tenth. Other scholars[5] do not accept Wace's redating, but follow his original assessment, that, despite the seventh-century material, the eleventh layer belongs mainly to the twelfth century.

If Mycenaean pottery had not received its absolute dates from Egypt, then, on the basis of that and other stratigraphical sections from Prosymna, Tiryns, Pylos, Athens, Sparta (Therapne), Kythera, Crete

---

[1] Cf. the very thick layer of wash from higher up the citadel overlying the cult center (Fig. 1, K) (A. H. S. Megaw: »Archaeology in Greece, 1964-65«, *Archaeological Reports* 1964-65, p. 11; W. D. Taylour: »A Note on the Recent Excavations at Mycenae, etc.«, *BSA* 68 [1973], p. 260), where the slope was much more precipitous. More to the point, the first Grave Circle (Fig. 1, D), which lies much closer to the Granary, also had a layer of washed debris above it (Wace, 1921-23, p. 126).
[2] Wace: *ibid.*, pp. 34-36, and fig. 4, p. 19.
[3] *Ibid.*, p. 34.
[4] Wace: »The Last Days of Mycenae«, in *The Aegean and Near East* (ed. S. Weinberg) (Locust Valley, NY, 1956), pp. 129-130.
[5] E.g., Desborough, 1973, pp. 99-100.

(Vrokastro), Chios, Troy, Italy (Taranto), etc.,[1] and also, as we shall presently see, on the basis of style, one might say – as numerous scholars once did – that LH III B-C pottery (1350 – 1100/1050 BC by Egyptian reckoning) immediately preceded the seventh-sixth century Orientalizing ware.

The Grave Circles

Immediately south of the Lion Gate and the Granary, Schliemann discovered a circle (Fig. 1, D), which contained six royal graves.[2] In the 1950s I. Papadimitriou and G. Mylonas discovered a second circle outside of, and to the west of the Lion Gate. That circle (Circle B), containing twenty-four more princely graves, is, for the most part, contemporaneous with Schliemann's (now called Circle A), beginning a bit before it and discontinued while Circle A was still in use. The two circles have furnished some of the richest and most exciting finds to come from Mycenae, or, in fact, from any prehistoric European site. Since the graves' contents are mainly contemporaneous with the early

---

[1] Prosymna: see n. below; Tiryns: for the debate over the twelfth- or seventh-century date of the "temple," see below, section »Tiryns«. For more recent discoveries of late eighth-century pottery immediately above, or mixed with, Late Helladic IIIB/C wares on the citadel, in the lower town, on the plain, and in a wall chamber, see W. Rudolph: »Tiryns 1968« in *Tiryns* V (ed. U. Jantzen) (Mainz, 1971), p. 93; U. Jantzen et al.: »Tiryns-Synoro-Iria 1965-1968«, *Archäologischer Anzeiger* (henceforth *Arch. Anz.*), 83 (1968), p. 371; W. Rudolph: »Tiryns: Unterburg 1968 etc.« in *Tiryns* VIII (ed. U. Jantzen) (Mainz, 1975), pp. 97, 99, 114; H. Doehl: »Tiryns Stadt: Sondage 1968« also in *Tiryns* VIII, pp. 152, 154. Athens: for eighth-century pottery mixed with LH III C in a well, see O. Broneer: »A Mycenaean Fountain on the Athenian Acropolis«, *Hesperia*, 8 (1939), pp. 402-403, 427-428; Therapne: see n. below; Kythera: for the lack of material between LH III B2 and the eighth century, see J. N. Coldstream in *Kythera* (ed. Coldstream and G. Huxley) (Park Ridge, N. J., 1973), pp. 305-306; Vrokastro: for late eighth-century ware immediately above, mixed with, and below Late Minoan III pottery, see E. H. Hall: *Excavations in Eastern Crete, Vrokastro* (Philadelphia, 1914), pp. 89-90, 108-109; Chios: for the abandonment of Emborio from LH III C till the late eighth century, see Snodgrass, (1971), p. 90; Troy: for an early eighth-century sherd beneath LH III C structures with no evidence of later disturbance, see C. Blegen et al.: *Troy* IV.1 (Princeton, 1956), pp. 231-233. For late eighth- and early seventh-century ware immediately above, mixed with, and beneath apparently uncontaminated LH III C layers, see *ibid.*, pp. 158, 181, 253, 265. For a fuller discussion, see below, section »Troy«; Scoglio del Tonno (near Taranto): for seventh-century ware mixed with LH III C, see T. J. Dunbabin: *The Western Greeks* (Oxford, 1948), p. 28, and idem: »Minos and Daidalos in Sicily«, *Papers of the British School at Rome*, 16 (N. S. 3) (1948), p. 10 and n. 77; other cases also exist.

[2] Schliemann found five of the graves. P. Stamatakes later found the sixth.

Eighteenth Dynasty of Egypt, archaeologists have assigned them to the seventeenth-sixteenth (or early fifteenth) centuries BC.[1]

Seeking the origin of such grave circles, N. G. L. Hammond recently maintained that they came to Mycenae from Albania. Comparing the Mycenaean examples to Albanian grave mounds, he saw "close analogies in the details of the burial customs, the structure of the mortuary chambers, and the contents of the graves."[2] Regarding the construction technique, "the similarities indeed are remarkably close."[3] The weapons from the Albanian graves also display "astonishing similarities" to those from the Mycenaean Grave Circles.[4] After considering several factors, Hammond concluded that "the answer can only be that the tumulus-burials of Albania ... are the antecedents" of the Mycenaean burials.[5]

There is a very serious drawback, however. F. Prendi, the excavator of the Albanian graves, at first claimed that, typologically, those burials belong no earlier than the eleventh century BC; he has continued to assign them 500-600 years later than does Hammond.[6] A. M. Snodgrass agreed that "at first sight Hammond's dating ... seems a natural one," because the earliest Albanian pottery and weapons do resemble material of, and immediately preceding the early Mycenaean Period.[7] Further analysis, however, ran Snodgrass "up against the fundamental difficulty of chronology."[8] Since Albania was extremely conservative throughout antiquity, he felt that there could have been a centuries-long "time-lag" between the creation of goods in Greece and their transmission to Albania, or, alternatively, that they could have arrived in Albania at the time of their manufacture in Greece, and remained

---

[1] Mylonas (1966, p. 236) set the dates at ca. 1650-1510 BC, while E. Vermeule: *The Art of the Shaft Graves at Mycenae* [Norman, OK, 1975], pp. 8, 49) lowered the final date to ca. 1450 BC.

[2] N. G. L. Hammond: *A History of Macedonia* I (Oxford, 1972), p. 275.

[3] Hammond: »Tumulus Burial in Albania, the Grave Circles of Mycenae, and the Indo-Europeans«, *BSA*, 62 (1967), p. 90.

[4] Hammond: *Epirus* (Oxford, 1967), p. 343.

[5] Hammond (1967), p. 91. See also his »The Dating of Some Burials in Tumuli in South Albania«, *BSA*, 66 (1971), pp. 229-241 and »Grave Circles in Albania and Macedonia« in *Bronze Age Migrations in the Aegean* (ed. R. Crossland and A. Birchall) (London, 1973), pp. 189-195.

[6] For the opinion of Prendi and other excavators of those tombs, see Hammond (1971), pp. 231, 240-241 and his references to the publications in Albanian.

[7] Snodgrass (1971), p. 259.

[8] *Ibid.*, p. 257.

in vogue in the north for centuries, without evolving as they had to the south.¹

Perplexed by the latest items from the Albanian grave mounds, some of which seemed to belong to the twelfth century, as Hammond claimed, while others seemed to be 600 years later, Snodgrass still decided to follow Prendi rather than Hammond. He thus assigned the Albanian graves not to the sixteenth-eleventh centuries, but to ca. 1100 – 600 BC.² More recently, Emily Vermeule, a noted Bronze Age archaeologist and art historian, and J. V. Luce gave credence to Hammond's case.³ If, however, Prendi and Snodgrass are correct in assigning the earliest Albanian material to ca. 1100 BC, then, despite "close analogies", "remarkably close", indeed "astonishing" similarities (Hammond), those graves obviously cannot be the "antecedents" and models for graves which are 500 years older at Mycenae.⁴

Over a number of the interments in the two Grave Circles of Mycenae stood twenty-two stone stelae, some plain, others decoratively carved. If they really belong to the seventeenth to sixteenth centuries BC, several authorities see a 500-year discontinuity before the custom of placing tombstones over graves resumed its vogue in Greece.⁵ More important than the 500-year problem is the subject matter on some of the sculpted stelae. The scenes of hunting and battle depicted, as well as the general carving technique, remind one very much of Syro-Anatolian relief sculptures – especially those six to seven centuries later in date.⁶ The ninth century "neo-Hittite" relief of a stag hunt

---

¹ *Ibid.*, pp. 173, 259.
² *Ibid.*, pp. 173, 257-261.
³ Vermeule (1975), pp. 13-14 n. 22, 26 n. 35, 49; J. V. Luce: *Homer and the Herioc Age* (London, 1975), pp. 31-32.
⁴ Of course, if the Eighteenth Dynasty were moved down by over 500 years, and along with it the contemporary Mycenaean Grave Circles, that problem vanishes.
⁵ There were later Mycenaean tombstones (E. Vermeule: *Greece in the Bronze Age* [Chicago, 1972], pp. 302, 304, fig. 47) and some scholars (e.g., G. Richter: *The Archaic Gravestones of Attica* [London, 1961], pp. 1-2 and M. Andronikos: *Totenkult* [*Archaeologia Homerica* III W] [Philadelphia, 1943], pp. 10-11), K. Friis Johansen (*The Attic Grave-Reliefs of the Classical Period* [Copenhagen, 1951], pp. 65-66), and D. C. Kurtz and J. Boardman (*Greek Burial Customs* [London, 1971] p. 38) reject such continuity, having a revival in the eleventh or tenth century. Actually, by the revised chronology those few stones now placed between the sixteenth/fifteenth century examples and the eleventh/tenth century ones, follow both.
⁶ A. H. Sayce: »The Inscriptions Found at Hissarlik« in H. Schliemann: *Ilios: the City and Country of the Trojans* (New York, 1881), p, 700; Vermeule (1975, pp. 16-18) cites sculpture of the "Hittite Empire" which Egyptian chronology places centuries earlier than

from Malatya in North Syria is strikingly close in iconography to the "sixteenth-century" stele above one of the graves at Mycenae.[1]

The burials inside the two Grave Circles consist of stone-lined shafts. In addition to the bodies of the Mycenaean rulers and their families, the graves contained much wealth in the form of gold masks, inlaid daggers and swords, gold and silver cups and goblets, gold jewelry and foil, etc. Almost immediately after the discovery of such objects in the first Grave Circle, dating controversies arose.

One of the graves produced a gold ring depicting warriors in a chariot hunting a stag with peculiar antlers, which one scholar compared to the ninth century Malatya relief, showing the same subject.[2] An authority on Greek art, P. Gardner, judged the golden breastplates, diadems, sword handles, buckles and patterned gold discs from the various graves to be products of the Geometric Age (so-named for the geometrical patterns on its pottery).[3] He made that assessment before the chronological sequence for pre-historic Greece received its dates from Egypt, which placed the Shaft Grave period some 500 years before the Geometric Age. He also described animal representations on the gold objects as "identical" in style to the seventh/sixth century examples.[4] Other late nineteenth-century authors noted still more similarities between the Shaft Grave artifacts and those of the seventh-sixth centuries BC.[5] Because of those similarities Gardner felt that the Shaft Graves were not far removed in date from the seventh

---

"Neo-Hittite" work, but which scholars originally dated on internal grounds to the ninth-sixth centuries BC (as they once did Mycenaean culture) – an attribution supported by Velikovsky's revision (I. Velikovsky: *Ramses II and his Time* [Garden City, NY, 1978] pp. 140-179).

[1] For other, though less striking, analogies, compare the stele to M. Vieyra: *Hittite Art 2300-750 B.C.* (London, 1955), pls. 48, 67, 77. As Velikovsky has shown (1978, pp. 165-168), scholars have dated the Malatya sculptures anywhere from the fourteenth century to the eighth because of the conflict between Egyptian and Assyrian criteria, but I follow Vieyra's ninth-century date (*ibid.*, p. 76) for the stag hunt.

Early ninth-century sculptures of the Assyrian King Assurnasirpal also show affinities to the Shaft Grave reliefs, but are of much finer execution (see R. D. Barnett and M. Falkner: *The Sculptures of Assur-Nasir-Apli II, etc.* [London, 1962], pl. 16, and E. Budge: *Assyrian Sculptures in the British Museum: Reign of Ashur-Nasir-Pal, 885-860 B.C.* [London, 1914], pls. 12, 42.)

[2] »Notes on Art and Archaeology«, *The Academy*, vol. 42, No. 1069 (29 Oct., 1892), p. 393, remarks by Heuzy. See C. Smith's cogent commentary in »Egypt and Mycenaean Antiquities«, *The Classical Review* 6 (1892) pp. 463-464. The Malatya relief, while similar in subject matter to the ring, more closely resembles the stele.

[3] P. Gardner in a book review of Schliemann's *Mycenae* in *Quarterly Review*, 145 (Jan. -Apr., 1878) p. 78.

[4] *Ibid.*, p. 80

[5] E.g. C. Schuchhardt: *Schliemann's Excavations* (tr. E. Sellers) (New York, 1891), pp. 180, 318.

century, but because much of the art was obviously more primitive, he decided to allow some time for development, thus assigning the graves to the twelfth-tenth centuries BC,[1] which is almost precisely where they would fall under the revised dates for the early Eighteenth Dynasty of Egypt.

H. R. Hall of the British Museum was so struck by the resemblance of the artifacts from Grave Circle A to "later" material, that he proclaimed that, "if we are not to throw aside all that we have learnt of the development of early Greek art," at least some of the objects belong to ca. 900 BC or later.[2] He proposed, therefore, that the Greeks re-opened graves dating to the early Eighteenth Dynasty after ca. 600 years, but instead of looting or re-using them, they piously deposited later material. His theory for those graves is universally rejected[3] – although, as we shall presently see, it has resurfaced for other graves at Mycenae. The burials and artifacts of Crave Circle A only span about three generations. If they really belong to the sixteenth (or early fifteenth) century, however, as most authorities now assume,[4] then their resemblance to later graves and objects seems all the more remarkable, since hundreds of years were to elapse before similar graves and artifacts supposedly re-appeared.

It is true that Gardner, Hall and others formed their opinions seventy-five to a hundred years ago, before anyone suspected that a centuries-long Dark Age followed the Mycenaean Period, separating it by an unbridgeable "gap of emptiness"[5] from the later objects which

---

[1] P. Gardner: »Stephani on the Tombs at Mycenae«, *Journal of Hellenic Studies* (henceforth *JHS*), I (1880), pp. 97, 101, 106.

[2] Hall: *The Oldest Civilization of Greece* (Philadelphia, 1901), pp. 16, 229.

[3] Hall himself later rejected that theory (*Aegean Archaeology*, [London, 1915], pp. 23-24). I hope to chronicle his dramatic turnabout at a later date. Accepting ninth-seventh-century dates for items from Enkomi on Cyprus, and convinced of their contemporaneity with some Shaft Grave artifacts, he sought to downdate the latter by over 500 years. Blasted by Arthur Evans for his heresy, Hall accepted the Egyptian-based dates for the Shaft Graves and all their contents, and added over 500 years to the dates of the Enkomi material.

[4] For their duration, see Hankey-Warren (1974), p. 150; Vermeule (1975) p. 8. For the dates, see p. 49.

[5] R. Carpenter: *Discontinuity in Greek Civilization* (Cambridge, England, 1966), p. 35. Shortly after Carpenter expressed that opinion, Desborough and Snodgrass each wrote extensive volumes on the Dark Age (1972). Both listed and sought to explain the material remains of the period. Both ran into numerous problems, of which we shall list some for Mycenae. Continued excavation reveals more material for the period; but, rather than forming a continuum, the latest Mycenaean artifacts do not flow into the earliest post-Mycenaean ones, with the former looking like and often mixed with 500-year later remains, the latter looking like and often mixed with 500-year earlier remains. That nobody realized the existence of

they considered to be similar or identical, and sometimes contemporaneous. Their observations on style are, nevertheless, still valid today. What they had "learned of the development of early Greek art"[1] had to be unlearned and re-learned. Even after nearly eighty years of re-education since Hall made that remark, the Shaft Grave contents, like the stelae and the circles themselves, still present "extraordinarily difficult" problems for, and "remain puzzling" to scholars today.[2]

Shaft Grave Art: Modern Problems

The Shaft Grave rulers, to judge by their more robust size than that of their followers, by their weapons and by their favorite scenes of art, were hunters and warriors who began consolidating the rather barbaric villages of Greece into a formidable empire. They brought their people from a comparatively backward Middle Helladic existence into the Late Helladic period, aptly named "the Mycenaean Age." Their houses, tombs and pottery were at first rather poor, since they preferred to lavish their wealth on precious weapons, bowls, ornaments, etc., which they took with them to their graves. At the start of the Eighteenth Dynasty of Egypt they imported and copied objects and ideas from many regions, but especially drew from the more sophisticated Minoans of Crete. By the time of the last interments in the Shaft Graves, during Pharaoh Thutmose III's reign, the Mycenaeans had not only embraced Minoan artistic trends, but had taken over former Minoan colonies throughout the Aegean, and had conquered Crete itself. By the end of the Eighteenth Dynasty and during the Nineteenth, the Greek rulers resided in palaces within fortified city-states, built sumptuous tombs, developed an intricate economic system supporting herders and farmers, merchants, soldiers, poets, scribes and skilled artisans, who produced beautiful poetry, jewelry, sealstones, ivory carvings, etc., which displayed artistic uniformity throughout Greece and her colonies. The Greeks had taken over the East Mediter-

---

such a Dark Age before Egyptian chronology transferred its dates to Mycenaean culture, see Snodgrass: *ibid.*, pp. 1-21. In the final words of his lengthy tome, meant to illuminate the period, Snodgrass (p. 436) confessed that it "seems to me to deserve the title of a dark age."

[1] Hall (1901), p. 16.
[2] Vermeule (1975), pp. 1, 51.

ranean trade routes, importing luxury items from every direction and exporting their own goods throughout the Aegean and Near East.[1]

One can trace all those developments during the span of the Grave Circles – from their inception towards the end of the Middle Helladic period till the special treatment accorded to Circle A during the Late Helladic III B period. We can relate those events to Egyptian history because of the culture contact – both direct and indirect (e.g., via Crete) – between Greece and Egypt throughout the Mycenaean Age. To illustrate that link during the Shaft Grave period, one need only look to the vases and metal objects from the two grave circles and from contemporary and only slightly later find-spots throughout the East Mediterranean.

Crete, which had enjoyed direct contact with Egypt for centuries before the Shaft Grave Period, sent many of the objects and provided much of the artistic inspiration found among the contents of the Grave Circles.[2] Both Crete and Greece entered the Late Bronze Age at about the same time, which one can firmly link to the beginning of the New Kingdom in Egypt. For example, several swords, daggers and vessels from the Shaft Graves display designs and scenes composed of inlaid gold, silver and niello (a black metallic compound), reminiscent of early New Kingdom Egypt, with some of the hunting scenes of definite Egyptian origin, though possibly acquired via Minoan intermediaries. In Egypt itself an ornamental axe head from the earliest years of the Eighteenth Dynasty depicts an Aegean griffin, and its companion piece, a dagger, shows animals at a "flying gallop" inspired by Aegean art, with the iconography of both weapons very closely related to the inlaid weapons of the Shaft Graves. Frescoes in the tombs of the Theban nobles who served Hatshepsut and Thutmose III portray foreign emissaries whose physiognomy, pigmentation, hair style and dress exactly resemble Aegean portraits of themselves. Those and later frescoes, along with Thutmose III's bas relief from Karnak, depict metal vessels which correspond in material, shape and decoration to the cups, goblets, pitchers, jars, conical pouring vessels, animal-headed containers and figurines which excavators have found in the rich graves of Mycenaean Greece, the mansions on Santorini, and the palaces and villas of Crete. The archaeologists of Egypt and the Levant have also discovered a number of actual Aegean exports of (and

---

[1] Vermeule (1972), pp. 82-279.
[2] Vermeule (1975), *passim*, esp, pp. 27ff.

slightly later than) the Shaft Grave Period in contexts which are clearly contemporaneous with Thutmose III.[1]

Since such firm links between the early Eighteenth Dynasty and the Shaft Graves establish a synchronism, Aegean archaeologists, who lacked a reliable dating system of their own, turned to their colleagues, the Egyptologists, who had employed the pharaonic lists of Manetho and astronomical computations to determine absolute dates for the New Kingdom. Transferring the results of their calculations to the Aegean, they assigned the Grave Circles to the seventeenth-sixteenth/early fifteenth centuries BC, and strapped Aegean archaeologists with a plethora of problems arising from such early dates. Velikovsky has already shown the highly dubious nature of the assumptions which the Egyptologists made in order to construct their dating system,[2] and set forth his case for subtracting over 500 years from the standard chronology of the Eighteenth Dynasty in accordance with Egyptian and Near Eastern circumstances.[3]

At the Aegean end, an author has recently made the same observation as struck Schliemann and Eduard Meyer in the 1880s while many of the vessels shown in the Eighteenth Dynasty frescoes correspond to Shaft Grave artifacts, some resemble Protogeometric and Geometric ware over 500 years later.[4]

Again like their nineteenth century precursors, modern scholars still compare some of the Shaft Grave artifacts to those of the Greek Archaic Period (seventh to sixth century). Schiering and Vermeule, for example, noted the similarities between the "second millennium" gold and electron masks from the Mycenaean Grave Circles and a seventh-century bronze mask from Crete and sixth-century gold masks from Bulgaria, each feeling that, despite the huge gap in time, an otherwise undetected continuity linked the Mycenaean and the much later examples.[5]

Many of the artifacts from the Grave Circles, including the stele and

---

[1] *Ibid.*, pp. 18-22; Vermeule (1972), pp. 109, 148-151; Hankey-Warren (1974), pp. 145-147 (with references to fundamental work by Evans, Kantor, Furumark and Vercoutter).

[2] I. Velikovsky: »Astronomy and Chronology«, *Peoples of the Sea* (Garden City, N.Y., 1977)

[3] I. Velikovsky: *Ages in Chaos* I (Garden City, N.Y., 1952) *passim.*

[4] E. Meyer: *Geschichte des Alterthums* I (Stuttgart, 1884), p. 245; H. Schliemann: *Tiryns* (New York, 1885), p. 89; T. Burton-Brown: *Third Millennium Diffusion* (Oxford, 1970), p. 184.

[5] W. Schiering: »Masken am Hals Kretisch-mykenischer und früh-geometrischer Tongefässe«, *Jahrbuch des deutschen archäologischen Instituts* (henceforth *JdI*), 79 (1964), p. 16 and figs. 17,18; E. Vermeule (1972), p. 108.

ring already mentioned, depict stags – a favorite subject of Mycenaean two-dimensional art.[1] In one of the richest graves of Circle A, Schliemann also found a three-dimensional silver stag having a hollow, barrel-shaped body and a spout on the back, probably used as a drinking vessel. Possibly an import from Anatolia, and certainly deriving inspiration from that region, where the stag had long been "a charged symbol," it seems to be a metallic copy of a ceramic model.[2] Excavations in Greece have, so far, produced only one other comparable grave offering in the form of a three-dimensional ceramic stag with a hollow, barrel-shaped body, probably used to hold liquid. Though different in material and in style from the Mycenaean example, it still reminded its discoverer of that find.[3] It comes from the Kerameikos cemetery of Athens, and is dated over 500 years after the Shaft Grave stag, at ca. 925 BC – a date which poses its own problems for those seeking to connect the Athenian model to similarly-made ceramic figurines of the Mycenaean Age, supposedly centuries earlier, with an apparent gap dividing them.[4]

Baltic amber first appeared in Greece in the Shaft Graves, and became characteristic of the Aegean during the early Mycenaean Age (sixteenth to fifteenth centuries), then lost its popularity for a long time,[5] returning near the end of the thirteenth century.[6] Five hundred years after the Shaft Grave period in the eleventh or tenth century, it again became "not uncommon", again disappeared for centuries, and again regained its popularity during the eighth century,[7] as it had in the late thirteenth. Roughly half a millennium separates the corresponding phases of its popularity and scarcity.

In addition to amber, northern burial rites, cultural traits and taste in art also found their expression in the Shaft Graves, with some scholars

---

[1] Vermeule (1975), pp. 15, 17, 23-26, 45.
[2] *Ibid.*, pp. 15-16.
[3] K. Kübler: *Kerameikos* IV (Berlin, 1943), p. 20, n. 19.
[4] R. Higgins (*Greek Terracottas* [London, 1967], p. 21) and Snodgrass ([1971], p. 401) both noted the similarity to Mycenaean works at least 200 years earlier, the former suggesting that the technique survived in Crete and Cyprus to return to Greece later. R. V. Nicholls ("Greek Votive Statuettes and Religious Continuity, ca. 1200-700 BC" in *Auckland Classical Essays Presented to E.M. Blaiklock* /ed. B. Harris/ [New Zealand, 1970], p. 13) believed in continuity in Greece itself, though he could only cite two examples which might belong to those two hundred years (Cf. Desborough (1972), pp. 282-283).
[5] Vermeule (1972), pp. 89, 114, 127-128, 131, 147, 227, 257.
[6] C. W. Beck et al.: "Analysis and Provenience of Minoan and Mycenaean Amber, II Tiryns", *Greek, Roman and Byzantine Studies* (Henceforth *GRBS*), 9 (1968), p. 15.
[7] Snodgrass (1971), pp. 248, 290, n. 34.

even speculating that the rulers of Mycenae may have been newly-arrived immigrants from the North.[1] Roughly half a millennium later, ca. 1100 BC, northern influence again spread into Greece.[2] In the tenth to ninth centuries, the tribes of Central Europe, especially Austro-Hungary, had a life-style and customs very similar to that of the Shaft Grave princes of Mycenae, and there are those scholars who look for such conditions in contemporary Greece, but fail to find them, since they assign the Shaft Graves 600 years earlier.[3]

Between the Danube and Mycenae lay the burials of Albania which Hammond considered the antecedents of the Shaft Graves, while Prendi and Snodgrass dated them 500 years later. At about the same latitude, to the east, in Macedonia was another cemetery site at Vergina. Like Mycenae, its earliest tombs were stone-lined shafts, roofed with wood, containing very primitive pottery, and enclosed by circles of stones. Once again Hammond assigned the first tombs earlier than the Grave Circles of Mycenae.[4] Responding to that assessment, Snodgrass[5] again noted that it was 500 years earlier than the excavator (M. Andronikos), Desborough, he himself, as well as most scholars had dated them on the basis of tenth century artifacts inside the tombs.[6] There are, however, still other similarities to the Shaft Graves, beyond those mentioned by Hammond, which pose problems for those convinced of Vergina's late date.

As at Mycenae, the people of Vergina were both wealthy and warlike, burying with them their weapons, amber trinkets, gold jewelry, long dress pins, spiral ornaments, spiral hair coils of bronze and gold wire, and many objects strongly influenced by the north[7] – all familiar features from the Shaft Graves. Contrasted with tenth-century Greece, however, their burials are without parallel,[8] their warlike society is "the first clear example of one,"[9] their wealth is "amazing," while "the most remarkable fact" is that the strong northern element did not

---

[1] Vermeule (1975), pp. 22-26, 28, 49; Luce (1975) p. 32.
[2] Snodgrass (1971), pp. 319-320.
[3] *Ibid.*, p. 392 (cp. Vermeule (1971); pp. 108-110); A. Mahr et al.: *The Mecklenburg Collection, etc.* (New York, 1934), pp. 9-11.
[4] Hammond (1972), p. 266.
[5] Snodgrass, review of Hammond's *A History of Macedonia*, JHS, 94 (1974), pp. 230-231.
[6] M. Andronikos: »An Early Iron Age Cemetery at Vergina, near Beroea«, *Balkan Studies*, 2 (1961), p. 89: ca. 1050-1000 BC (later revised to ca. 1000 BC); Desborough (1972), pp. 219-220: early tenth century; Snodgrass (1971), p. 133: late tenth century.
[7] Snodgrass: *ibid.*, pp. 253-254; Desborough: *ibid.* pp. 219-220.
[8] Snodgrass: *ibid.*, pp. 161-162; Desborough: *ibid.*, p. 220.
[9] Desborough: *loc. cit.*

"penetrate the rest of Greece at this period."[1] What is unique, "first," "amazing," and "most remarkable" for the tenth century fits well the Shaft Grave Period, currently placed 500 years earlier.

There was a number of special coils of gold wire in the Shaft Graves of Mycenae, as well as contemporary examples in gold or bronze at Kirrha and Eleusis, used for hair-rings, finger-rings, etc.[2] Not only at Vergina but elsewhere in Greece coils of bronze or gold wire, often indistinguishable from the Mycenaean examples, again became popular in the eleventh to tenth centuries, with the gold examples most noteworthy for their contrast to the general impoverishment and the particular scarcity of gold now seen for that period.[3]

Other gold ornaments from the Shaft Graves, which P. Gardner originally assigned to the Geometric Age, still cause problems for modern excavators who cannot bring them down that late. When publishing the early finds from the Kerameikos cemetery of Athens, K. Kübler characterized four ninth-century gold bands as having "closely related" (nahverwandte) and "completely similar forerunners" (völlig gleiche Vorläufer) in the gold work of Mycenae over 600 years earlier.[4] Quite recently he published a beautifully decorated T-shaped band, probably used as a garter belt, not earlier than the tenth century BC, and probably belonging to the eighth. He noted "comparable and unmistakable similarities" (vergleichbar und unverkennbar ähnlich) to a number of the golden garter belts from both grave circles, citing his example as still further proof of a "direct connection" (unmittelbarer Zusammenhang) between the metalwork of the Shaft Grave Period and that of the early first millennium.[5] With such finds separated by several centuries, it is easy to see similarities, but difficult to see any link, direct or indirect.

Several of the ornamental gold discs from Circle A showed "the frequent use of the compass" to form the embossed and engraved rosettes and concentric circle designs.[6] Compass-drawn, concentric cir-

---

[1] Snodgrass (1971), pp. 253, 257.
[2] H. Schliemann: *Mycenae* (New York, 1880) p. 353 No. 529 (from a plundered Shaft Grave south of Circle A); E. Bielefeld: *Schmuck* (Archaeologia Homerica I C) (Göttingen, 1968), p. 37, to which add G. Mylonas: »The Cemeteries of Eleusis and Mycenae«, *Proceedings of the American Philosophical Society* 99 (1955), p. 59.
[3] Bielefeld: *ibid.*, pp. 47-48; R. Higgins: *Greek and Roman Jewelry* (London, 1961), pp 72, 91, 93; Desborough (1972). pp. 304-305.
[4] K. Kübler: *Kerameikos* V. 1.1 (Berlin, 1954), pp. 185-186.
[5] K. Kübler: *Kerameikos* VI. 2. 2 (Berlin, 1970) pp. 403-404.
[6] F. Matz: *The Art of Crete and Early Greece* (tr. by A. E. Keep) (New York, 1962), pp. 174, 218 fig. 48; cf. Schliemann (1880), pp. 167 No. 241, 319 No. 481 (rosettes), 172 No. 252 (circles).

cles and semi-circles comprise "one of the most common features" of eleventh-century Protogeometric pottery. Desborough, who has made the most thorough study of that type of pottery, considered the sudden appearance of such precise motifs to be the result of a 500-year later "new Athenian invention,"[1] since compass-drawn patterns of any kind are difficult, if not impossible, to detect during the intervening half millennium.[2]

In Grave Circle A Schliemann discovered long dress pins, some with globular heads. In 1956 P. Jacobsthal, an authority on Greek art, wrote a book detailing the history of dress pins in Greece, which he felt did not begin prior to the late twelfth century BC, when women started to use long pins with globular pins to fasten thick clothing at their shoulders. Aware of the pins from Mycenae, two of which closely resembled the earliest ones of his series, he declined to include them in his survey. In a footnote he acknowledged the existence of Schliemann's finds and observed that two of them do "look like forerunners of the sub-Mycenaean pin-type. This must be coincidence: they are separated by an interval of 400 years, and this cannot be bridged."[3] Other scholars of about that time also agreed that the history of Greek pins ought to begin in the late twelfth century, not with the Shaft Grave examples.[4] N. Sandars, who speciallized in metallurgy, felt that the assumption that 400 years passed without any examples to connect the pins of Mycenae to the very similar ones which started Jacobsthal's series was "rather too sweeping."[5] Still there was an embarrassing gap.

During the course of that discussion, archaeologists found and published Grave Circle B at Mycenae and a cemetery only about seven miles away at Argos, both of which added new substance to the controversy, and made the gap even more embarrassing. Circle B produced still more "seventeenth-sixteenth-century" long pins with globular heads (some of rock crystal) clearly worn at the shoulders of women.[6] The excavator of Argos found similar long dress pins worn at the shoulders, but datable to the late twelfth century. He felt that since they were so similar in style and usage, and so close geographically,

---

[1] Desborough (1972), pp. 41-43, 145 (referring to the combination of the compass with a multiple brush).
[2] Snodgrass (1971), pp. 47, 99, n. 26.
[3] P. Jacobsthal: *Greek Pins* (Oxford, 1956) p. 1 and n. 1.
[4] H. Lorimer: *Homer and the Monuments* (London, 1950), p. 358; Higgins (1961), p. 92.
[5] N. Sandars: »A Minoan Cemetery on Upper Gypsades: The Bronzes«, *BSA*, 53-54 (1958-9), p. 235, n. 28.
[6] G. Mylonas: *Ancient Mycenae* (Princeton, 1957) pp. 144-145, 158.

there had to be a connection between the pins of Mycenae and Argos.[1] Desborough, granting that the shape and function were similar, and that Mycenae is very close to Argos and provides a "local predecessor" for the pins there, still felt that the time gap was too enormous for there to have been a conscious revival, and no evidence of survival. Despite the affinities of the Shaft Grave pins to those beginning in the late twelfth century, and becoming "a common feature" of the period, the later pins constituted a "radical change" from everything during the intervening 400 years. Desborough attached some importance to the later pins, since they "had a bearing on the vital matter of the origins of the whole sub-Mycenaean culture towards the end of the twelfth century,"[2] which, not only in regard to pins, bore numerous similarities to the culture of the seventeenth-sixteenth centuries,[3] but constituted "a radical change" from nearly everything which the present chronological scheme places between the two periods.

E. Bielefeld, unlike Desborough, did not want to connect the Shaft Grave pins to the later examples but, faced with the same centuries-long gap, suggested that there might have been a change in dress after the Shaft Grave period, possibly due to Minoan influence (or warmer weather), but at the end of the Mycenaean Age women again dressed as they had 400 years earlier. With no evidence that similar pins existed in Greece to span the gap, he suggested that the pins and dress might have survived in the East, only to return after 400 years, or, alternatively, that the pins and dress did survive in Greece itself, among the lower classes who did not embrace Minoan fashions, but that their remains have so far eluded excavators.[4]

Snodgrass, long concerned with metal work and the Dark Ages, noted that the later pins "appear somewhat abruptly," possibly due to a colder climate. He, too, saw the "clear ... antecedents" from the Shaft Graves, and felt some sympathy for the hypothesis of revival, but, like Desborough, was far less concerned with the short distance between the graves of Mycenae and Argos than the huge gap in time. Like Bielefeld he preferred to see the pins survive somewhere to bridge the gap, rather than view the similarities as merely coincidental. Since

---

[1] J. Deshayes: *Argos: les fouilles de la Deiras* (Paris, 1966), p. 205; see also B. C. Dietrich: »Some Evidence of Religious Continuity in the Greek Dark Age«, *BICS*, 17 (1970), p. 20

[2] V. Desborough: review of Deshayes' *Argos* etc. in *Gnomon*, 41 (1969), p. 217; cf. idem (1972), pp. 108, 295-299.

[3] Snodgrass (1971), pp. 383-385: cf. remark on p. 29.

[4] Bielefeld (1968), pp. 38-39.

Greece, despite so much excavation, has not produced the intermediate examples, he looked to more likely (and colder) areas to the north and northwest, but conceded that those regions show no evidence of spanning the gap either. He concluded that "the origins of the straight pin in Greece need to be reconsidered."[1] Bielefeld confessed a similar perplexity when he stated that the whole topic involves difficulties which at present are not fully resolved.[2]

Under the present chronology, either the Shaft Grave pins were some sort of aberrant phenomenon, which only incidentally resembled pins 400 years later, similar in function and style, and as close as ca. seven miles away, or else pins existed somewhere, as yet undetermined (to the North, the Northwest, the East, or in Greece itself – though even those who believe in survival do not agree where it took place, since the evidence is lacking or inconclusive for all areas), which span the centuries, centuries which Jacobsthal and others, who reject the notion of survival, considered unbridgeable.

We return to the vessels and daggers with inlaid designs and scenes of gold, silver and niello, which link the Shaft Graves to the early Eighteenth Dynasty. The inlay technique first appeared in Greece among the Shaft Grave artifacts, and continued through the early Mycenaean Age, and possibly until the destruction of the Late Helladic palaces towards the end of the LH period.[3] When describing the inlaid metal decoration of Achilles' shield in the *Iliad*, Homer gives such extensive details of the design and of its manufacture that late nineteenth and early twentieth-century scholars like C. Tsountas and K. Friis Johansen felt that the technique lasted until the poet's time.[4] Now that experts generally date Homer to the eighth century BC, while excavators have found no inlaid metal after the LH III B period, which Egyptian chronology assigns to the thirteenth century, scholars are forced to ask "how was it remembered?" during the intervening half millennium.[5] Some[6]

---

[1] Snodgrass (1971), pp. 226-228, 309-310 (climate).
[2] Bielefeld (1968), p. 39.
[3] Vermeule (1972), pp. 98-100, 128, 133, 151, 225; Luce (1975), pp. 61-63, 70-71, The inlaid silver cup found in the debris of the LH III B palace at Pylos, and often cited as LH III B in date of manufacture (e.g. Luce, p. 62), could have been an heirloom (Blegen-Rawson (1956) pp. 57-58, 62); nevertheless, it shows that such objects were still in use (possibly made) until the destructions marking the transition from LH III B to C.
[4] C. Tsountas and J. I. Manatt: *The Mycenaean Age* (New York, 1897), p. 324; K. Friis Johansen: *Les Vases Sicyoniens* (Rome, 1966 [reprint of 1923 edition]), pp. 159-160.
[5] Luce (1975), p. 63.
[6] D. E. Strong: *Greek and Roman Gold and Silver Plate* (Glasgow, 1966) pp. xxv, 53; D.H.F. Gray: »Metal-working in Homer«, *JHS*, 74 (1954), p, 4; see Vermeule (1972) p. 100.

postulate that individual pieces may have survived as heirlooms or been rediscovered centuries later, which would explain the description of the finished product but not of the manufacturing technique.[1] That is, in any case, purely hypothetical, since no inlaid objects have been discovered in contexts later than LH III B. Others doubt that possibility and prefer to believe that the tradition of oral poetry kept the memory of the objects and the technique alive[2] – a theory frequently employed to explain Homer's extensive knowledge of the culture which scholars now date half a millennium before his time. One of the Shaft Grave swords bore a geometric meander design on its hilt, which a recent writer considered "wholly untypical of Helladic workmanship at that time," and more akin to the decorative scheme which started to become popular some 500 years later.[3] A number of the swords had their handles attached by bronze rivets plated with silver or gold, as did other weapons during the early Mycenaean period. On present evidence, silver-plated rivets lasted from ca. 1550 –1400 then returned ca. 700 BC on Cyprus, which has provoked yet another debate among Homericists. Homer sings of gold-studded and "silver-studded swords" in his epics, with several classicists conjecturing that Homer chronicled weapons which had gone out of use centuries before his time, but which the metrical formulae of oral poetry kept fresh in the Greeks' memory.[4] Since the Cypriote swords with silver studs are contemporaneous with the rise of the epics, V. Karageorghis felt it more likely that Homer sang of the weapons of his own day.[5] Between the two groups of swords there is at present a gap of 700 years, with each

---

[1] Gray (ibid., pp. 3-4, 12-14) felt that Homer's description of the process was very erroneous and implied a long break. On one point, "kyanos" might designate niello rather than glass paste. Any misconceptions which Homer had about fabrication techniques – which were probably known only to a small guild of artisans – need have no chronological implications (cf. n. below), but if there was a temporal lapse, it need not have been several centuries in duration. The period between the probable manufacture date and time of deposition of the Pylos cup would be more than adequate, and, in fact, a generation or so would suffice.

[2] Luce (1975), p. 63; T.B.L. Webster: *From Mycenae to Homer* (New York, 1964), pp. 28-29, 213-214; G.S. Kirk: *The Language and Background of Homer* (Cambridge, 1964) p. 176; K. Fittschen: *Der Schild des Achilleus* (Archaeologia Homerica II. n. 1) (Göttingen, 1973), pp. 5-6, 17.

[3] Burton-Brown (1970), p. 184.

[4] Gray (1954) p. 14; Luce (1975), pp. 61-62, 101-102; Webster (1964), p. 92; Kirk (1964), pp. 176-183; Lorimer (1950), pp. 273-274; D. Page: *History and the Homeric Iliad* (Los Angeles, 1959), p. 278, n. 63; G.S. Kirk: *Homer and the Oral Tradition* (New York, 1976), pp. 20, 22, 42-43 (where he takes an even firmer stand than in his earlier work.)

[5] V. Karageorghis: »Homerica from Salamis (Cyprus)« in *Europa: Studien ... Ernst Grumach* (Berlin, 1967), pp. 167-168; idem: *Salamis in Cyprus* (London, 1969), p. 70

group of classicists championing examples on one side or the other of that lacuna[1] – a very familiar situation, as we shall see again and again in the present essay.

The earliest locally-made vases from the Shaft Graves are pretty homely compared to the metal work, the exotic imports and the much finer Mycenaean pottery which soon followed. Still, pottery is the major element which Aegean archaeologists employ to establish relative sequences and absolute dates for the pre-classical period,[2] so that the Shaft Grave vases deserve some consideration. They include goblets and storage vessels, the latter of which are of special interest. Although the "Submycenaean" pots of ca. 1125 BC supposedly followed immediately after the last phase of Mycenaean pottery (LH III C) in Western Attica, and Protogeometric pots of ca. 1050 – 900 BC supposedly followed LH III C at Mycenae and elsewhere in Greece,[3] there is "a striking difference" in the repertory of shapes between LH III C and sub-Mycenaean,[4] and both LH III C and sub-Mycenaean vases seem unlikely progenitors of protogeometric ware.[5] Those pots of ca. 1125 – 900 BC, which archaeologists now place centuries after the Shaft Grave period (despite some problems with that placement) show some marked similarities to the Shaft Grave pots, supposedly 400 – 600 years earlier.[6]

---

[1] A. Snodgrass: »An Historical Homeric Society?«, *JHS* 94 (1974) p. 123. Luce (1975, p. 102) suggested that Homer's poetry may have inspired the swords of Cyprus rather than vice versa, although one might wonder how familiar Homer was both to and with seventh-century Cyprus. Karageorghis (*Europa*, p. 168, and letter to me of Oct. 26, 1978) acknowledged the seven-hundred-year-gap in the evidence to date, but postulated that there were silver-studded swords during those centuries (as yet undiscovered) to bridge the lacuna (cf. scholars' similar beliefs on chariots, below »A Chariot Vase«, p. 201, n. 2 and p. 202, n. 3). In that regard, it is of interest to note that, so far, no one has discovered a silver-studded sword on Cyprus earlier than ca. 700 BC, and, of still greater interest, that, by the present chronology, there is a surprising gap from ca. 1400-1200 BC, when the Cypriots had no swords whatever (H. W. Catling: *Cypriote Bronzework in the Mycenaean World* [Oxford, 1964] pp. 110,113; L. Aström et al.: *The Late Cypriote Bronze Age: Other Arts and Crafts* [*Swedish Cyprus Expedition* (henceforth *SCE*) IV. 1D] [Lund, 1972], pp. 560, 762).

[2] E.G., for the Mycenaean Period see Vermeule (1972), p. 139; for the Dark Age see Snodgrass (1971), pp. 24-28, and Desborough (1972), p. 292.

[3] Snodgrass: *ibid.*, pp. 134-135.

[4] *Ibid.* p. 35. As he notes (*loc. cit.*), the repertory of pots called "Submycenaean" has both grown and shrunk due to new discoveries and reclassification (cf. Desborough (1972), p. 33). Some shapes clearly derive from the lates LH series, while others, currently seen as their contemporaries, do not, and seem to be 500-year throwbacks.

[5] V. Desborough: *Protogeometric Pottery* (Oxford, 1952), p. 126.

[6] Compare the shape (not handles) of *ibid.*, pl. 19 A 1452-1453 to Mylonas (1957), pls. 43a, 64 a-b; the shape of *ibid.*, pl. 35 IV.1 to Mylonas, p.. 81b; the handled kalathos (*ibid.*, pl. 8 No. 577.20) resembles an enlarged "Vapheio cup" (P.S. 224) for which note the gigantic

Numerous scholars have long noted resemblances of the earliest "Iron Age" pottery of Greece, with its distinctive shapes and geometrical designs, to the Middle Helladic (MH) ware at the time of, and immediately preceding the Shaft Grave Period, with the earliest writers, like Conze, Gardner, and Schliemann himself,[1] making them contemporaneous. Since the Shaft Graves showed a close link to the early Eighteenth Dynasty, however, Egyptian chronology discredited that notion, and separated the two sets of pottery by some 500 years. Despite that long interval, since the Middle Bronze Age ware of the Peloponnese and Boeotia still resembled the familiar Iron Age pottery from the Kerameikos cemetery of Athens, S. Wide proudly announced his discovery in 1894 of the long-sought "missing link" (das fehlende Glied) bridging the two groups at the site of Aphidna, less than fifteen miles northeast of Athens.[2] While his find did help geographically, chronologically it was still 500 years too old to connect with the Athenian Iron Age ware. Wide and J. Böhlau therefore proposed that while the upper classes used LH pottery, the humble folk continued to make and use their older style throughout those same 500 years, until the disappearance of the aristocracy and its cultural remains, at which point the native ware again came to the forefront.[3] Their idea that the older geometrical pottery coexisted with LH ware appealed to a number of contemporary scholars, even as late as 1935, since it explained the similarity of styles otherwise dated 500 years apart.[4]

---

cups carried by Aegeans in Egyptian frescoes; Amphora 590 (G. Karo: *Die Schachtgräber von Mykenai* [Munich, 1933], pl. 171) shows points of resemblance to C. G. Styrenius: *Submycenaean Studies* (Lund, 1967) pls. 49, 63, to C. W. Blegen et al.: *The Palace of Nestor III* (Princeton, 1973) pl. 298.14, and to K. Kübler & W. Kraiker: *Kerameikos* I (Berlin, 1939), pl. 55 No. 589; the amphoriskoi from Circle B (e.g. Mylonas: *Ho Taphikos Kyklos B ton Mykenon* [Athens, 1973], pl. 128B) show similarities to Styrenius, pl. 11 and Desborough (1952, p. 126.), pl. 31 (bottom center). The resemblances are generic, and I would not claim that the pots were made in the same place, at the same time, by the same men. They, along with many other artifacts and customs show similarities more easily explained by a closer link than scholars now see. The admitted differences are often slighter than those between contemporaneous Submycenaean pots from the same area with their "considerable variation" in shape and decoration (Desborough (1972), p. 33) and between contemporaneous groups of ninth-century pots made in different areas (Snodgrass (1971), figs. 42-44, 120-122).

[1] R. M. Cook: *Greek Painted Pottery* (London, 1972) p. 303; Gardner (1878), p. 78; Schliemann (1885), p. 89.

[2] S. Wide: »Aphidna in Nordattika«, *Athenische Mittheilungen* (henceforth *Ath. Mitt.*), 21 (1896) p. 407.

[3] *Ibid.*, pp. 400-403, 407-409. For Böhlau's contribution, see *ibid.*, p. 402, n. 1 and Cook (1972), p. 305.

[4] E.g. C. C. Edgar: »Excavations in Melos 1899: The Pottery«, *BSA*, 5 (1898-99), pp. 15-16;

More recently scholars have rejected the notion that geometrical MH pottery survived alongside LH ware in the Mycenaean world. Many, however, still see the earliest Iron Age pottery of Greece as "a clear break"[1] and a "separate entity" from the latest Mycenaean ware, which it supposedly succeeded directly, and as marking "a new era in the art of the Greek lands."[2] They still note closer similarities to MH ware 500 years earlier than to the intervening LH pottery, a matter which "raises a host of problems." Some regard the origin of the new Iron Age ware as "obscure", somehow "by-passing the Mycenaean phases" to link up with the 500-year-older MH tradition, possibly in some remote region to the north.[3] Desborough, who has made the most thorough study of the earliest Iron Age geometrical ware, rejected a derivation from such a source, although he, like others, was equally dissatisfied with a direct development from the latest Mycenaean ware.[4]

However one tries to solve the 500-year ceramic problem, the fact remains today, as in Schliemann's time, that some of the earliest Iron Age ware of Greece, with its distinctive fabric, its wheel made and handmade forms, and its incised and painted decoration, resembles the pottery which culminated in the Shaft Grave vases from Mycenae;[5]

---

idem.: »The Pottery« in *Excavations at Phylakopi in Melos* (JHS supplement 4) (London, 1904), pp. 97, 100, 103-106; H.B. Walters: *History of Ancient Pottery* I (New York, 1905), pp. 278-279; W. Dörpfeld: »Das Alter des Heiligtums von Olympia«, *Ath. Mitt.*, 31 (1906), pp. 205-218 (a view caustically attacked that same year by A. Furtwängler [»Das Alter des Heraion und das Alter des Heiligtums von Olympia«, reprinted in *Kleine Schriften* I (Munich, 1911) pp. 455-457], who had, as we shall see [below »Other LH III Figural Pottery«, p. 205, n. 2], proposed that Mycenaean ware lasted an extra 500 years, coexisting with the later geometrical ware); W. Dörpfeld: *Alt Olympia* I (Berlin, 1935), pp. 11-14.

[1] R. S. Folsom: *Handbook of Greek Pottery* (London, 1967), p. 21.
[2] Cook (1972), pp. 4-6; cf. M. Robertson: *A History of Greek Art* I (New York. 1975), p. 15.
[3] P. Demargne: *The Birth of Greek Art* (tr. by S. Gilbert and J. Emmons) (New York, 1964), p. 287; cf. V. Milojcic: »Die dorische Wanderung im Lichte der vorgeschichtlichen Funde«, *Arch. Anz.*, 1948-1949, p. 34; C. G. Starr: *The Origins of Greek Civilization* (New York, 1961), pp. 45, 93 and n. 1, 140. For the retention of MH ware in Albania and Macedonia supposedly 500 years after their disappearance in the south, see »The Grave Circles«, p. 174 footnotes, P. 175, ns. 1-2 and p. 182, ns. 4-6 above; for Thessaly see W. A. Heurtley and T. C. Skeat: »The Tholos Tombs of Marmariane«, *BSA*, 31 (1930-1), pl. 1, figs 4-7.
[4] Desborough (1952), p. 126; cf. Hall (1901), p. 39; Demargne (1964) p. 287, and Milojcic (1948-49), p. 34, against direct evolution from LH pottery.
[5] Snodgrass (1971) pp. 94-97, 384. In addition to those already cited above (last 8 ns.) cf. Lacy (1967), p. 171 on tea cups; Broneer (1939), pp. 418-419; E. Vermeule: »The Mycenaeans in Achaia«, *American Journal of Archaeology* (henceforth *AJA*), 64 (1960), p. 5 for MH vessels "skipping periods and occurring again after a lapse of time"; Skeat, Verdelis and others subscribed to that hypothesis to explain the ribbed pedestal on ninth-eighth-century vessels from Thessaly as derived from MH goblets, including those from Circle B at Mycenae, but J. N. Coldstream: *Greek Geometric Pottery* [London, 1968], p. 161 and n. 3 felt that

and at the site of Asine, less than twenty miles southeast of Mycenae, the excavators termed that resemblance "astounding."[1]

Later Use of the Grave Circles

Not very long after the Shaft Grave burials, a Mycenaean ruler disturbed one of the interments in Circle B, enlarging its shaft to form an entrance to a new "built tomb," with a stately chamber and saddle-shaped roof constructed of stone blocks. Enough ceramic material remained in the tomb, after its subsequent robbery, to indicate an LH II date for its fabrication and use. Since the LH II pottery phase corresponds to the reign of Pharaoh Thutmose III,.G. Mylonas, the tomb's excavator, assigned it to the fifteenth century BC. The tomb type is foreign to Greece, with the example from Circle B constituting its sole appearance in the country. Archaeologists have discovered the type at roughly the same period on Crete (also one example) and Cyprus and especially in Syria, where it originally developed. Mylonas saw "striking parallels" to the tombs of Syria and Trachonas on Cyprus;[2] but, as he had noted earlier, there was a problem with Trachonas since, despite its close proximity to Syria, its example is 500 years younger than those of Syria.[3] There are tombs of the "right" date on Cyprus, notably at Enkomi, but the 500-year problem still exists and has grown with time.

Excavations have found similar Iron Age built tombs in large numbers on Cyprus, in Asia Minor, Urartu, Palestine and at Carthage, none dating earlier than ca. 950 BC, and most belonging to the ninth-seventh centuries. Noting the same "striking parallels" between the examples of 1550 – 1200 BC and those from 950 – 600 BC, numerous archaeologists have tried to connect the two groups. A 250-year gap separates them, however, with the earliest Iron Age tombs resembling not the latest Bronze Age examples, but the earliest ones, ca. 600 years

---

the 600-700-year gap in the evidence invalidated that suggestion (see, however, p. 190, n. 5 above on Thessaly).

[1] O. Frödin and A. W. Persson: *Asine: Results of the Swedish Excavations 1922-1930* (Stockholm, 1938), p. 279.
[2] Mylonas: *Mycenae and the Mycenaean Age*, p. 107
[3] *Idem* (1957), p. 164; cf. Velikovsky, p. 183.

earlier, with developmental stages running parallel after a 600-year interval. Furthermore, although excavators assume that Syro-Phoenicia was the place of origin for both groups, especially since the Iron Age examples encircle that region and appear at Levantine colonies, there are, in fact, no such tombs known from Syro-Phoenicia during the second period.[1]

The built tomb of Circle B marks the last burial inside the Grave Circles. The Mycenaean rulers turned from simple, stone-lined shafts (and the one Syrian built tomb), sunk into the softer rock of the relatively flat land west of their citadel, to the neighboring hilly slopes to the west and southwest. There they excavated long, unroofed corridors into the hillsides, then hollowed out gigantic circular tombs which they lined with stone, capping them with corbelled, stone-built domes, resembling huge beehives, over which they heaped tremendous mounds of earth. They also began to protect their citadel with thick walls of stone.

In the LH III B period, which began towards the end of the Eighteenth Dynasty and extended through the subsequent reigns of the Ramesside pharaohs,[2] both Grave Circles, abandoned for centuries, experienced renewed activity. Circle B, the farthest from the citadel, and possibly silted over with wash and forgotten during the centuries of disuse, suffered an ignoble fate when the workmen excavating the last of the great beehive tombs (the so-called Tomb of Clytemnaestra, to which we shall return), sliced through the eastern portion of the Grave Circle, and heaped the earthen mound to cover that tomb over the rest of Circle B.[3]

---

[1] E. Sjöqvist: »Enkomi« in E. Gjerstad et al. *SCE* I (Stockholm, 1934) pp. 570-573; A. Westholm: »Amathus«, *SCE* II (Stockholm, 1935) p. 140; A. Westholm: »Built Tombs in Cyprus«, *Opuscula Archaeologica* (henceforth *Op. Arch.*) II (1941), pp. 30, 32-53, 57; E. Gjerstad: *SCE*, IV.2 (Stockholm, 1948), p. 239; Karageorghis (1967b), p. 123; C. Picard: »Installations cultuelles retrouvées au Tophet de Salambo«, *Rivista degli Studi Orientali* 42 (1967), pp. 189-199; G. C. and C. Picard: *The Life and Death of Carthage* (tr. by D. Collon) (London, 1968), pp. 47, 52; D. Ussishkin: »The Necropolis from the Time of the Kingdom of Judah at Silwan, Jerusalem«, *The Biblical Archaeologist*, 33 (1970), pp. 45-46; For a fuller discussion, see Isaacson (1974), pp. 14-15.

[2] Hankey-Warren (1974), pp. 147-148, 150.

[3] *Ibid.*, p. 145, 152, n. 2; Mylonas (1966), p. 98. The earthen mound of the beehive tomb, which also covered the Grave Circle, explains why no one knew of the circle, intersected by that tomb, after the discovery of the latter ca. 1807, or when workmen constructed the present road, a cistern and an aqueduct over the western side of the circle in modern times, until its chance discovery in the 1950s (Mylonas (1957), pp. 130, 143-144). If wash already covered the circle before LH III B, the apparent disrespect of that period might have the same explanation as more recent encroachments – ignorance of its existence.

Circle A, on the other hand, enjoyed a completely different lot during the same period.[1] Like Circle B, the beehive tombs, and all the other graves of rich and poor residents or Mycenae, Circle A originally lay west of, and outside the settlement proper, both during the period of its burials in MH – LH I, and at the time of the first extensive fortification of the city in LH III A. When the "thirteenth-century" Mycenaeans decided to enlarge their city, by building another, longer wall in the area of the "prehistoric cemetery" to the west, they faced the problem of what to do with Circle A. We already saw some evidence of the disrespect for their dead predecessors which the Mycenaeans displayed at Circle B, when the owner of the built tomb violated the earlier Shaft Grave he expropriated, only to have his own tomb pillaged after his death, and again when the excavators of the beehive tomb destroyed part of Circle B and heaped dirt over the rest of it. In fact, they were notorious for their lack of piety towards the deceased, building structures over earlier tombs, robbing the dead, and casting aside their bones.[2]

Unlike Circle B and so many other graves in the vicinity, the Mycenaeans treated Circle A, which lay directly in the path of their urban expansion, with a reverence singular for that age. They extended their fortification wall farther than mere concern for defense or for urban planning dictated, enclosing Circle A within the city proper. They made sacrifices and dedicated idols inside the circle.[3] Although space inside the citadel was at a premium, and the inhabitants crowded buildings around that area, many of them over older graves, some of which they plundered,[4] they spared Circle A. In fact, they decided to raise its level as a whole, to correspond to the higher grade of the city's interior – a massive engineering feat, requiring the construction of a giant retaining wall to the west over five meters high, adding tons of earth above the graves until they formed a higher, even surface, then raising the old grave stelae to the new level to designate the individual

---

[1] Mylonas and others have the activity at Circle A precede that at B by ca. 30 years, while Wace and others had the activity at Circle A follow that at B by ca. 50 years or more (Mylonas (1966), pp. 119-120). Still, all agree on an LH III B date for both.

[2] *Ibid.*, pp. 106-107, 109; Vermeule (1972), pp. 88, 299-230.

[3] Mylonas: *ibid.*, pp. 24, 28-31, 90, 94-96; idem: »The Cult of the Dead in Helladic Times«, in G. Mylonas (ed.): *Studies Presented to P.M. Robinson* I (St. Louis, 1951), pp. 96-99; Wace (1921-23), pp. 104-105.

[4] Mylonas (1966), p. 96; Wace: *Mycenae: An Archaeological History and Guide* (Princeton, 1949), pp. 51, 61, figs. 18, 69, plan 3; Vermeule (1972), p. 84.

burials below. At the new surface they constructed a new enclosure wall of two concentric rings of stone slabs filled with earth and capped by horizontal stone slabs.[1]

Considering the lack of respect for other, neighboring, tombs, the building all around but not above Circle A, the vast labor that went into deflecting the city fortification around the circle, and into creating the circle as it now appears, as well as the contemporary sacrifices and dedication of idols, some scholars have considered Circle A as a sacred burial precinct,[2] unique for thirteenth-century Greece. The next evidence of such a practice in Greece – again involving older graves sunk into the earth and lined with stone walls or stone slabs encircled by a later wall to form a sacred precinct – took place in Attica at Athens and at Eleusis roughly 500 years later.[3] Scholars regarded the latter two cases as the beginnings of hero shrines in Greece, stating that "respect for older burials is something quite new at this time [the eighth century]" and "foreign" to all earlier periods.[4] The similar instance from Circle A stands in isolation 500 years earlier. It is of further interest for the cult at Circle A itself, that, as with nearly every other example of real or presumed thirteenth-century cults throughout the Aegean, there is a sharp break soon after its initiation;[5] yet, again,

---

[1] Mylonas: ibid., 90-96; Vermeule: ibid., p. 84.
[2] Mylonas, following Wace, originally (1951, pp. 96-99) regarded it as such. He later changed his mind, since Circle B not only did not receive similar honor, but was violated at about the same time; and because Circle A, which did not have a doorway, showed no evidence of doors to bar the uninitiated and animals (1966, pp. 178-179). As to his first reservation, Circle B might not have suffered deliberate abuse if it was not visible at the time (see p. 192, n. 3); or, even if so, if the two circles represented two different groups, one might have been in esteem, the other in disfavor centuries later. As to the lack of doors, the Mycenaeans had other devices for blocking passages, such as skins, curtains, stone slabs, clay slabs, etc. (cf. Blegen-Rawson (1956), pp. 38, 111, 152, 161); they could have even used a fence or a rope cordon. Of far greater concern for the safety of the fortress as a whole is the fact that two entrances into the citadel from the Northeast (Fig. 1 P, Q) near the vital water supply, had no doors to bar them (Mylonas (1966), pp. 18-19, 32. Mylonas (loc. cit.) postulated that troops could protect them, and also envisioned an honor guard for Circle B (Mycenae: A Guide to Its Ruins and Its History [Athens, 1972], p. 57, fig. 25).The same could apply to Circle A. Whether sacred or not. Circle A was obviously very special to the people of Mycenae.
[3] Athens: H. A. Thompson: »Activity in the Athenian Agora: 1966-1967«, Hesperia, 37 (1968), p. 60; Eleusis: Mylonas (1955), p. 60; idem: Eleusis and the Eleusian Mysteries (Princeton, 1961), pp. 62-63.
[4] J. N. Coldstream: »Hero-cults in the Age of Homer«, JHS, 96 1976), p. 11; Cf. Kurtz-Boardman (1971), pp. 298-302.
[5] Some modern writers like Desborough (1972, pp. 278-287), Dietrich (1970, pp. 16-25) and N. D. Papachadzis (»Religion in the Archaic Period« in The Archaic Period [ed. G. Christopoulos and J. Bastias; tr. P. Sherrard] [London, 1975], pp. 25-26), bothered by the present

as in most other cults, people, apparently stirred by the same feelings as their predecessors, re-established worship and dedications at Circle A some 500 years later,[1] as if there suddenly arose "the revival of some kind of consciousness in a people who had previously lacked it" during the intervening half millennium.[2]

From the above account we see that the late nineteenth-century savants, who were forced to "throw aside all that we have learnt of the development of early Greek art" (Hall), when Egyptian chronology made the Shaft Graves of Circle A and all their contents no later than ca. 1450 BC,[3] were not alone in their problems. Even a century after Schliemann's fabulous discovery, and despite all the finds since then, including Circle B, still the stelae, grave construction, and many of the contents of the Shaft Graves of both circles, the built tomb of Circle B, and the cult at Circle A prove vexing to contemporary archaeologists. With the beginning of the Eighteenth Egyptian Dynasty redated by over 500 years, the Shaft Graves would belong to the eleventh-tenth centuries, the built tomb would fall into the late tenth century, and the special honor accorded to the dead of Circle A would date to the eighth century – all linked in time with similar items and traits of a supposedly later era. Under such a revision they no longer stand isolated from 400-600-year-later, but still comparable artifacts and customs of the eleventh-eighth (and later) centuries, with which some late nineteenth- and early twentieth-century scholars synchronized them, and with which even current scholars still compare, and seek (despite difficulties) to relate them.

---

lack of archaeological material to fill 500-year voids at numerous centers of religious activity – the one matter for which everyone believes in continuity throughout that half millennium – postulate that there was no break. Other recent authors, like Snodgrass (1971, pp. 130-131, 192-194, 275-279, 394-401, 408-409, 422; *Archaeology and the Rise of the Greek State* [Cambridge, 1977], pp. 25-32), Coldstream ([1976], pp. 8-17; *Knossos: The Sanctuary of Demeter* [London, 1973], p. 181), O. Dickinson (»Archaeological Facts and Greek Traditions«, *Bulletin of the Archaeological Society of the University of Birmingham*, 17.2 [1973-4], p. 40), and R. A. Tomlinson (*Greek Sanctuaries* [London, 1976], pp. 15, 20-21, 28, 64, 71, 78-80, 90, 124) are as perplexed as their colleagues, but do see a 500-year lacuna in the evidence (and cf. F. Grace: »Observations on Seventh-Century Sculpture«, *AJA* 46 (1942) p. 341).

[1] Coldstream (1976), pp. 9-10.
[2] Snodgrass (1971), p. 194.
[3] See above »The Grave Circles«, p. 174, n. 1 and p. 177, n. 2.

The Warrior Vase

In one of the buildings closest to Circle A (Fig. 1, F), Schliemann discovered the fragments of a large, decorative ceramic bowl, used for mixing water and wine. Because of its friezes of soldiers, he dubbed it "the Warrior Vase." It is probably the best known piece of Late Helladic pottery (Figs. 2, 4A).

Fig. 2: The Warrior Vase

Fig. 3: Krater signed by Aristonothos

For quite some time after its discovery, scholars dated the bowl to the seventh century BC. They regarded its peculiar bull's head handles as definitely derived from those found on eighth-century vases.[1] They likewise considered the registers of spearmen as a development from the eighth-century processional friezes on funerary jars found near the Dipylon Gate at the Kerameikos cemetery of Athens. They unhesitatingly attributed the soldiers on the bowl to the Protoattic Period (i.e., early seventh century BC) on the basis of style, comparing them to the warriors on another mixing bowl (Fig. 3) painted by a known seventh-century artist; some even ascribed both bowls to the same man.[2] They felt that still other technical and stylistic features of the bowl and its decoration indicated a date between 700 and 650 BC for the Warrior Vase.[3] That same vase is now firmly assigned to the early LH III C

---

[1] F. Dümmler: »Bemerkungen zum ältesten Kunsthandwerk auf griechischem Boden«, Ath. Mitt. 13 (1888), p. 291; E. Pottier: »Observations sur la céramique mycénienne«, Revue Archéologique 28 (1896) pp. 20-21; idem: »Documents céramiques du Musée du Louvre«, Bulletin de correspondance hellénique (henceforth BCH), 31 (1907) p. 248, n. 1.

[2] Pottier: ibid. (1896), pp. 19-23; (1907), pp. 245-248; Walters (1905), vol. I, pp. 297-298.

[3] Pottier: ibid. (1896), although not all of his considerations are valid for dating purposes.

period, which Egyptian chronology fixes at ca. 1200 BC,[1] leaving as problems the peculiar handles and the figural style. Over seventy years ago, D. Mackenzie replied to those who derived its bull's head handles from eighth-century prototypes, that the Warrior Vase itself proved that such a device "had a much earlier history."[2] Still, they stood in isolation from the much later handles, originally thought to be their prototype. The more recent discoveries of two other LH III C handles of the same type[3] has provided companion pieces, but has not alleviated the problem.

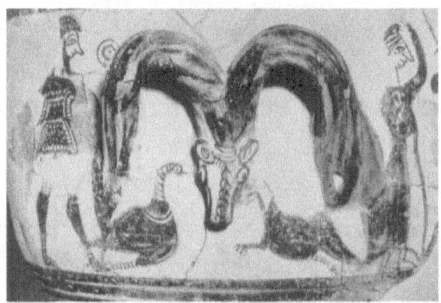 

Fig. 4A: Bull's head handles from the Warrior Vase   Fig. 4B: Bull's head handles on a seventh-century vase

Irrespective of the absolute dates for LH III C pottery, scholars had always considered bull's head handles as a later development from double-loop handles, now artistically rendered as horns surmounting a bovine face. In 1966 N. R. Oakeshott treated the topic in great detail. If the LH III C vases belonged to ca. 700 BC, as early scholars believed, there would be no problem in deriving the developed handles from the double loops on vases from the Protogeometric Period (i. e., no earlier than ca. 1050 BC) onward; but since scholars now assign LH III C to ca. 1200 BC, and since Oakeshott "searched in vain" for double loops earlier than that date, she concluded that the original idea, first seen in the three LH III C examples, was to fashion a fully-articulated bull's head attachment, both as a decorative and a functional device. She spoke of "a continuous tradition" from LH III C onward, but, reversing the previous consensus, she assumed that the Iron Age examples descended from those on the Warrior Vase, only

---

[1] S. Marinatos and M. Hirmer: *Crete and Mycenae* (New York, 1960) pls. 232-33 and captions; Lacy (1967), p. 224.

[2] D. Mackenzie: »Cretan Palaces and the Aegean Civilization III«, *BSA*, 13 (1906-07), p. 433.

[3] O. Broneer (1939), pp. 353-54; M. R. Popham and L. H. Sackett: *Excavations at Lefkandi, Euboea 1964-66* (London, 1968), p. 20, figs 38-39 (from another "Warrior Vase.")

later degenerating into mere double loops of clay.[1]

Oakeshott branded the early Iron Age handles "very debased," part of a "'holding operation,' almost a tactical retreat."[2] Her evidence for a "continuous tradition" is solid from perhaps 1050 BC (at the earliest) on, but there is a lacuna of at least 150 years between the developed LH III C bull's head handles and the earliest known "debased" double loops, which they supposedly engendered. Additionally, of all the numerous Iron Age handles from the Protogeometric Period onward, only the most developed forms of ca. 700 BC again began to look like articulated bull's heads, and were "very similar" to those of the Warrior Vase.[3] A vase from Cyprus displays not only "very similar" handles, but also a similar bird to those depicted on the Warrior Vase; the decoration of the Cypriote bird and the friezes of filling ornaments above the handle are also "very similar" to other LH III C pots.[4] Late nineteenth- and early twentieth-century scholars assigned the same dates to the Warrior Vase and the Cypriote pot. After Egyptian chronology set the former into the early twelfth century, while independent Cypriote chronology has fixed the latter in the early seventh, "the gap between the Cypriote products and the Warrior Vase, to which they are typologically closest, has widened" by half a millennium.[5]

Confronted by a lacuna of 500 years between the "typologically closest," "very similar" examples of bull's head handles, Oakeshott suggested "that a continuous tradition culminated in this area [Cyprus] in a revival."[6] We shall soon see that numerous scholars note a revival of LH III C pottery styles in Cyprus and throughout the East Mediterranean after a 500-year gap; still, Oakeshott, faced with a gap of at least 150 years, which unsettles the idea of "a continuous tradition" and observing the closest similarities between fully-developed bull's head handles of the seventh century (which went through ca. 350 years of continuous evolution from double loops) and 500-year-older handles (which were just as fully developed, but seem to have come about suddenly, and without any ascertainable forerunners) was in a quandary.

---

[1] N. R. Oakeshott: »Horned-head Vase Handles«, *JHS*, 86 (1966), pp. 114-115, 121.

[2] *Ibid.*, p. 121.

[3] *Ibid.*, p. 114.

[4] For similarly decorated LH III birds, concentric arcs, and zigzags, see A. Furumark: *Mycenaean Pottery* (Stockholm, 1941) motifs 7.48-52 (esp. 49), 44.10, and 61.17-18; M. Ohnefalsch-Richter in his *Kypros, the Bible and Homer* [tr. S. Hermann] [London, 1893], pp. 36-37, 63-64 long ago recognized those and other similarities to LH III C decoration.

[5] Oakeshott (1966), pp. 115-116.

[6] *Ibid.*, p. 114.

She concluded that "this is a feature of great interest that others must elucidate."[1] A chronological revision of 500 years not only elucidates the feature, but also eliminates the problems.

The turn-of-the-century scholars, who assigned the painted figures on the Warrior Vase to the seventh century, did so at a time, when there was a general consensus that the latest Mycenaean pictorial pottery lasted that late. After Egyptian chronology pushed the end of Mycenaean civilization some 400 years earlier than they believed (and the Warrior Vase 100 years still earlier), two problems arose, which remain today. The first is that, during the intervening centuries, there seems to have been what J. N. Coldstream has termed "the darkness of taboo on figured representation in Greek art." Because he felt that eighth-century painters who "revived" the figural style did so as a result of experimentation and "with no earlier models to guide them," and because he also considered that artistic revival to be the eighth century's "most striking innovation of all,"[2] one must explain how the style of ca. 700 BC, which was a natural development from an only-slightly-earlier "invention," came to resemble so closely the figural style of ca. 1200 BC after such a long break in the artistic tradition. The second problem is, why there should have been a centuries-long period when figures disappeared from art – a phenomenon which one recent observer considered both "strange" and "curious."[3]

Despite those problems, modern scholars, like Vermeule[4] still see analogies between the friezes of men on the Warrior Vase and those on eighth-century pottery. Unlike earlier commentators, who also saw that similarity, but who had the former develop from the latter, modern specialists must see the Warrior Vase as ca. 450 years earlier than, and devoid of historical connection with eighth-century figural pottery. O. W. von Vacano, like his predecessors impressed by the close similarity of the soldiers on that bowl to seventh-century figures, recently spoke of "an obvious link" between them.[5] If, however, 500 years really do separate the Warrior Vase from the later pottery, with nothing similar to fill the gap, there is, as everyone has noticed, an "obvious" similarity, but there can be no "link," obvious or otherwise.

---

[1] Ibid., p. 132.
[2] J. N. Coldstream (1968), pp. 357, 28 and 350 respectively.
[3] B. C. Dietrich (1970), p. 22.
[4] E. Vermeule (1972) p. 209 (endorsing the view of others).
[5] O. W. von Vacano: *The Etruscans in the Ancient World* (transl. by S. Ogilvie) (Bloomington, 1965) p. 81; cf. p. 88.

Fig. 5: Phrygian soldiers. Detail from a reconstruction of a Phrygian building at Pararli, Turkey, 7th-6th Centuries BC

The spearmen of the Warrior Vase not only resemble the men depicted on seventh-century Protoattic Pottery from Greece, but, as L. Woolley justly noted, they also look "remarkably" similar to soldiers painted on terracotta roof tiles from Phrygia in Asia Minor, currently dated sometime between the late eighth century and the sixth (Fig. 5).[1] Regarding Greek art, "one might almost say that the decorators of Protoattic pottery took up the animal [and human] designs where their predecessors of late Mycenaean times had left off. The similarity is very striking."[2] With 400 years separating the end of one from the beginning of the other, without anything comparable between the two, "the similarity is very striking" indeed!

---

[1] L. Woolley: *Mesopotamia and the Middle East* (London, 1961) pp. 166-168. Whereas he dated the tiles to the late eighth century, E. Akurgal: *Phrygische Kunst* [Ankara, 1955] p. 64, pls. 45-47; *Die Kunst Anatoliens* [Berlin, 1961] p. 100, pl. VII C assigns them to the sixth, an assessment with which M. Mellink (letter of Oct. 31, 1978) concurs. Whatever their true date, and irrespective of which region influenced the other, the Phrygian spearmen more closely resemble the art of seventh-century Greece than that of either the eighth or the sixth. [L. Woolley: *The Art of the Middle East* (NY, 1961), pp. 149, 166; S. Ferri: »Frigia, Arte«, *Enciclopedia Dell'Arte Antica* (Rome, 1960), p. 738, Fig. 905 – LMG]

[2] Broneer (1939), p. 361.

A Chariot Vase

Somewhere in the vicinity of the Warrior Vase was another LH III C mixing bowl, sporting a procession of chariot-borne troops. Only two tiny fragments of that vase are presently known – both retrieved from the heap of debris left behind by Schliemann's workmen. Each sherd depicts part of an open-work chariot transporting two soldiers. Although friezes of people in chariots were fairly common in Mycenaean art, on those two sherds both the spearmen and the drivers wear their shields in a manner "unique in chariot iconography" of the Myceanaean Age, but found again in eighth-seventh-century chariot scenes.[1] Regarding the chariots themselves, we have already alluded to their first appearance in Greece on the Shaft Grave ring and tombstones, where they are cumbersome box-like devices. Between that time and their appearance as swift, light-weight, manoeuverable vehicles on a mixing bowl, the so-called Chariot Vase of Mycenae ca. 400 years later, they had passed through a total of three developmental stages.

In eighth-century representations, supposedly another 400 or more years after the Late Helladic III Chariot Vase, chariots, showing no further modifications, look like "direct descendants" of the twelfth-century type. One would hardly object if the model was incapable of improvement, and thus remained unchanged for another 400 years, but there is no evidence of its existence during those intervening centuries;[2] and alongside the chariot which seems not to have changed for 400 years, other models make their first known appearance.[3]

The lack of evidence for chariots between the twelfth and eighth centuries, coupled with the impoverished picture of the Greeks, which modern scholars note during that "Dark Age," led Snodgrass to conclude that chariots disappeared from Greece for 400 years, then returned to their old form.[4] Despite that admitted lack of evidence for continuity, H. Catling preferred to follow those who believed that chariots did persist in their old form throughout the Dark Age, rather "than to add chariots to the long list of war-gear that failed to survive

---

[1] M. A. Littauer: »The Military Use of the Chariot in the Aegean in the Late Bronze Age«, *AJA*, 76 (1972), pp. 145-146 and »The Entrance to the Citadel«, p. 172, n. 4.

[2] H. W. Catling: »A Mycenaean Puzzle from Lefkandi in Euboea«, *American Journal of Archaeology* 72 (1968), p. 48.

[3] P. Greenhalgh: *Early Greek Warfare* (Cambridge, 1973), pp. 19, 29-39.

[4] Snodgrass: *Early Greek Armour and Weapons* (Edinburgh, 1964), pp. 159-163.

the Mycenaean period, and did not reappear in Greece until the eighth century or later."[1] Nevertheless, Snodgrass, who has specialized in, and been instrumental in compiling that "long list of war-gear," and who has also grappled with the problem of the Dark Age, which scholars place between the end of the Mycenaean Period and the eighth century, still believed that chariots disappeared for centuries, not to return until the eighth century.[2] The debate – at times rather heated – still continues.[3] Integrally related to that controversy is yet another one concerning Homer's references to chariots and chariot warfare, which some date to the thirteenth century, others to the eighth – which "raises a serious problem" for philologists as well.[4]

---

[1] Catling (1968), p. 48.

[2] Snodgrass: *The Dark Age of Greece* (Edinburgh, 1971), p. 433; idem: »An Historical Homeric Society?«, *Journal of Hellenic Studies* 94 (1974), p. 123, n. 40; idem: review of Greenhalgh's *Early Greek Warfare* in *Journal of Hellenic Studies* 94 (1974), p. 225.

[3] Greenhalgh (1973, pp. 19, 29-39), J. V. Luce (*Homer and the Homeric Age* [London, 1975] pp. 39-40) and O. Dickinson (»Archaeological Facts and Greek Traditions«, *Bulletin of the Archaeological Society of the University of Birmingham* 12.2 [1973-74], pp. 39-40) all concur with Catling, postulating that at least the aristocrats still used chariots during the Dark Age. Snodgrass (see n. 2) still held his original position that probably no one could afford such a luxury during the Dark Age, and the lack of evidence probably signalled a lack of real chariots – a conclusion with which G. Kirk (»The Homeric Poems as History«, *The Cambridge Ancient History*, Third ed., Vol. II, pt. 2 [Cambridge, 1975], p. 840) agreed. Greenhalgh: *Early Greek Warfare* [Cambridge, 1973], p. 19 noted that the absence of evidence seems entirely due to the lack of any figural representations in contemporary Greek art. That observation is certainly true for Greece and the Aegean – a source of consternation for art historians, as we shall soon see. Cyprus, however, was both part of the Greek world and in close contact with the Orient where the vehicle presumably persisted; it has produced some actual chariot remains (V. Karageorghis: *Salamis in Cyprus* [London, 1969] pp. 68-69, 78); its Mycenaean and Archaic pottery, and its terracotta models frequently depict chariots; its art continued to have figural representations at a time when Greece did not; its armies continued to employ war chariots long after the Greeks had ceased to use them; and all commentators, including Snodgrass (1964, p. 163), believe that chariots persisted in Cyprus throughout the Dark Age, with the seventh-century examples even resembling the Mycenaean model (Karageorghis, p. 69). Despite all that, both for actual remains and for representations of chariots, Cyprus has that same embarrassing gap from the twelfth century till the eighth/seventh (Karageorghis: »A propos des quelques representations de chars sur des vases chypriotes de l'Age du Fer«, *BCH* 90 [1966], p. 101; idem and J. des Gagniers: *La Céramique Chypriote de style figure* [Rome, 1974], pp. 15-17.

[4] G. S. Kirk: *ibid.*, p. 839. For discussions favoring Mycenaean times, see Snodgrass (1964, 1971); Kirk (1975); Greenhalgh (1973, p. 17); R. Hope Simpson and J. F. Lazenby: *The Catalogue of the Ships in Homer's Iliad* (Oxford, 1970), pp. 4-5. For discussions favoring the eighth century, see J. K. Anderson: »Homeric, British and Cyrenaic Chariots«, *American Journal of Archaeology* 69 (1965), pp. 349-352; idem: »Greek Chariot-borne and Mounted Infantry«, *American Journal of Archaeology* 79 (1975), pp. 175, 184 and »Shaft Grave Art: Modern Problems«, p. 190, n. 3; G. Ahlberg: *Prothesis and Ekphora in Greek Geometric Art* (Lund, 1971), p. 210; idem: *Fighting on Land and Sea in Greek Geometric Art* (Lund, 1971), pp. 70 and n. 34, 109-110. For discussions that waver between Mycenaean

Other LH III Figural Pottery

Throughout the area of Schliemann's excavation – south of Grave Circle A, as well as in Wace's trench beside the Lion Gate – there appeared vast quantities of ornamental LH III B-C pottery fragments. One system of decorating the LH III C pottery from that area (in fact, throughout the Mycenaean empire) is the "Close Style," a term which art historians use to describe compact designs arranged in friezes of water fowl, rosettes, triangles, loops, semi-circles and other motifs, which fill all the exposed surface area of the pots. Lacy recently found it "interesting to notice that the same phenomenon occurred again four hundred years later in the profusion of ornaments" that covered the so-called Dipylon pottery of the eighth century.[1] It is even more interesting that the individual motifs on the Close Style vases, as in the case of the Warrior Vase, find their most striking parallels to designs on the seventh-century "Orientalizing" pottery of Greece, Crete, Rhodes, Cyprus, Sicily, Italy and the Eastern Aegean. That interest heightens when we recall that at a number of excavations throughout that same area (including Wace's trench by the Lion Gate) eighth-seventh century pottery immediately overlay, was mixed with, or even lay beneath LH III B-C ware.[2]

In the late nineteenth and early twentieth century, a number of Aegean specialists believed that Mycenaean civilization immediately preceded the seventh century BC, but because the discovery of Late Helladic (soon followed by Minoan) remains was so fresh, they had little other than the better-known works of the first millennium with which to compare them. Egyptologists noted that the earliest Mycenaean artifacts in Grave Circle A corresponded to the early Eighteenth Dynasty; Flinders Petrie found a large quantity of LH III A – early LH III B pottery in Pharaoh Akhnaten's short-lived capital of Akhetaten in Egypt; and excavators outside Egypt began finding Eighteenth and Nineteenth Dynasty objects beside Mycenaean ware throughout the Levant and the Aegean. At Mycenae itself archaeologists discovered a number of Eighteenth Dynasty Egyptian objects, including some which bear the

---

times and the eighth century, see Kirk: *The Language and Background of Homer* (Cambridge, 1964), p. 176 and J. Wiesner: *Fahren und Reiten* (Archaeologia Homerica, I F) (Göttingen, 1968), pp. 92-110, esp. 93.

[1] Lacy (1967), p. 223.
[2] Cf. above »The Entrance to the Citadel«, p. 172 footnotes and p. 173, n. 1.

cartouches of Pharaoh Amenhotep II, Amenhotep III and his wife, Queen Tiy.[1]

Aegean archaeologists, confronted with Egyptian evidence, had to reassess their dates for Mycenaean culture. "Vehement disputes" erupted between those accepting Egyptian reckoning, and those challenging it as 500 – 700 years too early.[2] Some of these early controversies Velikovsky has chronicled above for Olympia, Tiryns, Enkomi and Mycenae. Those who rejected the Egyptian scheme usually branded the New Kingdom exports to the Aegean as centuries-old heirlooms.[3] That explanation was weak for a number of reasons: it assumed that the Mycenaeans only collected 500 – 700-year-old Egyptian artifacts to the complete exclusion of Egyptian items produced in their own day; it did not explain depictions of Mycenaean objects in Eighteenth-Dynasty murals; and it completely failed to explain the presence of LH pottery in bona fide Eighteenth Dynasty contexts in Egypt itself. None of those championing the heirloom theory even dared to consider that the very basis for dating the New Kingdom of Egypt might be incorrect. Cecil Torr was one Aegean specialist who did question the Egyptian chronological scheme,[4] but Egyptologists countered with strong and at times unfair retorts,[5] and Torr gained no appreciable following.

Most other Aegean prehistorians, realizing that the Late Helladic Period had to be as early as the Eighteenth-Nineteenth Dynasties of Egypt, and accepting the absolute dates furnished by the Egyptologists, pushed the beginning of the Mycenaean Age into the mid-second millennium BC. Many, who felt that the inception of the period had to be that old, still wanted the end of the era to last long into the first millennium, and thereby connect directly with the similar products of the eighth-sixth centuries BC. Beloch, and even Petrie who, through his discoveries and his writings was largely responsible for pushing back LH I – LH III A/early LH III B to the sixteenth-fourteenth

---

[1] J. D. S. Pendlebury: *Aegyptiaca* (Cambridge, 1930), pp. 53-57. More recently, see Hankey-Warren (1974).

[2] Demargne (1964), p. 8.

[3] E.g. A. S. Murray: *Excavations in Cyprus* (London, 1900), pp. 21-24; D. G. Hogarth: *Excavations at Ephesus* (London, 1908). p. 242.

[4] C. Torr: *Memphis and Mycenae* (Cambridge, 1896).

[5] E.g., H. Hall (1901), pp. 56-59 (to which see Torr's response in his review of Hall's book in *The Classical Review* 16 (1902), pp. 182-187 (esp. p. 187).

centuries, still had the remainder of the Mycenaean Age last into the eighth century.[1]

The LH III BC figural pottery, more than any other Mycenaean product, seemed to flow directly into the seventh-century ware of the Greek world. Since archaeologists agreed that Protogeometric and Geometric pottery also preceded the seventh century, many envisioned an overlap of LH III and Geometric styles, just as Böhlau, Wide and their followers had proposed a 500-year-earlier overlap of MH and LH styles. Furtwängler, one of the great pioneers in the study of pottery decoration was among that school's foremost proponents.[2] When further excavation revealed still more New Kingdom Egyptian material alongside the youngest Mycenaean vases, and showed that there was hardly enough LH III BC pottery to last from ca. 1350 – 700 BC, art historians had to abandon the notion that LH III co-existed with geometric ware as late as the eighth-seventh century in Greece itself.

Since the latest Mycenaean vases still resembled so closely 8th-7th century ones, and with Greece no longer a possible area of continuity, they postulated that somewhere in the far-flung Mycenaean empire, outside of the mainland, LH III pottery continued that late. They looked to islands like Sicily, Aegina, Melos, Crete, Rhodes, Cyprus and the east coast of Turkey as places where the tradition could have survived no matter what occurred in Greece proper.[3] Little by little, exploration of those areas revealed the same pattern as in Greece itself, with LH III C dying out by the late eleventh century, if not earlier still.[4]

According to Greek tradition, most of those places, like the Greek mainland itself, fell prey to Dorian invaders, whom early archaeologists – as well as some modern ones – have blamed for the obliteration of Mycenaean culture. Of all the places on the fringe of the Mycenaean world to which scholars looked for centuries-long retention of Mycenaean life and art, Cyprus afforded a unique setting for the contin-

---

[1] References in Tsountas-Manatt (1897), p. 321, n. 1.
[2] A Furtwängler: »Die Bronzefunde aus Olympia und deren Kunstgeschichtliche Bedeutung«, *Berlin Abhandlungen* 4 (1879), pp. 45-47 (reprinted in *Kleine Schriften* I (Munich, 1911), pp. 373-375); F. Dümmler: »Zu den Vasen aus Kameiros«, *JdI*, 6 (1891), pp. 270-271; Murray (1900), p. 23; Hall (1901), p. 36, n. 1; cf. Demargne (1964, p. 271) and Cook (1972, pp. 310, 312-313) for modern comments.
[3] Cook: *loc. cit.*; Hall (1901), pp. 36, 45, 62-63, III, 132, 137, 221-222, 229, 246, 255 n. 1, 259-260, 264-265, 274, 279, 283; A. Evans: »A Mycenaean Treasure from Aegina«, *JHS*, 13 (1892-3) pp. 224, 226.
[4] Snodgrass (1971), pp. 134-135.

uation of Mycenaean figural art, as both early and modern excavators have hypothesized.¹ It never fell victim to the Dorians;² it imported tremendous quantities of LH III pottery, and during the LH III C period it received numerous Mycenaean colonists, including skilled artisans steeped in the art of their homeland;³ it was far enough away from the Aegean centers to escape the turmoil which they encountered, and near enough Phoenicia to share in its presumed prosperity; its people were extremely conservative, reflecting many features of Mycenaean culture well into the eighth-seventh centuries;⁴ its late eighth-seventh century pottery shows some close similarities to LH III C shapes and especially decoration;⁵ and throughout the period between the end of LH III in Greece and the eighth century, Cyprus enjoyed a "special relationship" with the Aegean world, importing and exporting finished products (including pottery), and influencing the pottery shapes and decoration of Greece.⁶

Despite all those positive factors, Cyprus, for some reason not fully understood, followed the same pattern as the rest of the Mycenaean world at the transition from the Late Bronze Age to the Early Iron Age. It, too, suffered its own long period of destructions, abandonments, cultural desolation, archaeological obscurity, and historical darkness.⁷ P. Dikaios once claimed that its Iron Age ware, which scholars originally felt would continue the LH III tradition for centuries, in fact, made its appearance suddenly on the island, showing little connection with, and no evolution from the Late Bronze Age ware,

---

[1] H. Walters: »On Some Antiquities of the Mycenaean Age Recently Acquired By the British Museum«, *JHS*, 17 (1897), pp. 63-64, 77; Hall (1901), pp. 36, 63, III, 132, 137, 221, 229, 264-265; More recently, cf. P. Amandry: »Plaques d'or de Delphes«, *Ath. Mitt*, 77 (1962), p. 54, and C. Bérard: *Eretria* III (Bern, 1970), pp. 42-43; cf. ns. 4, 5 below.

[2] Hall (1901), p. 221; V. Karageorghis: *Cyprus* (London, 1970), p. 67.

[3] Karageorghis: *ibid.*, pp. 61-64; H. Catling: »Cyprus in the Late Bronze Age«, *CAH* 3 II. 2 (Cambridge, 1975), pp. 198-201, 207-213; Snodgrass (1971), pp. 29, 314, 365.

[4] H Karageorghis: *ibid.*, p. 67; idem: »Notes on Some Mycenaean Survivals in Cyprus During the First Millennium B.C.«, *Kadmos*, I (1962), pp. 72-77; idem (1967a), pp. 167-170 and (1969), p. 14; A. R. Burn: *Minoans, Philistines and Greeks, etc.* (London, 1968), p. 230.

[5] Gjerstad (1948), pp. 298-299; P. Dikaios: »Fifteen Iron Age Vases«, *Report of the Department of Antiquities. Cyprus* [henceforth *RDAC*], 1937-9 (pub'd, 1951), pp. 134, 137-138; idem: *A Guide to the Cyprus Museum* (Nicosia, 1961), p. 63; Karageorghis (1962), p. 76; idem: *Treasures in the Cyprus Museum* (Nicosia, 1962), pp. 4, 16-17; idem: »Some Cypriote Painters of Bulls in the Archaic Period«, *JdI*, 80 (1965), pp. I, 10-12, 14.

[6] Snodgrass (1971), pp. 94 (source of the quote), 444 (list of references); Desborough (1972), pp. 49-57, 145.

[7] Desborough: *ibid.*, pp. 49-57 (pace the disclaimer on p. 57); Catling (1968), pp. 53, 221, 301; idem (1975), pp. 193-196, 209-213; Karageorghis (1969), p. 23; idem (1970), pp. 66, 151.

which it supposedly superseded immediately. Even those who reject his opinion do not view it as a continuation of figural LH III.[1] Dikaios and others (including his critics) noted some instances where Cypriote Iron Age ware, like its counterpart in Greece, seems to have bypassed Late Bronze Age ceramics, resembling instead 500-year-older Middle Bronze Age pottery.[2]

Since countless authorities have long noted, and still note, that the late eighth-seventh century pottery of Greece, Sicily, Aegina, Melos, Crete, Rhodes, Cyprus and eastern Anatolia seems a direct continuation of LH III BC shapes and decoration;[3] since they have not found artistic continuity in any of those areas; and since they see too many close resemblances for the similarities to be merely "fortuitous,"[4] they

---

[1] Dikaios: »An Iron Age Painted Amphora in the Cyprus Museum«, *BSA*, 37 (1936-7), p. 58 n. 3. Others (e.g. Gjerstad (1948), pp. 282-287) disagree with that assessment. Again, as with Submycenaean (see above »Shaft Grave Art: Modern Problems«, p. 188, n. 4), some Late Cypriote (LC) III pottery and other artifacts obviously follow LC II, and some obviously precede the Cypro-Geometric period, but I would question the continuity within, and the homogeneity of LC III (cf. J. Du Plat Taylor: »Late Cypriot III in the Light of Recent Excavations, etc.«, *Palestine Exploration Fund Quarterly* [henceforth *PEFQ*], 88 [1956], p.30)

The Iron Age Cypriots did paint representations on some of their pottery, but those were not as common as, and did not directly continue the LH III C figures. There were gaps – some huge – during which many familiar forms disappeared entirely, or else bore little or no similarity to the earlier style; the closest resemblances to LH III B-C motifs belong not to the earliest "post-Mycenaean" ware of Cyprus but to the eighth-seventh centuries, as if a renascence only then took place (Snodgrass (1971), p. 94; Desborough (1972), p. 51; Karageorghis-des Gagniers (1966), pp. 4-6, 15, 47, 62, 94-95, 101, 107-112; cf. p. 206, n. 5).

[2] P. Dikaios: »Principal Acquisitions of the Cyprus Museum, 1937-1939«, *RDAC*, 1937-39 (pub'd, 1951), p. 200, idem (1961), pp. 203-204; Gjerstad (1948), pp. 216, 283 (for which, cf. *SCE* vol. II [Stockholm, 1935], p. 276), 293-294; J. F. Daniel: »Two Late Cypriote III Tombs from Kourion«, *AJA*, 41 (1937) pp. 71, 73-74 (to which see Catling's objection, (1964), pp. 52-53).

[3] In addition to the citations of p. 205, n. 2 and p. 206, n. 5, see inter alia Cook (1972), pp. 41, 44; Edgar (1904), p. 106; Starr (1961), p. 244; Broneer (1939), p. 361; Berard (1970), pp. 42-43; Friis Johansen (1966), pp. 5, 9, 19, 34, 48-50, 55-56, 63-64, 131; J. P. Droop: »Dipylon Vases from the Kynosarges Site«, *BSA*, 12 (1905-6), pp. 84-85, 90-91; D. Burr: »A Geometric House and a Proto-Attic Votive Deposit«, *Hesperia*, 2 (1933), p. 632; J. Pendlebury: *The Archaeology of Crete* (London, 1939) p. 335; R. Young: *Late Geometric Graves and a Seventh Century Well in the Agora* (Athens, 1939), pp. 49. 177, 186-187. 217; W. Taylour: *Mycenaean Pottery Italy and Adjacent Areas* (Cambridge, 1958), pp. 113, 116, 120, 136, 142, 157; E. Vermeule: »The Fall of the Mycenaean Empire«, *Archaeology* 13 (1960), p. 74; J. Boardman: *The Cretan Collection in Oxford* (Oxford, 1961) pp. 57-58, 144 (confusion and debates over dating), 151; E. Brann: *The Athenian Agora* VIII; *Late Geometric and Protoattic Pottery* (Princeton, 1962), pp. 15, 19, 43, 48, 51; E. Langlotz: *Ancient Greek Sculpture of South Italy and Sicily* (tr. A. Hicks) (New York, 1965), p. 15; G. K. Galinsky: *Aeneas, Sicily and Rome* (Princeton, 1969), pp. 82-84, 89; J. L. Benson: *Horse, Bird & Man* (Amherst, 1970), pp. 5-6 and *passim*; J. N. Coldstream: »The Cesnola Painter: A Change of Address«, *BICS*, 13 (1971), p. II; etc. etc.

[4] Vermeule (1960), p. 74.

view the phenomenon as a "renaissance."[1] Even so, with ca. 400 years separating the last LH III C figural ware from the earliest return to that bygone style, they need a mechanism to explain the revival. Since no corner of the Greek world kept the style alive during those centuries, some have conjectured that the Mycenaean ceramic and decorative traditions passed beyond the Greek world to Phoenicia, which provided the required continuity, and finally sent the Greek products, along with some Levantine accretions, in a "backwash" to their place of origin hundreds of years later. That theory is extremely popular[2] and explains why art historians refer to seventh-century Aegean ware with its Levantine and renascent Mycenaean elements as "Orientalizing."

The Levant did receive quite a bit of LH III pottery, and made its own imitation of LH III C shapes and decoration (the so-called Philistine ware);[3] it did send Oriental products (including the alphabet) to Greece in the ninth-seventh centuries; and it did inspire some of the decoration found on seventh-century Greek pottery. Between the Mycenaean Age and the ninth century, when Greece was undergoing a Dark Age, literary sources give a much brighter picture for Phoenicia. A Twenty-first Dynasty document from Egypt, which the accepted scheme places in the eleventh century,[4] indicates a very strong position for contemporary Lebanon; the Bible portrays tenth-century Phoenicia as an independent land, from which Kings David and Solomon purchased lumber and hired seafarers, stone masons, carpenters and a master craftsman.[5] Phoenicia therefore seemed an ideal place to foster LH III pottery until the seventh century.

The facts are that the Levant did not export painted pottery to seventh-century Greece; LH III shapes and decoration made only a very small impact on the Levantine ceramic industry as a whole, and even in Philistia, LH III C-type pottery did not last as long as it did in Greece

---

[1] Demargne (1964), p. 271.
[2] J. Droop: »The Pottery from Arcadia, Crete«, *Liverpool Annals of Archaeology and Anthropology*, 12 (1925), p. 11 (whence the term "backwash"); M. Hartley: »Early Greek Vases from Crete«, *BSA*, 29 (1930-1), pp. 62, 64, 86-37; D. Levi: »Early Hellenic Pottery of Crete«, *Hesperia* 14 (1945), pp. 1, 9-10; Cook (1972), p. 41; R. Higgins: *Minoan and Mycenaean Art* (New York, 1967), p. 190.
[3] Snodgrass (1971), pp. 107-109; F. Stubbings: *Mycenaean Pottery from the Levant* (Cambridge, 1951); V. Hankey: »Mycenaean Pottery in the Middle East«, *BSA*, 62 (1967), pp. 104-147; idem: »Mycenaean Trade with the South-Eastern Mediterranean«, *Mélanges de L'Université Saint Joseph*, 46.2 (1970), pp. 11-30.
[4] Velikovsky (1977, pp. 129-138 and 1978, pp. 80-81) has redated that document and the entire dynasty to the Persian Period.
[5] II Sam. 5:11; I Kings 5:15-32, 7:13-46; II Chron. 2:1-15.

itself – none of which helps the survival theory for the Levant any more than at all the other places suggested over the last century. Bothered by those facts some scholars, who still favor the theory, propose that Near Eastern metalwork, ivory carvings and decorated fabrics kept the designs (if not the pot shapes) alive over those centuries.[1] For continuity of decorative ivories and metalware the situation in the Levant presents as big an obstacle as in Greece (and as big a source of consternation), since there is no evidence of either product from ca. 1200 to 900 BC.[2] The only Levantine medium for continuity that is left is patterned fabric, which several people now see as the most likely source for LH III motifs' survival. While there certainly was ornamental cloth, and it could have preserved some LH III decoration, it lends itself more readily to geometrical patterns than to the curvilinear, naturalistic ornaments and figures of LH III C and seventh-century ware. Still, if one must limit oneself to only one medium for 400 years of

---

[1] Benson (1970), p. 5; Cook (1972), p. 41; Robertson (1975), pp. 23-24.
[2] For ivories, see below »Ivory Carvings«, p. 238, ns. 2-3; For metalware, many authorities have long noted that ninth-seventh-century Phoenician decorated bowls "continue the tradition" of similar bowls from Ugarit of Eighteenth Dynasty date (e.g., H. Frankfort: *The Art and Architecture of the Ancient Orient* [Baltimore, 1963], pp. 150, 195; Strong (1966), p. 53; S. Moscati: *The World of the Phoenicians* [tr. A. Hamilton] [London, 1968], pp. 67-68), and closely resemble Nineteenth-Dynasty metalware from Tell Basta in Egypt (e.g., W. K. Simpson: »The Vessels with engraved designs and the Repoussé Bowl from the Tell Basta Treasure«, *Journal of Near Eastern Studies* [henceforth *JNES*], 24 [1965], p. 28).
As in the case of Greek figural art (cf. pp. 189 and 190 footnotes, p. 191, n. 1 and the previous footnotes of this section), orientalists treating decorated metalware have split into two camps. Those who have championed survival attribute extraordinary conservatism to Phoenician artisans who, without leaving a trace, somehow continued to produce metalware in the ninth-sixth centuries, which differed little, if at all, from Eighteenth-Nineteenth Dynasty antecedents (e.g., Murray (1900), pp. 27-29; Hall (1901), pp. 137, 251-252; C. Schaeffer: *Ugaritica* II [Paris, 1949], p. 47). Those advocating revival proposed a conscious copying of 500-year-old forms (e.g., J. L. Myres: *Handbook of the Cesnola Collection of Antiquities from Cyprus* [New York, 1914], p. 275; cf. Hall: »Oriental Art of the Saite Period« in *CAH* 1 - III [Cambridge, 1925] [ed. J. B. Bury et al.], p. 327; Dikaios (1951), p. 137; Strong (1966), p. 53; for a fuller discussion, cf. Isaacson (1974), p. 15).
Some of the metal bowls from uncertain contexts have provoked heated debates between those who, seeing Minoan, Mycenaean and Egyptian New Kingdom analogies, have assigned them to the Late Bronze Age (e.g., Myres: *ibid.*, pp. 457-460; Fr. von Bissing: »Eine Bronzeschale mykenischer Zeit«, *JdI*, 13 [1898], p. 37; idem: »Ägyptisch oder Phoinikisch?«, *JdI*, 25 [1910], pp. 193-199; idem: »Untersuchungen über die 'phoinikischen' Metallschalen«, *JdI*, 38-39 [1923-1924], p. 190), and those who, acknowledging the 500-year-older elements, still insisted on ninth-sixth-century dates for those same items (e.g. Murray: *ibid.*, pp. 27-29; Hall: *ibid.*, [1901], pp. 137, 251-252, [1925], p. 327; F. Studniczka: »Der Rennwagen im syrisch-phoinikischen Gebiet«, *JdI*, 22 (1907), p. 75; H. Schäfer: *Ägyptische Goldschmiedearbeiten* [Berlin, 1910], p. 66; E. Gjerstad: »Decorated Metal Bowls from Cyprus«, *Op. Arch.*, 4 (1946), pp. 2-17). For similar problems with Aegean bronzes, cf. below »A Terracotta Figurine and a Terracotta Head«, p. 222, n. 4.

continuous patterning, and disregards its nonappearance in other media, Greece is as probable a candidate as Phoenicia;[1] in any instance, the case is completely unproveable, since all the cloth has vanished, and one can only speculate about its possible ornamentation. Yet another problem with Phoenicia, as the source of, retaining, then returning LH III decoration, is that some "Mycenaean" elements begin to appear in eighth-century Greece, before there are any signs of Oriental influence on Greek art; additionally many of the curvilinear motifs and naturalistic figures (especially human) found on seventh-century "Orientalizing" ware, and most reminiscent of the LH III C style, did not come from the Levant, but followed the same course as did the 500-year-earlier decorations, evolving directly from the stiffer forms of native Greek ornament which immediately preceded them.[2] Despite the popularity of the notion of a Phoenician link to explain the close similarities of two sets of Aegean vases now dated half a millennium apart, there is still no evidence that the Levant fared any better than did Cyprus or Greece in continuing the LH III artistic tradition until the seventh century.

---

[1] For decorated Phoenician textiles as the chief medium of continuous transmission, cf., inter al., H. Payne: *Necrocorinthia* (Oxford, 1931), p. 54; Benson (1970), pp. 55, 111-113, 122-123; Cook (1972), p. 41. From the extremely rare specimens of later Greek cloth that have survived, one sees that, at least by the classical period, the Greeks could and did transfer curvilinear and naturalistic designs to cloth from paintings on smooth surfaces, where such motifs are far quicker and easier to create (cf. G. Richter: *A Handbook of Greek Art* [New York, 1969], pp. 380-383).

It is somewhat hazardous to reconstruct the actual designs of textiles from their depictions in paintings, since the latter may show a style less rigid than, and possibly completely different from those on the cloth itself. (H. Kantor: »The Aegean and the Orient in the Second Millennium B.C.« *AJA*, 51 (1947), pp. 43-44); nevertheless, to judge by Mycenaean Age frescoes, Aegean textile workers had already begun to adorn cloth with representational designs including floral motifs, monsters and animals, which seem to have vanished from Dark Age pottery, only to "return" in the seventh century (cf. E. Evans (1935), vol. II [1928], fig. 456, pls. 25-27, and vol. III [1930], figs. 25-26 – if correctly restored and interpreted; Vermeule (1971), p. 193 and pl. 28A-B; S. Marinatos: *Excavations at Thera* VII [Athens, 1976], p. 36 and pl. 65).

While it is true that Homer mentioned "colorful" Phoenician cloth (II. VI; 289-295), he does not describe its design, which might merely have been woven stripes; he does, however, describe the representational adornments of battle scenes and flowers which Helen and Andromache created on cloth (II. III;125-128; XXII:441). If the "taboo" on figural pottery did not extend to textiles, Greek artisans could have kept the styles alive as easily as the Phoenicians allegedly did.

[2] Benson (1970), *passim*; Snodgrass (1971), pp. 54, 417-418; Cook (1972), pp. 41-43. But cf. J. Carter: »The Beginning of Narrative Art in the Geometric Period«, *BSA*, 67 (1972) pp. 25-58, who seeks to push back the earliest Oriental influence.

As an alternative to the still-popular hypothesis of survival, other scholars have postulated a native revival, whereby the Greeks of the late eighth-seventh centuries found 500-year-old vases, liked what they saw, and imitated some of the shapes and much of the ornamentation.[1] Such rediscoveries certainly fit the numerous cases where the later Greeks seem to have returned to cities, houses, wells, palaces, tombs and cult places supposedly abandoned for nearly half a millennium.[2] Still, one had to explain why only then, and at no time during the previous 500 years did the Greeks decide to return to those palaces and copy the bygone art. There is a popular notion, to which we shall return that the later Greeks, hearing Homer's epics, gained a new pride in their heritage, and consciously sought out the relics of the Trojan War heroes.[3] Taking that antiquarian devotion one step further, some observers have proposed that the later Greeks recognized the LH III BC ware in those places as belonging to the "Age of Heroes," and copied it to strengthen their ties of identity with their forebears.[4] K. de Vries has challenged that view reasoning that the eighth-seventh-century Greeks would not have been knowledgeable enough to identify the particular type of pottery used in the Heroic Age after so long a gap.[5]

C. G. Starr recently called the similarities of late eighth-seventh-century wares to LH III BC pottery "particularly puzzling and intriguing."[6] There have been several attempts to explain that phenomenon in terms of a fifth-century revival or survival, but none stands up to careful scrutiny. Some 75 years ago C. C. Edgar, who recognized that seventh-century ware resembled LH III C, just as eleventh-century Protogeometric resembled sixteenth-century Middle Bronze ware, felt that somehow the two revivals, after "obscure" 500-year gaps, followed the same pattern, and probably had the same explanation, whatever it happened to be.[7] Wide, Böhlau, Dörpfeld, Furtwängler and others, who favored survivals rather than revivals, sought to explain the similarities by synchronizing the Geometrical and Mycenaean styles, but

---

[1] Benson: *ibid.*, *passim*; Brann (1962), p. 19.
[2] Cf. p. 173, n. 1 and p.194, n. 5 ;p. 247, ns. 3-5 and p. 260, n. 3.
[3] Cf. n. below.
[4] Benson (1970) *passim*; Karageorghis (1962), pp. 72, 76-77.
[5] K. de Vries: review of Benson's *Horse, Bird & Man*, AJA,76 (1972), pp. 99-100.
[6] Starr (1961), p. 244.
[7] Edgar (1904), p. 106.

they also ran afoul of 500 years.¹ While I would not equate Middle Helladic with Protogeometric or LH III C with Orientalizing ware, since each group does have very distinctive shapes and designs which the other lacks, I would point out that, under a dating system which has eliminated 500 years, the early idea of co-existing styles would explain close similarities, which, under the current chronological framework, merely puzzle and intrigue.

Bronze Tripods

Somewhere in the area of Grave Circle A and the house which contained the Warrior Vase, Schliemann discovered fragments of a bronze cooking cauldron supported by three legs. Unfortunately, he did not record its exact provenience (which would have helped to fix its precise date),² but it is of more interest for its relative position in the history of Aegean metallurgy than its specific location inside the citadel of Mycenae.

Both its shape and its area of discovery help to define its chronological limits within the Mycenaean period. Stylistically the tripod cauldron could be as early as the LH III A period, which corresponds to the reigns of Pharaohs Amenhotep III and Akhenaten; both stylistically and stratigraphically it seems to be no later than the LH III C period, so that, in broad terms, archaeologists have assigned its date of fabrication and its subsequent burial sometime within the fourteenth-twelfth centuries.³ Snodgrass recently called its shape "particularly important," and noted its "close resemblance" to the bronze tripods of the eighth century from Olympia.⁴ Many archaeologists have long observed that close resemblance, and since it is essentially a utilitarian object, they believed that there must have been a continuous production of similar bronze tripods between the two ages.⁵

---

¹ Cf. p. 189, n. 4 and p. 205, n. 2.
² S. Benton: »The Evolution of the Tripod-Lebes«, *BSA*, 35 (1934-35), p. 76, n. 5.
³ *loc. cit.*; Catling (1968), pp. 169-170.
⁴ Snodgrass (1971), pp. 281-283.
⁵ A. Evans (1935), vol. II (1928), pp. 629, 637; W. Lamb: *Greek and Roman Bronzes* (New York, 1929). p. 44; Benton (1934-35), pp. 76-77; Catling (1968), pp. 169-170; idem in Popham-Sackett (1968), p. 29.

Today one sees that at the end of the Mycenaean Age there apparently occurred "a precipitous decline in the technique and employment of Bronze." Presumably, the Mycenaeans no longer had access to their sources of copper and/or tin ore to form new bronze, did not have enough old bronze artifacts and scrap to melt down to create new objects, and also lost the technology to cast the metal in complex molds.[1] Therefore, despite the close similarities of eighth-century bronze tripod cauldrons to Mycenaean specimens, all the excavation of the last century reveals no evidence for the continuous manufacture of bronze tripods of that distinct form, or, indeed, of any form during the Dark Age.[2] Catling, a specialist in the Aegean bronzework of the Mycenaean Age, felt that the close resemblance of eighth-century tripod cauldrons from Olympia and elsewhere in Greece to the Late Helladic examples, as well as the close resemblance of a highly developed eighth-century cuirass from Argos to an example from fourteenth-century Dendra (both places less than ten miles from Mycenae and from each other) implied continuous production for at least those two classes of bronze objects, despite the present gap of centuries in the evidence.[3] Snodgrass, also a specialist in metal work, and on the Dark Age as well, took the same position vis-à-vis Catling, with regard to tripods and body armor as he did with chariots, feeling that, despite the close similarities, a 400 – 600-year gap in the evidence indicated that the eighth-century items did not evolve directly from their Mycenaean antecedents.[4]

The tripod cauldrons were very effective for heating meals over a

---

[1] D. G. Mitten, and S. F. Doeringer: *Master Bronzes from the Classical World* (Los Angeles, 1968), p. 19; cf. Snodgrass (1971). pp. 237-238, 284, and Desborough (1972), pp. 314-318.
[2] Snodgrass: *ibid.*, pp. 281-285, 399.
[3] Catling in Popham-Sackett (1968), p. 29.
[4] Tripods: Snodgrass (1971), pp. 281-285; cuirass: *ibid.*, pp. 271, 345 and idem: *Arms and Armour of the Greeks* (Ithaca, New York, 1967), pp. 30, 41; idem (1974). p. 123. To bolster his case for the discontinuity of bronze tripods during the Dark Age, Snodgrass not only pointed to their absence but also to clay models manufactured during the eleventh-eighth centuries, as evidence that the Greeks of that era, between the two periods of similar bronze examples, experienced a bronze shortage, so that they turned to clay substitutes. Actually, clay tripods had a very long history in the Aegean before the advent of the Mycenaean Age, when bronze replaced clay. By a chronological revision, the "Dark Age" clay examples did not come after the Mycenaean Period and before the revived widespread use of bronze tripods in the eighth century; instead, they served as the original models before, and the poorer people's utensils during the time of Mycenaean metal examples, whose similarity to eighth-century bronze tripods is due to their rough contemporaneity.

cooking fire, but they had their disadvantages. Because of their massive size and weight, their boiling contents and their own heat over the flame, one could not remove them from the fire beneath them, but instead had to ladle what one could of the boiling liquid from their interior. In the LH III C period the Cypriots developed an improved model, consisting of a hollow tripod stand upon which one placed a separate cauldron, which one could remove from the fire, allow to cool, bring to the table, and from which one could pour the contents. Those tripods present similar chronological problems to the one-piece Mycenaean tripod cauldrons which they came to replace. Because there are numerous LH III C examples and a few precisely similar ones in contexts as late as the eighth century, Benson, endorsing earlier opinion, recently called the new tripods "one of the most often cited examples of continuity between the Late Bronze Age and the Geometric Period in the Aegean."[1]

Catling, who studied the numerous tripods, including the Dark Age stands, who noted the close similarity of an example from an eighth-century Athenian context to those of LH III C date, and who did believe, despite the complete lack of evidence, in the continuity of chariots, body armor, and tripod cauldrons during the Dark Age, which separates similar examples, nevertheless dated all the tripod stands to the LH III C period. Rejecting continuity of manufacture after that time, he postulated that all the tripod stands in later contexts were prized antiques.[2]

It is of no little interest that the bronze tripod stands of the LH III C period, replacing one-piece tripod cauldrons, then supposedly vanishing (except for rare heirlooms and much later clay models),[3] followed

---

[1] J. L. Benson: »Bronze Tripods from Koran«, GRBS, 3 (1960), p. 7 and cf. p. 16; cf. Hall (1914), pp. 132-135; Lamb (1929), p. 44; J. Charbonneaux: Greek Bronzes (tr. K. Watson) (New York, 1962), p. 54; Aström (1972), p. 563.

[2] Catling (1968), pp. 194, 216-217, 223; cf. Snodgrass (1971) pp. 119, 251, 271, 285, 325.

[3] For heirlooms, see Catling (1964), pp. 194, 216-217, 223; Snodgrass (1971), pp. 119, 251, 271, 285, 325. Regarding clay "substitutes," Catling (ibid., pp. 215-217), noted that they did not exist during the time of the twelfth-century bronze stands; "more surprisingly," rather than immediately replacing the bronzes at the end of the twelfth century, the clay models only started to appear in the late tenth century, but were still "remarkably close to their metal originals" (p. 215), whose production had supposedly ceased long before the clay "substitutes" ceased being made at the end of the eighth century, once bronze stands began to reappear in Greece. By a chronological revision, the latest "heirlooms" and all the clay "copies" preceded the bronze stands of LH III C date, whose resemblance to seventh-century bronze stands is due to their contemporaneity (cf. p. 214, n. 4).

the same course as, and physically resemble other Eastern tripod stands of the seventh century, which came to replace the eighth-century Greek tripod cauldrons,[1] as if history repeated itself with one 500-year throwback evolving from and supplanting another 500-year throwback. It is of still greater interest that a bronze bull's head attachment, presumably from a cauldron of LH III C date, looks very similar to animal-head attachments found on eighth-seventh-century Eastern cauldrons imported to Greece. Catling and others, noting that resemblance, believed that there must be some kind of connection, but felt perplexed that so many centuries, which offered nothing remotely similar, separated the Mycenaean Age example from its much later counterparts.[2] Furthermore, one of the most ornately decorated Cypriote tripod stands, presumably also of LH III C date, showed Levantine motifs which seemed to derive from somewhat earlier ivory carvings, but the one Levantine ivory carving, which Catling considered stylistically closest to that stand, probably belongs to the eighth century, while one of the closest Cypro-Levantine metalwork analogies dates to the seventh century BC.[3]

As in other cases that we have already seen, and still others as well, the archaeologists' impasse has also had a direct effect on Homeric scholarship, since Homer mentions bronze corselets and tripods in his epics. One group of scholars heralds those references as accurate memories of the Mycenaean Age, preserved through the centuries, while the other regards them as a reflection of the eighth-century world in which Homer and his audience lived.[4] Regarding two sources of literary controversy Homer refers to tripods as prizes at chariot races.

One particular passage, referring to an aborted chariot race for a tripod at or near Olympia shortly before the Trojan War (*Iliad* XI: 698-702) sparked one of the first chronological debates in Homeric

---

[1] Snodgrass (1971), pp. 321, 345; For the resemblance, cf. Boardman (1961), pp. 132-134.
[2] Catling (1968), pp. 154-155; E. Sjöqvist: review of Catling's *Cypriot Bronzework in the Mycenaean World*, Gnomon, 39 (1965), p. 400.
[3] Catling: *ibid.*, pp. 197, 222. The ivory carving from Assyria comes from a deposit whose limits are 824-703 BC. (R. Barnett: *A Catalogue of the Nimrud Ivories* [London, 1957], p. 49).
[4] Corselet: Mycenaean or eighth century: Snodgrass (1974), p. 123; idem (1964), pp. 171-177; probably Mycenaean: Dickinson (1973-4), p. 37; F. Stubbings: »Arms and Armour« in Wace and Stubbings: *A Companion to Homer* (London, 1962), pp. 506-510, 522n; probably eighth-century: P. Courbin: »Une tombe géometrique d'Argos«, BCH, 81 (1957), p. 356. Tripods: probably Mycenaean: F. Stubbings: »Crafts and industries« in Wace-Stubbings (*ibid.*), p. 535 (although see p. 419); probably eighth-century: Snodgrass (1971), p. 436; Dickinson (1973-4), p. 43.

scholarship. Writers of the Roman period argued whether or not the bard made a poetic allusion to the famous Olympic Games of his own day,[1] a problem which still troubles modern authors,[2] especially since some archaeologists feel that the eighth-century tripods found at Olympia, which so closely resemble the centuries-older Mycenaean examples, were, in fact, as Homer recounted, prizes for the winners of the early Olympic Games.[3]

The controversy, then as now, compounds itself because of two conflicting chronological schemes. The Greeks of the classical period attributed the foundation of the Olympic chariot races to a pre-Trojan War hero such as Pelops, Heracles or Atreus,[4] at a time when they had come to believe, via Egyptian reckoning, that the Trojan War fell sometime during the fourteenth-twelfth centuries BC. At the end of the fifth century the Greeks, using native accounts, calculated that the first recorded Olympic Games took place in 776 BC.[5] A dispute then

---

[1] Strabo VIII.3, 30; Pausanias V.8.2.
[2] W. R. Ridington: *The Minoan-Mycenaean Background of Greek Athletics* (Philadelphia, 1935), pp. 17-19, 23, 34, 50, 87; H. Schöbel: *The Ancient Olympic Games* (Princeton, 1966), pp. 19-21, 73, 75, 92, 137, 145.
[3] J. Sandys: *The Odes of Pindar* (New York, 1924), p. xxv; Benton (1934-35), pp. 114-115; Ahlberg (1971a, p. 198 and n. 1.)
[4] The east pediment of the early fifth century temple of Zeus at Olympia showed Pelops' chariot race, which many considered the first Olympic Game. Pindar (*Olympians* X: 55-59), at about the same date, attributed the Games to Heracles. For Atreus, see Velleius Paterculus I:8.1-2. For the Bronze Age in general, see Pausanias V:7.6-8.4, 10.6-7.
[5] J. Forsdyke: *Greece before Homer* (London, 1956), p. 62; G. Mylonas: »Priam's Troy and the Date of its Fall«, *Hesperia* 33 (1964), pp. 353, n. 3. The ceremonial date of 1184/3 BC was the estimate of Eratosthenes of Alexandria who, writing in the late third century BC, relied very heavily on the works of Ctesias (late fifth century) and Manetho (early third century). Modern authorities (e.g., Forsdyke: *ibid.*, p. 68; A. R. Burn: *Persia and the Greeks* [London, 1962], pp. 11-13) completely mistrust Ctesias' work. Without any direct knowledge, he purported to recount Assyrian history, pushing it back much too far. Even the fall of the neo-Assyrian empire in 612 BC (only about 200 years before Ctesias' own time), he dated some 265 years too early – actually to the period of its foundation (Forsdyke, pp. 68-74). Manetho's "history" of Egypt is roughly twice as long as modern scholars view it (A. Gardiner: *Egypt of the Pharaohs* [New York, 1972], pp. 61-62). Although even such respected Egyptologists as Hall, Breasted and Gardiner have noted gross errors in the number, order, dynasties, names and regnal years of Manetho's list of pharaohs, as well as irreconcilable discrepancies between different versions of the list, they still base much of the present chronological scheme for Egypt on his account (Velikovsky (1977), pp. 208-209 and ns. 3-5). Velikovsky (*ibid.*, pp. 205-244) has convincingly challenged Manetho's scheme and the modern one which it helped to create, and in the *Ages in Chaos* volumes has proposed his revision for the entire structure of later Egyptian history. Despite the faith that the ancients placed in those three late classical sources, even modern scholars, who adhere to the present chronological system, dismiss their calculations as worthless (in addition to those already

arose between those who assigned the foundation of the Olympics to the thirteenth century, and those who opted for the early eighth.[1] As happened with contemporary and analogous debates over the foundation dates of Rome and Carthage – either the era of the Trojan War heroes or the ninth/eighth century[2] – the ancients decided to resolve the arguments by accepting both traditions – all three were founded in the Heroic Age, abandoned for nearly half a millennium, then refounded at the later date. Pausanias, who over 1800 years ago related that compromise for the Olympics,[3] did not end the debate, and, in fact, created yet another 500-year problem for Olympia, which sparked the heated quarrel between Furtwängler and Dörpfeld, which Velikovsky has recorded above (»Olympia«).[4]

Rather than resolving ancient literary debates over Olympia, chari-

---

cited, cf. Dickinson (1973-4), pp. 34-35). As we shall see below, these three writers all drew on the still earlier texts of Herodotus, Hellanicus and Hecataeus, who also relied directly on fallacious Egyptian accounts to fix dates for events in Greek prehistory – generally four to five centuries too old.

[1] See Velleius Paterculus 1:8.1-2.
[2] For Rome, see Dionysius of Halicarnassus 1. 72.1-74.2; For references to Carthage, see G. C. and C. Picard (1968), pp. 30-33; Davis: *Carthage and Her Remains* (London, 1861), pp. 1-2. Of special interest, Appian (*Roman History* VIII:1,132), accepting both traditions, had Carthage's foundation both before the Trojan War and in the ninth century.
[3] Pausanias: V:4.5, 8.5. For recent discussions, see p. 216, n. 2 and D. I. Lazarides: »Greek Athletics« in *The Archaic Period* (1975), pp. 489-493.
[4] He assigned the earliest temple of Hera at Olympia to the reign of a king whose grandfather fought at Troy (*Ibid.*, V:3.6, 16.1). Contemporary archaeologists, who have studied the actual remains (A. Mallwitz: *Olympia und seine Bauten* [Munich, 1972], pp. 85-88; H-V. Hermann: *Olympia: Heiligtum und Wettkampfstätte* [Munich, 1972], pp. 93-94; E. Kunze: »Zur Geschichte und zu den Denkmälern Olympias« in *100 Jahre deutsche Ausgrabung in Olympia* [Munich, 1972], p. 11), date the foundation to the mid-seventh century, which is ca. 500 years later than Dörpfeld, trusting Pausanias, maintained. In addition to Velikovsky's treatment above, see H. E. Searls and W. B. Dinsmoor: »The Date of the Olympia Heraeum«, *AJA*, 49 (1945), p. 62.

Ancient debates between those advocating the Late Helladic Period and those championing the ninth-seventh centuries for various events were by no means rare. There are far more instances today, where the ancients unanimously attributed something to the Mycenaean Age, but modern archaeologists and historians can date it no earlier than the ninth-seventh centuries (e.g., Phrygians in Anatolia; Etruscans in Italy; Phoenicians in the Aegean; Phoenician colonization of the West Mediterranean; the Mycenaean [or Trojan] colonization of Sicily, South Italy, Cyrene, Chios, Thera [cf. n. below], Ionia [cf. below »The Design of the Palace«, p. 256, n. 2], and other regions, the unification of Attica, Athens' institution of the archonship and its participation in the league of Calauria [cf. below »The Design of the Palace«, p. 256 n. 4 and p. 257, n. 4]; the arrival of the alphabet [cf. n. below]; the first temples to Hera not only at Olympia, but also at Prosymna [cf. n. below], Perachora and Foce del Sele in Italy; the temple to Artemis in Brauron; the Isthmian, Pythian, Nemean and Olympic Games; the sculpture of Daedalus; the prominence of Argos; etc. etc.).

ots and tripods, modern philologists and archaeologists have run into the same problems (and still more) as their predecessors, and for the same reason – Egyptian chronology placed Mycenaean objects and institutions half a millennium before similar objects and institutions again appear.

A Terracotta Figurine and a Terracotta Head

Somewhere at Mycenae, and most probably in the same general region as the Grave Circle and the buildings to the south of it (Fig. 1, D-J), Schliemann discovered a fragmentary clay figurine which, along with a similar example that he found at the site of Tiryns, seems to represent someone kneading dough to form loaves of bread. He did not record the exact provenience (and the associated material) of either example, which would help to fix their date; both are fragmentary, unpainted and crude, which makes stylistic dating equally difficult; and there are many analogous breadmaker figurines from the Peloponnese (including examples from Tiryns and Prosymna, which lies between Mycenae and Tiryns), that belong to the Archaic period (i.e., seventh-sixth centuries). Despite all these considerations, archaeologists nevertheless felt that Schliemann's two finds were LH III in date, because of their discovery at citadels whose main period of occupation was the Mycenaean Age. Still, there were no similar LH III examples with which one could associate them.

C. Blegen published another breadmaker terracotta of unknown provenience, but definitely LH III A-B in modelling and decoration. Since his figurine did "at first glance" look "like a comparable piece" to Schliemann's finds, it could have helped to bolster the date which archaeologists had long believed, but could not prove for the examples from Mycenae and Tiryns, linking all three to form a tight little LH III group. Blegen realized that people did live in, and leave remains (including figurines) at both Mycenae and Tiryns during the Archaic period. He therefore felt that Schliemann's finds, which resembled the later examples and came from contexts that might as easily have been late as early, could have belonged to the archaic period. He finally decided to assign those two breadmakers to a time 500 years later than other archaeologists had assumed, but did connect them with the large group of seventh-sixth-century figurines, instead of leaving them cut off by centuries from the archaic group.

Blegen's example was certainly of LH III style, so he could not lower its date. Displacing the other two terracottas, the new one assumed their former, isolated position. It became the sole Mycenaean "antecedent" of the later group, "separated from them by a long interval" of 500 – 600 years, during which similar figurines seem not to have been made.[1] In fact, by the present chronological scheme, for nearly two of those intervening centuries, the Greeks seem to have made no figurines of any kind.[2] Blegen was not alone in his dilemma, however. For despite the break in continuity, many authorities note the remarkable similarity of eighth-sixth century terracottas to those of the LH III period – a matter which has elicited wonder and sparked debates involving 400 – 600 years over individual figurines.[3]

In 1896 C. Tsountas, excavating among the houses south of Grave Circle A, discovered a brightly painted, nearly-life-size terracotta head of a female (possibly a sphinx), which art historians have assigned to the thirteenth century BC. The monumental proportions of the head, contrasted with the more ubiquitous, tiny figures, led V. Müller to speculate whether the large-scale sculpture, which one finds from the seventh century onward in Greece, had a centuries-old tradition behind it, and with that question as his point of reference, he observed something in 1934 which is equally valid today: "The relationship of the Minoan-Mycenaean culture of the second millennium and the classical civilization of the first is one of the most pressing problems of present-day archaeology."[4]

---

[1] C. Blegen: »A Mycenaean Breadmaker«, *Annuario della Scuola Archeologica di Atene*, N. S. 8-10 (1946-48), p. 16. For a closer date for that figurine, see Furumark (1941), p. 88; Higgins (1967), p. 14; and Vermeule (1972), p. 222 (phi-shaped figurines). For numerous archaic breadmakers, see A. Frickenhaus: »Die Hera von Tiryns« in *Tiryns* I (Athens, 1912), p. 83.

[2] Higgins: *ibid.*, p. 17; Richter (1969), p. 229 (cf. above »Shaft Grave Art: Modern Problems«, p. 181, n. 4).

[3] For remarkable similarities, see C. H. Morgan II: »The Terracotta Figurines from the North Slope of the Acropolis«, *Hesperia* 4 (1935), pp. 194-195; Young (1939), p.194; C. H. Whitman: *Homer and the Heroic Tradition* (Cambridge, Mass, 1958), p. 52; Benson (1970), p. 123; Boardman (1964), pp. 61, 104. For some 400-600-year debates arising from those similarities, see Higgins (1967), pp. 24 and 141 (references), and Nicholls (1970), pp. 14-15. For related problems, cf. p. 222, n. 2, pp. 222, 223 footnotes, p. 224, n. 1 and »The Religious Center of Mycenae«, p. 228, ns. 2-8, p. 229 footnotes.

[4] *Metropolitan Museum Studies* 5 (1934), p. 158.

Art historians have long noted the close similarity of the first monumental Greek statues of the seventh-sixth centuries to the Eighteenth and Nineteenth Dynasty sculpture in Egypt. The Mycenaeans who visited Egypt at that time and copied other contemporary arts of their hosts, seem not to have imitated their sculpture. Apparently their descendants of the Archaic Period, returning to Egypt after centuries of allegedly broken contact, and seeing for the first time those same colossal works (by now quite ancient), did decide to copy them.[1] Müller observed that the Mycenaeans could and did create larger-scale sculpture, albeit non-Egyptian in inspiration, and cited literary statements that the later Greeks preserved early sculptures for centuries. He therefore considered it reasonable that native Greek sculpture, such as the terracotta head from Mycenae, might, like the contemporary Egyptian works, have been on constant display during the centuries of the Dark Age when, according to present evidence, the Greeks produced no other sculptures; he felt that the Mycenaean pieces could also have supplied an even more accessible, and just as natural a source of inspiration as Egypt did to seventh-century artists. He wanted to believe that, but in the end decided that the old statues "had no influence whatsoever on the new Greek types. Mycenaean civilization died ... classical art made a new beginning."[2] A few years later F. Grace like V. Müller: »The Beginnings of Monumental Sculpture in Greece«, also noted the nearly-life-size Mycenaean creations as possible models for monumental archaic sculpture. Unlike Müller, he doubted that the Greeks frequented cult centers throughout the Dark Age, rather than merely returning to them 500 years later, and felt it improbable that once they did return, there were still any Mycenaean sculptures on view. Like Müller, however, he felt that seventh-century Greeks, looking to Egypt and the Levant, rather than to older native works, "created their sculpture anew."[3]

More recent authorities have also noted the Mycenaeans' skill at producing monumental stone sculpture, such as the Lion Gate, the Shaft Grave stelae, the façades of the beehive tombs, and in modelling large-scale creations of clay, such as the terracotta head.[4] Like

---

[1] E.g., G. Richter: *Kouroi* (London, 1960), pp. 2-3, 28; idem: *Korai* (London, 1968), pp. 4, 23, and cf. Pl. I; idem (1969), pp. 56-57; Vermeule (1972), p. 214; Robertson (1975), pp. 39-41; E. Guralnick: »The Proportions of Kouroi«, *AJA*, 82 (1978), pp. 461-472.
[2] Müller (1934), pp. 164-165.
[3] F. Grace: »Observations on Seventh-Century Sculpture«, *AJA* 46 (1942) p. 341.
[4] Boardman (1964), p. 22; Mylonas (1966), p. 188; J. Barron: *Greek Sculpture* (New York, 1970), pp. 8-9.

Müller, they too ran into the problem of the huge gap separating the monumental thirteenth-century sculptures from those of the seventh century. E. Vermeule parodied the frequently-expressed sentiment that "the thrust toward monumental sculpture is somehow innate in [Mycenaean] Greece but will lie dormant" for over 500 years.[1] Still, the Dark Age of no similar sculpture forced such conclusions upon the art historians.

Not only the monumental size of the terracotta head looked to the seventh century. The shape of the face "seems to foreshadow," and "anticipates in an uncanny way the so-called 'Dedalic' style which was to emerge some six centuries later."[2] As if its own 600-year problems with size and morphology were not enough, that head has created still others. W. Schiering published a small terracotta face of unknown provenience, but noting its similar clay composition to Tsountas' discovery, he noted that it, too, probably came from the region around Mycenae. Observing the face's stylistic affinities to those on large-scale terracotta statues from the island of Kea, which are now dated to the sixteenth century, to the thirteenth-century head from Mycenae, and to a small head from the town of Asine, less than twenty miles southeast of Mycenae, now dated to the thirteenth or twelfth century, Schiering sandwiched the face between the latter two sculptures.[3]

Like the Mycenaean head, the Kean statues and the Asine head have their own 500-600-year problems – the former with stratigraphy,[4]

---

[1] Vermeule (1975, p. 6) actually refers to the Shaft Grave Stelae, but the point is valid for LH III sculpture.

[2] Higgins (1967), pp. 93-94.

[3] Schiering (1964), pp. 1-2.

[4] J. L. Caskey, the excavator of the temple at Kea, felt that it enjoyed uninterrupted attendance from its foundation late in the Middle Bronze Age until the Hellenistic period, with the room which contained the idols constituting the most revered part of the temple. He discovered the idols amid a fifteenth-century destruction layer, immediately above which was a continuous sequence of material which began only in the tenth century. Caskey assumed, on the basis of pottery finds from the "intervening" 500 years from other parts of the building, that tenth-century Keans had removed 500 years of floors from the room with the idols, which is the logical, and, indeed, the only reasonable conclusion, if there really were five "intervening" centuries (Caskey: »Excavations in Keos, 1963«, *Hesperia* 33 [1964], pp. 317, 326-333.) Similarly, see the supposedly continuous use of a religious sanctuary on Crete, where eleventh-century devotees performed the same rites and left identical offerings to those of the sixteenth century, which lay immediately below, with no intervening material to mark the half millennium which supposedly transpired [Evans (1928), pp. 123, 128, 134; Coldstream and Higgins in Coldstream (1976), p. 181]. Both those cases fit the pattern we have seen, and will see for the resemblance of buildings, tombs, pots, jewelry, etc. of the early Mycenaean Age to the early Iron Age, as well as the pattern for "continuity" of religious cults with a 500-year lacuna in evidence [most often between ca. 1200 and 700 BC]).

the latter with style.¹ Now the terracotta face, like its three companion pieces, has its own 600-year problem as well. Though its style does resemble the other problematical sculptures, its size fits well a series of seventh-century heads, but more importantly, its mode of manufacture also points to that same period. Distinct from all other Mycenaean terracottas presently known, the face was fashioned in a mold, something which scholars have traditionally considered an important invention of the early seventh century. If that face really belongs to the late thirteenth century, then the earliest-known Greek mold must go back that far, though its impact seems negligible; then it must have disappeared for ca. 500 years only to re-emerge in the seventh century,² at which time it "completely transformed" the Greek terracotta industry.³ Realizing the problem, Schiering counselled that, in order to follow the history of terracotta heads, one had to take "a long step" (einen weiten Schritt) from the end of the Mycenaean Age to their return ca. 700 BC.⁴

As we have seen, and shall continue to see, one must constantly take that "long step" whenever tracing the development of so many strikingly similar artifacts of two cultural phases supposedly separated by half a millennium. With specific regard to representational art, we already noted the "taboo" on figures on painted pottery of the Dark Age,⁵ and have just seen a similar "taboo" on stone and clay sculpture – both large and small. There is also a contemporary, cen-

---

[1] As others have noted, the Asine head bears a striking resemblance to a series of terracotta sculptures from post-Minoan Crete. Alexiou sought to connect a tenth or ninth-century Cretan head to the example from Asine, claiming that the latter example showed Cretan influence, while Schiering cited an eighth-century Cretan terracotta as proof of the revival of the Asine type of head (1964, p. 15). Nicholls (1970, pp. 5-6), who admitted the possibility of Cretan influence on the Asine head, asserted that it was "impossible chronologically" for the presently-known sequence of Cretan terracottas to have exerted any influence on the example from Asine, however non-Mycenaean and Cretanizing it appeared, since all the Cretan heads so far discovered are later than the Asine head.

[2] Schiering: *ibid.*, pp. 7, 14.

[3] Higgins (1967), p. 17. The Minoans, who used molds to form "eggshell" pottery during the Middle Bronze Age, seem to have continued their use into the Shaft Grave period for animal-shaped vessels, after which time they seem to have abandoned their use for centuries (*ibid.*, p. 12). In Greece itself, except for Schiering's example, which Egyptian chronology dates to ca. 1200 B.C, there is no other evidence for mold-made terracottas for another 500 years.

[4] Schiering (1964), p. 6; cf. Boardman's 500-year later date for a head which Evans classified as Minoan (Boardman (1961), p. 103).

[5] Cf. above »The Warrior Vase«, p. 199, n. 2.

turies-long lack of two-dimensional representations on carved gems and ivory plaques, and three-dimensional ivory and bronze statuettes, which separates the figures found in each of these media during the eighth to sixth centuries from the strikingly similar figures in each of those media during the LH III period.[1] The complete departure from all representational art in sculpture, glyptic and painting, immediately following a long period when such figures flourished, and immediately preceding the return of such similar specimens again seems "strange" and "curious". For bronze, ivory and semiprecious stones, one can postulate a shortage of raw material, or the loss of the skill to adorn them, or the lack of funds to commission the work; however, at a time when there was no dearth of clay and paint, and when artisans did continue to fashion ceramic objects and to adorn them, it is far more difficult to explain why the Greeks interrupted the flow of figural art for so long, only to revive it centuries later in forms so reminiscent of the Mycenaean Age.[2]

Specifically, terracotta figurines were "ubiquitous" during the LH III period, and became common again in the eighth-seventh centuries. Experts often have difficulties distinguishing examples of the two groups, and debates arise, as we have seen. At both periods the terracottas comprise one of the most conspicuous manifestations of Greek religion, which itself constitutes one of the few legacies of prehistoric Greece whose continuity throughout the Dark Age no one seriously

---

[1] Carved gems: p. 219, n. 4 and p. 220, n. 1; ivory plaques: see below »Ivory Carvings«, p. 238, ns. 2-3; ivory statuettes: see below »The Religious Center of Mycenae«, p. 227, n. 6; bronzes: for a gap in Greece during the Dark Age, followed by an eighth-century renewal, see Charbonneaux (1962), pp. 19, 79-80; Lamb (1929), pp. 29-30, 44; S. Casson: »Bronzework of the Geometric Period and Its Relation to Later Art«, JHS, 42 (1922), pp. 207, 219; Mitten-Doeringer (1968), p. 19; Snodgrass (1971), pp. 417-418. Despite that gap, some Mycenaean Age bronzes are strikingly similar to those 500-600 years later – something especially evident in the case of the youthful horned god from Enkomi on Cyprus, now dated to the twelfth century, but extremely similar to seventh-sixth century bronze statuettes in form and facial features (see R. Dussaud: »Kinyras, Etude sur les anciens cultes chypriotes«, Syria 27 [1950], pp. 74-75; Karageorghis (1962b), p. 16; idem (1970), p. 142; K. Hadjioannou: »On the Identification of the Horned God of Enkomi-Alasia« in C. Schaeffer: Alasia I [Paris, 1971], pp. 33-42). Similarly, although there is no evidence of continuity in Crete, some eighth-seventh century bronzes so closely resemble Late Minoan ones, that experts often cannot decide to which epoch individual pieces belong, which has led to consternation, equivocation and scholarly debates (Cf. Boardman (1961); pp. 5-9, 13, 47-48, 118-119); (cf. above »Other LH III Figural Pottery«, p. 209, n. 2, for Near Eastern bronzes.)

[2] Cf. above »The Warrior Vase«, p. 199, n. 3 and »Bronze Tripods«, p. 213, n. 1; For loss of skills except for modelling and decorating clay, cf. Snodgrass (1971), pp. 399-401.

questions. The fact that the later examples so closely resemble the earlier ones and that terracottas "disappear almost without a trace" between the two eras,[1] not only poses problems regarding art and religion, but is, once again, reminiscent of conditions 500 years earlier.[2]

The Religious Center of Mycenae

Starting in 1968, British and Greek archaeologists resumed excavations at and around a large structure southeast of Circle A (Fig. 1, K) which Tsountas and Wace had partly cleared long before. In the process they discovered an LH III B religious complex of altars and sanctuaries unlike any previously known in the Mycenaean world.[3] Until quite recently, scholars felt that the Mycenaean Greeks practiced their religion only at rustic shrines, or else in parts of the urban palaces where their kings served as priests. Those seeking to date the various institutions and objects which Homer described, decided that his references to an independent priesthood and to stone-built, roofed, freestanding urban temples, which he ascribed to the Mycenaean Age, were, in fact, anachronisms 500 years out of place.[4] The recent discoveries of Late Bronze Age temples inside the cult center of Mycenae, at Kition on Cyprus, Ayia Irini on the island of Kea (which began in the Middle Bronze Age), and most recently in the lower citadel at Tiryns, now vindicate Homer.[5]

Those discoveries also add urban temples and an independent clergy to a staggering list of Homeric references which one can ascribe as easily to the thirteenth-twelfth centuries as to the eighth-seventh, but not to the period between.[6] Archaeologists face the additional

---

[1] Snodgrass: *ibid.*, p. 192, and cf. p. 399; cf. p. 219, n. 2 above.
[2] *Ibid.*, p. 200, n. 34.
[3] W. Taylour: »Mycenae, 1968«, *Antiquity* 43 (1969), pp. 91-97; idem: »New Light on Mycenaean Religion«, *Antiquity* 44 (1970), pp. 270-280; G. Mylonas: »The Cult Center of Mycenae«, (English summary), *Pragmateiai tes Akademias Athenon*, 33 (1972), pp. 36-40.
[4] R. Carpenter: *Folk Tale, Fiction and Saga in the Homeric Epics* (Los Angeles, 1946), p. 85; Lorimer (1950), pp. 433-440; J. Myres: »Homer and the Monuments: A Review«, *Antiquity* 25 (1951), p. 73; M. I. Finley: *The World of Odysseus* (New York, 1954), p. 39; T.B.L. Webster in Wace-Stubbings (1962), p. 454; Dickinson (1973-4), p. 40; cf. Kirk (1964), p. 179.
[5] Hope Simpson-Lazenby (1970), p. 2; Mylonas (1972), p. 40; Snodgrass (1974), p. 12. For Tiryns, see M. E. Caskey: »Newsletter from Greece«, *AJA*, 81 (1977), p. 511, and *AJA*, 82 (1978), p. 339.
[6] Snodgrass: *loc. cit.*; idem (1971), p. 26. cf. p. 228, n. 1 below.

problem that the ground plan of temples starting in the eighth century seems to be a throwback to the groundplan of Mycenaean palaces and temples,[1] after a 400 – 500 year period which shows an abrupt abandonment of, and "an essential discontinuity" with Mycenaean architecture[2] – a Dark Age whose architectural forms also seem to be a 500-year throwback to pre-Mycenaean structures.[3] With regard to Homer's epics, for over a century now, archaeologists have "divided themselves into two parties as if engaged in a tug of war," either championing his references as accurate, 500-years-old Mycenaean reminiscences retained in the poems, or else viewing them as a reflection of eighth-century reality.[4]

Literary critics have, as we noted for tripods, engaged in the same tug of war for over 2000 years now.[5] Contemporary philologists, employing linguistic criteria in an attempt to determine the precise date of Homer's allusions, and thereby resolve the debates of their colleagues, find themselves as perplexed as the other disputants, since they cannot neatly separate the manifestations of eighth-century Greek from those which they judge to be 500 years older, and find numerous cases of "Mycenaean" language describing late material and late language describing Mycenaean material.[6]

The philologists, trying to aid the archaeologists to establish dates, readily confess their consternation that "'older' and 'younger' elements (whether archaeological, linguistic, or social) interlock,"[7] and

---

[1] Tsountas-Manatt (1897), p. 322; W. B. Dinsmoor: *The Architecture of Ancient Greece* (New York, 1950), p. 21; M. L. Bowen: »Some Observations on the Origin of Triglyphs«, *BSA*, 45 (1950), p. 123; W. McDonald: *Progress into the Past* (New York, 1967), pp. 423-424; Richter (1969), p. 22; B. Schweitzer: *Greek Geometric Art* (tr. P. & C. Usborne) (New York, 1971 [pub'd posthumously]), pp. 223-224; Robertson (1975), pp. 60-61; Cf. Snodgrass (1971), pp. 409, 424.

[2] Snodgrass: *ibid.*, p. 369; cf. H. Drerup: *Griechische Baukunst in geometrischer Zeit* (*Archaeologia Homerica* II,0) (Göttingen, 1969) p. 77.

[3] Snodgrass: *ibid.*, pp. 369, 383-384; Drerup: *ibid.*, p. 82; Dinsmoor (1950), p. 58; Starr (1961), pp. 247-248; D. M. Robinson: »Haus« in Pauly-Wissowa's *Real-Encylopädie*, Supp. 7 (1940), 235.

[4] M. P. Nilsson: *Homer and Mycenae* (London, 1933), p. 121.

[5] Cf. above p. 216, ns. 2-5 and p. 217, n. 1.

[6] Nilsson (1933), pp. 120, 159, 211; Gray (1954), p. 15; idem: »Homer and the Archaeologists« in *Fifty Years of Classical Scholarship* (ed. M. Platnauer) (Oxford, 1954), p. 29; Webster (1964), pp. 212, 226; J. Davison: »The Homeric Question« in Wace-Stubbings (1962), p. 257; G. F. Else: »Homer and the Homeric Problem« in *Lectures in Memory of L.T. Semple* I (ed. D. Bradeen et al.) (Princeton, 1967), p. 331; E. A. Havelock: »Prologue to Greek Literacy« in *Lectures in Memory of L.T. Semple* II (ed. C. G. Boulter et al.) (Princeton, 1973), p. 335; Kirk (1976), pp. 37-38, 42-43; for the problem of dating the language, cf. Whitman (1958), p. 61.

[7] Davison: *ibid.*, p. 257.

that those same components, which "differ in age by more than half a millennium ... are inextricably blended" – a fact which they term "most bewildering,"[1] and for dating purposes, even "fatal".[2] Since the linguists' attempts to separate the elements into distinct strata has met with failure,[3] they send the problem back to the archaeologists. As Snodgrass remarked, the whole matter is "a sorely vexed question, but it cannot be shirked. It remains as true today [1971] as it has been for some years past, that there are only two positively and widely identifiable historical 'strata' in the world described in the Homeric poems," the LH III period and the eighth century.[4] For temples specifically, and for each of a number of other items, he saw "a pattern ... emerging," wherein they belonged either to the thirteenth-twelfth centuries or the eighth-seventh, but not between."[5]

The dating controversy still rages over temples and an astonishing number of other matters,[6] with the recent discoveries of Mycenaean temples encouraging those who prefer to see all of Homer's references as genuine Mycenaean memories rather than eighth-century anachronisms.[7] But two gnawing questions arise: How did the LH III and eighth-century elements become so "inextricably blended" in the poems, if the epics grew through accretion; and why are those the only two periods in evidence? The second question goes to the very heart of the notion that oral poetry sustained Mycenaean memories through 500 years of illiteracy. If the epics in their original form were so sacrosanct that no poet, who transmitted them, altered them for centuries, why did an eighth-century bard feel that he could insert language, customs and objects of his own day in such a pervasive

---

[1] Nilsson (1933), p. 159.
[2] Else (1967), p. 331.
[3] Havelock (1973), p. 335.
[4] Snodgrass (1971), p. 389.
[5] Idem (1974), p. 123.
[6] *Loc. cit.*; Kirk (1964), pp. 176, 178; Nilsson (1933), pp. 121, 159, 211; Gray (1954), p. 15; Vermeule (1972), p. 309. In addition to the few items we already noted (silver-studded swords, chariots, tripods, corselets, temples) the list also includes references to Sicily, Egypt, Amazons, political geography, lamps, the brooch of Odysseus, helmets, greaves (leg guards), bows and arrows, thrusting spears, twin throwing spears, shields and shield devices, horse burials, hunting, fishing, farming, hording, overseas trade, ivory-inlaid furniture, even the principal characters in the poems and Homer himself – in fact nearly everything imaginable, where one side could favor the Mycenaean Age, the other the eighth/seventh century, and no one can make a good case for the intervening centuries.
[7] Hope Simpson-Lazenby (1970), p. 2.

manner? On the other hand, if it is true that no oral poet memorizes another bard's songs verbatim, or even sings his own tale twice the same way,[1] then one should expect that those transmitting enormous, unwritten secular sagas for 500 years would gradually omit or alter many of the Mycenaean details, which would only have confused or had no meaning to themselves or their audience during the Dark Age; one would further expect that the bards between the LH III period and the eighth century would have added contemporary language and references to make their epics more relevant and comprehensible to their own day and their own listeners:[2] yet they seem to have done neither of those things. Consequently, for Homer's temples, as for other matters, the "tug of war" across a 500-year chasm continues, and the entire situation remains "most bewildering."

Among the discoveries inside the cult center were two fairly large ivory figurines, representing a couchant lion and a very delicately modeled male head. Ivory carving in the round was very rare in Mycenaean times, and those two pieces struck the excavators "unique" among them. Since they come from a building of LH III 3 date, they can be no later than the thirteenth century BC.[3] The lion foreshadows a similarly-posed, late seventh-century sculpture from the island of Corfu,[4] and the face reminds one very much of archaic statuary of the seventh-sixth centuries, although, as we noted above, most critics agree that seventh-century sculptors began their art afresh, with no discernible ties to the bygone works of their ancestors.[5] As for the material itself, ivory statuettes vanished towards the end of LH III only to reappear in Greece ca. 750 BC.[6] There is, moreover, an important deposit of ivory figurines from Ephesus in Asia Minor, dating to the late seventh – early sixth century, including lions, one of which bears some resemblance to the specimen from Mycenae, and a statuette of a priestess (?), which shows close similarities to the ivory head from Mycenae in the shape and piercing of the head, the facial features, and the modeling of the hair. The peculiar rendering of the eyes on

---

[1] J. A. Notopoulos: »Homer, Hesiod and the Achaean Heritage of Oral Poetry«, *Hesperia*, 29 (1960), p. 187; A. Andrewes: *The Greeks* (London, 1967), p. 40.

[2] Cf. Dickinson (1973-4), pp. 36-37, 43-44.

[3] Taylour (1969), p. 96, cf. p. 97 n. 14; (1970), p. 275.

[4] Cp. Taylour: *ibid.*, (1970), pl. 41 a-b to Barron (1970), p. 16.

[5] Taylour: *loc. cit.* pl. 41 c-d; cf. above »A Terracotta Figurine and a Terracotta Head«, p. 220, ns. 2-3.

[6] Snodgrass (1971), p. 345.

the ivory face from Mycenae also foreshadows the similar, though slightly more realistic, eyes of an early seventh-century ivory sphinx from Perachora, less than twenty-five miles northeast of Mycenae.[1] Between the two "unique" LH III B ivories and comparable works of the late eighth-sixth centuries lies the centuries-long Dark Age.

Other cult objects include quite a few terracotta figurines whose lower bodies were formed on a potter's wheel as hollow tubes, in a typical Mycenaean process.[2] They range in date from LH III A – late LH III B, i.e., the fourteenth-thirteenth centuries BC. One of the thirteenth-century idols had a "curious" trait: the lips formed an "archaic smile"[3] – a feature which derives its name from its prevalence on seventh-sixth-century Greek sculpture, but is essentially unknown in Greece before that era.[4] After the manufacture of fourteenth-thirteenth-century Greek cylindrical idols of Mycenae, and the recently-discovered twelfth-century ones from a shrine at Tiryns,[5] there apparently follows a centuries-long break in their production throughout the Peloponnese, until ca. 700 BC., when "wheel-made work in the old technique" suddenly makes a "strange revival;" terracotta figurines in general then started to become "universal throughout Greece once more," as they had been during LH III, before their virtual disappearance during the Dark Age.[6]

In every case where the idols from the cult center still possessed their arms, they were "invariably raised,"[7] as were those on the more schematized specimens from the shrine at Tiryns,[8] and, in fact, most

---

[1] Cp. Taylour (1970), pl. 41 to Hogarth (1908), pls. 21.3, 25.12 (lion) and 21.6, 22 (priestess), and to T. J. Dunbabin et al.: *Perachora* II (Oxford, 1962), pi. 171 (sphinx).
[2] Taylour (1969), p. 92 and cf. Nicholls (1970), p. 3.
[3] Taylour: *loc. cit.*
[4] It appears much earlier in Egypt; the 18th and 19th Dynasty examples, by the revised chronology, inspired the Greek ones directly. It also appears on the Enkomi bronze mentioned above. (see »A Terracotta Figurine and a Terracotta Head«, p. 222, n. 4)
[5] Caskey (1977), p. 511 and fig. 7; (1978), pp. 339-340 and figs 2-4.
[6] Nicholls (1970), pp. 17-18. There were a very few Dark Age wheel-made figurines from Athens and Euboea, but despite their acknowledged similarity to Mycenaean specimens, they, too, seem to return to Greece after a centuries-long break – a fact which causes contention among experts (cf. above »Shaft Grave Art: Modern Problems«, p. 181, n. 4, to which add Dietrich (1970), pp. 21-22). Since the Greeks continued to fashion ceramic objects, including wheel-made pottery, and no one seriously doubts that their religious beliefs and practices remained essentially unchanged, the Greeks' failure to fashion wheel-made or even handmade figurines between the peak periods of production in LH III and the eighth-seventh centuries lacks a convincing explanation.
[7] Taylour (1970), p. 277 and cf. pl. 42.
[8] Cf. p. 228, n. 5 above.

of the numerous handmade and wheel-made figurines of the LH III B-C period. That pose presumably designates a worshipper in the posture of supplication, or a deity in the set of epiphany or benediction. The type suddenly became extinct at the end of the Mycenaean Age. With the return of the Peloponnesian wheel-made figurines and female idols ca. 700 BC., there is "a remarkable associated phenomenon, the reappearance of the goddess with raised arms," which, like other features of contemporary terra cottas, made a "strange revival."[1] They then "kept reappearing spontaneously in widely separated parts of the country without any direct continuity that can be traced among the votive statuettes themselves. Something much more than an archaeological zeal on the part of the faithful needs to be invoked to explain this!"[2]

Dark Age Burials

The cult center, along with much of the citadel, perished in a conflagration which swept through Mycenae towards the end of LH III B, i. e., the late thirteenth century, according to the accepted discovery.

---

[1] Nicholls (1970), pp. 17-18.
[2] *Ibid.*, p. 20; cf. Snodgrass (1971), pp. 192, 399, and Dietrich (1970), pp. 21-22. On Crete and Cyprus, the type did persist during the "Dark Age" (Desborough (1972), p. 285; V. Karageorghis: »The Goddess with Uplifted Arms in Cyprus«, *Scripta Minora* [Lund], 1977-1978 [2], pp. 5-44) – a fact which Nicholls (*ibid.*, p. 13) termed "inescapable." Nevertheless, as in the case of the wheel-made figurines from those islands (cf. above »Shaft Grave Art: Modern Problems«, p. 181, n. 4), he did not believe that the type returned from there after the 500-year gap in Greece itself. Closer to Mycenae, the sole intermediary example known is a crude bronze figurine from the island of Naxos, which falls sometime during the late eleventh-tenth century (Snodgrass: *ibid.*, pp. 200, n. 34, 399). By the revised chronology, the Naxian statuette, as well as the early Cretan and Cypriote specimens – none of which comes from Greece proper – precede the Mycenaean examples which they supposedly follow.
"The only simple explanation" for the revival which Nicholls offered (*ibid.*, p. 20) is that the later figurines copied wooden models, which spanned the Dark Age, but unfortunately failed to survive. The "perishables theory" is a favorite one among historians who note very similar non-perishable remains on either side of the Dark Age (e.g., figurines, statues, architectural forms, writing, decorative motifs, etc., etc.) and try to bridge the intervening centuries. By this very nature it is a hypothesis which is incapable of proof or refutation, and fails to explain why the Greeks, who still modeled, painted and incised clay, did not continue to make imperishable figurines during that period. Even if the gap was real, which is the main issue of the present essay a still simpler explanation would be that art imitated life, i.e, that people from Mycenaean times onward prayed with both hands uplifted, and that sculptors showed that pose at those times when they did produce figural art in permanent materials.

Digging through the debris of the temple compound, the excavators also found three graves of the eleventh-tenth centuries. All three were simple pits, though two of them had their sides lined and their roofs covered with stone slabs to form "cists."[1] Cist tombs were the most common type of grave at Mycenae, and throughout Greece, during the Middle Helladic period, ca. 500 years earlier. The sudden, widespread adoption of that type of burial and the rites that accompany it ca. 1125 BC. have struck several prehistorians as both an "innovation," when contrasted to Late Helladic burials, and, at the same time, "a resurgent phenomenon" when compared to the vogue 500 years earlier – a return to ancestral tomb types and burial rites after the destruction of Mycenaean civilization. That kind of grave became "the most characteristic form in both eras," and the graves of both periods are so closely similar that often excavators cannot decide to which age some cists belong, unless they contain the distinctive grave goods of one period or the other[2] – goods which, as we noted above, also, at times, look extremely similar, despite the 500 years separating them.

The tomb type did survive into the Mycenaean Period, but was not nearly as common then as before and after, and seems not to span the entire time between its two major peaks before ca. 1550 and after ca. 1125.[3] Because it is difficult to trace such continuity between the two ages, because the graves made "an almost universal take-over," supplanting the Mycenaean tomb types, and they constitute "one of the distinguishing features" of post-Mycenaean culture, which was "radically different from the old Mycenaean civilization" that it supplanted, those who reject a 500-year continuity or some strange revival after 500 years, postulate the influx of new people from the north, who retained burial customs whose popularity in Greece had been on the wane for half a millennium. Still, as we shall observe presently, the evidence for the hypothetical immigrants is highly questionable. Many archaeologists reject the notion, and even its adherents cannot show a spread of the new tombs from the north to the south, but they find

---

[1] Desborough (1973), p. 91

[2] Snodgrass (1971), pp. 153, 184, 384 respectively, and cf. pp. 183, 363; cf. Andrewes (1967), p. 35; N. Verdelis: »Neue geometrische Gräber in Tiryns«, *Ath. Mitt.*, 78 (1963), p. 56; Styrenius (1967), p. 161; C. Thomas: »Found: The Dorians«, *Expedition*, 20 (1978), p. 22.

[3] Snodgrass (1971), pp. 177-184, did try to bridge the period, but the examples are extremely few for so long a time, do not remain at any one locale throughout the period, and do leave some blanks, hence Desborough (1972, pp. 108, 266, 269) and Dietrich (1970, p. 20) remained unconvinced.

it easier to face "the present geographical gap in the evidence" than the chronological gap.[1]

The presence of the graves in the cult center, presumably destroyed long before, requires two assumptions: first, that the inhabitants of Mycenae decided to forsake their traditional cemetery grounds where for centuries they had interred their dead in the relatively soft ground away from their dwellings, outside and to the west of the citadel wall; and, second, that they chose, instead, to bury their dead inside the city itself, which required the more laborious task of digging the graves into a thick mantle of eroded debris and a cement-like mass of calcinated stones and fire-hardened brick within the former temple complex. Desborough, who published the graves, considered it "extremely unlikely that people living outside the walls" would enter the citadel for the sole purpose of burying their dead therein,[2] but the fact remains that there is no clear evidence that people inhabited the citadel at that time.[3]

The condition of the two cist tombs is also revealing. One of them showed the effects of a subsequent fire so intense that, in addition to the ashes it left over the grave, it bleached the stone cover slabs and the stone walls of the grave, and even burned the bones of the skeleton it contained.[4] Such a great burning over that spot is difficult to explain if the grave is later than the cult center,[5] but it would be much

---

[1] Desborough: *ibid.*, p. 269. For the dispute over northern immigrants, see ns. below.
[2] Desborough (1973), p. 101.
[3] Excavations have revealed no evidence of structures of the eleventh-ninth century over the cult center (*ibid.*, p. 91), or, for that matter, anywhere in the citadel. There are some potsherds from that period inside the city (*loc. cit.* p. 100; idem (1972, p. 365)), but as Desborough himself noted (1973, p. 100), they are negligible in quantity. He cited Mylonas' undocumented statement (*ibid.*, p. 101 and Sandars (1958-9, p. 235)) that there were dwellings of that date higher up on the citadel. In fact, Wace (1949, pp. 23-24, 84-85) carefully studied the area in question, and said that it was abandoned at that time, a conclusion with which Mylonas, on a later page of the same book that spoke of habitation, agreed, thereby effectively negating his earlier remark (1957, pp. 17, 63). More recently, Mylonas again noted that there was no evidence of Dark Age dwellings on the summit (*Mycenae's Last Century of Greatness* [London, 1968], pp. 30-31, 38.)
[4] Desborough (1973), p. 92; Megaw (1964-65), p. 10.
[5] It would take a lot of fuel to generate a blaze hot enough to scorch the stones and the skeleton in the grave, but there were no structures on the spot from LH III C times till the Hellenistic Period – supposedly some eight centuries later. Furthermore, since the area has constantly filled with debris from higher up the slope from the time of the LH III B destruction, there should have been a very thick protective mantle of earth and rubbish between the tenth-century grave and any flammable Hellenistic structures centuries later (cf. Desborough (1973), p. 91; Megaw: *ibid.*, p. 10; Taylour (1973), p. 260; K. A. Wardle: »A Group of Late Helladic III B Pottery, etc.«, *BSA*, 68 (1973), pp. 302-303).

easier to see as the result of the tremendous fire that destroyed the citadel towards the end of LH III B – if the tenth-century grave was, in fact, *earlier* than the LH III B[1] cult center. Desborough termed the second cist "sub-mural,"[2] because an LH III C wall rested over the eleventh-century grave – again easy to explain if the grave was older than the LH III C structure; if it was not, however, then one must conjecture that "the buriers decided – for some reason unknown – to destroy part of a wall" of the Mycenaean structure, and for some reason even more difficult to comprehend, they then decided to rebuild the wall of a structure long-since destroyed and abandoned and of no use to them, on top of the grave."[3]

The burial circumstances inside the temple complex reminded Desborough of the situation encountered by C. Tsountas at another spot inside the western extension of the citadel walls. To the northeast of the Lion Gate Tsountas excavated some LH III houses and discovered six cist tombs datable sometime within the eleventh – ninth centuries. The tombs lay *under* a deposit over six feet thick of LH III pottery and other remains, which by the accepted chronology should be older than the graves. To explain why LH III material lay over the graves, rather than the graves lying above it or cutting through it, Desborough speculated that even after tremendous fires supposedly flattened the city in the late thirteenth and mid-twelfth centuries, a few houses survived the conflagrations, remained intact for centuries until people entered their ground floors, not to inhabit them, but only to bury their dead, and that only sometimes thereafter the upper stories, still filled with LH III goods, which had somehow withstood earthquakes, fires and the ravages of time, then collapsed onto the graves.[4]

There is another way to view the "late" graves under the LH III buildings in the western citadel, which fits the special circumstances at the site, if one applies the revised chronology. The town of Mycenae was originally much smaller in size, and rested entirely on a hard limestone promontory. The inhabitants, in order to remove the deceased from the dwellings of the living, to perform burials with some ease, and to follow religious precepts, buried their dead outside of the first city

---

[1] Wardle: *ibid.*, p. 303.
[2] Desborough (1973), p. 100.
[3] *Ibid.*, p. 91.
[4] *Ibid.*, pp. 98-99.

wall, in the softer ground, and to the west – the region of sunset and death. When the rulers decided to enlarge the citadel in the LH III B period, they extended the fortification wall into the ancestral cemetery to the south and west. They enclosed the shaft graves of Circle A and accorded them special reverence, but built their structures over numerous other graves of the MH-LH II period (seventeenth – fifteenth centuries),[1] which, for the most part, were cist tombs – like "the 500-year-later" ones. In fact, the excavators of the temple complex found a Middle Helladic cist tomb inside the religious center and not far from the eleventh-tenth-century ones they discovered;[2] but because of the 500 years currently placed between them, they assumed the former cist was covered by the later structures, while the other cists cut into them (despite problems with fire and the overlying wall). If the LH III B period belongs not to ca. 1350 – 1200 BC., but some 500 years later, the discovery of the typologically identical, but supposedly 500-year-older cists beneath the LH III B buildings in the same area is no longer surprising.

Despite the 500 – 600 year problems we have already noted at the cult center regarding temples, Homer, ivories, idols, tomb types and stratigraphy, the excavators found one type of object there which, more than any other factor, has served to fix the absolute dates for Mycenae's period of greatness. Inside the temple was a faience plaque bearing the throne name of Pharaoh Amenhotep III. Quite a few identical plaques have turned up in Mycenae,[3] and the pattern of Eighteenth-Nineteenth Dynasty objects together with Mycenaean material throughout the Aegean, the Levant and Egypt itself, establishes a synchronism. Egyptologists assign that king's reign to the early fourteenth century BC, hence the dates for, and all the chronological problems with the Mycenaean Period. Velikovsky[4] places the same man in the ninth century. The direct effect of such redating for Mycenae is obvious.

---

[1] Cf. above »Later Use of the Grave Circles«, p. 193, ns. 2-4.
[2] J. P. Michaud: »Chronique des Fouilles en 1973«, BCH, 98 (1974), p. 604.
[3] Taylour (1969), pp. 95-96.
[4] Velikovsky (1952), pp. 229-33

The Northeast Extension

The city walls of the mid-LH III B period reached as far as wall O (Fig. 1) to the northeast. When the Mycenaeans realized that the citadel lacked an adequate supply of water to withstand a prolonged siege, they remedied the problem by extending the fortifications to the northeast (Fig. 1, P, Q, R), and transported water via a subterranean conduit from a natural spring to a cistern which they secretly excavated just outside the new walls, and to which they carved out an elaborate descending stepped passage with a hidden entrance just inside the wall (Fig. 1, S). The exact date of the undertaking is uncertain, because the original excavation was not fully published, but it was sometime shortly after the extension of the walls into the cemetery to the south and west, and before the end of LH III B, i.e., very late in the thirteenth century BC.[1] Mylonas called the system "the most striking construction in the citadel, a truly Cyclopean undertaking"[2] and "another wonder of the ancient world."[3] Probably spurred by Mycenae's example, both Tiryns and Athens constructed analogous underground reservoirs approached from inside the fortifications, also toward the end of LH III B (i.e., ca. 1200 BC).[4] Vermeule termed all three "marvellous feats of design," which inspire "admiration for the palace engineers ... tempered by awed respect."[5]

The concept of securing fresh water for a siege by such a clever device that early in human history impressed Tsountas as "astonishing."[6] Still, Karo felt that the system at Mycenae had a significance far greater than its mere construction, and that one could not view it in a historical vacuum. He noted comparable Greek water projects of the Archaic and Classical Periods and declared that, despite the huge gap in time, the similarities were not accidental, but that the Mycenaean system was the archetype for the much later undertakings.[7] In fact, one can think of the famous engineering marvel of Polycrates of Samos who, in the late sixth century, had spring water conducted into his city via a large tunnel.

---

[1] Wace (1949), pp. 99, 104; Mylonas (1957), pp. 32, 38-39; idem (1966), pp. 31-33.
[2] Mylonas: *ibid.*, (n. 6), p. 31.
[3] Idem (1957), p. 32.
[4] Idem (1966), pp. 14-15, 31-33, 41-43; Vermeule (1972), pp. 161, 268-270.
[5] Vermeule: *ibid.*, p. 161.
[6] Tsountas-Manatt (1897), p. 40.
[7] G. Karo: »Archäologische Funde u.s.w.«, *Arch. Anz.* (1933), pp. 227-228; idem: »Die Perseia von Mykenai«, *AJA*, 38 (1934), pp. 126-127.

When assessing the LH III B defensive architecture and water systems of Tiryns, Athens and especially of Mycenae, an example from beyond the Greek cultural sphere comes to mind. King Hezekiah of Judah, confronted by the Assyrian host, rebuilt the old walls of Jerusalem and erected new fortifications, hid natural springs and excavated a gigantic sinuous tunnel to carry spring water from Gihon to a reservoir at Siloam, most probably an underground cistern approached by a secret passage from inside the city. The Old Testament heralds that feat as one of his greatest secular accomplishments[1] and modern archaeologists have confirmed the Biblical account, in fact, K. Kenyon called the undertaking "an event in the history of Jerusalem which is of vital historical importance."[2] The Biblical description and the actual remains are very reminiscent of what took place at the northeastern extension of Mycenae. Hezekiah's defenses and water project belong ca. 700 BC, while the standard chronology places the ones at Mycenae, Tiryns and Athens ca. 500 years earlier.

Although it is certainly possible for the same idea to occur to different people in different locations at different times, under the revised chronology, the water systems of Mycenae, Tiryns and Athens are roughly contemporary with that of Jerusalem. It is therefore of interest to note that the three Greek tunnels seem so "astonishing," precisely because they appeared suddenly and fully developed, and constitute such a novelty for the region. Hezekiah's tunnel, on the other hand, was not only the successor to the earlier, less ambitious (and militarily disastrous) attempts by the Jebusites to channel spring water into Jerusalem, but also followed upon centuries of Israelite improvements which produced completely concealed water tunnels, making spring water accessible to besieged cities throughout Palestine at places such as Gibeon, Gezer, Megiddo and Hazor.[3]

---

[1] II Kings 20:20; II Chron. 32: 3-5, 30; Isa. 22:9-11.
[2] K. Kenyon: *Jerusalem* (London, 1967), p. 38, and cf. pp. 68-71, 77, 96-99 (pls. 37-44); cf. D. R. Ap-Thomas: »Jerusalem« in *Archaeology and Old Testament Study* (ed. D. W. Thomas) (New York, 1967), pp. 283-285.
[3] In accordance with the standard chronology, J. B. Pritchard (*Gibeon* [Princeton, 1962], p. 64), noting close similarities between the tenth (or ninth)-century water system at Gibeon and the late thirteenth-century examples from Greece, postulated that the idea might have traveled from Mycenae to Israel. That notion gained credence from the fact that scholars then dated the very similar, second, improved system at Megiddo to the twelfth century (e.g., J. N. Schofield: »Megiddo« in Thomas (1967), p. 320). Even without Mycenae, however, Palestine showed its own evolutionary process. Some archaeologists dated Megiddo's first water system, a covered gallery, to the fifteenth century BC, which would explain how the city withstood a seven-month siege by Pharaoh Thutmose III; that project was, nevertheless,

Of far greater importance in determining the date of the three contemporaneous Greek water systems is the fact that in the two excavations where the archaeologists did record their findings, the results correspond to Wace's trench by the Lion Gate. The Tirynthian and Athenian cisterns both contained pottery of the late eighth-seventh century immediately above, and mixed together with pottery from the transition of LH III B-C; they contained no ware from the "intervening" centuries and no layer of sediment to mark the passage of the five centuries which the standard chronology places between LH III B/C and the eighth/seventh century.[1]

---

far from ideal, since it left the spring exposed and at the mercy of attackers, who apparently killed the guard and cut off the city's water supply (*loc. cit.*), which presumably led to Megiddo's surrender (cf. J. Wilson in J. B. Pritchard [ed.]: *Ancient Near Eastern Texts, etc.* 2 [Princeton, 1955], pp. 234-238). There is also the problem of why the Jebusites of ca. 1000 BC felt so secure in the face of David's siege that they taunted his army, when they had also left their spring susceptible to poison or to blockage by the enemy, and even left their septem undefended. For those failings they lost Jerusalem when Joab's forces stormed their shaft and thereby took the city by surprise (II Sam 5:6-9; I Chron. 11:5-6; cf. Kenyon: *Royal Cities of the Old Testament* [London, 1971], pp. 25-26. Those elliptical passages are controversial, leaving it uncertain whether Joab's men entered Jerusalem via the shaft or merely cut off access to the water). The Jebusites' failure to safeguard the spring and the shaft is difficult to explain if their system followed the inadequate first system at Megiddo, and especially if it followed the completely protected second system, and the Greek examples which supposedly inspired it.

Today, after further excavation, the scenario for Israel is as follows: the unprotected Jebusite system was the earliest, followed by the first water project at Megiddo which, despite its guard, also proved vulnerable. Archaeologists have redated that project by 500 years from Thutmose III's reign to Solomon's (Y. Yadin: *Hazor* [New York, 1975], pp. 226-231) – two rulers who, under the revised chronology, were contemporaries (Velikovsky (1952), pp. 143-177). Then followed the completely concealed and protected second tunnel at Megiddo, and the systems at Gezer, Gibeon and Hazor, and finally the tunnel of Hezekiah. There is at present a 200-year gap between the Greek tunnels which were completely concealed and the first, exposed, Palestinian ones, which came into existence in an imperfect form long after the complete abandonment of the three Greek systems – which hardly points to direct influence from that quarter; the Greek tunnels, without any known Greek antecedents, most resemble the latest Israelite tunnels after their centuries of development and improvement from inadequate local prototypes. (See Ap-Thomas (1967), pp. 280-285; Kenyon (1971), pp. 25-26, 67-68, 102, 140; A. Negev: *Archaeological Encyclopaedia of the Holy Land* [New York, 1972], pp. 126, 129, 141, 204, 333; Yadin, pp. 226-231, 244, 247 for the Palestinian systems – to some of which material Rabbi J. Segal kindly referred me), (in an as yet unpublished essay, J. J. Bimson questions the Solomonic and Omrid dates for Palestinian material, reassigning it to ca. 700 BC which, if correct, would even more tightly cluster all the completely concealed water systems of Israel).

[1] Athens: Broneer (1939), pp. 402-403, 427-428; Tiryns: For the late eighth-century date of the earliest post-LH III C material among the debris which the Tirynthians dumped into their twin tunnels at a later date (N. Verdelis: »Anaskaphe Tirynthos«, *Archalocrikon Deltion* 18 [1963], p. 72 and 19 [1964], p. 110), see Rudolph (1971), p. 93. Of greater significance,

Ivory Carvings

Excavations in the eastern portion of the acropolis of Mycenae revealed a substantial structure (Fig. 1, U), which contained hundreds of scraps of ivory, gold leaf, and other precious commodities, obviously comprising the quarters and workshops of the palace artisans, who produced many of the ivory figurines and plaques, gold jewelry, and carved gems found throughout the Aegean, and the East Mediterranean.[1] Ivory, probably from Syria, first appeared in Greece as tiny ornaments applied to other objects in the Shaft Graves at the beginning of the Late Helladic Period. By the late Eighteenth Dynasty, the Mycenaean craftsmen were fashioning ivory sculptures and inlay plaques with intricate patterns and subjects, such as hunting scenes, combats with real and mythical beasts, warriors, heraldic and religious motifs, etc., which spread across the Aegean and Near East. They and their Syrian counterparts freely exchanged their creations, in the process mingling Eastern and Western decorative elements to form an international style.[2]

By the end of the Mycenaean Age, the importation of raw and finished ivory from the East, and its carving in the Aegean, apparently ceased, "making its first re-appearance" in Greece some 600 years after the Shaft Grave Period.[3] Greek artisans resumed the fashioning of intricate carved ivories in the eighth century,[4] with the motifs very reminiscent of Mycenaean work some five hundred years earlier.

Ivory carving is an extremely delicate craft, which only a small guild of artisans practised, passing the technique from master to apprentice, and probably from father to son; Greece itself had a centuries-long gap

---

note the stratigraphy of the chamber adjoining the southern tunnel, filled by sediment washed down from higher up in the city, wherein one stratum contained both LH III C and late eighth/early seventh-century sherds (mostly the former). That layer which, by the standard chronology, should represent 500 years of deposition, is only slightly thicker than the one immediately beneath it, which represents at most, only a few decades, and is significantly thinner than the layer above it which did represent a few centuries (Rudolph (1975), pp. 98-99, 114).

[1] G. Mylonas: *Mycenae and the Mycenaean Age*, (Princeton, 1966), p. 73.
[2] E. Vermeule: *Greece in the Bronze Age* (Chicago, 1972), pp. 218-221; H. Kantor: »Syro-Palestinian Ivories«, *Journal of Hellenic Studies* 15 (1956), pp. 169-174; idem: »Ivory Carving in the Mycenaean Period«, *Archaeology* 13 (1960), pp. 14-25; J.-Cl. Pursat: *Les Ivoires Mycéniens, etc.* (Paris, 1977).
[3] Snodgrass (1971), p. 248.
[4] R. Barnett: »Early Greek and Oriental Ivories«, *Journal of Hellenic Studies*, 68 (1948), pp. 2-3, 13-14, 24; J. N. Coldstream: *Greek Geometric Pottery* (London, 1968), p. 360.

in production, despite the close similarities of the later ivories to the Mycenaean ones; the Levant was the ancient source of the raw material as well as a center for ivory carving in antiquity; and the Levantine ivories of both the second and the first millennium BC displayed distinctive Mycenaean motifs. For all those reasons, students of ancient ivories looked to the East as the region which carried on the artistic tradition over the centuries when it had vanished from Greece. They believed, as did those who postulated the return of Mycenaean ceramic decoration from seventh-century Phoenicia, that thirteenth-century Mycenaean ivories influenced the Levantine artisans, who continued to fashion similar works without interruption until, centuries later, they sent the influence back to Greece.[1]

Those who look to the Orient as the place that preserved the artistic tradition meet the same difficulty there as they found for Greece, since from 1200 – 900 BC, both places have "a sudden gap ... in which no ivories are known."[2] Across those three centuries, one cannot detect any links to connect the ninth-eighth-century creations to the very similar examples of the fourteenth-thirteenth centuries, which were "now quite extinct," both in the Aegean and in the Near East. "Unlikely though it may seem ... this is yet the case."[3] Despite that gap, numerous authorities have long noted the close resemblence of the later group to the centuries-earlier one.[4] There are some cases (e.g., at Delos) where ivories from eighth-century contexts look Mycenaean in style, so that scholars proclaim them to be 500-year-old heirlooms,[5] and other cases which have sparked scholarly debates on whether the ivories stem from the thirteenth century or the eighth.[6] Still there is a perplexing gap.

In order to bridge the gap, M. Mallowan recently suggested that the Levantine artists turned from ivory to media such as textiles and wood

---

[1] Coldstream: *loc. cit.*; Barnett: *loc. cit.*; idem: »Nimrud Ivories and the Art of the Phoenicians«, *Iraq*, 2 (1935), pp. 195-196; idem: »Phoenician and Syrian Ivory Carving«, *PEFQ*, (1939), pp. 11, 13-15; J. W. & G. M. Crowfoot: *Early Ivories from Samaria* (London, 1938), pp. 36-37; Kantor (1956), pp. 169-174, (1960), p. 24; H. W. Catling: *Cypriote Bronzework in the Mycenaean World* [Oxford, 1964], p. 302; M. Mallowan: *Nimrud and Its Remains* II (London, 1966), pp. 480, 586; M. Robertson: *A History of Greek Art* I (New York, 1975), p. 32; I. Winter: »Phoenician and North Syrian Ivory Carving, etc.«, *Iraq*, 38 (1976), pp. 9-11.
[2] Kantor: *ibid.* (1956), p. 171.
[3] *Ibid.*, p. 174.
[4] Cf. p. 238, n. 1 above and p. 239, n. 5 below.
[5] Kantor (1956), p. 170; Webster (1964), pp. 28, 111, 139, 170.
[6] Kantor: *ibid.*, p. 156 and cf. below p. 239, n. 5, p. 240, n. 1.

– all examples have long since perished – to keep the tradition alive.¹ If one accepts that theory for the Levant, one can as readily apply it to Greece, in order to sustain the art there, without requiring a hypothetical Oriental interlude. The disadvantages of that idea are that it is completely unprovable, and, for the Levant, at least, where there was a native supply of the raw material, it provides no reason why the artisans stopped carving ivory, or how they managed to resume the art so skillfully, with motifs scarcely, if at all, changed from those of the earlier period, immediately after the break. Also recently, D. Harden observed that the two chronologically distinct sets of ivories are "closely akin in style" with "little or no gap in artistic tradition." With no stylistic break, the centuries-long gap in time troubled him. Whatever the effects of hypothetical invaders in Greece, or of raids on the Syrian coast, he could find no explanation for the art to cease in Phoenicia or further inland. He therefore concluded that, for the Levant, "there should not be such a hiatus in the evidence."²

Much to everyone's consternation, both the Aegean and the Orient presently have a very long "hiatus," which "should not" exist (in the latter region, at least), dividing two sets of very similar Aegeo-Levantine ivory carvings. H. Kantor, who chronicled many of these similarities, but also saw the gap that separated them, considered "the problem of the relationship" of the two displaced sets of material to be of "predominant importance."³ Yet that problem remains unresolved.⁴

That difficulty, of "predominant importance" today, did not trouble excavators at the turn of the century. A. S. Murray, then Keeper of Greek and Roman Antiquities at the British Museum, unearthed and published a number of Mycenaean Age ivory carvings at Enkomi on Cyprus. Observing the same close resemblances to ninth-seventh-century ivory and stone reliefs that still impress (and disturb) scholars today, he assigned his ivories, along with everything else he found at Enkomi, to that period. He did not believe in a Dark Age, and judged that the entire Mycenaean Age belonged that late, rather than five hundred years earlier.⁵ As Velikovsky has recorded above (»The Scandal of Enkomi«), other authorities, such as Arthur Evans, implicitly trusting in the dates furnished by Egyptologists for New Kingdom pharaohs, some

---

[1] Mallowan (1966), p. 480.
[2] D. Harden: *The Phoenicians* (New York, 1962), p. 184.
[3] Kantor (1956), p. 171.
[4] Very recently, see Winter (1976), pp. 9-11.
[5] Murray: *Excavations in Cyprus* (London, 1900), pp. 4-41. For ivories, specifically: pp. 10-14.

of whose exports were also at Enkomi, blasted Murray and the British Museum as well. They pushed back his dates by five hundred years,[1] in the process creating two similar, but chronologically disjointed groups of ivory carvings. The ensuing problem not only disturbs modern archaeologists and art historians but, once again, the philologists as well, since Homer's mention of furniture inlaid with carved ivory plaques strikes some classicists as a thirteenth-century memory preserved by epic poetry, while others view it as a reference to the material again becoming common in the poet's own day, five hundred years later.[2] The result of Egyptian chronology's triumph today are two epochs of ivory carving, showing similarities five hundred years apart, with a three-hundred-year break in the evidence, no way to bridge or even explain the gap, and a great many authorities who confess their bewilderment at the state of affairs which now confronts them.

Mycenaean Jewelry

Beginning in the Shaft Grave Period, the rulers of Mycenae not only patronized a guild of ivory carvers but also a guild of jewelers, who were probably inspired and instructed by, and perhaps originally were, Minoan artisans, who had had a venerable tradition in the art. The craftsmen of Mycenae fashioned gold rings with intricate designs of battle and hunting, and heraldic and religious scenes, and also produced lens-shaped and almond-shaped sealstones and gems of semi-precious materials, which they engraved with men, monsters and animals arranged in compositions similar to those on the ivories and gold rings.[3]

---

[1] A. Evans: »Mycenaean Cyprus as Illustrated in the British Museum Excavations«, *Journal of the Royal Anthropological Institute*, 30 (1900), pp. 199-200. The heated, and, at times, vicious attacks which Murray's publication generated form a very instructive chapter in the history of scholarly attitudes towards chronology, which I hope to document in greater detail at a later date.

[2] For Mycenaean times, see T. Webster: »Polity and Society«, pp. 460-461, and F. Stubbings: »Crafts and Industries«, p. 533, both in Wace-Stubbings (1962). *A Companion to Homer* (London, 1962). For the eighth century, see V. Karageorghis: »Homerica from Salamis (Cyprus)« in *Europa: Studien ... Ernst Grumach* (Berlin, 1967), pp. 168-170, and O. Dickinson: »Archaeological Facts and Greek Traditions«, *Bulletin of the Archaeological Society of the University of Birmingham*, 12.2 [1973-4], p. 43.

[3] Vermeule (1972), pp. 95, 128-133, 206, 223-225, 231, 289-290, 300-301.

Since the shaping, and especially the engraving, of such tiny, hard stones is an extremely precise and delicate craft which requires years of apprenticeship to master, and since both the shapes and the decoration of seventh-century gems and coins so closely resembled the jewels of the Mycenaean Age, late nineteenth-century archaeologists like Arthur Evans felt that there had been an uninterrupted tradition of Greek gem-carving from the Late Bronze Age until the historical period,[1] with Cecil Torr prepared to date the entire Mycenaean Period just prior to ca. 700 BC partly on the basis of carved gems.[2] Further excavation, plus chronological reconsiderations, seemed to refute their belief, as Evans later admitted, but since he still detected remarkable similarities of seventh-century gems to Minoan-Mycenaean ones, he dropped the idea of survival, and replaced it with one of revival.[3]

According to the current scenario, the jeweler's art perished toward the end of the Mycenaean Period. By ca. 750 BC "the native art of gem-cutting" returned to Greece, but since barren centuries separated one "native" manifestation from the other, art historians could not consider Greece itself as the source of the revival. Thus they once again turned to the Near East as a place for the Greeks to relearn the craft.[4] At first the Greeks used softer stones, formed various shapes, and engraved the gems by hand with the same type of geometrical patterns and figures as one finds on contemporary pottery. Within a few decades of their "relearning" the craft, the artisans created designs which, like seventh-century pottery, developed a more naturalistic, curvilinear appearance. Within seventy-five years of the re-introduction of the "native art," they again employed the cutting wheel used 500 years earlier, again standardized the shapes of the gems, mainly to the Mycenaean preference, and engraved themes extremely reminiscent of those belonging to the Mycenaean Age.[5] In carving technique, shaping and design, the early seventh-century jewelers "were in some mysterious way imitating the gems which had been made at least half a millennium earlier."[6]

In order to explain the "mystery," scholars now assume that sev-

---

[1] Evans (1892-93), p. 222; cf. J. Boardman: *Island Gems* (London, 1963), p. 13.
[2] Torr (1896), p. 69.
[3] Evans (1900), p. 209; idem (1935), pp. 539, 560-561.
[4] R. Snodgrass (1971), pp. 345-346, 399; J. Boardman (1963), pp. 94-95, 110; G. Richter: *Engraved Gems of the Greeks and the Etruscans* (New York, 1968), pp. 27-32.
[5] Richter (1969), pp. 245-246.
[6] Boardman (1963), p. 14.

enth-century artists not only followed a line of artistic progression similar to that of their ancestors, but that they actually found and imitated 500-year-old gems. They seem to have made such expert copies that even today, when the find-spots of individual gems are unknown, some experts cannot decide whether they fall into the Mycenaean Age or the seventh century, or else one group of scholars will champion Mycenaean dates for gems which other scholars place 500 years later. Even instances when the experts know the provenience and associated material of some gems are not always helpful, since they sometimes judge the gems to be half a millennium older or younger than the associated material, on the assumption that many gems are 500-year-old heirlooms, or else that late gems somehow slipped into (or were dedicated at) 500-years-older structures.[1]

Before Egypt provided absolute dates for the Mycenaean Period, late nineteenth-century scholars had none of the problems with Mycenaean gems (or, for that matter, with anything else) which beset modern specialists. Even after Egypt began to fix Mycenae's age, Cecil Torr had no problem, since he completely distrusted the Egyptologists' calculations,[2] but he was practically alone in his skepticism. Problems began for Evans and for everyone else from the turn of the century to the present, such that, even today, authorities freely admit that "there will always be some [engraved gems] which defy attribution" to one side or the other of the 500-year gap which now disrupts the sequence;[3] and debates continue between experts championing dates half a millennium apart for individual gems that they discover.[4]

Homer referred to Mycenae as "rich in gold," an epithet which is very appropriate when we recall the wealth of the Shaft Graves. In dealing with their masks, hair rings, diadems, pins, garters, discs, the chariot-hunt ring, etc., we already noted a number of 400-700-year problems. Other pieces of gold jewelry from Mycenae and across the Aegean have caused still more bewilderment for the excavators. As

---

[1] *Ibid., passim*, esp. 13-14, 20-21, 32-34, 52, 58, 64, 73-74, 92-95, 110 and n. 1, 153; cf. idem: *Archaic Greek Gems* (London, 1968), p. 169; Richter (1968), pp. 32, 38; idem (1969), pp. 245-246; Snodgrass (1971), p. 382; Evans (p. 241, n. 4 above); Higgins (1967), p. 190; De Vries (1972), p.100; Benson (1970), p. 121; R. M. Cook: *Greek Art* (New York, 1971), pp. 166-167; Robertson (1975), pp. 147-361.

[2] Torr (1896), *passim*.

[3] Boardman (1963), p. 14.

[4] For a recent case in point, see M. Vickers and J. M. Reynolds: »Cyrenaica, 1962-72«, *Archaeological Reports* 1971-2, p. 29.

was true of the gem-engravers, the first goldsmiths at Mycenae were probably trained by, or were themselves Minoan artisans, who had had a long history of craftsmanship on Crete. R. Higgins eloquently described "the superlative excellence of Mycenaean jewelry, in which the arts of filigree, granulation, inlay, enamelling, and repoussé work were carried to perfection."[1] Much of that work, at least in its final stages, apparently emanated from the royal workshop on the citadel (Fig. 1, U).

Towards the end of the Mycenaean Period there comes "a real break in continuity," with Greece too impoverished to create jewelry, except for rare pieces, which were "simple in extreme."[2] By ca. 850 BC, more intricate works, again showing filigree and granulation, start to reappear. Since jewelers engage in the "most conservative of all crafts," and there is a centuries-long break in the continuity of sophisticated jewelry in Greece, one could not assume that the Greeks began such delicate and intricate work again without the aid of non-Greek jewelers. Scholars therefore postulated that Mycenaean work which was exported to Cyprus and the Near East, had a profound impact on the artists there, who kept the tradition alive during the centuries when the Greeks themselves lost it, then re-introduced the old techniques and some jewelry types, which were popular in the bygone era.[3]

There is clear evidence of Near Eastern influence on Aegean jewelry of the ninth-seventh centuries,[4] but any evidence that the Orient adopted and continued the Mycenaean tradition from the twelfth-ninth centuries is almost as poor as that assumed for pottery painting, metal work, ivory carving and gem engraving.[5] In fact the earliest known "sophisticated jewelry" of ca. 850 BC from Athens, showing both filigree and granulation, looks less Oriental than it does native Greek; and the granulation does not resemble the Levantine type as much as it does Mycenaean work,[6] which flourished some 500 – 600 years earlier.[7] One therefore had to postulate that while Mycenaean techniques

---

[1] R. Higgins: »Early Greek Jewelry«, *BSA*, 64 (1969), p. 143; cf. idem (1961), pp. 69-70.

[2] Ibid., (1969), pp. 143-144; cf. idem (1961), p. 90.

[3] Ibid., (1969), pp. 144-146; idem (1961), pp. 70, 91, 95-96; Robertson (1975), p. 32.

[4] Ibid., (1969), pp. 145-146, 151; idem (1961), p. 95.

[5] Ibid., (1969)., p. 146; cf. K. P. Maxwell-Kyslop: *Western Asiatic Jewelry, ca. 3000-612 B.C.* (London, 1971), pp. 224-231.

[6] E. L. Smithson: »The Tomb of a Rich Athenian Lady, ca. 850 B.C.«, *Hesperia*, 37 (1909), pp. 111-112.

[7] Higgins (1961), pp. 70, 76.

may have returned from the Near East, the Greek jewelers probably also rediscovered and copied centuries-old pieces of native Mycenaean craftsmanship.[1]

The problem of gold jewelry is not confined to the Greek mainland. On Crete in the eighth or seventh century,[2] art historians are likewise "suddenly confronted with jewelry of great sophistication." One piece from contemporary Ithaca to the northwest displayed a complex pattern of filigree and granulation, which "inevitably recalls" a twelfth-century Cretan ring. Similarly a seventh-century Cretan ring resembles yet another twelfth-century Minoan ring. Such a repetition of designs after so long a period "leads to the question whether there can be any connection between the two groups ... Can this resemblance be due to chance?" Higgins, seeing such marked similarities between jewelry from Ithaca and Crete separated by 500 years, felt that they could not be fortuitous. He felt that there had to be a continuous tradition, but discounting the Near East as the intermediary, he suggested something which he hoped was not "too far-fetched" – that Crete itself kept the art alive during the Dark Age. Still, there were not only the problems of a 500-year difference in dates, and the sudden appearance of the later jewelry, but the additional one that for Crete, just as for Greece, "the record is a blank" for some two hundred years after the creation of the twelfth-century rings[3] – which hardly helps to support the notion of continuity.

Similar problems have beset a cache of jewelry now in the British Museum, purportedly from Aegina, which many scholars have long viewed as Mycenaean in spirit but ninth-seventh-century in date, while others, also aware of their affinities to ninth-sixth century Italian, Aegean and Oriental material of the first millennium, have assigned the hoard to the period of and just prior to the Shaft Graves, ca. 1700 – 1500 BC.[4] A gold and enamel scepter from Cyprus has also become

---

[1] Ibid., pp. 95-96; Cf. idem (1969), p. 145, and Robertson (1975), p. 32.
[2] J. Boardman (»The Khaniale Tekke Tombs, II«, BSA, 62 (1967), pp. 57-67) has recently re-dated much of the pertinent material from ca. 700 to ca. 800 BC, Higgins (1969, p. 150), who originally accepted the later date, follows Boardman, while Snodgrass ((1971), pp. 267, 293 n. 49) remained skeptical.
[3] Higgins: ibid., pp. 149-150.
[4] For the ninth-seventh centuries, see Evans (1892-93), pp. 197-226; F. Poulsen: Der Orient und die frühgriechische Kunst (Berlin, 1912), p. 60; Lorimer (1950), p. 71 and n. 1; C. Hopkins: »The Aegina Treasure«, AJA, 66 (1962), pp. 182-184. For dissatisfaction with such a late date for "Mycenaean" jewelry, see Myres (1951), p. 70 and S. Marinatos: »Nu-

the subject of a debate between those who see its analogies to jewelry of ca. 1200 BC, and those who see its resemblance to material of ca. 500 BC – again with a centuries-long gap separating the two groups, both for the jewelry technique and sophistication in general, and the manufacture of enamel in particular.[1] The difficulties which have beset archaeologists and art historians over actual jewelry have again provoked a 500-year "tug of war" between two schools of Homericists. Many commentators consider the Odyssey's description of its hero's golden brooch, depicting a hound attacking a fawn, to be a transplanted memory of Mycenaean jewelry design, while many others view it as an accurate reference to early seventh-century jewelry, and still others do not know which position to take.[2]

---

merous Years of Joyful Life«, *BSA*, 46 (1951), p. 114 and n. 36. For its redating to ca. 1700 – 1500 BC, see R. Higgins: »The Aegina Treasure Reconsidered«, *BSA*, 52 (1957), pp. 42-57; idem (1961), pp. 60, 64-67, 77, 82, 201 (but cf. p. 136 for the "striking likeness" to late seventh-century work); Demargne (1964), p. 110.

[1] For the twelfth century, see G. H. McFadden and E. Sjöqvist: »A Late Cypriot III Tomb from Kourion Kaloriziki No. 40«, *AJA*, 58 (1954), pp. 134, 141-142; Karageorghis: *Mycenaean Art from Cyprus* (Nicosia, 1968), p. 7; idem (1970), pp. 73, 156; Higgins (1961), p. 26; idem (1967), p. 180; A. Pierides: *Jewelry in the Cyprus Museum* (Nicosia, 1971), p. 23 (but see p. 3). For ca. 600 BC, see L. Buxton, B. Casson and J. Myres: »A Cloisonné Staffhead from Cyprus«, *Man*, 32 (1932), pp. 1-4; S. Casson: *Ancient Cyprus* (London, 1937), pp. 66, 157; G. Hill: *A History of Cyprus* I (Cambridge, 1940), p. 89, n. 6; P. Dikaios: *A Guide to the Cyprus Museum* (Nicosia, 1947), p. 107; idem (1961 ed. of same book), p. 159. Both groups point to the similarity of the scepter's scale pattern to contemporary pottery, although alternating rows of colored scales are characteristic only of the latter pots. Those who consider the scepter to be early point to the eleventh-century date of the tomb which allegedly contained it, and to similarly made twelfth-century Cypriote rings (although they must assume that the enamelling was an invention of that period, was used on the rings and scepter, and then vanished till ca. 600 BC). Those who date it late doubt that the scepter came from that early tomb (whose cremation burial presents yet another 400-year problem – cf. McFadden [1954], pp. 133-134; Karsgeorghis (1967b), p. 119; idem (1969), p. 9 [by M. Wheeler]), and point to similarly-made seventh-century jewelry. Most of them wrote before the discovery of the analogous twelfth-century rings; Dikaios, however, did know of them in 1961, but followed the same reasoning as Higgins (p. 244, n. 3 above), and Pieride (1971, p. 3), assuming some seventh-century jewelry reproduced twelfth-century patterns.

[2] Mycenaean Age: A. J. Evans: »The Minoan and Mycenaean Element in Hellenic Life«, *JHS*, 22 (1912), pp. 292-293; idem (1935), p. 524; H. P. and A. Wace: »Dress« in Wace-Stubbings (1962), p. 500; Webster (1964), p. 111; Hope Simpson-Lazenby (1970), p. 2; Probably early seventh century: Poulsen (1912), p. 117; F. Studniczka: »Die Fibula des Odysseus« in E. Bathe: *Homer 11.2 Odyssey* (Leipzig, 1929), pp. 145-148; Nilsson (1933), pp. 123, 25; Carpenter (1946), p. 55; Lorimer (1950), pp. 511-515; Jacobsthal (1956), p. 141; C. M. Bowra: »Composition« in Wace-Stubbings (1962), p. 41; probably early seventh century, but skeptical about the whole issue: Kirk (1964), p. 181; W. B. Stanford: *The Odyssey of Homer* II (New York, 1967), pp. 325-326; Bielefeld (1968), p. 68.

The Palace

In addition to the water system and the artists' quarters, the acropolis of Mycenae was also the site of the palace complex, including an eastern villa, called the House of Columns (Fig. 1, L, N). Both, at least in their final forms, belong to the LH III B period, and both, along with most of the rest of the city, as well as several other palaces and towns throughout the rest of the Aegean, perished in flames towards the end of the LH III B period (i.e., ca. 1200 BC). While there was a brief re-occupation of the House of Columns before its ultimate abandonment, the palace itself apparently became an uninhabited heap of rubble for the next five centuries, until the Greeks of the seventh (possible late eighth) century constructed a temple on the site.[1]

The palace was the abode of the king, whom the Greeks of the eighth century, and probably earlier as well, (like contemporary peoples in Egypt and Asia) considered to be semi-divine;[2] even though there was a separate religious complex in the lower city, presumably with its own priesthood, the king most probably still exercised much influence over the spiritual life of his subjects, performing sacred rites for the community as a whole inside the palace.[3] Since the palace grounds were

---

[1] There were some pottery fragments from the "intervening" centuries in the area, but no evidence of dwellings or other structures (cf. »Dark Age Burials«, p. 231, n. 3). By the revised scheme those Protogeometric and Geometric sherds, like the Middle Helladic and early Mycenaean ones found in the same area (Wace (1949), pp. 84, 87) antedate not only the temple, but also the destruction of the palace itself. The earliest pottery which Wace actually found above the LH III B destruction belongs to the seventh century (Wace: »The Palace«, BSA, 25 (1921-3), pp. 224, 226).

[2] Hesiod: *Erga*, lines 159f; Homer, *passim* (esp. Il. XII:23, 312; XVI:604; Od. XI:304, 602-603); Cf. Vermeule (1972), p. 307.

[3] Vermeule: *ibid.*, p. 233; Tomlinson (1976), p. 13. Mylonas (1972, p. 40) is correct to point out that the king was not in total control over the religious life of the city, nor was the palace the sole center of worship; but the separation of church and state, which he postulates, seems unlikely for Greece at such an early date. It is clear from Egypt and Near East that the kings exercised tremendous control over spiritual life – usually more than the clergy itself, which tended to act in concert with the kings, often owing their posts to royal appointments, and subject to dismissal or death at the whim of the king. The *Iliad* shows the royal house of Troy as more prominent than the priesthood itself in performing sacred rites for the good of the city (Bk. VI:86-98, 269-311); it further shows a Greek prophet afraid to offend his king (Bk. I:69-113), and demonstrates that the gods rendered more aid to the suppliant king than to their own priests (cp. Bk. I:393f. to 35-54). Likewise, the Oedipus trilogy of Sophocles shows a Greek prophet afraid of offending his kings, and demonstrates how important the kings' sets were to the well-being of the state (cp. the Old Testament accounts of good and bad fortune befalling the Hebrews' because of the piety and impiety of their kings, rather than that of the priests and prophets). Finally, the religious duties of the Athenian "king archon" of the historical period also points to the sacerdotal functions of the earlier kings.

the scene of religious activity in LH III B and from ca. 700 BC till the Hellenistic period, some recent authors have postulated that there was a continuous cult there, with the archaic temple and its Hellenistic replacement showing its more impressive manifestations at a later date.[1] As others have noted, however, if some 500 years actually transpired between the end of the palace and the erection of the first temple, with no evidence of cult activity during such a long interval, it is difficult to trace any continuity, and some even question whether the revival of religious activity on the site was a conscious one.[2]

The Greeks of ca. 700 BC erected temples over the ruins of LH III B palaces not only at Mycenae, but also at Athens, possibly at Prosymna,[3] and probably at Tiryns, a site which again generated a 500-year "tug of war" between two schools of archaeologists, making that case "problematical."[4] They also constructed shrines and temples over 500-year-older shrines and secular buildings on Aegina, Calauria, Crete, Delos and Samos; at Mycenae itself, Epidaurus, Olympia, Perachora, Therapne, Isthmia, Brauron, Eleusis, Delphi, Pherai, Thermon, and Tegea.[5]

Once again, those who noted clear evidence of religious activity at most of those sites before 1200 BC, and again in the eighth-seventh centuries, postulated an uninterrupted cult, while those who were disturbed by the lack of evidence for religious activity – in many cases of any activity – at those sites during the intervening Dark Age, believe, instead, that after a "prolonged lapse" of centuries, the Greeks of the eighth-seventh centuries sought a "deliberate communion" with their predecessors of the Mycenaean Age.[6] Since the evidence for religious activity not only at each of those places, but throughout the Aegean, is so meager during the Dark Age,[7] both those who believe in continuity of cult places, and those who do not, find it difficult to explain why "the huge increase in [religious and architectural] activity" occurred so

---

[1] Wace (1949), pp. 84-86; Dietrich (1970), p. 21.
[2] Mylonas (1957), pp. 63-64; Snodgrass (1971), p. 397: cf. Tomlinson (1976). The question is whether the Mycenaeans five centuries later had any memory of an LH III B cult there.
[3] Cf. n. below.
[4] Snodgrass (1971), p. 398; cf. Velikovsky's discussion of Tiryns, and my section on Tiryns, below, first published as Isaacson (1974), pp. 11-12.
[5] Cf. »Later Use of the Grave Circles«, p. 194, n. 5, to which add B. Berquist: *The Archaic Greek Temenos* (Lund, 1967), pp. 15f.
[6] Snodgrass (1971), pp. 343, 398 and cf. p. 194.
[7] Two exceptions are the shrines at Knossos and Kea, which have their own 500-year gaps (»A Terracotta Figurine and a Terracotta Head«, p. 221, n. 4).

late, and why "it had suddenly become so pressing a need" to erect temples to the gods only after some 500 years had elapsed since the destruction and/or abandonment of the earlier structures immediately beneath them.[1]

At Mycenae itself, Archaic and Hellenistic levelling and building operations as well as severe erosion, and the less sophisticated excavation, recording and publication techniques of the early archaeologists, who first cleared the area, make it impossible to ascertain the exact relationship of the Archaic Temple to the LH III B palace beneath it.[2] At other sites, such as Tiryns, Delos, and Prosymna, however, many scholars once believed – and some still do – that the temples of ca. 700 BC followed immediately after the destruction of LH III B buildings beneath them, but because 500 years ought to intervene, most authorities now reject that notion.[3]

Mycenae's palace, like most other opulent habitations of LH III B Greece, had its interior walls covered with a smooth facing of stucco, which fresco painters decorated with brilliantly-colored designs and scenes. Although Egypt and Crete had had a tradition of mural paintings for centuries, the Mycenaeans, probably under Minoan influence, only began to adopt the art during the late Eighteenth Dynasty.

---

[1] Snodgrass (1977), p. 32 and cf. pp. 25-26.

[2] The early excavators found some fragmentary late seventh-century sculptured stone slabs, presumably belonging to an altar, in the main court of the palace, along with a few architectural members of the Archaic temple re-used in the construction of its Hellenistic successor. (Wace (1949), pp. 85-86; F. Harl-Schaller: »Die archaischen "Metopen" aus Mykene«, Jahreshefte des österreichischen archäologischen Instituts 50 [1972-3], pp. 94-116). Wace (loc. cit.) felt that the archaic temple underlay the later Hellenistic one (Fig. 1, M), and overlay a major cult center of the palace, preserving its orientation and function.

Unfortunately, so little remains of the first temple that its exact location and orientation remain unknown. For that reason, along with his skepticism that the palatial apartment served a religious purpose, and that people returning after 500 years of abandonment to a huge heap of rubble from a complex system of rooms, could ascertain the putative religious section, Mylonas (1957, pp. 63-64) doubted any religious or architectural continuity. It is extremely unfortunate that we have forever lost the exact geographical, stratigraphical and orientational information concerning the temple's relation to the palace (and of both to the altar); by analogy to Tiryns, it is at least possible that the temple overlay the throne room of the palace, re-utilizing the base of its walls, and thus aligned E-W, rather than N-S, facing the altar to the West, rather than to the South.

[3] For immediate replacement, cf. inter al.: Frickenhaus (1912), pp. 31-40 (Tiryns), 119-120 (Prosymna); K. Müller: Tiryns III (Augsburg, 1930), pp. 213-215; H. Gallet de Santerre: Délos primitive et archaïque (Paris, 1958), pp. 89-91, 216, 278 and Webster (1964), p. 139 (Delos). Against immediate replacement: cf., inter al., Mylonas (1966), pp. 48-52 (Tiryns); Snodgrass (1971), pp. 395-396, 439, n. 36 (Delos), and, in general, cf. »Later Use of the Grave Circles«, p. 194, n. 5

Despite their late start, Vermeule judged the LH III A-B frescoes of Greece to be "perhaps the best of all Mycenaean arts."[1] After the destruction of the mansions and palaces during the late LH III B-C period, it seems that the Greeks abandoned that art form, along with so many others;[2] once again, as in so many comparable cases, they seem to have revived the craft some 500 years later, when they painted frescoes on the walls of early seventh-century temples.[3] Further west, some authors have detected marked similarities between Minoan-Mycenaean frescoes and sculpture of the Late Bronze Age, and Etruscan funerary murals of the seventh-fifth centuries, again confronted by the now-familiar centuries-long gap between the two groups.[4]

Mycenae's palace, like many other contemporary structures, was a multistoried building, with its walls formed by vertical and horizontal timbers, between which the builders packed rocks in a matrix of clay. As we noted above, the workmen covered the interior walls with a smooth layer of plaster, which painters decorated with beautiful frescoes. The outer faces of the palaces external walls presented a more difficult problem, since their wood and rubble composition was both aesthetically unattractive, and also too vulnerable to the elements. To remedy that situation, the Mycenaean builders decided simultaneously to mask, beautify, protect and strengthen the exposed exterior. Thus they quarried fairly large boulders of *poros* limestone, which they sawed into rectangular blocks, laying them in even courses, known 0.3 ashlar masonry, to present a solid architectural façade.

Although the Egyptians and Minoans had long been masters of monumental architecture in general and ashlar construction in particular, the Mycenaeans were again relatively late to adopt those skills, with the palace marking one of their last and finest accomplishments. Their

---

[1] Vermeule (1972), pp. 184-187.

[2] Snodgrass (1967), pp. 35-36; idem (1971), p. 399.

[3] O. Broneer: *Isthmia* I (Princeton, 1971), p. 34; H. Robinson: »Excavations at Corinth: Temple Hill, 1968-1972,« *Hesperia* 45 (1976), pp. 228-229. It is possible, as some (e.g., Broneer: *ibid.*, p. 35, n. 52) suggest, that the ornamented terracotta temple models of the eighth century show that the Greeks had already begun to decorate the exterior walls of the temples; but it is just as likely that the potters merely painted those clay models as they did other ceramics, such as vases, a model of a subterranean tomb stone (?), tripods, model granaries, figurines, etc. (Snodgrass (1971), figs. 57, 70, 100, 116, 119) with no particular concern for a faithful rendering of the original (cf. Higgins (1967), p. 21).

[4] E.g., Evans (1935), IV, pp. 187-191; M. Pallottino: *Etruscan Painting* (tr. M. Stanley & S. Gilbert) (Geneva, 1952), pp. 43-44; S. von Cles-Reden: *The Buried people; A Study of the Etruscan World* (tr. C. Woodhouse) (N. Y., 1955), p. 143.

earliest stone architecture of note consisted of the huge beehive tombs, at first constructed of rubble. With time they began to adorn them with ashlar façades and to line their entrances, which they had cut through earthen embankments, with ashlar retaining walls. Finally they changed from sawn *poros* blocks to much harder conglomerate rock, which they hammered into blocks not only for the façades and entrance walls, but also for the construction of the tombs themselves. Similarly, they began to employ huge, rectangular blocks of hastier-dressed conglomerate, laid in even courses, to sheath some portions of their older fortification systems, and as the exterior for new, thick, rubble-core walls which they added to the earlier enceintes, such as the Lion Gate. It was only relatively late that the Mycenaeans began to erect large buildings of stone and to face them with ashlar masonry.[1]

Despite that late start, the relatively short period of use, and their rather restricted application of monumental construction techniques, the Mycenaean builders "reached a high state of development" and "proved their greatness."[2] In fact, whereas Vermeule felt the highest esteem for those who painted the frescoes on the interior walls of buildings like the palace, Desborough considered that "above all ... the architects and stonemasons arouse one's admiration."[3]

As was true in the case of the frescoes, the Greeks seem to have suddenly lost the skills to shape some blocks, to create ashlar walls, or to erect impressive constructions of any kind by the end of the Mycenaean period. "Such artist and craft were not to be seen again in Greece" during the obscure centuries following[4] the destructions of the Late Helladic palaces. During the Dark Age the Greeks seem to have made only small structures of unbaked mud brick, at most having a low foundation of unworked pebbles set in mud – in many ways reminiscent of the architecture 500 years earlier. With time they again began to erect a few stone walls, but those usually consisted of unworked rocks in a matrix of mud, at best having only their outer faces squared.[5]

Suddenly, ca. 700 BC, the Greeks of Corinth and Isthmia, both less than twenty miles northeast of Mycenae, again erected large struc-

---

[1] Wace (1949), pp. 136-138; Mylonas (1966), pp. 16, 20, 33, 48, 67, 73-79, 119, 187; Vermeule (1972), pp. 116, 123.
[2] Mylonas: *ibid.*, p. 187.
[3] Desborough (1972), p. 16.
[4] *Loc. cit.*; cf. Boardman (1964), p. 22; Snodgrass (1971), p. 369.
[5] Snodgrass: *ibid.*, pp. 369, 383-384; cf. Desborough: *ibid.*, pp. 261-262; Tomlinson (1976), p. 28.

tures made of *poros* limestone, sawed into rectangular blocks, and laid in even courses:[1] "a striking token of the recovery of lost skills" employed half a millennium earlier.[2] Since both buildings are so early in the series of Greek temples, and follow 500 years of very meager architecture, one might expect them to be pretty "primitive", but the excavators found both structures to be surprisingly sophisticated.[3] Since the construction of large-scale buildings of rectangular *poros* blocks laid in the ashlar technique seems to have ended 500 years earlier, and there seems to be no intermediate stage after the mud-brick and pebble walls, and before the erection of those two temples, it is difficult to show that they continued the Mycenaean tradition or evolved from the intervening, native Greek works. In the present overview of Greek architecture, those two temples "appeared suddenly", as a "revolutionary innovation" by an ingenous, yet anonymous, Corinthian inventor.[4]

R. M. Cook and H. Thompson, noting that abrupt, unprecedented revival of ashlar masonry, the extreme proximity of Corinth and Isthmia to Mycenae, and the fact that some of Mycenae's ashlar walls (e.g., at the Lion Gate) are still extant, have recently suggested that those walls at Mycenae might have inspired the seventh-century architects to return to the techniques employed, then lost, some 500 years earlier.[5] While that view has its attractions, there looms the question of whether untrained people merely gazing upon the outer faces of 500-year-old walls, constructed of rectangular stone blocks, could successfully quarry, trim, transport, lift and set new blocks in the old manner. The Mycenaean ashlar masonry only form a façade to older walls behind it, to solid rubble cores, or to earthen embankments.

---

[1] Broneer (1971), pp. 1, 12-33, 55; Robinson (1976), pp. 225, 227 and n. 76, 234.
[2] Snodgrass (1971), p. 413 (referring to a mid-ninth century wall in Smyrna in Asia Minor, but equally applicable to the early seventh century temples of the Peloponnese. The Smyrna wall was "a revelation in that it finds no [contemporary] counterpart on the Greek mainland." [p. 298]).
[3] Broneer (1971), p. 55; Robinson (1976), pp. 225, 234.
[4] Cook (1971), p. 192.
[5] *Ibid.*, p. 178; H. Thompson: »The Tomb of Clytemnestra Revisited«, n. 36 (a paper as yet unpublished, but soon to appear in *Expedition*. Prof. Thompson has very graciously supplied me with an advance copy of his article, to which I owe some references to the more recent literature. He justly observes that the ready access to an abundant supply of *poros*, which one can shape with relative ease, would facilitate the move to ashlar work (letter to me of March 29, 1979). While that was the case for the Greeks of the thirteenth century and the seventh, those of the intervening period seem not to have taken advantage of the situation, which, along with other considerations, which we shall presently note, calls for some explanation); cf. J. W Graham: »Mycenaean Architecture«, *Archaeology* 13 (1900), p. 54

They did not have to bear the full weight of a roof and did not have to be perfectly plumb, since their solid backing supported them. The Mycenaean blocks were not always perfectly rectangular, and did not need to make precise joins, since only the outer face was of concern; the unseen inner faces might be left partly unworked or else splayed apart, leaving gaps to be filled with wood, rubble and clay.[1] The seventh-century blocks did not form a façade, but comprised the entire wall, only one stone thick, were perfectly rectangular, and had to join one another precisely on all contiguous faces; the walls had to be perfectly plumb to prevent collapse, and had to support heavy roofs. By ca. 700 BC the Greeks must have had a sizeable labor force of expert quarrymen, stone cutters, architects, engineers and masons, which seems to have arisen without any previous trace.

For all those reasons, some doubt that the seventh-century Greeks, merely-looking at 500-year-old walls, decided to copy them and immediately succeeded with no evidence of the kind of experimentation through trial and error that one would naturally expect if the Greeks taught themselves anew – and even surpassed the architectural accomplishments of the predecessors whom they sought to emulate. Since the gap from 1200 to 700 BC is so huge, and one can trace no development in Greece itself leading to the achievements of the temple-builders, once again scholars postulate that some area outside of Greece kept the tradition alive for 500 years, and served both to reeducate the Greeks in the long-forgotten construction techniques of their ancestors (whom, it seems, they immediately surpassed), and to instruct them in the mathematics required to shape stone blocks of precise dimensions, with their right angles, and their parallel and perpendicular faces and to lay out and erect the structures.[2]

The Egyptians had a centuries-long tradition of monumental architecture formed by regular courses of hard stone, sawn into rectangular blocks. Therefore, as in the case of monumental stone sculpture, some art historians once more look to the valley of the Nile as the region "of paramount importance" to which Greek craftsmen travelled to see the great buildings, and also to relearn the techniques first-hand at the large-scale construction projects in that land.[3] The fact is, however,

---

[1] (1956), pp. 35-36, 43.
[2] Drerup (1969, p. 104) noted the "new" concern for measurement, proportion and symmetry among the eighth-century designers of rectilinear buildings (to which one must add their familiarity with the principles of solid geometry).
[3] Tomlinson (1976), pp. 32-33; Cook (1971), p. 178.

that the ashlar temples of Corinth and Isthmia of ca. 700 – 675 BC antedate the re-opening of Egypt to Greek craftsmen by several decades.¹ A third possibility is that the Greeks of ca. 700 BC hit upon the idea of building monumental ashlar structures independent of any foreign or domestic models which might inspire them; and, untutored in the requisite techniques, quickly taught themselves how to create the blocks and erect the temples so successfully – admittedly the least compelling of the hypotheses.² Again, one is left to wonder how the Corinthians of ca. 700 BC came to recover the skills so suddenly and so perfectly, which the workmen and architects of Mycenae had employed and lost 500 years earlier, and less than twenty miles away.

The Design of the Palace

Approached through a large, open court, a covered porch, and a vestibule, there lies the large central room of the palace complex, called the "megaron," in which the king of Mycenae held court and conducted the affairs of state. In the middle of its floor is a large circular hearth surrounded by four columns which supported the roof. Against the no-longer extant south wall the king probably had his

---

[1] The first Greeks to re-enter Egypt came from Asia rather than the Peloponnese, were mercenaries rather than students of art and architecture, and arrived no earlier than ca. 664 BC. Merchants from Greece proper followed sometime thereafter, and tourists and "students" later still – cf. Herodotus II. 152-154 and A. B. Lloyd: *Herodotus, Book II; Introduction* (Leiden, 1975), pp. 14-60.
The Greeks did travel to the western coasts of Asia Minor long before reaching Egypt, but the Asiatic walls, like those of Greece itself, generally consisted of wood rubble, and/or mud brick. Such walls occasionally had a sheathing of stone ortho-stats, with their external faces rectangular and generally sculptured (Frankfort (1963), pp. 145, 169 and fig. 81, 171 and fig. 83). Some Levantine structures had roughly rectangular blocks, but their walls were usually very thick and laid out in headers and stretchers. Often in complete contrast to Mycenaean and Archaic Greek architecture, their exposed faces retained unworked and rough bosses. There were some instances of thick walls with smoothed, sawn, rectangular blocks as a facing, again in headers and stretchers, but those were not the norm, and soon gave way to the more pervasive use of rubble (Kenyon (1971), pp. 61, 76-78, 91, 95-96, pls. 30-32, 41-45, 63-64). It is of special interest that in the Biblical account of Solomon's building projects, we read that he generally used vast quantities of wood, and large stones which were roughly shaped at the quarry, but did not dress their faces during construction; the Bible emphasizes that he only used sawn stones to form quarters for the Egyptian princess whom he wed (I Kings 6:7-18; 7:8-12). The Levant is thus a far less likely area than is Egypt, for the Greeks to have learned the use of perfectly rectangular, sawn blocks, laid in even courses to form walls only one block thick (cf. Cook (1971), p, 178).
[2] Tomlinson (1976), pp. 32-33.

throne.¹ As Vermeule has justly observed, most people pay little attention to, and retain scant recollection of architectural details,² yet the LH palace designers obviously drew much inspiration from one another. Thus of the three best preserved LH III palaces at Tiryns, Pylos and Mycenae, the thronerooms all bear distinct similarities to each other, with those at Pylos and Mycenae almost identical in dimensions and arrangements.³ Since all three are roughly contemporary, separated only by geography, one assumes that, like their counterparts of the classical period, the LH architects made the relatively short journeys to study older plans and/or to design new buildings.

A more difficult problem presents itself when we consider that the throne rooms of those thirteenth-century palaces also bear many strking resemblances to the decoration, construction techniques, and the arrangement of eighth-seventh century temples. Despite the intervening gap, numerous authorities have sought to establish a direct connection between the eighth-seventh century temples and the 500-year-older palaces.⁴ Since a structure, which many scholars consider to be a seventh-century temple, rests directly above, copies the alignment and utilizes some of the features of the megaron of the palace at Tiryns, and since a number of archaeologists have felt that the later building succeeded the throne room immediately after its destruction, some writers therefore conjectured that the palace survived intact during those intervening centuries, and provided the required model for later builders.

There are problems with that notion, however. Some authorities regard the later structure as a dwelling of the twelfth century, rather than a temple of the seventh,⁵ whose existence on the site is certain, but whose location would then be undetected. Even those who do identify the structure with the temple generally concede that it is highly unlikely that the palace stood intact during the intervening half millennium. If it did survive the end of the Mycenaean Age, it must have been unin-

---

[1] The southeastern portion of the room has long since collapsed down the steep scarp of the ravine. Some (e.g., H. Wace et al.: *Mycenae Guide* [Meriden, Conn., 1971], p. 40, pls. C.P.) feel that the throne was in a separate room to the west of the court, but Mylonas (1972, pp. 30-31) believes that to be a guest room; by analogy to the completely preserved LH III palaces, he reconstructs the throne room in the megaron.
[2] Vermeule (1972), p. 186.
[3] Mylonas (1966), p.63 and fig. 16; Graham (1900), p. 52 and fig. 12
[4] Cf. above »The Religious Center of Mycenae«, p. 225, n. 1.
[5] C. Blegen: *Korakou* (New York, 1921), pp. 132-133.

habited, since there is no evidence of any occupation of the entire upper city, upon which the palace stood, from the late thirteenth century until the late eighth; there is also strong circumstantial evidence that the palace itself perished ca. 1200 BC in the same wave of conflagrations which destroyed Mycenae, Pylos and other seats of Mycenaean power, and which razed the rest of the upper city of Tiryns itself.[1]

With the case for continuity at Tiryns "problematical",[2] some authors have speculated that LH palaces may have survived intact for centuries in some other part of the Mycenaean world, which escaped the fate of the Peloponnesian centers. They therefore look to Athens and the Ionian coast of Turkey, since neither area fell victim to Dorian immigrants, whom many authorities have blamed for the destruction of Mycenaean civilization; and both became centers of refuge for Mycenaean Greeks, including artists, craftsmen and royal families, who fled their afflicted homelands. In such areas, under such circumstances, one would reasonably expect the old way of life, with its characteristic art, architecture, customs and institutions (such as palaces), to continue without the interruption that characterizes the Peloponnese.

Greek tradition maintained that the colonization of Ionia was a result of the Dorian invasion, occurring in some cases immediately, or, at most, a couple of generations thereafter;[3] it further ascribed the foundations of the Ionian settlements to princes who were, no doubt, accustomed to dwelling in palaces. During the late Archaic Period Ionia was a thriving center of science, philosophy and literature, which played a large part in inaugurating the classical age of Greece. Furthermore, that region has the strongest claim for the honor of producing Homer, and presumbably for keeping alive the memory of Mycenaean civilization which he chronicled. Since his epics contain detailed descriptions of LH palaces, which have struck numerous scholars as extremely accurate in their intimate knowledge of Mycenaean architecture (a matter to which we shall presently turn),[4] and since fourth century Ionian architects constructed buildings reminiscent of LH III palaces, it seemed, for all these reasons, quite possible that such edi-

---

[1] Cf. above »The Entrance to the Citadel«, p. 173, n. 1 and »The Palace«, p. 248, n. 3, and below, section »Tiryns«, for a fuller discussion (first published as Isaacson [1974]).
[2] Snodgrass (1971), p. 398.
[3] Ibid., p. 302; cf. p. 256, n. 2 below.
[4] Cf. n. below.

fices survived in Ionia.[1]

The facts are, however, that there is very little archaeological evidence for Greek settlement of that region prior to the eighth century – a date in keeping with some literary accounts[2] – and Ionia seems to have been a cultural backwater prior to its seemingly sudden bloom during the seventh century.[3] It has produced no evidence of palaces or of large buildings of any kind during the Mycenaean period or the subsequent Dark Age – only small, dingy, single storey, single-room dwellings made of pebbles, mud-brick, poles and thatch, whose very attribution to Greeks, rather than native Anatolians, one can question.[4]

Discouraged by the picture from Ionia, but still inclined toward architectural continutiy, some scholars have more recently looked to Athens,[5] which also escaped the Dorian onslaught and immediately

---

[1] D. Gray: »Houses in the Odyssey«, *Classical Quarterly* N. S. 5 (195), pp. I, II; cf. G. Kirk: *The Songs of Homer* (Cambridge, 1962), pp. 111-112; Lorimer (1950), p. 430.

[2] C. Whitman (1958, pp. 49-51, 322-323, ns. 16-21) made that assessment over twenty years ago. J. M. Cook conceded that most early evidence seemed to indicate an eighth-century date, but stated that new discoveries pushed the event back into the tenth century BC (»Greek Archaeology in Western Asia Minor«, *Archaeological Reports for 1959-1960*, p. 40), an assessment oft-repeated by Cook (e.g., »Greek Settlement in the Eastern Aegean and Asia Minor«, *CAH3* 11,2 [1975], pp. 780, 785) and echoed by others (e.g., Snodgrass (1971), pp. 127, 329, 373; Desborough (1972, pp. 183-184).
The fact is, as Cook's brother realized (1972, p. 11) that the amount of tenth-century material is rather meager to represent the major colonization which tradition attests. Besides those early imports need not indicate a Greek settlement as opposed to being trade goods sent to the natives (cf. the far larger quantities of LH III A-3 pottery found in Cyprus and sixth-century Athenian ware found in Etruria). Most instructive in that regard are the instance of Protogeometric pottery found in native Anatolian graves (Desborough: *ibid.*: p. 184) and the situation at Smyrna, where Cook interpreted the vast quantity of "Grey Ware" ceramics as belonging to Greek settlers (*ibid.* [1975], pp. 780, 785), while Coldstream (1968, pp. 338-339) and Desborough (*ibid.*, pp. 183-154) more reasonably judge them to belong to the indigenous population.
Despite the more recent discoveries and literature, the situation is still closest to Whitman's assessment – viz., that there is no compelling evidence for actual Greek colonization prior to the eighth century. Therefore the statement by the seventh-century Ionian poet Mimnermus that "we" came from Neleid Pylos to Colophon, and then sacked Smyrna (ca. 688 BC) (quotation in Strabo XIV.l.4) and Thucydides' pairing (1.12.4) of the Ionian migration with the late eighth century colonization of Sicily and Italy take on a new interest. Although modern scholars (e.g., Webster (1964), p. 148; Snodgrass (1971), p. 8) regard both accounts as highly compressed, since they take no account of the half millennium which supposedly intervened, they follow the same trend as other classical references which we have noted and shall note, which seem to indicate a centuries-later assignment for many events currently dated according to Egyptian chronology.

[3] Whitman: *loc. cit.*; Notopoulos (1960), pp. 185-186, n. 27.

[4] J. M. Cook: *The Greeks in Ionia and the East* (New York, 1963), pp. 31-32; Snodgrass (1971), pp. 369-370, 413; Desborough (1972), pp. 183, 262. For the question of who the inhabitants then were, cf. n. 2 above.

[5] E.g., Hope Simpson-Lazenby (1970), p. 2.

received numerous Mycenaean refugees, including artisans and royal families. Unlike Ionia, Athens had been a sizeable center of Mycenaean civilization, and had an LH III palace on its own acropolis. Unlike the other LH city states of the Peloponnese, there is no evidence that Athens' palace, or any part of the city, caught fire or fell victim to barbarians. Also, unlike practically every other contemporary site, there is ample proof of the continuous occupation of the city throughout the Dark Age. There is a native tradition that kings (who permanently dwelled in a palace) governed the city long after the Dorians conquered the other Mycenaean centers, and apparently as late as the eighth or early seventh century.[1] Finally, we know that the Athenians, like the people of Mycenae and Tiryns, erected an archaic temple over the LH III palace – a circumstance which conforms to the Homeric references to one structure replacing its predecessor.[2] Here, at least, one would expect the retention of Mycenaean civilization, whatever befell Athens' less fortunate neighbors.

What constantly surprises and perplexes archaeologists is that Athens, the one place where one should find continuity of culture, is the very place which, without any obvious reason, changed most drastically, abandoning its Mycenaean characteristics more quickly and more completely than every other region. While the old ways lingered on in the severely struck Peloponnese, Athens suddenly and inexplicably adopted a material culture and customs which scarcely resemble their immediate predecessors in Athens or their contemporary counterparts elsewhere in Greece,[3] but which in art, architecture, dress, burial customs, standard of living, etc., seem more closely akin to antecedents now placed 500 years earlier. Vermeule once stated that "without being burned, Athens faded away exactly like more obviously destroyed sites; neither architecture nor art continued, only people."[4] More recently, M. Robertson likewise concluded that by the end of the Mycenaean Age "in Greece the greatest cities were all devastated; and even in places which, like Athens, escaped the destruction, there is no monumental building, and the tradition of the major arts – architec-

---

[1] C. Hignett: *A History of the Athenian Constitution* (Oxford, 1958), pp. 38-46.
[2] Cp. *Od.* VII. 50-81, where Athena enters the house (sc. palace) of Erechtheus to *Il.* II. 526-551 where Erechtheus was placed in her temple. Cf. Webster (1962), pp. 454-455 and idem (1964), pp. 107, 143.
[3] T. C. Skeat: *The Dorians in Archaeology* (London, 1939), pp. 62-63; Demargne (1964), p. 287; Snodgrass (1971), pp. 31-40, 123, 134-135, 133-153, 179, 313-316, 326-329; Desborough (1972), pp. 32-33, 64-67, 76-79, 81-82, 106-111, 269-271, 293.
[4] Vermeule (1960), p. 71.

ture, sculpture, painting – dies out. This seems to be absolutely true" throughout the Greek world.[1]

The tradition of a continuous kingship until the period of temple construction conflicts with an equally firm account that it died out towards the end of the Mycenaean Age, several centuries earlier – the two seemingly contradictory accounts, as we noted for Olympia, becoming unsatisfactorily conflated.[2] The case for continuous occupation of the palace until its replacement by the archaic temple is almost precisely like that for Tiryns. Although people have inhabited Athens without any major interruption for the past 5,000 years, residing on the acropolis itself throughout early prehistory, and establishing a sizeable settlement thereon during the Mycenaean Period; and despite the fact that the settlement was neither invaded nor destroyed, its residents apparently deserted the entire upper city at the end of the Bronze Age.[3]

That abandonment not only poses a difficulty for those wishing to extend the duration of the palace's use, but raises even greater questions. Since one can find traces of every other period of human activity on the Acropolis from the Neolithic Age until today; since, by its very nature, it was well fortified – the more so when, during the Mycenaean Period, the Athenians ringed the summit with massive stone wall which, in some areas, still stands today;[4] and since scholars generally

---

[1] Robertson (1975), p. 14; cf. Desborough (1972), p. 289.

[2] Hignett (1958), pp. 38-46. Two other Athenian traditions regarding the unification of Attica and Athens' participation in a religio-political league on the island of Calauria (Poros) have similarly split modern scholars into two opposing camps, championing either the Mycenaean Age or the ninth-seventh centuries (for useful, though by no means exhaustive summaries of each case, cf. respectively, R. A. Padgug: »Eleusis and the Union of Attica«, *GRBS*, 13 [1972], pp. 135-150, and T. Kelly: »The Calaurian Amphictiony«, *AJA*, 70 [1966], pp. 113-122, esp. pp. 116-117 for the "striking" lack of continuity between thirteenth and eighth century remains).

[3] Broneer (1939), pp. 427-428; Idem: »What Happened at Athens«, *AJA* 52 (1948), p. 114; Snodgrass (1971), pp. 31, 316, 363; S. Immerwahr: *The Athenian Agora XIII; The Neolithic and Bronze Ages* (Princeton, 1971), pp. 154-155; J. Travlos: *Pictorial Dictionary of Ancient Athens* (London, 1971), pp. 52-53; Desborough (1972), p. 64; Tomlinson (1976), pp. 78-80.

After the twelfth-century abandonment, the next evidence of architecture and cult activity on the acropolis belongs to the seventh century (Travlos and Tomlinson). The earliest post-Mycenaean pottery belongs to the ninth-eighth centuries (Coldstream (1968), pp. 13, n. 2, 55, 399); but it is of interest that those ceramic finds come from the fountain, where they were mixed with, and lay beneath, pure Mycenaean war (Broneer (1939)), and from the area of the Parthenon, where they lay in the same "well defined" deposit as Mycenaean ware (W. Dinsmoor: »The Date of the Older Parthenon«, *AJA* 38 (1934), pp. 416-417, 426).

[4] Scholars, who noted the similarity of that wall (The Pelargikon) to the earliest defences of Acrocorinth, sought to date them both to the Mycenaean Age. R. Carpenter (in Carpenter and A. Bon: *Corinth III.2; The Defences of Acrocorinth and the lower Town* [Cambridge, Mass.,

portray the Dark Age as a period of anxiety and fear, one must wonder why it was precisely then that the people abandoned their bastion and moved to a "relatively unprotected" low-lying area "where there had been no previous Mycenaean buildings." "Astonishingly", whereas the Athenians seem to have forsaken their former stronghold, they followed the same practice as the Dark Age folk at Tiryns and Mycenae, using their deserted settlement solely as a place to inter a few of their dead.[1] As was true of the graves inside Mycenae's citadel, one might consider it "extremely unlikely" that people, who did not live on the acropolis, would scale it only to use it for burials,[2] especially since they then had a cemetery nearer their homes and in much softer ground.[3] Again, one should note that they used the same type of cist tombs on the acropolis as those in the same general area, but supposedly dug 500 years earlier.[4] Because of all those considerations, scholars generally conclude that even though Athens was not invaded or destroyed, its palace still ceased to be occupied after the end of the Bronze Age.[5] Neither is there any evidence that a new palace or mansion replaced the old palace, nor, in fact, that the Athenians erected any large-scale structures after the twelfth century and before the late seventh.[6]

Even if Tiryns' palace miraculously escaped the blaze that incinerated the rest of its citadel, and that palace and/or the one at Athens stood intact, though abandoned, after the end of the Mycenaean period, and even if other palaces still remain to be found at a later date (perhaps in Ionia), their very style of construction with rather thin walls, comprised of tremendous amounts of wood, small stones and clay, would render them, in the words of one author, "an insurance

---

1936], pp. 30-34 and n. 1), who also saw the resemblance – but could not assign the latter fortification earlier than the seventh century, decided to downdate the Pelargikon accordingly. O. Broneer (1939), p, 423, n. 177 showed that the Athenian wall did belong to the Mycenaean Age, that now one must interpose an interval of ca. 600 years (during which time the Greeks built nothing comparable) between the two similar fortification systems – a situation which we shall encounter again regarding the Cyclopean bridge at Mycenae (ns. below).

[1] Desborough (1972), p. 64; Snodgrass (1971), pp. 202, 316.
[2] Cf. above p. 254, n. 5 and p. 255, n. 1.
[3] Desborough (1972), p. 64; Snodgrass (1971), pp. 145-151.
[4] For MH graves on the acropolis, cf. Travlos (1971), p. 57, fig. 67. For the similarity of the earliest post-Mycenaean graves to their pre-Mycenaean counterparts, cf. above »Dark Age Burials«, p. 230, n. 2.
[5] E.g. Immerwahr (1971), pp. 154-155. Because Athens looms so large in every discussion of post-Mycenaean Greece, it has seemed appropriate to mention some of its problems not directly related to Mycenae's palace; we shall return to it when considering other sites at the end of this treatise.
[6] Cf. above p. 257, n. 4 and p. 258, ns. 1, 3.

company's nightmare."[1] The frequent seismic shocks of the region, termites, rot, crumbling clay, inclement seasons or some subsequent fire, singly or in any combination, would probably have reduced them to heaps of debris long before five centuries would have transpired.[2] Since eighth-seventh century temples still had a ground plan and other artistic and architectural details similar to those of the throne-rooms of Mycenaean palaces, which a few of those temples definitely overlay at Tiryns (?), Mycenae and Athens, some scholars decided that there must be a direct relationship. They have suggested that if the later architects did not see the palaces while they still remained intact, then they probably returned to the sites where the palaces had stood five centuries earlier and, poking through the piles of debris (cement-hard in many cases), discerned the older arrangement and details, liked them, and decided to reproduce them.[3] The fact is, however, that the later Greek architects "revived" the LH III arrangement before they erected temples over the Mycenaean palaces – even before people seem to have returned to the sites of those palaces –, and constructed their first monumental temples at places that had no palaces.[4]

Some suggest that the type may have persisted during the intervening period in monumental, rectilinear buildings of stone, which have so far eluded discovery, but most scholars reject that notion, because the examples of Dark Age architecture, which we do know, are not similar to the structures of either the thirteenth century or the eighth, but rather look back to buildings 500 years earlier still.[5] As they do with other phenomena which seem to show 500-year "revivals," some authors have suggested that the type did survive, but only in wood, which has long since vanished.[6] Such hypothetical structures should nevertheless have left at least some trace, even if only of their contents (e.g., pottery), and their post holes and wall trenches, but none has come to light. Additionally, in a land like Greece where massive rock formations, field stones and clay are far more common than suitable trees, the Greeks have always preferred to use those substances – which do leave traces – to the scarcer commodity; but, even if they did erect perishable buildings, it was their practice to make at least

---

[1] L. Pomerance: *The Final Collapse of Santorini (Thera)* (Göteborg, 1971), p. 17.
[2] *Ibid.*, pp. 16-17; Blegen (1921), pp. 132-133; Mylonas (1966), p. 49.
[3] Mylonas: *ibid.*, pp. 51-52; H. Plommer: »Shadowy Megara«, *JHS* 97 (1977), p. 82.
[4] Snodgrass (1971), pp. 409-412, 422-424.
[5] Cf. above »The Religious Center of Mycenae«, p. 225, ns. 2-3.
[6] E.g., G. Rodenwaldt: »Zur Entstehung der Monumentalen Architektur in Griechenland«, *Ath. Mitt.*, 44 (1919), pp. 179-180.

the foundation of stone to support the wall, and to safeguard against rot and erosion. The lack of evidence of large-scale megaron-shaped structures to span the centuries between the thirteenth-century palaces and the eighth-century temples thus seems significant.[1] Faced with those difficulties, some authorities have expressed an opinion that, by the time the canonical megaron returned to Greek architecture in the eighth-century temples, their builders must have lost all recollection of the Mycenaean palace. Nevertheless, the similar arrangement troubled them.[2]

Since most authorities now consider it highly unlikely that an LH III palace survived intact to inspire eighth-century builders; since those builders reproduced the megaron plan before they returned even to the ruins of the earlier palaces; and since one can trace no tradition of similar structures to bridge the gap – yet the eighth-century temples still resemble LH III throne rooms – one is left with two options. The first is to view the similarities as superficial or insignificant or coincidental. Experts, however, seem unanimous in considering the correspondences very close in many details, so that, in whatever way they try to explain them, they find them difficult, if not impossible, to attribute to mere chance.[3] Finally, some who view all the other alternatives as unproveable, improbable or impossible, have proposed another explanation. As in the case of the built tombs of the Mycenaean Age and their nearly identical, but 500-year-later, counterparts of the ninth-seventh centuries (cf. *supra*), they have suggested that Greek temples simply evolved from similar origins as, and in the same manner as, Mycenaean palaces, following a parallel development, separated by a 500-year gap, which precludes a conscious revival or even a direct survival of form.[4] But even proponents of that notion admit that it is intrinsically "less satisfying" than the other theories which they reject.[5]

For some reason(s) not fully understood, not universally accepted and not especially satisfying even to their proponents, the eighty-seventh century inhabitant of Mycenae and most of the Greek world decided to erect temples over the heaps of rubble of bygone palaces and religious centers, returned to fresco painting, somehow regained the lost skills

---

[1] Cf. Tomlinson (1976), pp. 15, 20-22, 28, 32.
[2] Rodenwaldt (1919), pp. 179-180; idem: »Mykenische Studien I«, *JdI*, 34 (1919), p. 95 and n. 2; Dinsmoor (1950), p. 58.
[3] Cf. »The Religious Center of Mycenae«, p. 225, n. 1 and n. 1 above.
[4] Dinsmoor (1950), pp. 35, 57-58; Tomlinson (1976), p. 28.
[5] Tomlinson: *loc. cit.* Cf. pp. 20-22 that, though continuity seems unlikely after a gap of centuries, it still offers "an attractive hypothesis."

of stone cutting, engineering, solid geometry and ashlar masonry, and copied the architectural details of LH III thronerooms – all after a 500-year period during which their predecessors made no similar attempts.

Chapter 2

Further Evidence

Tiryns

Travelling only a short distance southeast of Mycenae we arrive at another Late Helladic center, Tiryns.

Legend connected the Bronze Age hero Herakles with the site, while its fortifications, constructed of tremendous stones, were attributed to the mythical giants, the one-eyed Cyclopes. Tiryns, under the leadership of Odysseus' friend Diomedes, sent a contingent of men and ships to help regain Helen from the Trojans.

Excavation of the site began in 1884, when Schliemann, the first to excavate at Mycenae, turned his attention to Tiryns. The German Archaeological Institute in a number of prolonged campaigns has laid bare much more of the site and continues the work even today.

Before reaching Tiryns' palace, one must first pass through two monumental gate structures (propylaea) (Fig. 6 below: 11 and 12), built in the Late Helladic period. They, along with the entire (?) citadel, were destroyed in a violent conflagration dated ca. 1200 BC. For centuries thereafter there is no evidence for monumental architecture in Greece, and monumental propylaea were not to re-appear until the archaic period. When propylaea do "return," however, at the Aphaia temple on the island of Aegina and on the Athenian acropolis, they are said to copy the plan of the Tiryns gates. Some scholars are quite struck by the re-emergence of a model extinct for 700 years.[1] How

---

[1] H. Schliemann: *Tiryns* (New York, 1885), pp. 194, 197; Tsountas and Manatt: *The Mycenaean Age*, pp. 45, 322; Schuchhardt: *Schliemann's Excavations*, p. 105; W. A. McDonald: *Progress into the Past* (New York, 1967), p. 45; Robertson: *Greek and Roman Architecture*, p. 29; Dinsmoor: *The Architecture of Ancient Greece*, p. 18; W. Voigtländer: *Tiryns* (Athens, 1972), p. 10. See E. R. Fiechter: »Die mit dem Tempel gleichzeitig oder später entstandenen Bauten« in A. Furtwängler et al.: *Aegina: Das Heiligtum der Aphaia* (Munich, 1906), pp. 67, 83 for the date of the Aegina propylon, and p. 84 for its close similarity to those at Tiryns; J. A. Bundgaard: *Mnesicles* (Copenhagen, 1957), p. 191, n. 39 for lack of propylaea between those of Tiryns and those of late archaic date. Beneath the Mnesiclean Propylaea of Athens, traces of an earlier Propylon have been found. This building is variously dated between 520 and 480 BC. (See J. S. Boersma: *Athenian Building Policy from 561/0 to 405/4 B.C.* (Groningen, 1970), pp. 19, 21, 109, n. 232, 202.)

could the later Greeks have discerned the plan of the Tiryns gates if they had been buried beneath rubble for those 700 years, in fact, until Schliemann's excavations?

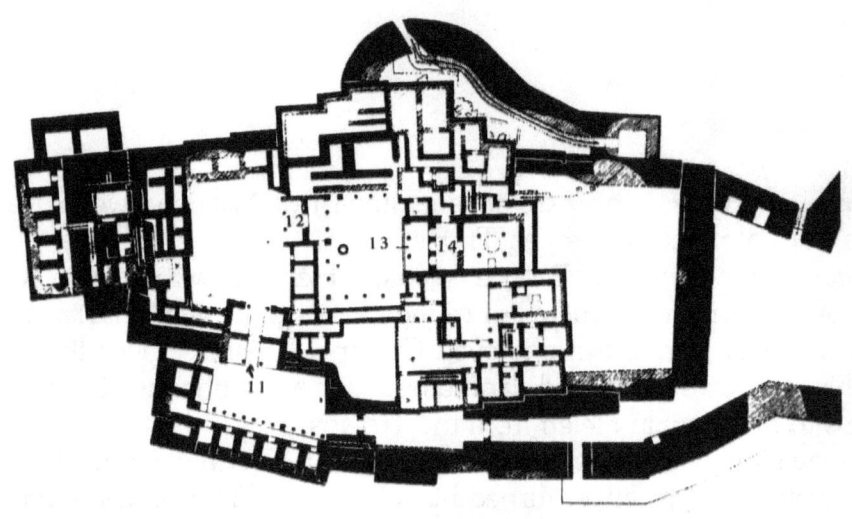

Fig. 6: Ground Plan of Tiryns.

After passing through the second propylon at Tiryns, then crossing a courtyard (Fig. 6 above: 13), one reaches the palace (Fig. 6 above: 14). "Along one side of the porch of the large megaron [the throne room and perhaps cult center of the palace] at Tiryns was found a curious series of seven interlocking blocks of alabaster ... inlaid with blue glass paste" forming "two elongated half-rosettes with inner patterns." The blocks' "resemblance to Doric triglyphs and metopes is very striking."[1] The bench formed by these blocks is "strikingly close to the triglyph and metope pattern of the later Doric order of architecture."[2]

One source sees the Doric triglyph altars as "a direct descendant" of this ritual stone bench at Tiryns,[3] while another author has the entire Doric order, including triglyph and metope friezes, "invented" "in about the middle of the seventh century" BC.[4]

---

[1] Robertson: *Greek and Roman Architecture*, p. 30.
[2] McDonald: *Progress into the Past*, p. 424.
[3] M. L. Bowen: »Some Observations on the Origin of Triglyphs«, *ABSA* 45 (1950); 124.
[4] R. M. Cook: »The Archetypal Doric Temple«, p. 17. See also p. 19 and Cook's earlier article: »A Note on the Origin of the Triglyphs«, *ABSA* 56 (1951); 52.

If the Doric altars are "a direct descendant," "how is it that we have no trace of the motif during the Dark Ages?"[1] Were such bench-altars made continuously between 1200 and 600 but only in perishable material, or did people return to Tiryns 500 – 600 years after it was destroyed, see, use, and then decide to copy the stone bench of the palace?[2]

If there is no direct descent, no copying of an extinct model, if the idea was invented afresh in the 7th century, how does one explain the "very striking" similarity of 7th-century altars to a 13th-century bench? On the other hand, how does one explain a decorative device with no functional nature or origin,[3] which, after its re-invention, "remained without variation for over four centuries" in altars and temple architecture? This fact, "it is argued, points to at least as long a period of development before its appearance in stone at the end of the seventh century."[4] Yet it is precisely the period before its appearance in stone, some 600 years, for which "there is at present no evidence to show that the Doric frieze was derived from this ancient scheme" as found at Tiryns.

"It is not impossible that the two forms have some real historical connexion."[5] While not impossible, if 600 years really separate the two forms, it is highly improbable. If 600 years did not transpire, as is the premise of the revised chronology, the similarity of the friezes is only natural and ceases to be "very striking."

It has been claimed that the Tiryns bench served as the model for triglyph altars. For the use of the triglyph and metope scheme on temples, a number of Bronze Age buildings and depictions of buildings with the triglyph and rosette frieze higher up are cited as prototypes.[6] Among these structures is the Treasury of Atreus at Mycenae. The position of the triglyph scheme above the columns (Fig. 7) is particularly notable, as this arrangement of Doric-like frieze surmounting

---

[1] M. L. Bowen: »Origin of Triglyphs«, p. 124.
[2] *Ibid.*, pp. 124-25.
[3] The Roman author Vitruvius (*De Architectura*, Book IV. 2-3) postulated that the stone frieze represented original wooden members. D. S. Robertson: *Greek and Roman Architecture*, p. 32, also believed in an early constructional origin. Both Bowen: »Origin of Triglyphs«, pp. 113-14, and Cook: »Origin of Triglyphs«, pp. 50-52, give good reasons for rejecting this notion.
[4] M. L. Bowen: »Origin of Triglyphs«, p. 113. Robertson: *Greek and Roman Architecture*, p. 32.
[5] *Ibid.* If the bench was used until the 8th century, both similarities to and differences with 7th-century friezes are easy to explain.
[6] Bowen: »Origin of Triglyphs«, pp. 121-22.

Doric-like columns is set centuries before the Doric order was "invented" in the 7th century. While this might remind one somewhat of a Doric temple façade, the chronological gap is hard to explain.

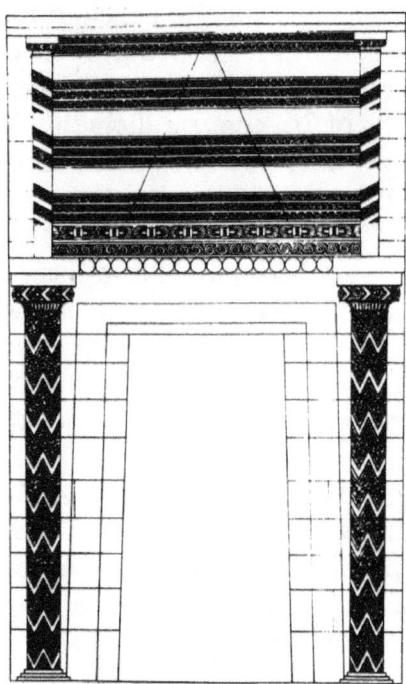

Fig. 7: Treasury of Atreus

We now come to a very thorny problem at Tiryns. The upper town was gutted by a fire dated ca. 1200 BC. Did the palace on the citadel miraculously escape the conflagration?

Many archaeologists have noted and been struck by the fact that the ground plan of a Mycenaean palace (especially the throne room or "megaron") is essentially the same as that for 8th-century and later temples. "How, for example, are we to explain the typical plan of the classical temple – with the two columns of the porch in line with the end walls and with the main shrine, or naos, and its central statue base – except as a carryover of the plan of the Mycenaean megaron?"[1]

---

[1] McDonald: *Progress into the Past*, pp. 423-24. See also Dinsmoor: *The Architecture of Ancient Greece*, p. 21; Bowen: »Origin of Triglyphs«, p. 123; Tsountas and Manatt: *The Mycenaean Age*. p. 322; B. Schweitzer: *Greek Geometric Art*, trans. by P. and C. Usborne (New York, 1971, published posthumously), pp. 223-24.

This could be explained very easily if there was continuity between the buildings of the 13th century and those of the 8th or 7th, but by the accepted scheme there is none. Immediately after the expiration of the Mycenaean period the "new" architecture displays an "essential discontinuity with Mycenaean architecture."[1] The change was quite abrupt.[2] Now, rather than monumental, rectilinear structures, we find oval-shaped huts and apsidal buildings (i.e., with one end rounded). The latter shape, however, is not new. Just as the 8th-century temple seems to be a 500-year throw-back to Mycenaean palaces, the "post-Mycenaean" apsidal house seems to be a 500-year throwback to Middle Helladic buildings.[3]

When the 8th-7th-century temples were built, the 13th-century palace plans must have been long forgotten,[4] unless some Mycenaean palace managed to survive intact until that time, or unless a ruined palace was cleared and its ground plan was then studied and copied. It is in the context of these two possibilities that Tiryns' palace becomes so important for those desiring to connect 13th-century palaces with 8th-7th-century temples.[5]

The palace of Tiryns has special significance for the Homericists as well. Now that Homer is assigned to the late 8th century while the destruction of the Mycenaean palaces is put in the late 13th, could

---

[1] A. M. Snodgrass: *The Dark Age of Greece*, p. 369. See also H. Drerup: *Griechische Baukunst in geometrischer Zeit* (*Archaeologia Homerica* II, 0, Göttingen: 1969), p. 77.

[2] Drerup: *Griechische Baukunst*, p. 77.

[3] *Ibid.*, p. 82; A. M. Snodgrass: *The Dark Age of Greece*, p. 369; Dinsmoor: *The Architecture of Ancient Greece*, p. 58; D. M. Robinson: »Haus« in Pauly-Wissowa's *Real-Encyclopädie*, Supplement 7 (1940), 235. (S. Sinos, however, in *Die vorklassischen Hausformen in der Ägäis* [Mainz, 1971], pp. 75-84, 87-90, 109-16 cites some examples of the co-existence of rectilinear, apsidal, and oval structures in the Middle, Late Bronze, and Dark Ages. He admits, p. 114, that there is no example of a megaron between Mycenaean times and the later temples.) A few apsidal houses do seem to have been built during the Late Helladic period but they were in vogue only during the Middle Helladic and "post-Mycenaean" times, were atypical in the Late Helladic period, and do not seem plentiful enough to span the time to connect the two peak periods. The most often-cited example is that at Thermon where the date is in dispute. As is so often the case, about 500 years are at stake. Elsewhere I will treat this case, and intend to show that essential discontinuity, and an abrupt change with a 500-year throw-back is not only true of "post-Mycenaean" architecture, but is also the case with the contemporary graves and the pottery.

[4] Dinsmoor: *The Architecture of Ancient Greece*, p. 58; G. Rodenwaldt: »Zur Entstehung der Monumentalen Architektur in Griechenland«, *Ath. Mitt.* 44 (1919), 179-180; G. Rodenwaldt: »Mykenische Studien I«, *Jahrbuch* (of the German Archaeological Institute) 34 (1919), 95 and n. 2.

[5] Robertson: *Greek and Roman Architecture*, p. 36; Schweitzer: *Greek Geometric* 224; G. Rodenwaldt: »Mykenische I«, p. 95, n. 2.

Homer have been influenced by Bronze Age palaces when he describes them in his *Odyssey*.

Since Homer is removed by 500 years from the palaces he described, "Mycenaean monuments ... will thus play no role" in any attempt to study the architecture that Homer actually knew.[1] So says one archaeologist.

Other archaeologists and Homericists disagree. They believe that Homer must have been familiar with at least one Mycenaean palace.[2] "No better succinct description could be given of the restored palace of Tiryns" than is found in Homer's *Odyssey*. "Buildings combining these characteristics [enumerated by Homer] are known in Greece at one period and one only, that known as Late Helladic III, and that is the period within which the action of the *Odyssey* is supposed to fall. Such a degree of coincidence can hardly be fortuitous, and it is now generally agreed that some connexion, however enigmatic, exists between the house of Odysseus and the Late Mycenaean palace."

"The extent to which the action of the *Odyssey* can be adapted to the stage of Tiryns must not, however, blind us to the extreme difficulty of accounting for the knowledge which the poet apparently possessed of architecture of the LH III type."[3] "How was the knowledge of the LH III type of palace preserved?"[4]

How can the palace at Tiryns help the Homeric archaeologists with their "extreme difficulty" of accounting for 13th-century details known so intimately by an 8th-century poet? How does it make the connection less "enigmatic"? How can it help the student of Greek architecture with his equally difficult problem of bridging the 500 years between Mycenaean Age palaces and 8th-century temples?

On the acropolis of Tiryns a large deposit of 8th-5th-century pottery and cult objects and 7th-century architectural fragments was unearthed.[5] It was thus reasonable to assume that an 8th or 7th-century temple existed on the citadel. A suitable spot, in fact the only possible spot, was chosen.

Above the megaron of the Mycenaean palace lay the walls of a some-

---

[1] H. Drerup: »Griechische Architektur zur Zeit Homers«, *Archäologischer Anzeiger* (1964), 180; "Mykenische Denkmäler werden also im Gegensatz zur Homerinterpretation keine Rolle spielen."
[2] H. L. Lorimer: *ibid.*, p. 407.
[3] *Ibid.*, pp. 408-10.
[4] For a brief list of finds see G. Karo: *Führer durch Tiryns*, 2nd ed. (Athens, 1934), pp. 47-49.
[5] A. Frickenhaus: »Die Hera von Tiryns«, *Tiryns* I (Athens, 1912), pp. 35f.

what smaller and less well-built structure, identified as the Greek temple. Since the temple seemed to have been built almost immediately after the palace perished in flames, and the builders were familiar with the palatial ground plan, it was decided that the palace miraculously escaped the conflagration of 1200 BC, and continued to stand until ca. 750 BC when it perished to a second fire on the citadel. Above its ruins the temple was then erected.

It was not only difficult for the excavators to imagine that the palace stood nearly half a millennium without alteration, but astonishing ("erstaunlich") to think that the Mycenaean elements of the palace (architectural, artistic, and stratigraphical) remained unchanged and visible to people 500 years later. Nevertheless, they felt compelled to accept this view, since the temple obviously followed immediately after the fire that razed the palace.[1]

If the palace of Tiryns stood 500 years longer than the other Bronze Age palaces, if it survived the fire of 1200 BC on the citadel and remained visible to 8th-century Greeks, then the architectural and Homeric problems are solved. The 8th-century temple builders and Homer were familiar with a 13th-century palace.

The conclusions of the excavators were challenged by Carl Blegen. He agreed that immediately after the palace burned down, the smaller structure was built by men intimately familiar with the palace when it stood;[2] but there was only one fire, ca. 1200, and it destroyed the palace with the rest of the citadel. Thus, to him, the smaller megaron-structure represents the remains of a 12th-century building, not a 7th-century temple. In support of his contention was the vast quantity of Mycenaean pottery around the site. He too found it difficult and astonishing to believe that the palace survived intact an extra 500 years, so he rejected the notion. Others also reject it as impossible, since the wooden beams within the walls would have rotted away long before.[3]

---

[1] C. Blegen: »The So-called Temple of Hera at Tiryns«, an appendix to *Korakou* (New York, 1921), p. 132.

[2] Ibid., 132-33; G. Mylonas: *Mycenae and the Mycenaean Age*, p. 49

[3] Bowen: »Origin of Triglyphs«, pp. 122-23. He incorrectly dates the Korakou example to Middle Helladic times (see Blegen: *Korakou*, pp. 80-83, 133). The only other Bronze Age examples he gives are a house from the VIth level at Troy, the archaeology of which we will soon examine, and the structure at Tiryns. (To this one should add an LH III example from Attica. See G. Mylonas: *Aghios Kosmas* [Princeton, 1959], »House T«, p. 55 and fig. 15.) Bowen rightly suspects the 9th-century date assigned to the Artemis Orthia temple at Sparta (see Snodgrass: *The Dark Age of Greece*, p. 277); more recently see H. Drerup: *Griechische Baukunst*, p. 89.

While this interpretation explains away many 500-year difficulties, it leaves the problem of the 8th-7th-century votive deposits and 7th-century architectural fragments. If this building, which followed immediately after the fire that destroyed the palace, belonged to the 12th century, where was the 7th-century temple?

If the palace did not stand an extra 500 years, how can it help with the problem of the 8th-century temples copying Mycenaean palaces and with Homer's knowledge?

A third solution is to have the palace destroyed in the great fire of 1200 BC, have the site abandoned, then rediscovered and cleared in the 8th or 7th century. Those clearing the debris would see the ground plan of the destroyed palace, thus pleasing the Homericists and architecture students. A temple could then be erected on that spot after a lapse of ca. 500 years. While this view eliminates many problems and explains much of the evidence, it neglects one very important item. Both of the other schools of thought regarded it as a fact that the smaller structure was built immediately after the palace burned – 500 years did not elapse between the destruction of the palace and the construction of its successor.

But these are stratigraphical problems. Perhaps the architectural form of the later structure will settle the dispute over its date – 12th century or 7th. Here again we find a difficulty. Its ground plan, a rectangular building with a single row of interior columns, can be found in a few structures of the 14th-12th centuries or in a long list of 8th-6th-century buildings. No intermediate examples seem to exist to connect these two groups.[1] To which group should we assign it?

What should one do? For the sake of helping the Homericists and students of architecture, does one presume that the palace stood intact an extra 500 years? Does one date the later structure to the 12th century, overlook the 8th-5th-century finds and see no temple here at all, thus destroying the one hope of the Homericists and architectural historians? As a compromise, does one have a 500-year-later rebuilding on an ancient site, partially pleasing, but partially displeasing both groups? This question has plagued Aegean scholars for over 50 years, has never been satisfactorily answered, and as long as 500 "ghost

---

[1] Drerup: *Griechische Baukunst*, p. 89.

years" exist, it will remain "problematical"[1] and defy explanation.[2]

Even the objects from the temple cult, while of certain date, are "problematical". Among these were terracotta figurines and grotesque masks of the 7th century BC. Like so many other 7th-century votive terracottas, they were produced on the wheel "in the old technique" the Mycenaeans had used 500 years earlier.[3] Such votives "kept reappearing spontaneously in widely separated parts of the country without any direct continuity that can be traced among the votive statuettes themselves. Something much more than an archaeological zeal on the part of the faithful needs to be invoked to explain this!" If we reject continuity, reject imitation of extinct models, and also reject the hypothesis that the type was preserved for centuries only in perishables now lost to us,[4] what is left for us?

At Tiryns we have run into 500-700-year problems with triglyphs, with propylaea, with Homer and 8th-century temple plans, with the architecture and archaeology of the palace, and with the temple votives.

The fire that destroyed the acropolis of Tiryns is of approximately the same date as the great fire that destroyed much of Mycenae, including its palace. If we accept the hypothesis that Tiryns' palace was destroyed then, not 500 years later (i.e., that the palaces of Mycenae and Tiryns burned down at about the same time), what was that time?

---

[1] Snodgrass: *The Dark Age of Greece*, p. 398.

[2] Since Velikovsky has released his chapter on Tiryns (*Pensée* [Winter, 1973-74], pp. 45-46), I have left out much detail in order not to repeat his points. In addition to Velikovsky's article, the reader is referred to H. Drerup: *Griechische Baukunst*, pp. 17-18, 89 for a succinct statement of the case and the opposing views. Drerup himself pointedly abstained from giving his own opinion. His bibliography is quite extensive, but by no means exhaustive.

A similar situation exists with two Mycenaean edifices on the island of Delos. The excavator claims that both of these – one, a sanctuary – stood until ca. 700 BC, and that the sanctuary was then converted into a Greek temple. Snodgrass (*The Dark Age of Greece*, pp. 395-96) and others (*ibid.*, p. 439, n. 36) reject this 400-year-long continuity.

[3] R. V. Nicholls: »Greek Votive Statuettes«, p. 17.

[4] *Ibid.*, p. 21. Nicholls seeks perishable (i.e., wooden) models to fill the gap here, as did Bowen for similarities of Doric triglyphs to Mycenaean friezes, as did some for connecting Linear B and the Phoenician alphabet. Likewise it had been proposed, and rightly rejected, that the connection between Mycenaean palatial architecture and 8th-century temples was to be found in monumental megaron-shaped wooden temples (G. Rodenwaldt: »Zur Entstehung«, p. 179f.). Why the Greeks should have used perishables exclusively during the Dark Age to connect similar non-perishable items separated by 500 years, when we know that they still fired clay, made metal objects, and used stone during that period is not adequately explained. Since they continued to make pottery on the wheel, they could quite easily fashion figurines in that way, rather than carving them from wood. The lack of wheel-made terracotta votives to span those 500 years requires another explanation.

We have seen arguments for making it the 8th or 7th century BC. We have also seen problems that crop up if we refuse to bring down the date that far.

Now let us travel across the Aegean Sea, and, like the "13th-century" kings of Mycenae, Pylos, and Tiryns, we will arrive at Troy.

Troy

The Trojan War was probably the single most significant event of the Mycenaean Age. The tale, immortalized in Homer's epics, is familiar to us moderns even millennia later. For the sake of the beautiful Helen, and to avenge her husband's indignation at her kidnapping, the Late Bronze Age Greeks mounted a massive campaign. Approximately 1200 troop-carrying vessels[1] were launched, and a war raged around the besieged city of Troy for 10 years, until the strategem of the wooden horse gave the Greeks access to the citadel. Once inside the city, they utterly destroyed it, slaughtering many inhabitants and enslaving all survivors who did not flee. This, at least, is the mythical account. When was that war fought?

The canonical Greek calculation was 1193/2 – 1184/3 BC. This number was arrived at by the 3rd-century BC chronographer, Eratosthenes of Alexandria, who apparently relied on the calculations of Ctesias and on Manetho's Egyptian king-lists. Ctesias, a late 5th-century author, is today viewed as "an amusing liar"[2] and "an ancient red herring".[3] Manetho's lists are the basis for modern calculations for Egyptian chronology. They are convincingly challenged by Velikovsky.[4]

---

[1] The number of ships is commonly (but incorrectly) said to be 1,000. Thucydides (1.10.4) speaks of 1200, while the sum preserved in the *Iliad* (II. 494-750) is 1186.

[2] J. Forsdyke: *Greece Before Homer* (London, 1956), p. 68.

[3] A. R. Burn: *Persia and the Greeks* (London, 1962), p. II; see pp. 11-13.

[4] I. Velikovsky: »Astronomy and Chronology«, *Pensée* (Spring-Summer, 1973), 38-49 {reprinted as Supplement in *Peoples of the Sea* (NY, 1977)}. Other ancients also dated the war early. We have already seen that the most ancient source, Herodotus, also got his date from the Egyptians, who were obviously lying to him (see »Shaft Grave Art: Modern Problems«, p. 186, n. 2). Other estimates ranged from the 14th – 12th centuries BC (see Forsdyke: *Greece Before Homer*, p. 62 and G. Mylonas: »Priam's Troy and the Date of its Fall«, *Hesperia* 33 [1964]; p. 353, n. 3). These dates are challenged as too early even by adherents to the accepted chronology. I hope to treat this topic in detail at a later date.

The archaeologists also have a date for that war, ranging sometime between ca. 1260 and 1200 BC.[1] This date is assigned to a conflagration layer (stratum VIIa) at the site of Hissarlik in Northwestern Turkey, which, in the excavator's opinion, marks the Greek destruction of Troy. The date depends on the time of the Mycenaean pottery found in this layer. That in turn is based solely on Egyptian chronology.[2] Thus, if the Egyptian scheme is off, both the Greek calculations and the archaeological date must be changed.

It is a simple task to show that the Greek calculations are of no worth and that the Greeks themselves made the Trojan War contemporaneous with many events that we now know to be of the 8th century BC. Elsewhere I will show this in some detail. Only the archaeological problems will here concern us.

It is conceded that no artistic representations of any event connected with the Trojan War appear before the 8th century BC.[3] We have already seen that cults to the Greek leaders of that war do not seem to have sprung up until then. Homer is invoked to explain both these and many other phenomena, but Homer was almost universally regarded by the ancients as composing his epics very shortly after Troy's fall.[4] In our attempt to resolve this dilemma, we shall examine the archaeological findings from Hissarlik to see why they were assigned an early date, and whether the stratigraphy and other archaeological consid-

---

[1] C. W. Blegen, the latest excavator of the site, pushed the date progressively back (see »New Evidence for Dating the Settlements at Troy«, *ABSA* 37, [1936-1937], 12 for 1200 BC; *Troy* IV. I [Princeton, 1958], p. 9 for pre-1230 BC; »Troy«, *Cambridge Ancient History* [henceforth *CAH*], fascicle 1 [1961], p. 14 for 1250 BC; *Troy and the Trojans* [London, 1964], p. 174 for 1260 BC). Other archaeologists lean more toward Blegen's original assessment of ca. 1200 BC (See Blegen: *CAH* fascicle, p. 14, n. 1; C. Nylander: »The Fall of Troy«, *Antiquity* 37 (1963), 7, 10, II; G. Mylonas: »Priam's Troy«, pp. 362-66). The problems are complex: how much earlier than the destruction of Pylos the destruction of Troy should be; whether certain potsherds from Troy VIIa are very late LH III B or very early LH III C; the time of the transition from LH III B to LH III C. These need not detain us here. For our purposes, the archaeological date falls sometime within the 13th century BC.

[2] Blegen: *Troy and the Trojans* (henceforth *T & T*) pp. 159-61, 174.

[3] K. Friis Johansen (*The Iliad in Early Greek Art* [Copenhagen, 1967, p. 36]) sets the influence of the *Iliad* on art at ca. 700. J. N. Coldstream (*Greek Geometric Pottery* [London, 1968], p. 351) has one scene appear early in the 8th century, but Johansen, pp. 23-25, does not think that the *Iliad* itself is responsible for that scene. The subject, Siamese twins, need not be connected with Nestor's account in Book XI of the *Iliad*, or even be connected with Nestor. In any case, no example exists before the 8th century. Of course, the lack of figural representation during the Dark Age could account for this, and this is not prima facie evidence that the war was fought this late.

[4] See »Shaft Grave Art: Modern Problems«, p. 186, n. 2.

erations support a 13th-century date for the great war. The Homeric problem and mythical matters relating to the war will await discussion until another time.

Just as at Mycenae and Tiryns, the first large-scale excavation of the site was undertaken by Heinrich Schliemann in the 1870s – 1890. His collaborator, Wilhelm Dörpfeld, continued the work after Schliemann's death in 1890. From 1932 – 1938, yearly excavation of the site was undertaken by an expedition from the University of Cincinnati. Their findings, published in final form in the 1950s, provide the principal scientific data about the site.

Nine major habitation levels, ranging from the Early Bronze Age (stratum 1) to Roman times (stratum IX) were distinguished, of which only levels VI – VIII will concern us.

As was pointed out in my earlier paper, the 8th-century Phrygians, who, according to Homer, were allies of Troy during its siege, copied the architectural style of the fortifications of Troy VI when they built their great gate at Gordion. Since the end of Troy VI is put at ca. 1300 BC, its walls must have been buried by 500 years of debris, making them invisible in the 8th century. The excavator of Gordion, faced with this 500-year problem and no intermediate examples, still saw close similarities and was hard pressed to explain them.[1] A house of Troy VI, destroyed in the great earthquake that leveled the site, assigned to ca. 1300 BC, is of the same type as buildings beginning in the 8th century BC after a supposed break of centuries during which no similar houses are known.[2] The end of the sixth layer of Troy is dated by the presence of Mycenaean pottery, which, in turn, receives its place in time from Egyptian chronology.

Between the 7th and 8th strata of Hissarlik, it is said that 400 years transpired, during which the site was "a ghost-town in the gloom of the Dark Ages of the ancient world." "There is nothing at Troy to fill this huge lacuna. For 2000 years men had left traces of their living there; some chapters in the story were brief and obscure, but there was never yet a chapter left wholly blank. Now at last there is silence, profound and prolonged for 400 years; we are asked, surely not in vain, to believe that Troy lay 'virtually unoccupied' for this long period of time."[3]

---

[1] Isaacson: »Carbon 14 Dates«,"p. 28, see n. 33, p. 32 for references.
[2] See »Later Use of the Grave Circles«, p. 192, n. 3.
[3] D. Page: »The Historical Sack of Troy«, Antiquity 33 (1959), 31.

Why are we asked to believe this? The eighth settlement began ca. 700 BC. The seventh, however, contained Mycenaean pottery, which, of necessity, should be centuries earlier. At a tell such as Hissarlik one would expect a layer of wash and/or humus to mark this 400-year abandonment.[1] There is none.

Recalling the legend of Troy, we would hardly object to an abandonment after the Greek sack of that city; it would be only natural, and is, in fact, attested in ancient sources.[2] But the settlement said to mark the Trojan War is VIIa, and we are here dealing with the second sub-stratum above this, VIIb2.[3]

Why should people who tenaciously remained on the site for 2000 years, despite fires, earthquakes and all-out war, abandon the town now? Was there another sack of the city, this time more devastating than the earlier destruction by the Greeks, yet, unlike its predecessor, lost forever to human memory?[4]

Let us examine this 400-year gap in some detail. Was the end of settlement VIIb2 marked by a destruction layer so intense that abandonment could be rationalized? Reading the official publication of the most recent excavation, we find that it was not known what caused the end of stratum VIIb2.[5]

If there is no sterile layer marking the desertion and no obvious cause for such action, we are certainly justified in asking if the site really was

---

[1] Since most of the material from Troy VIII was found on the lower slopes of the mound, one would expect the erosion of the upper mound to deposit a layer of the dissolved remains of the mud brick houses, etc., from higher up the slope. Such a layer should be found above the last deposits of Troy VII and below the first of Troy VIII. For just such an instance from another mound and a good explanation of the process see K. M. Kenyon: *Digging up Jericho* (London, 1957), pp. 44-45, 171, 259-60, 261; and M. Wheeler: *Walls of Jericho* (London, 1958), pp. 43, 55, 124.

[2] Those authors (Lykurgus: *In Leocrantem*, 62; and Strabo, XIII.1, 41-42) make it quite clear that the abandonment lasted at least till the Roman period. Strabo considered Hissarlik not to be the Troy of Homer (XIII.1. 25, 35, 37, 38). For these and other literary, archaeological, stratigraphical, geographical, and topographical reasons, this writer is unconvinced that Hissarlik is the site of the Homeric Troy. He is further unconvinced that the burning of layer VIIa was the work of the Greeks, or, in fact, of invaders. J. L. Caskey, a participant in the Cincinnati expedition, who does believe that Hissarlik is the site of Troy, states some of this writer's reservations very well (»Archaeology and the Trojan War«, *Journal of Hellenic Studies* 84 [1964], 9). Since it is generally accepted that the Trojan War was fought at Hissarlik, its archaeology is important.

[3] There is, in fact, no sign of abandonment or marked population loss or change after the conflagration of level VIIa. On the contrary, the original inhabitants quickly rebuilt the town (Blegen: *T & T*, pp. 165f)

[4] Blegen (*T & T*, p. 172) suggests this.

[5] C. W. Blegen, et al.: *Troy IV. I* (Princeton, 1968), p. 147.

abandoned. If level VIII immediately overlay level VII, why could it not have begun immediately after the end of VII? The answer is that Troy VIII began in the early 7th century BC while Troy VI and VII contained Mycenaean pottery. Between VII and VIII "some four centuries *must* have elapsed."[1]

If, by redating Egyptian chronology, we reduce the age of Mycenaean pottery by centuries, could Troy VIII have followed immediately after Troy VII without any gap?

Surprisingly, perhaps, for those accepting the old chronology, such a revision fits the circumstances of the two layers. In 1893 Dörpfeld, the great German excavator of Troy, more interested in stratigraphy and architecture than in pottery, treated Troy VII and VIII as a single unit, and, in some cases, could not differentiate between the two phases.[2] With the results of over 20 years of excavations before him and an additional 8 years to reflect on matters, he still had Troy VIII follow immediately after Troy VII, and, at times, noted the presence in Troy VII of the 7th-century pottery characteristic of Troy VIII.[3]

Dörpfeld assigned the task of analyzing the pottery from all levels of the site to Hubert Schmidt. Schmidt noted obvious Greek wares in level VIII, marking a Greek colonization, while the material from layer VII seemed to represent a different culture. He nevertheless placed VIII immediately after VII. Noting Mycenaean imports in Troy VII, he still put this layer at ca. 1000-700 BC, rather than 500 years earlier.[4]

These were early excavators and could be forgiven for their opinions as they did not know any better. Egyptian chronology had not yet established firm absolute dates for Mycenaean pottery.[5] What did the modern excavators find?

After completing seven seasons of excavation at Troy, Carl Blegen, the chief archaeologist of the Cincinnati expedition of the 1930s, saw no break between layers VII and VIII.[6] After several more years had

---

[1] *Ibid.*, emphasis added
[2] W. Dörpfeld: *Troja 1893, Bericht über die im Jahre 1893 in Troja veranstalteten Ausgrabungen* (Leipzig, 1894), p. 64.
[3] W. Dörpfeld: *Troja und Ilion* (Athens, 1902), pp. 31, 201.
[4] H. Schmidt: »Die Keramik der verschiedenen Schichten« in Dörpfeld: *Troja und Ilion*, pp. 296-98.
[5] Blegen: *Troy IV.1*, p. 4.
[6] Blegen: »New Evidence«, p. 12. Although he set the division at 900, rather than Dörpfeld's 700 BC, he still had one layer follow immediately after the other. The journal for 1936 – 1937 was not released until 1940, two years after excavations at Troy had ceased. From the article (p. 10) it is clear that Blegen wrote after the end of his last season, and, whenever

elapsed, allowing additional time to reflect on the dig, to study the pottery more carefully, and especially after Mycenaean pottery dates became more firmly entrenched,[1] it was realized that a gap of centuries should exist between the two layers. Nevertheless, even in their official publication, the excavators were so impressed by certain facts relating to the mound itself that they left open the possibility that there was no gap.[2] By the accepted chronology there had to be a lacuna, as they acknowledged, but they hesitated on this point. Their reasons are interesting.

The new excavations showed that the locally-made pottery of Troy VIII was "obviously akin" to that of Troy VII.[3] The local grey ware pots of Troy VII (i.e., of the Mycenaean Age) were looked upon as the "direct ancestors" of the local ware not only of Troy VIII but also of 7th-6th-century Northwestern Turkey and the off-shore island of Lesbos as well.[4] With a 400-year gap in the evidence, how can one connect this widespread 7th-6th-century ware with that of the Mycenaean Age?

At the very time that there was supposed to be a 400-year abandonment of Hissarlik, one house seemed to show continuity between the end of layer VII and the time of VIII, as if no one had left and only a few years had passed.[5]

In several deposits of Troy VIII there were sherds from Troy VII.[6] There was finally, however, a more serious problem. Although the excavators were meticulous in their method of digging stratified layers and labelling and recording all finds and their provenience,[7] in sub-strata of Troy VII that seemed to be undisturbed, sherds were found of the imported Greek pottery of the early 7th century.[8] "The only explanation we can find is to suppose that, in spite of our efforts to isolate and certify the deposits we examined, contamination had somehow been

---

the article was submitted between 1938 and 1940, there is no evidence that he changed his mind before publication of the volume (there is no postscript, or corrigendum attached).

[1] A. Furumark's monumental work of dating Mycenaean pottery by Egyptian associations came out shortly after the Troy excavations had ended.
[2] Blegen et al.: *Troy I.1* (Princeton, 1950), p. 23; Blegen: *Troy IV.1*, p. 250.
[3] Blegen: *Troy IV. 1*, p. 251. Also see pp. 147, 252-53, 257.
[4] W. Lamb: »Grey Wares from Lesbos«, *Journal of Hellenic Studies* 52 (1932), 1-2. See Blegen: *Troy IV.1*, p. 253.
[5] Blegen: *Troy IV.1*, p. 250, 291-93.
[6] *Ibid.*, pp. 253, 265.
[7] Blegen: *Troy I.1*, pp. 20-21.
[8] Blegen: *Troy IV.1*, pp. 158, 181.

effected and brought about the intrusion of the later wares into strata of Troy VIIb."[1] The discovery of these 7th-century sherds "in several areas in the strata of Troy VIIb1" stratified below layer VIIb2, which is supposed to represent the 12th century, "presents a perplexing and still unexplained problem."[2]

After all the digging by Schliemann, Dörpfeld, and Blegen at Hissarlik, only one sherd has turned up which could conceivably fall within the 400-year gap postulated for the site. Stratigraphically, however, it was not found where it should have been. A rim fragment from a "Protogeometric" cup was found "with sherds of Phase VIIb1, but probably out of context." The reason it was probably out of context is that it was covered over by "two successive buildings of Phase VIIb2"[3] which of necessity belong to the 12th century BC. The sherd beneath those two buildings is seen as part of a body of material found from Palestine to Macedonia[4] which, beginning perhaps ca. 900 BC, was in vogue until the 8th or 7th century BC.[5] It is stratigraphically impossible to have a 7th, 8th, or even 9th-century BC item below the floor of a 12th-century BC building, unless contamination occurred. "There was apparently no contamination from disturbance or later intrusions," however.[6]

---

[1] *Ibid.*, p. 181.
[2] *Ibid.*, p. 158. Blegen, as we saw in my previous article (*Pensée* [Spring-Summer, 1973], p. 27) was faced with the same problem of 7th-century sherds in bona fide Mycenaean strata at Pylos and was again at pains to account for this state of affairs.
[3] *Ibid.*, p. 233.
[4] *Ibid.* Blegen compares it to V. R. Desborough's low-footed skyphoi with pendent semicircles. See Desborough (*Protogeometric Pottery* [henceforth *POP*] (Oxford, [1952], p. 192).
[5] For scholarly opinions on the Euboean and/or Cycladic manufacture and the range of dates for this type of cup, see Desborough: *POP*, pp. 192-94; Desborough: »A Group of Vases from Amathus«, *Journal of Hellenic Studies* 77 (1957), 218; Desborough: »The Low-Footed Skyphoi with Pendent Semicircles«, *Archäologischer Anzeiger* (1963), cols. 204-205; Desborough: *The Greek Dark Ages* (London, 1972), pp. 186, 197 and see 199; O. T. P. K. Dickinson in Popham and Sackett's *Excavations at Lefkandi*, etc., p. 28; J. N. Coldstream: *Greek Geometric Pottery*, p. 330; A. M. Snodgrass: *The Dark Age of Greece*, pp. 71, 98, n. 4, 335 and index p. 448; H. W. Catling: »A Pendent Semicircle Skyphos from Cyprus and a Cypriote Imitation«, *Reports of the Department of Antiquities of Cyprus*, 1973 (Nicosia, 1973), 184-85.
Most exports of this ware to the East Mediterranean (presumably including the example from Troy) are thought to belong to the early 8th century (Desborough: *PGP*, pp. 192-94; Snodgrass: *The Dark Age of Greece*, p. 335) but possibly continued into the 7th century (Snodgrass: *The Dark Age of Greece*, p. 98, n. 4). To my knowledge, no one has treated the example from Troy to determine its date within the 9th-7th-century range, but wherever it falls, its find spot still poses a serious stratigraphical problem for the standard chronology.
[6] Blegen: *Troy IV.1*, p. 231. If Troy VIIb2 really ended ca. 1100 BC, this sherd of the 9th, 8th, or 7th century ought to lie above this layer. Instead, it was found stratified ca. 1/2 m

In time these "perplexing and still unexplained" problems were brushed aside, and reservations about a 400-year gap were abandoned, because, by the accepted chronology, that gap had to exist. All the work of the excavators, their failure to detect any physical sign of abandonment, their belief that Troy VII ended immediately before Troy VIII began (i.e., sometime around 700 BC), their detection of continuity of culture, their discovery of a house that seemed to span the ghost years, their finds of "12th-century" pottery just beneath or mixed in with 7th-century strata, their finds of 7th-century pottery in and sometimes under "12th-century" layers which seemed undisturbed (a situation quite similar to but more disturbing than what we saw for the stratified section just inside Mycenae's Lion Gate), the opinions they held, the problems that upset them – all became secondary to making the evidence fit the accepted chronology. Archaeological facts were forced to fit a historical theory.

Then a new theory was needed. If there was indeed a 400-year gap, something must have caused it. The cause for the end of layer VIIb2 was unknown when no gap was seen,[1] but when the gap became necessary, it was decided that Troy VIIb2 must have perished by fire and sword more terrible in their effect than the Trojan War which ended Troy VIIa. Why else would people too stubborn to leave despite 2000 years of great hardships abandon their site now?

Only revision of the Egypto-Mycenaean dates can explain the "still unexplained" problems at Hissarlik. Only then do they cease to be "perplexing."

Pylos

Near the modern town of Pylos in Messenia in the southwestern Peloponnesus, a Mycenaean palace and town, taken to be the ancient Pylos of which Homer sang, were uncovered. According to legend, Nestor, its aged king, fought in the Trojan War. Carl W. Blegen, the excavator of both Troy and Pylos, assigned absolute dates to a burned

---

below, and two buildings were constructed over the spot where the sherd was found. Since no contamination was detected, these buildings assigned to the 12th century BC should postdate this 9th, 8th, or 7th-century sherd, and the "12th-century" Mycenaean pottery they contained ought to postdate the sherd as well. See Fig. 359 of *Troy IV.2*.

[1] See »The Warrior Vase«, p. 198, n. 4, p. 199, n. 4, p. 200, n. 1.

layer at the site of Hissarlik in Northwestern Turkey, which he assumed to represent the Greek destruction of King Priam's Troy, and to the Palace of Nestor, also destroyed by fire. The absolute dates were furnished by Mycenaean pottery in and under both destructions. Blegen found Mycenaean pottery in the destruction layer of Pylos obviously representing "the ceramic shapes and styles that were in normal current use on the very day the palace was set afire and destroyed."[1] "The collection as a whole reflects chiefly the latest stage in the style of Mycenaean III B" but there were quite a few pieces belonging to the III C period.[2] Arne Furumark set the transition from the one style to the other at ca. 1230 BC, about the time of the death of Pharaoh Ramses II.[3] Blegen revised this downward by about 30 years, setting the date of Pylos' destruction at ca. 1200 BC.[4]

In the debris of the palace he also found a great deal of pottery which was dated not by Egyptian criteria but on the internal evidence from Greece itself. This ware he ascribed to ca. 600 BC.[5] Blegen saw that after the fire "the site was obviously abandoned and thenceforth left deserted."[6] To account for the mass of later pottery he acknowledged that ca. 600 BC "there was fairly widespread activity on the site."[7]

This later pottery appeared in many rooms of the palace, often, in fact, in the same layer as the pottery dated 600 years older[8] so that the earlier sherds must have percolated up. In one case the later sherds were found together with the earlier ones in a layer "which

---

[1] C. W. Blegen: *The Mycenaean Age, The Trojan War, The Dorian Invasion, and Other Problems* (Cincinnati, Ohio, 1962), p. 18.

[2] C. W. Blegen and M. Rawson: *The Palace of Nestor at Pylos in Western Messenia* (henceforth *PN*), vol. I (Princeton, 1966), p. 421.

[3] A. Furumark: *The Chronology of Mycenaean Pottery* (Stockholm, 1941), p. 115.

[4] *PN* 421. S. E. Iakovides: *Perati*, vol. B (Athens, 1970), p. 468, brings down the date a bit further. The evidence for reducing the date is not at all secure, and, if anything, the change now seems to me to have preceded Ramses' death.

[5] In »The Palace of Nestor Excavations of 1956«, *American Journal of Archaeology*, 61 (1957), 130, Blegen cautiously said, "perhaps of the seventh century B.C.," but see *PN* 177, 184 for his most recent view. He constantly called these sherds "late Geometric" (*PN* 64, 175, 229, 294-6, 300, 329, 332 and see *AJA* 1957, p. 130). More recent analysis by J. N. Coldstream: *Greek Geometric Pottery* (London, 1968), p. 330, established ca. 750 – 680 BC as the limits for the Late Geometric phase in this area, but Coldstream seems unsure whether Blegen's finds are "late Geometric" (408) – either the term is incorrect in the light of this more recent analysis or the pottery precedes 680 BC.

[6] *PN* 422.

[7] *PN* 294.

[8] *PN* 181, 184, 185, 294, 300, 303.

rested on the stucco pavement of the court" and "unquestionably represents the latest phase of occupation of the palace." Since, by the accepted chronology, they are six centuries too young to have been in use "on the very day the palace was set afire and destroyed",[1] they "must somehow have penetrated from above"[2] through however much dirt settled and vegetation grew over 600 years, then slipping through "a compact layer of smallish stones closely packed in blackish earth"[3] 0.15 – 0.25 m thick, they finally forced their way into a 0.03 – 0.10 m thick "clayey deposit",[4] for how else could they have gotten there?

Two sets of pottery are involved here: a group dating to the 7th century on internal grounds, and a group dating to the 13th century on external grounds – the time of Ramses II of Egypt, with whose scarabs Mycenaean III B and C pottery is found.[5] Though the two groups were found together in the same strata, because of the supposed passage of 600 years, the "late Geometric" pottery was branded part of "an intrusive deposit"[6] and the Mycenaean was used as a dating criterion for the fire. Velikovsky has postulated that Ramses II reigned ca. 600 BC, not in the 13th century BC.[7] This would solve a problem at Pylos. No pottery percolated. None "penetrated from above." The two styles were contemporaneous. Both were used in the palace before the fire and buried by the debris.

---

[1] C. W. Blegen: *The Mycenaean Age, The Trojan War, The Dorian Invasion, and Other Problems* (Cincinnati, Ohio, 1962), p. 18.
[2] *PN* 294.
[3] *AJA* (1957), p. 130. Above the black layer the earth was plowed (*PN* 294) and much disturbed (*AJA*, 1957, p. 131) and there is a discrepancy whether the black layer was "immediately below the surface" (*AJA* 130) or under "a stratum of plowed earth, ca. 0.15 m deep" (*PN* 294) or if the two descriptions mean the same thing. This being the case, especially since the surface down to perhaps 0.15 m was disturbed (*PN* 294, *AJA* 131) it would be difficult to say how much dirt would settle and vegetation grow over the 600 years (see *PN* 422 for vegetation growth) but one would expect both processes to have occurred if 600 years really did transpire. The small stones in the black layer were presumably from the collapse of rubble walls within the palace (*PN* 177). Such walls would most certainly have fallen at or soon after the time of the fire, not standing six centuries to topple onto later pottery.
[4] *PN* 294.
[5] A. Furumark: *The Chronology of Mycenaean Pottery* (Stockholm, 1941), pp. 114-15. Iakovides: *Perati*, vol. A (1969), pp. 166, 382; vol. B (1970), pp. 467-68.
[6] *PN* 175.
[7] I. Velikovsky: *Ramses II and His Time* (New York, 1978).

Ugarit

We now leave Asia Minor's northwest coast and travel to the area where its south coast meets northern Syria, to Ugarit and Alalakh.

In the published volume of *Ages in Chaos*, Velikovsky made a strong case for challenging Ugarit's conventional dates.[1] He pointed out many 500-year problems in the literary texts uncovered at the site, and shows the difficulty relating to vaulted Cypriote tombs constructed in the style of those from Ugarit but set 500 years later. For those who have not read or were not already convinced by the material presented by Velikovsky for Ras Shamra-Ugarit, perhaps a couple of additional problems will suffice.

Let us again look at the vaulted tombs of Cyprus. Velikovsky has already mentioned some of these, especially the 7th-century example from Trachonas. The island of Cyprus has an "astonishing" number of these tombs[2] which divide neatly into two series: those assigned to 1550 – 1200 BC, and those beginning in 950 BC and continuing for some time.[3] The first group of vaulted tombs (at Enkomi) corresponds closely in date and style to the Ugaritic tombs, and the type is thought to have come from Syria to Cyprus.[4] The second group of Cypriote tombs corresponds to both the Ugaritic and earlier Cypriote examples, but a 250-year gap separates the inception of the second group from the end of the Bronze Age tombs. More important than the 250-year period when no tombs were built in Syria or Cyprus to connect the later tombs to the earlier ones, is the fact that the earliest tombs of each group (i.e., those of 1550 and 950 BC), separated by 600 years, are most similar.[5]

The Cypriote vaulted tombs from 950 – 600 BC seem to undergo the same development as the Enkomi and Ugaritic tombs with 600 years separating the corresponding phases. It has been postulated that the later tombs somehow copied the earlier Cypriote or Syrian ones, but the tombs presumably copied must have been buried and invisible for some 600 years.[6]

---

[1] I. Velikovsky: *Ages in Chaos*, pp. 179-222.
[2] A. Westholm: »Built Tombs in Cyprus«, *Opuscula Archaeologica* II (1941), p. 30.
[3] *Ibid.*, pp. 32-51.
[4] *Ibid.*, p. 57.
[5] *Ibid.*, pp. 52-53. See also A. Westholm: »Amathus«, in E. Gjerstad et al.: *The Swedish Cyprus Expedition* (henceforth *SCE*) II (Stockholm, 1935), p. 140, and E. Sjöqvist: »Enkomi« *SCE* I (Stockholm, 1934), pp. 570-73.
[6] E. Gjerstad: *SCE* IV.2 (Stockholm, 1948), p. 239; V. Karageorghis: *Excavations in the*

Similar tombs are found in Jerusalem, Asia Minor, and Urartu of the 9th – 7th centuries, and again it is thought that they originated in 9th-7th-century Syro-Phoenicia.[1] But the only tombs of this type in that region, notably the ones from Ugarit, are placed centuries earlier.

Leaving behind the regions bordering Syro-Phoenicia, we shall travel briefly to an actual Punic colony. In the 9th or 8th century BC,[2] a group of Phoenicians sailed to North Africa and founded Carthage. One of the oldest archaeological discoveries from the site is a late 8th-century BC built tomb "closely related" to the Ugaritic tombs in architectural plan.[3] It is a "faithful miniature rendering" of the Syrian tombs both in design and, apparently, in arrangements for religious rites.[4] It would hardly be surprising for 8th-century Phoenician colonists to bring over current tomb type and burial customs from their motherland. The only similar tomb type and burial customs that their motherland can produce, however, are put 500 years earlier. By the accepted scheme, the colonists' ancestors would have been very familiar with these matters, but by the 8th century BC, the Ugaritic tombs must have been buried over, invisible, and forgotten.[5]

How did these tombs of Ugarit serve as models for Cypriots, Israelites, Urartians, Anatolian peoples, and Phoenician colonists, if contemporaneity is denied, and they went out of use and were thus forgotten 500 – 600 years earlier?

The final items we will examine from Ugarit are a gold bowl and a gold plate, both beautifully decorated. Stratigraphically, they belong shortly before the destruction of the city during the Amarna period,

---

Necropolis of Salamis I (*Salamis*, vol. 3) [Nicosia, 1967], p. 123.

[1] D. Ussishkin: »The Necropolis from the Time of the Kingdom of Judah at Silwan, Jerusalem«, *The Biblical Archaeologist* 33 (1970), 45-46.

[2] The foundation date was disputed in antiquity. Most ancient estimates fell within the range of 846 – 751 BC. Of particular interest for our purposes is the fact that a number of ancient authors stated that Carthage was founded before the Trojan War.

[3] G. C. and C. Picard: *The Life and Death of Carthage*, trans. from the French by D. Collon (London, 1968), p. 47.

[4] *Ibid.*, p. 52, and see C. Picard: »Installations Cultuelles Retrouvées au Tophet de Salammbo«, *Rivista degli Studi Orientali* 42 (1967), 189-99.

[5] Picard: »Installations«, sees close relations between the Ras Shamra and Carthage tombs but recognizes the chronological difficulty. His suggestion, pp. 197-98, that this tomb type came from Cyprus does not help matters. The Carthaginian settlers were primarily Syro-Phoenicians, not Cypriots. Besides, he seems not to realize that the type did *not* survive in Cyprus from Bronze Age times (contra, p. 197). Like the Carthaginian example, it "came back" after a mysterious chronological gap. Even if we make the Carthage example depend on Cyprus, not Syria, we are still left with the puzzle of how and why the Cypriots copied, yet did not copy, the 600-year extinct tombs of Ras Shamra or Enkomi.

and are thus assigned a date somewhere between 1450 – 1365 BC.[1] Stylistically, as well, they belong to the Mitannian-Amarna period and show scenes reminiscent of late 18th Dynasty Egypt, notably the time of King Tutankhamen.[2] Both stratigraphically and stylistically, then, a late 18th Dynasty date is necessitated. Since Velikovsky lowers that date by over 500 years, how are the gold bowls affected?

These two pieces are called "remarkable antecedents of the use of the frieze of animals on metal bowls" of Phoenician workmanship, firmly dated to the 9th – 7th centuries BC.[3] What is more "remarkable" than the Ugaritic examples' manufacture and burial over 500 years before the "later" series began, is the subject matter of the two items. Extraordinary conservatism was attributed to the Phoenicians, since the later group faithfully reproduced similar scenes and arrangement of the decoration,[4] after a lapse of 500 years.

The chariot scene on the 14th-century gold plate is compared to similar scenes of the 9th-century Neo-Hittites and of the Assyrian King Assurnasirpal II (883 – 859 BC).[5] The elongated gallop of the horse is seen to be quite similar to depictions on Assyrian reliefs, but Assyrian influence "is chronologically impossible, all the Assyrian monuments presently known where horses are depicted at gallop being about half a millennium later than our plate" (174). The gold bowl with its combination of Aegean, Egyptian, Mesopotamian, and Levantine motifs is "an excellent example of Phoenician syncretism, half a millennium before Phoenicians in the proper sense are known."[6]

Surely, it was thought, these golden objects, remarkably foreshadowing by 500 years similar metal bowls and similar scenes, "may be claimed as ancestors of the series of 'Phoenician' bowls of the ninth-seventh centuries B.C."[7] How can they be ancestors if they were

---

[1] C. F. A. Schaeffer: *Ugaritica* II (Paris, 1949), pp. 5, 47. See H. Frankfort: *The Art and Architecture of the Ancient Orient* (Baltimore, 1963), p. 149 for their assignment to the Mitannian period, p. 140 for his dates for that period; D. E. Strong: *Greek and Roman Gold and Silver Plate* (Glasgow, 1966), p. 53.
[2] Frankfort: *Art and Architecture*, p. 150.
[3] P. Dikaios: »Fifteen Iron Age Vases«, *Report of the Department of Antiquities of Cyprus, 1937-1939* (Nicosia, 1951), 137, 172; Schaeffer: *Ugaritica* II, p. 47.
[4] M. Vieyra: *Hittite Art*, pp. 45-46.
[5] Schaeffer: *Ugaritica* II, pp. 22-23: "Une influence de ce côté est chronologiquement impossible, tous les monuments assyriens actuellement connus où figurent des chevaux au galop étant postérieurs de près d'un demi-millénaire à notre patère."
[6] Frankfort: *Art and Architecture*, p. 149 (p. 257, ill. 296 in the paperback version).
[7] Strong: *Gold and Silver Plate*, p. 53.

buried and unseen for 500 years before the later series began, and the art was lost over those 500 years?

If metal bowls reproduced similar scenes in similar arrangements for 500 years, that would indeed be "extraordinary conservatism." That 9th-7th-century Phoenicians should imitate so closely 14th-century bowls they never saw, after a 500-year gap, is merely "extraordinary."

When their date is reduced by half a millennium, these bowls fit beautifully into the later series. If one keeps high dates for the Mitannians and the 18th Egyptian Dynasty, then this is yet another mystery to add to our list.

Alalakh

Traveling a bit farther inland and to the north, one reaches Tell Atchana, the ancient Alalakh.

The uppermost levels VI-I of the site, the ones of most concern to us, depend solely on Egyptian chronology, and the dates for imported Late Cypriote and Mycenaean pottery, Hittite New Empire and Mitannian material.[1] The four latter sets of material owe their dates solely to Egyptian chronology, and maintain them by floating on mysterious Dark Ages, which are archaeologically empty, or, at best, very obscure. It is thus an easy matter to find some 500-600-year puzzles of the type met over and over again in this paper. For the sake of brevity we will treat here only two.

During part of the period of the 18th Egyptian Dynasty, Alalakh was ruled by King Niqmepa. His royal palace is thus assigned to the 15th-14th centuries BC. Only a short distance north of Alalakh lies the site of Zinjirli with its 5th-century palace.

According to H. Frankfort there are no monuments, in fact, no works of art to fill the gap between ca. 1200 and 850 BC in this part of the ancient Levant. He was nevertheless struck by the resemblances of the 8th-century palace of Zinjirli to the 14th-century palace of Alalakh.[2]

---

[1] L. Woolley: *Alalakh* (Oxford, 1955), p. 384-99.
[2] H. Frankfort: *Art and Architecture*. On p. 166 he speaks of the Dark Age. He saw similarities between Alalakh and Zincirli in constructional technique employed by the architect but invisible to onlookers (p. 145), and in ground plan (p. 167). He was, in fact, so struck by these similarities that he disbelieved a break in architectural continuity during the Dark Age

How was the tradition of monumental architecture kept alive for 600 years, if the Niqmepa palace was covered over and invisible by the 14th century, and if there is absolutely no continuity in this or any of the other arts between the two periods?[1]

Many large fragments of sculpted stone lions were also unearthed at Alalakh. These were found re-used in the last phase of the "temple",[2] but presumably guarded the doors to this structure at an earlier date. According to the excavator,[3] these lions have great "importance as monuments for the history of art. In the 'Syro-Hittite' period gateway lions of this sort are so regular a convention as to be almost the hallmark of North Syrian art." Such lions are normally assigned to the 9th – 7th centuries BC,[4] but because Egyptian chronology provides the absolute dates for Alalakh, "now for the first time we have a series of lion sculptures which cannot be later than the fourteenth century B.C."

Should we view the Alalakh lions as "early forerunners of the whole series of Syro-Hittite lions"?[5] Were they also the model for the guardian lions of Assyrian palaces, "anticipating [both sets] by five hundred years"?[6] Could they have provided the inspiration for the 500-year-later sculptures?

If, by the 9th century BC, the Alalakh lions were completely buried over by debris and long forgotten,[7] and no similar lions exist to span the Dark Age in this region, "how can we explain why the system of flanking gates with large, guardian figures and stone reliefs in the

---

(p. 163). Yet he himself has shown that, by the accepted scheme, the palace at Alalakh and other contemporary buildings were all destroyed long before Zincirli's palace was built, and he fails to cite any intermediary structures to fill the gap between 1200 and 850 BC (pp. 163-66).

[1] W. F. Albright's attempt (»Northeast-Mediterranean Dark Ages and the Early Iron Age Art of Syria« in *The Aegean and the Near East*, ed. S. Weinberg [Locust Valley, New York, 1956], pp. 144-65) to bridge the chronological gap fails. While many of his remarks are quite cogent, he disregards much evidence for dating some finds, and, as was his custom, chose dates to suit his own scheme.

[2] Frankfort (*Art and Architecture*, p. 162) believed that the building called a temple by Woolley may have been a palace.

[3] L. Woolley: *A Forgotten Kingdom* (London, 1959), pp. 132-33.

[4] Woolley (ibid., p. 132) pushes the lions back to the 10th century, but Frankfort (*Art and Architecture*, p. 166) shows that they only go back to the 9th century.

[5] Woolley: *A Forgotten Kingdom*, p. 133.

[6] S. Lloyd: *The Art of the Ancient Near East* (New York, 1961), p. 274. Lloyd is actually speaking of stone sphinxes from the Hittite capital of Boghaz Koy foreshadowing Assyrian bulls and lions, but the quotation fits the Alalakh lions as well.

[7] Woolley: *A Forgotten Kingdom*, p. 152.

ninth-century Assyrian palaces resembles so much that employed"[1] here at Alalakh and other contemporary centers some 400 – 500 years earlier?

Résumé

In this work the reader has traveled to six ancient cities to study some of the buildings and artifacts that modern excavators have unearthed. These six places were referred to as stumbling blocks for the revised chronology. We were told that they could not come down by centuries in time, thus the revised chronology, a nice enough theory, was disproved by archaeological facts. What did we see?

At Mycenae, Tiryns, Troy, Pylos, Ugarit and Alalakh, we found numerous 500-700-year problems for the excavators and for those trying to trace the development of artistic and architectural types. We have examined palaces, temples, tombs, pots, pins, carved slabs, bowls, figurines, etc. We have come across stratigraphical sections that do not conform to the expected and accepted sequence of events. Everywhere we went we found unanswered questions, perplexing problems, and always these involved 500 – 700 years.

In this article only five places were visited, and these but briefly. The number of 500-700-year problems studied by this writer is quite large, and the more he reads, the greater the number swells. No ad hoc theory has yet been advanced which adequately explains any one of the cases, let alone all of them. Only a revision of ancient history, a shortening of Egyptian chronology, works for all the cases mentioned in this paper, and, in fact, for all others which this writer has researched.

If there were no problems, or only a couple of minor points not yet fully understood, it would be simple, indeed necessary, to accept the

---

[1] W. S. Smith: *Interconnections in the Ancient Near East* (London, 1965), p. 109. Smith actually refers to Hittite art, but the situation is the same for the Alalakh lions. See also Lloyd: *Art of the Ancient Near East*, pp. 193-94, and Woolley: *A Forgotten Kingdom*, p. 133. Smith, Lloyd, and Woolley all wanted to connect the "early" lions with the "late" ones, but they could not bridge the Dark Age pointed out by Frankfort (*Art and Architecture*, pp. 164-66), which should separate the two groups. It is true that the Alalakh lions are less sophisticated than other lions from this region, but that need not be a sign of a very early date. Frankfort (*Art and Architecture*, p. 254, n. 7) speaks of various degrees of success, or lack of it, in local carvings of the 9th century, citing the Alalakh sculptures as an earlier precedent.

standard chronology. When, however, major "exceptions to the rule" appear in great numbers, and these form a consistent pattern,[1] it becomes very difficult to brush them aside and have faith in "the rule". One must make a choice. Should archaeological evidence be forced to fit the Procrustean bed of historical theory, or should a new scheme be put forth to explain all the facts?

A few problems from a handful of sites do not prove that the revision is valid. Volumes could and need to be written to enumerate all the problems faced by the old scheme, which act as confirmations for the new. One article need not convince the skeptical reader that Velikovsky is right, but anyone reading this might start wondering: Just how sound is the accepted chronology?

---

[1] As merely one case of consistency, let us reconsider the "12th-century" LH III C period. At Pylos we found 7th-century pottery mixed with the 12th. We have seen that stylistically LH III C figural pottery most resembles 7th-century ware. Stratigraphically 7th-century sherds were mixed with LH III C inside the Lion Gate of Mycenae. At Troy two LH III C structures were built over a 9th or 8th-century sherd, while 7th-century pottery was found stratified directly above, mixed with, and under LH III C. Many more cases exist (e.g., the perplexing mixture of LH III C with early 7th-century pottery in a stratum of Scoglio del Tonno near Taranto in South Italy). Why don't stylistic and stratigraphical considerations cause the redating of this period? As was pointed out above, this period is connected with Pharaoh Ramses II. Utilizing other evidence, Velikovsky has redated this king from the 13th to the late 7th century BC.

Supplement II

New Light on the Dark Age of Greece

(by Jan Sammer)

New Light on the Dark Age of Greece

The Tombs at the Argive Heraion

Argos, in the south of the Argive valley, or Argolis, was, according to Greek tradition, a very ancient city. It stood four miles from the sea at the foot of a steep hill, which formed its acropolis. In the days of the Trojan War it was reputedly ruled by Diomedes, one of the heroes of that war. In historic times, during the reign of King Pheidon, in the first half of the seventh century, Argos was the leading city in the Peloponnesos; but later it surrendered its supremacy to Sparta.

To the north of the city stood a temple dedicated to Hera: Legend has it that it was at this Heraion in the Argive plain that the leaders of the Trojan War assembled and took an oath of loyalty to their cause.[1] Legend has it also that this center of worship of Hera was founded at least thirteen generations before Agamemnon and the Trojan expedition.

Close to the Heraion a cemetery of Mycenaean Age was excavated by Carl Blegen early in his distinguished archaeological career.[2] We shall follow him through a series of tombs and see whether Furtwängler's scheme did insure the archaeologist against any conflicting evidence. We can say at the start that this journey along the graves will not be as problem-free as it should be if the accepted scheme is all true and if the centuries between the Mycenaean and Ionic ages are real and not fictitious.

The cemetery was ascribed by Blegen to the Mycenaean Age, in round numbers, from -1600 to -1200. The only object "definitely datable through foreign analogies was the Egyptian scarab found in Tomb XIV, which may be attributed to the reign of Queen Hatshepsut, not much later than 1500 B.C."[3]

Here, as in all other places of early Greece, chronology is established through contact with Egypt. And it stands only if, as in this case, Hatshepsut reigned about -1500. Since, however, as was shown in *Ages*

---

[1] *Dictys Cretensis* 116.
[2] C. W. Blegen: *Prosymna, The Helladic Settlement Preceding the Argive Heraeum*, vol. I (Cambridge, 1937).
[3] *Ibid.*, p. 261.

in *Chaos*, vol. I, Hatshepsut was a contemporary of King Solomon and lived in the tenth century, we are prepared for all kinds of embarrassing finds and strained solutions.

The problem which Blegen faced almost wherever he dug was "the recovery in so may tombs of objects dating from the Geometric period[1] – a time separated by centuries, actually by more than half a millennium, from that of Queen Hatshepsut – this on the conventional timescale. We can start our survey with any one of the fifty-two excavated tombs, since the problem is not confined to one or to several among them.

"Tombs IX, XIX and L had ... clearly been disturbed, and the discovery of geometric pottery on or just above the Floor permitted the disturbance to be approximately dated...?" What kind of disturbance was it? "There was nothing to suggest that the tombs had been deliberately rifled,"[2] and, as we shall presently see, even had the tombs been rifled, the perplexing problem would persist.

Tomb IX is most instructive: "The tomb had been entered and disturbed in the Geometric Period. ... Practically all braces of Mycenaean occupation had been removed and the earth filling the chamber contained objects of Geometric date, which continued down to the floor itself, at a depth of 2.90 meters below the surface of the grounds. ... Just above the floor were recovered two spherical beads of glass paste, probably dating from the Mycenaean period."[3] Where geometric ware was found in the fill it was thought to have a later date of deposition, but how with the Mycenaean ware in the fill, above the geometric ware on the floor?

Let us turn to tomb XIX and once more quote Blegen, since the issue is of decisive importance. The tomb "was opened and entered in post-Mycenaean times, and the objects which were then deposited in the chamber make it clear that the date of the intrusion is to be assigned to the later part of the Geometric Period."[4] But for what purpose were the tombs opened? "The purpose of this reopening of the tomb in Geometric times was not definitely ascertained. No traces of bones came to light, and it did not look as if this deposit of bronzes and other objects was of a sepulchral character." Then, what moved

---

[1] *Ibid.*, p. 262.
[2] *Ibid.*, p. 262.
[3] *Ibid.*, p. 165.
[4] *Ibid.*, pp. 59-60.

people to deposit their pottery and bronze in tombs over half a millennium old? "The tomb may have become in effect a simple shrine" of the cult of the dead. There was no rifling of the tomb, nor a second burial: The objects were deposited to honor ancestors whom nobody could remember.

About tomb L Blegen wrote: "Most of the fill of Mycenaean times, except for a few centimeters above the floor, had disappeared, and the earth and the debris removed in the course of our excavations contained many Geometric sherds and a few fragments of bronze."[1]

In all the three cases cited above the sole basis for claiming disturbance was the finding of Geometric pottery – and not only in the fill of the tombs, but "on or just above the floor." If the "disturbance" is of a later date than the time the sepulchers were made, how could the ware have come to lie under the fill, on the floor? If the tombs were opened in the Geometric period, how could the objects put in by the disturbers find their place with the Mycenaean ware, on the floor?

"In eight further instances [tombs VIII, X, XXVI, XXXIV, XXXVII, XL, XLIII and XLIX] similar deposits came to light."[2] Let us examine them one by one.[3]

The Geometric deposit in tomb XXVI "was apparently not of a sepulchral nature, but in all respects similar to that brought to light in the chamber of tomb XIX"[4] – that is, a votive deposit – though here it did not rest on the floor itself. It looked as if the roof had caved in; but instead of pilfering the contents of the thus-exposed tombs, the pious Geometric people, descendants of five centuries, added objects of their time to the ancient funerary equipment.

The contents of tomb XXXIV evoked the following admission on the part of the excavator: "The date of this [Geometric] deposit is more easy to determine than its significance. The oenochoe for "wine pourer" ... is of the Geometric style; the skyphosis a typical Protocorinthian fabric ... the unpainted vessels and the bronzes are of types one might expect in the same association and the whole deposit might be as late as the end of the eighth century."[5]

---

[1] *Ibid.*, p. 140.
[2] *Ibid.*, p. 262.
[3] Tomb VIII "...The earth filling it contained a considerable number of objects dating from the Geometric period" on top of a shallow Mycenaean deposit, (*ibid.*, p. 161) The situation in tomb X was very similar.
[4] *Ibid.*, p. 93.
[5] *Ibid.*, p. 112.

In tomb XXXVII "a number of small Protocorinthian sherds and many fragments of bronze, bronze wire and a bronze pin of a Geometric type were found down to within half a metre of the floor."[1] The roof was found to have collapsed.

In tomb XL Blegen found the roof in its place, but the drop of the lintel opened access into the chamber – "the opening above the walled door must have been large enough for a man to enter: A number of objects of post-Mycenaean date, at any rate had been deposited inside the chamber and were found in the fill at a height of 1 m to 1.60 m above the floor. These objects included a small Corinthian jug, a number of fragments of Proto-Corinthian pottery, representing several skyphoi, a bronze bowl, and a bronze pin." Blegen concluded: "This deposit of post-Mycenaean objects in the chamber is, I believe, to be interpreted as evidence for a continuing cult of the dead."[2] But is it likely, or even imaginable, that a man would squeeze through a hole in the lintel of a grave in order to put objects in – and that no one else, seeing the opening, would break in to steal the ancient artifacts? Yet this is what Blegen had to assume on the basis of the accepted chronology.

The tombs numbered XLIII and XLIX also contained Geometric deposits besides those identified as Mycenaean.

The finds of Protocorinthian skyphoi in tombs XXXIV and XL were especially on Blegen's mind. "What is the significance of these objects?" he asked.[3]

Their significance is in their perturbing the accepted historical time table. Since the tombs were not reused, how good is the explanation that the disturbers – riflers they were not – deposited bronze and pottery of their own age in so many graves? It was absolutely clear to Blegen that none of these graves had ever been reused for burial or second interment.

In the absence of a more reasonable answer to the startling state of things Blegen, as we have seen, arrived at the conclusion that the eighth or seventh century inhabitants of the place were devotees of an ancestors' cult. Therefore "what we have in a high level in these Late Helladic tombs [-1600 to -1200] are clearly votive offerings which were deposited at some time in the Geometric Period. This evidence,

---

[1] *Ibid.*, p. 124.
[2] *Ibid.*, p. 133.
[3] *Ibid.*, p. 262.

it seems to me," Blegen continued, "can only mean that the cult of the dead, some traces of which we have already seen within the sepulchers themselves, was still flourishing in the cemetery at the Heraeum long after the Mycenaean age had passed away."[1] But the words "we have in a high level" in the tombs conflict with Blegen's observation and description: In several tombs the Geometric ware was clearly the earliest – it was on the floor of the tombs – in others mixed with the Mycenaean ware. And since no repeated burials were found in these tombs, Blegen admitted that they presented "a puzzling problem."

"In tombs IX, XIX and the main chamber of XXVI, the presence of Geometric objects on the floor of the chamber, or near it, suggested that the disappearance of some Mycenaean remains was due to later disturbance ... In almost every instance recorded or a skeleton lying in order in the tombs at the Heraeum it is clear that the body of the person buried had been laid directly on the floor of the chamber."[2] Is it, then, thinkable that the late worshippers of the dead in some instances added their ware to the Mycenaean ware and in other instances replaced the Mycenaean ware by one of their own time, surrounding the skeleton of the dead with objects five centuries more recent than himself?

Should we try, on the basis of contact with Egypt, to establish the true age of the cemetery at the Heraion? First, the already mentioned scarab found in tomb XIV – what is its evidence?

"The cartouche apparently reads, 'the good favour of Amen'... It is of a type common in the time of the eighteenth dynasty and is almost exactly similar to some scarabs of Queen Hatshepsut's reign, recently found by Mr. Winlock in the excavations of the Metropolitan Museum at Deir el-Bahari. The chronological evidence supplied by this scarab is of no little value in confirming the date of our tomb." It belonged to a type "used in the early XVIII Dynasty as amulets or charms."[3]

"Other Egyptian objects dating from the XVIII Dynasty were found in the Tholos [beehive] tomb at the Heraeum and from the slope below the Second Temple."[4]

---

[1] *Ibid.*, p. 263.
[2] *Ibid.*, p. 262.
[3] *Ibid.*, p. 169.
[4] *Ibid.*, p. 281. Blegen dated the Second Temple to post-Mycenaean times (p. II). Besides objects attributed to the Eighteenth Dynasty, scarabs of "a much later" date, belonging to the Twenty-sixth Dynasty, were found there, too.

It is not excluded that the older of the tombs date from the time of Hatshepsut of the Eighteenth Dynasty; yet the scarab found and attributed to her reign was not a royal signet, but a charm or amulet, and could be from a later part of the Eighteenth Dynasty. It appears that the cemetery dates from sometime in the tenth or, more probably, the ninth to sometime in the eighth century.[1]

The state of things at the cemetery of the Argive Heraion calls for a vindication of some of the views of W. Dörpfeld and some of A. S. Murray. But before we reverse the verdict, we will follow Carl Blegen to Troy and to Pylos.

The Identification of Troy

When Alexander crossed the Hellespont, setting foot in Asia for the first time, he paused briefly at what he believed to be the site of the Homeric Ilion – the hill we know today as Hissarlik. A Greek and after it a Roman town named 'Ilion' grew up on the site, and few ancient writers doubted that here once stood the "well-towered" citadel of Priam. The Roman geographer Strabo, however, questioned the identification, and brought many arguments to show that 'Ilion' was in all respects unlikely to have been the site of the Homeric city.[2] Uncertainty about the identification of Troy continued into modern times, and even Schliemann's spectacular discoveries at Hissarlik did not end it. Several years after the publication of *Troy and Its Remains*, Professor R. C. Jebb, one of the foremost classicists of the age, proclaimed that Schliemann had not uncovered Homer's Troy at all and, further, that it was vain to expect that a city such as Homer sang of lay hid-

---

[1] Blegen published a more complete survey of what he considered later or intrusive deposits in the tombs in an article in the *American Journal of Archaeology* 43 (1939), titled »Prosymna: Remains of Post-Mycenaean Date«. Cf. also p. 293, n. 3 above. J. N. Coldstream assumes widespread cult surrounding the Mycenaean tombs five centuries after they were abandoned and forgotten. It is much more likely that the Greeks of the late eight century remembered ancestors who had not been buried more than a few decades. Cf. also idem: *Geometric Greece* (London, 1977) pp. 346 ff.

[2] Strabo: *Geography*, Book XIII, ch. 1. Strabo draws chiefly on information supplied by Demetrios of Skepsis; cf. Schliemann's refutation of Strabo in *Troy and Its Remains* (London, 1875), pp. 41-42. Cf. also W. Leaf: *Strabo on the Troad* (London, 1923). For a recent geological survey of the site, see John C. Kraft, Ilhan Kayal, Oguz Erol: »Geomorphic Reconstructions in the Environs of Ancient Troy«, *Science* 209 (15 August 1980), pp. 776-782.

den beneath the soil of the Troad. Hissarlik, in any case, could not accommodate any fortress on the scale envisaged by the poet: "The spatious palaces, and wide streets of the Homeric Troy point to a city totally different, both in scale and in character, from anything of which traces exist at Hissarlik." Although in his view "no one site in the Troad satisfies all the Homeric data for the position of Troy," yet Bali Dagh, a nearby hill looking over the village of Bunarbashi, was, according to Jebb, a much better choice: "'Troy ought to have been here' is one's feeling when, coming from Hissarlik, one mounts the hill above Bunarbashi."[1]

Jebb's objections would continue to weigh on the minds of those who followed Schliemann in his identification, as well as those who disagreed: The area of Hissarlik, even at its widest extent, was barely a twentieth of the size of the great citadel conjured by the poet. Even Schliemann expressed his dismay:

> I am extremely disappointed at being obliged to give so small a plan of Troy; nay, I had wished to be able to make it a thousand times larger, but I value truth above everything, and I rejoice that my three years' excavations have laid open the Homeric Troy, even though on a diminished scale, and that I have proved the Iliad to be based upon real facts.[2]

By the early 1890s new discoveries at Hissarlik had shown that Troy II, where Schliemann had found the great treasure, and which he confidently identified as the fortress of Priam, was in fact much more ancient: It was as old as the Pyramids, and it met its fiery end at the same time as the Egyptian Old Kingdom collapsed into anarchy. The finding of Mycenaean pottery in Troy VI made Wilhelm Dörpfeld, Schliemann's pupil and leader of the new campaign of excavations, claim that city as the most likely to have been the Ilion of Homer.[3] Dörpfeld found evidence that Troy VI had been destroyed by a violent earthquake; the damage was partly repaired and the city rebuilt, though on a much smaller scale. Such evidence, in the view of Carl Blegen, who conducted the most recent excavations on the site, could hardly be reconciled with the Homeric account of a city whose walls

---

[1] R. C. Jebb: »I. The Ruins of Hissarlik. II. Their Relation to the Iliad«, *Journal of Hellenic Studies* 3 (1882), pp. 195-217. But cf. p. 299, n. 1 below that Bunarbashi was, in fact, not inhabited that early.

[2] H. Schliemann: *Troy and Its Remains*, p. 344.

[3] W. Dörpfeld: *Troja und Ilion: Ergebnisse der Ausgrabungen in den vorhistorischen und historischen Schichten von Ilion 1870-1894* (Athens, 1902).

were breached by an enemy after a lengthy siege and which, on being plundered and denuded of its inhabitants, was for a long time left deserted. Blegen disagreed with Dörpfeld about the identity of the Homeric city; looking for a fortress that fell not due to an earthquake, but by siege and assault, he identified the Troy sung by Homer in Troy VIIa.[1]

Troy II was a stronghold; Troy VI was also a well-built fortress, girded by thick walls embracing an even larger area. Yet even in Troy VI "you could still saunter from side to side in less than two minutes; and a moderate sprinter could cover the ground in less than twenty-five seconds."[2] But Troy VIIa was smaller still. Before Blegen identified it as Priam's citadel, it had been known as a settlement of squatters. It is still described as "degraded and altogether pitiable." Poor huts with earthen floors, "sheepish cubicles," huddled against the walls of the little town.[3]

"The very poverty and insignificance of Troy VIIa," wrote C. Nylander in criticism of the conclusions of Blegen's expedition, "make it a less likely object of a large scale military enterprise from far away across the sea by a coalition of Mycenaen states, such as depicted by Homer." In his view the pottery found in this settlement is not of as early a date as was assigned to it by excavators – the evidence indicates that Troy VIIa was destroyed in the same series of catastrophes which overtook the palaces of Mycenae, Tiryns and Pylos together with so many other cities in all parts of Greece and the ancient East as a whole. The citadel of Priam, in Nylander's opinion, must have succumbed earlier than this, when the Mycenaean cities were yet strong. Thus, he concluded, if a Homeric city did exist it had to be Troy VI.[4]

This view, however, has not found general acceptance.[5]

Whichever level scholars may agree to identify as Homer's Troy, the wider problem of relating the Homeric geography to the site of Hissarlik remains. Some years ago Rhys Carpenter put the matter

---

[1] C. W. Blegen: »New Evidence for Dating the Settlements at Troy«, *Annual of the British School at Athens* 37 (1936-37), pp. 8-12; idem: *Troy and the Trojans* (New York, 1963).
[2] D. Page: *History and the Homeric Iliad* (Berkeley, 1959), p. 54.
[3] Idem: »The Historical Sack of Troy«, *Antiquity* 23 (1959), p. 27.
[4] C. Nylander: »The Fall of Troy«, *Antiquity* 37 (1963), pp. 6-9. A similar view was earlier expressed by F. Schachermeyr in *Poseidon* 1950, pp 189ff. and in *Minoica*, p. 368.
[5] V. R. d'A. Desborough: *The Last Mycenaeans and Their Successors* (Oxford University Press, 1964), pp. 164-65; G. Mylonas (»Priam's Troy and the Date of Its Fall«, *Hesperia* 33 [1964], pp. 352-380; *Mycenae and the Mycenaean Age* [Princeton, 1966], p. 215) also argues in favor of Blegen's identification of Troy VIIa as the Homeric city.

very succinctly: "There are obvious indications," he wrote, "that Hissarlik does not agree with the situation demanded by the Iliad, which speaks of a great walled city with streets, houses and palaces, rising to a temple-crowned acropolis, at an approachable distance from the Hellespont [Straits of Dardanelles] and apparently invisible from it, situated across the Scamander, with abundant springs of deep-soil water gushing close at hand. Actually, Hissarlik is in plain sight of the Hellespont, on the same side of the river, without any running springs, and enclosed within its walls an area of less than five acres."[1]

From the *Iliad* it transpires that the Achaeans could not effectively besiege Troy because of its great size – the Trojans were able to receive aid from all the nations of Asia Minor until the very end of the war.

Whether or not Troy has really been found, the mound of Hissarlik remains one of the most carefully excavated sites of Mycenaean times: And it is to the stratigraphic sequence that we shall now turn.

The Archaeology of Hissarlik

Any modern discussion of the stratigraphical situation at Troy must lean very heavily on the work of the University of Cincinnati expedition which dug at the site between 1932 and 1938 under the direction of Carl W. Blegen. The need for a new and definitive survey of Hissarlik arose in the 1920s because of continuing uncertainties about the dating of the various strata identified earlier by Schliemann and Dörpfeld.

Schliemann's great trenches, dug in haste in his relentless drive to reach the lower layers of the mound, where he firmly believed he would find the remains of Priam's fortress, ironically resulted in the irretrievable loss of large portions of the higher levels which scholars were later to identify as the Ilion of Homer. Dörpfeld's campaigns, though executed and organized on a much more scientific basis, nevertheless

---

[1] *Folk Tale, Fiction, and Saga in the Homeric Epics* (Los Angeles, 1946), p. 49. Carpenter argues that Homer construed the *Iliad* without knowledge of the true site of the city of which he sang, and with the assumption that Bali Dagh represented the remains of Ilion. If Homer did make such an assumption, archaeology does not bear him out – J. M. Cook (*The Troad: An Archaeological and Topographical Study* [Oxford, 1973]) failed to find any evidence of Bali Dagh being inhabited so early.

dismantled additional portions of the hill without really resolving some of the most urgent problems facing Homeric scholarship. While a few definite conclusions could be drawn on the basis of Dörpfeld's work – such as the realization that Troy II belonged to the Early Bronze Age, and could not therefore be the Homeric city – many new problems arose, especially concerning the relation of the Late Bronze Age city to its seventh-century Greek successor.

It was left to Carl Blegen, whose careful work at Korakou, Zygouries, and Prosymna had earned him a well-deserved reputation for accuracy and thoroughness, to undertake a new examination of what remained of Hissarlik in the hope that the troubling chronological questions could once and for all be resolved.

Before turning to the results of the American excavations, let us briefly glance at the stratigraphic situation as it was understood before Blegen.

Schliemann's interpretations have already been reviewed – his identification of Troy II with the Homeric Ilion led him to describe the sixth city with its characteristic Gray Minyan ware as a "Lydian" settlement, "contemporary with the colonization of Etruria by the Lydians."[1] Yet in his last campaign at Troy, conducted in 1890 with the assistance of Wilhelm Dörpfeld, he found this same Gray Minyan pottery belonging to Troy VI mixed with Mycenaean ware of a sort familiar to him from his diggings at Mycenae and Tiryns. Further discoveries by Dörpfeld in the years following Schliemann's death confirmed the fact that Troy VI in its later phases belonged to the Mycenaean Age.

When in 1902 Dörpfeld published his results,[2] he argued for the sixth city to be identified as Priam's, and had Troy VII follow immediately after. After about the year -700 the appearance of "advanced Geometric pottery" marks the transition to Troy VIII. "We can thus take approximately the year 700 as the boundary between the VIIth and VIIIth strata."[3] H. Schmidt in his ceramical study in the same

---

[1] Schliemann: *Ilios, The City and Country of the Trojans* (New York, 1961). Herodotus (I.94) put the migration of the Lydians to Etruria some time before the Trojan War; but archaeologists find no sign of the Etruscans in Italy prior to about the beginning of the eighth century, a discrepancy of ca. 500 years. Cf. T. Dohrn: »Stamnoi und Kratere aus grauem Ton, Nachahmungen von Metallgefässen (Civilta Castellana)« in W. Helbig and H. Speier: *Führer durch die öffentlichen Sammlungen klassischer Altertümer in Rom* (revised edition, Tübingen, 1969), p. 701, Nr. 2791; H. G. Buchholz: »Gray Minyan Ware in Cyprus and Northern Syria« in *Bronze Age Migrations in the Aegean* (Park Ridge, NJ, 1974), p. 180.

[2] *Troja und Ilion. Ergebnisse der Ausgrabungen in den vorhistorischen Schichten von Ilion 1870-1894* (Athens, 1902).

[3] Ibid., p. 201: "Die VIII lassen wir mit den entwickelt-geometrischen Vasen beginnen und

publication viewed the two phases of the seventh stratum as "a long period of transition" from the Homeric sixth city to the Greek eighth. The seventh stratum could be linked to the sixth by the presence in both of imported Mycenaean pottery and of Gray Minyan ware; the manufacture of Gray Minyan pottery continued into the eighth phase. "In about the year 700 B.C. belongs the approximate boundary between the latest phases of the seventh stratum and the oldest of the eighth."[1] No break in the occupation of the site was noted by either Schliemann or Dörpfeld. Even Blegen at first found no reason to postulate any hiatus – in an article published soon after the completion of his excavations he put forward some of the new insights presented by his discoveries, outlining the areas where he found it necessary to differ with Dörpfeld's scheme.[2] Troy VIIa was made to span the thirteenth century, and thus became the obvious choice as the city of Priam. Troy VIIb, where imported Mycenaean pottery of a late phase was still in evidence, was assigned to the years from ca. -1200 to ca. -900, the latter date marking, in Blegen's view, the beginning of the eighth city with its Gray Minyan and Geometric pottery.

The final publication of the findings of the Cincinnati expedition was only completed in 1958, twenty years after the end of the excavations. By then it had become evident that the solution advocated by Blegen in his earlier article was no longer tenable: Troy VIIb could not have lasted for three centuries – its span was halved to ca. 160 years – and Troy VIII showed no sign of being any earlier than ca. -700.[3] Blegen's final conclusions can be summarized as follows: After the destruction of the sixth settlement in an earthquake ca. -1300, the survivors rebuilt the town, though poorly, and on a much-reduced scale. Troy VIIa was destined to be short-lived, succumbing to an enemy attack ca.-1260, and was replaced by Troy VIIb, whose two phases lasted until about -1100. The eighth settlement, built atop the remains of this last Bronze Age city, was unmistakably a Greek town, and was assigned to the beginning of the seventh century. What transpired in

---

können daher als Grenze zwischen der VII. und VIII. Schicht rund das Jahr 700 annehmen."
[1] *Ibid.*, p.298.
[2] C. W. Blegen: »New Evidence for Dating the Settlements at Troy«, *Annual of the British School at Athens* 37 (1936-37).
[3] According to J. N. Coldstream (*Greek Geometric Pottery* [London, 1968], p. 376) some vases from Troy VIII belong to ca. 720-700, but a few sherds may be slightly earlier. In *Geometric Greece* (London, 1977), p. 246, he dates the re-settlement of Troy "from ca. 750 B.C. onwards."

the meantime? Archaeology could provide no clue, no trace of any human habitation between the extinction of Troy VIIb, supposedly ca. -1100, and the beginning of the Greek city slightly before -700. Thus a Dark Age was called upon to envelop Troy.

The lack of any deposits between the levels of the Late Bronze and Greek cities would normally be interpreted as indicating that there was no break in the occupation of the site, and it was so understood by Dörpfeld, as we have seen; but here, a diametrically opposite conclusion was reached purely because of the need to conform to the strictures of an extraneous chronological system. The imaginary break in the stratigraphic sequence was then claimed to signify a total desertion of the hill during the Dark Age.

An even more puzzling problem arose when it was realized that the inhabitants of the eighth, or Greek, settlement were linked to their predecessors in the seventh, or Helladic, settlement by numerous and strong cultural ties, despite the supposed gulf of some four centuries separating the one from the other: There was "a continuity of transmission" of an "abundant heritage, cultural and historical."[1] Most perplexing was the fact that the new settlers used the same type of pottery as their Helladic predecessors. "In the seventh century B.C. the Trojan citadel, which had been virtually deserted for some four centuries, suddenly blossomed into life once more with occupants who were still able to make Gray Minyan pottery."[2] Gray Minyan ware made up "the great bulk of the pottery of Troy VIII,"[3] and was characteristic also of the earlier Late Bronze Age settlements, Troy VI and Troy VII. The survival of the tradition at Troy itself was ruled out since Blegen's scheme required a 400-year abandonment of the site – but, the excavators speculated, was it not possible that the artisans carried on their peculiar style elsewhere during the dark centuries and then returned? Some remnants of the Trojans perhaps survived on the near-by hill of Bali Dagh, where they could have "maintained a foothold for several centuries in virtual isolation until 700 B.C." There the survivors would have "clung to their customs and traditions through the troubled period from about 1100 to 800 or later, and thus transmitted their ancestral gray pottery to successors in the eighth and seventh centuries."[4] Such

---

[1] C. W. Blegen, J. L. Caskey, M. Rawson: *Troy*, Vol. IV, pt. I (Princeton, 1958) p. 10.
[2] Blegen: *Troy and the Trojans* (New York, 1963), p. 172.
[3] Blegen et al.: *Troy*, vol. IV, pt. I, p. 251.
[4] *Ibid.*, p. 147. Surveys of Bali Dagh carried out in 1959 and 1968 revealed "nothing earlier

remarkable tenacity of tradition is all the more questionable, being devised specifically to evade the conclusions that would normally follow from a straightforward interpretation of the stratigraphical situation. Even so, it is not explained why the Trojans would have found Bali Dagh any more hospitable than their own hill during the Dark Age, and why, once settled elsewhere, they would have seen fit to reoccupy bare and desolate Hissarlik.

The strata exposed by Blegen's team reveal a city of the Late Bronze Age (Troy VIIb) remade ca. -700 into a Greek settlement (Troy VIII), with considerable continuity between the two phases. Even the boundary between the two settlements could not always be clearly delineated – thus in undisturbed strata belonging to the Late Bronze Age Settlement were found fragments of pottery assigned to "the very beginning of the seventh century." "As far as we could judge [the sherds] seem to be of exactly the same kind as the late Geometric pottery from the archaic [seventh-century] strata." Such finds were unacceptable in the standard chronological scheme; as a way out the excavators pleaded mea culpa: "The only explanation we can find is to suppose that, in spite of our efforts to isolate and certify the deposits we examined, contamination had somehow been effected, and brought about the intrusion of the later wares into the strata of Troy VIIb."[1] In another part of the site, in the level of the Late Bronze Age settlement, pieces "indistinguishable from types that are common in Troy VIII and are usually attributed to the seventh century" were found; and the excavators acknowledged that "their occurrence in several areas in the stratum of Troy VIIb, below the deposits of Knobbed Ware [pottery characteristic of the last Bronze Age settlement] presents a perplexing and still unexplained problem."[2]

In the Greek city the archaeologists came upon the remains of a house (no. 814) which, as became evident with the progress of digging, had been originally a Late Bronze Age building belonging to Troy VIIb – yet its seventh-century Greek owner apparently could re-occupy the place and re-use the still-standing walls and intact foundations of the previous structure. Parts of the walls of the Greek house were "indistinguishable from the earlier construction," and the excavators "could

---

than 600 B.C." – J. M. Cook: »Bronze Age Sites in the Troad«, *Bronze Age Migrations in the Aegean*, p. 38.
[1] Blegen et al.: *Troy*, vol. IV, pt. I, p. 181.
[2] *Ibid.*, p.158.

not follow any clearly marked stratum throughout the building"[1] – in other words, they could not distinguish supposedly twelfth-century features from seventh-century ones.

The continuing doubts and misgivings, raised by finds such as these, finally evoked the following admission from Blegen's team – this after seven years' digging and decades of careful analysis:

> ...It has been argued that Troy VIIb came to its end about 1100 B.C. Generally considered, our evidence leads us to believe that a gap of 400 years exists between the end of Troy VIIb and the beginning of Troy VIII, but the *possibility of a contrary view* is established by the evidence of several successive floors of house 814, and also by the presence of Geometric sherds in a context of Troy VIIb.[2]

What the "contrary view" might be they did not spell out; but the question would not be laid to rest: Did not the Greek city follow the Homeric directly, with no abandonment of four centuries' duration intervening?

Blegen at Pylos

Pylos in Messenia, in the western Peloponnese, had a rather brief existence – according to tradition, no more than four kings were its rulers from its founding to its destruction. It was Neleus, the father of Nestor, who built the city, having come from Iolcus when his brother Peleus expelled him, and settled there a mixed population of his own followers.[3]

Neleus brought great renown to Pylos; but later in his reign, when his sons were still only young men, some unexplained disaster overtook the city, remembered in tradition as the destruction of Pylos by Heracles.[4] A large part of the population perished: Of Neleus' twelve

---

[1] *Ibid.*, pp. 291-92.

[2] *Ibid.*, p. 250 (emphasis added).

[3] Diodorus IV. 68. 6; Pausanias IV. 36. 1.

[4] The *Iliad*, XI. 689; "Heracles" may be an allusion to the planet Mars (Hyginus: *Fabulae* II.42: "Tertia est stella Martis quam alii Herculis dixerunt." Cf. Macrobius: *Saturnalia* III.12.5-6, reporting the opinion of Varro). The excavators of Nestor's palace found also remains of an earlier settlement whose violent destruction they attributed to Neleus' occupation of the site (C. W. Blegen and M. Rawson: *The Palace of Nestor in Western Messenia*, vol. I, pt. I. (Princeton, 1966), p. 423). However it is more likely to represent the city of Neleus destroyed by "Heracles". Diodorus differs from Pausanias in asserting that Neleus was the founder of Pylos.

sons Nestor only survived; but the people of Pylos rebuilt the city on an even grander scale, including a spatious palace for Nestor, who followed Neleus on the throne. Afterwards the city became involved in bitter warfare with neighboring Elis, and Nestor distinguished himself at the head of the Pylian forces.[1] But by the time of the Achaean expedition against Troy Nestor's age no longer permitted him to lead his warriors in battle. Homer tells in the *Iliad* that this king of Pylos had seen two generations of men pass – "those who had grown up with him, and they who were born to these in sacred Pylos, and he was king in the third age."[2] From this we can judge that some four or five decades separated the time of the disaster which overtook Pylos in Nestor's youth from the siege of Troy. Of those who came to Troy with Agamemnon, Nestor's was one of the few safe returns; once again he seated himself upon the marble bench in his palace, "scepter in hand, a Warden of the Achaean race."[3] Homer describes the visit of Telemachus, Odysseus' son, to Nestor at Pylos, ten years after Troy's fall – the prince from Ithaka found a prosperous city at the head of a peaceful realm, unruffled by any whiff of danger. Yet it is worth noting that Nestor took care to placate Poseidon the "earthshaker" with frequent sacrifices.[4]

The end of Pylos came in the second generation after Nestor: "After the end of the war against Ilium, and the death of Nestor after his return home, the expedition of the Dorians and return of the Heracleidae two generations afterwards drove out the descendants of Neleus from Messenia."[5] That there was an influx of Doric-speaking peoples into the Peloponnese after the downfall of the Mycenaean centers is certain – the distribution of Greek dialects in classical times attests to this; but the old view that they were the cause of the widespread catastrophe that marks the end of the Late Bronze Age in Greece now finds few supporters. The Dorian bands descended on the weakened Mycenaean kingdoms, taking possession of a depopulated land.[6] The Heraclids, as their name shows, were worshippers of Mars. Having been expelled from the Peloponnese one or two generations before the Trojan War, they settled in northern Greece. However, the dis-

---

[1] *Iliad*, XI. 682, 698-701.
[2] *Iliad*, I. 250-252.
[3] *Odyssey* III.
[4] *Odyssey*, III. 3f. For evidence of the cult of Poseidon at Pylos see also M. Ventris and J. Chadwick: *Documents in Mycenaean Greek*, second ed. (Cambridge, 1973), p. 279.
[5] Pausanias, IV, 3.
[6] See above, section »A Gap Closed«, p. 113, n. 3.

locations and upheavals which marked the eighth and early seventh centuries uprooted them once again and brought them back to claim possession of their ancient homeland. But this was no mass displacement of populations; as Pausanias records, only the royal family, "the descendants of Neleus" were expelled. "The old Messenians were not turned out by the Dorians, but agreed to Cresphontes being their king, and to the partition of the land among the Dorians. And they were brought over to this compliance by suspicion of their former kings, because they were Minyae who had originally sprung from Iolcus."[1]

The route by which the Heracleidae reached Pylos appears to have been this: They were advancing from the north towards the Peloponnesos, but were dissuaded from crossing the Corinthian Isthmus;[2] instead they took to the sea, directing their ships westward through the Corinthian Gulf, and disembarked on the unprotected northern coast of Achaia. Thence they advanced south through Arcadia towards Elis, and then on to Pylos. The unprotected palace of Nestor was seized and put to the torch.[3] The conquest completed, Pausanias relates, the Heraclid king who received Messenia as his share did not establish himself at Pylos, but "changed the royal residence to Stenyclarus."

Thus Pylos was abandoned and remained deserted – even the knowl-

---

[1] Pausanias, III. 3. The exile of the Neleids to Attica is mentioned in numerous ancient sources. For an evaluation of these traditions in the context of recent archaeological evidence, see Ch. Sourvinou-Inwood: »Movements of Populations in Attica at the End of the Mycenaean Period« in *Bronze Age Migrations in the Aegean* (1974), pp. 215-222.

[2] Pausanias: *Elis* I, iii.6. The massive wall built across the Isthmus of Corinth in late Mycenaean times may have been a factor in forcing the Heracleidae to put to the sea. Cf. O. Broneer: *Hesperia* 28 (1959), pp. 298ff.; G. Mylonas: *Mycenae and the Mycenaean Age* (Princeton, 1966), pp. 219-220.

[3] The conflagration in which Nestor's palace perished preserved many clay tablets with inscriptions in Linear B, dating from the palace's last days; they have been interpreted to indicate preparations for an enemy attack from the sea (L. Palmer: *Minos*, vol. IV, d. 22; idem: *Mycenaeans and Minoans* (London, 1962); Ventris and Chadwick: *Documents in Mycenaean Greek* n. 138) but this view has been questioned (D. Page: *History and the Homeric Iliad*, pp. 193ff.; V. R. d'A. Desborough: *The Last Mycenaeans and Their Successors* (Oxford, 1964), p. 223). Blegen's team found no traces of any fortifications, in contrast to strongholds such as Mycenae, Gla and Tiryns which were heavily fortified. The lack of defence preparations within the palace has been noted by several authors: F. J. Tritsch: »The Women of Pylos« in *Minoica* (ed. E. Grumach) (1958), pp. 406-410; L. Palmer: *The Interpretation of Mycenaean Greek Texts* (Oxford, 1963), pp. 116-120; L. Deroy: *Les leveurs d'impôts dans le royaume mycénien de Pylos* (Incunabula Graeca 24) (Rome, 1968); R. Schmitt-Brandt: »Die Oka-Tafeln in neuer Sicht«, *Studi Micenei ed Egeo-Anatolici*, 7 (Incunabula Graeca 28) (1968), pp. 69-96. On balance the evidence does not necessarily imply destruction by a human agent, and seems consistent with the effects of some natural cause.

edge of the site of Nestor's palace was lost; it became a matter of discussion already in antiquity. Most ancients and moderns, however, have agreed in placing Nestor's palace somewhere in the vicinity of the Bay of Navarino in western Messenia.[1] This was also the conviction of Carl Blegen when in 1939 he came to Messenia to search the countryside for any sign of the ancient city of Pylos with Nestor's famous palace, celebrated by Homer.

#[2] Blegen selected for his first dig a prominent hilltop, a short distance from the sea, which seemed to him eminently suitable to be the site of a royal palace; and really, as soon as he began to lift the earth from his first trench, extensive structures began to appear, and much pottery of Mycenaean time.

Here, without doubt, was Nestor's great palace. The excavations at Pylos were hardly even started when war intervened; it was not until 1952 that Blegen was able to return with a team from the University of Cincinnati and organize a thorough campaign of excavation – he was to stay for a dozen years.

Already in 1939 in the very first trench he dug

Blegen unearthed scores of tablets written in Linear B – and soon there were hundreds of them. Such profusion made the archaeologists question whether the script was Minoan or had its origins on the mainland of Greece; and when subsequently more tablets inscribed with these characters were found at other sites on the Greek mainland – at Mycenae and at Thebes – the name "Mycenaean" came rather regularly to be applied to the script.

For over a decade after their discovery the tablets were neither

---

[1] The major dissenter was Strabo who placed Pylos farther north in Triphylia, and his case was taken up in modern times by Wilhelm Dörpfeld. But Blegen's excavations in Messenia re-solved the debate in favor of the southern Pylos. Cf. Blegen and Rawson: *The Palace of Nestor*, I, pt. I, pp. 3ff.; W. A. McDonald: *Progress into the Past* (Indiana University Press, 1967), pp. 229-242.

[2] The passages marked by # are by Velikovsky. The section on Pylos is one of several that were written as a collaborative effort between Jan Sammer and Velikovsky; Velikovsky wanted to highlight the work of Blegen and the chronological problems this archaeologist faced at each site where he dug. The sections on Blegen's excavations at the Argive Heraion and at Troy were also parts of that collaborative effort, although the actual writing is entirely by Jan Sammer. The collaboration involved his writing of certain passages based on research by Velikovsky, Schorr and himself, Velikovsky's editing of those writings, subsequent rewritings, etc. In 1980, at the request of Velikovsky's Estate, Jan Sammer separated out the parts written by himself from the rest of the manuscript. However, some Velikovsky passages are integral and inseparable from Jan Sammer's work; they have therefore been kept and marked by #.

published nor read;[1] but when read, they were found to contain no literary text: They were regularly archive notes, dealing with taxation or conscription, or human and animal census or storage inventory. Nevertheless, interesting parallels could be drawn with the Homeric epics: Pylos is mentioned at the head of nine towns that profess allegiance to it – in Homer and on the tablets – even some of the names of the towns are the same in both sources.[2] And to Blegen's great satisfaction Pylos was found repeatedly mentioned on the tablets retrieved from the palace he identified as Nestor's.[3] Nestor's name, however, was not found.

The tablets, originally not fired but only dried, would have disintegrated long ago, were it not for the fire that destroyed the palace and baked the tablets. A great conflagration raged over the structure; it came rather suddenly, since neither furniture, nor pottery, nor the contents of the storage rooms and archives were removed, nor were the animals led away: But humans all fled.[4] Blegen placed the destruction not long after the Trojan War, at the close of the Mycenaean age.[5] However, no signs of warfare, siege, occupation by people of another culture or occupation in general were found.[6]

The palace and the temple next to it, a sanctuary of Hera, presented Blegen and his collaborators with problems not unlike those that had already occupied him at the cemetery of Argos and then at Troy.

The time of the destruction of the palace of Nestor was determined by the Mycenaean pottery found in the ruins, sealed by the layer of ashes and debris of the final conflagration. Comparing the designs on the pottery in use at the time of the palace's destruction with the established stylistic sequence of Mycenaean pottery, calibrated according to the Egyptian time-scale, the excavators decided that the end of Pylos came ca. the year -1200.[7] But this date was reached at the cost of ignoring the evidence of other pottery pointing to a much later time. In the main building of the palace, among sherds from Mycenaean vases "a not inconsiderable number stood out as of a dif-

---

[1] They were published in 1951 (*The Pylos Tablets; A Preliminary transcription*) and the decipherment was completed by 1953. See below, section »Linear B Deciphered«.
[2] *Iliad*, II. 591-594; Blegen & Rawson: *The Palace of Nestor*, vol. I pt. 1, p. 419.
[3] *The Palace of Nestor*, loc. cit.
[4] *Ibid.*, p. 424.
[5] *Ibid.*, p. 422.
[6] *Ibid.*, p. 422.
[7] *Ibid.*, p. 421.

ferent character: From this material it was possible to reconstruct in whole or in part four pots which may be assigned to a late geometric phase ..."[1] Nor was this an isolated case – such finds were common throughout the palace: "In some places ... in the upper black layer [the level of burning] ... were found, along with the usual Mycenaean pottery, a few glazed sherds of Late Geometric Style as in so many parts of the site, where similar deposits were encountered."[2] If Late Geometric sherds were found next to Mycenaean ones in the level of burning, the question must arise: When was the Palace of Nestor destroyed, ca. -1200 or in the seventh century? To escape this dilemma Blegen postulated "fairly widespread activity on the site in late geometric times"[3] after five centuries of abandonment – this despite his assertion that the conflagration marked "the end of human occupation of the site."[4] But such an explanation is hardly tenable in the light of the stratigraphic situation. If the Late Geometric pottery had been left by new occupants of the hill five hundred years or more after the burning of Nestor's palace, the remains of these vases would not have been found mixed with the ware used by the occupants of the palace at the time of its destruction. The exact position of the Late Geometric pottery merits a closer examination. The pavement of the court was covered by a thin "yellowish-white clayish deposit"; immediately above it was an "extremely black layer" less than a foot deep. In "the yellowish-white stratum [which] unquestionably represents the latest phase of occupation of the palace" were found, besides fragments of Mycenaean pottery "also some pieces of glazed Geometric ware."[5] But how could fragments of seventh-century Geometric ware have come to rest on the floor of Nestor's palace? They "must somehow have penetrated from above." How they could possibly have achieved this, however, finds no easy answer. After the palace's destruction "vegetation spread its mantle over the whole area."[6] To penetrate to the floor

---

[1] *Ibid.*, p. 124. Blegen dates the style "perhaps to the turn from the seventh to the sixth century." The date may have to be revised upwards by a few decades on the basis of the work of J. N. Coldstream (*Greek Geometric Pottery* (London, 1968), p. 330) who dates the Late Geometric Style to between -750 and -680. However the workmanship of the vases is very rough with hardly any design distinguishable; they are not given to precise dating.
[2] *Palace of Nestor*, p. 300.
[3] *Ibid.*, p. 294.
[4] *Ibid.*, p. 424.
[5] *Ibid.*, p. 294.
[6] *Ibid.*, p. 422.

of Nestor's buried palace the sherds would have had to find their way not only through the layer of earth and vegetation but also through the black stratum of the final burning, "a compact layer of smallish stones closely packed in blackish earth."[1] These small stones within the burnt stratum were clearly remains of the roof and walls which had collapsed in the conflagration and covered whatever deposit was left on the floor at the time. A stratigraphic situation such as this allows only one conclusion: The Geometric ware belonged, as did the Mycenaean, to the last occupants of the palace and was left behind when they fled. The collapse of the building in the course of the raging conflagration sealed the deposit in place.

Most of the smaller towns in Messenia suffered a similar fate, and only a handful survived into the subsequent Archaic age.[2]

The Trojans and their Allies

As the host of the Achaeans, gathered from every part of Greece, stepped out of their "curved ships" and filled the plain before Troy till they seemed like "sands of the seashore" to the anxiously watching Hector, the allies of Priam, who had come to his aid, were arrayed opposite them, an army of many nations' and divers tongues. There were Dardanians, led by Anchises, father of Aeneas, Pelasgians and Thracians; tribes from Paphlagonia and Mysia, also Phrygians, Lycians and Carians "of the outland speech", and many others from every region of Asia Minor.

Of all these peoples it is the Phrygians in particular that shall concern us – not only because of the prominent role they are assigned in defending Priam's citadel, but because the time of their presence and influence in Asia Minor is well known from ancient authors and is attested also by numerous archaeological investigations.

"Phrygian art first originated at the beginning of the eighth century" – so wrote Ekrem Akurgal, who devoted a lifetime to the study of the ancient cultures of Anatolia, adding that there is no sign of the Phry-

---

[1] C. W. Blegen in *American Journal of Archaeology* 61 (1957).
[2] Imre Tegyey: »Messenia and the catastrophe at the end of Late Helladic III B« in *Bronze Age Migrations In the Aegean*, pp. 227-232.

gians or any other people in central Asia Minor in the four centuries prior to ca. -800.[1]

The eighth century before the present era, starting in -776, was, together with the beginning of the seventh, a period of great natural upheavals. These changes in nature moved entire nations to migrations in the hope that beyond the horizon fertile lands, not damaged by unchained forces of nature, awaited the conquerors.

It seems that in one of the earliest waves of the eighth-century migrations the Phrygians moved from Thrace over the Hellespont or the Bosporus into Asia Minor. Xanthus the Lydian is said by Strabo to have held the view that the Phrygians arrived in Asia Minor sometime after the Trojan War; but Strabo himself, noting that already in the *Iliad* they are listed among Priam's allies, was of the opinion that the Phrygians' migration must have taken place before the siege of Troy. Then, Strabo wrote, "after Troy was sacked, the Phrygians, whose territory bordered on the Troad, got mastery over it."[2] Arrian, the biographer of Alexander, explained the Phrygians' crossing into Asia Minor as resulting from their being harassed by the Cimmerians.[3] A few decades afterwards these same nomads were to destroy the short-lived Phrygian kingdom. The tradition of how Gordias, the first king of the Phrygians in their new domicile, selected his new capital, Gordion, is a well-known legend.[4] Under Midas, the son of Gordias, the Phrygian kingdom reached the peak of its power;[5] while Midas, even more than his father, was an object of legendary motifs – whatever he touched turned to gold, he had the ears of an ass – he was also a historical person, and is attested in contemporary documents.[6]

---

[1] E. Akurgal: *Phrygische Kunst* (Ankara, 1955), p. 112; cf. idem in *Hittite Art and the Antiquities of Anatolia* (Arts Council of Great Britain, London, 1964), p. 35.

[2] Strabo: *Geography*, transl. by H. L. Jones (*Loeb Classical Library*, 1917), Bk. X, ch, iii.22. Modern scholarship has also attempted to put the Phrygians in Anatolia in time to succor Priam in the thirteenth century (e.g. *The Cambridge Ancient History*, vol. I, 1970, p. 108). The lack of archaeological evidence for their presence there before the eighth century is a serious« drawback to this view. Cf. M. J. Mellink: »Postscript on Nomadic Art« in *Dark Ages and Nomads c. 1000 B.C.; Studies in Iranian and Anatolian Archaeology*, ed. by M. J. Mellink (Leiden, 1964), p. 64.

[3] Arrian, quoted by Eusthates in Denys Periegetes, 322.

[4] Arrian: *The Anabasis of Alexander* 11.3; Justin, XI.7; G. & A. Körte: *Gordion* (Berlin, 1904), pp. 12ff.; R. Graves: *The Greek Myths* (1955), no. 83.

[5] R. S. Young: »Gordion: Preliminary Report, 1953« in *American Journal of Archaeology* 39 (1955), p. 16.

[6] M. Mellink: »Mita, Mushki, and the Phrygians« in *Anadolu Arastirmalari* (Istanbul 1955); cf. Akurgal: *Die Kunst Anatoliens*, pp. 70-71.

He reigned, according to the chronicle of Hieronymus, preserved by Eusebius, from -742 to -696;[1] his prosperity and growing power involved him in international intrigue: He conspired with the rebellious king of Carchemish against Sargon II of Assyria (-722 to -705), and the curbing of Midas was the aim of Sargon's campaign of the year -715.[2] But eastern Anatolia was not yet pacified, and continuing disturbances brought Sargon several more times to the defense of his northeastern frontier; he finally met his death there in battle in -705.

The Phrygian kingdom in Asia Minor had an ephemeral existence.[3] As we saw, no Phrygian presence can be recognized in the archaeology till the beginning or even the middle of the eighth century – and soon after the start of the seventh, about the year -676, the Phrygian kingdom was destroyed in the catastrophic Cimmerian invasion. This is also when Midas met his end[4] and his capital Gordion was burned to the ground.[5] Of the royal tumuli (kurgans) excavated by the Körte brothers, only three are antecedent to the Cimmerian invasion; this suggests that not more than three generations of kings reigned in Gordion from its founding to its destruction.[6]

"The Phrygian kingdom was thus at the apex of its power toward the end of the eighth century, when it apparently extended as far southeast as the Taurus and was in contact with Assyria. This period of power was apparently the time of the adornment and fortification of its capital city."[7] In 1953 a team from the University of Pennsylvania led by Rodney Young, in the course of their work at Gordion, exposed to view a large double gateway with a central courtyard, belonging to the Phrygian period. Its date, like that of most of the Phrygian

---

[1] *Eusebius Werke*, ed. R. Helm (Leipzig, 1913), vol. VII, pp. 89, 92.
[2] Mellink: »Mita, Mushki, and the Phrygians«; Akurgal: *Die Kunst Antoliens*, P. Naster: *L'Asie Mineure et l'Assyrie*, p. 37.
[3] R. S. Young, the excavator of Gordion, estimated a period of "a half century" or more for the flourishing of Phrygian culture at the site – »The Nomadic Impact: Gordion« in *Dark Ages and Nomads*. p. 54.
[4] By suicide according to Eusebius (*Chron.* p. 92) and Strabo (*Geography* I.3.21.).
[5] The Cimmerian destruction level was found in 1956, see Young: »Gordion 1956: Preliminary Report« in *American Journal of Archaeology* 61 (1957), p. 320. Cf. also idem: »The Nomadic Impact: Gordion« pp. 54-56.
[6] Cf. Young: »The excavations at Yassihuyuk-Gordion, 1950« in *Archaeology* 3 (1950), pp. 196-199. The non-royal tumuli were much more numerous. A royal tomb, perhaps of Gordias, was excavated in 1957 – Young: »The Royal Tomb at Gordion«, *Archaeology* 10 (1957), pp. 217-219.
[7] Young: »Gordion 1953: A Preliminary Report«, p. 16.

constructions at Gordion, was put sometime in the eighth century.[1] The manner of construction of the walls of the gateway reminded the excavators of the fortifications at another Anatolian site: The walls of the sixth city at Troy appeared to be nearly duplicated in those of the Phrygian Gate at Gordion. In his report of the discovery Young wrote:

> In their batter as well as their masonry construction the walls of the Phrygian Gate at Gordion find their closest parallel in the wall of the sixth city of Troy ... Though separated in time by five hundred years or thereabouts, the two fortifications may well represent a common tradition of construction in north-western Anatolia; if so, intermediate examples have yet to be found.[2]

The search for intermediate examples is bound to be fruitless since the time gap between Troy VI and Gordion is unreal, a phantom construct of historians. Whereas the Trojans had a long tradition building in stone, the Phrygian gateway appears as if out of nowhere, without any visible antecedents; yet at the same time it displays technical skills that speak of a long period of development. This apparent contradiction is also noted by Young:

> ... The planning of the [Phrygian] gateway and the execution of its masonry imply a familiarity with contemporary military architecture and long practice in the handling of stone for masonry. The masonry, in fact, with its sloping batter and its more or less regular coursing recalls neither the cyclopean Hittite masonry of the Anatolian plateau in earlier times, nor the commonly prevalent contemporary construction of crude brick. The closest parallel is the masonry of the walls of Troy VI, admittedly very much earlier. If any links exist to fill this time-gap, they must lie in west Anatolia rather than on the plateau.[3]

The Trojan fortifications belong according to the revised chronology, in the eighth century, and thus were roughly contemporary with the Phrygian.

A little light is thus shed on the alliance between Phrygians and Trojans, known to Homer; and the date of the Trojan War is delimited by the period when the Phrygians were a power in Asia Minor, between the years -750 and -676.

---

[1] *Ibid.*, loc. cit.
[2] *Ibid.*, p. 13.
[3] Idem: »The Nomadic Impact: Gordion«, p. 52.

Regarding the Cimmerians and the extent of Homer's knowledge of them, the question was already discussed by various ancient authors. Strabo, for one, was certain that Homer was acquainted with the historical Cimmerians, "for surely if he knows the name of the Cimmerians [*Odyssey*] he is not ignorant of the people themselves – the Cimmerians who in Homer's own time, or shortly before his time, overran the whole country from the Bosporus to Ionia. At least he intimates that the very climate of their country is gloomy, and the Cimmerians, as he says, are 'shrouded in mist and cloud, and never does the shining sun look upon them, but deadly night is spread o'er them.'"[1]

The Cimmerians are not mentioned in the *Iliad* by name, only in the *Odyssey*,[2] but it is rather probable that the Amazons who are mentioned in the *Iliad* as well as in later authors like Diodorus,[3] were the historical Cimmerians. Quite possibly the tales about the Amazons arose from accounts of the warlike Cimmerian womenfolk who used to accompany the men in battle.[4]

After destroying the Phrygian kingdom and pushing the Phrygians toward the Bosporus, the Cimmerians ravaged the western regions of Asia Minor settled by Greeks – Aeolis and Ionia,[5] attacking Smyrna, Miletus, Sinope and other coastal cities.[6] It appears that Homer refers to the Cimmerian invasion of Phrygia in the passage where he has Priam recall how once he "went into vine-clad Phrygia" and there saw "the Phrygian men with their gloaming horses, most numerous, encamped by the bank of the Sangarios. For I was mustered as an ally among them on that day when the Amazons came. But even so, they were not as many as are the glancing-eyed Achaeans." Rhys Carpenter, discussing this passage in his *Folk Tale, Fiction and Saga in the Homeric Epics* reasoned thus:

> "... it is quite possible, and even probable, that the last stand [against the Cimmerians] was made behind the long, curving barrier of the great

---

[1] Strabo: *Geography* I.1.10 (transl. by H. L. Jones, *Loeb Class. Libr.*, 1917). Cf. ibid., III.2.12.

[2] However, the fact that some of the *variae lectiones* in the manuscripts give different readings of the name throws some doubt on Strabo's argument. Cf. Rhys Carpenter: *Folk Tale, Fiction and Saga in the Homeric Epics* (University of California Press, 1946), pp. 148-149.

[3] Diodorus Siculus II. 45.

[4] This was the view expressed by Emile Mireaux in his *Les poèmes homériques et l'histoire grecque* (Paris, 1948-49).

[5] Strabo III.2.12.

[6] Herodotus IV.12.

Phrygian river, the Sangarios. Here all the forces of western Asia Minor would have gathered to stop the terrible archers on horseback, who nonetheless overwhelmed them and rode westward to the sea. In the pages of the Greek historian Diodoros, centuries later, these same horsemen are the Amazons. If they were already Amazons for Homer, the date of Priam's reference must be the year of Midas' downfall, 676 B.C. ... If the author of the Iliad was an Ionian Greek of the early seventh century, the most impressive and tremendous political event of his lifetime must have been the Cimmerian destruction of the Phrygian empire. Of what else could he have been thinking when he made Priam speak of Phrygian armies gathered against the Amazons on the banks of the Sangarios?"[1]

According to Herodotus the Cimmerians were originally displaced from the Asiatic steppes by the Scythians: But it was not until the second half of the seventh century that the Scythian hordes themselves arrived on the scene and, after decimating the Cimmerians with the aid of Assyria, pushed southward to the very border of Egypt, engulfing Palestine. The population fled in terror before "the noise of the horsemen and bowmen."[2]

The Scythians at that time were worshippers of Mars, whom they represented as a sword, for a while leaving their ancient worship of Saturn in abeyance. They were called Umman-Manda, or "People of Saturn" in Akkadian and in the so-called Hittite literary texts.

If the author of the *Iliad* composed his poem in the early decades of the seventh century, he may or may not have known of the Scythians. At one point in the *Iliad* there is mention of a people named "the proud Hippemolgoi, drinkers of milk" and of "the Abioi, the most righteous of all men."[3] A scholium on Homer considers these to be tribes of Scythians[4] as does Strabo: "How then," he asked, "could the poet be ignorant of the Scythians if he called certain people 'Hippemolgi' [mare-milkers] and Galactophagi' [curd-eaters]? For that the people of his time were wont to call the Scythians 'Hippemolgi'. Hesiod

---

[1] Carpenter: *Folk Tale, Fiction and Saga in the Homeric Epics*, pp. 175-176. Cf. Strabo 1.2.9: "The writers of chronicles make it plain that Homer knew the Cimmerians, in that they fix the date of the invasion of the Cimmerians either a short time before Homer, or else in Homer's own time."

[2] Jeremiah 4:29.

[3] *Iliad* XIII.5-6. A scholium takes the description "righteous' to refer to the Scythian custom of holding all property in common (*Venetus A*). Cf. Herodotus' description of the nomadic Massagetae (1.216.1), Nasamones (IV.172.2) and Agathyrses (IV.104). See also F. Buffière: *Les mythes d'Homère et la pensée grecque* (Paris, 1956), pp. 362-363.

[4] *Venetus A* to Iliad XIII.6.

too is witness in the words cited by Eratosthenes: 'the Ethiopians, the Ligurians; and also the Scythians, Hippemolgi'."[1] That the *Iliad* is referring to some nomadic tribes appears certain. Whether it is the Scythians who are meant and whether they had by then already left the plains of South Russia cannot be decided on the basis of the vague Homeric reference.

In the tenth year of the siege, after the action described in the *Iliad*, Priam was said to have received a contingent of Ethiopians under the leadership of Memnon. The brave Ethiopians fought valiantly against the Greeks and caused them much hardship, till Achilles finally slew Memnon and caused them to depart. Some of these traditions are very ancient, in the *Odyssey* Nestor recalls the death of his son Antilochos,[2] who died by the spear of "the glorious son of shining Dawn",[3] which is an epithet of Memnon. Later in the *Odyssey* the Ethiopian warrior is mentioned by name as "great Memnon".[4] The epic *Aethiopis*, a sequel to the *Iliad*, recounted the deeds of Memnon and of the Ethiopians at Troy – it is considered to be among the earliest of the post-Homeric epics, possibly as early as the seventh century.[5]

The heyday of Ethiopian power lasted a little over half a century, from the end of the eighth to the middle of the seventh centuries; following their emergence out of Nubia, they fought repeatedly and at times successfully with the Assyrians for control over Egypt. The Ethiopian host mentioned in the *Iliad* suggests an Ethiopian attempt to outflank the Assyrian enemy by sending an expeditionary force in support of the Phrygians, under pressure from the Ionians in the West

---

[1] Strabo: *Geography* VII.3.7.
[2] *Odyssey*, III.111-112.
[3] *Odyssey*, IV.185-202.
[4] *Odyssey*, XI.522.
[5] We know of the contents of the *Aethiopis* only from the summary of it made by Proclus (*Chrestomathia* ii), preserved by Photius. It was ascribed to Arctinus of Miletus "who is said to have flourished in the first Olympiad (776 B.C.)" – H. G. Evelyn-White: *Hesiod, The Homeric Hymns and Homerica*, Loeb Classical Library, (1914), p. xxxi. For several reasons this date appears much too early – writing was only re-introduced into Greece in the second half of the eighth century, and the *Aethiopis* is not likely to be earlier than the *Iliad*. A seventh-century date thus appears more probable. Later classical writers wrote extensively about Memnon, and it is not excluded that the *Aethiopis* was among their sources. Notable among these were the so-called "chronicles" of Dictys of Crete (lv. 5-8. VI. 10) and of Dares the Phrygian (25, 33), both apparently-composed in the first century (see the translation by R. M. Frazer (Indiana University Press, 1966)), and the *Posthomerica* of Quintus Smyrnaeus. (Bk. II) dating most probably from the fourth. The accounts of Diodorus Siculus (11.22.1ff) and Plato (*Laws* III.685C) are of less value being contaminated by the tabulations of Ctesias.

and the Assyrians and Cimmerians in the East.[1]

Again and again we are brought to the same period – the time of Phrygian power in Asia Minor, of its destruction by the Cimmerian invasion, and of the Ethiopian rule in Egypt is the end of the eighth and beginning of the seventh centuries before the present era. Then this is the historical background of the Trojan War, and if there be any core of truth to the story it must be seen in relation to these events.

The Western Colonies

Greek literary tradition recounts many tales of the "returns" of the heroic generation that fought at Troy – but few of the plunderers of Priam's citadel reached home safely, and those who did kept their thrones for only a little while; most were condemned to years of wandering in the far reaches of the known world until finally, in despair of ever again seeing their homes, they settled on distant shores from one end of the Mediterranean to the other. It was as if the return home was blocked – not just by stormy seas, but by upheavals and dislocations that deprived the returnees of shelter in their own land. Following the disasters that afflicted the Greek lands, the last of the heroic generation turned into wanderers and pirates, seeking for living space far from their own ravaged habitations.[2] Strabo, the Roman geographer, thus described the situation that ensued in the wake of Troy's fall:

> For it came about that, on account of the length of the campaign, the Greeks of that time, and the barbarians as well, lost both what they had at home and what they had acquired by the campaign; and so, after the destruction of Troy, not only did the victors turn to piracy because of their poverty, but still more the vanquished who survived the war. And indeed, it is said that a great many cities were founded by them along the whole seacoast outside of Greece, and in some parts of the interior also.[3]

---

[1] Mireaux: *Les poèmes homériques et l'histoire grecque*. Mireaux sees many parallels between Homer's Ethiopians and the rulers of Egypt's XXVth Dynasty, most notably their bountiful sacrifices to the gods (*Il.* I.423-425; *Od.* I.22-26). As several authors have noted it was these feasts that gave rise to Herodotus' story of the Table of the Sun (III.18), located on the upper reaches of the Nile. The parallel with Homer's Ethiopians is drawn also by A.D. Godley in a note to his translation of Herodotos (*Loeb Classical Library*, 1921). In Mireaux's view the verses of *Od.* I.23-24 that tell of the Ethiopians as divided into two groups, western and eastern, is an interpolation based on later geographical knowledge.

[2] Cf. above, section »A Gap Closed«.

[3] Strabo: *Geography*.

Excavations in Sicily over the past one hundred years have revealed evidence of extensive contact with Greece in the Mycenaean Age. As to the people with whom the Mycenaeans traded, their remains attest to a prosperous culture, beginning in the Early Bronze Age and lasting for many centuries; but then, after the latest style of imported Mycenaean ware had run its course,[1] no new pottery, actually no sign of any human presence, appears until the late eighth century. Scholars conclude that Sicilian civilization of the Late Bronze Age "came to an abrupt end about the end of the thirteenth century B.C."[2] Were the same causes which brought to a close the age of Mycenaean greatness also active on the far-removed island of Sicily? Archaeologists can only speculate about causes; but on one point their verdict is clear – "A real Dark Age set in only to be brought to an end five centuries later with the Greek colonization of Sicily and Southern Italy."[3] Regarding the new Greek settlements, archaeology and tradition agree that the first ones were established near the end of the eighth century and the beginning of the seventh. The founding of colonies in the western Mediterranean was one of the earliest achievements of the historical Greeks as they emerged out of the ruins of the Mycenaean Age. Syracuse, on the eastern coast of Sicily, was founded, according to the almost universally accepted tradition, ca. 735 BC;[4] Thucydides wrote that "Gela was built in the forty-fifth year after Syracuse by Antiphemus, that brought a colony out of Rhodes."[5] This yields a date of ca. -690 for the founding of Gela on the island's southern shore.[6] A tradition preserved by Eusebius has Gela founded in the same year as the city of Phaselis in Asia Minor. Eusebius' date for both cities is -690, closely matching that of Thucydides.[7] These traditions were set

---

[1] The latest style was Late Helladic III B with a small number of exemplars of Late Helladic III C. See W. Taylour: *Mycenaean Pottery in Italy and Adjacent Areas* (Cambridge, 1958) p. 74; H.- G. Buchholz: »Ägäische Funde und Kultureinflüsse in den Randgebieten des Mittelmeers«, *Archäologischer Anzeiger* 89 (1974) pp. 343, 345, 346, 349-350. Thapsos, near Syracuse and Agrigento, are the two main find spots.

[2] L. B. Brea: *Sicily Before the Greeks* (New York, 1966) p. 130.

[3] *Ibid., loc. cit.*; cf. M. Guido: *Sicily: An Archaeological Guide* (New York, 1967) pp. 133, 196-198.

[4] M. Miller: *The Sicilian Colony Dates: Studies in Chronography I* (SUNY Press, Albany, 1972) pp. 13, 21, 32, 33, 41, 42, 110, 182.

[5] Thucydides: *The Peloponnesian War* VI.4.

[6] Cf. A. G. Woodhead: *The Greeks in the West* (London, 1962) pp. 51-52; P. Griffo and L. von Matt: *Gela: The Ancient Greeks in Sicily* (Greenwich, Conn., 1968).

[7] This tradition is given in the version of Eusebius' *Chronicle* preserved by Jerome, Dionysius and Barhebraeus; cf. Miller: *The Sicilian Colony Dates*, pp. 14, 187.

forth in greater detail by a Greek historian whose works are no longer extant except for fragments preserved by other ancient writers. In one surviving fragment from his book *On the Cities of Asia*[1] Philostephanos wrote that Antiphemos, the founder of Sicilian Gela, was a brother of Lacius who founded Phaselis in Asia Minor, both brothers hailing from Rhodes – they had been in the company of Mopsus as he made his way into Cilicia in the years following the Trojan War. In the chronology of Philostephanos, then, Gela was founded in the same generation that saw the fall of Troy, by one of the warriors who took part in that war; and since, as we have seen, the historical date of Gela's establishment is acknowledged by the best authorities to be ca. 690 BC, Priam's city could not have fallen more than two or three decades earlier.[2]

If the Sicilian Late Bronze Age, contemporary with the Mycenaean Age in Greece, ended abruptly about the time of the Trojan War, the stratigraphic sequence yields no evidence about the dark centuries supposedly separating it from the Geometric Age. After only a few decades the Geometric Age was interrupted by the arrival of Greek colonists, bringing their own distinctive culture from Corinth and Rhodes and other places in Greece. Despite the marked changes in the archaeological finds after the cessation of imported Mycenaean ware, many of the old Mycenaean influences continued to flourish both in the native settlements of the late eighth and early seventh centuries and in the Greek colonies – the examples are very numerous.

"The strength of 'Mycenaean' influence in Sicily [in Late Geometric times] is attested by a tholos tomb at Sant-Angleo Muxaro, north of Agrigento [an ancient port on Sicily's southern coast]; but it can scarcly be appreciated without knowledge of the Mycenaean royal tombs."[3] The "large and unusual tholos tombs"[4] at Muxaro "are, in fact, real tholoi, comparable with the Mycenaean ones"[5] even though they are dated "much later than Mycenaean times"[6] – this because of the Geo-

---

[1] In Athenaeus: *Deipnosophistae* VII. 298.
[2] A Cretan named Entimus is said to have assisted Antiphemos in the founding of the city; and traces of Minoan influence at Gela have been noted by E. Langlotz (*Ancient Greek Sculpture of South Italy and Sicily* [New York, 1965], transl. by A. Hicks, p. 15) and by many others.
[3] Langlotz: *Ancient Greek Sculpture*, p. 15.
[4] Guido: *Sicily*, p. 102.
[5] Brea: *Sicily Before the Greeks*, p. 174.
[6] Guido: *Sicily*, p. 102; the author dates them "probably from the VIII to the middle of the V" pre-Christian centuries (p. 129).

metric pottery found inside. How the Sicilians were able to imitate the dome-shaped tholos tombs half a millennium after such constructions ceased to be made in Greece, and despite being "cut off from contact with the Aegean" during the same period[1] is a puzzling question, especially if we consider that scholars deny that any such tombs were built in Sicily in the five preceding centuries, though they were common in the Late Bronze Age.[2] But let us enter some of the tombs and examine the objects found inside. Little pots with geometric and orientalizing designs indicated a period not earlier than the beginning of the seventh century.[3] Among them the excavators discovered two "splendid gold rings with animal figures incised in their settings."[4] One of these "shows a cow suckling a calf, the other a strange feline animal, or perhaps a wolf,"[5] depicted in a way clearly descended "from remote Mycenaean traditions."[6] Not only the rings, but gold bowls found in the same tomb "derive from Mycenaean gold-work."[7] "Perhaps here again we have a far-distant echo of the Mycenaean world."[8]

The same puzzling survivals from Mycenaean times appear also at another Sicilian site – at Segesta, in the western part of the island. The founding of Segesta was dated by tradition to the years following the Trojan War, and was ascribed to a Trojan named Aegestes.[9] The eighth and seventh-century Geometric pottery from Segesta displays startling Mycenaean influences. "A good example is the schematized drawing of a bull, moving from the left to the right, with horns butting against an unidentified object. This motif was a common one on Mycenaean and, more generally, Aegean pottery." Other motifs of Mycenaean derivation include stylized floral patterns and tassels with meandering lines; these motifs "are not paralleled in Geometric pot-

---

[1] T. J. Dunbabin: »Minos and Daidalos in Sicily«, *Papers of the British School at Rome*, Vol. XVI (New series, vol. III [1948]) p. 9: "The complete absence of Protogeometric, and of Geometric older than the second half of the eighth century, makes it clear that the Minoan-Mycenaean contacts were quite broken."
[2] E.g., at Thapsos, Cozzo del Pantano and Caltagirone; cf. Woodhead: *The Greeks in the West*, p. 22.
[3] Brea: *Sicily Before the Greeks*, p. 174; but cf. above p. 319, n. 6.
[4] *Ibid.*, p. 175.
[5] G. K. Galinsky: *Aeneas, Sicily, and Rome* (Princeton, 1969) p. 86.
[6] Brea: *Sicily Before the Greeks*, p. 175. For photographs of the ring, see E. Sjöqvist: *Sicily and the Greeks* (Chicago University Press, 1973) fig. 1 on p. 5.
[7] Langlotz: *Ancient Greek Sculpture*, p. 15.
[8] Guido, quoted in Galinsky: *Aeneas, Sicily, and Rome*, p. 86.
[9] Strabo: *Geography* 6.2.5; 6.1.3. Another name for Segesta was Aegesta.

tery."[1] The examples are many; and they are all the more remarkable since the last Mycenaean pottery on the island is said to have gone out of use some four or five hundred years earlier. These observations caused much amazement among art historians, but brought no viable suggestion as to how the motifs could have been transmitted through the Dark Age to influence the Geometric ware of Segesta half a millennium later. Could the Phoenicians perhaps have preserved the Mycenaean tradition and, on establishing themselves on the island, have imparted them to the native people of Sicily?, wondered one scholar; but he rejected the thought, for the earliest Phoenician settlement in Sicily dates from the seventh century, and what was found there "of course is not Mycenaean."[2]

Wherever the archaeologists turned they found a blank in the archaeological sequence where five centuries should have left at least a trace. At Gela "there is a gap ... between the Bronze Age sites, belonging at the outside to the middle of the second millennium, and the objects from the first Greek occupation in the seventh century B.C." And the explanation? "This is one confirmation that the native peoples left the coastal regions at the close of the age when, at the dawn of the Greek world, the Mycenaeans and other seafarers who came in their wake brought piracy, violence and looting along with trade." [3] At Thapsos, in the vicinity of Syracuse, "Mycenaean imports ... cease towards the end of Mycenaean IIIB, and this implies that the coastal villages were abandoned by about 1270 B.C. ... In the late VIII century Thapsos was occupied again for a short time by Greek colonists ..."[4] If the coast was abandoned during the Dark Age, did life continue in the interior? At Morgantina in central Sicily, "below the earliest defences put up by the colonists ... late Mycenaean XIII century ware and Ausonian pottery of the XII century [was followed] by VII century pottery of Sant'Angelo Muxaro type."[5] Between the levels, nothing at all was found.

The responsibility for creating the Dark Age of Sicily lies with the erroneous Egyptian timetable. Some of the Mycenaean ware found

---

[1] Galinsky: *Aeneas, Sicily, and Rome*, p. 83.
[2] *Ibid.*, p. 89.
[3] Griffo and von Matt: *Gela*, p. 56.
[4] Guido: *Sicily*, pp. 196-198.
[5] *Ibid.*, p. 133. On the excavations at Morgantina, cf. the reports in *American Journal of Archaeology*, vols 62, 64, 65 and 66.

on the island "is exactly the same pottery as that found in Egypt in the ruins of Tell el-Amarna, the capital of Amenophis [Akhnaton]."[1] All the indications from Sicilian sites showing direct succession of the Late Bronze Age and Greek colonial periods counted for nothing when an absolute time scale, introduced from Egypt, demanded the insertion of five empty centuries. As one scholar admitted in another context, "the Aegean prehistorians have no choice but to adapt themselves to the Egyptologists."[2]

The Date of Carthage's Founding

The Phoenicians, who are credited with imparting the alphabet to the Greeks, themselves left few documents, though we know that they had their historians and kept official chronicles. Apart from the laconic testimony of some scattered inscriptions carved in stone, Phoenician writings have perished; for what we know of their history we depend on the reports of Greek and Roman authors who were not kindly disposed towards them. A grim struggle was waged for centuries between the Greeks and Romans on the one hand, and the Phoenicians and their western offshoot, the Carthaginians, on the other, in which the prize was nothing less than the political and commercial control of the Mediterranean. It began as early as the Orientalizing period of the eighth and early seventh centuries with the rivalry of Greek and Phoenician settlers in the West, and culminated with Alexander's capture of Tyre in the fourth century, Rome's defeat of Carthage after the exhausting Punic wars of the third, and Carthage's destruction in the second. Carthage had been the focus of Phoenician presence in the West for many hundreds of years before it was leveled to the ground by the Romans in -146. The Roman historian Appian gave a round figure of seven centuries for Carthage's existence, which would imply a date for its founding about the middle of the ninth century. Timaeus, the Greek chronographer, gave the year -814 as the date of Carthage's founding[3] by Dido or Elissa, who had fled with a group of

---
[1] Brea: *Sicily Before the Greeks.*
[2] G. Cadogan: »Dating the Aegean Bronze Age Without Radiocarbon« in *Archaeometry* 20 (1978) p. 212.
[3] *The Antiquities of the Jews*

followers from the hands of her murderous brother Pygmalion, king of Tyre. Josephus dated Dido's flight 155 years after the accession of Hiram, the ally of David and Solomon, that is, in -826. Another tradition, associated with the fourth-century Sicilian chronographer Philistos, placed Carthage's founding "a man's life-length" before the fall of Troy. Despite the fact that Philistos' dating of the Trojan War is unknown, scholars have assumed that he put the date of the founding of Carthage in the thirteenth century.[1]

Yet Appian, who followed Philistos in dating the founding of Carthage "fifty years before the capture of Troy"[2] knew that the city, destroyed in -146, had had a lifetime of not more than seven hundred years.[3] Thus Appian dated the Trojan War to ca. -800, and there is no reason to think that Philistos did not do likewise.

Archaeology, however, does not support a mid- or late-ninth century date for Carthage's founding. After many years of digging archaeologists have succeeded to penetrate to the most ancient of Carthage's buildings. P. Cintas, excavating a chapel dedicated to the goddess Tanit, found in the lowest levels a small rectangular structure with a foundation deposit of Greek orientalizing vases datable to the last quarter of the eighth century. These are still the earliest signs of human habitation at the site; although Cintas originally held out hope that there would be found remains of the earliest settlers of the end of the ninth century, the years have not substantiated such expectation.[4] Scholars are now for the most part ready to admit that the ancient chronographers' estimate of the date of the city's founding was exaggerated.[5] But if Carthage was founded ca. -725 the Trojan War would, in the scheme of Philistos and Appian, need to be placed in the first quarter of the seventh century.

---

[1] Pauly's *Realencyclopädie*, article »Karthago«; G. C. Picard: *The Life and Death of Carthage* (London, 1968), p. 30.

[2] Bk. VIII, pt. I. *The Punic Wars* I.1.

[3] Bk. VIII, ch. 132.

[4] J. N. Coldstream: *Geometric Greece* (London, 1977) p. 240; Picard: *The Life and Death of Carthage*, pp. 34ff.

[5] Picard: *The Life and Death of Carthage*, pp. 34, 37; Coldstream: *Geometric Greece*, p. 240. A. R. Burn long ago pointed to this tendency of the ancient chronographers to give inflated estimates of past dates. See his »Dates in Early Greek History«, *Journal of Hellenic Studies* 55 (1935), pp. 130-146. Cf. R. Carpenter: »A Note on the Foundation Date of Carthage«, *American Journal of Archaeology* 68 (1964) p. 178.

Tarshish

According to the picture which emerges with the removal of the dark centuries from ancient history, the Late Minoan civilization finds its place at the beginning of the first millennium before the present era alongside the Mycenaean culture of mainland Greece and the New Kingdom in Egypt. In Israel the corresponding period gets underway with the anointing of Israel's first king, David, and the brilliant reign of his son and successor, Solomon; it continues with the divided monarchy till the time of Isaiah.

The impressive power of Minoan Crete, whose ships plied the sea-lanes of the ancient Mediterranean and regularly called at Levantine ports, and whose rulers were for a time uncontested masters of the busy, and vital, trade routes, could not have passed unnoticed on the pages of the Old Testament. And indeed, in several books of the Scriptures frequent reference is made to a trading nation called Tarshish. Biblical scholars widely disagree on the whereabouts of Tarshish: But Minoan Crete is not among the suggested sites.

The debate had an early start: The *Septuagint*, the Greek version of the Old Testament, translated Tarshish as Carthage;[1] Josephus and others with him identified Tarshish with Tarsus in Cilicia;[2] Julius Africanus thought it was a name for Rhodes or for Cyprus;[3] Eusebius and Hippolytus conjectured that the city of Tartessos in Iberia, mentioned by Herodotus and other ancient writers[4] was the Biblical Tarshish.[5] Modern authors are divided between Tartessos in Iberia[6] and Tarsus in

---

[1] Cf. Jerome (St. Hieronymus) in his Latin translation of the Scriptures, the Vulgate, in the passage Ezekiel 27:2.

[2] Josephus: *Jewish Antiquities* I. vi. 1; the Scholiast to Lycophron's *Cassandra*, 653; Stephen of Byzantium: 'Ligystiné', Cod. A; Eustathius to Dion, 195.

[3] Quoted in G. Syncellus: *Chronography*, 380.

[4] Herodotus 1.163; IV 152, 191; Sfesichorus (fl. -608) in Strabo 3.2.11; the Scholiast to Aristophanes, Ranae, 475; Eustathius to Dion, 337.

[5] Eusebius: *Chronicle* 11.17 in Syncellus: *Chronography*, 91; Hippolytus: *Chronicon Paschale*, II. 98.

[6] S. Mazzarino: *Fra Oriente e Occidente* (Florence, 1947), p. 272; G. Charles Picard: *La vie quotidienne à Carthage au temps d'Hannibal* (Paris, 1958), p. 265, n. 7; A. Schulten: *Tartessos*, second ed. (Madrid, 1945), pp. 54ff.; A. Garcia y Bellido: *La Peninsula Ibérica en los comienzos de su Historia* (Madrid, 1954), pp. 170ff.; the last-named author professes not to be absolutely certain about this identification. Cf. D. Harden: *The Phoenicians* (London, 1962), p. 160. P. Bosch-Gimpera considers it very doubtful: *Zephyrus* 13 (1952), p. 15; *La nouvelle Clio* 3 (1951).

Cilicia[1] – although some would regard the expression "ships of Tarshish" as a general term for ships sailing on long-distance voyages;[2] others consider the name Tarshish to refer to foreign lands in general[3] and William F. Albright and several others with him, suggested that it referred to mines for precious ores and was applied to certain countries which produced them.[4] However, as another scholar rightly remarks, Tarshish is for the writers of the Old Testament a specific land[5] – it is mentioned in the company of Lud (Lydia) and Javan (Ionia).[6] The great perplexity of scholarship on this question and the fact that none of the suggested locations for Tarshish was compelling enough to have produced a general concensus, result from a mistaken chronological scheme which eliminated the possibility of a correct identification before it was ever suggested.

I will attempt to bring evidence in support of Velikovsky's view that Tarshish was the name employed by the writers of the Old Testament to designate Crete as a whole, or its chief city Knossos.[7]

The first mention in the *Book of Kings* of this geographical location refers to the activities of Solomon: "The king had at sea a navy of

---

[1] G. Conteneau: *La civilization phénicienne* (Paris, 1949), p. 235; Bérard: *L'expansion et la colonization grecques jusqu'aux guerres médiques* (Paris, 1960) p. 129; H. L. Lorimer: *Homer and the Monuments* (London, 1950), pp. 65ff. On Tarsus see also J. Boardman in *Journal of Hellenic Studies* 85 (1965), pp. 16ff. Cf. U. Täckholm in *Opuscula romana* 5 (1965), pp. 143ff. and W. Culican: *The First Merchant Ventures* (London, 1966), pp. 77ff.

[2] Garcia y Bellido, Bosch-Gimpera and Conteneau, cited above.

[3] Conteneau: *La civilization phénicienne*.

[4] Albright: *Bulletin of the American Schools of Oriental Research* 83 (1941), pp. 14ff.; Cintas: *Céramique punique* (Paris, 1950), p. 578; Hitti: *History of Syria* (London, 1951), p. 104.

[5] J. M. Blazquez: *Tartessos y Los Origenes de la colonizacion fenicia en Occidente* (Universidad de Salamanca, 1975), p. 18. This fact should be remembered in connection with C. Gordon's attempt to interpret the name "Tarshish" with the "wine-dark sea" of Homer – *Journal of Near-Eastern Studies* 37 (1978), pp. 51-52.

[6] Isaiah 66:19; cf. Psalm 72:10: "The kings of Tarshish and of the isles shall bring presents: the kings of Sheba shall offer gifts."

[7] The name for Crete in the Bible is generally assumed to have been Caphthor (Keftiu of the Egyptian texts). Velikovsky has already indicated that Caphthor is the Biblical designation for Cyprus (*Ages in Chaos*, vol. I, section »Troglodytes or Carians?«, n. 17). It follows that the tribute bringers from Keftiu depicted on the walls of Egyptian tombs of the Eighteenth Dynasty were in reality Cypriots, and not Cretans, and that the homeland of the Philistines was Cyprus, and not Crete. The idea that Caphthor refers to Cyprus was long ago expressed by Birch (»Mémoire sur une patère égyptienne du Musée du Louvre [1857]«, *Mém. Soc. Imp. Ant, Fr.* XXIV [1858]) but found little support. Cf. H.R. Hall: »The Peoples of the Sea« in *Recueil d'études égyptologigues dédiées à la mémoire de Jean-François Champollion* (Paris, 1922), p. 300.

Tharshish with the navy of Hiram: once in three years came the navy of Tharshish bringing gold and silver, ivory and apes, and peacocks."[1]

These precious or exotic items were brought from Ophir, a land whose location is uncertain – but it must have been a rather distant place, considering that the return voyage took three years.[2]

In the next, ninth, century, King Jehoshaphat "made ships of Tharshish to go to Ophir for gold: but they went not; for the ships were broken at Ezion-geber."[3] The parallel account in the *Book of Chronicles* explains the destruction as being due to the Lord's wrath at Jehoshaphat's alliance with the wicked Ahaziah of Israel.[4] It would thus appear that the Minoans had a fleet on the Red Sea which participated with the Phoenician navy in trading ventures to far-away lands. Ezion-geber also must have been the harbor whence the ships of Tarshish set out on their long journey to Ophir in the time of Solomon.[5] The ill-fated attempt by Jehoshaphat to resume the voyages to Ophir was cut short by the intervention of nature, if we may so understand the verse in the forty-eighth Psalm: "Thou breakest the ships of Tarshish with an east wind."[6]

The destruction of the fleet from Tarshish at Ezion-geber did not stop

---

[1] I Kings 10:22; cf. I Chron. 9:21.

[2] Suggestions for the site of Ophir have ranged over the five continents, and this is not the place to discuss their relative merits. Some part of Africa or India could furnish the products listed as coming from Ophir; both are accessible from Ezion-geber on the Red Sea. The three-year return voyage is compatible with a journey around Africa (cf. Herodotus IV. 42 for the three year duration of the circumnavigation of Africa in the time of Pharaoh Necho II, i.e., the late seventh or early sixth centuries. Since King Hiram of Tyre, in association with Solomon, also sent his own ships, unassisted by the Tarshish fleet, to Ophir [Kings 9:27-28, 10:11; II Chron. 8:17-18, 9:10], it is not unthinkable that the Phoenician sailors despatched more than three hundred years later by Necho II, had prior knowledge of the route.) In recent years R. D. Barnett has made a detailed and plausible case for locating Ophir in India – though his placement of Tarshish in the same region is untenable. See Barnett: *A Catalogue of the Nimrud Ivories in the British Museum* (London, 1957) pp. 59-60, 168; *Antiquity* 32 (1958), p. 230. For a general discussion of Solomon's trading ventures, see O. Eissfeldt: *The Hebrew Kingdom* (Cambridge, 1965), pp. 56ff.

[3] I Kings 22:48.

[4] II Chronicles 20:35-37. The words "to make ships to go to Tarshish" should likely be understood as meaning ships of the navy of Tarshish which were being readied for the voyage to Ophir. The passage may be based on a misunderstanding of a tradition more accurately recorded in the Book of Kings.

[5] Cf. n. 2 above.

[6] Psalm 48:7. The passage may, however, refer to a later event. Whether the storm alluded to in the Psalm has any connection with the very violent eruption of the volcano on the island of Thera north of Crete (which, by the revised chronology, belongs in the mid-ninth century) must remain an open question.

that nation's commercial activity, for in the next century we again hear of the ships of Tarshish frequenting the port of Tyre in Phoenicia. The prophet Isaiah in his message to Tyre refers to some overwhelming disaster which overtook the city in his time;[1] and since Tyre had been a major base for the ships of Tarshish, they are said to bemoan their loss: "Howl ye, ships of Tarshish, for it [Tyre] is laid waste, so that there is no house, no entering in ..." The inhabitants of the devastated city are invited to "pass over to Tarshish" – possibly indicating that some of Tyre's citizens resettled on Crete. As a sign of the two countries' commercial interdependence Tyre is called a "daughter of Tarshish". The ships of Tarshish are said to be fatally weakened by the loss of their chief port of call: "Howl ye, ships of Tarshish, for your strength is laid waste."

The tradition of the close links which had existed, ever since Hiram's expeditions to Ophir, between the ships of Tarshish and the merchant city of Tyre was re-echoed down the centuries. In the time of the Babylonian exile Ezekiel wrote in his message to Tyre: "Tarshish was thy merchant by reason of the multitude of all kinds of riches ... the ships of Tarshish did sing of thee in thy market: and thou wast replenished and made very glorious in the midst of the seas."[2]

The trade between Tarshish and the Levant continued in the mid-seventh century, as is shown by the story of Jonah, who was able to board at Joppa (Jaffa) a ship making a regular commercial run to Tarshish.[3]

So far we have based our discussion of the identity of Tarshish on Biblical sources; but there also exists an allusion to that land in another source, a cuneiform text found about a hundred years ago at Assur on the Tigris. The text is part of the annals of the Assyrian king Esarhaddon, who ruled over Assyria from -681 to -669. It reads:

> All the kingdoms from (the islands) amidst the sea – from the country of Iadanan and Jaman as far as Tarshishi bowed to my feet and I received heavy tribute.[4]

---

[1] Isaiah, chapter 23.
[2] Ezekiel 27:12, 25.
[3] The Book of Jonah purports to deal with events of the mid-seventh century when Nineveh, Assyria's capital, was still standing, but in paramount danger of destruction by hostile armies. Although the book was written much later than this, some of the background of the story, such as the Tarshish-bound ship which Jonah boards at Joppa, probably preserve memories of actual seventh-century conditions.
[4] J. Pritchard: *Ancient Near Eastern Texts Relating to the Old Testament* (Princeton, 1955), p. 260.

The identities of the first two countries mentioned by Esarhaddon are known: Iadanan is Cyprus and Iaman is the Ionian coast of Asia Minor; the location of Tarshishi, however, became the subject of some debate, for this statement by Esarhaddon is the only time the name appears in any Assyrian text. It was noted that "Tarshishi" has the determinative māt for "country" in front of it, as do Idanana, or Cyprus and Iaman, or Ionia. The only clue to its location was its being described as a kingdom "amidst the sea", apparently somewhat farther removed from Assyria than either Cyprus or Ionia.

When Esarhaddon's text was first published and transliterated the name was read as "Nu-shi-shi."[1] At that time there were several conjectures as to the identification of this land. The city of Nysa in Caria was one suggestion; another was that the word refers to "nesos" for Peloponnesos. In 1914 D. D. Luckenbill ventured that "Knossos, for Crete, would fit better."[2] Three years later B. Meissner made a fresh examination of the cuneiform tablet and found that the original transliteration of the name had been mistaken, and that "Tar-shi-shi" was the correct reading.[3] The new reading took away Luckenbill's chief reason for his identification; yet he had the right solution, even if he reached it on wrong grounds. More recent scholarship identifies the land of Tarshishi mentioned by Esarhaddon with the city of Tarsus in Cilicia.[4] Had Tarshishi been a city the name would have been preceded by the determinative URU; however, as mentioned above, it has māt for "country". It is also difficult to see how a place in Cilicia would fit the description "from Iadanana and Iaman as far as Tarshishi." Clearly Tarsisi was farther west than either Cyprus or Ionia. These criteria are filled admirably by Crete.

Velikovsky sought to support this identification by the following facts: In the work of the ancient Greek grammarian Hesychius, who composed his biographical lexicon in the fourth century of the present era, it is said that "Tritta" was another name for Knossos.[5] A double t is

---

[1] Messerschmidt in *Keilschrifttexte aus Assur historischen Inhalts* vol. I, Nr. 75, vs. 10f.
[2] D. D. Luckenbill: »Jadanan and Javan (Danaans and Ionians)«, *Zeitschrift für Assyriologie* 28 (1914), pp. 94-95, n. 3.
[3] B. Meissner in *Orientalistische Literaturzeitung* (1917), p. 410; Cf. F. Hommel: *Ethnologie und Geographie des Alten Orient*, p. 1001.
[4] S. Mazzarino: *Fra Oriente e Occidente*, pp. 132f.; Blazquez: *Tartessos*, p. 21.
[5] Pauly-Wissowa's *Realencyklopädie der Altertumswissenschaft*, article »Knossos«; cf. v. C. Bursian: *Geographie von Griechenland*, vol. II (Leipzig, 1868-72), p. 559 n. 1; see also Diodorus V. 70, 72.

often substituted in ancient Greek by a double s.[1] From Trissa could have been derived the name Tarshish, and the designation may later have been extended to cover the whole island of Crete.

Whoever held sway over the island in the early part of the seventh century, the motive for sending gifts to Esarhaddon is clear. After the subjugation of Sidon and the imposition of a treaty of vassalage on Tyre, the sealanes of the Levant were under Assyrian control; and the gifts may have been intended to gain access for the ships of Tarshish to their traditional ports of call; Crete could hardly have felt itself directly threatened by the land-based power of Assyria.

The reason why the identification of Tarshish with Crete, so evident from the texts quoted above – the Old Testament narrative of the trading ventures of Solomon and Hiram, the prophecies of Isaiah and Ezekiel, the story of the voyage of Jonah, as well as the annals of Esarhaddon – was not made before is due to the fact that the end of Minoan Crete is considered by scholars who follow the accepted chronology to have occurred some four to six hundred years before these texts were written. In the days of Solomon, as in those of Isaiah and of Esarhaddon, Crete is said to have been immersed in its own Dark Ages, without the possibility of a high civilization, with no question of a far-ranging fleet. Only when the disarrayed centuries are brought to their proper order does the identity of Tarshish with Minoan Crete emerge into the light of history: the solution to an old puzzle.

The Dark Age Spanned

Of all the excavated sites in Greece and the Aegean region, it was to Athens that the archaeologists pointed as the one place which preserved a continuity from the end of the Mycenean age down to classical times, and where a sequence of pottery spanning the Dark Age could be followed. Athens thus became the site by which the finds at all other excavated places were identified and placed in time. We are therefore bound to examine the actual stratigraphic situation at Athens.

The sequence of pottery styles at Athens – and thus in all the Greek lands – is usually given thus:

---

[1] E.g. Attic thalatta, meaning "sea," becomes thalassa in Doric.

Middle Helladic	to ca. -1550
Mycenean (Late Helladic)	to ca. -1230
Submycenean	to ca. -1050
Protogeometric	to ca. -900
Geometric	to ca. -680

It must immediately be said that neither in Athens nor at any other site in Greece has a stratified sequence such as this been uncovered. Then on what basis was the scheme built?

There are three ways of determining the relative position of pottery in time:

1) *Relationship of motifs*: Determining the sequence from a study of the way decorative motifs merge into one another. This method is of necessity a rather uncertain one but can be useful if employed together with other methods.

2) *Juxtaposition of finds*: If different styles are found in a common undisturbed deposit, this is strong evidence that they were contemporaneous. If they are found at different levels in a stratified deposit, this indicates their relative position in time.

3) *Links with outside chronologies*: If a certain style of Greek art can be associated with, for instance, Thutmose III and another style with Akhnaton, then at least a relative chronology can be established, even if the absolute chronology is in dispute.

The final stages of the Mycenean period at Athens were illuminated by Broneer's excavations on the Acropolis in the late 1930s. Broneer found that emergency measures had been taken to fortify the city and prepare it for withstanding a siege: One of the measures was the construction of a deep well on the Acropolis with a wooden stairway leading down the shaft. At some point the stairway collapsed and the well was abandoned and filled with discarded sherds of late Mycenean pottery.[1] Following the destruction of the fountain (Plato in his *Kritias* attributes it to "earthquakes") occupation on the Acropolis ceased; only in the seventh and sixth centuries did building activity resume on the site.

---

[1] O. Broneer: »A Mycenean Fountain on the Athenian Acropolis« in *Hesperia* 8 (1939).

Where did the people go during the dark centuries? This is a question which baffles the archaeologists. From the end of the Mycenean age till the seventh century there will be no dwelling places in Athens[1] – only a necropolis, or "city of the dead." Where was the city of the living?

The series of burials which are supposed to fill the dark centuries between the end of the Mycenean age and the time of the Proto-Attic ware of the seventh century are located near the north-western Dipylon gate of Athens and in the Kerameikos cemetery next to it. Other tombs were excavated in the Agora, or marketplace, north of the Acropolis. The burials in the Kerameikos are associated with the style named "Protogeometric" – characterized by a narrow band of decoration around the middle of the vase, with the rest of the vessel having a black glaze. The decoration inside the band consists of concentric circles drawn by some sort of multiple compass. The relationship of this ware with the latest Mycenean pottery found inside the fountain on the Acropolis cannot be judged for "it is a significant fact that the pottery from the fountain extends to, but does not overlap, the period represented by the early graves in the Kerameikos cemetery."[2] This brings into question the usual assertion that the Protogeometric ware followed the Mycenean and sub-Mycenean styles. If there is no overlap, how can a sequence be established? Beside the fact that no dwelling places have been found for the people buried in the Kerameikos, there is another important indication that the Protogeometric pottery and the population associated with it are incorrectly placed following the Mycenean: All of the Protogeometric burials are inside cist-tombs of the type used in the pre-Mycenean or Middle Helladic age. These tombs are not derived from Mycenean tombs, but, where dated to Middle Helladic times, are considered antecedent to them.[3] This, together with other factors to be discussed below, is a strong clue to the true placement of the Protogeometric pottery and the population group associated with it. The archaeologists should look to the Middle Helladic (pre-Mycenean) settlements for the houses of those buried in the Kerameikos.

---

[1] E. A. Gardner and M. Gary: »Early Athens« in *The Cambridge Ancient History* Vol. III (New York, 1925), p. 597.

[2] Broneer: »A Mycenean Fountain«, p. 427.

[3] A. Andrewes: *The Greeks* (London, 1967) p. 35; cf. C. G. Styrenius: *Submycenaean Studies* (Lund, Sweden, 1967), p. 161.

The Kerameikos burials continue into the Geometric period, but the bulk of Athenian Geometric pottery has been found near the Dipylon gate. Other Geometric sherds were found in a stratified deposit south of the Parthenon mixed together in one and the same stratum with Mycenean ware. A terrace filling yielded eight distinct layers, the lowest "well-defined stratum" dating from Mycenean and Geometric times and the one above it, taking in the period up to the burning of the Acropolis by the Persians at the beginning of the fifth century.[1] But the Mycenean and Geometric periods are said to be separated by some four centuries. If the deposit had been accumulating for this length of time, how is it that none of the Protogeometric wares that supposedly followed the Mycenean and preceded the Geometric was found in it? The problem should be seen in the light of the solution proposed above, that the Protogeometric ware belongs to the pre-Mycenean, Middle Helladic settlement. As was noted long ago by Gardner, "fragments of Geometric vases, indistinguishable from the Dipylon type, have been found on various sites in Greece together with later examples of Mycenaean pottery."[2] On the Acropolis itself fragments of Mycenaean vases were found mixed with Geometric sherds.[3] The find south of the Parthenon, taken together with the discoveries at other sites from Troy to Pylos to Olympia, tends to show that Geometric ware was in fact contemporary with Mycenean, a case also very forcefully argued by W. Dörpfeld, as Velikovsky pointed out his discussion of »Olympia«.

Evidence amounting to proof that Protogeometric and Geometric pottery preceded and was contemporary with Mycenean ware was unearthed by C. C. Edgar at Phylakopi on the Aegean island of Melos. He found Geometric pottery under Mycenean, and mixed with it until the very end of the Mycenean deposit.[4] Thus it would seem that while Protogeometric ware is contemporary with Middle Helladic and early Mycenean pottery[5] the Geometric style coexisted with the Mycenean.

---

[1] W. B. Dinsmoor: »The Date of the Older Parthenon« in *American Journal of Archaeology* 38 (1934), pp. 416-417.
[2] E. Gardner: *Ancient Athens* (London, 1902), p. 157.
[3] *Ibid.*, p. 154.
[4] C. C. Edgar: »The Pottery« in *Excavations at Phylakopi in Melos* [Supplementary Paper no. 4 of *Journal of Hellenic Studies* (London, 1904)], pp. 85-107, and 159-163.
[5] This seems to be implied by a find at Kos of Protogeometric and Mycenean IIIA vessels in the same undisturbed deposit, the Mycenean IIIA style was found at el-Amarna and therefore belongs to the ninth century according to the revised chronology.

An added proof of this is in the fact that in Egypt, in tomb paintings of the time of Thutmose III (tenth century according to the revised chronology) foreigners are shown bringing geometric pottery.[1]

The designs on the geometric vases from the vicinity of the Dipylon gate display features which strongly indicate that they were indeed made at the same period as Mycenean vases. They show "two-horse chariots, with very primitive horses, and with men whose wasp-waists remind one of Minoan and Mycenean art; and in some cases much of the human figure is concealed by the great Mycenean or Minoan figure-of-eight shield. ... The women are dressed much in the same fashion as the Minoan and Mycenean women, in tight bodices and bell-shaped skirts." Thus, "everything seems to point to a civilization at Athens in the Dark Age something like the old Mycenean. ..."[2] The Mycenean civilization survived till the beginning of the seventh century and merged with the orientalizing and proto-Attic styles.

---

[1] Schliemann: *Tiryns* (New York, 1895), p. 39.
[2] H. B. Cotterill: *Ancient Greece* (New York, 1913), pp. 99-100.

Supplement III

Additional Light on the Dark Age of Greece

(by Lewis M. Greenberg)

The Lion Gate at Mycenae Redux

For more than a century and a quarter, the academic community – by and large – has accepted the putative dates for the monuments of pre-Hellenic Mycenaean Greece which were first established via synchronisms with Dynastic Egypt. Despite challenges to the chronological reliability of the latter, the current schema of Egyptian history remains the primary standard for assigning dates to pre-Classical civilisations.
The present chapter, which focuses on the most notable work of Mycenaean art – the Lion Gate, reexamines both the basis and sources of its chronological placement and artistic achievement. In the process, the role of Egypt is seriously questioned and tested.

Introduction

The citadel of Mycenae and its famous "Gate of Lions" lies in the northeast sector of the Peloponnesian peninsula of Greece midway between the ancient cities of Corinth and Argos where, by its strategic position, it dominated the Argive plain.[1]

In 1876 Heinrich Schliemann,[2] a successful German businessman, entrepreneur and self-made archaeologist, became the first person to excavate the site in modem times. Utilising the accounts of Classical authors such as Pausanias[3] among others, whose historical authenticity he never doubted, Schliemann eventually revealed a brilliant world of pre-Hellenic culture hitherto unsuspected.[4]

The main entranceway to Mycenae, known as the Lion Gate, is surmounted by two sculptured and now headless feline figures – rampant, heraldically opposed and separated by a central column. As things now stand, this stone relief is the oldest extant example of monumental sculpture on Greek soil; and, in the words of Boardman, "more

---

[1] See the *Atlas of the Classical World*, A.A.M. Van Der Heyden & H.H. Scullard, eds. (NY, 1959), pp. 20, 24-26; *Lost Civilizations*, F. Bourbon & V. M. De Fabianis, eds. (NY, 1998), pp. 36-41; F. Durando: *Greece: A Guide to the Archaeological Sites* (NY, 2000), pp. 130-137.
[2] See D. A. Traill: *Schliemann of Troy* (NY, 1995), pp. 141-176.
[3] Pausanias, II. 15. 16. 17.; J.L. Fitton: *The Discovery of the Greek Bronze Age* (Cambridge, MA, 1996), pp. 71-95.
[4] H. Schliemann: *Mycenae* (NY, 1880); C. Schuchhardt: *Schliemann's Discoveries of the Ancient World* (NY, 1891/1979), pp. 134-298.

than five hundred years were to pass before Greek sculptors could command an idiom which would again satisfy [the same] monumental aspirations in sculpture and architecture."[1] In fact, the traditional time frame for this sculptural achievement is closer to 600 years.[2] Vermeule was likewise surprised by this situation.

> Monumental stone sculpture is almost missing in [pre-Hellenic] Greece, except for the Lion Gate at Mycenae ... In Greece the absence of a sculptural tradition is particularly odd because good stone was quarried and used in monumental architecture and masons were highly trained.[3]

Thus, the Lion Gate remains a key – albeit unique – monument in the history of ancient art serving, so to speak, as a kind of singular portentous prelude to the later sculptural works of the Classical Greeks.[4]

Of Potsherds and Pharaohs

Almost from the moment of its rediscovery, the Lion Gate and other adjacent material gave rise to "vehement disputes between 1880 and 1890 about the dating of the Mycenaean finds"; dates were put forward assigning the monuments to either the years 1400 – 1100 BC or 800 – 700 BC.[5] It is these dates which now require careful re-examination. It was the discovery of sherds beneath the threshold of the Lion Gate – identified as Late Helladic IIIB – that ultimately fixed the chronological placement of the gate and its attendant sculpture in the mid-13th century BC.[6] However, it was Egypt which provided the dates for LH IIIB as well as LH IIIA.[7]

---

[1] J. Boardman: *Greek Art*, 4th ed. (London, 1996), p. 31.
[2] W.-H. Schuchhardt: *Greek Art* (NY, 1972), pp. 65-67; B.S. Ridgway: *The Archaic Style in Greek Sculpture*, 2nd ed. (Chicago, 1993), pp. 21ff.; G.M.A. Richter: *A Handbook of Greek Art* (London, 1965), pp. 47-48.
[3] E. Vermeule: *Greece in the Bronze Age* (Chicago, 1972), p. 214.
[4] See F. Matz: *The Art of Crete and Early Greece* (NY, 1962), *inter alia* and concluding remarks on pp. 226-227 but cf. commentary by R. Carpenter in *Greek Art* (Phila., 1962), pp. 27-30.
[5] P. Demargne: *The Birth of Greek Art* (NY, 1964), p. 8.
[6] P. MacKendrick: *The Greek Stones Speak* (NY, 1966), p. 73; G. Mylonas: *Mycenae and the Mycenaean Age* (Princeton, 1966), pp. 20-21, 236; W.A. McDonald: *Progress into the Past* (NY, 1967), p. 262; A.J.B. Wace: *BSA*, 25 (1921-23), p. 13.
[7] Lord W. Taylour: *The Mycenaeans* (NY, 1964), pp. 45-59; R. Higgins: *Minoan and Mycenaean Art*, rev. ed. (NY, 1997), pp. 12-14; A.J.B. Wace: *Mycenae: An Archaeological History and Guide* (NY, 1964), pp. 10-12.

Fig. 1: The Lion Gate at Mycenae (Schliemann excavation)

The work of Furumark[1] further entrenched the absolute chronology of the pottery categories but once again this resulted primarily from

> the synchronisms that can be established by comparison and correlation of Mycenaean objects found in datable Egyptian contexts and of Egyptian objects recovered in observed Mycenaean stratigraphic associations.[2]

As far back as 1897 Tsountas[3] warned scholars not to ignore "the unsettled state of Egyptian chronology" when enlisting the aid of

---

[1] A. Furumark: *The Chronology of Mycenaean Pottery* (Stockholm, 1941). But see S. Deger-Jalkotzy: *The Aegean Bronze Age*, ed. by C.W. Shelmerdine (NY, 2008), pp. 392-393: "... Furumark needs revision."

[2] C. W. Blegen: *Troy and the Trojans* (NY, 1963), pp. 159-160; also see A. Samuel: *The Mycenaeans in History* (Englewood Cliffs, 1966), pp. 47-48.

[3] C. Tsountas and J.I. Manatt: *The Mycenaean Age* (NY, 1897), p. 317, n. 2; cf. I. Velikovsky: *Ages in Chaos* (NY, 1952), p. 181 & n. 7.

Egyptology in dating Mycenaean products and, in 1960, Cook[1] again reminded students of Greek pottery of the difficulties concerning the establishment of relative and absolute chronologies and their "reconciliation". As it happens, the dating of LH IIIB pottery was established via the putative date for the reign of Ramesses II.[2] Pottery displaying elements of the IIIB style was "found [by Petrie] at Gurob in the Fayyum in association with Egyptian objects that were in fashion not long before Ramses II came to the throne";[3] and LH IIIB ware was also discovered in the tomb of the Phoenician king Ahiram in Byblos along with Egyptian artefacts bearing the cartouche of Ramesses II.[4] The time of Ramesses II is therefore crucial to our present study since it was the actual determinant for the date of the Lion Gate, even though iconographical and aesthetic factors pointed elsewhere.[5]

At this juncture, it should be stressed that the pottery specimens excavated at Gurob and other Delta sites were fragmentary and spotty. Petrie's account and interpretation of his archaeological activity was also frequently disjointed and highly conjectural; and the material he collected was collated and dated at a time when the chronology of Egypt itself was in a state of flux. Moreover, Petrie's position did not go unchallenged; Cecil Torr vigorously questioned and debated his methodology and conclusions but to no avail. Petrie's "solution" to the problem of the absolute dating of Mycenaean chronology prevailed.[6] However, the influence of Gurob was not finished. Only a few years later, a parallel and related art historical problem involving glass vases

---

[1] R. M. Cook: *Greek Painted Pottery* (London, 1960), pp. 261- 270; Matz: *op. cit.*, pp. 74-75; Velikovsky: *ibid.*, pp. 180-183, 221-222; S. Hood: *The Arts in Prehistoric Greece* (NY, 1978), p. 18; also see comments by M.I. Finley in *Early Greece: The Bronze and Archaic Ages* (NY, 1981), p. 50.

[2] According to a most recent source on Ramesses II [see J. Tyldesley: *Ramesses: Egypt's Greatest Pharaoh* (Penguin, NY, 2001), p. xxiii]: "His precise calendar dates are by no means certain but on current evidence 1279-13 BC (or less likely 1290-24 BC) seem the most probable; 1304-1238 BC, which may be found in some older references, is now known to be incorrect." Cf. T. Wilkinson: *Ramesses The Great* (London, 2023), 191-194.

[3] Taylour: *op. cit.*, p. 57; Tsountas: *op. cit.*, pp. 318-320. Cf P. James et al.: *Centuries of Darkness* (London, 1991), pp. 23.-24.

[4] C. G. Starr: *The Origin of Greek Civilization* (NY, 1961), p. 54 and n. 5; H. Frankfort: *The Art and Architecture of the Ancient Orient* (Penguin, NY, 1988), p. 271.

[5] L. M. Greenberg: »The Lion Gate at Mycenae«, *Pensée* IVR III, Winter, 1973, pp. 27-29; I. Velikovsky: »The Lion Gate at Mycenae«, *ibid.*, p. 31; and *infra* in the present paper.

[6] W. M. Flinders Petrie: »The Egyptian Bases of Greek History«, *JHS* 11 (October 1890), pp. 271-277; for a full account of the debate between Torr and Petrie as well as a reprint of Petrie's and Torr's writings, see C. Torr: *Memphis and Mycenae*, ed. D. Rohland M. Durkin, *ISIS Occasional Publication* No. I, 1988, pp. I-LXIX for *The Debate* and pp. 1-63 for *M and M*.

developed at Enkomi, a possible site of Cyprus's ancient capital. In 1974 Velikovsky published a meticulous exposé of this controversial situation.[1]

Under the direction of A.S. Murray, the British Museum conducted excavations at Enkomi in 1896. Among the many objects of art that came to light were vases of variegated glass. At first it appeared that these could be favourably compared and dated via a comparison with others "obtained from the tombs of Cameiros [in Rhodes], and dating from the seventh and sixth centuries, or even later in some cases". Yet, a subsequent comparison with similar examples found by Petrie in Gurob forced Murray to accept a much earlier date for his finds even though – in the words of Murray –

> Professor Petrie's date (about 1400 BC) [was] based on scanty observations collected from the poor remains of a foreign settlement in Egypt.

Murray wanted to lower his dating for the artistic finds at Enkomi but was hamstrung by Egyptian chronology; once again Gurob and Egypt had carried the day. As for Ahiram's tomb, its disputation will be dealt with below.

For now, it is important to note that, independent of Egypt, Edwin M Schorr (writing under the name of Israel M. Isaacson in 1974) clearly delineated the difficulty in ascribing LH III B-C pottery to the 14th-12th centuries BC. By analysing Mycenaean stratigraphy in the vicinity of the Lion Gate, Schorr revealed the probability that "LH IIIC pottery ... lasted until the 7th-6th centuries BC".[2] "Stratigraphically 7th-century sherds were mixed with LH IIIC inside the Lion Gate of Mycenae" along with similar "anomalies" at Pylos, Troy, and Scoglio del Tonno near Taranto in southern Italy.[3] James et al. have likewise cited problematic relationships between Protogeometric and Geometric deposits vis-à-vis Mycenaean material. Notable examples include Delphi, Samos, and Pylos.[4] Thus, LH IIIB could have been dated to the late 8th or early 7th centuries BC were it not for Egyptian synchronisms.

---

[1] I. Velikovsky: »The Scandal of Enkomi«, *Pensée* IVR X (Winter, 1974-75), pp. 21-23.

[2] I. M. Isaacson (E.M.S.): »Applying the Revised Chronology«, *Pensée* IVR IX (Fall, 1974), p. 7 and n. 13, p. 16, n. 11, p. 17, n. 43; cf. Suppl. I of the present book.

[3] *Ibid.*, p. 33, n. 187. Also see commentary by R.M. Cook: *op. cit.*, p. 16 on the Geometric and Orientalising styles.

[4] James et al.: *op. cit.*, pp. 92 and 358, n. 83. Once again, James fails to cite a significant predecessor researching the same area – in this case, Isaacson/Schorr.

The Tomb of Ahiram

In *Ramses II and His Time*, Velikovsky reserved an entire section for a detailed discussion of the tomb of Ahiram. In an exhaustive survey, Velikovsky exposed the inherent problems relevant to the dating of Ahiram's tomb and concluded that the tomb, its contents and the time of Ramesses II should all be assigned a date closer to 600 BC.[1] It is of more than passing interest to note that, while Sabatino Moscati – an authority on the Phoenicians – ascribed the Ahiram sarcophagus to the 13th or 12th century BC and its inscription to the 10th, he also observed that "after Ahiram new sarcophagi are only found in the *fifth* century";[2] later, Moscati said that "this sarcophagus is a unique case since no others have appeared prior to the *6th-5th* century".[3] The eclectic character of Phoenician sarcophagi also permits a downdating of Ahiram's coffin.

Barnett also discerned that the sarcophagus of Ahiram "obviously reproduces in stone a contemporaneous wooden chest decorated with carved panels; it is the earliest example of what later became the established type of Phoenician funerary furniture, *continuing with little change* through stone sarcophagi such as the *late-6th – and early-5th century* pieces from Amathus, Tamassos, and Athienou [on Cyprus] on to the Satrap and Alexander sarcophagi and that of the 'Mourning Women' at Carthage".[4]

One is entitled to ask: Where are the intervening examples that should pre-date the 6th century BC? Once again, we seem to be looking at a chain with missing links.

Frankfort, who stubbornly adhered to a 13th century BC date for the sarcophagus of Ahiram, also made one very relevant and interesting observation:

---

[1] I. Velikovsky: *Ramses II and His Time* (NY, 1978), pp. 63-83. (Also see the summary of Velikovsky's discussion in *SISR* VI:1-3, special *Ages in Chaos?* issue (1982), pp. 80-81.); Velikovsky's proposed dating scheme for the tomb of Ahiram has recently been upheld by Emmet Sweeney: see E.J. Sweeney: »Ramessides, Medes and Persians«, *The Velikovskian* V:2 (2000), pp. 44-46, and E. Sweeney: *Egypt's Ramesside Pharaohs and the Persians* (2021), pp. 100ff.
[2] S. Moscati: *The World of the Phoenicians* (NY, 1970), p, 60 (emphasis added).
[3] S. Moscati, et al.: *The Phoenicians* (NY, 1999), p. 355 (emphasis added).
[4] R. D. Barnett: »Phoenician-Punic Art«, *Encyclopedia of World Art*, XI (NY, 1966), p. 307 (emphasis added).

Fig, 2a: Ahiram's Sarcophagus

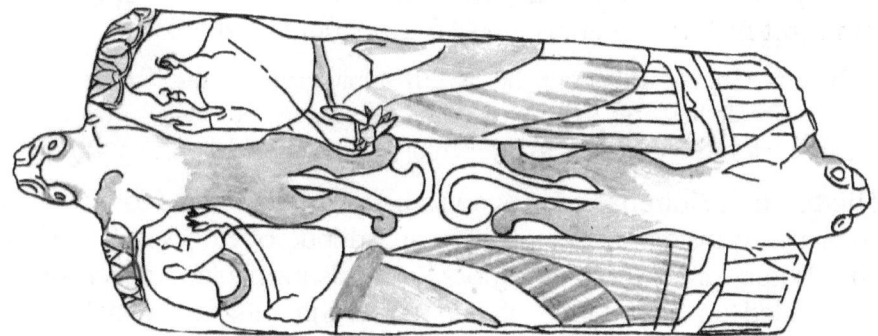

Fig. 2b: Cover of Ahiram's Sarcophagus

Un-Egyptian are the four supports of the sarcophagus, shaped as lions, and a similar shape is given to the two projecting knobs which allowed the lid to be put into place. These lions, crudely carved like the whole of the sarcophagus, seem to anticipate Syro-Hittite sculpture of the *eighth century BC*.

However, Frankfort was dismissive and quickly went on to conclude that "the resemblance is merely due to an unskilled rendering of a common subject".[1] Here is a case where aesthetic subjectivity may have influenced chronological judgement.

Aside from any revisionist theory, the idea that the Ahiram coffin is a 13th century work that must have been reused in the 10th[2] is no

---

[1] Frankfort: *op. cit.*, pp. 271-272 (emphasis added).
[2] E.g., D. Harden: *The Phoenicians* (NY, 1962), pp. 118, 182, and 303, n. 15 as well as plate 15; S. Smith: *Alalakh and Chronology* (London, 1940), p. 46, n. 117.

longer universally accepted. Markoe, for one, has opted for a 12th century date which he relates to the time of Ramesses III[1] while Porada has argued against its reuse, maintaining that it was actually carved in the 9th century.[2] Woolley dated the sarcophagus to c. 975 BC without mentioning anything about "reuse".[3] More importantly, the archaeological contradictions seen in the tomb of Ahiram do not comprise an isolated incident. James et al. noted a like situation in the "Gold Tomb" at Carchemish[4] and Schorr cited similar phenomena at Mycenae and Sparta.[5]

In the case of the latter, Late Helladic tombs contained material which is indisputably dated to the 8th-7th centuries BC; and architectural features found in 14th or 13th century BC contexts have their counterpart in 8th-7th century structures. The separation of 500-700 years is art-historically unjustified.[6] Schorr rightly asked:

> Did the Greeks wait until the 500th anniversary of the Trojan War to honor their leaders? Why were 8th-7th century objects placed in 13th century tombs? Why were 13th century rulers honored only ca. 700 BC?[7]

The tomb of Ahiram has proven to be a veritable archaeological can of worms. In his trenchant review and critique of *Ramses II and His Time*, Peter James tended to gloss over this particular subject though he provided an abundance of counter arguments to the balance of the book's contents.[8] However, in *Centuries of Darkness*, James et al. discussed the sarcophagus of Ahiram in much more detail leading to the conclusion that the coffin could be dated some time between the late 9th to early 7th centuries BC with no intrusion after the interment of Ahiram.[9] The importance of that last point is telling, for

---

[1] G. E. Markoe: *Phoenicians* (Los Angeles, 2000), pp. 144 & 216, n. 4 and plate v. J. Teixidor ascribes "a date at the end of the eleventh century BCE" for Ahiram's sarcophagus (*The Oxford Encyclopaedia of Archaeology in the Near East*, 1, ed. E.M. Meyers (NY, 1997), pp. 31-32).

[2] E. Porada: »Notes on the Sarcophagus of Ahiram«, *Journal of the Ancient Near Eastern Society of Columbia University*, 5 (1973), pp. 355-372.

[3] L. Woolley: *The Art of the Middle East* (NY, 1961), pp. 107, 110.

[4] James et al.: *op. cit.*, p. 128.

[5] Isaacson/Schorr: *op. cit.*, pp. 9-10; cf. Suppl. I of the present book.

[6] *Ibid.*, pp. 9-10, 18, notes 66-81.

[7] *Ibid.*, p. 10; A.M. Snodgrass: *The Dark Age of Greece* (Edinburgh, 1971), pp. 192-194 and the rationalisation of V.R. d'A. Desborough: *The Greek Dark Ages* (London, 1972), p. 283.

[8] P. James: »A Critique of *Ramses II and His Time*«, *SISR* III:2 (Autumn, 1978), pp. 48-55, esp. p. 50.

[9] James et al.: *op. cit.*, pp. 249-251, 383, n. 103.

if the Ahiram tomb should be dated to the first millennium BC then the Ramesside material found in the tomb would have to be several hundred year-old "heirlooms" according to conventional chronology. The alternative is to reconsider the date for Ramesses II, making him a possible contemporary of Ahiram's tomb. The latter prospect, proposed by Velikovsky, is far more plausible. Indeed, the dates proposed in *Centuries of Darkness* for Ahiram's coffin are much closer to that put forward by Velikovsky than the generally accepted one.

Will the Real Shishak Please Stand Up?

For James et al., who would place Ramesses II in the 11th century and Ramesses III in the 10th century – making the latter the Biblical Shishak who looted the Temple of Solomon[1] – there is still a problem. The alabaster remains from the time of Ramesses II in Ahiram's tomb would still have been more than 200 years old at the least; and one might also wonder why something from the time of Ramesses III – given his suggested closer proximity in time and proposed Levantine activity – wasn't included in the tomb of Ahiram. One must also consider what effect the dating of Ramesses II in the 11th century would have on Mycenaean art and its relative position in Eastern Mediterranean archaeology.

To make matters more confusing, David Rohl has also presented a strong argument in favour of Ramesses II as the candidate pharaoh who sacked Solomon's Temple.[2] However, neither James nor Rohl deigned to acknowledge or respond to Velikovsky's earlier proposal that it was Thutmoses III who plundered the Great Temple of Solomon[3] – a thesis fundamentally supported by Eva Danelius in a lengthy

---

[1] *Ibid.*, p. 257.
[2] D. M. Rohl: *Pharaohs and Kings (aka A Test of Time)* (NY, 1995), pp. 162-163. In 1994, Bob Porter discussed the question of "Ramses II or Ramses III?" regarding the identification of Shishak. His conclusion really doesn't help: " ... the easiest course seems to be to opt for Ramesses III as Shishak, and this is certainly more likely to find support in the scholarly world simply due to its smaller reduction. My own preference remains firmly with Ramesses II" [R.M. Porter: »Shishak-Ramesses II or Ramesses III?«, *C&CR* XVI (1994), p. 13]. For a full discussion of the Shishak=Shoshenq equation, see J. Bimson: *C&CR* VIII (1986), pp. 36-46 and articles by C. Jansen-Winkeln & P. van der Veen in *JACF* Vol. 8 (1999), pp. 17-25.
[3] Velikovsky: *Ages, op. cit.*, pp. 143-177.

and scholarly article published in the very pages of the SIS Review [1] and also ignored by James and Rohl in a remarkable oversight.

More recently, Dale Murphie has challenged Rohl's identification of Ramesses II as the Biblical Shishak;[2] and, in a lengthy essay of his own, Murphie reaffirmed Velikovsky's identification of Thutmoses III as the Shishak of the Bible.[3] In turn, Eric Aitchison has written a lengthy criticism of Murphie, proposing Ahmose – the first pharaoh of Dynasty XVIII – as Shishak, after previously proffering Kamose as said Shishak.[4] The repercussion of Aitchison's proposal is the necessary down-dating of Ramesses II from his current placement in the 13th century BC (1279-1213) to the 7th century BC (675-611). The Lion Gate would then date to either the late 7th century or early 6th century by both Aitchison's and Velikovsky's scheme. In effect, Aitchison would be de facto supporting Murphie's, Sweeney's, and Velikovsky's dating of Ramesses II regardless of which identification of Shishak is correct. On the other hand, James' identification of Shishak would put the Lion Gate in the late 11th or early 10th century BC, while Rohl's chronology would place the Lion Gate in the late 10th or early 9th century BC. James did allude to the Lion Gate in *Centuries of Darkness* but merely referred to Ramsay's and Hogarth's comparison with the Phrygian Lion Tomb at Arslan Tash. No suggested date of his own was given for the Lion Gate. Rohl never even mentioned the Lion Gate in *Pharaohs and Kings* (published as *A Test of Time* in the UK). Therein lies the conundrum. The redating of Ramesses II or the reidentification of Shishak by revisionists – whether in agreement

---

[1] E. Danelius: »Did Thutrnose III Despoil the Temple in Jerusalem?«, *SISR* II:3 (Special Issue 1977/78), pp. 64-79 and Velikovsky's response in *Ibid.*, p. 80. Also see Danelius' Appendix to her earlier articles on Hatshepsut and Thutmose III in *SISR* VII, Part A (1982/3), pp. 29-31. Despite the highlighting of nascent awareness in mainstream circles of Danelius' "Velikovskian papers" in that same issue of *SISR* (p.30), she remains unacknowledged by those revisionists working in the same area, except for John Bimson's citations in his critique of the Hatshepsut=Sheba equation (*C&CR* VIII (1986), pp. 12, 23, 24 & 26). It is appropriate at this time to call attention to David Lorton's unpublished *Hatshepsut, the Queen of Sheba and Immanuel Velikovsky*, written in 1984 and revised for publication on the WWW in 1999. It is some 37 pages in length. Lorton disputes the identification, but is now fully rebutted along with Bimson in the most recent issues of *CHRONOLOGY & CATASTROPHISM REVIEW* by both Sweeney and Greenberg.

[2] D. F. Murphie: »Testing Rohl's Test of Time«, *Aeon* V:l (Nov. 1997), pp. 88-98; Idem: *C&CR* 1997:1, pp. 31-33.

[3] D. F. Murphie: »After 200 Years It's Time to Get Serious About Dynasty XVIII and Tuthmose III«, *Aeon* V:3 (Dec. 1998), pp. 69-95.

[4] E. Aitchison: »Thutmose III: A Different Perspective«, *Aeon* V:6 (Aug. 2000), pp. 47-61; Idem: »Egyptian C14 Dates«, *C&CR* 1997:2, p. 59, *C&CR* 1998:1, Correction, p. 56.

with Velikovsky or not – creates a serious fluctuation in Mycenaean art history by as much as 400 years. Therefore, more caution must be exercised when moving various pharaohs all over the chronological chessboard.[1]

Fig. 3: Sculptured Lions from Phrygian tomb, Arslan Tash, 8th century BC

Additionally, Murphie's support for Velikovsky's dating of Ramesses II – a dating already criticised and rejected by James[2] and Jonsson[3] – has come under fire from Michael Reade. In an effort to alleviate the problem of "duplicate dynasties" and "alter egos", Murphie had proposed two Nechos,[4] one Biblical and one Dynastic, the former being the pharaoh who best fits the historical description of Ramesses II. Reade will have none of it and, in a brief rebuttal, dismissed Murphie's "resurrection" of Velikovsky's Ramesses II = Necho II equation, concluding from various conventional synchronisms that it is "impossible that Ramesses II and Necho (whether biblical or dynastic) could be one

---

[1] See, e.g., M. G. Reade: »Shishak, the Kings of Judah and Some Synchronisms«, C&CR 1997:2, pp. 27-36.

[2] James: »A Critique ...«, loc. cit.

[3] C. O, Jonsson: »Nebuchadrezzar and Neriglissar«, SISR III:4 (Spring 1979), pp. 93-97.

[4] D. F. Murphie: »Another Velikovsky Affray«, C&CR 1991:1, pp. 31-34.

and the same."[1] Yet, this would appear to contradict Reade's own earlier position that "the picture as a whole is favourable to Velikovsky's suggestions (Necho = Ramesses II, etc.)."[2]

Adding yet another dimension to the equation is Jonsson's earlier suggestion that, while "the XIXth Dynasty (to which Ramesses II belongs) is not identical with the XXVIth Dynasty (664-525 BC), ... the evidence speaks in favour of a placement for Ramesses II in the 8th century BC, as has been suggested by Donovan A. Courville."[3] Back in 1971, Courville argued for both a reordering as well as redating of pharaonic reigns. Thus, Ramesses II was identified as a member of the XVIIIth Dynasty and his accession date to the throne was placed in the years 792-791 BC.[4] The revised regnal years for Ramesses II would then be ca. 792-725 BC. Courville's proposal, seconded by Jonsson, fits the suggested chronological parameters first put forth by Ramsay in the late 19th century and reiterated by Velikovsky and the present author in the late 20th century for the dating of the Lion Gate.[5] Moreover, back in 1978, James, Gammon, and Bimson all presented a case for placing more than 60 years of Ramesses II's reign in the 8th century.[6]

In an earlier position than the one taken in *Centuries of Darkness*, James concluded that "if Velikovsky's dates for the XVIIIth Dynasty are correct, then a revised date for the XIXth Dynasty (keeping it in sequence) must place it largely in the 8th century"; Gammon provisionally arrived at regnal dates for Ramesses II of 804 – 738; and Bimson supported Gammon by confirming late 8th century dates for Merneptah. While the chronological positions of the aforementioned scholars have changed over the years, an 8th century BC date for the Lion Gate is tempting. Yet a late 7th century BC date fits even better with Velikovsky's proposed date for the time of Ramses II considering the possible Phrygian, Assyrian, and Archaic Greek links along with relevant gateway ceramic finds.

---

[1] M. G. Reade: »Necho = Ramesses II?«, *C&CR* 2000:2, p. 67.
[2] Reade: »Shishak...«, *op. cit.*, p. 31.
[3] Jonsson: *op. cit.*, p. 93.
[4] D. A. Courville: *The Exodus Problem and its Ramifications* (Loma Linda, 1971), I, pp. 279ff., especially pp. 292 and 302. Unfortunately, Courville contradicts himself between pp. 292 and 302. The former has Ramesses II acceding to the throne in 792-791 BC while his chart on the latter has 793 BC.
[5] Velikovsky & Greenberg, *supra* and *Pensée* III (1973), pp. 29-31.
[6] *SISR* III:2 (Autumn 1978), pp. 54, 56-59.

Chronological and Historical Considerations

In 1945,[1] and again in the 1950s,[2] Velikovsky maintained that the buildings and fortifications of Mycenae and Tiryns should be dated to the 8th century BC. Ramsay had already proposed a similar dating in 1888[3] and again in 1889[4] for the Lion Gate as a result of comparisons made with art in Phrygia.[5] There, two sculptured lions, somewhat worn by weather, flank the opening to a tomb at Arslan Tash, whose entrance was high up on the side of a cliff. The huge heads, gaping jaws and devouring aspects of the beasts must have been quite imposing and ominous when viewed from below, which would suit their purpose well as the guardians and protectors of the deceased within.[6] The overall resemblance to the Lion Gate was so complete that Ramsay was forced to conclude that the Mycenaean monument was either the work of Phrygian artists or copied from Phrygian art.[7] In 1892, Gardner also observed close analogies between Mycenaean and Phrygian lions[8] and, in that same year, Murray – like Ramsay – placed the Lion Gate and walls of Mycenae in the 8th to 7th centuries BC on the basis of Mycenaean gem comparisons and apparently believed in the possibility of following a "stream of Greek art backward without interruption to a powerful source in an age of great popular activity."[9] It

---

[1] I. Velikovsky: »Theses for the Reconstruction of Ancient History«, *Scripta Academica Hierosolymitana* (1945/46), p. 11.

[2] Velikovsky: *Ages, op. cit.*, p. 182; I. Velikovsky: *Worlds in Collision* (NY, 1950), pp. 216-217 & 245-253 ; I. Velikovsky: *Earth in Upheaval* (NY, 1955), »The Supplement«, p. 277.

[3] W. M. Ramsay: »A Study of Phrygian Art (Part 1)«, *JHS* 9 (1888), pp. 351, 369-371; Tsountas: *op. cit.*, p. 31.

[4] W. M. Ramsay: »A Study of Phrygian Art (Part II)«, *JHS* 10 (1889), p. 147.

[5] W. M. Ramsay: »Studies in Asia Minor«, *JHS*, 3 (1882), pp. 19- 25 & 256-263; James et al.: *Centuries, op. cit.*, pp. 93-94, discussed and illustrated the comparison between Mycenaean and Phrygian relief sculpture but failed to cite either Velikovsky or Greenberg, almost treating the matter as a dead issue from 1925 until the time of their own writing. Their statement on p. 94 that "no one today could seriously contemplate the lowest dates for Mycenaean civilization experimented with by late 19th century scholars" leaves the present author speechless. Velikovsky, myself and Schorr have been doing exactly that for a number of decades now. Also see S. Ferri: »Arte Frigia«, *Enciclopedia dell'arte Antica* III (Rome, 1960), pp. 739-741, fig. 909; G. Garbini: *The Ancient World* (NY, 1966), p. 108.

[6] Note the compositional similarity to the Lion Gate. See E. Akurgal: »Asia Minor, Western«, *Encyclopedia of World Art*, I (NY, 1959), pp. 884-888 and plate 528. Akurgal prefers a date after the 6th century BC, while H. Hall: *The Oldest Civilization of Greece* (London, 1901), p. 274, suggested an 8th century BC date.

[7] Velikovsky: »Lion Gate ...«, *op. cit.*, p. 31.

[8] P. Gardner: *New Chapters in Greek History* (NY, 1892), pp. 81-82.

[9] A. Murray: *A Handbook of Greek Archaeology* (NY, 1892), pp. 177-179; Tsountas: *op. cit.*, pp. 31 & 254.

should be noted that both Gardner and Murray held to their own convictions even after Flinders Petrie supposedly resolved the Mycenaean chronological problem in 1890/91.[1]

If, in fact, the lions (actually lionesses[2]) of the Lion Gate at Mycenae do indeed date from the 8th to 7th centuries BC, what would or could have been their source of artistic inspiration and execution? There are no known monumental antecedents or descendants on Greek soil for the Lion Gate according to its present placement in time, which would rule out the concept of stylistic convergence.

Ramsay[3] argued that the Mycenaean gateway most likely belonged to the 8th century BC due to the lively intercourse which took place between Argos and Asia Minor at that time, during which the Argives would have learned "to fortify their city in the Phrygian style with lions over the gate." He also raised the logical question,

> is it probable that all traces of the greatest period in Argive history have altogether disappeared, while numerous remains exist of Argive glory during the unknown period 1500-1000 BC, and again of Argive bronze work of the sixth century BC?[4]

As previously noted, Velikovsky has also supported this same view; and Perrot and Chipiez saw the "relations between Phrygian and Mycenian [sic] art [as] a question of vital interest for archaeology."[5] Unfortunately for Velikovsky, he overlooked the fact that by supporting Ramsay's chronological viewpoint he was negating his own dating for Ramesses II. It is chronologically impossible for the Lion Gate to be dated to the 8th century BC while Ramesses II occupies the 6th. The same caveat that applies to Velikovsky also applies to James and Rohl and anyone else who plays the revisionist game. Historical revisionism automatically engenders a falling domino effect. To his credit, Velikovsky must have realised this and that is probably the reason why he took so long before finalising his revised chronology in print.

---

[1] Petrie: »The Egyptian Bases of Greek History«, op. cit., pp. 271-277; W.M. Flinders Petrie: »Notes on the Antiquities of Mykenae«, JHS 12 (1891), pp. 199-205. Contra Petrie, see Torr: op. cit., pp. I-XXXVIII.

[2] Ramsay: »A Study ...«, Part I, op. cit., p. 369; D. Preziosi & L.A. Hitchcock: Aegean Art and Architecture (NY, 1999), p. 189: " ... an increasing number [of scholars] prefer lionesses, citing the interpretation of lions as indicative of a sexist bias."

[3] Ramsay: ibid., p. 370 and n. 3; Ramsay: »A Study ...«, Part II, op. cit., p. 148.

[4] Ibid., Part I, pp. 370-371.

[5] G. Perrot & C. Chipiez: History of Art in Phrygia, Lydia, Caria and Lycia (NY, 1892), p. 395.

In 1972, I suggested – almost as a mischief – the possibility that the Lion Gate sculpture might not be contemporaneous with the gateway itself. In 1999, Preziosi and Hitchcock implied the same thing when they stated the following: "[The Lion Gate's] uniqueness on the mainland has indicated to some that the relief was brought from elsewhere and recarved to fit it into the relieving triangle."[1] The "elsewhere" was never identified by the authors of that statement. Neither was the identity of the sculptors. A closer examination of Mycenaean and Asiatic contacts may provide a solution.

In the late 8th and early 7th centuries BC, the greater Eastern Mediterranean World was being exposed to the expanding cultural and artistic influence of the powerful Neo-Assyrian Empire. What was occurring was the "Assyrianization" of the lands along its northwestern border and beyond; and just as Phoenician artistry reached Greece earlier, there were significant Greek encounters with the Neo-Assyrian Empire resulting in definite influential effects on the former. The concept of Oriental vs. Occidental and the idea of the "Other" is a modern fallacy. The ancient Greeks and others along the far flung northeastern regions of the Assyrian Empire were highly receptive to the lifestyles and products of the Orient.[2] The dramatic felines that surmount the Lion Gate of Mycenae, from both an iconographical and stylistic standpoint, might actually have been carved by a Near Eastern sculptor who was all too familiar with the scenic "lion hunts" that adorned the palace walls of the Assyrian potentates as well as the "antithetical" motifs of Ancient Near Eastern art.

There seems to be no doubt of Greek and Anatolian, as well as Levantine contacts in the 8th or 7th century BC on the basis of literary[3]

---

[1] Preziosi & Hitchcock: *op. cit.*, p. 188. P. P. Betancourt: *Introduction to Aegean Art* (Phila., 2007), pp. 162-163 independently came to the same conclusion. "On the other hand," Hood has suggested that "the relief may be *earlier* than the gate, which appears to have been erected in the thirteenth century, and it may even have been designed to occupy some other position such as the relieving triangle over the entrance of a tholos tomb" (Hood: *op. cit.*, p. 101 & n. 106, emphasis added).

[2] Ann C. Gunter: *Greek Art and the Orient* (NY, 2012), pp. 1-70. Also see W. Burkert: *The Orientalizing Revolution – Near Eastern Influence on Greek culture in the Early Archaic Age* (London, 1992), pp. 14-25; T. J. Dunbabin: *The Greeks and Their Eastern Neighbours* (Chicago, 1979), pp. 46-48; J. M. Barringer: *The Art and Archaeology of Ancient Greece* (Cambridge, 2014), pp. 43-45; M. D. Stansbury-O'Donnell: A *History of Greek Art* (Chichester, 2015), p. 57.

[3] D. L. Page: *History and the Homeric Iliad* (Berkeley, 1959), p. 40, n. 63.

as well as artistic[1] documentation, but as to the specific identity of these "Greeks" there is still considerable debate.[2] Michael Grant summed it up best when discussing the Mycenaeans of conventional chronology:

> ... in spite of all [the] traceable links with other countries, it is still impossible to discover who these rich and fierce, somewhat barbarous but culturally acquisitive rulers were, or even whether they descended from earlier settlers in Greece or had immigrated themselves.[3]

Grant, of course, assumed that he was referring to people who belonged to the mid-2nd millennium BC. Ramsay assumed that they were Mycenaeans who were artistically influenced by their Asiatic (Phrygian) neighbours but he was referring to people now placed 500-600 years earlier in time. Unfortunately, there is a terrible confusion over "who was where, when" and "who was influenced by whom" owing to the existing state of historical/chronological affairs.[4] The Gordion knot of art historical controversy is not so easily cut, either. As Demargne has put it:

> To what extent was the Mycenaean world influenced by Syria or Egypt either directly or via Cyprus ... Conversely, to what extent were the civilizations of the Syrian towns, of the Egypt of Amarna and the XIXth Dynasty, accessible to Aegean influences?[5]

Nevertheless, one thing is certain and that is the fact that according to the now accepted art historical framework, we have a renowned work of monumental sculpture which timewise exists in apparent splendid isolation and alien in spirit to the Cretan artistic temperament:[6]

> For a long time it was believed that Mycenae had been under Cretan domination, almost as if it were the colonial outpost of a seafaring nation. This has proved to be a misconception and although the cultural and political relationship between these rival powers remains obscure and the historical causes of the rise of the one, and the decline of the oth-

---

[1] E. Akurgal: *The Art of Greece: Its Origins in the Mediterranean and Near East* (NY, 1966), pp. 162f.; S.P. Morris: *Daidalos and the Origins of Greek Art* (Princeton, 1992), pp. 101-149; W. Burkert: *The Orientalizing Revolution* (London, 1992), pp. 141f.; G. Hoffman: *Imports & Immigrants* (Ann Arbor, 1997), pp. 1-151.
[2] Page: *op. cit.*, p. 40, n. 63; also see H.E.L. Mellersh: *The Destruction of Knossos* (London, 1970), p. 157.
[3] M. Grant: *The Ancient Mediterranean* (NY, 1969), p. 102.
[4] Frankfort: *op. cit.*, pp. 236-237.
[5] P. Demargne: »The Aegean World«, *The Larousse Encyclopedia of Prehistoric and Ancient Art* (NY, 1962), p. 195.
[6] Higgins: *op. cit.*, p. 91.

er are beyond our grasp, it is clear that Mycenae had a cultural individuality of its own and that its remains must be dealt with on their own merit.[7]

Fig. 4: Lion Hunt from Palace of Ashurbanipal, Nineveh (ca. 668-630 BC)

Aesthetic Considerations

Matz[8] was also quick to point out the un-Minoan characteristics of the Lion Gate and yet, despite the trend toward Mycenaean emancipation from Cretan influence in the minds of scholars,[9] Platon once stated that "the technique of the execution [of the Lion Gate] is clearly inspired by Cretan sculpture."[10] Vermeule also felt that the paucity of monumental pre-Hellenic Greek sculpture was somehow related to Crete and believed that "it was the lack of Minoan prototypes which probably delayed this branch of art [large-scale sculpture in Mycenaean Greece] so long, because sculptural instinct was already present in the Shaft Grave stelai."[11] However, the latter-mentioned works them-

---

[7] H. A. Groenewegen-Frankfort and B. Ashmole: *Art of the Ancient World* (NY, 1972), p. 141; also see Boardman: *op. cit.*, pp. 30-31; P. Strong: *The Classical World* (NY, 1965), p. 16.
[8] Matz: *op. cit.*, pp. 202-203.
[9] See, e.g., comments of S. Marinatos: *Crete and Mycenae* (NY, 1960), p. 81 and J. Boardman et al.: *Greek Art and Architecture* (NY, 1967), p. 119.
[10] N. Platon: »Cretan-Mycenaean Art«, *Encyclopedia of World Art*, IV (NY, 1958), p. 109.
[11] Vermeule: *op. cit.*, p. 214.

selves may also be incorrectly dated.[1] They make a good deal more art historical sense when compared, for example, with the hunting scenes of Ashurnasirpal II from Nimrud, which are dated in the 9th century.

Special note should be made of the thematic and compositional similarities apparent in the hunting scene on a grave stele over Grave V from Mycenae and the depiction of mastiffs hunting wild onagers on an alabaster relief from the North Palace at Nineveh (668-630 BC). The subject of a lion chasing a stag or a goat, found on a six-sided wooden box with gold plaques, also from Grave V, is likewise noteworthy. A military subject such as the one portraying Mycenaean soldiers storming a town, found on the upper part of a silver funnel-shaped rhyton from Grave IV, also accords artistically well with a like battle scene proclaiming the victory of King Ashurbanipal to be seen on a relief from the Southwest Palace of Sennacherib at Nineveh (704 – 681 BC).[2]

Fig. 5: The Lion Gate at Boghazkoy (Hattusa)

---

[1] Matz: *op. cit.*, p. 170, suggested a 16th century BC date while Higgins put forth dates ranging from the 16th to the 13th centuries BC for the Shaft-Grave stones. Our present study would indicate the possibility that these dates are still way too high.

[2] Marinatos: *op. cit.*, plates 146, 147, 174, 198-199; cf. A. Parrot: *The Arts of Assyria* (NY, 1961), p. 54, figs. 62-74. Vermeule: *op. cit.*, p. 92, thought that Grave Gamma "probably has Near Eastern models behind it."

The very idea of decorating a citadel gateway with apotropaic animal guardians such as those which occur on the Lion Gate finds its universal parallel at Nimrud (883-859 BC), Khorsabad (721-705 BC), Babylon (604-562 BC) and perhaps even in Nineveh.[1] In Asia Minor, the Lion Gate of Hattusa (c. 1300 BC) – the Hittite capital – and the gateway from Malatya (1050-850 BC) offer additional parallels. It must be emphasised, however, that the Hittite examples depend upon Egyptian chronology for their dating and may prove to be considerably later. This is especially true for Hattusa.[2] Schorr has already pointed out the striking similarities between some of the hunting and battle scenes depicted on Mycenaean grave stelae of the Mycenaean Grave Circles and those seen on Neo-Hittite relief sculpture some 6 - 7 centuries later in date.[3] To the Greeks, lions, composite beasts and other fabulous creatures initially derived from other artistic traditions. In the case of the lion, the model for this animal "can often be identified with precision: [it] is first Hittite and later Assyrian in form."[4] Nancy Sandars actually compared the sculpture of the Lion Gate to that of the Hittite lions which guarded the gate at Hattusa and even speculated that the former may have been "perhaps learnt from Anatolian mason."[5] Sandars was, of course, thinking in terms of a 13th century BC date.

In any event, the key question that must be asked and was indeed posed by Preziosi and Hitchcock is:

> Where did the Mycenaeans get the idea for the subject of the gate? From the Minoans, the Hittites, or another Near Eastern people? ... If we

---

[1] E. Strommenger: *5000 Years of the Art of Mesopotamia* (NY, 1964), plates 198, 200 220.
[2] For good examples of Hittite gateway sculpture, see J.G. Macqueen: *The Hittites*, rev. ed. (NY, 1986), pp. 138-144; on the subject and problems of Hittite chronology, see T. Bryce: *The Kingdom of the Hittites* (NY, 1998), pp. 408-415 and J. Lehmann: *The Hittites* (NY, 1977), pp. 202-207. On Hattusa/Bogazkoy, see remarks by J.D. Hawkins: »Bogazkoy«, *The Dictionary of Art*, 4, ed. by Jane Turner (NY, 1998), pp. 229-230; also see Sweeney: *op. cit.*, pp. 11-12. Velikovsky's downdating of the Hittite Empire (*Ramses II, op. cit.*, pp. 140- 179) has been disputed, though he too concluded that the Lion Gate of Malatya should be dated to the second part of the 8th century BC (pp. 167-168). James et al.: *op. cit.*, also presented an excellent argument for lowering the dates of the Hittite Empire (pp. 113-141).
[3] Isaacson/Schorr: *op, cit.*, pp. 7-8; cf. Suppl. I of the present book.
[4] O. Murray: *Early Greece*, 2nd ed. (Cambridge, MA, 1993), p. 85.
[5] N.K. Sandars: *The Sea Peoples* (London, 1978), pp. 64-65. So, too, Rhys Carpenter: "Large reliefs such as the heraldically opposed lionesses which still guard the gateway of the citadel at Mycenae presumably reflect Anatolian examples" (R. Carpenter: *Greek Sculpture* (Chicago, 1971), p. 4).

Fig. 6: Pair of lions displaying Assyrian influence, Kayseri, Turkey (c. 700 BC)

choose to focus our attention on the significance of the antithetical group and the effect of the entablature we should be aware of the fact that the antithetical group can be inserted into a 2,000-year history of meaning that spans the Bronze Age Mediterranean in its entirety."[1]

At this point, taking into consideration all of the historical and archaeological data relating to the Lion Gate so far presented, we are inevitably forced to alter our chronological, geographical and cultural focus away from currently accepted beliefs. It would appear that we are dealing with a work of sculpture essentially and unquestionably different from Minoan workmanship which reasonably and sensibly fits into a much later artistic koine whose source was the art of the Neo-Assyrian Empire which dominated the Near East from 883 to 626 BC.[2] Stylistically, the felines of Mycenae are reminiscent of the

---

[1] Preziosi and Hitchcock: *op. cit.*, p. 190.
[2] Akurgal: *Art of Greece, op. cit.*, p. 25; W. Stevenson Smith: *Interconnections in the Ancient Near East* (NY, 1965), pp. 53-55, also see U.B. Alkim: *Anatolia I (Archaeologia Mundi)* (NY, 1968), pp. 150-177; A. Moortgat: »Mesopotamia«, *Encyclopedia of World Art* IX (NY, 1964), pp. 775-780. The Archaic Greek sculpture of Samos (ca. 575 BC) was greatly influenced by Assyrian sculpture and other artistic evidence has revealed close connections

Dying Lioness from Nineveh and other leonine as well as canine figures from that site, all datable to the 7th century. An even more interesting, if not compelling, comparison can be made between the Lion Gate figures and two rampant bulls on either side of a central pole depicted on enameled brick from Fort Shalmaneser, dating from the 9th century.[1] "The imposing sculptures that adorned Assyrian palaces became the Classical style of the ancient Near east and were taken as models by all neighboring peoples."[2]

Fig. 7: Wounded lioness on a relief, now in the British Museum, from the Neo-Assyrian North Palace of Ashurbanipal at Nineveh, generally believed to date from the 7th century BC

From the Bronze Age on, contacts between the Greek mainland and Mesopotamia were considerable; and "long before the seventh century, Mesopotamian culture began to influence Greek-speaking people."[3] A number of cylinder seals have been found in Mycenaean

---

between Samos and Mesopotamia (see Parrot: *op. cit.*, pp. 11-69, figs. 70-71; *The Legacy of Mesopotamia*, ed. S. Dalley et al. (NY, 1998), p. 98).

[1] P. Amiet: *Art of the Ancient Near East* (NY, 1980), p. 274, plate 114; also see pp. 414-415, figs. 624-631. A recent author (D. Evely) described the Lion Gate in these terms: "... overall the work creates a naturalistic impression of raw power", an apt description that could be applied to the leonines of Assyria as well – see »Helladic, V, 2(iii)« in *The Dictionary of Art*, ed. J. Turner, Vol. 14 (NY, 1998), p. 353.

[2] Akurgal: *op. cit.*, p. 25 and plates 5, 9-11; also see E. Akurgal: *The Art of the Hittites* (NY, 1962), pp. 130ff., and plates 124, 132, 135-137; *Hittite Art and the Antiquities of Anatolia*, The Arts Council (London, 1964), pp. 34-35 and plate 215; K. Bittle: »Hittite Art«, *Encyclopedia of World Art*, VII (NY, 1963), pp. 573-575 and plate 285; L. Woolley: *op. cit.*, pp. 161-199.

[3] S. Dalley et al.: *op. cit.*, p. 92.

sites; and interaction between the Near East and the Aegean World intensified during the Neo-Assyrian period (ca. 900 – 612 BC). Greeks came into contact with Assyrians through diplomatic and commercial activity as well as commonplace encounters from Syria to Egypt.[1] Mesopotamian bronzes have also been found in several Greek sites, ranging from Athens, Delphi, Olympia, Rhodes and Samos.

Aside from aesthetic considerations, the iconography of the Lion Gate is readily traceable to Mesopotamia.[2] The rampant lions of the Mycenaean gateway repeat a motif long familiar in the art of the ancient Near East and seen also in the Predynastic art of Egypt from Gebel-el-Arak and Hierakonpolis.[3]

Fig. 8: Predynastic knife handle from Gebel-el-Arak

---

[1] *Ibid.*, pp. 87-98. Cf. M. Bernal: *Black Athena*, II (New Brunswick, 1991), pp. 472-494.

[2] Greenberg: *op. cit.*, p. 29.

[3] W. Stevenson Smith: *The Art and Architecture of Ancient Egypt*, rev. by W. K. Simpson, 3rd ed. (London, 1998), p. 14; K. Michalowski: *Art of Ancient Egypt* (NY, 1968), p. 359, fig. 180, p. 540, fig. 919. Also see S. Lloyd: *The Art of the Ancient Near East* (NY, 1961), pp. 17-43; H.W. Muller: »Egyptian Art«, *Encyclopedia of World Art*, IV (NY, 1961), p. 622 and plates 320-324; W.H. McNeill: *The Rise of the West* (Chicago, 1963), pp. 67, 190-191; S. Mark: *From Egypt to Mesopotamia* (London, 1997), pp. 76-79.

The disagreements among scholars over the dating of the Lion Gate at Mycenae and its cultural and historical relationships within the milieu of the Ancient World continue even into the domain of aesthetic evaluation and iconographical understanding. One almost gains the impression of a Rashomon story when examining the opinion of various individuals concerning the stylistic merits of the Lion Gate and its meaning.

Boardman described the lions as monsters[1] "rather poor as animal sculpture" which, "in their conventions and proportions ... are hardly more than Mycenaean seal engravings or ivories monstrously enlarged. It was probably this inability to find an adequate idiom or technique which inhibited further attempts at major sculpture in stone."[2]

Matz found the character and perfection of the work astonishing in light of the fact that it was the product of a very weak tradition of craftsmanship.[3] He also felt that the gap between Minoan pictorial representation, with its radial composition on the one hand, and the Lion Gate, with its tectonic structural qualities on the other, presented a point of view almost indicative of a fresh start.[4]

Higgins saw, in the Lion Gate, "the effective translation of a miniature theme into a major sculptural creation" in which "we must acknowledge the Mycenaean, rather than the Cretan genius."[5]

MacKendrick described the lions as "noble beasts"[6] and Taylour noted that while "there are differing interpretations as to the symbolism of this famous relief, some emphasizing the religious aspects, others the secular ... all are agreed in recognizing in this early example of Greek sculpture a great monument, noble and majestic in conception, and a worthy precursor of later Greek genius."[7]

Much analysis has also dealt with the symbolic significance of the Lion Gate, with almost as many divergent explanations put forward as there are critics. Schliemann[8] followed the opinion that the central column of the Lion Gate represented Apollo Agyieus, "the guardian

---

[1] See D. H. Fischer: *Historians' Fallacies: Toward a Logic of Historical Thought* (New York, 1970), 244 for a discussion of "the fallacy of insidious analogy."
[2] J. Boardman: *Pre-Classical: From Crete to Archaic Greece* (Baltimore, 1967), pp. 48-50.
[3] F. Matz: *The Art of Crete and Early Greece* (New York, 1962), 202.
[4] *Ibid.*, 203-04. And see R. Scranton: *Aesthetic Aspects of Ancient Art* (Chicago, 1964), pp. 159-84: H. Frankfort: *The Art and Architecture of the Ancient Orient* (Baltimore, 1958), 166, also discusses North Syrian art of the first millennium as representing a fresh start.
[5] R. Higgins: *Minoan and Mycenaean Art* (New York, 1967), 92.
[6] P. MacKendrick: *The Greek Stones Speak* (Mentor Books, New York, 1966), 73.
[7] Lord W. Taylour: *The Mycenaeans* (New York, 1964), 128.
[8] H. Schliemann: *Mycenae* (New York, 1880), 33-35.

of the gateway" which had been united with the two lions "either as the sacred animals of Rhea or as the symbol of the powerful dynasty of the pelopids." It should be noted that Pelops supposedly migrated from Phrygia and was the son of the Phrygian king Tantalus.

Demargne[1] saw in the relief as a whole a sort of "heraldic badge of the city of Mycenae," while Matz asserted that "the old identification of the lion relief as a royal coat-of-arms misses the point. It is anything but an emblem or ornament. It is a powerful symbol which conjures up the protecting deity at the site."[2]

The lions themselves press downward on two objects termed altars[3] which Luce has viewed as a potent symbol of Minoan cultural conquest over Mycenae since "the royal lions of the house of Atreus support themselves against a Minoan pillar standing on a Minoan altar base."[4] However, Marinatos interpreted the altars as a "Sea" symbol on the basis of a comparison made with similar objects seen on a Cretan fresco from Amnisos and "thus the blazon of Mycenae might be read as the Union of ... two Sea-powers" with the "second" power possibly being Crete.[5] Employing the same fresco, Galanopoulos presented a case for a possible link between Crete and Atlantis.[6]

By now, it should be obvious to the reader that we are dealing with a veritable kaleidoscope of scholarly speculation with the same thing meaning different things to different people. The same situation exists to some extent when considering the artistic source for the theme of the Lion Gate.

Evans noted the constant recurrence in Crete of "the sacral 'antithetic' subject of a male or female figure between pairs of lions," which also acted "as supporters of the Minoan Rhea on the ceilings of the Central Palace sanctuary at Knossos."[7] Also at Knossos, the Cretan Mother Goddess appeared on a seal impression standing atop a mountain between two guardian lions.[8] This particular iconograph-

---

[1] P. Demargne: *The Birth of Greek Art* (New York, 1964), 203.
[2] Matz: *op. cit.*, 202.
[3] S. Hood: *The Home of the Heroes: The Aegean before the Greeks* (New York, 1967), p. 97.
[4] J. V. Luce: *Lost Atlantis* (New York, 1969), p. 175 and plates 91 and 92. On relations between Crete and Mycenae, see H. J. Kantor: *The Aegean and the Orient in the Second Millennium B.C.* (Bloomington, 1947).
[5] S. Marinatos: *Crete and Mycenae* (New York, 1960), p. 11, footnote 39. This is certainly a direct contradiction to Luce's interpretive theory.
[6] A. G. Galanopoulos and E. Bacon: *Atlantis: The Truth behind the Legend* (New York, 1969), pp. 152-55.
[7] Sir A. Evans: *The Palace of Minos at Knossos*, 3 (London, 1921-35), pp. 126-27.
[8] *Ibid.*, 3. p. 414; Taylour: *op. cit.*, 63, figure 17.

ic portrayal probably had some symbolic connection with the Great Mother Ninhursag of Mesopotamia, who was known as the "Lady of the Mountain".[1]

Ramsay found similar lion and pillar groups in Phrygia and in one instance the goddess Cybele assumed the place of the pillar.[2] In addition, a Cretan intaglio displayed two lions in the same heraldic pose as those of the Lion Gate except that an eight-pointed star was substituted for the pillar between them.[3] The presence of the eight-pointed star again points to the Orient since it was the symbol for the goddess Ishtar with whom the Minoan Goddess could have been identified. To assume that the Lion Gate was merely a symbolic representation of the Minoan Goddess flanked by her guardian lions, the result of some sort of cultural and theological transliteration, would be far too simplistic.

The rampant lions of the Mycenaean gateway repeat a motif long familiar in Mesopotamian art and seen also in the pre-dynastic art of Egypt from the sites of Gebel-el-Arak and Hierakonpolis.[4]

Additional Considerations and Questions

Our study of the Lion Gate at Mycenae has inevitably led us back to the art of the Ancient Near East, regardless of what aspect of that monument was under discussion. Thus, its artistic debt to that part of the world cannot be denied. Nor can we neglect its Minoan heritage. Yet, the cultural legacy of the former would obviously appear to be far greater than that of the latter, which also possessed certain elements of Egyptian and Mesopotamian origin.[5]

---

[1] Frankfort: *op. cit.*, 6.
[2] W. M. Ramsay: »Sepulchral Customs in Ancient Phrygia«, *JHS*, 5 (1884), 241-51.
[3] G. Perrot and C. Chipiez: *History of Art in Primitive Greece*, 2 (London, 1894), pp. 214, 246.
[4] See W. S. Smith: *The Art and Architecture of Ancient Egypt* (Baltimore, 1958), p. 19, figure 5; W. H. McNeill: *The Rise of the West* (Chicago, 1963), pp.67, 190-91; H. W. Muller: »Egyptian Art«, *EWA*, 4 (New York, 1961), 622 and plates 320-24. For a general sculptural survey of the lion in ancient art, see L. M. Greenberg: *The Animal and Mythical Creature in Greek Art - A Study in Symbolism* (unpublished thesis), Rutgers Univ. Library (New Brunswick, New Jersey, 1961).
[5] See Marinatos: *op. cit.*, 81-82 for a discussion of Egyptian connections with Mycenae on the basis of similar mummification practices and quantities of gold whose source was most likely Egypt.

To view the Lion Gate as a mere overblown version of Cretan glyptic art[1] is an archaic oversimplification of the history of art and a basic underestimation of the cultural interaction of ancient civilizations in general and Mycenaean accomplishments in particular. To assume that the sculptural portion of the Lion Gate can be dated on the basis of a handful of broken pottery (itself dependent upon a fluctuating chronology) found beneath the gateway threshold also displays a bit of scholarly laxity. Even if the pottery is correctly dated, it only yields a terminus a quo[2] for the gateway and guarantees no positive date for the sculpture, which theoretically could have been carved or substituted for something else at a much later period in time.[3]

The whole problem of the continuity between the various cultures of Greece and the link between Mycenaean and Classical Greek civilization[4] rests directly upon a redating of the Lion Gate and other Mycenaean objects as well as a reconsideration of several other key factors, such as who the Ahhijawa[5] really were, the date of the Trojan War[6] (if in fact there ever was one), and whether or not a "Dorian invasion" of Greece ever took place.[7]

Despite the supposed final destruction of Mycenae around 1100 BC[8] and Schliemann's belief that Mycenae "must have been destroyed at

---

[1] Boardman: *Pre-Classical, op. cit.*, 48.
[2] A. J. B. Wace: *Mycenae. An Archaeological History and Guide* (New York, 1964), 50, 132-34.
[3] For a full discussion of current theories and problems dealing with Mycenaean Civilization, see W. A. McDonald: *Progress into the Past* (New York, 1967), 361-426; E. Vermeule: *Greece in the Bronze Age* (Chicago, 1964), vii-viii; G. Mylonas: *Mycenae and the Mycenaean Age* (Princeton, 1966), 223. The Lion Gate was added at a later date to the original enciente of Mycenae. See p. 351, n. 1 *supra*.
[4] McDonald: *ibid.*, 421-22; G. Becatti: *The Art of Greece and Rome* (New York, 1967), pp. 10-11.
[5] See McDonald: *ibid.*, 393; J. P. Cohane: *The Key* (New York, 1969), pp. 100-04; Page: *op. cit.*, 40, footnote 63; S. Barr: *The Will of Zeus* (New York, 1961), pp. 11ff.; O. R. Gurney: *The Hittites* (Baltimore, 1954), pp. 46-58.
[6] See McDonald: *ibid.*, 403-06; Velikovsky: *Worlds in Collision, op. cit.*, 245-53; A. R. Burn: *The Pelican History of Greece* (Baltimore, 1966), p. 70; *The Greek World*, H. L. Jones, ed. (Baltimore, 1965), p. 24; C. W. Blegen: *Troy and the Trojans* (New York, 1963), 13-20; Mylonas: *op. cit.*, 215-18; Vermeule: *op. cit.*, 274ff.
[7] See Mylonas: *ibid.*, 218-29; McDonald: *ibid.*, 406-17; H. Hall: *The Oldest Civilization of Greece* (London, 1901), 41ff., 221ff.; R. Carpenter: *Discontinuity in Greek Civilization* (New York, 1966), pp. 34ff.; L. Palmerance: »The Final Collapse of Santorini (Thera) 1400 B.C. or 1200 B.C.?« *Studies in Mediterranean Archaeology*, 26 (Goteborg, 1970), pp. 26 and 28-32.
[8] Taylour: *op. cit.*, 178.

a period of great antiquity ... too strongly confirmed by the monuments,"¹ problems of art historical resolution and traditional continuity still remain. "How, for example, are we to explain the typical plan of the classical temple – with the two columns of the porch in line with the end walls and with the main shrine, or naos, and its central statue base – except as a carry-over of the plan of the Mycenaean megaron?"² How can we account for the similarity between the early Doric column and capital and the Lion Gate column, the resemblance between "stone-carved and fresco examples of Minoan-Mycenaean friezes of split rosettes alternating with groups of vertical fasciae [which] are strikingly close to the triglyph and metope pattern of the later Doric order of architecture,"³ and the awareness of the Classical Greeks of the "many nonmaterial facets of their heritage?"⁴ In addition, the relationship between the theme and compositional arrangement of the Lion Gate at Mycenae and the sculptural program of the pediment of the Temple of Artemis at Corfu (ca. 600 BC)⁵ offers yet another logical reason for assuming an unbroken artistic tradition on the Greek mainland.

If the basic premise of this paper, namely that the Lion Gate at Mycenae is sculpturally an eighth or seventh century BC monument, should prove to be correct and other Mycenaean problems are resolved as a result of an alteration of chronology in favor of a later dating, then the "Dark Ages" of Greece⁶ would be instantly swept away. This would not be the first time a "Dark Age" had vanished in the light of new discoveries and willing critical reevaluation.⁷

---

[1] Schliemann: *op. cit.*, 373 and 366ff. Mycenae may actually have been occupied without interruption until 468 BC, if no "Dark Age" exists. See Mylonas: *op. cit.*, 236-37 for the chronology and events of Mycenaean history as they now stand and Vermeule: *op cit.*, 323-25.

[2] McDonald: *op. cit.*, 423-24.

[3] *Ibid.*, 424 and figure 101.

[4] *Ibid.*, 425; Vermeule: *op. cit.*, 63-64.

[5] See R. Lullies and M. Hirmer: *Greek Sculpture* (New York, 1960, rev. ed.), pp. 56-57, plates 16-19; The Gorgon motif was also found in Mycenae – see Perrot and Chipiez: *History of Art in Primitive Greece, 2, op. cit.*, 249.

[6] See V. R. Desborough and N. G. L. Hammond: »The End of the Mycenaean Civilization and the Dark Age«, *CAH* Fascicle 13, 1962; V. R. Desborough: *The Greek Dark Ages* (New York, 1972); A. M. Snodgrass: *The Dark Age of Greece* (Chicago, 1971).

[7] See V. Karageorgis: *The Ancient Civilization of Cyprus* (New York, 1969), pp. 103ff.; P. Verzone: *The Art of Europe: The Dark Ages* (New York, 1967); Frankfort: *op. cit.*, 166.

Conclusion

It would appear that Ramsay's initial dating of the Lion Gate to the 8th century BC had considerable merit. His comparison of that monument to Phrygian sculpture grows even more credible when considered in conjunction with the application of a viable revised chronology and a close examination of Assyrian relief sculpture. Perhaps Ramsay merely lacked the historical perspective necessary to carry his observations to their possible conclusion.[1] In this study, all roads eventually led back to the ancient Near East and the Lion Gate's debt to that part of the world cannot be ignored.

Nevertheless, many problems remain: The date for the time of Ramesses II seems up for grabs, with as many as 5 or 6 competing chronologies; the dating of Mycenaean pottery offers its own difficulties;[2] who and to what Age do the Hittites belong is a question whose answer continues to be elusive;[3] sherds found beneath Mycenaean thresholds are not always indisputable;[4] the so-called 'Dark Age' of Greece along with any number of other inexplicable historical lacunae is troublesome to conventional chronology;[5] the exact date and locale of the Trojan War (if in fact there ever was one) is still uncertain;[6] the validity of the Ahhiyawa=Achaeans equation is debatable;[7] and the

---

[1] But see W. Ramsay: »A Study of Phrygian Art (Part I)«, *op. cit.*, p. 366.

[2] C. D. Fortenberry: »Helladic, I, 4«, *The Dictionary of Art, op. cit.*, pp. 334-335; Hood: *op. cit.*, p. 18; Taylour: *op. cit.*, pp. 45-59; I. Velikovsky: »Olympia«, *Kronos* I:4 (April 1976), pp. 3-7 for a very specific problematic example.

[3] E.g., E. Sweeney: »Were the Hittites Lydians?«, *The Velikovskian* V: 1 (2000), pp. 44-52; L.M. Greenberg: »Hittites and their Skulls«, *Pensée* IVR V (Fall, 1973), pp. 35-36; James et al.: *Centuries, op. cit.*, pp. 113-141.

[4] See the comments by H.R. Hall: *The Civilization of Greece in the Bronze Age* (NY, 1927), pp. 146-149 for the disagreement between Wace and Evans (p. 149).

[5] E.g., C. G. Thomas and C. Conant: *Citadel to City-State* (Bloomington, 1999), pp. xv-xxxii; Demargne: »Birth ...«, *op. cit.*, pp. 279-281; S.B. Pomeroy et al.: *Ancient Greece: A Political, Social, and Cultural History* (NY, 1999), pp. 41-81; V. Karageorgis: *The Ancient Civilization of Cyprus* (NY, 1969), pp. 65-67; Akurgal: *Art of the Hittites, op. cit.*, pp. 124-126.

[6] The literature is vast but see e.g., »The New Trojan Wars« and »Greeks vs Hittites: Why Troy is Troy and the Trojan War is Real« in *Archaeology Odyssey*, 5:4 (July/Aug. 2002), pp. 16-35; H. G. Jansen: »Troy: Legend and Reality«, *Civilizations of the Ancient Near East*, II (NY, 1995), pp. 1121-1134; F. Vinci: »Homer in the Baltic«, *Aeon* VI:2 (Dec. 2001), pp. 95-109; J.V. Luce: *Celebrating Homer's Landscapes* (New Haven, 1998), *passim*; D. Easton: »The Quest for Troy«, *Mysteries of the Ancient World*, ed. by J. Flanders (London, 1998), pp. 66-77; P. James & N. Thorpe: *Ancient Mysteries* (NY, 1999), pp. 415-419.

[7] Bryce: *op. cit.*, pp. 59-63; R. Drews: *The End of the Bronze Age* (Princeton, 1993), pp. 216-217, n. 12; Jansen: *ibid.*, pp. 1129-1130.

authenticity of many of the pre-Hellenic finds is controversial.¹ Yet, for all that, to quote Lynn E. Rose and Raymond C. Vaughan, "We do not stand before a wall: we stand before a door."²

The effective downdating of the Lion Gate and other Mycenaean artefacts would certainly help in solving the vexing problem of Greek cultural continuity and the question of linkage between Mycenaean and Classical Greek civilization.³ Given the subject matter and compositional arrangement of the Lion Gate, a lowering of its date would bring it more in line with the format and theme of early Archaic Greek pedimental sculpture, such as that found on the Temple of Artemis at Corfu (ca. 600 BC)⁴ and the oldest poros and peripteral temples built on the Athenian Acropolis (ca. 575-550 BC);⁵ and, more importantly, the ultimate acceptance of a revised chronology for Mycenaean art would constitute a significant step towards ending the tyranny of Dynastic Egypt over the dating of nearly two millennia of Ancient Mediterranean civilisations.

Fig. 9: The Lion Gate at Mycenae today

---

[1] Traill: op. cit., inter alia; S.H. Allen: Finding the Walls of Troy (London, 1999), pp. 180-184; James and Thorpe: ibid., pp. 515-518; K. Lapatin: Mysteries of the Snake Goddess (Boston, 2002), p. 37; W. A. Calder et al.: »Behind the Mask of Agamemnon«, Archaeology 52:4 (July/August 1999), pp. 51-59.

[2] L.E. Rose & R.C. Vaughan: »Velikovsky and the Sequence of Planetary Orbits«, Pensée IVR VIII (Summer, 1974), p. 34.

[3] McDonald: op. cit., pp. 361-426; G. Becatti: The Art of Greece and Rome (NY, 1967), pp. 10-11; New Perspectives in Early Greek Art, ed. D. Buitron-Oliver (London, 1991), pp. 99-104.

[4] Boardman et al.: Greek Art... , op. cit., p. 163; R. Lullies: Greek Sculpture (NY, 1960), plates 16-17 and p. 57. The Mycenaean lions are naturalistically far more advanced than their Greek Archaic counterparts – see R. Hampe and E. Simon: The Birth of Greek Art (NY, 1981), plates 444-453 & pp. 279- 280.

[5] Boardman et al.: ibid., p. 164 & p. 188 for the Temple of Apollo (V) at Delphi.

Ramesses II and Greek Archaic Sculpture

Introduction

The current, generally accepted dates for the reign of Ramesses II are 1279-1213 BC.[1] Velikovsky, in *Ramses II and His Time*, presented an extensive case for repositioning Ramesses II primarily in the late 7th and early 6th centuries BC with a solitary regnal period of some 30 years (ca. 610-580 BC).[2] Any attestation of additional regnal years was postulated to reflect a co-regency with Seti the Great and Merneptah.[3] Thus, Ramesses II might have actually reigned from ca. 630-570 BC according to Velikovsky's chronological scheme.[4]

The dramatic downdating for the time of Ramesses II, first proposed by Velikovsky, has been greeted with a highly mixed response, ranging from outright acceptance to downright rejection. This is not the place, however, to enter into that debate.[5] Instead, what is offered here is a kind of "litmus test". Since the dates for Ramesses II put forth by Velikovsky coincide with the early Archaic period of Greek art, it is of intellectual interest – at the least – to see what transpires when we compare various examples of Ramesside art with Greek Archaic sculpture.

Egypt and Greece

It has long been accepted that Greek Archaic sculpture – particularly the kouros type – owes a certain debt to Egypt,[6] though Greek art could never be termed derivative. Egyptian artistic and architectural achieve-

---

[1] See K. A. Kitchen: *Pharaoh Triumphant: The Life and Times of Ramesses II* (Warminster, 1982), pp. 43-210; M.G. Hasel: *Domination and Resistance: Egyptian Military Activity in the Southern Levant* (Leiden, 1998), pp. 151, 152. Also see p. 344, ref. 2, *supra*.

[2] I. Velikovsky: *Ramses II and His Time* (NY, 1978), pp. 212-217.

[3] *Ibid.*, pp. 212-213, 217. Cf. T. Wilkinson: *Ramesses The Great* (London, 2023), pp. 191-194.

[4] *Ibid.* and the Synchronical Table on p. 254. The text is a bit unclear and seems to contradict the ST which itself appears to be incomplete.

[5] Already documented in »The Lion Gate Redux« by the present author. See *supra*.

[6] J. M. Hurwit: *The Art and Culture of Early Greece, 1100- 480 BC* (Ithaca, 1985), pp. 190-197; J. Whitley: *The Archaeology of Ancient Greece* (NY, 2001), pp. 215-224.

ments were inspiring for the Greeks but did not lead to mere imitation.[1] Rhys Carpenter, long ago, incisively summed up the situation:

> ... the origin of Greek monumental sculpture must be sought elsewhere than in Greece itself. And since the date of the oldest surviving examples of the art seems provably coincident, within rather close chronological margin, with the Greek resumption of commercial relations with Egypt of the Nile Delta, and since it was Egypt which at that time most conspicuously practiced monumental sculpture, it is both natural and logical to look to Egyptian examples for the necessary initial inspiration.[2]

In the late 7th century BC, Ionian Greeks led by Milesians were encouraged to settle in the Egyptian delta city of Naukratis.[3] Situated along the Canopic branch of the Nile, Naukratis was only 10 miles from Sais, the capital of Dynasty XXVI, and some 75 miles northwest of Giza.[4] Conventional history places the Greeks in Naukratis during the reigns of Psammetichos I, Necho II, Psammetichos II, Apries and Amasis, nearly all of whom Velikovsky has identified with the pharaohs of Dynasty XIX. It is Ramesses II and the art produced under his aegis that concerns us here.

Perhaps the finest and most exquisite existing portrait of Ramesses II as a youth is the seated statue of his likeness carved in black granite and currently in the Turin Museum.[5] In the refined appearance of the facial features and the smooth planes of the face (Fig. 1), we see an individual who (in the words of Lange) "possesses characteristics of human warmth, readily appreciated virtue and a sweet bearing [along with] an expression of inner piety ... his expression withdrawn into itself and the hint of a *gentle smile* playing round the corners of his mouth."[6] A most unusual description of a ruler known for his

---

[1] B.S. Ridgway: *The Archaic Style in Greek Sculpture*, 2nd ed. (Chicago, 1993), pp. 33-43.
[2] R. Carpenter: *Greek Sculpture* (Chicago, 1960), p. 7.
[3] For a full discussion of Naukratis, see J. Boardman: *The Greeks Overseas* (Baltimore, 1964), pp. 133.ff. The founding date is arguable but appears to be ca. 640-630 BC; also see M.M. Austin: »Greece and Egypt in the Archaic Age«, *Proceedings of the Cambridge Philological Society*, Supplement No.2, 1970, pp. 22-25; for a most recent and comprehensive discussion, see A. Moller: *Naukratis* (NY, 2001), *passim*.
[4] J. Baines and J. Malek: *Cultural Atlas of Ancient Egypt*, rev. ed. (NY, 2000), pp. 50-51, 166-167.
[5] K. Lange and M. Hirmer: *Egypt*, 4th ed. (London, 1968), plates 232-233. For a full discussion of the Turin statue's physiognomy, see J. Malek: *Egyptian Art* (London, 1999), p. 325. While I agree with Malek that this image of Ramesses II "does not conform to the standard facial type" of that Pharaoh, I disagree with his aesthetic description of the facial features and his conclusion.
[6] Lange: *ibid.*, p. 496 (emphasis added).

quantitative building activity and general bombast. The general feel of this statue is evocative of the youthful male figures of Greek Archaic sculpture – more specifically, the Kouros from Melos[1] for one (Fig. 2; ca. 575-550 BC), with its smiling countenance and confident bearing who, as described by one scholar, evinces a "delicacy of the facial features which brings to mind that 'sweet Naxian melody' ... exemplified by several torsos from Delos."[2] Even its curlicues of hair seem to echo the circular decorations of Ramesses' war helmet. Additionally, the garb of the Turin Ramesses, especially in the chest and shoulder area, is reasonably comparable to that seen in the statue of Queen Karomama II, wife of Takelot II (ca. 850-825 BC),[3] thereby providing yet another more sensible fit with far later art styles than those of 13th century BC Egypt.

Fig. 1: Ramesses II, Turin Museum

Fig. 2: Kouros from Melos, Athens Nat. Mus.

Of further related interest is the fact that the bronze bust of a pharaoh from Qantir – once thought to be Ramesses II but now considered to

---

[1] R. Lullies & M. Hirmer: *Greek Sculpture*, rev. ed. (NY, 1960), plates 34-35 & p. 61.
[2] J. Charbonneaux, R. Martin & F. Villard: *Archaic Greek Art* (NY, 1971), p. 132.
[3] P. A. Clayton: *Chronicle of the Pharaohs* (London, 1994), p. 187.

be of a much later date[1] – brings to mind the black granite head in the Louvre of the Pharaoh Apries (ca. 580 BC).[2] Another black granite statue from Tanis – presumed to be Ramesses II – of which only the upper torso survives, also displays the "round face, high cheekbones, slightly bulging almond-shaped eyes, and sweet smiling mouth"[3] that one can associate with Greek Kouros figures such as Cleobis and Biton (ca. 590 BC) found at Delphi,[4] or the Kouros from Attica (ca. 540-515 BC)[5] – all of whom reveal the high cheekbones, almond-shaped eyes and typical smile of Greek Archaic sculpture. Surely, these comparisons appear to be more art historically valid than the standard ones employed, such as *The Cambridge Illustrated History of Ancient Greece*'s juxtaposition of the Metropolitan Kouros (ca. 600 BC) and the Vizier Bakenrenef (ca. 635 BC).[6] Or Hurwit's illustration of the diorite statue of Ir-khonsu-aat (Dynasty XXV – early 7th century) for purposes of comparing it to the Kouros from Sounion (600-590 BC),[7] or that old chestnut – the statue of Mentuemhet from the reign of Taharka (ca. 675 BC) which one sees in various books on Greek Archaic sculpture.

Another masterpiece from Dynasty XIX is the painted limestone statue of Meryetamun, daughter and wife of Ramesses II, now in the Cairo Museum.[8] The highly colouristic aspects of the work combined with its overall stylised aesthetic elegance evoke several Korai figures from the Acropolis in Athens, especially Kore 675 originally from Chios (ca. 520 BC).[9] Both depicted below also display the typical Archaic smile.

---

[1] Baines & Malek: *op. cit.*, p. 175.
[2] Clayton: *op. cit.*, p. 196.
[3] R. E. Freed: *Ramesses the Great* (Boston, 1988), p. 132; also see J. Tyldesley: *Ramesses: Egypt's Greatest Pharaoh* (Penguin, NY, 2000), fig. 19.
[4] Lullies: *op. cit.*, plates 14-15 & p. 56.
[5] G.M.A. Richter: *A Handbook of Greek Art*, 4th ed. (London, 1965), p. 67, fig. 81; also see K. Papaioannou: *The Art of Greece* (NY, 1989), pp. 232-234, plates 66-68.
[6] *The Cambridge Illustrated History of Ancient Greece*, ed. P. Cartledge (Cambridge, 1998), p. 49.
[7] Hurwit: *op. cit.*, pp. 193-195.
[8] Freed: *op. cit.*, pp. 134-135 & p. 28; Lange: *op. cit.*, plate LIV & p. 502.
[9] Papaioannou: *op. cit.*, pp. 242-249, plates 72-77 and pp. 374-377; Lullies: *op. cit.*, p. 13, plate III & pp. 66-67; also see Charbonneaux, Martin & Villard: *op. cit.*, pp. 233.ff.

Fig. 3: Meryetamun, Cairo Mus.

Fig. 4: Kore 675, Athens Mus.

A granite statue of Tuyu (Vatican Museum), mother of Ramesses II, a Dynasty XIX wooden statuette of Ahmes Nofretari (The Louvre) and a standing female figure nestled between the colossal granite legs of Ramesses II in the first courtyard of the Karnak temple[1] all convey a similar feeling and artistic approach when placed alongside the Archaic Greek Korai. Allowing for differences in fashion and material, both the Egyptian and Greek examples have a convincing resemblance in stance, arm position and rhythm of coiffure.[2] The Ramesside examples also accord well when matched with an alabaster statue of Queen Amenirdis I (Cairo Museum),[3] wife and aunt of the Pharaoh Shebitku (ca. 702-690 BC) from Dynasty XXV.

Even making allowance for the inherent conservatism of Egyptian sculpture, it is quite difficult to imagine that 600-700 years elapsed between the sculpture produced in the time of Ramesses II and that of the Greek Archaic period as well as Egyptian Dynasty XXV.

An interesting concluding comparison between Ramesside art and

---

[1] K. Michalowski: *Art of Ancient Egypt* (NY, 1968), p. 407, figs: 527-528 & p. 456; Clayton: *op. cit.*, p. 149.

[2] Papaioannou: *op. cit.*, pp. 374-375.

[3] Clayton: *op. cit.*, p. 192.

Greek Archaic sculpture involves the Tomb of Nefertari[1] – favourite queen of Ramesses II – and the Treasury of the Siphnians at Delphi (ca. 525 BC).[2] Nefertari's death probably occurred somewhere between Years 24 and 30 of Ramesses II's reign or sometime around 1252 BC, according to conventional chronology. Applying Velikovsky's chronological approach, Nefertari's passing could have occurred ca. 580 BC with the completion of her tomb occurring shortly thereafter. Given its more than 5,000 square feet of painted decoration, this tomb in the Valley of the Queens must have required a veritable army of artisans. Since there were a significant number of foreigners already in Egypt at the time of Ramesses II's accession, with additional foreign "labourers conscripted to work on pharaoh's monuments" during his reign, it is highly probable that this group consisted of a number of Greeks.[3]

Fig. 5: A painted scene in Nefertari's tomb, QV66, Egypt

---

[1] J. K. McDonald: *House of Eternity; The Tomb of Nefertari* (Los Angeles, 1996), pp. 66-67, 84 & 100; A. Siliotti: *Egypt: Splendors of an Ancient Civilization* (NY, 1998), pp. 216-225.

[2] The island of Siphnos was almost midway between Crete and the Greek mainland as one proceeds due north [see P. Levi: *Atlas of the Greek World* (NY, 1982), p. 45] and Herodotos called it the richest of the islands. For the Treasury of the Siphnians, see Lullies: *op. cit.*, pp. 63-64, plates 48-55; Papaioannou: *op. cit.*, pp. 378-379 & pp. 508-509. An attempt to downdate the Siphnian Treasury by Francis and Vickers has been soundly rebuffed – see Ridgway: *op. cit.*, pp. 16-17; Whitley: *op. cit.*, pp. 72-74; Hurwit: *op. cit.*, p. 295.

[3] Tyldesley: *op. cit.*, pp. 56 & 64.

A close examination of some of the painted scenes in Nefertari's tomb reveals a variety of seated figures comprising a rather distinctive composition. From the north wall of Chamber K, we see Anubis, Hathor and Osiris receiving adoration from Nefertari.[1] In Recess E, just beyond Chamber G, Nefertari is led before seated images of Re'Horakhty and the Theban Hathor. The goddess raises her arm as if to touch the headdress or, perhaps, the shoulder of the god seated in front of her.

If we look at the east frieze of the Siphnian Treasury (Delphi Museum), we can observe two groups of seated deities – one favouring the Trojans, the other the Greeks – placidly facing each other.[2] The overall compositional feel of the Archaic relief, its rhythmical flow, combined with the gestural activity and richly patterned drapery of the divine figures (e.g., Aphrodite, Artemis, and Apollo or Athena, Hera, and Demeter) echoes the stately seated and elegant divinities of Nefertari's tomb. Of special interest is the possibility that the sculptor of the Siphnian Treasury frieze was also "equally at home in ... painting."[3]

Fig. 6: A sculpted scene from the Siphnian Treasury frieze, Delphi, Greece

Similar seated group compositions from the time of Ramesses II are also to be found on one of the walls of the pronaos of the temple at Abu Simbel where a standing Ramesses II offers Ethiopian and Nubian

---

[1] McDonald: *op. cit.*, p. 100.
[2] Lullies: *op. cit.*, plates 48-49. Note the comments about this frieze by R.M. Cook: *Greek Art: Its Development, Character and Influence* (Penguin, NY, 1972), p. 103.
[3] M. Robertson: *A History of Greek Art I* (Cambridge, 1975), p. 157.

prisoners to a seated Amen-Re and Mut as well as the deified image of himself seated between them,[1] and on the façade of the Ramesseum in Thebes where the intaglio-like kneeling figure of Ramesses II ritually makes an offering to the seated and like-sculpted figures of Amen-Re, Mut and Khons.[2]

Conclusion

Accepting the contemporaneity of Ramesses II and Archaic Greece as a point of departure, this speculative essay has dealt with the art historical "fallout" from such a premise. As it happens, some provocative artistic parallels have come to the fore while no insurmountable contradictions arose. We may even conjecture whether Greek artists and artisans were actually employed in the Egypt of Ramesses II and, if so, whether they were the ones who carried certain necessary skills back to Greece after honing their craft in the Land of the Pharaohs.[3]

The relationship between Egypt and Greece regarding the origins and evolution of Archaic Greek art is complicated and controversial.[4] As Spivey so aptly put it:

> It seems inconceivable that Egypt did not play a great part in the early formation of Greek art ... But attempts to arrive at forensic proof concerning the origins of monumental Greek art and architecture are generally fruitless and perhaps even pointless.[5]

The Land of the Nile was not the only source of inspiration for early Greek art but nothing in the Near East could compare with the life-

---

[1] Siliotti: *op. cit.*, pp. 36-37; Idem: *Egypt Lost and Found* (NY, 1999), pp. 208-209.
[2] Michalowski: *op. cit.*, p. 410, fig. 548; W. MacQuitty: *Abu Simbel* (NY, 1965), p. 58.
[3] Two renowned Greek sculptors of the 6th century BC were "said to have spent time among the Egyptians" (see Diodoros: *Library* 1.98.5-9 and the evaluation by R. Osborne: *Archaic and Classical Greek* Art (NY, 1998), p. 79). However, conventional chronology is not thinking of the period of Ramesses II.
[4] Cook: *Greek Art ..., op. cit.*, pp. 85-93; M. Bernal: *Black Athena Writes Back* (London, 2001), pp. 289-317; G.M.A. Richter: *The Sculpture and Sculptors of the Greeks* (New Haven, 1962), rev. ed., pp. 51-52; B. Ashmole: »Archaic Art«, *Encyclopedia of World Art*, I (NY, 1959), pp. 587-590.
[5] N. Spivey: *Greek Art* (London, 1997), pp. 117. Also see the erudite comments by C. G. Starr: *The Origins of Greek Civilization* (NY, 1961), pp. 258-260 and those of Hurwit: *op. cit.*, pp. 190-197.

size and colossal standing and seated figures of Egypt; and it was the latter that exerted such a profound effect on the nascent sculpture of Archaic Greece. Boardman described the circumstances quite well:

> Given that no Greek statuary answering these new concepts [of monumentality] can be securely dated before [any] attested interest in Egypt, given the existence of the models for them in Egypt ... and the absence of such models in the east where even major statuary is basically decorative or architectural rather than freestanding monumental, it is impossible not to associate this new era in Greek sculpture with influence from Egypt.[1]

Yet, for all that, an identifiable specificity of Egyptian monumental influence on Greek Archaic sculpture has eluded the best of scholarly scrutiny. The exceedingly rapid transformation of Greek sculpture away from Egyptian paradigms as the former achieved its own unique distinctiveness has also made meaningful comparisons that much more difficult.[2] Could the sculpture of Dynasties XXV and XXVI have been sufficiently influential on the Greeks, or did the art of Dynasty XIX also contribute? If so, should we believe that a 700-year gap made no difference, especially considering the fact that, by conventional chronological reckoning, a great deal of Ramesside material would have been sealed away, buried, or ruined by the time Greeks settled in the Nile Valley?

---

[1] J. Boardman: *Greek Sculpture: The Archaic Period* (NY, 1978), p. 18. For additional detailed discussion on this matter, see J. G. Pedley: *Greek Art and Archaeology*, 2nd ed. (London, 1998), pp. 143-145.

[2] Osborne: *op. cit.*, pp. 76-79; A. Stewart: *Greek Sculpture: An Exploration*, Vol. I (New Haven, 1990), pp. 12-13, 34, 38, 108-109, & esp. 312-313; A. Snodgrass: *Archaic Greece: The Age of Experiment* (Los Angeles, 1980), pp. 186-187. The influence of Egyptian architecture and sculpture, in a generalised and generic way, on Greek architecture and sculpture of the Archaic period has been noted [see e.g., C. Freeman: *Egypt, Greece and Rome* (NY, 1996), pp. 135-138]: "The inspiration to be more creative and ambitious with [limestone] possibly came from Egypt. The opening of Egypt by King Psamtek I (Psammetichus) (664-610 BC) encouraged the first major incursion of Greeks [who] inevitably ... came into direct contact with its vast array of stone monuments. The pyramids of Giza, for instance, were only 120 kilometres from the Greek trading post of Naucratis ... It is interesting that the majority of Greeks who settled Naucratis were Ionians, and a taste for monumental art seems to be found largely in the Ionian cities. The temple of Artemis at Ephesus with its double row of columns may be an echo of the columned halls of Egypt, while the famous row of marble lions at Delos seems an almost direct copy of the traditional sacred processional routes of the Egyptian temples." "The Ionians may not have been the only Greeks who borrowed from the Egyptians. Much of the ornament in the Doric order seems to develop directly from earlier Greek timber models ... but a comparison can be made between the columns of the shrine of Anubis at the temple of Hatshepsut at Deir el-Bahri and the temples to Hera at Olympia (590 BC) and to Apollo at Corinth (540 BC)."

For the moment, we may be at an impasse but, hopefully, the eventual answer to our dilemma may prove to be a way around the poetic words of Shelley uttered in a different context:

> My name is Ozymandias, king of kings:
> Look on my works ... and despair! ...

You Can't Have Amnesia if There's Nothing to Forget

"With the possible, but dubious exception of Homer ..., ancient authors preserved no memory of the four or so centuries that followed the collapse of the Mycenaean palaces."[1]

A major problem if not *the* problem when it comes to dealing with the Greek Dark Age is the inability to explain with exact certainty why or how the Mycenaean or "Heroic Age" came to an end and when it did. Various dates ranging from 1200 to 1100 BC have been proffered for its demise.[2] But that chronological factor still depends upon both Egyptian correlations, which are suspect, as well as the speculative date for the Trojan War which is fluid. Natural disasters such as volcanic eruptions, earthquakes, floods, and climate change have been proposed. Famine, disease, and human invasions are others. Indeed, it is accepted that there *was* destruction and disruption. It is the duration of the hiatus that was created which is in dispute. A four or five hundred-year Dark Age leaves us with too many contradictions, puzzles, and questions.

In the words of one scholar: "As far as accurate historical knowledge went ... the Greeks of later periods suffered from a *virtual amnesia* about the Bronze Age. They knew very little about Mycenaean civilization and its fall, and some of the major things that they thought they knew seems not to have been true. They believed, for example, that, following the collapse of Mycenaean civilization, a Greek-speaking group from the north, called the Dorians, began to invade central and southern Greece. ... Strikingly, however, modern archaeology has not discovered any distinctive remains attesting a Dorian invasion, and

---

[1] J.M. Hall: *A History of the Greek Archaic World 1200-479 BCE* (2nd ed., Chichester, 2014), pp. 59-60.

[2] R. Drews: *The End of the Bronze Age* (Princeton, 1993), *inter alia*. Drews offers multiple possibilities for the final destruction of the Mycenaean Age in 1200 BC; Lord William Taylour: *The Mycenaeans* (Folio Society, London, 2004), p. 163, opts for 1100 BC.

many scholars reject this ancient idea as a fiction. ..."[1] That may all be true. Yet it doesn't take centuries for traditional knowledge and information to be lost. What do those of a certain age living in the early 21st century really know about WWI or WWII? It does not require a long term Dark Age to create a memory vacuum. Yet therein lies the conundrum. How to reconcile a prolonged Dark Age from which purportedly little is remembered with Homeric epics that apparently contain so much relevant and specific cultural information. An oral tradition of poetry, storytelling, music, and song have been proposed. But this is being transmitted via a supposed Dark Age. This is not a place where we might find a comparable counterpart to a late Medieval troubadour going from town to town, not convulsed in some way, where its people eagerly and attentively await the latest news.

How can we account for the shapes of particular 7th century seals made in Melos or the reappearance of particular technical processes and decorative motives from Mycenaean art in the Greece of the 7th and 8th centuries BC? For the former, Reynold Higgins would have us believe that "lentoid and amygdaloid shapes of seals made in Melos in the seventh century BC can only be explained as being inspired by Minoan and Mycenaean seals found in tombs on that island." The latter he "explained as reintroductions from the East, where they had been adopted in the days of the Mycenaean empire and kept alive through the Dark Age."[2] Are we to believe, therefore, that people went tomb exploring during a Dark Age in search of trinkets? Or that neighboring regions acted as "care givers" for foreign artistic and centuries old motifs and techniques without any change so as to return them to their original creators?

With regard to the above Rodney Castleden has posed an intriguing question:

> Was Homer an historian or a pseudo-historian?...There is some evidence from the Linear B tablets to suggest that elements of the story were authentic survivals from the bronze age. The phrase 'Athana potnia' which is found on bronze age Linear B tablets of the thirteenth and fourteenth centuries BC is very close to Homer's phrase 'Potni Athenaie', and means the same thing, 'the Lady Athena'. If the story of the Trojan

---

[1] T. R. Martin: *Ancient Greece From Prehistoric to Hellenistic Times* (London, 1996), pp. 37-38 (emphasis added).
[2] R. Higgins: *Minoan and Mycenaean Art* (New Rev. Ed., London, 1997), p. 190.

War as told in the *Iliad* is fact, when is it likely to have occurred, how and why? Were Atreus and Agamemnon historical figures, real rulers of Mycenae?[1]

Margalit Finkelberg has also raised some relevant and provocative points:

> ... the narrative of the past adopted by the new Greek civilisation that replaced Mycenaean Greece was the narrative of the Heroic Age and its end in the Trojan War. ... [While it] is obvious indeed that, whatever the nature of the historic events underlying the Trojan saga, they cannot account for the destruction levels and depopulation in mainland Greece. The momentous events that brought about the end of the Mycenaean civilisation were replaced in the mainstream Greek tradition by the story of the Trojan War ... a war specially designed by Zeus to put an end to the Race of Heroes – a mythological construction that was apparently considered as offering a more satisfactory explanation of the transition of Greece from prehistory to history.[2]

And so it came to pass, as Finkelberg concluded,

> it was the Trojan War rather than the population movements [among other things] that shook Greece at the end of the second millennium BC that became universally envisaged as the main if not the only factor responsible for the catastrophe that brought about the end of the Heroic Age.

Continuing, Finkelberg had this to add:

> It is not out of the question that at least to some extent this remarkable instance of *collective amnesia* was due to what Jack Goody defined as *'homeostatic transformation'*, or selective forgetting and remembering, which he regards as a characteristic feature of oral societies.[3]

---

[1] R. Castleden: *Mycenaeans* (NY, 2005), p. 199; Cf. H.J. Kantor: *The Aegean and the Orient in the Second Millennium B.C.* (Boston, 1997), p. 86, Plate XXIII.

[2] M. Finkelberg: *Greeks and Pre-Greeks* (Cambridge, 2005), pp. 167-169. Sequence of some sentences have been reversed.

[3] *Ibid.*, p. 169 (emphasis added) and 10-11; See J. Goody: *The Power of the Written Tradition* (London, 2000), pp. 44-45. Also see I. Velikovsky: *Worlds in Collision* (NY, 1950), pp. 298-300 – »A Collective Amnesia«, and the excellent treatise by Mircea Eliade: *Myth and Reality* (NY, 1968).

Memories of Yesteryear

"During the Mycenaean period there was much contact [with neighboring regions]. According to the Linear B texts Cyprus, Egypt, and even Ethiopia to the south of Egypt were known to the Mycenaeans. ... Now the classical Greeks called these same lands by the same names as their Mycenaean forebears. If one were to assume that the Greeks during the Dark Age lost all contact with these lands, then it would surprise that when the Greeks allegedly rediscovered these lands sometime in, say, the eighth century BC, they applied to these lands the *exact same names which had been in currency five centuries earlier.*"[1]

The best explanation from some is that the Greeks in the Dark Age retained contact with these lands. If so, then why call it a "Dark Age"? And how could this contact have enabled the retention of exact appropriate nomenclature by an illiterate society which existed for centuries without the ability to record it? – A better explanation is that there was no gap of five centuries and therefore *no Dark Age*.

---

[1] V. Parker: *A History of Greece 1300-30 BC* (Chichester, 2014), pp. 65-66 (emphasis added).

Lefkandi

"At the beginning of the eleventh century, Greece seems to have been a depopulated country. The number of known inhabited sites drops appreciably from 320 sites in the thirteenth century to 40 sites in the eleventh century. However, this depopulation – a loss of three-quarters of the population – did not affect all regions of Greece in a uniform manner. Argolis and Messenia seem to have lost more inhabitants than Attica and Euboea, for example."[1]

Afterwards a new pottery style came into vogue, iron gradually replaced bronze, funerary practices changed, and Greeks emigrated from mainland Greece and settled along the coasts of Asia Minor.

"All these were important innovations, and they suggest that a totally dark and negative view of these centuries would be inappropriate. The tendency today is to rehabilitate this period and emphasize its elements of continuity rather than those indicating a break. In some regions that appear to have been deserted because of the scarcity of archaeological data there, cultural elements in fact did survive, as if dormant, to reappear at the beginning of the archaic period. To account for the contradictory evidence of, on the one hand, severe depopulation and, on the other, cultural continuity, some historians now put forward the hypothesis that the Greeks of this period switched to a pastoral mode of life. ... It is a hypothesis that does provide an explanation as to how it was that there was not a total break between the Mycenaean and the archaic worlds. ... However, the hypothesis does little to resolve what remains the principal puzzle: What kind of a society and what kind of structures of power existed?"[2]

The authors of the above statements should have applied the theory of Occam's Razor: the simplest solution is probably the correct one. They needlessly backed themselves into a conundrum corner and were unable to take that one final "simple" and logical step – reject the concept of a "Greek Dark Age". Rather than hopefully seeking that one point of light in a 400-500 years long Dark Age, go back to the beginning and consider what it was that led to such a span of

---

[1] C. Orrieux and P. S. Pantel: *A History of Ancient Greece* (translated by J. Lloyd, 1999), p. 23.
[2] *Ibid.*, pp. 23-24.

time with its "contradictory evidence" of simultaneous depletion and cultural continuity. There is a one word answer: Egypt. If you discount the links to a questionable Egyptian chronology, not to mention the subjectivity of pottery sequence, this would allow the discarding of the assumptive "Greek Dark Age", thereby rendering the gap closure.

There still could have been a relatively brief period in Greece where there was temporary upheaval, dislocation, and retardation that lasted for, say, 50 years without anything to do with Egypt. Then came renewal along with partial continuity of the old. There was no elongated "Dark Age" – merely a most likely interregnum caused by all the human and natural catastrophes already cited whose rebirth seems astonishing. Yet what appeared after it was over should hardly surprise anyone living in the 21st century. Take the period in world history from 1914 – 1970. A rapidly expanding plague early on, two consecutive world wars, civil and regional wars, depressions, famine, assassinations, uprisings, and desolation. Some thought it would be the end of civilization as we know it. A world destroyed! However, by 1970, many countries were well on their way to full recovery. In that same time span we moved from horse and buggy to automobiles, from the first successful air flight to jet planes and space ships, space exploration and putting a man on the Moon, from radio to TV, movies with sound and color, the arts and live theater flourished, entered the Atomic Age for war and peace, new medicines, new vaccines, standard telephones, the beginning of computers. – That's Astonishing!

But for now we must return to Ancient Greece and the site of Lefkandi which inspired my digression. Lefkandi was a coastal village on the island of Euboia, northeast of Athens. The first archaeological activity began here in the mid 1960s. In 1981 a diverse and significant assemblage of burial objects was uncovered at an adjacent settlement site called Xeropolis. What was found were the remains of four horses, two people, a miniature terracotta centaur, iron weapons, unusual architecture, an "ancient" Babylonian necklace (suggested by one author to be early 2nd millennium with no citation), and other sundry goods. Lacking a more exact date for the Babylonian neck piece, which might have been somewhat helpful, an approximation of when it could have been deposited – such as the early eighth century during the time of the Neo-Assyrian Empire? – would have been welcomed.

Almost immediately, Lefkandi was looked upon as a kind of beacon light in the midst of a Dark Age. This singular discovery has been blown all out of proportion. It's as if what was found there somehow vitiates the idea of a Greek Dark Age. Associated pottery of the LH IIIC type has been found at the site which has then been further classified into particular Phases. Theoretical dates ranging from 1200 – 700 have been applied, but continuity on the site is unproven. Surrounding later activity apparently from the Protogeometric and Geometric periods has supposedly destroyed any other remnants that might have been on the site. This, however, is pure guesswork. Not only are the suggested dates for Lefkandi quite fluid, the objects found there are somewhat confusing. Of special interest is a horseshoe-shaped structure, fully rectangular except for one short rounded end. "Built of mudbrick on a stone foundation, this building is the largest yet known in the Greek world between LH IIIC and the *eighth century BCE*."[1] As it happens, the reliability of LH IIIC chronology has recently been questioned as previously cited;[2] additionally "the survival of 'Mycenaean' types in various ways in different parts of Greece makes it impossible to give a universally applicable end-date for Late Helladic IIIC."[3] Indeed, the establishment of an agreed upon definition of Late Helladic IIIC is fraught with difficulty.[4]

Despite many unanswered questions, Lefkandi is the

> "site most frequently invoked by those who deny that there was a true Dark Age in Greece ... however, the apparent exceptionality of Lefkandi only indicates that in the Dark Age an aggregately lower amount of wealth was distributed less evenly between communities than was the case in either the Mycenaean period or the period from the eighth century onwards. Lefkandi hardly serves to refute the concept of a Dark Age."

---

[1] R. T. Neer: *Greek Art and Archaeology* (NY, 2012), p. 72 (emphasis added). Also consider the words of J. Camp & Fisher: *The World of the Ancient Greeks* (London, 2002), pp. 60-61, employing the conventional chronology: This structure "dated to the tenth century ...is the largest building we know of built in Greece for *a period of 500 years, between 1200 and 700 BC*." (emphasis added); so, too, R.T. Neer: *Greek Art and Archaeology* (NY, 2012), p. 73.

[2] S. Deger-Jalkotzy: *The Cambridge Companion to the Aegean Bronze Age*, edited by C. W. Shelmerdine (Cambridge, 2008), p. 392.

[3] O. Dickinson: *The Aegean from Bronze Age to Iron Age* (NY, 2007), p.21.

[4] *Ibid.*, pp. 21-23.

"Unless, that is, the *Dark Age is simply a historiographical mirage, generated by faulty chronological reasoning. This is precisely the suggestion made in 1991 by a consortium of historians and archaeologists.*" The latter were both "*struck by the seemingly seamless resumption, after three or four centuries,*" of so many diverse key societal and cultural activities that "they wondered whether the palatial destructions [of the Mycenaean period] may not have taken place considerably later, thereby compressing the period of time normally allotted to the Dark Age. In their view the *source of the problem lies with Egyptian chronology, upon which all the dating-systems of the Mediterranean and Near East are, to a greater or lesser degree, dependent.*"[1]

But they never acted upon their observation.

Additional Relevant Sources:

- *The Oxford Handbook of the Bronze Age Aegean* (ed. E. H. Cline, Oxford, 2010), *inter alia*.
- D. Plantzos: *Greek Art and Archaeology c. 1200-30 BC* (Atlanta, 2016), pp. 48-49.
- L. Schofield: »Lefkandi«, *The Dictionary of Art* 19 (ed. J. Turner), pp. 67-68.
- G. Shipley: »Archaic Into Classical«, *Greek Civilization* (ed. by B. A. Sparkes, Oxford, 1998), pp. 54-56.

---

[1] J. M. Hall: *A History of the Greek Archaic World ca. 1200-479 BCE* (2nd ed., Chichester, 2014), pp. 62-65 (emphasis added).

Thera

The Aegean island of Thera/Santorini is arguably the most beautiful of all the Greek islands. Whitewashed, cube-shaped buildings, some capped with blue colored domes and turquoise swimming pools hug the side of what is left of the original mountain top that once crowned the island. It is positively resplendent in the daylight sun and a major tourist attraction for so many reasons.

Looking downward from the heights of Santorini who could ever suspect that the huge basin of water or caldera below, surrounded by the remnants of the original island, is the watery scar of one of the greatest volcanic eruptions to occur in historical times. It wasn't until 1939 that Spyridon Marinatos linked the destruction of the late Minoan Palaces on Crete to the titanic eruption of the island of Thera which he dated at the time to ca. 1500 BC.[1]

In 1960 and then again in 1972 Marinatos reaffirmed his conviction that a natural cataclysm brought on by the eruption of Thera, sometime between 1550 and 1525 BC, devastated Crete.[2] His dates were based upon pottery finds, fresco fragments, and seal impressions that could be linked with Egypt and Egyptian artifacts of a supposedly known date. A Homeric reference to Achaeans, the Trojan War, and Knossos may have also been a factor. A cautionary note here. External historical, archaeological, and literary associations with Crete and Thera have chronological problems. The latter two have their own independent ones. Any necessary change on one side of the equation affects the other.

It has now been estimated that the Theran eruption was four times greater than that of Krakatoa. Unlike Pompeii, known for the eruption of Mt. Vesuvius in 79 AD, it appears that there was enough warning to the inhabitants of Thera, perhaps from initial minor earthquakes, that most left before the volcano reached a critical explosive point. Thus we do not find evidence of a buried populace the way we do for

---

[1] S. Marinatos: »The Volcanic Eruption of Minoan Crete«, *Antiquity* 13 (1939), pp. 425-439.
[2] S. Marinatos: *Crete and Mycenae* (NY, 1960), pp. 20, 22; *National Geographic* 141 (May, 1972), p. 715. Also see D. Ninkovich and B. Heezen: »Santorin Tephra«, *Colston Papers*, Vol. 17 (1965), pp. 413-452 for comprehensive information on all aspects of the Theran eruption and its consequences published up to 1965.

excavations at Pompeii. The entire matter of the Theran eruption is still a puzzlement to this day.[1] First and foremost is the problem of *chronology*.

> On the basis of stylistic examination of the pottery [found there in conjunction with Egyptian correlations], the date of the disaster on Thera coincides with the completion of the development of Late Minoan IA pottery in Crete. Indeed, both imported Minoan pottery at Akrotiri, as well as local imitations, are restricted to the style prevailing in Late Minoan IA Crete; so far, pottery of the subsequent Late Minoan IB phase, the characteristic 'Marine style', is *entirely absent*. Having these two very distinctive and stratigraphically distinct styles as *termini post and ante quem*, the date of the end of Thera must be placed towards the end of the Late Minoan IA period in Crete, the absolute chronology of which is generally accepted to be c.1500 BC.

– the beginning of the Egyptian 18th Dynasty if not earlier.[2] LM IB could then be affiliated with the time of Thutmosis I, II, Hatshepsut, and Thutmosis III, but *not* found in Thera.

In 1999, S. W. Manning emphasized the point about LM IB in his book *A Test of Time*. Continued efforts to conflate late LM IA with LM IB and other efforts both theoretical and archaeological changed nothing. "Despite many, many thousands of ceramic finds, *nothing was LM IB in style*. This was clear in 1970 when Hood ... wrote that 'none of the pottery found ... has decoration characteristic of Late Minoan IB', and remains true nearly 30 years later."[3] The clear cut separation of LM IA and LM IB has important ramifications for Velikovsky's revised chronology for the end of the Middle Kingdom, Second Intermediate Period, and beginning of the 18th Dynasty (see *infra*). Before proceeding further with our discussion of LM IA and LM IB we must, for now, consider the suggested revised dates for the eruption of Thera. Later, the possible connection between its eruption and a cosmic encounter between the Earth and another planetary body will be posited at the very end of this entire Section.

---

[1] For a summary of the different types and amounts of destruction see C. G. Doumas: *Thera: Pompeii of the Eastern Aegean* (London, 1983), pp. 147-150.

[2] *Ibid.*, pp. 138-139 (emphasis added); see the section titled »Shaft Grave Art: Modern Problems« by Schorr on p. 178 in this book. Also see W. L. Friedrich: *Fire in the Sea: The Santorini Volcano: Natural History and the Legend of Atlantis* (Cambridge, 2000), Chapter 7, pp. 82-93 for a detailed survey of more recent scientific methodology being employed to date the Thera eruption.

[3] S. W. Manning: *A Test of Time* (Oxford, 1999), pp. 16-17 (emphasis in original).

The dispute over the date of Thera's eruption has become quite heated. There is no testimony by an eye witness such as Pliny the Younger's for Pompeii nor any connective reference to a contemporary ruler as we have for the reign of the Emperor Titus. The one debate involving the latter volcano has dealt with the time of year for Pompeii's eruption – now set in mid-Autumn. Why has the dating of Thera's eruption become so disquieting and controversial? The answer is to be found in Egyptian chronology which provided the original dates for LM IA; neither Crete nor Greece did.

Thanks to new scientific methods for dating purposes such as calibrated C14 dating, dendrochronology, ice cores, and even thermoluminescence new dates for the eruption of Thera have been proposed beginning in the 1980s.[1] These new dates range from 1664 – 1601 BC with ca. 1628 – 1617 BC being the likeliest probability. Some Egyptologists have rejected this outright. One particular individual, M. Bietak, was especially outraged over the possible implications. "If we were to adopt the more recent high chronology for the Santorini (Thera) explosion at about 1628 BC, based on radiocarbon and dendrochronology, we would have to raise the dates of Egyptian chronology by some 130 years ... no Egyptologist would accept such a proposition."[2] Manning immediately jumped in and claimed that "in fact, on examination, this is not the case." What is lacking, he said, is a proper integration of science and archaeology which should be done. And if it was, what would Egyptologists do if the same new dates continued to appear? Are the absolute dates for Ancient Egypt never to be adjusted regardless of the new scientific evidence for that possibility? One wonders what the reactions of Torr and Ramsay would be to this entire matter if they were alive today.

Today the new dates for the Theran eruption are categorized as the "high chronology" (see Betancourt for one – *Introduction to Aegean Art*), a euphemistic term for what cannot be fully accepted by either Aegeanists or Egyptologists. This reminds me of the situation regarding two radiocarbon datings gleaned from material taken from the tomb of Tutankhamen and finally tested back in 1971. British Museum samples consisting of reed and palm nut kernels were dated to ca. 846 BC and ca. 899 BC, dates that could have supported Velikovsky's

---

[1] en.wikipedia.org/wiki/Minoan_eruption#Magnitude
[2] Manning: *op. cit.*, p. xxx and ref. 15. A revised edition from 2012 is available.

revised chronology for the time of Tutankhamen. But they were never officially published after announcing and giving assurance that they would be released as part of a group. Then, after a number of letter inquiries back and forth between various individuals and museums, someone from the British Museum replied that "this laboratory has made no measurements on material from the tomb of Tutankhamun."[1] As for Bietak, someone needs to remind him how much of Egyptian chronology was in a state of flux well into the 20th century and the fact that "fine tuning" is going on even today. (Consider the Hyksos period in Egypt.) The following list of dates proposed for the Second Intermediate Period by highly qualified individuals during the 65 years from 1839-1904 is especially appropriate given the fact that the new "high chronology" for Thera would probably affect the current accepted dating and length of the Second Intermediate Period the most. Here is that compiled table taken from R. Weill: *Bases, Méthodes et Résultats de la Chronologie Egyptienne* (Paris, 1926), pp. 3-4 and reprinted in *Kronos* I:3 (Fall, 1975), p. 16:

EGYPTOLOGIST	YEAR	INTERVAL OF TIME	ABSOLUTE DATE FOR 18TH DYNASTY BEGINNING
Champollion-Figeac	1839	1595 years	1822 BC
Wilkinson	1842	1595	1575
Boeckh	1845	1589	1655
Bunsen	1845	1009	1625
Lepsius	1858	676	1591
Brugsch	1859	893	1706
Unger	1867	1359	1796
Lieblein	1873	618	1490
Mariette	1876	695	1703
Brugsch	1877	533	1700
Lauth	1879	600	1585
Wiedemann	1884	1500 (?)	1750
Maspero	1897	1306	?
von Bissing	1904	1299	?
Meyer, Eduard	1904	210	1580

[1] *Pensée* VI (Winter 1973-74), *ASH*, pp. 18-19. In a reply to Bruce Mainwaring, G. W. Van Oosterhout of Delft University had this to say: "Apparently Mr. Barker does not know what's going on in his laboratory, to say it kindly. This is much worse than what you said. Deviating results are not only not published, it is even denied that they have been found ..."; also see B. Feldman: *Kronos* II:1 (August, 1976), p. 83 and ref. 43.

As one can clearly see from all of the above, the duration of the Second Intermediate Period and the accepted absolute date for the start of the 18th Dynasty were not established by much of a consensus. It was Eduard Meyer's chronology that prevailed though Maspero, von Bissing, and Petrie did not accept it. Apparently it was Breasted's support and acceptance of Meyer's proposal that led to it being embraced. However, Meyer's "Sothic" theory of dating remains controversial to the present day. The late Eva Danelius's brilliant and lucid commentary on this entire matter in the above cited issue of *Kronos*, pp. 4-7, summarizes the problem exceedingly well. Furthermore, there is another factor that is all too often overlooked. Very frequently a theory becomes "canonized" because the opposition to that theory dies. Given the ages of all of the above when these chronological debates were going on, add to it the average life span then, the "Spanish" flu, and WWI, and even disciples of the aforementioned could have been swept away. If "history is written by the victors" then the "acceptance of theories is often won by those who survive."

While we're on the subject of Egyptian chronology it is worthwhile to turn our attention back to the book by Manning. Afterwards, we will conclude our survey of Thera by considering a possible cause for the timing of its eruption, and the significance of the presence of LM IA on Thera without any LM IB ware being found there.

After Manning concluded the main text of *A Test of Time*, he proceeded to offer a most detailed and rigorous Appendix (1) with a nearly 50 page discussion of Egyptian chronology. He admitted that, for the second millennium BC, "a complete chronology from a fixed point does *not* exist."![1] He then went on to cite a variety of discrepancies that make a firm absolute chronology so problematic for that period of time. His focus then became very specific. First he turned his attention to the subject of Sothic-astronomical dating. Alas, nothing really new was brought up, only the same old chestnuts – Sirius, Censorinus, the Papyrus Ebers, and the "era of Menophres". The latter is given a new twist, but in the end Manning was forced to conclude that even for this approach (S-a dating) "the problems, however, are also plentiful" – the more so had he ever considered the Sothic-astronomical revelations put forth by Velikovsky, Rose, Long, Courville, Mage, Sammer, Day-

---

[1] Manning: *op. cit.*, p. 368 (emphasis in the original).

ton, Greenberg, Gammon and James in the pages of *Kronos*.[1]

Instead, Manning referenced Kitchen, von Beckerath, Parker, Hornung, Redford, Spalinger, and Neugebauer, along with several others – excellent and renowned scholars all, yet wedded irreversibly to the conventional chronology put forth for Ancient Egypt. Manning, to his credit, rightly pointed out the inherent weaknesses in "dead-reckoning and dependence upon king-list tradition" for absolute Egyptian, Israelite, Babylonian, Assyrian, and Hittite chronology; even linkage dates are suspect. Nevertheless, he surprisingly sticks by the conventional chronology even though he is well aware of the revisionist Egyptian historical framework presented by Velikovsky, James, and Rohl.[2]

Regarding the last three, Manning deals with them in a second Appendix, all of 4(!) pages long, whose title alone could make one squirm: "Why the standard chronologies are approximately correct, and why radical redatings are therefore incorrect". Where Velikovsky's reconstruction is concerned, Manning displays no real interest and perpetuates an old canard with the dismissive words: "Often there is also an underlying agenda: the most common is the attempt to create reality for the Old Testament. Velikovsky and his book *Ages in Chaos* (1953 [sic], and subsequent volumes, London: Sidgwick & Jackson) is seminal."[3] No mention even of the titles! As an aside, *Peoples of the Sea* neither contains the word "Bible" in the text nor is it listed in the Index. Neither does *The Dark Age of Greece*. Rohl is criticized and marginalized because he "essentially pursues the same approach" as Velikovsky while "the work of James et al. instead has scholarly pretensions". Ironically, the word "seminal" applied to Velikovsky's oeuvre is usually meant as a compliment. Manning's attitude and generalized approach to revisionist history unfortunately reflects the view of others as well. The profound brevity and tone of Manning's Appendix 2 may well also reflect a present day syndrome – in this case, the politicization of Egyptology.

For Velikovsky's reconstruction the new radiocarbon dates for the Theran eruption and the classification of the pottery found beneath the ash and pumice may have brought very good news. As stated earlier in this section, it is LM IA and LMIA only that was found at the site.

---

[1] See *Kronos* VI:1 (Fall-1980), Special Supplement, pp. 51-85.
[2] Manning: *op. cit.*, Appendix 1, pp. 367-413.
[3] *Ibid.*, pp. 415-416.

At this time I am going to take the liberty of quoting myself from the last article I wrote for the last issue of the journal *Kronos* (XII:3,1988) which I co-founded in 1975:

> ... LM IA began before the start of the 18th Dynasty of Ancient Egypt, perhaps around 1600 BC according to present conventional chronology [P.M. Warren: »Absolute Dating of the Aegean Late Bronze Age«, *Archaeometry*, 29, 2 (1987), p. 207.] LM IB relates to the time of Thutmosis III. ... Thus, the eruption of Thera is easily divorced from the time of the Egyptian New Kingdom and the 18th Dynasty; and the linkage between Thera and Velikovsky's revised chronology is broken. As a result, the mid-second millennium BC date for Thera's explosion can still stand while the New Kingdom of Egypt is downdated according to Velikovsky's chronological scheme as it was presented in *Ages in Chaos*.
>
> To an objection that LM IB is too close by conventional dating to LM IA for the kind of chronological lowering proposed by Velikovsky, with its resultant ceramic style gap, the following may be offered. According to G. Cadogan, an expert on dating Aegean Bronze Age material, "there is ... the problem of how much time elapsed between an object's being made and its being deposited. In an extreme case of ... early third millennium Egyptian stone vases, found in tombs at Knossos and the Argolid of c.1400 BC, it can be as much as fifteen hundred years [!]" [G. Cadogan: »Dating the Aegean Bronze Age without Radiocarbon«, *Archaeometry* 20 (1978), p. 211, e.a.]

Furthermore, according to P. Betancourt, an authority on Late Aegean Bronze Age ceramic ware, since

> LM IIIA:1 vases were already in use during the reign of Thutmosis III, then it is highly likely the LM IB pottery from this period represents *heirlooms*, buried some years after their manufacture. [P.P. Betancourt: »Dating the Aegean Late Bronze Age with Radiocarbon«, *Archaeometry, 29* (1987), p. 47, emphasis added].

A final thought that I alluded to at the close of one of the first paragraphs that introduced the subject of this entire Section will now be addressed. The destruction of Thera and the damage it wrought on Crete have created a puzzling scenario. L. Pomerance raised a critical question in a letter he wrote to the NYT (8/9/87, p. 14): "What finally destroyed Zakro and the rest of the Minoan centers – resulting in a 'dark age' – is a puzzle not yet solved." J.W. Graham, too, "has wondered at the destruction which occurred to high Cretan sites well above the reach of the ravaging waves."[1] It has to do with the way the waters of the Mediterranean affected different land masses, how they were directed, and how some areas were able to escape the eruptive wrath of Thera while others were obliterated. Was Thera alone responsible? Those who are familiar with Velikovsky's catastrophic scenario know that Velikovsky had proposed a near encounter of the Earth with Venus when the latter was still in its cometary phase ca. 1500 BC.[2] There may even have been two near encounters separated by fifty years. Thera has also presented some contradictory evidence indicating that it may have had two consecutive eruptions separated by the same length of time.

What was not considered by the archaeologists, geologists, and seismologists were two additional key questions: 1) Could another agent independent and in concert with Thera have caused the widespread destruction that was found on Crete and elsewhere in the Eastern Mediterranean? 2) Why did Thera erupt when it did and with such unprecedented force? C. Wilson has actually suggested that the cause of "... the eruption of Santorin [Thera] ... may well have been Velikovsky's comet [Venus]" and "in matters of this sort, where science knows almost as little as anybody else, it is well to keep the mind open."[3] In *Worlds in Collision* Velikovsky had in fact discussed the possible relationship between torsion of the global crust and "the direct attraction of a cosmic body when in a close contact" with the Earth.[4] In *Earth in Upheaval* he even went so far as to state that "volcanic activity is generally considered as connected with seismic activity; and the latter appears to be a response to a stress; and stress appears to have its origin in forces outside our Earth."[5]

---

[1] L. M. Greenberg: »Atlantis«, *Pensée* VI, *op. cit.*, p. 53; J. W. Graham: *The Palaces of Crete* (Princeton, 1972), p. 12; D. L. Page: *The Santorini Volcano and the Desolation of Minoan Crete* (London, 1970), pp. 35-44; F. Schachermeyr: *Die ägäische Frühzeit*, Bd. 2, *Die mykenische Zeit und die Gesittung von Thera* (Vienna, 1976), pp. 84-87 – he noticed an unusual pattern to the destruction wrought by Thera and questioned particular explanations as to why it happened the way it did. Finally, he theorized that the explosive catastrophe was implemented by something working "from both above and below."

[2] I. Velikovsky: *Worlds in Collision* (NY, 1950), pp. 39ff.

[3] Greenberg: *ibid.*; C. Wilson: *The Occult* (NY, 1971), pp. 163-166; see *Science News*, 13 January 1973, p. 26 for a proposed correlation between eruptions of mud volcanoes and the positions of the Sun and Moon.

[4] Velikovsky: *ibid.*, pp. 126-131, 273-278.

[5] I. Velikovsky: *Earth in Upheaval* (NY, 1955), pp. 147-153, 283-292.

The last word should be Plato's in *Timaeus* 22c:

> There is at long intervals a variation in the course of the heavenly bodies and a consequent wide-spread destruction by fire of things on the earth.

For Velikovsky "these words of Plato received the least attention, though they deserved the greatest."[1]

---
[1] The passage is quoted from Lee: *Plato: Timaeus and Critias*, p. 35.

Hercules

For people familiar with the exploits of the demi-god Hercules they are generally most aware of his famous Labors. Less well known is an experience he purportedly had with the city of Troy several years prior to the Trojan War.

After Poseidon and Apollo finished building the walls of Troy, Laomedon the king of Troy reneged on a deal he had made previously with the two gods and failed to pay them. As a result Poseidon sent a sea-monster to ravage the land all around the city.

In order to halt the destruction Laomedon was instructed by an oracle to offer his daughter Hesione to the monster as the only way to stop the carnage. Laomedon did so but also promised a gift of immortal horses to anyone who killed the beast. Thus it was that Hercules, with the help of Athena, accomplished the feat.[1]

Never one to learn a lesson Laomedon substituted mortal horses. Upon discovering the trick, Hercules returned to Troy, sacked the city and claimed his original reward. A depiction of this event appears on a Corinthian krater of ca. 560 BC as well as the east pediment of the temple of Aphaia at Aegina ca. 580-480 BC. The second sacking of Troy, the Trojan War, appears on the west pediment.[2]

After entering Troy, Hercules slaughtered Laomedon and his sons. He then offered Hesione to Telamon, one of his youthful companions. Hesione was also allowed to choose any captive to accompany her. She chose her only surviving brother, Podarces. He, however, decided to remain and rebuild Troy. Hesione agreed but she changed his name to Priam which means "paid for" or "to buy" from the Greek *priamai*. This, because she had given a ransom payment to Hercules who had demanded it for her brother's freedom.[3]

When the stories about Hercules and his first appearance originated are long time subjects of debate. The theory that Hercules was imported in some way into Greek lore has been rejected. Current opinion

---

[1] E. Stafford: Herakles (NY, 2012), pp. 70-72.
[2] See J. M. Barringer: *The Art and Archaeology of Ancient Greece* (Cambridge, 2014), pp. 199-201; Stafford: *ibid.*, p. 73.
[3] A. Blanshard: *Hercules A Heroic Life* (London, 2005), pp. 137-138; P. Matyszak: *Hercules The First Superhero* (Canada, 2015), pp. 120-121.

holds "that stories were being told about Herakles [Hercules] in the Dark Age of Greece, which preceded Homer (ca. 1100-750 BC), but we cannot be sure exactly what these stories included, or how far back they went. ... [E]arly twentieth-century scholars argued that Herakles originated within Greece itself, either in the Mycenaean period or in the Dark Age, *more specifically in eighth-century Argos.*"[1]

So, apparently, the story of Hercules sacking and his destruction of Troy may have originated some 450 years *after* it was destroyed for the *second time* during the Trojan War. In that case, the latter may have also occurred in the eighth century.

Hercules has also been credited with clearing the field prior to the holding of the first Olympic Games. Since the latter occurred sometime in the 8th century BC between 776 and 700 we run into another problem if he is placed in Latium in the 13th century BC. (See the sections: »Celestial Events in the *Iliad*« by Velikovsky (p. 105) and »Carthage, Rome, Dido, And Aeneas« by Greenberg (p. 399), particularly reference 2 on p. 406.)

---

[1] Stafford: *op.cit.*, p. 11 (emphasis added).

Carthage, Rome, Dido, And Aeneas

The city of ancient Carthage was located on what is today the northeast coast of Tunisia. It was founded by Elissa/Dido, a Phoenician princess fleeing Tyre to escape her malevolent brother Pygmalion. Both the historicity of Dido and founding date for Carthage have been debated at length. Several dates based upon literary sources alone have been proffered for the founding of that city. They range from 846 BC, 826-25 BC, or 814 BC.[1] It is the last which has become the putative date.[2] However, while archaeology has failed to fully support the literary sources, the dates garnered from each discipline are getting closer. In a very recent book (2020) by G. Woolf: *The Life and Death of Ancient Cities*, the author states that "the first occupation levels there have been dated between 835 and 800 B.C."[3]

Given what the Romans did to Carthage after their ultimate triumph it's a wonder that any helpful archaeological remains can be found. Though it must be stated that the Romans most likely avoided the sacred area concerned only with obtaining worthwhile secular goods. The main hill-citadel, called Byrsa by the Greeks and Romans, was the primary first site of occupation. Due to a "warning omen" it was quickly abandoned and the early Carthaginians settled nearby instead. "It has been suggested that the [cattle and sheep] bones found near the shore below Byrsa and carbon-dated to the late 9th century, yet with [Greek Late Geometric] pottery fragments dated a century later, may have been dislocated from an initial settlement higher up the hill, perhaps in the course of urban development."[4] Regarding all the various dates that have been proposed, Picard & Picard had this to say: "Myth and fact have become inextricably entwined and the founding of Carthage is one of the most difficult problems of history."[5] The same could be said for the date of the Trojan War.

A succinct question posed by Serge Lancel gets to the heart of the matter: "Can one really break free from the chronological framework

---

[1] See B. Feldman: »Pygmalion, Prince of Tyre and the El-Amarna Correspondence«, *Kronos* II:1 (August-1976), p. 81 (with a caveat).
[2] Many authors.
[3] G. Woolf: *The Life and Death of Ancient Cities* (NY, 2020), p. 151.
[4] D. Hoyos: *The Carthaginians* (NY, 2010), p. 9.
[5] G. C. Picard & C. Picard: *The Life and Death of Carthage* (NY, 1968), p. 29.

of Greek pottery for dating the earliest evidence of the Punic metropolis? Generally speaking, one would shy away from doing so, as from taking a leap in the dark."[1] Lancel should have looked to Egyptian chronology instead. The same holds true for B. H. Warmington.

While writing his book on Carthage, Warmington strongly criticized the Greeks and Greek authors for their shabby approach to chronology. He then chastised Virgil for placing Aeneas in the early years of Carthage's founding without considering all the possible implications. According to Warmington, "there were several different versions of the story of Dido until Virgil effectively swept them away with his tale of the love of Aeneas. It may be noted that Virgil, probably following an earlier Roman poet Naevius, put the story centuries earlier than the accepted foundation date [of Carthage] in order that it might be introduced into the saga of Aeneas fleeing from the sack of Troy on his way to Italy ... thus to confront in romantic fashion the founders of the two cities who later disputed the mastery of the Mediterranean. The variants of the tradition, its highly romantic character and *ruthless* disregard for chronology and probability indicate well enough the facility with which classical antiquity constructed or altered legends to take the place of exact [sic] knowledge of the distant past."[2] Warmington never thought of lowering the date for the Trojan War thus placing Aeneas in the latter part of the 9th century or very early 8th century BC. Instead he assumed that Virgil had thrown Carthage and Dido back in time to the early 12th century. Yet Virgil never committed to any date. Perhaps he intended Carthage and Dido should remain where they were while moving Aeneas *downward* in time. Later events in Italy seem to support that view.

It's true that Eratosthenes had put forward a date of 1184 BC for the Trojan War. But he also "stated that Romulus was son of Ascanius, and so grandson of Aeneas ... an obvious chronological problem,"[3] to put it mildly, since Timaeus proposed a date of 814/13 for the foundation of Rome, 748/47 for Fabius Pictor, 751/50 for Cato, and 753 for Varro, with the latter becoming the canonical date. The "Sicilian historian Alcimus ... provides the first mention of Romulus, saying that he was the son of Aeneas and Tyrrhenia ... and the grandfather

---

[1] S. Lancel: *Carthage A History* (Oxford, 1995), p. 31. Also see pp. 1-77.
[2] B. H. Warmington: *Carthage A History* (NY, 1969), p. 31 (emphasis added).
[3] S. Casali: »The Development of the Aeneas Legend«, *A Companion to Virgil's Aeneid and Its Tradition* (ed. by J. Farrell & M.C.J. Putnam), p. 47.

of Rhomus (if that is the correct emendation of the text), the founder of the city."[1]

On top of all that there is even doubt regarding the historical reality of Romulus. While the myth surrounding his existence was prevalent in the third century BC that "doesn't necessarily prove that he ever existed." The "earliest extant fragmentary mentions of Romulus appeared 400 or more years subsequent to Rome's supposed founding date. ... There is no known written record of an eponymous Roman founder until around the mid-fourth century BC," when Alcimus referenced him.[2]

From all of the above, it is quite apparent that Warmington's outrage over Virgil's placement of Aeneas is overly harsh and misplaced given the dates put forth by other ancient poets, writers, and chronographers re cities, persons, and wars – be they Greek or Roman. Warmington never thought to question or criticize the basis for the date of the Trojan War as calculated by Eratosthenes. Others had put forward a variety of similar dates as well, ranging from 1300 to the tenth century BC. Virgil was composing his epic poem two hundred years after Eratosthenes. Knowledge of the chronological setting for Dido and Aeneas as well as that presented by Eratosthenes for the Trojan War certainly would have been well known by the educated Roman elite. What did Virgil know? Yet no contemporaries of Virgil that I am aware of questioned any possible anachronisms. As it happens, among the dates proposed for the Trojan War, a mid or late 9th century BC possibility was one of them and considered plausible (see Sammer elsewhere in this book (p. 323)). That would fit neatly with the founding and early days of Carthage as well as the time of Aeneas re the *Aeneid*.

The *Aeneid* was Virgil's masterpiece and arguably also the greatest example of Latin poetic literature. But how true was it? At this point in time it makes no difference. It is firmly embedded in the cultural history of the West and an integral part of its literary and art historical tradition. In the words of one scholar, "the structure of Virgil's poem is that of a journey toward an historical destiny that is already fulfilled." What most concerns us here are the chronological implications of Virgil's *magnum opus*. A needless "Dark Age" of 500 years was forcibly in-

---

[1] G. Bradley: *Early Rome to 290 BC* (Edinburgh, 2020), pp. 85 & 97.
[2] M. Hyden: *Romulus* (Padstow, Cornwall, 2020), p. 235-237; T. J. Cornell: *The Beginnings of Rome* (London, 1995), pp. 68-71.

serted into the very early history of the West, despite protests, because the rediscovery of its archaeological and art historical remains were harnessed to a newly built unstable chronological framework based upon the dynastic reigns of Oriental despots. Thrown back in time, an inexplicable gap was created; and the more entrenched the controlling chronology became the more locked in the "Dark Age" became even though numerous anomalies kept appearing. The *Aeneid* enables the possible detachment of one more block from the wall that disrupts what should be the normal flow of Eastern Mediterranean history beginning with the early Bronze Age period possibly all the way down to the 5th century BC. By any other name, someone founded Carthage and someone founded Rome. The role that each played in the other one's history was absolutely critical for determining the path that Western civilization would take over the millennia leading up to the present. As for Aeneas, the highly germane bibliographical references in this Section cited below pertaining to Virgil and the *Aeneid* validate that point.[1] The final victory of Octavian, who became Augustus, over Antony and Cleopatra sealed the deal – something else that Virgil was acutely aware of and referred to.

The story of Dido and Aeneas has "captured the imagination of readers from Saint Augustine, who in his *Confessions* scolds himself 'because I wept for Dido who killed herself for love,' to Harvard graduates who, sympathizing with the jilted quote, voted Aeneas 'the epic hero least likely to succeed'."[2] Putting aside the attempted and misguided humor of the latter, the importance of Aeneas's amorous encounter with Dido – brief as it was – set the stage for two key historical events to come: Dido's curse on the suddenly departing Aeneas thereby guaranteeing the perpetual enmity between Rome and Carthage which

---

[1] M. Tanner: *The Last Descendant of AENEAS* (Dexter, MI, 1993); P. Hardie: *The Last Trojan Hero* (NY, 2014); R. Waswo: *The Founding Legend of Western Civilization (From Virgil to Vietnam)* (Hanover, NH, 1997); A. Adolph: *Brutus of Troy* (Bridlington, 2015); D. Comparetti: *Vergil in the Middle Ages* (Princeton, 1997, originally 1885); C. David Benson: *The History of Troy in Middle English Literature* (Woodbridge, Suffolk, 1980); T. Ziolkowski: *Virgil and the Moderns* (Princeton,1993), "... in the nineteenth century the westward expansion ...of the United States [was] regularly equated with Aeneas's journey to establish a new Troy in Italy" (p. ix); M. C. J. Putnam: *VIRGIL'S AENEID (Interpretation And Influence)*, (London, 1995); L. M. Greenberg: *The Reign of the Swastika* (Wynnewood, PA, 1997), Chapter IV: Aeneas, Augustus, and Adolf, pp. 20-27.

[2] P. MacKendrick: *The North African Stones Speak* (Chapel Hill, 1980), p. ll; K. W. Gransden: *Virgil: The Aeneid* (Cambridge, 2nd ed., 2004), p. 98; P. Fredriksen: *Augustine and the Jews* (NY, 2008), for an excellent background to Augustine and his relationship with "pagan" authors. (Also see pp. 379, ref. 1 and 430.)

resulted in the Punic Wars and Carthage's ultimate destruction; Aeneas's landing in Italy, hence becoming the progenitor of Rome and its "Empire Without End". And it didn't stop there. Aeneas became the prime source and model over the next 2500 years for those individuals and nation-states of the northern latitudes who competed with each other and laid claim to being Rome's sole heir and successor, wishing to assert full legitimacy for the newly acquired dominion and power they now possessed. Forget Caesar, Tsar, and Kaiser. It was Aeneas and Virgil's *Aeneid* that held sway from Charlemagne to Adolf Hitler.[1]

A key question must be asked at this time: Were Dido and Aeneas real people? For starters, Elissa/Dido does appear to have an historical basis thanks to the meanings of her alter ego names and what we know about Phoenician history; the activity details about her in the *Aeneid* appear so precise that they also support that possibility and deserve careful consideration.[2] A significant predecessor of Virgil, the aforementioned Naevius, who lived in the time of the first war with Carthage (264 – 241 BC), wrote the first Roman national epic. It was an account of that war and "began with the flight of Aeneas from Troy after its destruction by the mainland Greeks. His work was called the *Bellum Poenicum*, or *The Punic War*, and we know that it mentioned both Aeneas and Dido."[3] Moreover, a near contemporary of Virgil, Pompeius Trogus, wrote an account of Dido's life and death

---

[1] L. M. Greenberg: *op. cit.*, pp. 7-9 for Charlemagne and additional European royalty. Regarding Hitler, eight tapestries depicting the story of Dido and Aeneas which had been taken from Vienna were hung in the Reich Chancellery, one of which hung in Hitler's study. Hitler's private thoughts on monarchy and any regnal aspirations he had were not out of line with the monarchical climate of the 20th century. As a temporary successor to Habsburg, Hohenstaufen, Hohenzollern, and Carolingian secular authority, Adolf Hitler – like it or not – incidentally and subreptitiously took his place for a time as "the last descendant of Aeneas" (pp. 26-27). After I published those words in my 1997 book I came across a 1988 book by Desmond Seward titled *Napoleon and Hitler: A Comparative Biography*. There, Seward had this to say: "Hitler was himself a species of monarch. 'In the National Socialist form of State, the title Führer is the most suitable. ... He termed the concept of a leader elected by the people 'German democracy' ... but basically the Führerprinzip was not so very different from that of Napoleon's concept of the 'People's King'. Significantly, he felt a certain kinship with the elected Kaisers of the medieval Reich, apparently regarding them as his forerunners" [p. 121].

[2] G. Herm: *The Phoenicians* (NY, 1975), pp. 182ff.; D. Hoyos: *The Carthaginians, op. cit.*, pp. 7-12; M. E. Aubet: *The Phoenicians and the West* (Cambridge, 1996), pp. 187-190.

[3] D. Soren et al.: *Carthage: Uncovering the Mysteries and Splendors of Ancient Tunisia* (NY, 1990), pp. 23-25; *The Oxford Handbook of the Phoenician and Punic Mediterranean*, Ed. by C. Lopez-Ruiz and B. R. Doak (NY, 2019), pp. 281-282, 679-680.

independent of Virgil's narration and based upon an older version that he possessed. "Trogus never doubted for a moment that Dido really lived, and his account fits squarely with what we have come to know of Phoenician culture. The account differs from that of Virgil in a number of points, not the least of which is the utter absence of Aeneas."[1] I find that final comment most intriguing because of my own reaction to the rendezvous d'amour of Dido and Aeneas. Given the brevity of their relationship, a mere dalliance, its intensity up to and after the sudden departure of Aeneas, it seemed as though each saw in the other an imagined phantasm of their dead spouses – Acherbas for Dido, Creusa for Aeneas – who were killed just before the two future lovers were forced to leave their own separate homelands. I wondered if they ever truly met corporeally. Once Aeneas was gone and cursed, Dido immolated herself with Aeneas's sword (a phallic symbol? – "a strand of eroticism runs carefully through the poem" in the words of one author) and hurled herself into a fiery pyre of her own making leaving behind nothing but ashes. As for Aeneas, after a stopover at Sicily, he arrived near Cumae, then traveled with his companions up the Tiber where he landed at the site of future Rome. There he met Evander the Arcadian (more on him *infra*). After a series of exploits – one involved the slaying of a nemesis named Turnus, another his marriage to Lavinia – Aeneas suddenly disappeared without a trace as if he never was, thereby mirroring the end of Dido.

Raymond Bloch, author of *The Origins of Rome*, missed the significance of the above points completely when he avoided even mentioning Dido and totally downplayed the role of Aeneas in Rome's founding. Unable to break away from the conventional chronology, Bloch was dismissive of the "Aeneas legend". "There is no archaeological evidence to support the theory of immigrants arriving on the plains of Latium, nor of the presence in the region of a fairly advanced culture at the date when, according to legend, Aeneas arrived in Italy."[2] But Virgil did not put Aeneas in the 12th century. Bloch merely assumed he did because of the date for the Trojan War. However, Virgil only recounted the story of Dido and Aeneas while carefully omitting any dates. Bloch wrote what he did back in 1960. More recent scholarship says otherwise (see *infra*); but it too has problems since it depends upon the conventional chronology.

---

[1] Soren et al.: *ibid*. See ref. 10, *Introduction*, Pease (1935), pp. 11-21 for Dido.
[2] R. Bloch: *The Origins of Rome* (NY, 1960), pp. 44-45.

Nevertheless, Bloch does admit that "the archaeological material found in Etruria, which includes illustrations of Aeneas fleeing from his country, shows that the Aeneas-figure was known to the Tuscan people as early as the sixth century B.C."[1] Other artifacts, including 58 terracotta statuettes of Aeneas bearing his father, Anchises, on his shoulders clearly indicate that "the Trojan warrior must have been known in central Italy before 500 B.C." How much earlier than 500 BC is the question. Bloch also asks: "But why and how did it grow up in Etruria? In the absence of definite evidence the question is difficult to answer."[2] It certainly is; however, another question which may provide an answer is why would objets d'art bearing the image of Aeneas appear more than 500 years after his supposed appearance in Italy with nothing of him in between? This is also similar to what Schorr pointed out pertaining to the honoring of Achaean heroes on mainland Greece 500 years after the time of the Trojan War (see Schorr elsewhere in this book).

In 1980 a book titled *Mycenaeans In Early Latium* by Emilio Peruzzi appeared and attempted to make a case for what was advertised on the book's title. Employing literary sources and archaeological evidence, a conclusion was reached that an individual named Evander fleeing from Arcadia in Greece with a few others arrived in Italy a little more than sixty years before the Trojan War, eventually interacting with the likes of Hercules and Aeneas. Fragments of Mycenaean pottery found in Latium, some of which were attributed with a high degree of certainty to the period designated as LH III B (ca. 1300 – 1200 BC) appeared to substantiate that conclusion. Yet the author of *Mycenaeans* did issue a cautionary note shortly afterwards: "... the few Mycenaean sherds found in Latium do not allow a univocal interpretation."[3] Added

---

[1] *Ibid.*, pp. 45-46.

[2] *Ibid.*, p. 47.

[3] E. Peruzzi: *Mycenaeans in Early Latium* (Rome, 1980), pp. 2 and *inter alia*. The subject of Aeneas and Latium was totally dismissed by David H. Trump in his book *Central and Southern Italy Before Rome* (1966): "The story of Aeneas leading a band of Trojan refugees to found a new home in Latium must be regretfully dismissed as the literary fiction it is" (p. 169). More recently, T. J. Cornell: *op. cit.*, (1995), has not been any more charitable: Unlike southern Italy and Sicily, the "precious little Mycenaean material ... found in central Italy ... does not justify the conclusion that the heroic legends are based on fact. One might just as well argue that the presence of Mycenaean sherds in southern Britain confirms the medieval legend of Brutus the Trojan, a descendant of Aeneas who founded London and became the ancestor of the British" (p. 40). It must be emphasized that Trump and Cornell were both thinking in terms of the conventional chronology.

to this is the fact that the date for the Trojan War is highly suspect. Not only has Eratosthenes' date been treated with skepticism, the very existence of such a war has been questioned.[1] Furthermore, Schorr has also convincingly argued elsewhere in this book (p. 171 ff) that "the LH III B period belongs not to ca. 1350-1200 BC, but some 500 years later." That would bring Evander, Aeneas, and even Hercules[2] (whose exploits in Italy are associated with Evander) down to the late 9th or early 8th century BC, further reinforced by the posited time for Aeneas' love affair with Dido. Of course there are some scholars who would have none of the above, dismissing it all as pure legend.[3]

A later chapter in *Mycenaeans* deals with Mycenaeans and Etruscans. A group of exiles coming from Tegea, the town of Evander's father only six miles away from Pallanteion, the home of Evander, theoretically could have been part of "two waves of the same migratory process." However, that group arrived in Etruria. But the Etruscans didn't arrive into that area until after the 8th century BC.[4] Of further interest is the fact that Tarquinia which became one of the greatest of Etruscan cities began receiving colonial Greek contacts "about 750 BC, and consequently that date serves as the end of Villanovan I; the beginning of Villanovan I is harder to fix. [Hencken's] inclination is to place it about the tenth century BC, though here we are in the Dark Age of the Aegean when absolute dates are no better than the vague and scanty evidence on which they are based."[5]

What we are left with here is a confluence of contradictory mytho-historical stories and events that serve as a specific microcosm of the greater general problem that contemporary scholarship faces – chronology – surprisingly not unlike the same problem faced by our ancient historian counterparts.

---

[1] See M. I. Finley: *The World of Odysseus* (NY, 1978), p. 177. "Homer's Trojan War, we suggest, must be evicted from the history of the Greek Bronze."
[2] For an excellent survey of Heracles (Hercules) and his activities in the central and western Mediterranean, see R. Miles: *Carthage Must Be Destroyed* (NY, 2010), *inter alia*; Peruzzi: *inter alia*; Cornell: *op. cit.*, see Index. The context for his exploits would appear to place him in the 8th century BC and outnumber those that would indicate a much earlier period. These contradictory dates reflect the same situation that involves other individuals and events.
[3] Cornell: *ibid.*, pp. 40, 70-74.
[4] R. Bloch: *The Etruscans* (NY, 1960), pp. 51-64; M. Pallottino: *The Etruscans* (London, 1975), pp. 91-101; *The Etruscan World*, ed. by J. M. Turfa (NY, 2013), pp. 88-104.
[5] H. Hencken: *Tarquinia And Etruscan Origins* (NY, 1968), pp. 45-46.

The *Aeneid* was meant to be a paean to Augustus the first Emperor whose reign heralded a new Golden Age for Rome. Augustus was looked upon as a second Aeneas, the second founder of a New Rome that "straddled the known world like a colossus." A century of civil war was ended and Imperial Rome was the center of that world remaining that way for almost half a millennium. "All roads led to Rome," absorbing multiple peoples and cultures into the fabric of Roman society while radiating its own influence in every direction ... and it was Aeneas and Romulus as seen on the Ara Pacis Augustae who stood out as the founders of all of this – even if it required a chronological manipulation. Or not.[1]

---

[1] See my section: »The Ara Pacis Augustae: New Perspectives«. (p. 409)

The Ara Pacis Augustae: New Perspectives

In 13 BC the Roman senate decreed that an altar should be built to honor the new Roman Emperor Augustus. It was also intended to simultaneously celebrate his safe return to Rome after a three-year absence visiting and pacifying the provinces of Gaul and Spain.

For the first time in several decades the Empire was in a state of relative peace. There were always disturbances along the eastern frontiers, but nothing was seriously menacing. On 30 January 9 BC, Livia's birthday, the altar was completed and dedicated. It was formally named the Ara Pacis Augustae (the Altar of Augustan Peace) and in a serious and deliberate way was the visual counterpart of Virgil's *Aeneid*. The altar itself was actually surrounded on all sides by a wall of Carrara marble almost 15 feet high. The southern and northern sides were nearly 38 feet long while the slightly narrower east and west sides were some 35 feet wide which included two entrances. Inspiration for the Ara Pacis was most likely the great Altar of Zeus at Pergamon (see Castriota, figs. 47-54b). There, the main sculptural program was the battle of gods and giants. The Ara Pacis represented so much more. Combining the sculptural techniques and full classicizing style of the Hellenistic period with the verism and iconographic formulas of Roman art, the Ara Pacis was a triumph of Roman Imperial monumental architectural sculpture.

External scenes represented a variety of programs in high relief which were originally painted in vivid colors that added a brilliant luster to the whole. Six figurative panels decorated the upper part of the marble wall. Combined, they displayed an eclectic iconographical mix that successfully merges the past, present, and future of Rome and the Roman people. A continuous dado incorporating lush vegetation, flowers, small animals and birds runs all around the Ara Pacis separated from the panels above and contained by the dado rail and skirting board. There is also a continuous sculptured border between the upper and lower registers that consists of a complex meander pattern. Embedded within the latter is a repetitive swastika motif that has possible Trojan associations since that symbol was found a number of times by Schliemann when he excavated the presumed site of Troy.[1] What we have here is the consummate marriage of mythohistory and history. The legacy of Troy prevails and Trojan destiny fulfilled.

The scenes that we see reflect foundation events, dynastic intent, victory, triumph, renewal, and abundance. Nowhere is Pax depicted, though it may be implied by the subjective interpretation of the totality of the combined imagery that can be observed. We must now examine and discuss in particular two of the panels, beginning with the one on the southwest side. It has long been accepted as a depiction of the preeminent progenitor of Rome – the Trojan prince Aeneas, son of the goddess Aphrodite-Venus and his mortal father Anchises – making a sacrifice to the penates or household gods. Some authorities have even considered Aeneas to be the father or grandfather of Romulus. Here, we must pause for a moment to consider a chronological problem. Ordinarily, Aeneas has been assigned to the late 13th or early 12th centuries BC depending upon the putative date for the Trojan War. However, Virgil had Aeneas in the late 9th century or early 8th century depending upon the accepted foundation date for the city of Carthage. And he was/is not alone. Ovid (*Fasti* III, 543-656) put Aeneas and the Trojan War "contemporary with Carthage's founding". Alfred de Grazia, in his 1984 book *The Burning of Troy*, stated "that Aeneas was a Trojan noble, active around -800" (p. 48). John Lascelles in 2005 (*Troy The World Deceived*) calculated that Aeneas met Queen Dido in 802 BC (p. 169). These suggested dates for Aeneas (and some revisionist dates for Hercules) cast additional doubt on the existence of a Dark Age beginning in pre-Classical Greece.

*****

Returning to the relevant panel, "Aeneas, founder of the Julian family, is portrayed as a bearded older man, the pater Aeneas as recreated by Virgil for the Romans. Aeneas's presence here suggests Augustus's divine descent from Venus through Aeneas. Aeneas is depicted in roughly the same position as Augustus in the south frieze. ... Augustus's return to Italy after a trip to Spain and Gaul is paralleled

---

[1] O. Rossini: *ARA PACIS* (Rome, 2009), p. 22; L. M. Greenberg: *The Reign of the Swastika* (Wynnewood, PA, 1997), p. 25. Examples of the swastika employed as a decorative devise in Schliemann's palatial home in Athens can be seen on the gates and elsewhere in his home as well as the National Numismatic Museum. See other pictures online as well.

by Aeneas's arrival in Italy. In the scene on the Ara Pacis, Aeneas is followed by his adult son, Julus-Ascanius, from whom the Julian family received its name." It was Mars, however, via the person of Romulus who "was thus ultimately the father of the Roman people."[1]

Recently, the above identification was challenged by the late Paul Rehak in 2001 who suggested that it was not Aeneas but Numa Pompilius, the second of seven kings who ruled Rome until it became a Republic ca. 509 BC.[2] Rehak's contention was based upon a more nuanced examination of the panel's foreground and background details, the assumed deeds of Numa, and the aged appearance of the figure identified as Aeneas. At best I would tentatively accept this proposal as simply one more example of yet another one of the several double entendres that exist in the multi-layered meanings that are embedded in the reliefs of the Ara Pacis and other examples of Roman art. Indeed. When we come to the *"Tellus"* relief which will be the second and final panel to be discussed in our new analysis of the Ara Pacis, the terms "polysemantic" and "polyvalent" have already been applied by previous scholars.

Fig. 1: The "Aeneas" Panel

---

[1] Diana E. E. Kleiner: *Roman Sculpture* (New Haven, 1992), p. 96.
[2] P. Rehak: »Aeneas or Numa? Rethinking the Meaning of the Ara Pacis Augustae«, *The Art Bulletin*, Vol 83, No. 2 (June, 2001), pp. 190-208.

When it comes to a definitive identification of the key figure in the "Aeneas" panel, we have no way of knowing what Aeneas actually looked like. He was conventionally described as handsome, was probably around 40 years of age when he arrived in Italy based upon the duration of the Trojan War and the number of years traveled afterward. He certainly would not have been considered a young man by the standards of the time. In any case, the fact that the figure is shown with a beard is meaningless for age. Look at the number of young men today with facial hair. As it happens, the figure of Mars across the way in the Lupercal panel is also bearded and faces Aeneas thereby creating a fully balanced composition when the two are viewed as a unit. These are the two progenitors of Rome, its people, and the *gens Iulia* – one patriarchal (Mars) and one matriarchal (Venus).

The appearance of Aeneas in this panel is critical for it serves as a pendant to the one right across from it. Numa does not. To remove Aeneas from the Ara Pacis would also remove him from being a comparative figure to Augustus who leads the procession of Julio-Claudian royalty and nobility on the south frieze; and that would change one of the key rationales for building the Ara Pacis – asserting the divine ancestry of the Imperial Dynasty to come. Finally, Augustus – even though he was now *Imperator* (Emperor) went to great pains to avoid the idea of kingship and promoted the concept of the principate with his position as *primus inter pares* – "first among equals" – though assuredly he was "more equal than others."

For the Romans it was the combination of Troy, Aeneas, Virgil's *Aeneid*, and even Carthage that became the quintessential archetypal foundation blocks for Rome and its eventual imperium. It was during the reign of the Emperor Augustus that Roman origins as depicted on the Ara Pacis were codified once and for all.

> Augustus changed everything, redefining Rome's Trojan past and adding new meaning to it. [Aeneas] became identified with the imperial family and his story became a myth of the Roman Empire as a whole; it was no longer one shared only between Greeks and Romans. The Augustan [Aeneas] could be found from one end of the Mediterranean to the other.[1]

*****

---

[1] A. Erskine: *Troy Between Greece and Rome* (Oxford, 2001), p. 255 & *passim*.

A Master's Thesis (1950) written by a Jesuit, John Patrick Beall of Loyola University, that I came upon while composing this very Section lends considerable support and credence to what I have been presenting so far re Aeneas. Rev. Beall's primary focus was why Virgil chose Aeneas over Romulus as the basis for what became the *Aeneid*. According to Beall, "the reason which most influenced Virgil to choose Aeneas was the claim of the Julian House to be descendants of Aeneas and Venus. Aeneas had already at the time of Virgil become a very important part of Roman tradition. ... the official recognition of Aeneas as founder of Rome, his recognition in literature, the claim of the Julian House, and many other claims of the Roman elite to be descendants of Aeneas, influenced Virgil in his final choice of Aeneas as the hero of his epic."[1]

The piety and inner strength of Aeneas could not be denied. He was epic; and Virgil needed an epic hero for his literary epic. Furthermore, "Augustus in order to accomplish his religious revival, wished to assume the title *Divus*. If Virgil were to grant this title to the emperor, he would have to choose for his hero a man who could claim the gods as his ancestors. Virgil found such a man in the character of Aeneas."[2] In his Thesis, Rev. Beall also introduced us to a noted Greek lyric poet named Stesichorus who lived sometime between ca. 632 – 555 BC. He was born in either southern Italy or Sicily, but his adult life was spent in the latter. His real name was Teisias so Stesichorus may have been a title. He composed twenty-six books of verse most of which dealt with the cycle of myths relating to Troy – the *Story of Orestes*, *Helen*, *The Wooden Horse*, *The Sack of Troy*, and *The Homecomings of the Heroes*. Removed from Homer by anywhere from approximately 120 to 200 years his "language is often Homeric, though the dialect is Doric. We know Stesichorus' work only through quotations by other authors and from fragmentary papyri. ... His poems were substantial, often longer than a thousand lines." He also wrote about the myths of Hercules and others.[3] Stesichorus is known to be the earliest authority and originator of the tradition that Aeneas wandered from

---

[1] J. P. Beall: *Virgil's Choice of Aeneas in the Light of His Purpose in Writing the Aeneid*, A Master's Thesis (Loyola University, 1950), *inter alia*.
[2] *Ibid*.
[3] J. Hazel: *Who's Who in the Greek World* (London, 2000), »Stesichorus«, p. 229; *Who Was Who in the Greek World*, ed. by Diana Bowder, »Stesichorus« (Oxford, 1982), p.195; W. E. Sellar: *Roman Poets of the Augustan Age* (Oxford, 1897).

Troy to Latium.[1] Greek mariners arriving in Sicily some time ca. the 8th and 7th centuries BC were also responsible for the growth of the Aeneas legend as their influence took hold at various ports along the Mediterranean. Shrines dedicated to the worship of Aphrodite Aineias were credited to Aeneas by Greek merchants, though Aineias was *not* the same as Aeneas. The epithet "Aineias" indicated that Aphrodite, goddess of love, was also the *patroness of sailors*. However, the homonymic similarity became persuasive. Moreover, a good many of those shrines, built by earlier Phoenician seafarers,[2] were taken over from ones already there that had been dedicated to the Phoenician goddess Astarte, a deity comparable to Aphrodite in other aspects.

The city of Eryx (modern Erice), situated in the western part of Sicily, was famous for its temple of Venus Erycina, the goddess of fertility; "... at the Sanctuary of the Venus of Erice, a Phoenician dedication to the goddess Astarte [was found there] as well as a Greek inscription to Aphrodite and fragments of one in Latin to Venus – *three divinities sharing the same identity*,"[3] a most significant fact that will have a key bearing on our later promised discussion of the *"Tellus"* panel.

Many independent legends of Aeneas grew up around the various shrines for Aphrodite and it was these legends that played such an important part in the final formulation of the legend that was received and told by Virgil. Multiple shrines attributable to Aeneas have also been found at different locations as individual cities vied with each other by claiming each had a connection to Aeneas. The bigger question is why were these shrines erected 500 or more years *after* the fall of Troy and the death of Aeneas – a similar question posed by Schorr pertaining to the construction of a late honorific shrine built by the people of Mycenae for Agamemnon their king and "supreme commander of the Greek forces at Troy" and another near Sparta for his brother Menelaus and his wife Helen, both of which date to ca. 700 BC. With the Trojan War currently assigned to the 13th century BC, "Did the Greeks wait until the 500th anniversary of the Trojan War to honor their leaders?"[4] Another related question is: Why did the Romans build an altar in the early Roman Forum honoring Hercules

---

[1] Beall: *op. cit.*, pp. 28-31; C. H. Heithaus: »The History of the Aeneas Legend«, *Historical Bulletin* (Jan., 1930), p. 27.
[2] M. E. Aubet: *The Phoenicians and the West* (NY, 1996), pp. 167-198.
[3] wondersofsicily.com/erice.htm; Also see G. K. Galinsky, APPENDIX, pp.243-257.
[4] E. M. Schorr writing as Israel M. Isaacson: »Applying the Revised Chronology«, *Pensée* IX, Vol. 4, No. 4 (Fall, 1974), pp. 9-10; cf. Suppl. I of the present book.

more than 500 years after his supposed exploits in Latium? Returning to Stesichorus one last time, it should be noted that – as far as we can deduce – in all his oeuvres which were quite expansive even compared to Homer there is not a hint or awareness of any Dark Age in Greece. The Trojan War subjects that he deals with certainly have more of a contemporary feel about them than one that transcends the passage of 600 years. For example, his treatment of Helen of Troy. In a first telling of her story, *Helen*, Stesichorus followed a traditional path wherein she was abducted and raped by Paris. Because of this he was blinded or made blind by Helen herself who was angry over that version of her story. He later had his eyesight restored by composing a *Palinode* or recantation which was a second *Helen* denying that Helen ever went to Troy. Thanks to Hera her virtue was saved when the goddess whisked Helen away to Egypt and replaced her with a replica phantom that went to Troy in her stead.[1] In some places Helen was even viewed as a goddess by the populace. The main point here is that Stesichorus is treating Helen as if she were alive – human, goddess, or otherwise – and a contemporary of his own time, the 6th century BC, as opposed to being an object of storytelling from 500 or more years earlier.

*****

It is now time to turn to one last panel on the Ara Pacis, the best preserved and most discussed and debated by scholars over the course of many decades – a seated goddess or personification that has most frequently been identified as *Tellus* or *Italia*. But first some prelude material must be presented.

On the first of August 30 BC – a date that would be celebrated time and time again by the Romans – the city of Alexandria founded by Alexander the Great fell before the forces of Octavian. The Queen city of the Mediterranean and all of Egypt would soon become the private property of the Roman Emperor to be, Augustus Caesar. Upon entering the city and witnessing first hand its architectural and sculptural splendor, the Roman troops must have felt like Alaric the Goth centuries later when he and his own troops entered and sacked the city of Rome in 410 AD. As the Romans made their way to the palace,

---

[1] *The Oxford History of the Classical World*, ed. by J. Boardman et al. (Oxford, 1987), pp. 80-107.

this marked the beginning of the end for Cleopatra and Antony whose war with Octavian to see who would reign supreme over the Mediterranean world was coming to a close.

The night before Octavian and his men entered Alexandria, strange music accompanied by a frenzy of singing, shouting, and Dionysian type dancing could be heard in the streets. The noise began to recede and diminish as the group of unseen revelers approached the city gate and were apparently leaving Alexandria. But this was interpreted as a sign that the god Dionysus of whom Antony thought himself the living counterpart was now abandoning him and leaving as well. "What really happened is not beyond conjecture. There was an ancient Roman custom, the *evocatio* of the gods of an enemy city before a battle: The Roman general would call them out and invite them to take up a new friendly Roman home. The rite was probably enacted before the fall of Carthage in 146; it was also used in the routine capture of a Cilician town, Isaura Vetus, in 75 B.C. Octavian was always sensitive to the use he could make of antique custom." (C. Pelling: *CAH* X, »The Augustan Empire, 43 B.C. – A.D. 69«, 2nd ed. (Cambridge, 2004), p. 63.) In the chaos and confusion that followed, Antony was misled into thinking that Cleopatra was dead. A botched attempt at suicide on his part then left him mortally wounded. Cleopatra, who was hiding in her mausoleum at the time, was informed as to what had happened and gave orders to bring Antony to her. He was hauled up on a makeshift litter into the mausoleum and then died shortly afterward right before her eyes. Members of Octavian's inner circle secretly obtained a way into the mausoleum and facilitated Cleopatra's arrest. There she was held captive.

Later on Octavian met privately with Cleopatra. The sources differ as to what passed between them. One claims that she was appropriately dressed and might have attempted to seduce Octavian, but to no avail. Another, that she was disheveled and extremely upset over the loss of both Antony and her realm. No doubt each tried to bluff the other and thought they had succeeded. Octavian promised that he would treat Cleopatra properly, but she found out he had lied. When Cleopatra then attempted to starve herself to death Octavian threatened her children if she didn't reverse her course and allow herself to be restored. He very much wanted her alive for his future victory parade in Rome. He even brought in a medic at one point to attend to her. Octavian did have one problem. He desperately wanted her for his triumph, but Cleopatra had been popular when she was in Rome fifteen years before, arriving with Caesar's son Caesarion and as Caesar's paramour. Additionally, an earlier triumphal procession involving her despised sister Arsinoe did not turn out so well. A few authors claim that Octavian hated her. I strongly disagree. On the contrary, and this is important, I believe that he obsessed over her and did so for decades to come long after she was gone; and I intend to support my claim later on.

When Cleopatra did commit suicide with some type of poison, Octavian supposedly reacted in a contradictory way and expressed his frustration. To this day, for a variety of reasons, no one is absolutely certain as to how Cleopatra administered the poison. The canonical story involving an asp or two of them does not stand up under close scrutiny nor any other theories as to what happened during Cleopatra's final moments.[1] It remains a mystery though a new theory as to what type of snake it was has been proffered.[2] Octavian then presided over the funeral of Cleopatra. Her mummified body was interred next to that of Antony in her mausoleum which remains undiscovered to this day. Octavian proceeded to tour Alexandria, visited Alexander's tomb, saw his preserved body and, much to the dismay of the accompanying priests, accidentally broke off a part of his nose when he touched it. Soon, on the 13th of August, Octavian left Egypt never to return. Before that, while Cleopatra was still a prisoner, Octavian displayed his ruthless side by having the eldest son of Antony – Antyllus – hunted down, captured, and beheaded. Based on a tip, his soldiers then went southward after a fleeing Caesarion who was attempting to escape to India. When caught he was immediately executed. Any would-be challengers to Octavian's right to rule were thus eliminated.

*****

---

[1] E.g., see D. Stuttard & S. Moorhead (among others): *Antony, Cleopatra and the Fall of Egypt* (London, 2012), pp. 164-171 for one of the most detailed and vivid descriptions of Cleopatra's last days.

[2] But see P. de Ruggiero: *Mark Antony: A Plain Blunt Man* (Barnsley, 2013), p. 277, for a new theory as to what type of snake known as "Cleopatra's Asp" really was.

Returning to Rome, Octavian began making celebratory plans for his recent triumphs. The third of three was the Alexandrian victory. On the 13th of August 29 BC, the ceremonies began. First came Octavian's triumph over the Illyrians; the next day marked the victory at Actium; then on the third day came the grand finale, the triumphal parade celebrating Octavian's victory over Antony and Cleopatra and the annexation of Egypt. Cleopatra's children by Antony, the twins – Alexander Helios and Cleopatra Selene – barely ten years old, marched in chains followed by Ptolemy Philadelphus their six year-old brother likewise in chains. The deceased Cleopatra also appeared but in the form of a wax effigy lying on a couch with a fake snake attached to her bosom. Then came Octavian in a chariot drawn by four horses. The crowd roared and cheered, but I cannot believe that many weren't turned off by the lurid and distasteful spectacle of young children laden in chains and a waxen image of a still admired semi-nude Cleopatra clasping a deadly serpent to her breast. If the appearance of her sister in chains during Caesar's earlier triumph for his successes in Egypt did not go over well with the Roman populace at that time, one can only imagine what went through the minds of those who were forced to put on a "happy face" for this one. I would suspect that the lavish treasures of Egypt that were also conspicuously displayed served as some kind of palliative.

As for Antony, every effort had already been made to erase his memory and very existence. He suffered a *damnatio memoriae* (a damnation of memory), his titles removed, property destroyed, and his birthday of 14th January marked as *nefastus* (unholy). Meanwhile his remaining children by Cleopatra were eventually placed in the care of Octavia, sister of Octavian, despite their forced participation in the latter's triumphal parade.

****

Our focus now shifts to the main point of this entire Section – a detailed examination of the Tellus panel on the southeast side of the Ara Pacis where a female figure is depicted sitting upon a throne-like rock embracing two babies. The sumptuous vegetation, birds, and small animals that cover the entire bottom register will also be shown to have a bearing on the identification of the aforementioned female figure.

But first we must return to Octavian and consider his mindset and behavior regarding both Antony and Cleopatra. While the former and Octavian were compatriots and allies at one time, their falling out was over the usual thing – the desire for power. They were different in many ways, but also alike in others. Octavian was 20 years younger than Antony who was born sometime between 86 and 81 BC with 83 chosen as the compromised date. Octavian was a sickly child and continued to have bouts of illness during his lifetime. Yet he was considered quite handsome (his portraits support this) and managed to live to the hoary age (for its time) of 77.

His favored deity and chosen protector was Apollo, the god of masculine beauty above all others; god of the Sun, of medicine, music, and poetry. The god Apollo was on the side of Troy during the Trojan War and his aim with the bow and arrow was deadly. Known as the "far darter" he once made the other Olympian gods tremble as he went through the domain of Zeus. Nevertheless, a darker side would have him a god of plague and pestilence, often seen to be haughty who bore a close resemblance to the Latin war god Mars; in fact, "the cults of Apollo and Mars were fundamentally analogous" and both gods were identified with the planet Mars.[1] A few of Apollo's attributes could aptly fit those of Augustus who was responsible for erecting a temple to Mars Ultor (Mars the Avenger) in his new Forum of Augustus; and also built his huge family mausoleum in the Campus Martius (the field of Mars) near the Tiber river. His devotion to Mars may have been a way to appropriate that which once belonged to Antony. The latter thought of himself as a descendant of Hercules or Hercules incarnate; and, additionally, Hercules was associated with the planet Mars.[2] Augustus's homage to Mars would usurp what Antony had claimed for himself. There's also more. Antony was a notorious womanizer and drinker. He identified with the god Dionysus and was hailed in the Greek east "as the new Dionysos, an appropriate divinity for Antony, the god of wine and beneficence ... and sometimes as Hercules."[3]

---

[1] E. Cochrane: *Martian Metamorphoses: The Planet Mars in Ancient Myth and Religion* (Ames, IA, 1997), p. 57, footnote 29; I. Velikovsky: *Worlds in Collision* (NY, 1950), pp. 238ff. The Greeks seem to have viewed Apollo as a distinct planet at first, but then realized it was one and the same as Mercury, with Apollo as a kind of "Mercury Morning Star" and Mercury (Hermes) as a "Mercury Evening Star".

[2] Cochrane, pp. 4ff.; Velikovsky, p. 294.

[3] Ruggiero, pp. 235-276; P. Southern: *Mark Antony* (Stroud, 1998), pp. 86, 73.

> Octavian deliberately chose to adopt sober Roman attitudes and behaviour, and sober gods to promote his cause, such as Apollo and Mars. Antony was, and had always been, far from sober himself, and he adopted far from sober gods such as Dionysus and Hercules to promote his cause.[1]

For all his faults, Antony was not the only one who carried a lot of baggage. In response to Octavian's criticism that he had betrayed Roman traditions, chose a foreigner for his lover, worshipped foreign gods, and named his children after them, Antony responded in kind.

> Octavian's sexual behaviour and preferences were two of his favorite topics. Suetonius specifically points to Antony and his brother Lucius as the source of the gossip which had Octavian earning the adoption by Julius Caesar by prostituting himself to him, just like he had lain with Aulus Hirtius in Spain for 300,000 sesterces. ... Octavian's penchant for young boys [was] an accepted truth. ...[2]

On the heterosexual front, Octavian was also quite active and even guilty of immorality, but his approach there according to some was supposedly motivated by his need to gain political information.[3]

> Others were not so sure. A man as promiscuous as Augustus was reputed to be seemed, to many citizens, lacking the self-control that was properly the mark of a Roman. Unchecked sexual appetites, while only to be expected in a woman – or, of course, a Greek – were hardly appropriate to a citizen steeled in the noblest traditions of the city. Energies devoted to sleeping around were better suited to serving the glory of the Roman people. Augustus's reputation as a serial adulterer, far from boosting the aura of his machismo, cast him instead in an effeminate and sinister light. No man could be reckoned truly a man who was the slave of his own desires. Playboys who chased after married women were well known to be womanish themselves.[4]

Antony's affair with Cleopatra became Octavian's primary target. She was considered the *femme fatale* and "the other woman". In the meantime, what you have are two alpha males jockeying for power and position. Human nature, probably the one constant in this world of ours, certainly rings true here. Take away claims of divinity and their dress finery and you have basic quarrels involving sex and territory.

---

[1] P. Southern: *Mark Antony A Life* (Stroud, 2010), pp. 165, 206.
[2] Ruggiero, p. 249.
[3] Ruggiero, pp. 250-251.
[4] T. Holland: *Dynasty* (NY, 2015), p. 100.

Antony was physically fit and an experienced soldier; Octavian was slight, often sickly, had virtually no real battle experience, but highly intelligent. From what we read about their relationship there always seemed to be an underlying tension that appeared to be something other than just political; and they were always squabbling over trivial matters so much so that Octavia, Octavian's sister, had to intervene and berate him over it. One time when Antony told Octavia to remain in Athens as he sauntered off to be with Cleopatra, Octavian who had set up the deliberate provocation was about to make a public display over the insult to his sister. Octavia would have none of it. "[D]emonstrating great political savvy and balance, [she] did her best to placate her brother by proclaiming that the *true scandal was not that Antony had snubbed her, but that the two most important men in the Republic were fighting over matters of women and jealousy.*"[1] And there you have it. Lest the reader of all this think that I am merely making a prurient digression, you could not be more wrong. Too often historians and art historians overlook what truly lies beneath the surface of great art. The relationships between Octavian and Antony, Antony and Cleopatra, and Cleopatra and Octavian were very complex, and created an unusual *ménage à trois* that not only determined the future course of the Roman Empire, but a significant portion of the art and architecture of Rome itself that was created in the final decades of the Augustan Age.

*****

Let us begin with Octavian vs. Antony & Cleopatra. Though the former had been adopted by Caesar, a victory by Antony would have left the throne to Caesarion, the capital of the Empire moved to Alexandria, and its future would have been a hybrid of Greco-Egyptian culture and mores. Rome would have reverted to being a rustic backwater. Antony and Cleopatra would have most likely acted as regents until their own children came of age thereby starting a renewed Ptolemaic Dynasty. Any further speculation is irrelevant at this time. Octavian did win, but what did he *really* want and how did he handle *not* getting it.

The double suicides by Antony and Cleopatra doubly deprived Octavian of something he wanted most – to take them alive in chains

---

[1] Ruggiero, p. 229 (emphasis added).

back to Rome. The triumph he did have for his Alexandrian victory consisted of young children in chains and a wax mannequin. Not quite the same thing. (It was actually mocked in private.) As stated earlier, I believe that Octavian was obsessed with Cleopatra. Moreover, I also believe he had a kind of love-hate relationship with the two of them. Had he even been able to take just Cleopatra back to Rome that most likely would have led to considerable gratification. She would have been his to do as he pleased. Once alone with Cleopatra he could have ravaged her at will. However, that spiteful act would not have been all of it. Remember that Cleopatra was married to Antony according to Egyptian law and he was still an upper class free born Roman; and she was, after all, Queen of Egypt. However, here's the kicker: "... of all the offenses that an unchecked sexual appetite might prompt a citizen to commit, there was none so unsettling to his fellows as adultery. To cuckold a man was not merely to take possession of his wife; *it was also to shaft the husband himself.*"[1]

The ring has still not been completely closed. Recall that Antony was married to Octavia, Octavian's sister. She was only a year older than her brother and most likely resembled him in many ways. What was going through Antony's mind as he was intimate with Octavia? As for Augustus, he supposedly "feigned love for Cleopatra as a ploy when trying to capture her; a love note was allegedly delivered to Cleopatra by Augustus's freedman Thyrsus as a way of discouraging her from burning her treasury before Augustus could appropriate it."[2] Even if it was feigned (totally?), the thought of possessing Caesar's queen and Antony's royal wife must have been extremely appealing to one who had such high political aspirations and a voracious sexual appetite.

*****

Despite having completely defeated Antony and Cleopatra, Octavian was unable to achieve the kind of triumph and triumphal monument that he surely desired. Though a tri-partite triumphal arch, the first of its kind, was built across the Via Sacra in honor of his Actium victory (only the base stumps remain today), no arch could be built for his Alexandrian victory. Neither Octavian nor the Roman people were

---

[1] Holland, p. 107 (emphais added).
[2] Diana E. E. Kleiner: *Cleopatra and Rome* (London, 2005), p. 264.

anxious to celebrate another civil war triumph with any monument; Antony no longer existed and in no way could be depicted in either a visual or inscriptive way while any references to Cleopatra would have been unnecessarily redundant after the third triumphal procession of 29 BC ... unless it was done *sub rosa* and symbolically.

Keeping the above in mind, in 1995 David Castriota, then an Assistant Professor of Art History at Sarah Lawrence College, published his masterpiece on the Ara Pacis Augustae. In his book Castriota clearly demonstrated how the lush vegetation, birds, and floral decoration that blanketed the lower register of the Ara Pacis wall that was the altar enclosure

> was profoundly significant, operating as a visual counterpart to the technique of metonymy in language. It utilized an array of realistic plants and flowers as allusive elements associated with various gods and goddesses, which together symbolized the support and blessing of the Roman divinities for the Augustan regime.[1]

 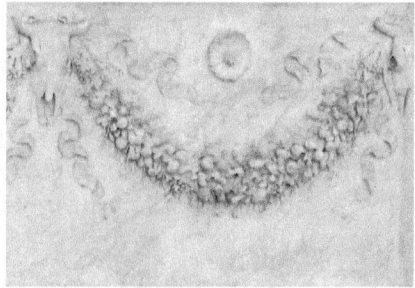

Fig. 2: Vine Scroll Motifs (with vegetal, floral, bird, and animal motifs on the side dadoes below)

Fig. 3: Garland Motif

---

[1] D. Castriota: *The Ara Pacis Augustae and the Imagery of Abundance in Later Greek and Early Roman Imperial Art* (Princeton, 1995), inside cover summary. The true pioneer in this area was H. P. L'Orange: *The Roman Empire Art Forms and Civic Life* (Milan, 1985), »The Floral Zone of the Ara Pacis Augustae«, pp. 211-228 (translated by Donald Mills); originally first published in Oslo in 1962 (see source opposite Contents page). The brilliant dissection, and skeptical analysis of the Ara Pacis Augustae (which will be cited again later) by Wayne Andersen: *The Ara Pacis of Augustus and Mussolini* (Boston, 2003), must also be referenced here.

In other words, the striking and surprising preponderance of ivy and grapevines appearing there pointed to a strong Dionysian presence; and it was Antony who transformed himself into the New Dionysus. Augustus followed an Apolline tradition and chose Apollo as his patron and protector. However, in time the two gods became united and "the poet Lucan could effectively refer to both gods as a *numen mixtum*, a mixed or united divinity ... the Apolline and Dionysian plants on the Ara Pacis have achieved a new quality of integration reflecting [that] conception of mixed divinity."[1] The Ara Pacis was a public monument with a definite message. What that message was depended upon the sophistication and understanding of its audience. There was no news person interviewing the populace in search of a particular response. Even now with hindsight one can only make an educated guess as to what was fully intended. From my own perspective the Ara Pacis Augustae (the Altar of *Augustan* Peace) served as a substitute for the triumphal arch that Augustus could not have (or refused).[2] The metonymic symbolism of the Dionysian and Apolline iconography allowed him to celebrate his Alexandrian victory by having a botanically camouflaged Antony securely implanted onto the surrounding marble wall of the Altar – a viable alternative to the marble exterior of an arch he was never going to have. There were many arches in Rome and in the Roman Empire, but only one Ara Pacis Augustae. Furthermore, the *numen mixtum* of Dionysus and Apollo nullified the singular potency of the former regardless of numbers and allowed the latter to become the dominant one. The following line from the Actian *Elegies* of Propertius, IV, 6, 76: "Bacche, soles Phoebo fertilis esse tuo", "O Bacchus, you are accustomed to be fertile for your Phoebus" emphasizes a theoretical speculation I inferred earlier in this Section regarding the sexuality and plausible relationship of Dionysian-Antony to Apolline-Augustus and vice versa.

*****

We now turn our attention to the Tellus panel. In 1960 G. Karl Galinsky published his book *Aeneas, Sicily, and Rome*.[3] A final chapter attempts to identify the central female figure as Venus, but in a much

---
[1] Castriota, pp. 4-10, 87-89, 121-122.
[2] M. Torelli: *Typology and Structure of Roman Historical Reliefs* (Ann Arbor, 1982), p. 33.
[3] G. K. Galinsky: *Aeneas, Sicily, and Rome* (Princeton, 1969), pp, 191- 241.

broader sense. It is Galinsky's erudition that enables us to see the polysemantic and multi-layered meanings of a given individual or scene. As an example, Galinsky cites the armor of the Prima Porta Augustus where

> Tellus, Magna Mater, and Italia are symbolized by the same figure. Because of the link between Magna Mater and Venus, the symbolism of the Ara Pacis figure is even more extensive. By choosing what is primarily a Venus figure, the sculptor of the relief tried to realize to the fullest possible extent the complex web of associations which gives the frieze its unity.[1]

There is, however, one more goddess that would make even more sense and also give the frieze its unity; and that would be *Isis* of the myriad names. Better yet, I would propose *Isis-Cleopatra* as the central figure. That solves a number of problems and adds still more meaning to the Ara Pacis. The hybrid conflation is fully appropriate. First of all, Cleopatra was the living Isis.[2] Secondly, it was her demise that brought a conclusion to the Roman wars of the first century BC and allowed Pax to reign and the Augustan Age to flourish. Let us examine a number of facts that led to my conclusion.

The Romans were very number conscious, as are so many nations and people today. Why the Ara Pacis was decreed in 13 BC has always bothered me. Augustus's return from Gaul and Spain was not the first time he had been there and returned safely. The dedication day and date were 30 January 9 BC – Livia's birthday (possibly her 50th). If that was significant, what about the earlier one? As it turned out, thanks to dealing with Carthage, Dido, and the *Aeneid*, the answer came to me. 13 BC marked the 250th anniversary of the First Punic War, the beginning of Rome's mastery of the Western Mediterranean, just as Cleopatra's death marked the completion of the conquest of the Eastern Mediterranean. The 13th of January was also the birthday of Cleopatra. Octavian left Egypt on the 13th of August in 30 BC and celebrated his triumph there exactly one year later on the 13th of August in 29 BC; 13 BC would also be the 800th year anniversary of the founding of Carthage by some reckonings; and the 50th birthday of Augustus as well.

*****

---

[1] Galinsky, p. 240. For an excellent conventional discussion of the Ara Pacis and the "Tellus" relief, see D. Earl: *The Age of Augustus* (1968), pp. 113-116.

[2] For Cleopatra as Isis, the New Isis, etc., there are numerous sources.

Fig. 4: The Ara Pacis Augustae "Tellus" Panel

What first drew me to the goddess Isis was Galinsky's reference to a swan in the *Tellus* relief when it came to supporting his identification of Venus as the central figure. But it wasn't a swan; it was a *goose*,[1] sacred to Isis.[2] Going over the relief step by step is most revealing. The central female holds two babies, one on each side, which I would identify as Alexander-Helios and Cleopatra-Selene, the twin children of Cleopatra and Antony. The vegetation that surrounds the central figure as well as that which appears in the foreground seems to be more Nilotic than anything found along the Tiber. The agricultural elements that are pictured which helped Spaeth in 1994[3] to identify the central figure as Ceres could even be more properly applicable to

---

[1] P. Zanker: *The Power of Images in the Age of Augustus* (Ann Arbor, 1990), p. 174.

[2] M. D. Donalson: *The Cult of Isis in the Roman Empire* (Lewiston, NY, 2003), pp. 4, 67. The debate over the bird's identity has been considerable and heated at times: See Galinsky, p. 207, ref. 56; Galinsky fully accepted "swan" because he apparently could not think of any substitute for Aphrodite. Yet Isis also fulfills more of the requirements for the *balance* of the iconography in the Tellus relief than Aphrodite; see Andersen, pp. 138-140 and Chapter 12, The Tellus Panel.

[3] B. S. Spaeth: *The Roman Goddess Ceres* (Austin, 1996). Spaeth makes a strong case for Ceres, but her status and range are hardly sufficient to warrant being the central figure on the Tellus panel. An attempt to connect Ceres to Venus and Tellus (p. 133) in a polysemantic interpretation does not really work either. In fact, Ceres is almost closer to being a personification rather than a goddess. Associating her with Livia (pp. 169-173) and awarding Livia a possible place in the Tellus relief is interesting but strained. Again, I would refer the reader to Andersen's incisive comments regarding identifications and conclusions that appear in so many discussions of the Ara Pacis – see his Chapter 13, »The Perils of Polysemy«, and the thoughtful and detailed commentary in his Addendum and Notes.

Isis and Egypt. The latter, known for its agriculture, became the breadbasket and granary for Rome; and it was Isis myrionymos as Demeter, the Greek goddess of agriculture who comes closest to Isis. Both were goddesses of the crops and giver of men's daily bread. As Isis Lochia, she was patroness of fertility and childbirth who was well-known in Greek and Roman circles.[1] The iconography of Ceres actually belongs to Isis. The so-called sea dragon or sea serpent that we see on the extreme right looks very much like one of those Egyptian crocodiles that we see depicted in Roman sculpture found in the Met, British Museum, Capitoline Museum or in the Palestrina mosaic, and a first century BC mosaic from Pompeii,[2] among others. Sobek, the crocodile deity, was worshipped in Egypt.

When it comes to the bull positioned beneath the rocky throne of the goddess it could have been associated with *Italia*. However, it also could have been an allusion to the many bulls that were worshipped throughout Egypt from the earliest times, the Apis bull in particular whose mother was said to be Isis.

> Isis was particularly worshiped as a cow-goddess and identified with Hathor who had a cow's likeness. ... As a cow-goddess she was also easily a lunar deity, but while the horns of her statues and paintings represent the crescent moon, the disk held between them represents the sun.[3]

If one looks closely, the curved horns of the bovine figure set against the backdrop of the rocky throne even create the *appearance of a disc* between them – a concealed image of the Apis bull? The *suovetaurilia* (the sacrifice of specific animals) would ordinarily have consisted of pig, lamb, and calf. The *greater suovetaurilia* would have consisted of boar, ram, and bull. The Tellus panel presents just a sheep situated next to a resting bovine, both of which were found in Ancient Egypt as well as Italy. The combination we see is neither one of the above. Interestingly, the pig was found in Egypt but the Egyptians did not favor it because they considered it unclean. The two Aurae are easily attributable to Isis. The one on the right as we face the panel is associated with the sea. Going as far back as hoary antiquity, Isis was associated with the barque of the gods. One of the most popular festivals in Egypt involved a sacred procession that moved by sea and was

---

[1] Donalson, pp. 4-7, 125.
[2] For one example, see M. Grant: *Cleopatra*, fig. 43; also see R.E.Witt: *Isis in the Ancient World* (London, 1971), pp. 20-69.
[3] Donalson, p. 4; Witt, p. 123.

known as the *Navigium Isidis* – "the Ship of Isis". Ships were named for Isis. She "was called *Isis Pharia*, with the last term interpreted as referring to a cloak, or a cloth – most likely here the sail and/or Isis' own cloak, shown frequently as *billowed by the wind* on coins. She was the guardian of the harbor itself, the sailors and the ships at sea; the guarantor of the safe return, the prosperous voyage; and she was the hope for plentiful cargo, with special reference to grain ships. ... The *Pharia* title was also connected to the great lighthouse in the harbor of Alexandria. ..."[1]

> The identification of the goddess Hathor with Isis enhanced the latter's reputation at sea, since Hathor was herself known as 'Mistress of the Barque,' as well as 'Lady of Byblos'.[2]

Another voyage of Isis enabled her to be called *Isis Pelagia*, "Isis of the Sea". When Cleopatra first met Antony at Tarsus upon the river of Cydnus she traveled on her Egyptian-style barge with her Isis-like appearance. According to Plutarch "...word spread on every side that Aphrodite had come to revel with Dionysus for the happiness of Asia". Indeed – this was no ordinary meeting. Stage-crafted carefully by Cleopatra, the New Isis was about to meet the New Dionysus, counterpart of the Egyptian Osiris. As such, there was now a meeting between two powerful gods – Osiris and his sister-wife, the divine Isis. Their encounter has been described as *archetypal* by one author, thereby echoing the exact term that this author once employed about the meeting of Solomon and Sheba-Hatshepsut (according to Velikovsky's revised chronology) who, through comparative theology and symbolism, could also be compared, respectively, to a previous encounter between Osiris and Isis.[3]

> The incarnation of Isis upon earth was Cleopatra herself, and her consequent identification with Aphrodite seemed abundantly right and clear.[4]

The second of the two Aurae to our left on the Tellus panel has been identified by Galinsky as Aphrodite herself; and he did discuss briefly the debate over the identity of the bird she sits upon along with other relevant depictions of Aphrodite. Yet, for all that, by the time of the

---

[1] Donalson, pp. 67-68, 71, 74-75 (emphasis added).
[2] Donalson, pp. 68, 125.
[3] L. M. Greenberg: »The 'Land of Punt' Redux«, *Chronology & Catastrophism REVIEW* 2018:1, pp. 32-34.
[4] Grant, pp. 117-118.

construction of the Ara Pacis, Aphrodite had been irrefutably merged or subsumed with Isis.[1] We know that Ptolemaic queens of Egypt were deified as Isis and Aphrodite simultaneously. Therefore, with the airborne goose beneath her along with the billowing cloak above, Aphrodite-Isis-Cleopatra is not difficult to accept. The central figure may be Cleopatra as the living Isis while the two Aurae represent different aspects of Isis. All meaningful imagery on the Tellus relief has now been accounted for in a sensible and fully supportive way. Since a disguised Antony was symbolically referenced by the Dionysian images on the lower friezes that surround the Ara Pacis, one should expect to find some reference to Cleopatra as well; and in fact her appearance in anthropomorphic form as Isis-Cleopatra comes as no surprise. She suffered no *damnatio memoriae*. Deprived of or unwilling to have a triumphal arch for his Alexandrian victory, Augustus realized a substitute surrogate in the Ara Pacis for that which he couldn't have absent a triumphal arch. For there, frozen in the splendor of the Carrara marble, were Antony and Isis-Cleopatra – forever prisoners of the victorious Augustus as they appeared in what ever form on the Ara Pacis Augustae. The general populace were not expected to recognize all of this, but that didn't matter since it certainly would have been self-satisfying for Augustus. Besides, the educated elite could have. And that's what counted. I don't believe that Augustus' motives were totally vindictive. He also wanted to capture their essence and power (see *infra*), undoubtedly recognized as formidable opponents. Augustus must have felt some sort of deep inner respect for who and what they stood for. While the Ara Pacis has long been associated with Pax, it seems to be merely a cover for something far more significant. The late S. Weinstock, who was roundly rebutted by Toynbee and Torelli, may have been on to something.[2] Weinstock concluded that the altar "may have served the aims of the dynasty" but did not believe that the Altar was an Altar of Augustan *Peace*. Aside from not appearing on the Ara Pacis even once, Pax Augusta was never depicted on a single coin of Augustus during his lifetime. It may have been implied by the totality of the Ara Pacis' iconography, but that was a very thin veneer for what really existed beneath the surface.

---

[1] Witt, pp. 122ff.
[2] Torelli, pp. 29-30, ref. 9; S. Weinstock: »Pax and the 'Ara Pacis'«, *Journal of Roman Studies*, 50 (1960), pp. 40ff.; J.M.C. Toynbee: »The Ara Pacis Augustae«, *Journal of Roman Studies*, 51 (1961), pp. 153ff.

For the Romans, *gloria* and *victoria* were everything. The encryption of Isis on the Ara Pacis was not only appropriate but could be appropriated by Augustus. According to Donalson, "Isis had already been a victory goddess early in Egyptian history."[1] Along with the armed image of Roma seated upon a throne of armor, depicted in the pendant panel on the east side of the Ara Pacis, the two female figures represented the combined might of Rome the city, its people as well as the Roman Empire – the latter an empire built on conquest. As the conqueror of Egypt, Augustus became the new Pharaoh immediately acquiring a familial association with Isis, Osiris, and Horus. Isis was already known as Athena (Neith), "the victorious" in Egypt; Roma was both a personification and war goddess; Minerva was the Roman counterpart of Athena in her martial form; Bellona – sister, wife, and daughter of Mars – was the national War Goddess. All were merged into the all-goddess, the Panthea from Egypt who was none other than Isis herself "among whose countless titles were 'triumphalis' and 'victrix', the *triumphant* and *victorious*."[2] Actually, in one of the most complex examples of polysemic merging, this was a superb way of achieving a uni-directional approach for a politico-religious situation that existed in a polytheistic society. Perhaps the Ara Pacis Augustae should be renamed the Ara Victrix Augustae.

> For a culture imbued not only with aspirations for a manifest destiny (as articulated by Vergil), but also a cultic preoccupation with victory, and associated deities, Isis provided a natural choice. From early times in Egypt she had been known as protectress of her native country against invasion – a 'mistress of battle'... [Later on she] became a part of Roman victory lore [and] hailed as *Invicta* ... ('unconquered').[3]

In his concluding remarks for his excellent analysis of the imagery on the Ara Pacis, Galinsky maintained that it is actually Venus *Victrix* who is portrayed in the Tellus relief. And – "Because Venus and Roma share many of the same characteristics [that is why] the Venus and Roma reliefs join together the two halves of the Altar more closely than do the slabs with Aeneas and Mars. This is [also] why Venus and Roma are represented on the front of the Ara Pacis."[4] However, Galinsky *assumes* that it is Venus *Victrix* because he *needs* her to be

---

[1] Donalson, p. 12.
[2] Witt, pp. 122-123.
[3] Donalson, p. 18.
[4] Galinsky, pp. 237-238.

that for his concluding identification that the central figure on the relief is Venus. However, the act of making peace or being the preserver of *pax* does not automatically allow that identification, especially when it is a secondary attribute of Venus compared to the sustained history of Isis as *Victrix* and *Invicta*. With all due respect, Galinsky seems to be invoking a bit of contortionist pleading in order to make his case. This becomes even more apparent when he reminds his readers that "Pax is not represented on the Ara Pacis. This should not surprise us: the Ara frieze is suggestive rather than explicit, as is much of Augustan poetry."[1]

Putting all this together, one is tempted to describe the Ara Pacis by the old revelatory phrase: "A Wolf in Sheep's Clothing."

*****

We must now consider a relief that was found in Carthage, now in the Louvre, that is very similar to but not an exact replica of the Tellus relief on the Ara Pacis. Once again we see a central female figure embracing two babies as she sits on a rocky ledge with a sheep and resting heifer beneath her. Toynbee dismissed it in one sentence; Zanker in one brief paragraph, primarily discussing the two figures that replaced the Aurae in the Ara Pacis version which he identifies as Triton (our right) and Diana Lucifera (our left). Galinsky goes into much more detail, but again more time is spent on analyzing and identifying the ancillary figures on either side. For Galinsky, they represent Sol (our right) rising from the sea and Venus (on our left) as the morning star.[2] Other scholars have either totally ignored or passed over it with barely a word. That was most unfortunate because this relief may hold a key clue regarding the final victory of Augustus over Cleopatra and Antony and that of Scipio Aemilianus, the adopted grandson of Scipio Africanus, over Carthage. It was the youthful Scipio Aemilianus who brought Carthage to its end in 146 BC and purportedly wept as he saw in the flames that engulfed what was left the preordained eventual end of Rome as well. "With the obliteration of its greatest rival, Rome had arrived as a world power, while at the same time setting in motion

---

[1] *Ibid.*

[2] J.M.C. Toynbee: *The Ara Pacis Reconsidered And Historical Art In Roman Italy* (1953), p. 81; Zanker, pp. 313-314; Galinsky, pp. 203ff. *Cf.* L.H. Martin: *Hellenistic Religions* (NY, 1987), pp. 10, 59, 72ff.

the cycle that would eventually lead to its own destruction."[1]

One most important question must be asked before we resume our study of this "Tellus" replica. Why was it placed in Carthage and how did it relate to the one in Rome? The Carthage relief was evidently part of an altar, a series of which were scattered along the North African area. If it was decreed and planned simultaneously with its Roman counterpart (which I believe was the case) what might have been its rationale. As I stated earlier, 13 BC marked the 250th anniversary of the start of the Punic Wars. The triumph over Cleopatra and Antony brought a final closure to Rome's conquest and domination of the Mediterranean world. The two events just referred to were like bookends to an inevitable march towards the acquisition of total power. If it was a time for Pax then it was also a time for *reconciliation*. First thwarted in a plan to do something new with the Temple of Concord in Rome, Augustus proceeded with a second idea. In 29 BC, when Augustus celebrated his Alexandrian triumph, he put forward a proposal first made by Julius Caesar back in 44 BC to rebuild Carthage as a new *Roman* city. When done it "was reborn as Colonia Iulia Concordia Carthago, the administrative capital of the Roman province of Africa Proconsularis." If this was to be the beginning of a new Golden Age, then it was time to heal old wounds even if they were inflicted by Rome's rapacious appetite for conquest and the spoils of war. Carthage was certainly high on the list. Moreover, the appearance of Virgil's *Aeneid* brought renewed attention to both Carthage and Aeneas; and he helped to create a different view and appreciation of Dido. She was no longer the culprit and was fully exonerated. Aeneas' later attitude towards her and meeting with Dido in the underworld reinforced that. An examination of the Carthaginian relief provides further evidence. But what could that evidence be? It was one thing to relate the two altar reliefs, yet it was more essential to find an appropriate iconography for each. We know what the Ara Pacis purportedly stood for. Let us now proceed with an identification analysis of the one found in Carthage in order to learn what it most likely stood for. Galinsky has already paved a possible pathway.

---

[1] R. Miles: *Carthage Must Be Destroyed* (NY, 2010), pp. 346-347; also see the comments made by Miles on p. 369. B.H. Warmington: *Carthage* (NY, 1969), p. 242. The destruction of Corinth in the same year (146 BC) may also have affected Aemelianus and caused him to think that way.

Galinsky concluded that the central figure on the Carthaginian relief "probably symbolizes Venus under her cosmic aspect. This impression is confirmed by her companion figures, which, as on the Ara Pacis, are of considerable significance for the interpretation of the main figure."[1] Galinsky thus maintained that the figure to her right (to our left) "resembles that of Venus [as] the morning star, *stella Veneris genitalis et roscida et prospera et salutaris*. It is no coincidence, therefore, that the vegetation below her grows somewhat more copiously than the reeds under the corresponding figure on the Ara Pacis."[2] Galinsky accepted "the often suggested interpretation of the figure [to our] right as Sol is probably correct: Hellenistic speculation connected Sol with Apollo and Augustus [though] in the Carthage relief, Sol is primarily the cosmic nature deity."[3]

I would agree with Galinsky up to a point, but only in a generic sense. What Galinsky has failed to do is to take into account that this is a *Carthaginian* relief and should have a *Carthaginian* reference. He also avoids *specifically* identifying the two children, but does say that they were "chosen to parallel the representation of the twins Romulus and Remus in the former relief." While it's true that Romulus and Remus do appear in the Lupercal panel, Galinsky *never* affirmed nor even suggested that they were the two children on the lap of the female figure in the Tellus panel. Indeed – I would now go so far as to say that Romulus and Remus *are* the two children on the lap of the central figure in the Carthaginian relief; and the female figure is none other than Tanit-Dido. The figure on her right (our left) is Astarte and the one on her left (our right) is none other than Baal-Hammon, a possible counterpart to Sol. Except for their names, the aforementioned Carthaginian deities all equate with the identifications made by Galinsky.

---

[1] Galinsky, p. 232 and fig. 162.
[2] *Ibid.*
[3] *Ibid.*

Fig. 5: The Carthaginian "Tellus" Panel

*****

Beginning in the 5th century BC, the goddess Tanit (now Tinnit preferred) superseded along with her consort Baal Hammon the cults of Astarte and Melqart in the Punic pantheon of the gods. Tanit did retain an association with Astarte, the latter being an equivalent of Aphrodite, Venus, Ishtar, and Innana. Thus Tanit was viewed in multiple hypostatic ways. She was a warrior goddess, a goddess of fertility, and later melded with Juno Caelestis to show her position as a sky goddess. An important added epithet was *"Pene Baal"*, meaning "Face of Baal" whose epithet Hammon meant something like "burning" or "fiery". That may have derived from one of his characteristics as a *solar deity*.[1] Tanit's association with Astarte and those other goddesses linked her with the same specific attributes; only a name change occurred due to a difference in cultural provenance. It was a small step thereafter for Tanit as well to be worshipped as Venus the Morning Star which preceded Baal Hammon as the rising Sun. This is one possible meaning of the expression *"Pene Baal"*. The iconography of the Carthaginian relief, now suggested, consists of valid examples of appropriate and meaningful polysemantic as well as other possible counterparts to the figures on the Tellus relief as put forth by Galin-

---

[1] Warmington, pp. 145-146; Miles, p. 69.

sky and myself. We have Aphrodite to Astarte, Venus-Isis-Cleopatra to Tanit-Dido, Sol to Baal-Hammon, and the twins Alexander-Helios and Cleopatra-Selene to the twins Romulus and Remus.[1] Interestingly, when discussing the Ara Pacis, Toynbee had this to say about its Carthaginian counterpart: "The relief from Carthage in the Louvre, depicting Tellus *or a local goddess* ..."

Dido was not a goddess, but her association with the divine Tanit combined with her role and influence on the mythohistory and actual history of Rome would have elevated her well above the mortal pale. The locus of Tanit and all that she stood for at that time served as a cosmic *éminence grise* for the founder of Carthage. Though Tanit rose late in importance at Carthage and "evidence of the cult of Tanit is equally late ... she is often considered to be a barely modified avatar of a Cypro-Phoenician Mother-Goddess which Dido would have introduced."[2] That justifies her transcending the centuries to be attached to Dido on this marble relief from the late first century BC.

> It seems likely that [Tanit's] popularity was due to the acquisition of the rich African land and the feeling of the need to worship a deity who brought life and fertility. She probably owed much to the cult of Hera among the Greeks of the west, and also to that of Demeter. Symbols of fertility such as the palm tree, pomegranates and doves appear on numerous stelae in her honour, but she was more than a fertility goddess. ... [a] most important function, the assurance of fertility, was taken over by Tanit.[3]

The abundant vegetation that surrounds the central figure in this relief as well as the considerable fruit on her lap that is front and center emphasizes the above comment.

Since some of what I proposed, of necessity, is purely theoretical and speculative, nonetheless, it is based upon a reasonable and knowledgeable interpretation of Roman history, art, and political and reli-

---

[1] Miles, p. 275, for what happened at the Sicilian city of Eryx involving a multivalent cult of Venus Erycina. Also see A. Strong: *The Phoenicans in History and Legend* (2002), p.144: "Tannit is usually associated with Astarte especially in Sarepta, Carthage and Malta, as a warrior goddess...The Tannit of Hadrumentum and Ibiza is associated to Osiris in the role of Isis. In the coins and later in a stele from Hadrumentum she is assimilated to Artemis and becomes later in the Roman period the 'Nurse of Saturn' when she is depicted as mother (Nutrix)." Also, J.M.C. Toynbee: *The Ara Pacis Reconsidered and Historical Art in Roman Italy*, p. 81 (emphasis added).

[2] G. C. Picard & C. Picard: *The Life and Death of Carthage* (NY, 1968), p. 1.

[3] Warmington, pp. 146-147.

gious symbolism. I would also add human behavior. My analysis and conclusions are certainly not that far removed, if at all, from those of my scholarly predecessors who have discussed and debated this part of the Ara Pacis for more than *eighty* years with no absolute resolution! I tip my pen to them for they certainly opened a door despite possibly having more constraints placed upon them than I had. When dealing with the subject of "Peace" it is more than a physical reality. It is also a state of mind that arguably may be more difficult to achieve yet more profound. When it comes to the replica "Tellus" panel in Carthage, the identifications and interpretations applied to it *parallel* the one in Rome, but do *not* duplicate it exactly. Both panels point in the direction of Pax which is depicted in neither one; and the directional line is quite different. In the Roman example, Pax is implied more by the ending of endless war and the resulting bountiful resources now available to the Roman people. I also tried to prove that particular parts of the Ara Pacis served as a symbolic replacement for the Triumphal Arch that Augustus could not have for his Alexandrian victory.

*****

As far as the Tellus counterpart in Carthage is concerned its solution may be more complex, but more satisfying. If, as I posited, the central figure does represent Dido with the twins Romulus and Remus, then we have a childless and despairing Dido who, in the words of Adrian Goldsmith, "regrets that her lover has not given her a 'little Aeneas' as consolation for his abandonment of her," now symbolically compensated by being allowed to embrace and care for what could be either the children or grandchildren of Aeneas – one of whom becomes the legendary founder of Rome itself. Is this not the ultimate reconciliation? I should now like to quote the words of Richard Miles, an authority on Carthage, who independently arrived at a similar conclusion by taking a different approach:

> In many ways, the Dido and Aeneas episode within the *Aeneid* concerns the impossibility of reconciliation between Carthage and Rome. The cruel and faithless rejection of Dido by Aeneas in favour of his preordained fate functions as a commentary on the brutality of the Roman quest for empire – a quest similarly ordained by the gods. Just as Aeneas crushes Dido in order to fulfill his divine mission, so too will Rome crush

Carthage in its pursuit of empire. Nevertheless, just as Aeneas as a character matures, and comes to regret his treatment of the Carthaginian queen (whom he later confronts in the underworld), so too does the *Aeneid* mourn the necessary but nonetheless lamentable destruction of Carthage, and preempt its eventual, Augustan, restoration as a city of the Roman Empire. By subverting centuries of Carthaginian stereotypes (and presenting Dido as more Roman than Aeneas), Vergil points not only to the impropriety of such stereotypes in the new Augustan world, but also to the potential of the Carthaginians to be good Romans. Even at the point at which future enmity is set in train, therefore, the reader is given a clear sight of future *reconciliation*. Like Augustus's new city, the *Aeneid* stood simultaneously as a monument to the restoration of Carthage as a symbol of *concord* and as a reminder of the discord that had prompted its destruction.[1]

And there you have it. Concord (a form of Pax if you will) and Reconciliation. That is what the Carthaginian relief represents; and that is why Dido appears on a monument in *Roman* Carthage. The similarities between Dido and Cleopatra reinforce the links between the Roman and Carthaginian versions; and also give more credibility for my theoretical identifications. Virgil actually referred to Cleopatra in the *Aeneid*. She primarily appears on the shield of Aeneas, crafted by Vulcan, for his final battle with Turnus. There, we see the figure of Augustus engaging the forces of Antony and Cleopatra at the battle of Actium where the Trojan past, Aeneas, and Augustus "are thus linked through clear verbal reminiscence. Recent critics have shown with what care for minute detail Virgil makes these interconnections between the ancient past and his Augustan present."[2] A comparison of Dido to Cleopatra is most revealing; and Virgil obviously referenced his contemporary world when he composed the *Aeneid* because he was insightful enough to see what that would conjure. The two were North African Queens who were considered representative of the Orient, dominant yet foreign in their respective realms (one Phoenician in origin, the other Macedonian-Greek), had a life and death struggle with a brother, both stood in the way of Rome's ultimate destiny, and then very deliberately committed suicide after being rejected. Dido and Cleopatra symbolized the Alpha and Omega of the first 750 years of Rome's mythohistory and history from its tentative foundation begin-

---

[1] Miles, pp. 369-370 (emphasis added).
[2] Michael C. J. Putnam: *Virgil's Aeneid* (Chapel Hill, 1995), p. 163 & *inter alia*.

nings to completion of its Imperial Supremacy over all the Mediterranean lands as it created "mare nostrum". I also find it interesting that the name Lavinia chosen for Aeneas' wife in the *Aeneid* sounds so similar to Livia, the name of Augustus' last wife.

*****

Afterword: Earlier, I wrote that Octavian was *obsessed* with Cleopatra. I should now like to present some interesting facts about his behavior all the way down to the end of of his reign as Augustus to make my point. When the Ara Pacis Augustae was completed it was placed in the Campus Martius not far from what was the Via Flaminia, according to the wishes of Augustus. It was located at the center of an open plateau where various exercises and maneuvers were regularly performed by both the army and cavalry. A direct line eventually connected the Ara Pacis to the Mausoleum of Augustus which was situated northwest of the altar. The completion of the Mausoleum preceded the Ara Pacis by possibly as much as 14 years and was the first Augustan structure to be built in the Campus Martius. As a funerary monument, technically it could not be within the *pomerium*, the sacred border of Rome itself. It was the Horologium Solare Augusti, a huge open air plaza that was basically a large sun-dial in the form of a double axe that loosely connected the two structures and was more closely connected to the Ara Pacis, almost adjacent to it on its eastern side.

> The concept of military success [that we have been discussing above] was further emphasized by the fact that in 10 B.C.E. Augustus set up and dedicated to the sun-god Sol an Egyptian obelisk to serve as the *gnomon* (pointer) of his colossal sundial, the Solarium (or Horologium) Augusti, which was designed to measure the length of the year. The Solarium was also a victory monument celebrating the year of the *vicennalia* (twentieth anniversary) of his great military success over Egypt in 30 B.C.E., marking the end of the civil war period.
> The Solarium with its obelisk was planned in conjunction with the Ara Pacis, which was constituted in 13 B.C.E., the year of the fiftieth anniversary of Augustus' birth in 63 B.C.E., and dedicated in 9 B.C.E. on January 30, the birthday of his wife Livia. Together, both commemorative monuments served as a visual metaphor for *parta victoriis pax* ('peace brought forth by victories' or 'peace through victory'), an ideo-

logical shibboleth that was reiterated directly and indirectly in a number of Augustus' representational programs.[1]

The obelisk (think Washington Monument), an upright stone with a pyramidal top some 100 feet tall, was originally commissioned by the Egyptian Pharaoh Psammetichus II. When it arrived in Rome it was reinscribed with Octavian's name and placed in the center of the aforementioned Solarium. D. Kleiner expressed the view that this obelisk was "something more than a clock; it might well be interpreted as a victory monument over Egypt and Cleopatra, and Mark Antony, at the Battle of Actium." Not satisfied with just the one obelisk, Octavian ordered a sequence of additional obelisks to be brought back to Rome. The result was that Rome eventually ended up with more obelisks than remained in Egypt. Pollini has made a most provocative suggestion pertaining to the obelisk:

> The Latin word *obeliscus* derives from the Greek *obeliskos*, meaning 'small spit' or 'skewer', which undoubtedly also had sexual overtones, given its obviously phallic shape. Since such associations would have been known to the educated Roman elite, one wonders whether there was an intentional pun associated with the shadow of a phallic, male-gendered *obeliskos* piercing the western opening of the female-gendered Ara Pacis. Sexual overtones in the context of cosmic birth and rebirth are to be found, after all, in Augustus' own expression *parta victoriis pax* ('peace brought forth by victories') in his *Res Gestae* (13), since the Latin perfect passive participle parta is from parire ('to procreate,' 'to give birth to,' 'to bring forth').[2]

*****

If the image of Cleopatra was indeed concealed within the iconography of the Tellus relief as I previously proposed (see *supra*) then Pollini's remarks sound very similar to that which I suggested earlier regarding subliminal interactions between Octavian and Cleopatra as well as Octavian and Antony. As we shall read shortly, J. Fletcher was of a similar mind when it came to the Forum of Augustus (see *infra*). Two more obelisks were brought to Rome from Egypt and each placed

---

[1] J. Pollini: *From Republic to Empire* (Norman, OK, 2013), p. 210 (emphasis added). Cleopatra's birthday was on 13 January 69 BC.

[2] *Ibid.*, p. 216.

on either side of the main entryway to Augustus' Mausoleum. The structure outwardly looked like a splendiferous version of an Etruscan Tumulus, but it had features similar to what August surely saw in the construction of Cleopatra's Mausoleum. He had presided over the funeral of Cleopatra and Antony where they were entombed and had plenty of opportunity to admire it. In the words of Fletcher, "Beneath the domed top, the tomb was essentially a step pyramid in cross-section, and as Egyptomania took hold of Rome wealthy men such as Gaius Cestius even built their own pyramid-shaped tombs in the middle of the eternal city." The location of his Mausoleum was next to the Tiber. Cleopatra's was close to the Mediterranean sea. Furthermore, the Mausoleum was not that far from the great *Iseum*,which may or may not have been built yet at that time. There is some confusion over that. Octavian, along with Antony and Lepidus, had earlier pledged funds to build the *Iseum*. Supposedly, it was destroyed by Tiberius and then rebuilt by Caligula. The cult of Isis and the *Iseum* had a checkered history. My own feeling is that it did exist at the time that Augustus was completing his Mausoleum, and its location not that far from the *Iseum* (or a significant Isis cult locale if not yet built) was deliberate. Augustus had a very strange relationship with both Isis and Serapis, the former's divine male consort. A bronze coin from Sabratha in North Africa depicts the bust of Serapis on its reverse and Augustus on its obverse. When in Alexandria, Augustus also venerated Serapis. A *Serapium* in Rome was right next to the *Iseum*. While some consider Augustus' contradictory behavior to be good politics I believe that it went further than that. Cleopatra's tomb was deliberately located next to a Temple of Isis; and here in Rome we have Augustus' tomb located within a reasonable distance from the *Iseum*. Yet, for all that, Augustus suppressed the cult of Isis and would not allow it to function in the city of Rome proper. But that did not involve the Campus Martius.

The very name "Augustus" appears to have been stolen from Cleopatra. For a brief period of time Augustus considered using the name "Romulus". That was rejected in favor of the now familiar one. A man named

> Munatius Plancus suggested the name 'Augustus', quoting an epigram which stated 'when glorious Rome had founded been, by augury august'. Although ground consecrated by the augurs was indeed known as 'august', it seems more than coincidental that Plancus, who had once

danced before Cleopatra, the New Isis, would have known that another of her divine titles was 'Isis Augusta' meaning majestic and sacred. So it was that the banker's son Gaius Octavianus became Augustus Caesar in 27 BC after lifting a name from the goddess persona of Cleopatra.[1] [Cf. *infra* to what Augustus did in the Pantheon.]

Moreover, women "favored addressing Isis as *Isis Augusta*" and the term *Pax Augusta* derived from the latter as well. Name changes did not end there.

It was also decided that a month should be named to celebrate Octavian's new name in the same way that the fifth month, Quinctilis, had been renamed July in honour of Julius Caesar's birth month. Yet instead of selecting his own birth month, September, the newly named Augustus claimed Sextilis as the month of Augustus, ordering 'that the month renamed in his honour should be the one in which he brought down Cleopatra' and the first day August, the day Alexandria had surrendered, was declared a public holiday.[2]

Then fully acting the role of *Imperator* while claiming not to be, Augustus forbid any Romans from visiting Egypt and the reverse for those Egyptians desiring to visit Rome. Egypt was his and his alone. Later Emperors did visit Egypt, enjoying the sites and traveling up the Nile to observe the cities of the south. The most notable Emperor who visited Egypt was Hadrian whose youthful lover Antinous drowned under mysterious circumstances in the Nile. He was then deified and his idealized statues spread throughout the Empire.

*****

Around the same time that the Mausoleum of Augustus was being completed, Agrippa was putting the finishing touches to the first Pantheon (ca. 25 BC). This building, that has been classified as a Roman temple, is something of an enigma. The original one burned down and was rebuilt by the Emperor Hadrian. The one we see today with its dramatic Dome was not a part of the first one. The orientation was also different, though its location is apparently the same. As such, it forms an exact triangle with a connecting line between the Mausole-

---

[1] J. Fletcher: *Cleopatra the Great* (NY, 2008), p. 330; Also see Donalson, pp. 8-10.
[2] Fletcher: *ibid*.

um, the Ara Pacis, and the Pantheon. All of this may have something to do with the goddess Isis. According to E. S. Shuckburgh, "It was dedicated to Mars and Venus, mythical ancestors of the Iulian gens, but its name may be derived either from its numerous [sic] statues of the gods, or from the supposed likeness of its dome to the sky [sic]. Its purpose – beyond being a compliment to Augustus – is still a subject of dispute. Nor have we any record of its use except as the meeting-place of the Arval brothers."[1] MacDonald considered the Pantheon to be "both a religious building and a *secular imperial monument* [and because of] the universality of its forms belongs to everyone. This is why it is the temple of the whole world."[2]

Octavian's involvement in the Pantheon is very interesting. Upon its completion he placed a new statue of Venus within its confines.

> Keen to reclaim the goddess for Rome and to symbolise Cleopatra's defeat, he adorned his new statue with her remaining huge pearl 'cut in two pieces, so that half a helping of the jewel might be in each of [Venus'] ears'. He even took for his new statue the pearl necklace [Cleopatra] herself had placed on Caesar's statue of Venus in his family temple in the Forum.[3]

It is my belief that Augustus was a secret devotee of Isis who, by that act was actually reclaiming *her* for Rome and himself. By putting the jeweled objects that he took off the statue of Cleopatra, the *New Isis*, on to that of Venus, Augustus effected a sympathetic magic transformation. Do not forget that Isis was "she of the countless names" and *Panthea*, the "All-goddess". Ultimately "she merited the title *Pantokrator* and that of *Panbasileia*, both signifying the 'All-ruler'."[4] As Witt wrote: "It can hardly have been an accident that Hadrian built his Pantheon to replace Agrippa's in the Campus Martius not far from the home of Isis Panthea." There, *en passant*, we have a possible explanation for the name "Pantheon" whose meaning has been so elusive for so long for so many. As it happens, in addition

---

[1] E. S. Shuckburgh: *Augustus Caesar* (NY, 1995 reprint), p. 106. Some of what Shuckburgh says was picked up second hand from Dio who was not correct in the first place. The "numerous" gods probably came later, if at all. See L. Richardson Jr.: *A New Topographical Dictionary of Ancient Rome* (London, 1992), p. 283.

[2] W. L. MacDonald: *The Architecture of the Roman Empire* (New Haven), pp. 119, 121 (emphasis added). Also see J. Rupke: *Pantheon* (Princeton, 2016), pp. 262-27

[3] Fletcher, p. 328.

[4] Donalson, p. 10; Witt, pp. 111-129. *Cf.* W. L. MacDonald: *Pantheon* (Cambridge, 1976), *inter alia*

to the Mausoleum of Augustus, there is a proposed link regarding "parallels in the architecture and topography of Alexandria [which] have also been cautiously advanced for the Pantheon." Furthermore, there is a recent alternate proposal for why this structure was called the Pantheon, but with a caveat. "The name 'Pantheon' probably derives from the Greek *pantheion*, a term that conveyed different but related meanings, whether a temple of all the gods, a temple of the 12 Olympian gods, or a temple in which the image of a ruler stood in the company of such divinities. For although there are textual clues, it is tradition more than anything else that explains our use of this name for a structure whose original purpose *remains uncertain*. In truth, we cannot even be absolutely sure that the Pantheon was a temple, as most scholars believe on account of some temple-like characteristics, most notably the great pedimented front. It is also significant that several ancient sources do refer to the building as a temple, yet a passage from the life of Hadrian cites buildings that he restored, and it includes the Pantheon with wording that could be read to mean that it was not in the category of temples."[1] As Emperor, Augustus was also Pharaoh with all of its accompanying divine and secular authority. His attachment to Egypt was now even more profound.

For all that, Augustus was not done with Cleopatra (and possibly even Caesar). Once again the unflinching words of Fletcher drive home a point:

> Although mindful of his pledge [to Archelaos who had paid Augustus 2,000 talents to leave all of Cleopatra's statues intact] ... Octavian ... changed [the immediate surroundings of the Caesar's Forum] by creating a much larger Forum with a somewhat phallic layout. Two semi-circular galleries or exedrae appear to form testicles and a long projecting forecourt extended into the area of Caesar's Venus temple so that 'the buildings could be imagined as having sexual intercourse' in a very subtle,

---

[1] *The Pantheon: From Antiquity to the Present*, edited by T.A. Marder & M.W. Jones (NY, 2015), Marder & Jones: »Introduction«, p. 4 & References for long quote (emphasis added); pp. 49-159 by E. La Rocca, L.M Hetland, G. Martines & G. Waddell, all on many key aspects of the Pantheon. Martines in particular is noteworthy for bringing up the subject of corbelling techniques employed in Roman architecture that are reminiscent of Mycenaean false domes and corbelling layers. He makes reference to Apulia and Sardinia (see the section titled »Further References« *supra* (p. 127)) where this type of architectural construction displays a supposed continuity from the early second millennium BC until ancient Roman times. The Etruscan "Tomba dei Carri" in Populonia, 7th century BC, with its Tholos-type structuring is cited as well (pp. 127-131, emphasis added, where key pictures of a corbelled vault and corbelled dome from different sites is also illustrated).

albeit disturbing, use of architectural domination.[1] [Cf. to my comments and those of Pollini *supra*.]

Was Augustus now giving the proverbial shaft to Caesar as well as Cleopatra as he continued to relentlessly pursue and consolidate his power? After all, he accomplished what his two predecessors had attempted to do and failed – namely, the conquest and control of the entire Mediterranean world with all the monarchical titles that went with it. Except for the building activity and implications involving the Forum of Augustus which occurred near the end of the first century BC, all other structures that may have had anything to do with Egypt, Cleopatra, and even Antony preceded the Forum construction. Given the sub-text for the Pantheon, the Mausoleum, and the Iseum, they all lend greater credence for the Ara Pacis identifications both in Rome and Carthage that I proposed.

Ironically, the progeny of Antony and Cleopatra extended well beyond that of anything that emerged from the Augustan bloodline. Antony's endured until the latter part of the 3rd Century AD. The veneration given to Cleopatra and the cult of Isis continued all the way into the 6th Century AD at the sites of Dendera and Philae in southern Egypt. It even outlasted the collapse of the Western Roman Empire. All of this was finally terminated during the reign of the Byzantine Emperor Justinian.

---

[1] Fletcher, p. 328. The gift of Archelaos notwithstanding, "in B.C. 28 however Octavian had his revenge on the cult of Isis. 'He did not allow the Egyptian rites to be celebrated inside the pomerium' at Rome. In Egypt Cleopatra's memory long remained." (J. Lindsay: *Cleopatra* (1971), p. 436.)

Epilogue

Looking back at the vast extent of the Roman Empire, a saying originated and evolved in the Medieval period: "All roads lead to Rome" – a fitting metaphor. When studying the chronology of the Ancient Eastern Mediterranean littoral from the mid-second millennium BC until the late seventh century BC the phrase "All roads lead to Egypt" is also highly appropriate.

And therein lies the key to dealing with the problem of the Dark Age of Greece as previously set forth in the many pages of this book. Starting with the first archaeological efforts of Schliemann in the 1870s, when he brought ancient Troy and Mycenae to light, the question of how to date these two citadels and other related sites in Greece that came to the fore was immediately problematic. "Not until the fifth century BC did the historic Greek world come to date even contemporary events in a coherent scheme."[1] Because the Aegean world and Greece itself lacked a coherent and viable internal chronology scholars had to look elsewhere for the answer to the chronological question. They assumed, wrongly as it turned out, that pharaonic chronology was the answer. But that chronology was in its own infancy and fluid. Despite protests and disagreements as elucidated earlier, an Aegean chronology began to be formulated.

"In attempting a history of the Mycenaean age we are still largely confined to the history of material culture. ... For the Mycenaean rulers did not, like the Egyptians, record their names and exploits in inscriptions or public monuments."[2] Given the absence of written records, an attempt to establish an independent chronology through the use of retro-calculation based upon genealogies was doomed to failure. Those genealogies were often inflated, corrupted, too short and fundamentally inexact. As an example, "genealogies of the royal Lacedaimonian families ... were the most stable pedigrees that the Greeks possessed, though they were partly fictitious."[3]

---

[1] C. G. Starr: *The Origins of Greek Civilization* (NY, 1961), p. 67.
[2] F. H. Stubbings: *CAH* II:1, »The Rise of Mycenaean Civilization« (Cambridge, 2004), p, 627; also see »The Egyptian Connexion«, pp. 633-635.
[3] J. Forsdyke: *Greece Before Homer* (NY, 1957), pp. 67-68; B.H. Warmington: *Carthage A History* (NY, 1969), pp. 27-28.

One effort to demonstrate that a number of genealogies, thirty years to a generation, if reckoned backward from a time in the fifth century BC could culminate at a possible significant historical date beginning around the tenth century BC proved to be untrustworthy. This "process of creation involved many misinterpretations and distortions, in addition to anything that may have happened during the transmission of the material previously. ... It would be unwise to believe that even as accounts of descent such genealogies represent information transmitted intact from the past, and this must discredit any dating system based on them."[1] "The archaeological material, then, must be the only basis for establishing some kind of framework for the [Third Palace Period]."[2]

With no other options, two related sources were brought into play – Egyptian synchronizing applied to Aegean pottery finds – each imbued with its own inherent weaknesses. Simply put, ceramic objects found in an Egyptian context are dated accordingly while the reverse is also true – Egyptian artifacts found in an Aegean context are also responsible for the dating of the latter. But this is not a double-blind situation. Challenges to this approach have been rebuffed or ignored. Egyptian absolute dates are a modern construct based upon multiple sources each with its own shortcomings as highlighted in previous sections of this book. As for pottery, here is the testimony from various individuals pertaining to its reliability for absolute dating sequences:

> Cross-dating depends on finding objects of a known date from one culture in one level of another. Thus a well-dated Egyptian artifact from a known dynasty when found in a stratum of a Minoan or Mycenaean site can be used to establish the date of that stratum, assuming that the Egyptian artifact is not an heirloom or antique (always a risky assumption). Key cross-dates were established in this way early in Aegean Bronze Age archaeology, and they still underpin the entire chronology of the period.[3]

> The most objective evidence for the Dark Age is provided by archaeology – the settlements which have been excavated, unfortunately very few for this period, and the innumerable artifacts which have been unearthed. Of these, pottery, as usual, because of its almost indestructible nature,

---

[1] O. Dickinson: *The Aegean from Bronze Age to Iron Age* (NY, 2007), pp. 11-12.
[2] A.M. Snodgrass: *The Dark Age of Greece* (Edinburgh, 1971), pp. 10-15.
[3] C. Runnels & P. M. Murray: *Greece Before History* (Stanford, 2001), p. 160. On heirlooms, see Snodgrass: *op. cit.*, pp. 382-383.

> is the most abundant and important. ... Pottery is such an important historical source for this period that a warning about accepting the evidence squeezed from it may be salutary. A vase is an objective fact, but the interpretation of its significance, even by an expert in ceramics and archaeology, is bound, of course, to be somewhat subjective.[1]

> ... Furumark's establishment of a chronology of Mycenaean pottery ... was perhaps the most important single contribution in the struggle for a chronology but also because it best exemplifies the difficulties today.
> Even archaeologists have constantly to be reminded, though they of course know it, that a pottery chronology such as Furumark's is not the equivalent of a chronology of the kings of England.[2]

Consider the question and self-given answer by O. Dickinson:

> How then did the idea of a Dark Age arise? In part, it seems to derive from the establishing of a more accurate chronology of the LBA and the succeeding period. This made it clear that Mycenaean civilisation, now perceived to have superseded the older Minoan civilisation as the dominant force in the Aegean, reached its height in the fourteenth and thirteenth centuries, while the most striking material of the EIA belonged in the ninth and eighth centuries. Very little material could be placed in the intervening period, and what there was seemed notably unimpressive.[3]

Is this an answer? This is a *testamonium paupertatis*. Dickinson's response to himself was fundamentally vague and generic. He never deigned to even mention what specific artifacts were utilized to determine a dating. Nor did he indicate what methodology was applied that supposedly could reveal an absolute date for the material being scrutinized. Not one word regarding Egypt or an Egyptian synchronism or anything else for that matter.

Yet there is one noted authority who did acknowledge Egypt at the outset when dealing with the earliest days of the problem with Mycenaean chronology – Chrestos Tsountas. Back in 1897, after a brief discussion involving the dating of Mycenaean culture and the "upheaval which buried Thera," Tsountas had this to say:

> Here we call in the aid of Egyptology. In Greece we find datable products in Mycenaean deposits, and conversely in datable Egyptian deposits we find Mycenaean products.

---

[1] John V. A. Fine: *The Ancient Greeks A Critical History* (Cambridge, MS, 1983), p. 28.
[2] M. I. Finley: *The World of Odysseus* (NY, 1978), p. 172.
[3] Dickinson: *op. cit.*, p. 3.

In using the word 'datable', we do not ignore the unsettled state of Egyptian chronology; but it would seem safe to conduct an inquiry like this – on ground that is otherwise hopelessly dark – on the basis of a reckoning in which such authorities as Meyer, Ermann and Petrie substantially agree. Down to the twelfth dynasty there is still a wide divergence, but from the eighteenth dynasty on – and these are our chief concern – the variation is but slight, as the following shows:

Dynasty	Flinders-Petrie	Meyer-Ermann
XII	2700-2500 BC	2130 BC
XVIII	1450-1250	1530-1320
XIX	1250-1150	1320-1180
XX	1100 – ?	1180-1050

Cecil Torr indeed brings the twelfth dynasty down to 1500 B.C., 'at latest;' the eighteenth to 1271; the twentieth to 1000; but it will be time to reckon with this chronology when experienced Egyptologists have given it a hearing.[1]

Torr's dates are difficult to pin down because he had dynasties ruling concurrently and overlapping (see *Memphis and Mycenae*, Chapter III.)

At this point in our discussion of dynastic dates, the reader should be reminded of Velikovsky's position on this matter as expressed in *Ages in Chaos*. He placed the Exodus at the close of the Middle Kingdom which he dated to ca. 1447 BC (p. 7) and the beginning of the Eighteenth Dynasty to ca. the early tenth century BC.

Later on in this Epilogue we shall once again present some of the critical observations made by Tsountas regarding the end of Mycenae and possible cultural continuities from before the "Dark Age" to the time after it ended.

One more note about ceramic material. Greece was not a unified polity during the time of the Mycenaean Age. The inherent difficulty of judging style differences aside, a highly subjective topic, it should be emphasized that different sites could have had different styles with a varying chronology or a single site could have had older and newer objects at the same time; consider the carry over and mixture of fine china in our own contemporary societies; there could have been imitations or heirlooms (see Snodgrass: *The Dark Age of Greece*, pp. 382-

---

[1] C. Tsountas & J. I. Manatt: *The Mycenaean Age* (Chicago, 1969, unchanged reprint of 1897 edition), pp. 317-318 and ref. 2; C. Torr: *M&M, op. cit.*, Chapter V, »The Connection of Egypt with Greece«.

383), or antiques at a site. People did not necessarily throw away older pottery when new shapes and designs were created and available. Strata were not uniform and had no guarantee of being undisturbed. Before we leave the subject of pottery as a means of establishing the chronology of the Ancient Aegean World, we should reaffirm the considerable importance of the Supplement sections of this book written by Edwin M. Schorr (pp. 165 ff) which are so germane to the study of ceramics and stratigraphy in that world. His lengthy and meticulous detailed analysis of this archaeological procedure is a challenging exposé of the inexplicable anomalies that exist or could exist – e.g., older material found above younger material, stratigraphic layers that are not the proper density that one would expect to find, etc.

Furthermore, aside from Egypt, "datable Oriental records which refer unmistakably to Aegean events are virtually absent down to 500 BC."[1] Nonetheless, there is strong circumstantial evidence of possible contact between Aegean sculptors and artisans with the artistry of the seventh century Neo-Assyrian Empire as previously discussed in the section on the Lion Gate at Mycenae. Why no records exist prior to 500 BC is a puzzlement. Perhaps they were destroyed during the Persian conquest of the Near East.

We must now turn our attention to Mycenae and Troy. Both stand as signifiers of the Greek Aegean World; both stand at the beginning of the Dark Age of Greece. The former under the leadership of its king, Agamemnon, led a major coalition assault on the latter; the latter was ultimately destroyed by it.[2] Did they exist? Was their end ca. 1200 BC truly final? To add to the confusion, some findings indicate that Mycenae may have been destroyed before it attacked Troy. Such are the problems of dating the Aegean past without any written records.

Beginning in the 1870s AD, Heinrich Schliemann, a wealthy German entrepreneur, uncovered their remains proving that they once indeed did exist. But ... did he discover Homer's Troy? And what of Mycenae? And when did all this destruction happen, if it happened at all? Let us examine the time of the Trojan War first, bearing in mind that any dramatic chronological change should affect that of Mycenae and other sites of that period. What is about to be presented is funda-

---

[1] Starr: *op. cit.*, p. 65.
[2] Homer's *Iliad* and *Odyssey*; Quintus of Smyrna: *The War at Troy* (Univ. of Oklahoma, 1968).

mentally a summation and reiteration of what preceded the Epilogue in the many pages of this book. Additional source material and perspectives have been brought in to emphasize and enhance what has gone before.

Were it not for Homer, there probably would be neither a Troy nor a Trojan War to captivate us through the millennia. Though Homer's story only dealt with the last few weeks of a supposed ten year war that ended with the death and funeral of Hector, he gave us much to contemplate and reflect upon. Because of Homer, Schliemann was moved to open an archaeological door that first led him to the mound at Hisarlik and then to Mycenae – a world without a history, yet sophisticated, cultured, human, and engaging in so many ways. Troy, in particular, because of its location, was wealthy from the tariffs it imposed on the east-west trade that moved through the Hellespont. It was this monetary prize far more that appealed to the Achaean confederacy which attacked Troy than reclaiming the fair Helen who may or may not have left willingly in the arms of the Trojan Paris away from Menelaus and Sparta.

Be that as it may, it was Homer's Troy that served as the touchstone for the Mycenaean Age as well as numerous future generations that invoked Troy for political expediency and legitimacy. Troy became the stage which allowed the notable "actors" of the time to "play their part" and make their individual and collective appearances. Their influence and importance from that period on the mythohistory, history, art, literature, theater, and films of Western Civilization cannot be overstated. But who was Homer? When did he compose the *Iliad* and the *Odyssey*? Where was he from? When was the Trojan War, if indeed there was one?

The last question has already been dealt with by Velikovsky and Sammer elsewhere in this book. Suffice it to say that the date most often cited – 1184/83 BC – is that given by Eratosthenes ca. 220 BC when he was the chief librarian at the great Library-Museum of Alexandria. How it was obtained was presented in an excellent scholarly article written by N. Kokkinos in *AWE (Ancient West & East)* 8 (2009), pp. 37-56. That doesn't mean that 1184/3 BC was the actual date or that it helped in identifying the Troy of Homer in any way. Moreover, there are other competitors for that date which lie on either side of the chronological divide.[1] Eratosthenes was under pressure from his Greco-Macedonian rulers to push Greek history back in time due to the decades' earlier simultaneous appearance of both Manetho's *Aegyptiaca* and Berossus' *Babyloniaca* – where each made a case for the great antiquity of their respective civilizations, Egypt and Babylonia, in order to override the greatness of their new conquerors.

It should once again be emphasized that Manetho's original version, wherein he established the dynastic framework still in vogue today, did not make it through the millennia untouched. It passed into several different hands already removed by several centuries from Manetho. We will never know what was lost or what changes were made by later scribes. The version that did survive contained an assortment of errors with adjustments and corrections already made by contemporary scholars. Yet Manetho's history is all too often treated as if it were some kind of sacred document. (Consult the excellent book *BEROSSOS and MANETHO, Introduced and Translated* by G. P. Verbrugghe & J. M. Wickersham (Ann Arbor, 1996), with an outstanding specialized Bibliography, pp. 213-215, and a key Fig. 1 on p. 118 illustrating how Manetho was preserved and transmitted through a period of more than an entire *millennium*.)

Eratosthenes "sought to date events by contemporary evidence", but stopped his story with the death of Alexander the Great in 323 BC. Apollodoros of Athens who was an immediate successor to Eratosthenes carried the story down to his own time, 140 BC. Then "Castor, in the first century BC, compiled a comparative chronology of the world, Oriental, Greek and Roman. In order to establish *some equality with the much older Egyptian and Asiatic histories*, he carried Greek chronology back to the earliest *legendary or imaginary* events."[2]

As of now, dates for Homer when he theoretically converted an oral story of the Trojan War into written form vary between ca. 800 BC and ca. 670 BC while a majority of scholarly opinion takes a middle ground of 750-730 BC.[3] Various cities competed for Homer's origins, Smyrna being one of them. A good choice given the fact that Quintus of Smyrna, sometime in the third century AD, wrote *The War At Troy* which picks up the story where Homer ends the *Iliad*.[4]

---

[1] Forsdyke: *op. cit.*, p. 62, where 11 different dates are listed; Starr, p. 66.
[2] Forsdyke, p. 29 (emphasis added).
[3] R. Lane Fox: *The Classical World* (NY, 2006), p. 18.
[4] Quintus of Smyrna: *op. cit.*

The question of Homer's time and place of origin have recently taken a back seat to the question: Is the mound at Hisarlik the *true* location for Homer's Troy regardless of what stratum Schliemann may or may not have uncovered? Several other locations have been proposed, some with an extreme geographical and credibility difference. Two authors, Lascelles and Crowe, have made compelling cases for locating Homer's "Troy" on the site of Anatolia's Pergamum.[1] This is all based upon comparing Troy's civic, topographical, and geographical features, as put forward in the *Iliad*, to other locales – Korfmann's archaeological evidence to the contrary notwithstanding. This is not a new phenomenon. Criticism of designating Hisarlik as the site of Homer's Troy has been ongoing for decades. Even determining which of the many strata found at Troy is applicable to Homer's has proven difficult and controversial. Evidence of destruction does not square with warlike activity. Natural causes appear to be the answer. Currently, Troy VIIa almost by default is the prime candidate, but doesn't check all the boxes.[2]

John V. A. Fine put it most succinctly:

> Although archaeology furnishes no evidence, beyond the presence of some contemporary Mycenaean pottery, that the Mycenaeans were responsible for this destruction, most scholars agree that Troy VIIa was the city made famous by Greek epic. Since the literary source for the Trojan War, from which the whole later tradition was derived, is Homer, and since Homer lived some five [sic] centuries after the supposed date of the war, a definitive decision on the actuality of the Trojan War will probably never be possible.[3]

---

[1] J. Lascelles: *Troy The World Deceived – Homer's Guide to Pergamum* (Victoria, BC, 2005). Lascelles convincingly argues for a date for the fall of Troy in 808/7, the founding of Carthage in 824 by Dido, who then met Aeneas in 802/1. See pp.142-151. John Crowe: *The Troy Deception* (Leicester, 2011), follows Lascelles, whom he acknowledges. Crowe is much more detailed and the book is almost 300 pages. A promised second volume on the citadel of Pergamon has not yet appeared to my knowledge. Iman Wilkens: *Where Troy Once Stood* (NY, 1990) opts for Western Europe, Northwest Africa all the way to the Caribbean for the location and sources of the *Iliad* and *Odyssey* – a text that goes beyond density and no Index. Felice Vinci: *The Baltic Origins of Homer's Epic Tales* (Rochester, VT, 2006) takes M. I. Finley as a start and does present an interesting case, but an entirely different book would be needed to make a proper response and evaluation. Chao C. Chien: *In Search of Troy* (US, 2019, 2nd Edition), places Troy somewhere in Central Asia. He throws everything at you but the kitchen sink which, for all I know, may actually be in there as well. NB: *Troy From Homer's Iliad to Hollywood Epic*, ed. by Martin M. Winkler (Singapore, 2007), pp. 25-26 & *passim*.

[2] C. Blegen: *Troy and the Trojans* (NY, 1963), p. 164. Also see the sections by Sammer on Troy and Hisarlik elsewhere in this book (p. 296 ff).

[3] Fine: *op. cit.*, p. 9.

For all that, it should be noted that Troy VIIb "obviously represents a direct survival of the culture that prevailed in Troy VIIa. The fortification wall evidently still continued to stand, or was repaired [and] the main street leading straight to the upper part of the acropolis followed the line of its forerunner; ... As for the pottery, Grey Minyan and Tan Wares still retain their dominant position with hardly any perceptible alteration." The area remained settled, but by the time of Troy VIIb 2 the settlement and its citadel were looted and destroyed by fire. What remained of its populace fled to another site. The tradition of the Grey Minyan pottery was purportedly continued so "that in the seventh century BC the Trojan citadel, which had been virtually deserted for some four centuries, suddenly blossomed into life once more with occupants who were still able to make Grey Minyan pottery."[1]

But did four hundred years really go by? While the exact location of Troy may have nothing to do with repudiating a non-existent Dark Age, the ever present pottery types certainly do. So too any related art forms whether it be sculpture, the architecture of city walls, the construction and decoration of city gates, scarabs, or jewelry – all were subjected to the absolute dates of Egyptian chronology, the latter remaining unmoved for the most part by any new external historical, logical, or scientific challenges.

Ironically, no Egyptian artifacts have been found at Troy; no Trojan artifacts have been found in Egypt. It is Mycenaean pottery found at Troy or fragments representing the style of particular Mycenaean ceramics as well as age estimates based upon stratum thickness that have been responsible for assigning absolute dates. But one site is still not sufficient for applying absolute dates which are recognized as fluid, something Blegen admitted almost sixty years ago. A few more things need to be said here before we proceed to Mycenae: The need to date something appears to be endemic to the Western mind. If something doesn't have a date it's as if it only exists in some kind of void. A date gives it life, gives it a place in the scheme of things. The Western mind thinks only in linear terms. "Tomorrow, and tomorrow, and tomorrow ..." There is a line spoken by Laurence Olivier as Crassus in the movie *Spartacus*: "Rome is an eternal thought in the mind of God." Forget for the moment the Hollywood dialogue. When we think of Troy and the Trojan War, in truth we don't concern ourselves with its physical

---

[1] Blegen, pp. 171-174.

location or its dates as a primary focus. We think of it in terms of a dramatic martial contest like no other, one in which even the gods and goddesses of Greece participate – all of which began with a divine beauty contest and ended after ten years of a life and death struggle by mere trickery. The story of Troy is timeless. It too exists primarily in the mind.[1]

Compare the following evaluations of Bronze Age Troy by various scholars:

> Troy was not merely a place of antiquarian interest, but the ancestral homeland of the Roman nation, whence came the lineal ancestor of their emperor. ... According to Lucan, an epic poet of the first century AD, Julius Caesar visited the site after his victory over Pompey the Great at Pharsalus in Thessaly on 29 June 48 BC. [This may be a dubious claim.] ...There is, however, no doubt that Caesar became a benefactor of the site [and because of him] Troy rose to high prominence in the Roman world.

Augustus never traveled to Ilium (Troy), but did support the city and made considerable use of its "history" via Virgil to support his new imperial position.

> Tiberius' nephew and adopted son Germanicus visited Ilium in the year 18 AD ... [Nero praised Ilium and exempted it from taxes.] In 124, the emperor Hadrian graced it with his presence. And ninety years later, Caracalla stopped at Troy on his expedition to the east against the Parthians. ... Constantine the Great considered making it or the nearby site of Sigeum his new capital [but decided on Byzantium instead]. ... the apostate emperor Julian visited the site in 355 [and it may have even endured up to the time of the emperor Justinian]. ... the Ottoman sultan Mehmet II, conqueror of Constantinople in 1453 ... ten years after his conquest ... visited the site and 'glorified in the fact that he had defeated the descendants of those who had destroyed the city. They had, at last, he declared, paid the debt they owed the people of Asia.[2]

---

[1] N. M Sweeney: *Troy – Myth, City, Icon* (London, 2018), pp. 3-4. Sweeney would have Troy "a fully functioning community from the start of the Bronze Age until the seventh century CE, a period of almost four millennia. ... However, Troy is more than merely a city or a myth. It is also an idea – an abstract concept that resonates today just as it has resonated through the twenty-eight centuries that separate us from Homer. This idea extends beyond the individual city itself, or the specific legend of the Trojan War. It has resulted in Troy being depicted in works of literature and art across numerous countries and cultures, and deployed in popular culture for everything from computer programmes to condoms."

[2] T. Bryce: *The Trojans and their Neighbors* (NY, 2006), pp. 177-179.

The site of Troy, "contrary to what Blegen believed, even during the 'dark ages' that followed the end of the second millennium BC, ... was never completely abandoned. The oldest houses of Greek Ilion are from the end of the 8th century BC ... The city of Ilion prospered during the Hellenistic and Roman periods, not least by exploiting its ties with a mythical past politically and as a source of income from travelers. After all, even Roman emperors believed their ancestors descended from Troy's royal family."[1]

With the oldest city dating from the 8th century BC, this is further confirmation of continuity in Mycenaean chronology. Indeed, it is Troy which offers the best example of legitimate continuity although its earliest dates do appear to be spurious and do deserve additional scrutiny and revision. This also casts more doubt on any "historical" date for the Trojan War. While the Troy VII phase "is commonly known as 'the Homeric city' [Joachim Latacz considered] that it is merely a convention and in no way a historical statement. ... so far not a single piece of written evidence that definitely originates in Troy has come to light. Troy itself remains mute. There is not so much as one mention of its name."[2]

In 2001, a professor of ancient history at the University of Tübingen named Frank Kolb even took his associate Manfred Korfmann, both of whom shared the running of a research group on Anatolia, to task for "misleading the public". "Troy, [Kolb] asserted, had never had the importance claimed for it by the research team in their thirteen years of investigation and now upheld" in a current public exhibition of the time.[3]

Yet, before all that, "When Alexander the Great visited Troy to pay homage to the heroes in 334 BC, it was to Hisarlik that he came – and nowhere else. The Ilians who lived there showed Alexander their temple of Athena. ..."[4] Prior to Alexander, Xerxes I on his way to conquer Greece in 480 BC stopped at Troy, ascended its citadel and there upon sacrificed 1,000 oxen to the goddess Athena of Ilion. It served as an excellent piece of propaganda with repercussions and also provided a considerable feast for his massive army and anyone else enticed into joining his vast force.[5]

---

[1] *The Oxford Handbook of the Bronze Age Aegean*, p. 856.
[2] J. Latacz: *Troy and Homer* (NY, 2004), p. 9.
[3] *Ibid.*, p. ix.
[4] R. Castleden: *MYCENAEANS* (NY, 2005), p. 224; Latacz, p. 5.
[5] Bryce: *op. cit.*, pp. 154-158.

To summarize this part of the Epilogue: The continuity and longevity of Troy alone, the most famous of all sites from the Mycenaean Age casts considerable doubt on a 500 year-old "Dark Age". Yes, there could have been breaks, but none so specific nor definitive as to implicate a "united Greece" carrying on a ten year-old war against this singular city – if, *de facto*, it was even Homer's Troy. Schliemann himself had his doubts during his darker and more frustrated moments; he also didn't believe in a "Dark Age".

> Archaeology cannot give proof of the Trojan War if we are not sure that this was the site of Troy. So far nothing has proved this. We have no late Bronze Age written evidence, no cuneiform or Linear B tablets, no stones inscribed with hieroglyphs, nothing that might really say to us, 'Here lies Troy'. Nor is there anything relevant in the Linear B texts from other sites.[1]

The lack of any absolute identification for Hisarlik-Troy may have profound chronological, historical, and archaeological consequences, but ... it has generated much, much more in a positive way to the total equation.

> The Bronze Age city of Troy (or at least the Turkish site many people now believe to have been Troy) thrived for nearly 2000 years. We may never know the extent to which Troy was a real city and the extent to which it was a mythic city made unforgettable by Homer's poems. However, Troy has had an extraordinary impact on the cultural history of the Greeks and on subsequent Western civilization. Whatever Troy's reality may have been, its importance to the history, literature, and arts of later civilizations has been unprecedented. Even today, Troy is a powerful mythic emblem of a great city destroyed by lust, greed, and foolish errors.[2]

> The *Iliad* is Europe's first work of literature – no other language of Europe possessed any literature at this early date – and to this day it is the only written work to tell at length of the 'Trojan War', that war which to the Greeks was never a myth but a factual event in their early history.[3]

A final word on Troy deserves to be given to M. I. Finley. When it came to the relationship between literary sources and historical-archaeological ones, Finley firmly believed that the latter "have no great

---

[1] Latacz, p. 18.
[2] Diane P. Thompson: *The Trojan War* (Jefferson, NC, 2004), p. 13.
[3] Latacz, p. viii.

relevance to the literary merits of the poems [*Iliad* and *Odyssey*], or to their entertainment value. In return, [he insisted] that the literary merits have no relevance to matters of historicity."[1] He then criticized Blegen for drawing unwarranted chronological conclusions and over-stating the value of what he found or, better yet, what he didn't find from his archaeological activity at Hisarlik. Finley went on to say:

> Yet the plain fact is that Blegen found nothing, literally nothing, at either place [Troy and Pylos] to warrant his *historical* conclusion. Not a scrap was uncovered at Troy to point to Agamemnon or any other conquering king or overlord, or to a Mycenaean coalition or even to a war.

He then quoted the authority of Caskey, who wrote:

> the physical remains of Troy VIIa do not prove beyond question that the place was captured at all. ... The archaeology of Troy has added nothing.[2]

A previous statement made by Finley and cited earlier needs to be repeated:

> Homer's Trojan War, we suggest, must be evicted from the *history* of the Greek Bronze Age.[3]

We must now say farewell to Mycenae along with some concluding remarks regarding the Dark Age of Greece. The reasons for the collapse of the Mycenaean kingdoms is still inconclusive. One thing is now certain, however. We can now say goodbye to the "Dorian Invasion". There never was one, at least not one that affected Greece in a transformational way that would have brought about a Dark Age. Evidence for a Dorian Invasion is virtually nil;[4] and modern archaeology has been unable to uncover the necessary remains that would attest to such an invasion. In fact, the whole idea of the Dorian Invasion has been rejected by many scholars as a fiction.[5] Osborne, for one, believes that the archaeological record unequivocally fails to support such an event.

---

[1] Finley, p. 169.
[2] *Ibid.*, pp. 170, 173.
[3] *Ibid.*, p. 177.
[4] *CAH* II:2 (3rd Edition), *Middle East and Aegean c. 1380-1000 B.C.*,V. R. d'A. Desborough: »The End of Mycenaean Civilization and the Dark Age« (Cambridge, 2000), pp. 660ff.
[5] T. R. Martin: *Ancient Greece* (New Haven, 1996), p. 38.

In the face of this, and of the silence of Homer and Hesiod, we are obliged to conclude that the Greeks of the archaic period knew nothing about the Dark Age. ... None of our earliest literary records from archaic Greece, the Homeric epics, the *Iliad* and the *Odyssey*, and the two extant long poems by Hesiod the *Theogony* and the *Works and Days*, knows anything about, or shows any concern with, the Dark Age.[1]

Archaeological surveys were carried out in the 1980s and 1990s "in the Nemea Valley, the southern Argolid, and the Berbati and Limnes Valleys, all of which are within sight of Mycenae itself, and collectively they produced no evidence of human occupation in the Dark Age."[2] *"No evidence of human occupation in the Dark Age."* Then who was there to hear the song of the bard singing his tune of Mycenaean days gone by? Apparently no one. Not even an audience much less a bard. According to Finley, "Now it is more than probable that the *Iliad* and *Odyssey* as we know them were composed in writing, and not orally."[3] Finley does go on to say, however, that "Even if the bards who composed the *Iliad* and *Odyssey* did so in writing, the diffusion of the two poems was still primarily oral."[4] Yet those "oral traditions ... are invariably misleading in chronological matters."[5]

Turning now specifically to Mycenae, which was supposedly destroyed around ca. 1200 BC, we no longer can attribute any destruction to the non-existent Dorian Invasion. The demise of Mycenae at that time is told in vague and nondescript terms by conventional historians. Pure speculation and meaningless phrases are employed: e.g., the words of Desborough in *The Cambridge Ancient History* (Third Edition), II, Part 2, *The Middle East and the Aegean Region c. 1380-1000 B.C.*: "... the whole fabric of the Mycenaean system collapsed. The spirit was no longer there." What does that even mean? On the contrary there is evidence that continuity is found all the way down to 800 BC and beyond. Desborough himself, immediately after the statement quoted above, goes on to list "several instances of later sanctuaries or cults occupying sites known to have been sacred to the Mycenaeans. At Mycenae itself, the temple of historic times overlay the sanctuary attached to the palace ..." (p. 670), and many more

---

[1] R. Osborne: *Greece in the Making 1200-479 BC* (NY, 1996), p. 37.
[2] C. Runnels & P. M. Murray: *Greece Before History* (Stanford, 2001), p. 121.
[3] Finley, p. 30 (emphasis added).
[4] *Ibid.*, p. 36.
[5] *Ibid.*, p. 170.

examples are enumerated. One observation in particular stands out (pp. 670-671):

> In no case is there any archaeological evidence of continuous use from Mycenaean times onwards, but it must be stressed that this is an aspect where archaeology may present less than the true picture, since at Amyclae, for example, there is undeniable literary evidence that the pre-Greek deity Hyakinthos was still worshipped in historical times alongside Apollo. Even on archaeological grounds, however, a reasonable claim for continuity can occasionally be made, as for the Artemisium on Delos, for the shrine of Dionysus on Ceos, where the earliest cult evidence belongs to the fifteenth century B.C., and perhaps for the Heraeum on Samos, on the basis of the types of figurine dedicated.

The question must be asked: How can so many different Mycenaean sites retain the reputation and usage of the same sacred areas and build on them without any habitation over a period of five centuries?

Back in the late 19th century, Tsountas had already noted a tendency to lower the date for the Mycenaean age on the part of others, but he personally backed away partly on the basis of the limited amount of iron that was found in Mycenaean tombs compared to what was already known in Egypt from much earlier times.

> For the lower limit of the Mycenaean age we [Tsountas] have taken the twelfth century, though certain archaeologists and historians are inclined to a much more recent date – some [Beloch and Flinders-Petrie] even bringing it three or four centuries farther down.[1] This is not only improbable on its face, but at variance with the facts. To take but one test, the Mycenaean age hardly knew the use of iron; at Mycenae itself it was so rare that we find it only in an occasional ornament such as a ring. ... In Egypt, on the other hand, iron was known as early as the middle of the second millennium B.C., and if the beehive and chamber-tombs at Mycenae are to be assigned to a period as late as the ninth century, the rare occurrence of iron in them becomes quite inexplicable.[2]

It is here that we must bring in two overlooked relevant published items by Velikovsky on the subject of bronze and iron: 1) »Metallurgy and Chronology« in *Pensée* V (Fall, 1973), pp. 5-9; 2) »Bronze and Iron«, *Ramses II And His Time* (NY, 1978), pp. 221-237, especially

---

[1] Tsountas, p. 321 & ref. 1.
[2] *Ibid.*, pp. 321-322.

232-237 where the Mycenaean Age is discussed as well as Egypt and the Near East. The metallurgical questioning raised by Tsountas (not mentioned) is answered therein.

The final collapse of Mycenae supposedly occurred sometime ca. 1200 BC. But as we shall see it wasn't as final as some people think. Because they accept a literal Dark Age, Runnels and Murray find it difficult to accept the fact that the "staggering scale of the disaster that overtook the Mycenaeans and expunged their culture cannot be explained by one or even many natural disasters. It was so comprehensive that the memory of the Mycenaeans appears to have been nearly wiped out. ... Homer's great epic poems, which appear to be wholly about the world of the Mycenaeans, tell more about Homer's own world of the Early Iron Age. This *cultural amnesia* remained unexplored and unquestioned for nearly three millennia [until the discoveries of Schliemann] brought the Mycenaeans and the Bronze Age world back to the light of day. ... [and] In our view an explanation for the catastrophe must be sought in the realm of human affairs. ..."[1] Perhaps there was nothing to forget and Runnels and Murray were looking at the wrong century. "Homer, we too easily forget, had no notion of a Mycenaean Age, or of the sharp break between it and the new age that followed its destruction. The Mycenaean Age is a *purely modern construct*."[2] There is absolutely nothing about Mycenae from the time of its supposed destruction until the *fifth century* BC. According to Dickinson there is "the almost total lack of anything striking in the archaeological record over several centuries" for Mycenae and the other related sites of the Aegean World. In his view, then, "what has been called the 'Dark Age' was like the Collapse that brought about the conditions for its onset, a real phenomenon."[3]

Let us assume for a moment that there was NO "Dark Age". That would certainly explain the absence of material goods in a period that didn't even exist. Let us further assume that Mycenae continued to flourish down to and after the time of Homer. The latter, who lived and wrote ca. 750 BC, could not have written about something that came after him. (See Velikovsky and Greenberg elsewhere in this book pertaining to Mycenae, the Lion Gate, and Ramses II.) But if Homer did

---
[1] Runnels & Murray, p. 121 (emphasis added).
[2] Finley, p. 45 (emphasis added).
[3] Dickinson: *op. cit.*, p. 239.

live in the mid-eighth century BC and wrote about an Age of Heroes from long ago that would certainly explain the anachronisms. Once again it must be emphasized that the *Iliad* and *Odyssey* are NOT history. Homer has even been referred to as a "pseudo-historian". Homer was a poet, not an historian. Between Homer, absolute reliance on Egyptian chronology, highly questionable genealogies, and pottery finds subjectively categorized, the entire Aegean Age is built on sand. Homer is considered by many to be the greatest poet of all time when it comes to his genre. But he also had certain constraints. Regarding epic poetry, we once again invoke the words of Finley. Afterwards, I intend to present a new hypothesis regarding the survival and final destruction of Mycenae.

> The glorification of insignificant incidents is common in heroic poetry. The French *Song of Roland* tells of a great battle at Roncevaux in the year A.D. 778, between the hosts of Charlemagne and the Saracens. Like Homer, the poet of the French epic is unknown, but he certainly lived in the twelfth century, at the time of the Crusades. Unlike Homer, he could read and he had access to chronicles, which he explicitly says he used. But the facts are these; the actual battle of Roncevaux was a minor engagement in the Pyrenees between a small detachment of Charlemagne's army and some Basque raiders. It was neither important nor crusade-like. The twelve Saracen chieftains of the poem and their army of 400,000 are pure invention, with German, Byzantine or made-up names; there is even a strong case for dismissing Roland himself as an imaginary person. The *Song of Roland* can be checked against written records. The *Iliad* and the *Odyssey* cannot, and, in so far as historical detail is concerned, there is no way of reversing the process of distortion and re-establishing the original kernel.[1]

And there you have it. Now look at Homer in the same light.

And now for Mycenae. Back in 1897 once again, we can read Tsountas' description of its last days as the Mycenaeans fell before the onslaught of the Dorian [sic] hordes. Their massive walls gave way, the castles collapsed, and the palaces perished in flames. But a remnant survived; and more than 600 years later in 480 BC eighty of their descendants joined the Spartan forces at Thermopylae led by Leonidas and temporarily held off a mighty force of Persians under

---

[1] Finley, p. 47.

the command of Xerxes I. And one year later, Mycenae together with Tiryns contributed a total of 400 men to the Greek army that defeated the Persians once and for all at Plataea with Herodotus as a source for the latter. In 1961 Starr (p. 65) mentions it in passing, citing Massimo Pallottino – one of the foremost scholars on the Etruscans as a source – who "suggests that the physical destruction of Mycenae took place early in the fifth century B.C., at the time of the Argive conquest." Starr then goes on to say: "It is a great pity that solid stratification is really lacking at Mycenae." In 1966 Mylonas repeated the same story: "For centuries after [LBA] destruction, the fortunes of Mycenae remain *unrecorded*. We next hear of the city when another menace threatened Greece, when Persian armies of Xerxes poured over Greece like the uncontrolled waters of a mountain torrent. A contingent of eighty Mycenaeans is recorded as having joined the small force of Leonidas at Thermopylai. A year or so later Mycenae, along with Tiryns, contributed [400 total] men to the battle of Plataia" which the Greeks won.[1]

In 2005 Castleden reported the "later fall of Mycenae in 468 BC", citing Mylonas. He then went on to compare that fall to the assumed centuries' earlier one and cited Pausanias. But Pausanias lived in the second century AD, removed from Mycenae's "final" fall by nearly 600 years. Without realizing it Pausanias was probably observing the destruction wrought by the Argives. The reason that Mycenae was destroyed in 468 BC was due to a surprise Argive assault on that city after the Mycenaeans announced particular expectations and made some demands based upon their recent victory over the Persians, an event the people of Argos had not participated in. This aroused the envy and enmity of the Argive people who laid siege to Mycenae and destroyed it so thoroughly that according to Diodoros "Mycenae remained uninhabited until our day" and Strabo wrote that "not a trace of the city was to be seen" in his time.[2] So, too, the simultaneous destruction of Tiryns – Mycenae's ally during the Persian wars – by the selfsame aggrieved Argives in -460 as noted by Velikovsky in his section on Tiryns (pp. 77, 78). However, coins in large quantity from the third century BC, the Hellenistic period, were discovered by Tsountas near the end of the 19th century. Sundry items discovered at the site

---

[1] G. E. Mylonas: *Mycenae and the Mycenaean Age* (Princeton, 1966), p. 7.
[2] *Ibid.*; also see Tsountas, p. 17.

also indicate probable Roman occupation of Mycenae even in Imperial times.

Now, I shall attempt to clarify that enormous hodgepodge of Mycenaean history and chronology which was just offered and present a new hypothesis regarding the real history and chronology of Mycenae. First of all, there were *no* Dorians to destroy Mycenae at any time. The so-called Dorian Invasion is now considered to be a phantom. Mycenae was not destroyed ca. 1100. On the basis of Schorr's detailed examination of numerous Mycenaean artifacts and tombs, Velikovsky's revised chronology, and the information I provided regarding the Lion Gate, Ramses II and Greek Archaic sculpture, Mycenae continued to exist and flourish down to the beginning of the 6th and early 5th centuries BC. How else to explain how that city – after half a millennium of seemingly non-existence – could easily supply the manpower for not just one but *two* contingents against what was then the Eurasian world's major super power? It was the vindictive and sudden attack by the Argives in 468 BC which left Mycenae in a state of almost unrecognizable ruin specifically attested to by Classical authors who observed the destruction first hand. It was that ruin that Schliemann, Tsountas, Wace, and others came upon. It was only the dating of those objects dependent upon Egyptian synchronisms that created the confusion. And how is it that so many noted scholars failed to question how a city such as Mycenae, believed to be deceased for nearly 600 years, could suddenly emerge out of nowhere and have the resources to provide a total somewhere between 250-280 hardy troops to help battle – on no less than two occasions – the vast armies of the Persian Empire?!

To this day, a chronological methodology first introduced by Flinders-Petrie and Arthur Evans towards the end of the 19th century still has a controlling grip on the dating of Aegean material from a time that all too often has been classified as pre-history. The term itself carries a certain stigma that appears to allow a convenient latitude when it comes to analyzing and drawing various conclusions. What constitutes true history? Is it like beauty – it's in the eye of the beholder? When a book suddenly appears and its title proclaims: "A New History of ..." – what do we do with it and the previous ones on the same subject? It is the hope of the authors of this book that it will provide a possible answer to a problem that has existed for nearly 140 years – the so-called Dark Age of Greece. *There wasn't one!* Even now Aegean chronology remains in a state of constant partial flux. Its "dates continue to be adjusted as new data appear through internal Aegean ceramic 'fine tuning', although not always keeping up to date with Egyptian refinements. ... Recently, radiocarbon dating and other scientific means have been employed to independently realize a variety of 'absolute' dates for certain Aegean archaeological events (especially the Thera eruption) that have yet to be entirely reconciled with Egyptian dating."[1]

Compare and ponder the following words of Pierre Demargne from almost 60 years ago:

> When we remember that the chronology of the Mycenaean age has now been established with some certainty by correlating it with that of Egypt, and that with the Late Bronze Age we virtually enter historical times, we are likely to be perplexed by the 'Dark Age' which follows. A gap of over four centuries lies between the traditional Greek dates for the fall of Troy (1183 B.C.) and the founding of the Olympic games (776 B.C.).
> ... Whereas the history of the Ancient East proceeds without a break after a relatively brief spell of violent destruction, the phase of Greek history extending from about 1200-1150 to 750 B.C. is ... one of the most obscure in all ancient history. There is no means of reducing this long hiatus, for Mycenaean datings are definitively correlated with the Eighteenth and Nineteenth Dynasties of Egypt, and the Subgeometric art of Archaic Greece cannot be carried back any earlier than 750 B.C. With the Mycenaean civilization we were almost on the threshold of historical times, yet now we are plunged into a protohistoric epoch which seems almost a complete blank. To describe it as the 'Homeric period' is absurd; Homer's world corresponds either to the Mycenaean or to the Archaic period, surely not to the interval between them. To describe it as the Geometric period is more correct, but tantamount to confessing that our knowledge of it remains purely archaeological. ... it remains none the less true that Greek Archaic art was born in an epoch that is almost 'dateless'.[2]

---

[1] J. Phillips: *Oxford Handbook of the Bronze Age Aegean* (Oxford, 2012), p. 822.
[2] P. Demargne: *The Birth of Greek Art* (NY, 1964), pp. 279, 281, 279.

Now read the reflective thoughts of Chester Starr also from 60 years ago:

> A modern observer who today walks about the glittering showcases of the Mycenaean room in the National Museum, Athens, or stands at the Lion Gate of Mycenae must have somber thoughts when he considers the fate of Greece in the twelfth century B.C. *Not for half a millennium to come* were men of these lands again to be organized so firmly in political units, to practice such varied and skillful arts, or to have the intangible and physical strengths which must underlie an advanced civilization – and by that point the Greek heart was to beat in a different rhythm.[1]

The elimination of the Dark Age of Greece restores the integrity and cohesiveness of Greek history. Though the Mycenaean Age is frequently referred to as "prehistory", nevertheless it now exists as a wondrous uninterrupted prelude to the glory of a Greece that stands as the fountainhead of Western civilization.

Lewis M. Greenberg

---

[1] Starr, pp. 63-64 (emphasis added).

Index

(**Hint for the user:** Page numbers followed by 'f' or 'ff' refer to the following page(s) as well, usually indicating a more detailed reference to the topic.)

A

Achaeans 36f, 47f, 94, 97ff, 109, 149, 159, 227, 299, 305, 310, 314, 364, 387, 405, 450
Achilles 35, 37, 45, 47, 94, 159ff, 186, 316
Acrocorinth 258
Adrastos 95
Aegean 12, 18f, 25, 36f, 42ff, 49, 51f, 59, 65f, 72ff, 80ff, 88, 97, 109, 112, 122f, 130, 139ff, 147, 167ff, 172-181, 188f, 194, 197, 201-217, 237ff, 242f, 246f, 256, 270ff, 284ff, 300, 303, 306, 310, 320ff, 329, 332, 339, 350ff, 358, 360, 379, 385-393, 406, 445-449, 455-464
Aegina 113, 205ff, 244ff, 263, 397
Aegylips 97
Aeneas 37, 47, 52, 85f, 95, 135-139, 146, 149, 154ff, 161, 207, 310, 320f, 398-414, 424, 430ff, 436ff, 452
Aeneid 37, 85, 139, 146, 400ff, 407, 412f, 425, 432, 436ff
Aeschylus 36f
Afghanistan 86
Afyonkarahisar 57
Agamemnon 36ff, 47, 51, 92, 95, 108, 150f, 159, 161, 169, 305, 379, 414, 449, 457
Agrigento 85, 318f
Agrippa 155, 441f
Ahab 30, 100
Ahaz 106, 108, 326
Ahhijawa 362

Ahiram 340-345
Ahmes Nofretari 371
Ahmose 346
Aigyptos 95
Ajax 94f
Akhenaten, s. Akhnaton
Akhet-Aton 38, 73, 123
Akhnaton 28, 30ff, 38, 59, 66, 70ff, 86, 123f, 212, 322, 330
Akurgal, Ekrem 42f, 48f, 58, 129f, 310ff, 349
Alalakh 282, 285ff
Alba Longa 52
Alberg 114
Albright, W. F. 129, 286, 325
Alcimus 400f
Alektryon 95
Alexander 30, 37, 51, 119, 153, 296, 311, 322, 342, 415, 417f, 426, 435, 451, 455
Alexander Helios 418
Alexandria 31, 121, 153, 216, 272, 415ff, 440ff, 450
Alexiou 222
Altan Oba 87
Amalekites 29
Amarna 15, 28ff, 67, 73, 86, 130f, 134, 283f, 322, 332
Amasis 368
Amber 181f
Amenhotep 28ff, 38, 59, 69ff, 124, 204, 212, 233
Amenirdis 371
Amenophis s. Amenhotep
Amphiaros 95
Amu 29

Amyclae 459
Amythaon 95
Anapha 110
Anatolia 42f, 56, 60, 91, 98, 128-134, 167, 175, 181, 207, 217, 256, 283, 310ff, 351, 355ff, 452, 455
Anchises 52, 310, 405, 410
Andronikos, M. 175, 182
Antenor 95
Anthemos 94
Antilochos 51
Antinous 441
Antiphemos 85, 318f
Antissa 110f
Antony 402, 416-426, 428f, 432, 437-440, 444
Antyllus 417
Aphidna 189
Apollo 94, 137, 359, 365, 373, 375, 397, 419f, 424, 433, 451, 459
Apollodorus 54, 107, 451
Appian 118, 217, 322f
Apries 368, 370
Araxus 86
Archaic 44, 68, 75f, 79, 82, 97f, 153, 175 ,194, 202, 206, 217ff, 227, 234, 242, 247f, 253ff, 257f, 263, 303, 310, 338, 340, 348, 351, 356, 359, 362, 365-377, 383, 386, 458, 463f
Ares 47, 106, 108, 150, 161
Argive 35, 38, 58, 76, 291, 296, 307, 337, 350, 462f
Argolis 291, 383
Argonaut 36, 147
Argos 36, 58, 97, 184f, 213, 291, 308, 337, 350, 398, 462
Aristonothos 67, 84, 196
Aristotle 44, 111
Arno 83
Arrian 48, 311
Arslan Tash 57f, 346f, 349
Artemis 94, 137, 217, 269, 363, 365, 373, 375, 435, 459
Ascanios 52
Ashmolean Museum 80

Ashurnasirpal 354
Asia Minor 25, 36, 42ff, 48ff, 53, 57ff, 87, 97f, 105, 109, 112, 117, 121, 128ff, 140-145, 149, 153, 160, 191, 200, 227, 251ff, 256, 282f, 299, 310-319, 349f, 355, 383
Asine 191, 221f
Assurbanipal 50f
Assurnasirpal 68, 176, 284
Assyria 32, 49ff, 56, 58, 67f, 72, 74, 86, 116, 123, 128, 130ff, 176, 215f, 235, 184ff, 312, 315ff, 327ff, 348, 351, 354-358, 364, 384, 392, 449
Astarte 414, 433ff
Athena 137, 257, 319, 358, 373f, 378, 397, 430, 455
Athene 47, 53, 94, 106, 160
Athens 31, 35f, 63ff, 68, 74-79, 84, 150, 171ff, 181, 183, 189, 194, 196, 207, 210, 2174, 219, 234ff, 243, 247, 255-263, 268, 276, 290, 297ff, 329ff, 358, 369ff, 384, 410, 421, 451, 465
Atreus 36, 107ff, 152, 216, 265f, 360, 379
Attica 188, 194, 217, 258, 269, 306, 370, 383
Augustine 108, 402
Augustus 143, 153ff, 402, 407, 409f, 412ff, 419-444, 454
Avaris 29
Ayia Irini 224

B

Baal-Hammon 433
Babylon 27, 119, 131, 152, 355, 384, 392, 451
Bakenrenef 370
Bali Dagh 297, 299, 302
Barhebraeus 318
Basque 92, 461
Beall, John Patrick 413
Bellona 430
Beloch 204, 459
Berosus 119f

Bietak, M. 389f
Bimson, J. J. 236, 345f, 348
Bissing, Fr. von 390f
Biton 370
Black Sea 36, 47, 141
Blawatsky, Vladimir 140
Blegen, Carl 37, 41, 46, 55, 77ff, 89ff, 103, 111, 218f, 269, 273, 276, 278ff, 291-310, 453-457
Bloch, Raymond 143, 404ff
Blytt, A. 116
Boardman, John 60, 40, 170, 244, 337, 359, 375
Boeotia 36, 97, 99f, 110f, 189
Boethius, Axel 153
Böhlau, J. 189, 205, 211
Borovka, Gregory 87f
Bosporus 111, 311, 314
Brauron 217, 247
Breasted, J. R. 216, 391
Broneer, O. 330
Bronze Age 40, 45, 72, 74, 81f, 114, 122f, 133, 135, 137, 139ff, 150, 169, 179, 188f, 191, 206f, 214, 221ff, 249, 258f, 263, 265, 268f, 272, 274, 282f, 300-306, 318ff,3 56f, 377f, 393, 402, 446, 454ff, 460, 464
Bryce, T. 131ff
Bulgaria 87, 141, 180
Bunarbashi 297
Bura 111
Burkert, W. 128
Byblos 129, 340, 428

C

Cadmus 99ff, 136
Caere 67
Caesarion 417, 421
Calauria 217, 247, 258
Calvisius, Seth 26
Cameiros 67, 69, 341
Canaan 27
Caphthor 325
Carbon-14 15, 131, 274, 322, 389, 392f, 399, 464
Carchemish 49, 131, 312, 344

Caria 87, 328, 350
Carians 42, 50f, 310, 325
Carpenter, Rhys 101, 112ff, 177, 298f, 368
Carthage 52f, 149, 156, 191f, 217, 283, 322ff, 342, 398-403, 410ff, 416, 425, 431-437, 444f, 452
Caskey, J. L. 221, 275
Castleden, Rodney 136, 378f, 462
Castor 451
Castriota, David 423
Catling, H. 201f, 213ff
Cato 149, 400
Caucasus 49f, 86, 103
Centaurs 94, 162
Cerveteri 84
Chadwick, John 39, 94, 96, 98
Chaldean 32, 86, 119, 123
Champollion 26, 390
Charlemagne 403, 461
China 106, 157
Chios 36, 173, 217, 370
Chronicles 27, 30, 50, 315f, 326, 461
Cimmerians 49ff, 58, 115, 311-317
Clazomenae 67
Cleobis 370
Cleopatra 153, 402, 416-444
Clytemnaestra 192
Colchis 36
Coldstream, J. N. 199
Collon, D. 134
Colonna, Giovanni 150
Colophon 36, 256
Confucius 107
Conze 189
Corinth 77, 111, 250ff, 306, 319, 337, 375, 432
Corinthian Isthmus 35, 306
Courville, Donovan A. 348, 391
Crete 25, 31, 35, 38, 52, 58, 60, 71f, 80-85, 89, 91, 94, 112-116, 121, 123, 159, 172f,178ff, 191, 197, 203, 205, 207f, 221ff, 229, 243f, 247f, 291, 316, 324-329, 338, 353, 359f, 372, 387ff, 393f
Crimea 49, 87

Crowe, John 452
Ctesias 121, 216, 272, 316
Curtius, E. 62
Cybotus 111
Cyclopes 169, 263
Cyprus 25, 66, 70-75, 88, 103,
  110, 121, 177, 181, 187f, 191f,
  198, 202-210, 223f, 229, 239f,
  243ff, 256, 278, 282ff, 300,
  324f, 328, 341f, 352, 363f, 381

D

Damascus 30
Danaans 48
Danelius, Eva 345f, 391
Dardanelles 37, 103, 299
Dardanians 310
Darius 51
David 29, 208, 236, 323f
Deir el-Bahari 29, 295
Delos 110, 238, 247f, 271, 369,
  375, 459
Delphi 247, 341, 358, 365, 370ff
Deluge 27
Demargne, P. 352, 360, 464
Democles 109
Dendrochronology 16, 389
Desborough, V. R. d'A. 113, 177,
  182ff, 190, 232, 250, 256ff, 458
Dickinson, O. 447, 460
Dictaean Cave 80, 82
Dido 52, 135, 155f, 322f, 398-406,
  410, 425, 432-437, 452
Dikaios, P. 206, 245
Diodorus 44, 110f, 304, 314ff, 328,
  462
Diomedes 263, 291
Dionysius 143, 146, 154, 217, 318
Dionysus 94, 136, 416, 419f, 424,
  428, 459
Dipylon Gate 63f, 196
Dodwell, Edward 153
Donalson, M. D. 430
Dörpfeld, W. 55, 61-65, 75, 79,
  101, 111, 122, 211, 217, 274-
  278, 296-302, 307, 332

E

Early Bronze 104, 274, 300, 318,
  402
Edgar, C. C. 211, 332
Egypt 11-19, 24-33, 50f, 55, 59f,
  63, 65,f, 69-75, 79, 83, 86f, 93,
  95, 104f, 114, 118-124, 128-
  132, 139, 142ff, 146ff, 157, 162,
  169-180, 186, 189, 195-199,
  203ff, 208f, 216-222, 226ff, 233,
  239ff, 246ff, 252f, 256, 272-287,
  291, 295ff, 308, 315ff, 321-325,
  333, 337-346, 350ff, 355, 358ff,
  365-375, 377, 381, 384-393,
  400, 415-418, 421f, 425-430,
  438-453, 459-464
el-Amarna 28f, 31, 67, 73, 86, 134,
  322, 332, 399
el-Arish 28f
Eleusina 111
Eleusis 183, 194, 247
Elice 111
Elis 53f, 63, 305f
Elissa 322, 399, 403
Enispe 97
Enkomi 60, 66-75, 88, 177, 191f,
  223, 228, 239f, 282f, 341
Entimus 319
Epidaurus 247
Eratosthenes 118ff, 216, 272, 316,
  400f, 406, 450f
Eryx 414, 435
Esarhaddon 327ff
Eteocles 95
Ethiopian Dynasty 51
Ethiopians 48, 51, 114, 316f, 373
Etruria 67, 83f, 122, 136, 140, 143-
  149, 153-157, 256, 300, 405f
Etruscans 83f, 143-150, 153, 156f,
  199, 217, 241, 300, 406, 462
Euphorbos 67
Euripides 36f, 107
Eurystheus 169
Eusebius 49, 118f, 312, 318, 324
Eusthates 311

Evander 137, 157, 404ff
Evans, Arthur 38, 60, 71ff, 79ff, 89ff, 115, 177, 221f, 239-245, 249, 360, 364, 463
Exile to Babylon 27
Exodus 26ff, 32, 123, 348, 448
Ezra 27

F

Fabius Pictor 52, 400
Famagusta 66
Finkelberg, Margalit 379
Finland 106
Finley, M. I. 138f, 406, 447, 452, 456-461
First Intermediate Period 27
Flavius, Josephus 27
Flinders Petrie, W. M. 12, 59, 69f, 203, 340, 350, 463
Foce del Sele 217
Frankfort 284, 361
Frankfort, Henri 129, 285ff, 342f
Freret, Nicolas 143
Frickenhaus, A. 75ff
Furtwängler, A. 62ff, 79, 111, 122, 205, 211, 217, 291
Furumark, Arne 280, 339, 447

G

Galinsky, G. Karl 425-433
Gardner, E. A. 64, 331f
Gardner, P. 176f, 183, 189, 349f
Gebel-el-Arak 358, 361
Gela 85, 318ff
Gelzer, H. 50
Genesis 27
George, King 38
Gere, C. 150ff
Gezer 235f
Gibeon 235f
Gibraltar 110f
Goldsmith, Adrian 436
Gordias 48f, 311f
Gordion 48f, 55ff, 58, 122, 130ff, 274, 311ff, 352
Gray 225

Grotta Campana 83
Grotta Regolini Galassi 83
Gurob 69f, 340f
Gyges 50f

H

Hadrian 441ff, 454
Hala Sultan Tekke 73
Hall, H. R. 72ff, 177
Halone 110
Hammond, N. G. L. 174f, 182, 363
Harden, D. 239
Hatshepsut 29, 179, 291f, 295f, 346, 375, 388, 428
Hattusa 133, 354f
Hattusilis 26
Hazor 235f
Hecataeus 217
Hector 52, 67, 94, 159, 161, 310, 450
Hedjaz 29
Hekataeus 121
Heliacal rising 26
Helladic 30f, 35, 46, 51, 60, 75, 80, 84, 112, 116, 147, 169, 171, 173, 178f, 186ff, 193, 201, 203f, 213, 217, 230ff, 237, 246, 250, 263, 267ff, 291, 294, 302, 310, 318, 330ff, 338, 344, 357, 364, 385
Hellanicus 217
Hellenic 30ff, 35, 44, 58f, 76, 80, 86, 92ff, 118, 149, 169, 177, 202, 208, 237, 245, 275, 277f, 297, 323, 325, 332, 337f, 353, 365
Hellenistic 25, 30f, 37, 119, 149, 221, 231, 247f, 378, 409, 433, 455, 462
Hellespont 47f, 51, 110, 296, 299, 311, 450
Helos 97
Hera 62, 76ff, 94, 106, 109, 137, 160, 217, 219, 269, 291, 308, 373, 375, 415, 435
Heracles 26, 53f, 72, 110, 137f, 147, 162, 169, 216, 263, 304, 398, 406

Heraion 62ff, 75, 190, 291, 295f, 307
Hermes 94, 137, 419
Herodotus 25, 44, 50, 70, 86, 94, 100f, 112, 114, 118, 120f, 136, 143, 217, 253, 272, 300, 314ff, 324, 326, 462
Heroic Generation 48
Hesiod 93f, 159, 227, 246, 316, 458
Hesione 397
Hesychius 328
Hezekiah 106, 108, 235f
Hierakonpolis 358, 361
Hieroglyphs 26, 456
Hieronymus 49, 312, 324
Higgins, R. 243f, 359
Hiller 116
Hine 97
Hippolytus 107, 324
Hiram 323, 326f, 329
Hissarlik 37, 46, 55, 133, 175, 273-280, 296-303, 450, 452, 455ff
Hitchcock, L. A. 350f
Hitler 403
Hittite 26, 43, 56, 91f, 128-134, 175f, 284ff, 311, 313, 315, 343, 355ff, 362, 364, 392
Holland, T. 420
Homer 23, 32, 35-51, 54f, 58, 61, 65, 68, 78, 89-98, 106, 108, 111, 118, 121f, 128, 133ff, 141f, 150ff, 158-163, 175, 183-188, 194, 198, 202f, 210f, 215f, 219, 224ff, 233, 240, 242, 245, 255-275, 279, 296-301, 304ff, 313-317, 325, 351, 364, 377f, 387, 398, 406, 413, 415, 449-464
Hood, S. 388
Hyksos 28f, 390

I

Iakchos 95
Ialysos 69
Iceland 106
Iliad 23f, 36f, 40f, 45ff, 53f, 89f, 94ff, 105-111, 118, 136f, 141, 151f, 157-162, 186f, 202, 215, 246, 272f, 297ff, 304-308, 311, 314ff, 351, 379, 398, 449ff, 456-461
Ilion 37, 55, 296-300, 455
India 106, 141, 157, 326, 417
Iolcus 304, 306
Ionia 11, 30f, 35, 44, 50f, 58, 67, 71, 91, 93, 96-100, 109, 112, 117, 124, 217, 255ff, 314ff, 325, 328, 368, 375
Ipuwer 28f
Ir-khonsu-aat 370
Iron Age 40, 42f, 112, 122, 128, 139, 142, 144ff, 151, 182, 189ff, 197f, 206f, 221, 284, 286, 385, 446, 460
Isaiah 50, 107, 324-329
Isis 425-431, 435, 440-444
Israel 25ff, 49, 106, 235f, 324, 326, 392
Isthmia 217, 247, 249-253
Italy 25, 47, 52, 83, 85f, 110, 115, 127, 137, 139, 143-149, 153-157, 203, 207, 217, 256, 288, 300, 318f, 341, 400-406, 410ff, 427, 431, 435
Ithaca 47, 95, 244

J

Jacobsthal, P. 184, 186
James, Peter 18f, 129, 341, 344-350, 392
Japan 106
Jebb, R. C. 296f
Jehoshaphat 29f, 326
Jerome 318, 324
Jerusalem 29, 50, 108, 155, 192, 235f, 283, 346
Joab 29, 236
Johnson, M. J. 153f
Jonsson, C. O. 347f
Josephus 27, 119, 323f
Joshua 27
Judah 29, 107, 192, 235, 283, 347
Julius Africanus 119, 324

K

Kamose 346
Karatepe 43
Karnak 29, 179, 371
Karomama II 369
Kastor 94
Kea 221, 224, 247
Kerameikos 181, 183, 189, 196, 331f
Khorsabad 355
Kirrha 183
Kition 224
Kleiner, D. 439
Knossos 38, 71, 82, 84, 94f, 115, 247, 325, 328, 360, 387, 393
Kolb, Frank 455
Korakou 77, 269, 300
Korfmann, Manfred 452, 455
Körte, G. & A. 49, 311f
Kos 113, 332
Kurgans 49, 312
Kythera 172f

L

Lacius 319
Lacy, A. D. 203
Lake Urmia 86
Lancel, Serge 399f
Laodokos 95
Laomedon 397
Lapland 106
Larnaka 73
Lascelles, John 410, 452
Late Bronze Age 40, 59, 64, 133, 150, 169, 179, 201, 206ff, 214, 224, 241, 249, 272, 300-305, 318ff, 393, 456, 464
Late Kingdom 27
Latium 52, 398, 404f, 414f
Lavinia 404, 438
Layard 67
Lazarides, D. I. 217
Leighton, R. 139
Lepsius 26, 390
Linear A 39, 89
Linear B 24, 33, 39f, 89-94, 98, 101, 122, 127, 252, 260, 306ff, 378, 381, 456
Lion Gate 57ff, 170ff, 203, 220, 232, 236, 250f, 279, 288, 337-341, 346-367, 449, 460, 465
Liparus 150
Lozengrad 87
Lucan 424, 454
Luce, J. V. 175, 360
Lycians 42, 310
Lydian 49f, 132, 143, 300, 311, 364
Lykurgus 275

M

Macedonia 48, 174, 182, 190, 278, 437, 451
Malatya 176, 355
Manetho 14f, 25ff, 119ff, 180, 216, 272, 451
Manning, S. W. 19, 388ff
Marinatos, Spyridon 116, 360f, 387
Mark, S. 358
Mars 53f, 106ff, 130, 157, 161, 304f, 315, 411f, 419f, 430, 442
Megiddo 235f
Melos 113, 205, 207, 332, 369, 378
Melqart 434
Memnon 51, 316
Menelaus 35f, 47, 67, 151, 414, 450
Mentuemhet 370
Merneptah 28, 348, 367
Mersin 43
Meryetamun 370f
Mesha 100
Mesopotamia 14, 25, 105, 119, 200, 284, 355-361
Messe 97
Messenia 89, 279f, 304ff, 310, 383
Mexico 106, 116f
Meyer, Eduard 180, 390f, 448
Midas 49, 311f, 315
Mid-Century Report 92
Middle Kingdom 27f, 103, 123, 388, 448
Midianites 29

Miller, M. 318
Mimnermus 256
Minerva 430
Minoan 23, 25, 31, 35, 38, 53, 60, 72f, 76-93, 97, 101, 110, 113-118, 122f, 139, 156, 173, 178ff, 184f, 203, 206, 208f, 216, 219, 222f, 240-249, 306f, 319, 324, 326, 329, 333, 338, 353ff, 359-363, 378, 387ff, 393, 446f
Minos 72, 115, 148
Minotaur 94
Mireaux, Emile 50f, 314, 317
Mitannians 285
Mopsus 319
Morgantina 321
Mount Sipylus 109
Munatius Plancus 440
Murphie, Dale 346f
Murray, A. S. 58, 66, 69-74, 79, 204, 239f, 296, 341, 349f
Mycenae 11ff, 23ff, 30ff, 35-47, 57-100, 107f, 112-118, 121ff, 131f, 136, 139ff, 146-153, 156ff, 169-310, 318-324, 331f, 337-341, 347-365, 377-387, 398, 405f, 414, 443-465
Mylonas, G. 173f, 191ff, 234, 462
Mysia 310

N

Naevius 400, 403
Naukratis 368
Naxos 139, 229
Nea 110
Necho 64, 326, 347f, 368
Nefertari 372f
Nehemiah 27
Neith 430
Neleus 54, 304ff
Neritos 95
Nestor 35, 45, 47, 51, 53f, 89f, 95, 135f, 148f, 189, 273, 279f, 304-310, 316
New Kingdom 27ff, 55, 179f, 204f, 209, 239, 393

Nile 95, 114, 252, 317, 368, 374f, 441
Nilsson 78
Nimrud 67ff, 326, 354f
Niqmepa 285f
Numa Pompilius 411
Numitos 52

O

Oakeshott, N. R. 197f
Odysseus 35f, 45ff, 108, 224ff, 245, 263, 268, 305, 406f
Odyssey 24, 36f, 45, 50f, 89, 95, 108, 137, 245, 256, 268, 305, 314ff, 364, 449ff, 457f, 461
Old Kingdom 55, 104, 297
Olosson 97
Olympia 26, 52ff, 61ff, 75, 121, 137f, 141, 157, 190, 204f, 212-217, 247, 258, 332, 358, 364, 375, 419, 443
Olympiad 52ff, 114, 316
Ophelestas 94
Ophir 326f
Orestes 169, 413
Osborne, R. 457f
Osorkon 114
Oxus 86
Oxylus 63

P

Page, Denys L. 40f, 96f
Palestine 105, 191, 207, 235, 278, 315
Pallanteion 406
Pallottino, M. 143ff, 249, 406, 462
Palmer, Leonard R. 80, 92
Pamphilius 119
Papadimitriou, I. 173
Paphlagonia 310
Pausanias 44, 62f, 217, 306, 337, 462
Pedasos 95
Pelargikon 258f
Pelasgians 310
Peleus 304

Peloponnese 53f, 62, 89, 112f, 121, 150f, 169, 189, 218, 228f, 251, 253, 255, 257, 279, 304f, 318, 328, 337
Pelops 53, 216, 360
Pentateuch 27
Perachora 217, 228, 247
Pergamum 452
Perseus 169
Persia 64, 86, 103, 105, 120, 132, 151, 208, 216, 272, 332, 342, 461ff
Peru 106
Phaselis 318f
Phegeus 95
Pheidon 97, 291
Pherai 247
Philistos 52, 323
Philostephanos 319
Phoenicia 17, 40, 53, 59, 66, 69f, 93, 99ff, 127, 135f, 144, 148, 192, 206, 208ff, 217, 238f, 271, 283ff, 321-327, 340-344, 351, 399, 403f, 414, 435, 437
Phrygia 42f, 48-60, 115, 122, 129-134, 200, 217, 274, 310-317, 346-352, 360f, 364
Pictor, Fabius 52, 400
Plato 107, 110, 114, 119, 316, 330, 395
Pliny 109ff, 389
Pnyx 74
Podarces 397
Pollini, J. 439
Polyphontes 95
Pomerance, L. 116, 260, 393
Pompeius Trogus 403
Pontus 87, 110
Popham 278
Populonia 83, 443
Poseidon 94, 109, 161, 298, 305, 397
Pottery 16, 25, 35, 38, 41, 59-69, 72, 72, 74ff, 79, 81, 85f, 89f, 131, 142, 146f, 150, 157, 169, 171-178, 182, 184, 188ff, 196-211, 221ff, 236f, 241-246, 256-260, 267-281, 285, 288, 292ff, 297f, 300ff, 307ff, 318, 320ff, 329-333, 339ff, 362, 364, 383-388, 392f, 399f, 405, 446ff, 452f, 461
Prendi, F. 174f, 182
Preziosi, D. 351
Priam 37f, 46-51, 55, 89, 94, 216, 272f, 280, 296-301, 310f, 314-319, 397
Pritchard, J. 327
Propertius 424
Prophets 27, 116, 246
Prosymna 172f, 217f, 247f, 291, 296, 300
Psammetichos 50f, 64, 368, 375, 439
Ptellos 97
Ptolemy 118f, 418
Pygmalion 323, 399
Pylos 39, 47, 53f, 89ff, 94f, 121, 136, 172, 186f, 254ff, 278, 272f, 278ff, 296, 298, 304-308, 332, 341, 457
Pyrasos 94
Pyrrha 111

Q

Queen of Sheba 29
Quintus of Smyrna 449, 451

R

Radiocarbon 15, 123, 131, 322, 389, 392f, 464
Ramesses 26, 28, 64, 70, 128, 130f, 144, 176, 280f, 288, 340-350, 355, 367-374
Ramsay, W. M. 58ff, 61, 346-352, 361, 364, 389
Ramses s. Ramesses
Ras Shamra 72, 103, 282f
Rehak, Paul 411
Reinach, Solomon 58, 87f
Renaissance 45, 208

Renfrew, Colin 18
Rhodes 36, 67, 69, 85, 110, 203, 205, 207, 318f, 324, 341, 358
Risch, E. 99
Rohl, David 345f, 350, 392
Roman 37, 44f, 52f, 71, 107f, 118, 120, 138, 141ff, 147ff, 153ff, 161f, 181ff, 186, 212, 216f, 239, 263-267, 274f, 284, 296, 317, 322, 325, 398-445, 451, 453ff, 463
Romulus 52, 107f, 400f, 407, 410ff, 433ff, 440
Runnels 460
Rupke, J. 442
Rusellae 83
Russia 49f, 86f, 115, 316

S

Sais 119ff, 368
Salamis 36
Samaria 49, 100
Samos 247, 341, 356ff, 459
Sandars, Nancy 60, 184, 231, 355
Santillana, Giorgio de 161
Santorini 179, 387, 389, 394
Sardis 50f
Sargon 49, 86, 312
Saul 29
Scaliger, Joseph 25f
Schaeffer, Claude F. A. 103ff
Schliemann, Heinrich 37f, 41, 55, 63, 65, 75, 92, 169, 173, 180, 184, 189f, 195f, 201, 203, 212, 218, 263f, 274, 278, 296-301, 337ff, 359, 362f, 410, 445, 449f, 452, 456, 460, 463
Schorr, Edwin M. 21, 127, 131, 141, 146, 151, 167, 307, 341, 344, 349, 355, 405f, 414, 449, 463
Scipio Aemilianus 431
Scipio Africanus 431
Scoglio del Tonno 288
Scythia 50, 86ff, 122, 140f, 153, 155, 315f

Second Intermediate Period 27, 29, 388, 390
Segesta 139, 320f
Selenos 95
Seleucus 119
Seneca 107, 110f
Sennacherib 50, 106ff, 120, 354
Serapis 440
Sethos 120
Seti 367
Shabaka 114
Shebitku 371
Sicily 44, 52, 84ff, 110f, 138f, 148f, 173, 203ff, 217, 226, 256, 318-322, 404f, 413f, 424
Simoeisios 94
Siphnos 372
Sipylus 109, 111
Sirius 26, 161, 391
Smyrna 36, 251, 256, 314, 316, 449, 451
Snodgrass, A. M. 174f, 181ff, 201f, 212ff
Sobek 427
Sodom and Gomorrah 27
Solomon 29, 236, 253, 292, 323ff, 329, 345, 428
Solon 114, 119
Sophocles 36f, 246
Sothic 14, 19, 26f, 131, 138, 391
Spaeth, B. S. 426
Sparta 47, 71, 113, 120, 151, 172, 269, 291, 344, 414, 450, 453, 461
spdt 26
Sprenger, Maja 144f
Stamatakes, P. 173
Stesichorus 413, 415
Strabo 54, 109ff, 148, 158, 296, 311-317, 462
Sudanese 51
Sumerian 92
Syria 25, 103, 110, 129, 131, 133f, 167, 176, 191f, 237ff, 282-286, 300, 352, 358f

T

Taharka 114, 370
Takelot 369
Tanit 323, 433ff
Tantalis 111
Tantalus 109, 360
Tarchon 150
Tarquinia 406
Tarsus 43, 324f, 328, 428
Tegea 247, 406
Teisias 413
Telamonian 94f
Telemachus 305
Tell Atchana 285
Tell Basta 209
Tell el-Amarna s. el-Amarna
Thebes 36, 51, 70, 89, 95, 99f, 136, 307, 374
Thera 14, 74, 110, 116, 217, 326, 362, 387-394, 447, 464
Therapne 172f, 247
Therasia 110
Thermon 247, 267
Theseus 95
Thetis 47
Tholos 83, 85, 141, 190, 295, 319f, 351, 443
Thrace 48, 52, 87, 113, 140ff, 153, 155, 311
Thracians 141ff, 310
Thucydides 44, 98, 256, 272, 318
Thutmose 27, 29, 178ff, 191, 235f, 330, 333, 345f
Thyestes 36, 107f, 110
Tiber 83, 404, 419, 426, 440, 454
Timaeus 119, 322, 400
Timaios 52f
Tirhaka 51
Tiryns 38, 63, 65, 67, 75-79, 83, 121f, 151, 172f, 180f, 204, 218f, 224, 228, 230, 234ff, 247f, 254-260, 263-274, 287, 298, 300, 306, 333, 349, 462
Tiy 31, 38, 59, 73, 123f, 204, 215ff, 272ff, 279-293, 291, 300, 305, 308, 311, 313, 317, 319f, 323, 344, 362, 364, 377, 379, 387, 397-401, 404ff, 410, 412, 414f, 419, 449-457
Tomlinson 250
Torr, Cecil 12ff, 204, 241f, 340, 350, 389, 448
Tower of Babel 27
Trachonas 191, 282
Troad 48, 50, 109, 121, 296ff, 303, 311
Troilos 95
Trojan War 12, 17, 36f, 42, 44, 48, 50-55, 63, 72, 85, 89f, 100f, 106ff, 112, 118ff, 127, 133-138, 142, 148ff, 157, 159-163, 211, 215
Tros 94
Troy 23, 30, 36-56, 63, 65, 85, 89-93, 96, 100, 103-111, 118, 122, 127-136, 148f, 158ff, 169, 173, 193, 216f, 231f, 246, 255, 257ff, 263, 265, 269-281, 286ff, 296-319, 323, 332, 337, 339, 341, 362ff, 384f, 393, 397-403, 410-415, 419, 445, 449f
Tsarskij Kurgan 87
Tsountas, Chrestos 186, 219, 221, 224f, 232, 234, 447f, 459ff
Turkey 37, 141, 205, 255, 273, 277, 280, 356
Tutankhamen 70, 73, 284, 389f
Tuyu 371
Tyndaris 111
Tyre 322f, 326ff, 399
Tyrrhenus 146, 150

U

Ugarit 29, 103, 209, 282ff, 287
Umman-Manda 315
Urartu 191, 283

V

Vapheio 71, 188
Varro 52f, 304, 400
Veii 83f

Velikovsky, I. 11, 13, 18f, 21, 23f, 127-132, 136ff, 144, 146, 150, 152, 157-162, 167, 170, 176, 180, 204, 216f, 233, 236, 239, 247, 271f, 281f, 284, 288, 307, 325, 328, 332, 341f, 345-350, 355, 362, 364f, 367, 372, 388-398, 428, 448, 450, 459f, 462f
Ventris, Michael 92ff, 98
Venus 14, 53, 107f, 131, 137, 158, 160, 394, 410-414, 424ff, 430-435, 442f
Vergina 182f
Vermeule, Emily 175, 180f, 199, 221, 234, 249f, 254, 353
Vespasian 27
Vetulonia 83
Virgil 37, 52, 85, 146, 400ff, 409-141, 432, 437, 454
Volga 86

W

Wace, A. J. B. 39, 170ff, 203, 224, 236, 463
Wanax 95
Warmington, B. H. 400f
Webster 95
Winlock 295

X

Xanthus 311
Xenophon 44
Xeropolis 384
Xerxes 455, 462

Y

Young, Rodney 55f, 312f

Z

Zerah 29
Zeus 47, 94, 106, 137, 160, 216, 362, 379, 409, 419
Zinjirli 285
Zygouries 300

Bibliography

(**Hint for the user:** Sources marked by * are listed for the purpose of a complete bibliography, but are not quoted elsewhere in this book.)

A Companion to Ancient Egypt (ed. A.B. Lloyd) (2014), »Chronology«, xxxvii, ff
A Companion to Ancient Thrace (eds. J. Valeva et al.) (Chichester, 2015)
A Companion to Greek Art (eds. Smith, Tyler Jo, Plantzos, Dimitris) (2018)
A Companion to Sport and Spectacle in Greek and Roman Antiquity (eds. Christesen, P. and Kyle, D. G.) (Singapore, 2014)
Adolph, A.: *Brutus of Troy* (Bridlington, 2015)
Adrados, F. R.: »Les Institutions religieuses mycéniennes« — III »Les dieux et leur culte« in *Minos* XI (1972)
Ahlberg, G.: *Prothesis and Ekphora in Greek Geometric Art* (Lund, 1971)
Ahlberg, G.: *Fighting on Land and Sea in Greek Geometric Art* (Lund, 1971)
Aitchison, E.: »Thutmose III: A Different Perspective«, *Aeon* V:6 (Aug. 2000)
Aitchison, E.: »Egyptian C14 Dates«, *Chronology & Catastrophism Review* 1997:2
Akurgal, E.: *Phrygische Kunst* (Ankara, 1955)
Akurgal, E.: »Asia Minor, Western«, PHRYGIA, *Encyclopedia of World Art I* (Rome, 1959)
Akurgal, E.: *Die Kunst Anatoliens von Homer bis Alexander* (Berlin, 1961)
Akurgal, E.: *The Art of the Hittites* (NY, 1962)
Akurgal, E.: *The Art of Greece: Its Origins in the Mediterranean and Near East* (NY, 1966)
Akurgal, E.: *Ancient Civilizations and Ruins of Turkey* (Istanbul, 1970)
Albright, W. F.: *Bulletin of the American Schools of Oriental Research* 83 (1941)
Albright, W. F.: »Northeast-Mediterranean Dark Ages and the Early Iron Age Art of Syria« in *The Aegean and the Near East* (ed. S. Weinberg) (Locust Valley, New York, 1956)
Alexander, Caroline: *The War That Killed Achilles – The True Story of Homer's Iliad and the Trojan War* (2009)
Alin, Per: *Das Ende der mykenischen Fundstätten auf dem griechischen Festland* (Lund, 1962)
Alkim, U.B.: *Anatolia I (Archaeologia Mundi)* (NY, 1968)
Allen, S.H.: *Finding the Walls of Troy* (London, 1999)
Amandry, P.: »Plaques d'or de Delphes«, *Ath. Mitt*, 77 (1962)
Amiet, P.: *Art of the Ancient Near East* (NY, 1980)
Andersen, Wayne: *The Ara Pacis of Augustus and Mussolini* (Boston, 2003)

Anderson, J. K.: »Greek Chariot-borne and Mounted Infantry«, *American Journal of Archaeology* 79 (1975)

Anderson, J. K.: »Homeric, British and Cyrenaic Chariots«, *American Journal of Archaeology* 69 (1965)

Andrewes, A.: *The Greeks* (London, 1967)

Andronikos, M.: *Totenkult (Archaeologia Homerica* III W) (Philadelphia, 1943)

Andronikos, M.: »An Early Iron Age Cemetery at Vergina, near Beroea«, *Balkan Studies*, 2 (1961)

Ap-Thomas, D. R.: »Jerusalem« in *Archaeology and Old Testament Study* (ed. D. W. Thomas) (New York, 1967)

Aristotle: *Meteorologica*

Arrian: *The Anabasis of Alexander*

Ashmole, B.: »Archaic Art«, *Encyclopedia of World Art*, I (NY, 1959)

Astour, M. C.: *Hellenosemitica* (Leiden, 1967)

Aström, L. et al.: *The Late Cypriote Bronze Age: Other Arts and Crafts (Swedish Cyprus Expedition* IV. 1D) (Lund, 1972)

Atlas of the Classical World (eds. A.A.M. Van Der Heyden and H.H. Scullard) (NY, 1959)

Aubet, M. E.: *The Phoenicians and the West* (Cambridge, 1996)

Augustine: *The City of God*

Austin, M.M.: »Greece and Egypt in the Archaic Age«, *Proceedings of the Cambridge Philological Society*, Supplement No.2 (1970)

Bachvarova, M. R.: *From Hittite to Homer* (Cambridge, 2016)

Baines, J. and Malek, J.: *Cultural Atlas of Ancient Egypt*, rev. ed. (NY, 2000)

Bard, Kathryn A.: *An Introduction to the Archaeology of ANCIENT EGYPT* (2008)

Barker, G. and Rasmussen, T.: *The Etruscans* – The Peoples of Europe series (Oxford, 1998)

Barnett, R. D.: *A Catalogue of the Nimrud Ivories* (London, 1957)

Barnett, R. D.: »Early Greek and Oriental Ivories«, *Journal of Hellenic Studies*, 68 (1948)

Barnett, R. D.: »Nimrud Ivories and the Art of the Phoenicians«, *Iraq*, 2 (1935)

Barnett, R. D.: »Phoenician and Syrian Ivory Carving«, *Palestine Exploration Fund Quarterly* (1939)

Barnett, R. D. and Falkner, M.: *The Sculptures of Assur-Nasir-Apli II, etc.* (London, 1962)

Barnett, R. D.: »Phoenician-Punic Art«, *Encyclopedia of World Art*, XI (NY, 1966)

Barringer, J. M.: *The Art and Archaeology of Ancient Greece* (Cambridge, 2014)

Barron, J.: *Greek Sculpture* (New York, 1970)

Barr, S.: *The Will of Zeus* (New York, 1961)

Bathe, E.: *Homer 11.2 Odyssey* (Leipzig, 1929)

Beall, J. P.: *Virgil's Choice of Aeneas in the Light of His Purpose in Writing the Aeneid*, A Master's Thesis (Loyola University, 1950)

Beattie in *Journal of Hellenic Studies* 76 (1956)

Becatti, G.: *The Art of Greece and Rome* (New York, 1967)

Beck, C.W. et al.: »Analysis and Provenience of Minoan and Mycenaean Amber, II Tiryns«, *Greek, Roman and Byzantine Studies*, 9 (1968)

*Beckwith, C. I.: *The Scythian Empire* (2023)

Benson, C. David: *The History of Troy in Middle English Literature* (Woodbridge, Suffolk, 1980)

Benson, J. L.: »Bronze Tripods from Koran«, *Greek, Roman and Byzantine Studies*, 3 (1960)

Benson, J. L.: *Horse, Bird &Man* (Amherst, 1970)

Benton, S.: »The Evolution of the Tripod-Lebes«, *Annual of the British School at Athens*, 35 (1934-35)

Benveniste, E. in *Etudes myceniennes* (Paris, 1956)

Bérard, J.: *L'expansion et la colonization grecques jusqu'aux guerres médiques* (Paris, 1960)

Bérard, C.: *Eretria* III (Bern, 1970)

Bérard, V.: *Les Phéniciens et l'Odyssée* (Paris, 1927-28)

Bernal, M.: *Black Athena*, II (New Brunswick, 1991)

Bernal, M.: *Black Athena Writes Back* (London, 2001)

Berosus: *Babyloniaca*

Berquist, B.: *The Archaic Greek Temenos* (Lund, 1967)

Betancourt, P. P.: »The End of the Greek Bronze Age«, *Antiquity* 50 (1976)

Betancourt, P. P.: *Introduction to Aegean Art* (Phila., 2007)

Betancourt, P. P.: »Dating the Aegean Late Bronze Age with Radiocarbon«, *Archaeometry*, 29 (1987)

Bianchi Bandinelli, R.: *Enciclopedia Dell'Arte Antica* - III, »Etrusca, Arte« (Rome, 1960)

Bielefeld, E.: *Schmuck (Archaeologia Homerica* I C) (Göttingen, 1968)

Bimson, J.: *Chronology & Catastrophism Review* VIII (1986)

Biot, E.: *Catalogue général des étoiles filantes et des autres météors observés en Chine après le VIIe siècle avant J.C.* (Paris, 1846)

Birch: »Mémoire sur une patère égyptienne du Musée du Louvre [1857]«, *Mém. Soc. Imp. Ant, Fr.* XXIV (1858)

Bissing, Fr. von: »Ägyptisch oder Phoinikisch?«, *Jahrbuch des deutschen archäologischen Instituts*, 25 (1910)

Bissing, Fr. von: »Eine Bronzeschale mykenischer Zeit«, *Jahrbuch des deutschen archäologischen Instituts*, 13 (1898)

Bissing, Fr. von, »Untersuchungen über die 'phoinikischen' Metallschalen«, *Jahrbuch des deutschen archäologischen Instituts*, 38-39 (1923-1924)

Bittle, K.: »Hittite Art«, *Encyclopedia of World Art*, VII (NY, 1963)

Blanshard, A.: *Hercules A Heroic Life* (London, 2005)

Blawatsky, Vladimir: »Greco-Bosporan and Scythian Art«, *Encyclopedia of World Art* VI (NY, 1962)

Blazquez, J. M.: *Tartessos y Los Origenes de la colonizacion fenicia en Occidente* (Universidad de Salamanca, 1975)
Blegen, C. W.: »A Mycenaean Breadmaker«, *Annuario della Scuola Archeologica di Atene*, N.S. 8-10 (1946-48)
Blegen, C. W.: *Korakou, a Prehistoric Settlement near Corinth* (American School of Classical Studies at Athens, Boston, 1921)
Blegen, C. W.: »The So-called Temple of Hera at Tiryns«, an appendix to *Korakou* (New York, 1921)
Blegen, C. W.: »New Evidence for Dating the Settlements at Troy«, *Annual of the British School at Athens* 37 (1936-1937)
Blegen, C. W.: *Prosymna, The Helladic Settlement Preceding the Argive Heraeum*, vol. I (Cambridge, 1937)
Blegen, C. W. et al.: *Troy*, vol. I. 1 (Princeton: 1950)
Blegen, C. W.: »The Palace of Nestor Excavations of 1956«, *American Journal of Archaeology*, 61 (1957)
Blegen, C. W., Caskey, J. S., Rawson, M.: *Troy*, vol. IV (Princeton, 1958)
Blegen, C. W. et al.: *Troy, Settlements VIIa, VIIb and VIII*, vol. IV (Princeton, 1958)
Blegen, C. W.: »Troy«, Cambridge Ancient History, fascicle 1 (1961)
Blegen, C. W.: *The Mycenaean Age, The Trojan War, The Dorian Invasion, and Other Problems* (Cincinnati, Ohio, 1962)
Blegen, C. W.: *Troy and the Trojans* (London, 1964)
Blegen, C. W. and Rawson, M.: *The Palace of Nestor at Pylos in Western Messenia*, vol. I (Princeton, 1966)
Blegen, C. W. et al.: *The Palace of Nestor* III (Princeton, 1973)
Bloch, Raymond: *The Etruscans* (NY, 1960)
Bloch, Raymond: *The Origins of Rome* (NY, 1960)
Boardman, J.: *The Cretan Collection in Oxford* (Oxford, 1961)
Boardman, J.: *Island Gems* (London, 1963)
Boardman, J.: *Greek Art* (New York, 1964)
Boardman, J.: *The Greeks Overseas* (Baltimore, 1964)
Boardman, J. in *Journal of Hellenic Studies* 85 (1965)
Boardman, J.: *Greek Art*, 4th ed. (London, 1996)
Boardman, J.: *Pre-Classical: From Crete to Archaic Greece* (Baltimore, 1967)
Boardman, J.: »The Khaniale Tekke Tombs, II«, *Annual of the British School at Athens*, 62 (1967)
Boardman, J.: *Archaic Greek Gems* (London, 1968)
Boardman, J.: *Greek Sculpture: The Archaic Period* (NY, 1978)
Boersma, J. S.: *Athenian Building Policy from 561/0 to 405/4 B.C.* (Groningen: 1970)
Boethius, A. and Ward-Perkins, J. B.: *Etruscan and Roman Architecture* (Baltimore, 1970)
Boethius, A.: *Etruscan and Early Roman Architecture* (NY, 1978)
Borovka, Gregory: *Scythian Art* (London 1928)

Borrelli, F. and Targia, M. C.: *The Etruscans Art, Architecture, and History* (LA, 2004)
Bosch-Gimpera, P. in *Zephyrus* 13 (1952)
Bosch-Gimpera, P. in *La nouvelle Clio* 3 (1951)
Bowen, M. L.: »Some Observations on the Origin of Triglyphs«, *Annual of the British School at Athens*, 45 (1950)
Bowra, Sir Maurice: *Homer and His Forerunners* (Edinburgh, 1955)
Bowra, Sir Maurice: »Composition« in Wace-Stubbings (1962)
Bradley, G.: *Early Rome to 290 BC* (Edinburgh, 2020)
Brann, E., The Athenian Agora VIII; Late Geometric and Protoattic Pottery (Princeton, 1962)
Brea, L. B.: *Sicily Before the Greeks* (New York, 1966)
Breasted, J. R.: *The Ancient Records of Egypt* (Chicago, 1906)
Broneer, O.: »A Mycenaean Fountain on the Athenian Acropolis«, *Hesperia*, 8 (1939)
Broneer, O.: »What Happened at Athens«, *American Journal of Archaeology* 52 (1948)
Broneer, O. in *Hesperia* 28 (1959)
Broneer, O.: *Isthmia* I (Princeton, 1971)
Bronze Age Migrations in the Aegean (ed. R. Crossland and A. Birchall) (London, 1973)
Brooks, C. E. P.: *Climate through the Ages*, 2nd edition (New York, 1949)
Bryce, T.: *The Kingdom of the Hittites* (NY, 1998)
Bryce, T.: *The Kingdom of the Hittites* (New Edition) (NY, 2005)
Bryce, T.: *The Trojans and their Neighbors* (NY, 2006)
Bryson, R. A., Lamb, H, H. and Donley, D. L.: »Drought and the Decline of Mycenae« in *Antiquity* 48 (1974)
Buchholz, H. G.: »Gray Minyan Ware in Cyprus and Northern Syria« in *Bronze Age Migrations in the Aegean* (Park Ridge, NJ, 1974)
Buchholz, H. G.: »Ägäische Funde und Kultureinflüsse in den Randgebieten des Mittelmeers«, *Archäologischer Anzeiger* 89 (1974)
Budge, E.: *Assyrian Sculptures in the British Museum: Reign of Ashur-Nasir-Pal, 885-860 B.C.* (London, 1914)
Buffière, F.: *Les mythes d'Homère et la pensée grecque* (Paris, 1956)
Bundgaard, J. A.: *Mnesicles* (Copenhagen, 1957)
Burgess, J. S.: *The Tradition of the Trojan War in Homer and the Epic Cycle* (Baltimore, 2001)
Burkert, W.: *The Orientalizing Revolution – Near Eastern Influence on Greek culture in the Early Archaic Age* (London, 1992)
Burn, A. R.: *Minoans, Philistines and Greeks: B.C. 1400-900* (London, 1930)
Burn, A. R.: »Dates in Early Greek History«, *Journal of Hellenic Studies* 55 (1935)
Burn, A. R.: *Persia and the Greeks* (London, 1962)
Burn, A. R.: *The Pelican History of Greece* (Baltimore, 1966)
Burn, A. R.: *Minoans, Philistines and Greeks, etc.* (London, 1968)

*Burney, C.: *Historical Dictionary of the Hittites*, 2nd ed. (2018)
Burr, D.: »A Geometric House and a Proto-Attic Votive Deposit«, *Hesperia*, 2 (1933)
Bursian, C.: *Geographie von Griechenland*, vol. II (Leipzig, 1868-72)
Burton-Brown, T.: *Third Millennium Diffusion* (Oxford, 1970)
Buxton, L., Casson, B. and Myres, J.: »A Cloisonné Staffhead from Cyprus«, *Man*, 32 (1932)
Cadogan, G.: »Dating the Aegean Bronze Age without Radiocarbon«, *Archaeometry* 20 (1978)
Calder, W. A. et al.: »Behind the Mask of Agamemnon«, *Archaeology* 52:4 (July/August 1999)
Cambridge Ancient History I- III, (ed. J. B. Bury et al.) (Cambridge, 1925)
Camp, J.: »A Drought in the Late Eighth Century B.C.« in *Hesperia* 48 (1979)
Camp, J. and Fisher, E.: *The World of the Ancient Greeks* (London, 2002)
Carpenter, R.: »The Antiquity of the Greek Alphabet«, *American Journal of Archaeology* 37 (1933)
Carpenter, R. and Bon, A.: *Corinth III.2; The Defences of Acrocorinth and the lower Town* (Cambridge, Mass., 1936)
Carpenter, R.: »The Greek Alphabet Again«, *American Journal of Archaeology* 42 (1938)
Carpenter, R.: *Folk Tale, Fiction and Saga in the Homeric Epics* (Los Angeles, 1946)
Carpenter, R.: *Greek Sculpture* (Chicago, 1960)
Carpenter, R. in *Greek Art* (Phila., 1962)
Carpenter, R.: »A Note on the Foundation Date of Carthage«, *American Journal of Archaeology* 68 (1964)
Carpenter, R.: *The Discontinuity in Greek Civilization* (Cambridge University Press, 1966)
Carpenter, R.: *Greek Sculpture* (Chicago, 1971)
Carter, J.: »The Beginning of Narrative Art in the Geometric Period«, *Annual of the British School at Athens* 67 (1972)
Cartledge, P.: *Thebes* (London, 2020)
Casali, S.: »The Development of the Aeneas Legend«, *A Companion to Virgil's Aeneid and Its Tradition* (ed. by J. Farrell and M.C.J. Putnam) (Malden, Oxford, 2010)
Caskey, J. L.: »Excavations in Keos, 1963«, Hesperia 33 (1964)
Caskey, M. E.: »News Letter from Greece«, *American Journal of Archaeology* 81 (1977)
Caskey, M. E.: »News Letter from Greece«, *American Journal of Archaeology* 82 (1978)
Casson, B., and Myres, J.: »A Cloisonné Staff-head from Cyprus«, *Man* 32 (1932)
Casson, S.: *Ancient Cyprus* (London, 1937)
Casson, S.: »Bronzework of the Geometric Period and Its Relation to Later Art«, *Journal of Hellenic Studies* 42 (1922)
Castleden, R.: *The Attack on Troy* (2006)
Castleden, R.: *Mycenaeans* (NY, 2005)

Castriota, D.: *The Ara Pacis Augustae and the Imagery of Abundance in Later Greek and Early Roman Imperial Art* (Princeton, 1995)
Catling, H. W.: *Cypriote Bronzework in the Mycenaean World* (Oxford, 1964)
Catling, H. W.: »A Mycenaean Puzzle from Lefkandi in Euboea«, *American Journal of Archaeology* 72 (1968)
Catling, H. W. in Popham-Sackett (1968)
Catling, H. W.: »A Pendent Semicircle Skyphos from Cyprus and a Cypriote Imitation«, *Reports of the Department of Antiquities of Cyprus*, 1973 (Nicosia, 1973)
Catling, H. W.: »Cyprus in the Late Bronze Age«, *Cambridge Ancient History* 3 II. 2 (Cambridge, 1975)
Chadwick, J.: *Documents in Mycenaean Greek* (1956)
Chadwick, J.: *The Decipherment of Linear B* (Cambridge, 1958)
Chadwick, J.: »The Linear Scripts« in *The Cambridge Ancient History*, vol. II, ch. XIII (1971)
Chadwick, J.: *Minos* (1975)
Charbonneaux, J.: *Greek Bronzes* (tr. K. Watson) (New York, 1962)
Charbonneaux, J., Martin, R. and Villard, F.: *Archaic Greek Art* (NY, 1971)
Chien, Chao C.: *In Search of Troy* (US, 2019, 2nd Edition)
Chrystal, Paul: *War in Greek Mythology* (Barnsley, 2020)
Cintas, P.: *Céramique punique* (Paris, 1950)
Civilizations of the Ancient Near East, Volumes One & Two (editor in Chief J. M. Sasson) (NY, 1995)
Clarke, L.: *The War at Troy* (NY, 2004)
Clayton, P. A.: *Chronicle of the Pharaohs* (London, 1994)
Cles-Reden, S. von: *The Buried People; A Study of the Etruscan World* (tr. C. Woodhouse) (N.Y., 1955)
Cochrane, E.: *Martian Metamorphoses: The Planet Mars in Ancient Myth and Religion* (Ames, IA, 1997)
Cohane, J. P.: *The Key* (New York, 1969)
Coldstream, J. N.: *Greek Geometric Pottery* (London, 1968)
Coldstream, J. N.: »The Cesnola Painter: A Change of Address«, *Bulletin of the Institute of Classical Studies* (Univ. of London) 13 (1971)
Coldstream, J. N. in *Kythera* (eds. Coldstream, J. N. and Huxley, G.) (Park Ridge, N.J., 1973)
Coldstream, J. N.: »Hero-cults in the Age of Homer«, *Journal of Hellenic Studies* 96 (1976)
Coldstream, J. N.: *Geometric Greece* (London, 1977)
Colonna, G.: »The Original Features of the Etruscan Peoples«, *The Etruscans* (ed. M. Torelli) (NY, 2000)
Comparetti, D.: *Vergil in the Middle Ages* (Princeton, 1997, originally 1885)
Conteneau, G.: *La civilization phénicienne* (Paris, 1949)
Cook, J. M.: »Greek Archaeology in Western Asia Minor«, *Archaeological Reports for 1959-1960*

Cook, J. M.: *The Greeks in Ionia and the East* (New York, 1963)

Cook, J. M.: *The Troad: An Archaeological and Topographical Study* (Oxford, 1973)

Cook, J. M.: »Bronze Age Sites in the Troad«, *Bronze Age Migrations in the Aegean* (eds. R. A. Crossland and Ann Birchall) (London, 1973)

Cook, J. M.: »Greek Settlement in the Eastern Aegean and Asia Minor«, *Cambridge Ancient History* 3 11,2 (1975)

Cook, R. M.: »A Note on the Origin of the Triglyphs«, *Annual of the British School at Athens* 56 (1951)

Cook, R. M.: *Greek Painted Pottery* (London, 1960)

Cook, R. M.: »The Archetypal Doric Temple«, *Annual of the British School at Athens* 65 (1970)

Cook, R. M.: *Greek Art* (New York, 1971)

Cook, R. M.: *Greek Painted Pottery* (London, 1972)

Cook, R. M.: *Greek Art: Its Development, Character and Influence* (Penguin, NY, 1972)

Cornelius, F.: *Berossus und die Altorientalische Chronologie*, KLIO 35 (1942)

Cornell, T. J.: *The Beginnings of Rome* (London, 1995)

Corpus der minoischen und mykenischen Siegel, ed. F. Matz and H. Bisantz (Berlin, 1964)

Cotterill, H. B.: *Ancient Greece* (New York, 1913)

Courbin, P.: »Une tombe géometrique d'Argos«, *Bulletin de correspondance hellénique* 81 (1957)

Courby, F.: *Les Vases grecques à relief* (Paris, 1922)

Courville, D.: *The Exodus Problem and its Ramifications*, V.2 (Loma Linda, 1971)

Crowe, J.: *The Troy Deception* (Leicester, 2011)

Crowfoot, J. W. & G. M.: *Early Ivories from Samaria* (London, 1938)

Cryer, F. H.: »Chronology: Issues and Problems«, *Civilizations of the Ancient Near East*, Volumes One & Two (Editor in Chief J. M. Sasson) (NY, 1995)

Culican, W.: *The First Merchant Ventures* (London, 1966)

Cunliffe, B.: *The Scythians Nomad Warriors of the Steppe* (Oxford, 2019)

Danelius, Eva: »Did Thutrnose III Despoil the Temple in Jerusalem?«, *SIS Review* II:3 (Special Issue 1977/78)

Danelius, Eva in *SIS Review* VII, Part A (1982/3)

Danelius, Eva in *Kronos* I:3 (Fall, 1975)

Daniel, J. F.: »Two Late Cypriote III Tombs from Kourion«, *American Journal of Archaeology* 41 (1937)

Davis, N.: *Carthage and Her Remains* (London, 1861)

Davison, J.: »The Homeric Question« in Wace-Stubbings (1962)

Deger-Jalkotzy, S. in *The Cambridge Companion to the Aegean Bronze Age* (ed. C. W. Shelmerdine) (Cambridge, 2008)

Degrassi, N.: »Taranto« in the *Enciclopedia Dell'Arte Antica* - VII (Rome, 1966)

Demargne, P.: »The Aegean World«, *The Larousse Encyclopedia of Prehistoric and Ancient Art* (NY, 1962)

Demargne, P.: *The Birth of Greek Art* (tr. by S. Gilbert and J. Emmons) (New York, 1964)
Dennis, G.: *The Cities and Cemeteries of Etruria* (London, 1878)
Deroy, L.: *Les leveurs d'impôts dans le royaume mycénien de Pylos (Incunabula Graeca* 24) (Rome, 1968)
Desborough, V. R. d'A.: *Protogeometric Pottery* (Oxford, 1952)
Desborough, V. R. d'A.: »A Group of Vases from Amathus«, *Journal of Hellenic Studies* 77 (1957)
Desborough, V. R. d'A. and Hammond, N. G. L.: »The End of the Mycenaean Civilization and the Dark Age«, *Cambridge Ancient History* Fascicle 13 (1962)
Desborough, V. R. d'A.: »The Low-Footed Skyphoi with Pendent Semicircles«, *Archäologischer Anzeiger* (1963)
Desborough, V. R. d'A.: *The Last Mycenaeans and Their Successors* (Oxford, 1964)
Desborough, V. R. d'A.: review of Deshayes' *Argos* etc. in *Gnomon*, 41 (1969)
Desborough, V. R. d'A.: *The Greek Dark Ages* (London, 1972)
Desborough, V. R. d'A. in *The Cambridge Ancient History* (Third Edition), II, Part 2, *The Middle East and the Aegean Region c. 1380-1000 B.C.* (1975)
Deshayes, J.: *Argos: les fouilles de la Deiras* (Paris, 1966)
Dickinson, O.: »Archaeological Facts and Greek Traditions«, *Bulletin of the Archaeological Society of the University of Birmingham*, 17.2 (1973-4)
Dickinson, O.: *The Aegean from Bronze Age to Iron Age* (NY, 2007)
Dietrich, B. C.: »Some Evidence of Religious Continuity in the Greek Dark Age«, *Bulletin of the Institute of Classical Studies* (Univ. of London) 17 (1970)
Dikaios, P.: »An Iron Age Painted Amphora in the Cyprus Museum«, *Annual of the British School at Athens* 37 (1936-7)
Dikaios, P.: *A Guide to the Cyprus Museum* (Nicosia, 1947)
Dikaios, P.: "Fifteen Iron Age Vases," *Report of the Department of Antiquities. Cyprus*, 1937-9 (pub'd, 1951)
Dikaios, P.: »Principal Acquisitions of the Cyprus Museum, 1937-1939«, *Report of the Department of Antiquities. Cyprus*, 1937-39 (pub'd, 1951)
Dikaios, P.: *A Guide to the Cyprus Museum* (Nicosia, 1961)
Dikaios, P.: *Treasures in the Cyprus Museum* (Nicosia, 1962)
Dikaios, P.: »Some Cypriote Painters of Bulls in the Archaic Period«, *Jahrbuch des deutschen archäologischen Instituts* 80 (1965)
Dinsmoor, W. B.: »The Date of the Older Parthenon«, *American Journal of Archaeology* 38 (1934)
Dinsmoor, W. B.: »The Date of the Olympia Heraeum«, *American Journal of Archaeology* 49 (1945)
Dinsmoor, W. B.: *The Architecture of Ancient Greece* (New York, 1950)
Diodorus Siculus: *Bibliotheca historica*
Dionysius of Halicarnassus: *Roman Antiquities*
Doehl, H.: »Tiryns Stadt: Sondage 1968« in *Tiryns* VIII (ed. U. Jantzen) (Mainz, 1975)
Dörpfeld, W.: *Troja 1893, Bericht über die im Jahre 1893 in Troja veranstalteten Ausgrabungen* (Leipzig, 1894)

Dörpfeld, W.: *Troja und Ilion* (Athens, 1902)
Dörpfeld, W.: "Das Alter des Heiligtums von Olympia," *Ath. Mitt.*, 31 (1906)
Dörpfeld, W.: *Homers Odyssee, die Wiederherstellung des ursprünglichen Epos* (Munich, 1925)
Dörpfeld, W.: *Alt-Olympia* I (Berlin, 1935)
Dohrn, T.: »Stamnoi und Kratere aus grauem Ton, Nachahmungen von Metallgefässen (Civilta Castellana)« in W. Helbig and H. Speier: *Führer durch die öffentlichen Sammlungen klassischer Altertümer in Rom* (revised edition, Tübingen, 1969)
Donalson, M. D.: *The Cult of Isis in the Roman Empire* (Lewiston, NY, 2003)
Donley, D. L.: »Drought and the Decline of Mycenae« in *Antiquity* 48 (1974)
Doumas, C. G.: *Thera: Pompeii of the Eastern Aegean* (London, 1983)
Drees, L.: *OLYMPIA Gods, Artists, and Athletes* (NY, 1967)
Drerup, H.: »Griechische Architektur zur Zeit Homers«, *Archäologischer Anzeiger* (1964)
Drerup, H.: *Griechische Baukunst in geometrischer Zeit (Archaeologia Homerica* II,0) (Göttingen, 1969)
Drews, R.: *The End of the Bronze Age* (Princeton, 1993)
Droop, J. P., "Dipylon Vases from the Kynosarges Site," BSA, 12 (1905-6)
Droop, J. P., "The Pottery from Arcadia, Crete," Liverpool Annals of Archaeology and Anthropology, 12 (1925)
Dunbabin, T. J.: »Minos and Daidalos in Sicily«, *Papers of the British School at Rome* 16 (New series, vol. III) (1948)
Dunbabin, T. J.: *The Western Greeks* (Oxford, 1948)
Dunbabin, T. J. et al.: *Perachora* II (Oxford, 1962)
Dunbabin, T. J.: *The Greeks and Their Eastern Neighbours* (Chicago, 1979)
Dümmler, F.: »Bemerkungen zum ältesten Kunsthandwerk auf griechischem Boden«, *Ath. Mitt.* 13 (1888)
Dümmler, F.: »Zu den Vasen aus Kameiros«, *Jahrbuch des deutschen archäologischen Instituts* 6 (1891)
Duncker, M.: *History of Greece* ... (V.1, London, 1883-86)
Durando, F.: *Greece: A Guide to the Archaeological Sites* (NY, 2000)
Durn, R. in *Jahrhefte der k. Arch. Instituts zu Wien*, X (1907)
Dussaud, R.: »Kinyras, Etude sur les anciens cultes chypriotes«, *Syria* 27 (1950)
Earl, D.: *The Age of Augustus* (1968)
Early Rome Myth and Society (ed. J. Neel) (2017)
Easton, D.: »The Quest for Troy«, *Mysteries of the Ancient World* (ed. by J. Flanders) (London, 1998)
Edgar, C. C.: »Excavations in Melos 1899: The Pottery«, *Annual of the British School at Athens* 5 (1898-99)
Edgar, C. C.: »The Pottery« in *Excavations at Phylakopi in Melos (Journal of Hellenic Studies* supplement 4) (London, 1904)
Edwards, R. B.: *Kadmos, the Phoenician* (Amsterdam, 1979)
Eissfeldt, O.: *The Hebrew Kingdom* (Cambridge, 1965)
Eliade, Mircea: *Myth and Reality* (NY, 1968)

Else, G. F.: »Homer and the Homeric Problem« in Lectures in *Memory of L.T. Semple* I (eds. D. Bradeen et. al.) (Princeton, 1967)
Eratosthenis catasterismorum reliquiae (ed. C. Robert) (1878)
Erskine, A.: *Troy Between Greece and Rome* (Oxford, 2001)
Etruscan Italy (ed. J. F. Hall) (Provo, 1996)
Euripides: *Electra*
Euripides: *Orestes*
Europa: Studien zur Geschichte und Epigraphik der frühen Aegaeis (Festschrift für Ernst Grumach) (ed. William C. Brice) (Berlin, 1967)
Eusebius: *Werke* (ed. R. Helm) (Leipzig, 1913)
Evans, A. J.: »A Mycenaean Treasure from Aegina«, *Journal of Hellenic Studies* 13 (1892-3)
Evans, A. J.: »Mycenaean Cyprus as Illustrated in the British Museum Excavations«, *Journal of the Royal Anthropological Institute* 30 (1900)
Evans, A. J.: »The Minoan and Mycenaean Element in Hellenic Life«, *Journal of Hellenic Studies* 22 (1912)
Evans, A. J.: *The Palace of Minos at Knossos* (1921-1935)
Evans, A. J.: *The Palace of Minos* (London, 1935)
Evely, D.: »Helladic, V, 2(iii)« in *The Dictionary of Art* (ed. J. Turner), Vol. 14 (NY, 1998)
Evelyn-White, H. G.: *Hesiod, The Homeric Hymns and Homerica, Loeb Classical Library,* (1914)
Feldman, B.: »Pygmalion, Prince of Tyre and the El-Amarna Correspondence«, *Kronos* II:1 (August-1976)
Ferri, S: »Arte Frigia«, *Enciclopedia dell'arte Antica* III (Rome, 1960)
Fiechter, E. R.: »Die mit dem Tempel gleichzeitig oder später entstandenen Bauten« in Furtwängler, A. et al.: *Aegina: Das Heiligtum der Aphaia* (Munich, 1906)
Fine, John V. A.: *The Ancient Greeks A Critical History* (Cambridge, MS, 1983)
Finkelberg, Margalit: *Greeks and Pre-Greeks* (Cambridge, 2005)
Finley, M. I.: *The World of Odysseus* (New York, 1954)
Finley, M. I.: *The World of Odysseus* (New York, 1978)
Finley, M. I. in *Early Greece: The Bronze and Archaic Ages* (NY, 1981)
Finley, M. I. et al.: *A History of Sicily* (NY, 1987)
Fischer, D. H.: *Historians' Fallacies: Toward a Logic of Historical Thought* (New York, 1970)
Fitton, J. L.: *The Discovery of the Greek Bronze Age* (Cambridge, MA, 1996)
Fittschen, K.: *Der Schild des Achilleus (Archaeologia Homerica* II. N. 1) (Göttingen, 1973)
Fletcher, J.: *Cleopatra the Great* (NY, 2008)
Flinders Petrie, W. M.: »The Egyptian Bases of Greek History«, *Journal of Hellenic Studies* 11 (October 1890)
Flinders Petrie, W. M.: »Notes on the Antiquities of Mykenae«, *Journal of Hellenic Studies* XII (1891)
Flinders Petrie, W. M.: *Illahun, Kahun and Gurob* (London, 1891)

Fol, A. and Marazov, I.: *Thrace and The Thracians* (NY, 1977)
Folsom, R. S.: *Handbook of Greek Pottery* (London, 1967)
Forsdyke, J.: *Greece before Homer* (London, 1956)
Fortenberry, C. D.: »Helladic, I, 4«, *The Dictionary of Art*, Vol 14 (1998)
Fowler, W. W.: »Mars« in *Encyclopaedia Britannica*, 14th ed.
Fox, R. Lane: *The Classical World* (NY, 2006)
Frankfort, H.: *The Art and Architecture of the Ancient Orient* (Baltimore, 1963)
Frankfort, H.: *The Art and Architecture of the Ancient Orient*, 4th ed. (New Haven, 1970)
Fredriksen, P.: *Augustine and the Jews* (NY, 2008)
Freed, R. E.: *Ramesses the Great* (Boston, 1988)
*Freely, J.: *Children of Achilles* (2010)
Freeman, C.: *Egypt, Greece and Rome* (NY, 1996)
Frickenhaus, A.: »Die Hera von Tiryns«, *Tiryns* I (Athens, 1912)
Friedrich, W. L.: *Fire in the Sea: The Santorini Volcano: Natural History and the Legend of Atlantis* (Cambridge, 2000)
Frödin, O. and Persson, A. W.: *Asine: Results of the Swedish Excavations 1922-1930* (Stockholm, 1938)
Furtwängler, A.: »Das Alter des Heraion und das Alter des Heiligtums von Olympia«, *Sitzungsberichte der Philosophisch-Philologischen Klasse der Königlich Bayerischen Akademie der Wissenschaften*, 1906, reprinted in *Kleine Schriften* (Munich, 1912)
Furtwängler, A.: »Die Bronzefunde aus Olympia and deren Kunstgeschichtliche Bedeutung«, *Berlin Abhandlungen* 4 (1879), reprinted in *Kleine Schriften* I (Munich, 1911)
Furtwängler, A. et al.: *Aegina: Das Heiligtum der Aphaia* (Munich, 1906)
Furumark, A.: Mycenaean Pottery (Stockholm, 1941)
Furumark, A.: *The Chronology of Mycenaean Pottery* (Stockholm, 1941)
Galanopoulos, A. G. and Bacon, E.: *Atlantis: The Truth behind the Legend* (New York, 1969)
Galinsky, G. K.: *Aeneas, Sicily and Rome* (Princeton, 1969)
Gams, H. and Nordhagen, R.: »Postglaziale Klimaänderungen und Erdkrustenbewegungen in Mittel-Europa«, *Mitteilungen der geographischen Gesellschaft in München*, vol. XVI, no.2 (1923)
Garbini, G.: *The Ancient World* (NY, 1966)
Garcia y Bellido, A.: *La Peninsula Ibérica en los comienzos de su Historia* (Madrid, 1954)
Gardiner, A.: Egypt of the Pharaohs (New York, 1972)
Gardner, E. A.: *Ancient Athens* (London, 1902)
Gardner, E. A. and Gary, M.: »Early Athens« in *The Cambridge Ancient History* Vol. III (New York, 1925)
Gardner, P.: book review of Schliemann's *Mycenae* in *Quarterly Review*, 145 (Jan.-Apr., 1878)
Gardner, P.: »Stephani on the Tombs at Mycenae«, Journal of Hellenic Studies, I (1880)
Gardner, P.: *New Chapters in Greek History* (NY, 1892)

Gere, C.: *The Tomb of Agamemnon* (2006)
Ghica, Ion: *Istoriile lui Erodot*, vol. II (Bucuresti, 1912)
Ginzberg, L.: *The Legends of the Jews* (Philadelphia, 1929)
Gjerstad, E. et al.: *The Swedish Cyprus Expedition, 1927-1931* (Stockholm, 1934)
Gjerstad, E.: »Decorated Metal Bowls from Cyprus«, *Op. Arch.* 4 (1946)
Gjerstad, E.: *The Swedish Cyprus Expedition*, IV.2 (Stockholm, 1948)
Goody, J.: *The Power of the Written Tradition* (London, 2000)
Grace, F.: »Observations on Seventh-Century Sculpture«, *American Journal of Archaeology* 46 (1942)
Graham, A. J.: »The colonial expansion of Greece«, *The Cambridge Ancient History* III, 2nd ed., part 3 (Cambridge, 2002)
Graham, J. W.: »Mycenaean Architecture«, *Archaeology* 13 (1900)
Graham, J. W.: *The Palaces of Crete* (Princeton, 1972)
Grandazzi, Alexandre: *The Foundation of Rome Myth and History* (Ithaca, 1997)
Gransden, K. W.: *Virgil: The Aeneid* (Cambridge, 2nd ed., 2004)
Grant, M.: *The Ancient Mediterranean* (NY, 1969)
Grant, M.: *Cleopatra*
Graves, R.: *The Greek Myths* (London, 1955)
Gray, D.H.F.: »Metal-working in Homer«, *Journal of Hellenic Studies* 74 (1954)
Gray, D.H.F.: »Homer and the Archaeologists« in *Fifty Years of Classical Scholarship* (ed. M. Platnauer) (Oxford, 1954)
Gray, D.H.F.: »Mycenaean Names in Homer«, *Journal of Hellenic Studies* 78 (1958)
Gray, D.H.F.: »Houses in the Odyssey«, *Classical Quarterly* N.S. 5 (1959)
Grazia, Alfred de: *The Burning of Troy* (1984)
Greenberg, L. M.: *The Animal and Mythical Creature in Greek Art – A Study in Symbolism* (unpublished thesis), Rutgers Univ. Library (New Brunswick, New Jersey, 1961)
Greenberg, L. M. and Sizemore, W. B.: »Cosmology and Psychology« in *Kronos* I:1 (April, 1975)
Greenberg, L. M. and Sizemore, W. B.: »From Microcosm to Macrocosm: The Fearful Symmetry of Catastrophism« in *Kronos* I:2 (June, 1975)
Greenberg, L. M.: »Astronomy and Chronology: An Assessment«, *Kronos* II:4
Greenberg, L. M.: »The Lion Gate at Mycenae«, *Pensée* IVR III (Winter, 1973)
Greenberg, L. M.: »Hittites and their Skulls«, *Pensée* IVR V (Fall, 1973)
Greenberg, L. M.: »Atlantis«, *Pensée* VI
Greenberg, L. M.: *The Reign of the Swastika* (Wynnewood, PA, 1997)
Greenberg, L. M.: »The 'Land of Punt' Redux«, *Chronology & Catastrophism Review* 2018
Greenhalgh, P.: *Early Greek Warfare* (Cambridge, 1973)
Green, P.: *A Concise History of Ancient Greece to the Close of the Classical Era* (London, 1973)
Griffo, P. and Matt, L. von: *Gela: The Ancient Greeks in Sicily* (Greenwich, Conn., 1968)
Grimal, Pierre: Preface to *The Foundation of Rome Myth and History* by Alexandre Grandazzi (Ithaca, 1997)

Groenewegen-Frankfort, H. A. and Ashmole, B.: *Art of the Ancient World* (NY, 1972)
Guido, M.: *Sicily: An Archaeological Guide* (New York, 1967)
Gunter, Ann C.: *Greek Art and the Orient* (NY, 2012)
Guralnick, E.: »The Proportions of Kouroi«, *American Journal of Archaeology* 82 (1978)
Gurney, O. R.: *The Hittites* (Baltimore, 1954)
Hadjioannou, K.: »On the Identification of the Horned God of Enkomi-Alasia« in C. Schaeffer: Alasia I (Paris, 1971)
Hall, E. H.: Excavations in Eastern Crete, *Vrokastro* (Philadelphia, 1914)
Hall, E. H.: »Oriental Art of the Saite Period« in *Cambridge Ancient History* 1 - III (Cambridge, 1925)
Hall, H. R.: The Oldest Civilization of Greece (London, 1901)
Hall, H. R.: *Aegean Archaeology* (London, 1915)
Hall, H. R.: »The Peoples of the Sea« in *Recueil d'études égyptologigues dédiées à la mémoire de Jean-François Champollion* (Paris, 1922)
Hall, H. R.: *The Civilization of Greece in the Bronze Age* (NY, 1927)
Hall, J.M.: *A History of the Greek Archaic World 1200-479 BCE* (2nd ed., Chichester, 2014)
Hammond, N. G. L.: *Epirus* (Oxford, 1967)
Hammond, N. G. L.: »Tumulus Burial in Albania, the Grave Circles of Mycenae, and the Indo-Europeans«, *Annual of the British School at Athens* 62 (1967)
Hammond, N. G. L.: »The Dating of Some Burials in Tumuli in South Albania«, *Annual of the British School at Athens* 66 (1971)
Hammond, N. G. L.: *A History of Macedonia* I (Oxford, 1972)
Hammond, N. G. L.: »Grave Circles in Albania and Macedonia« in *Bronze Age Migrations in the Aegean* (eds. R. Crossland and A. Birchall) (London, 1973)
Hampe, R. and Simon, E.: *The Birth of Greek Art* (NY, 1981)
Hankey, V.: »Mycenaean Pottery in the Middle East«, *Annual of the British School at Athens* 62 (1967)
Hankey, V.: »Mycenaean Trade with the South-Eastern Mediterranean«, *Mélanges de l'Universite Saint Joseph*, 46.2 (1970)
Hankey, V. and Warren, P.: »The Absolute Chronology of the Aegean Late Bronze Age«, *Bulletin of the Institute of Classical Studies* (Univ. of London) 21 (1974)
Hanson, Victor Davis and Heath, John: *Who Killed Homer?* (1998)
Harden, D.: *The Phoenicians* (New York, 1962)
Hardie, P.: *The Last Trojan Hero* (NY, 2014)
Harl, K. W.: »The Greeks in Anatolia from the Migrations to Alexander the Great« in *The Oxford Handbook of Ancient Anatolia* (eds. S.R. Steadman and G. McMahon) (NY, 2011)
Harl-Schaller, F.: »Die archaischen "Metopen" aus Mykene«, *Jahreshefte des österreichischen archäologischen Instituts* 50 (1972-3)
Hasel, M. G.: *Domination and Resistance: Egyptian Military Activity in the Southern Levant* (Leiden, 1998)
Haspels, Emilie: *Highlands of Phrygia* (Princeton, 1971)
Hartley, M.: »Early Greek Vases from Crete«, *Annual of the British School at Athens* 29 (1930-1)

Havelock, E. A.: »Prologue to Greek Literacy« in Lectures in Memory of L.T. Semple II (ed. C.G. Boulter et. al.) (Princeton, 1973)
Hawkins, J. D.: »Bogazkoy«, *The Dictionary of Art* 4 (1996)
Haynes, S.: *Etruscan Civilization A Cultural History* (LA, 2000)
Hazel, J.: *Who's Who in the Roman World* (NY, 2001)
Heithaus, C. H.: »The History of the Aeneas Legend«, *Historical Bulletin* (Jan., 1930)
Helbig, W. and H. Speier: *Führer durch die öffentlichen Sammlungen klassischer Altertümer in Rom* (revised edition, Tübingen, 1969)
Hencken, H.: *Tarquinia And Etruscan Origins* (NY, 1968)
Hermann, H-V.: *Olympia: Heiligtum und Wettkampfstätte* (Munich, 1972)
Herm, G.: *The Phoenicians* (NY, 1975)
Herodotus: *The Histories* V. 58 (transl. by A. de Selincourt) (1954)
Heubeck, A.: *Aus der Welt der frühgriechischen Lineartafeln* (Göttingen, 1966)
Heurtley, W. A. and Skeat, T. C.: »The Tholos Tombs of Marmariane«, *Annual of the British School at Athens* 31 (1930-1)
Higgins, R.: »The Aegina Treasure Reconsidered«, *Annual of the British School at Athens* 52 (1957)
Higgins, R.: *Greek and Roman Jewelry* (London, 1961)
Higgins, R.: *Greek Terracottas* (London, 1967)
Higgins, R.: *Minoan and Mycenaean Art* (New York, 1967)
Higgins, R.: »Early Greek Jewelry«, *Annual of the British School at Athens* 64 (1969)
Hignett, C.: *A History of the Athenian Constitution* (Oxford, 1958)
Hiller, S.: »Die Explosion des Vulkans von Thera«, *Gymnasium* 82 (1975)
Hill, G.: *A History of Cyprus* I (Cambridge, 1940)
*Hoddinott, R. F.: *The Thracians* (1999)
Hoffman, G.: Imports & Immigrants (Ann Arbor, 1997)
Hoflmayer, F.: »Establishing a Chronology of the Middle Bronze Age« in *The Oxford History of the Ancient Near East*, V. II, (eds. K. Radner et al.) (NY, 2022)
Hogarth, D. G.: Excavations at Ephesus (London, 1908)
Holland, T.: *Dynasty* (NY, 2015)
Homer: *Iliad*, transl. by R. Lattimore (1951)
Hommel, F.: Ethnologie und Geographie des Alten Orient (1926)
Hood, S.: *The Home of the Heroes: The Aegean before the Greeks* (New York, 1967)
Hood, S.: *The Arts in Prehistoric Greece* (NY, 1978)
Hopkins, C.: »The Aegina Treasure«, *American Journal of Archaeology* 66 (1962)
Hoyos, D.: *The Carthaginians* (NY, 2010)
Hurwit, J. M.: *The Art and Culture of Early Greece, 1100- 480 BC* (Ithaca, 1985)
Hyden, M.: *Romulus* (Padstow, Cornwall, 2020)
Hyginus: *Fabulae*
Iakovides, S. E.: *Perati*, vol. A (1969)
Iakovides, S. E.: *Perati*, vol. B (Athens, 1970)
Immerwahr, S.: *The Athenian Agora XIII; The Neolithic and Bronze Ages* (Princeton, 1971)
Isaacson, I. M.: »Applying the Revised Chronology«, *Pensée*, IVR IX (1974)
Jacobsthal, P.: *Greek Pins* (Oxford, 1956)

James, P. et al.: *Centuries of Darkness* (London, 1991)
James, P. and Thorpe, N.: *Ancient Mysteries* (NY, 1999)
Jansen, H. G.: »Troy: Legend and Reality«, *Civilizations of the Ancient Near East*, II (NY, 1995)
Jansen-Winkeln, C.: »Dating the beginning of the 22nd dynasty« in *Journal of the Ancient Chronology Forum*, 8 (1999)
Jantzen, U. et al.: »Tiryns-Synoro-Iria 1965-1968«, *Archäologischer Anzeiger* 83 (1968)
Jantzen, U.: *Führer durch Tiryns* (Athens, 1975)
Jebb, R. C.: »I. The Ruins of Hissarlik. II. Their Relation to the Iliad«, *Journal of Hellenic Studies* 3 (1882)
Jeffrey, L. H.: *The Local Scripts of Archaic Greece* (Oxford, 1961)
Johansen, K. Friis: *The Attic Grave-Reliefs of the Classical Period* (Copenhagen, 1951)
Johansen, K. Friis: *Les Vases Sicyoniens* (Rome, 1966, reprint of 1923 edition)
Johansen, K. Friis: *The Iliad in Early Greek Art* (Copenhagen, 1967)
Johnson, M. J.: »The Mausoleum of Augustus: Etruscan and Other Influences on Its Design« in *Etruscan Italy* (ed. J. F. Hall) (Provo, 1996)
Jonsson, C. O.: »Nebuchadrezzar and Neriglissar«, *SIS Review* III:4 (Spring 1979)
Josephus: *Jewish Antiquities*
Kambouris, M. E.: *The Trojan War as Military History* (Phil., 2023)
Kantor, H.: »The Aegean and the Orient in the Second Millennium B.C.« *American Journal of Archaeology* 51 (1947)
Kantor, H.: »Syro-Palestinian Ivories«, *Journal of Hellenic Studies* 15 (1956)
Kantor, H.: »Ivory Carving in the Mycenaean Period«, *Archaeology* 13 (1960)
Karageorghis, V.: »Notes on Some Mycenaean Survivals in Cyprus During the First Millennium B.C.«, *Kadmos*, I (1962)
Karageorghis, V.: *Treasures in the Cyprus Museum* (Nicosia, 1962)
Karageorghis, V.: »A propos des quelques representations de chars sur des vases chypriotes de l'Age du Fer«, *Bulletin de correspondance hellénique* 90 (1966)
Karageorghis, V.: *Excavations in the Necropolis of Salamis* I (Salamis, vol. 3) (Nicosia, 1967)
Karageorghis, V.: »Homerica from Salamis (Cyprus)« in *Europa: Studien ... Ernst Grumach* (Berlin, 1967)
Karageorghis, V.: *Mycenaean Art from Cyprus* (Nicosia, 1968)
Karageorghis, V.: *Salamis in Cyprus* (London, 1969)
Karageorghis, V.: *Cyprus* (London, 1970)
Karageorghis, V. and Gagniers, J. des: *La Céramique Chypriote de style figure* (Rome, 1974)
Karageorghis, V.: »The Goddess with Uplifted Arms in Cyprus«, *Scripta Minora* (Lund, 1977-1978)
Karo, G.: *Die Schachtgräber von Mykenai* (Munich, 1933)
Karo, G.: »Archäologische Funde u.s.w.«, *Arch. Anz.* (1933)
Karo, G: »Die Perseia von Mykenai«, *American Journal of Archaeology* 38 (1934)
Karo, G: *Führer durch Tiryns*, 2nd ed. (Athens, 1934)
Kelly, T.: »The Calaurian Amphictiony«, *American Journal of Archaeology* 70 (1966)

Kenyon, K. M.: Digging up Jericho (London, 1957)
Kenyon, K. M.: *Jerusalem* (London, 1967)
Kenyon, K. M.: *Royal Cities of the Old Testament* (London, 1971)
Kirk, G. S.: *The Songs of Homer* (Cambridge, 1962)
Kirk, G. S.: *The Language and Background of Homer* (Cambridge, 1964)
Kirk, G. S.: »The Homeric Poems as History«, *The Cambridge Ancient History*, Third ed., Vol. II, pt. 2 (Cambridge, 1975)
Kirk, G. S.: *Homer and the Oral Tradition* (New York, 1976)
Kitchen, K. A.: *Pharaoh Triumphant: The Life and Times of Ramesses II* (Warminster, 1982)
Kleiner, Diana E. E.: *Roman Sculpture* (New Haven, 1992)
Kleiner, Diana E. E.: *Cleopatra and Rome* (London, 2005)
Klengel, H.: »Anatolia (Hittites) and the Levant«, *The Oxford Handbook of the Archaeology of the Levant c. 8000-332 BCE* (eds. M. L. Steiner amd A. E. Killebrew) (Oxford, 2014)
Knossos, The Sanctuary of Demeter (London, 1973)
Körte, G. and A.: Gordion (Berlin, 1904)
Kokkinos, N. in *Ancient West & East* 8 (2009)
Kraft, John C., Kayal, Ilhan, Erol, Oguz: »Geomorphic Reconstructions in the Environs of Ancient Troy«, *Science* 209 (15 August 1980)
Kübler, K. and Kraiker, W.: *Kerameikos* I (Berlin, 1939)
Kübler, K.: *Kerameikos* IV (Berlin, 1943)
Kübler, K.: *Kerameikos* V. 1.1 (Berlin, 1954)
Kübler, K.: *Kerameikos* VI. 2. 2 (Berlin, 1970)
Kunze, E.: »Zur Geschichte und zu den Denkmälern Olympias« in *100 Jahre deutsche Ausgrabung in Olympia* (Munich, 1972)
Kurtz, D. C. and Boardman, J.: *Greek Burial Customs* (London, 1971)
Kyle McCarter Jr., P.: *The Antiquity of the Greek Alphabet and Early Phoenician Scripts* (Ann Arbor, 1975)
Kyle, D. G.: »Greek Athletic Competitions: The Ancient Olympics and More« in *A Companion to Sport and Spectacle in Greek and Roman Antiquity* (eds. Christesen, P. and Kyle, D. G.) (Singapore, 2014)
Lacy, A. D.: *Greek Pottery in the Bronze Age* (London, 1967)
Lamb, W.: *Greek and Roman Bronzes* (New York, 1929)
Lamb, W.: »Grey Wares from Lesbos«, *Journal of Hellenic Studies* 52 (1932)
Lancel, Serge: *Carthage A History* (Oxford, 1995)
Lange, K. and Hirmer, M.: *Egypt*, 4th ed. (London, 1968)
Langlotz, E.: *Ancient Greek Sculpture of South Italy and Sicily* (tr. A. Hicks) (New York, 1965)
Lapatin, K.: *Mysteries of the Snake Goddess* (Boston, 2002)
Lascelles, J.: *Troy The World Deceived – Homer's Guide to Pergamum* (Victoria, BC, 2005)
Latacz, J.: *Troy and Homer* (NY, 2004)
Lazarides, D. I.: »Greek Athletics« in *The Archaic Period* (1975)

Leaf, W.: *Strabo on the Troad* (London, 1923)
Legge, J.: *The Chinese Classics*
Lehmann, J.: *The Hittites* (NY, 1977)
Leighton, R.: *Sicily Before History* (Ithaca, 1999)
Levi, D.: »Early Hellenic Pottery of Crete«, *Hesperia* 14 (1945)
Levi, P.: *Atlas of the Greek World* (NY, 1982)
Lindsay, J.: *Cleopatra* (1971)
Littauer, M. A.: »The Military Use of the Chariot in the Aegean in the Late Bronze Age«, *American Journal of Archaeology* 76 (1972)
Lloyd, A. B.: *Herodotus, Book II; Introduction* (Leiden, 1975)
Lloyd, S.: *The Art of the Ancient Near East* (New York, 1961)
Long, R. D.: »A Re-examination of the Sothic Chronology of Egypt«, *Kronos* II:4 (Summer-1977); reprinted with permission from *Orientalia*, Vol. 43 (Nova Series – 1974)
L'Orange, H. P.: *The Roman Empire Art Forms and Civic Life* (Milan, 1985)
Lorimer, H. L.: *Homer and the Monuments* (London, 1950)
Lorton, David: *Hatshepsut, the Queen of Sheba and Immanuel Velikovsky*, written in 1984, unpublished and revised for publication on the WWW in 1999
Lost Civilizations (eds. Bourbon, F. and De Fabianis, V. M.) (NY, 1998)
Luce, J. V.: *Lost Atlantis* (New York, 1969)
Luce, J. V.: *Homer and the Heroic Age* (London, 1975)
Luce, J. V.: *Celebrating Homer's Landscapes* (New Haven, 1998)
Luckenbill, D. D.: »Jadanan and Javan (Danaans and Ionians)«, *Zeitschrift für Assyriologie* 28 (1914)
Lucretius: *De Rerum Natura*
Lullies, R. and Hirmer, M.: *Greek Sculpture* (New York, 1960, rev. ed.)
Lykurgus: *In Leocrantem*
MacDonald, W. L.: *The Architecture of the Roman Empire* (New Haven, 1982)
MacDonald, W. L.: *Pantheon* (Cambridge, 1976)
MacKendrick, P.: *The Greek Stones Speak* (NY, 1966)
MacKendrick, P.: *The North African Stones Speak* (Chapel Hill, 1980)
Mackenzie, D.: »Cretan Palaces and the Aegean Civilization III«, *Annual of the British School at Athens* 13 (1906-07)
Macqueen, J. G.: *The Hittites and their contemporaries in Asia Minor*, rev. ed. (NY, 1986)
MacQuitty, W.: *Abu Simbel* (NY, 1965)
Macrobius: *Saturnalia*
Mahr, A. et al.: *The Mecklenburg Collection, etc.* (New York, 1934)
Malek, J.: *Egyptian Art* (London, 1999)
Mallowan, M.: *Nimrud and Its Remains* II (London, 1966)
Mallwitz, A.: *Olympia und seine Bauten* (Munich, 1972)
Manetho: *Aegyptiaca*
Manning, S. W.: »Chronology and Terminology« in *The Oxford Handbook of the Bronze Age Aegean* (ed. E. H. Cline) (Oxford, 2010)

Mansuelli, G. A.: The Art of Etruria and Early Rome (New York, 1965)
Manuel, Frank: Isaac Newton, Historian (Harvard University Press, 1963)
Marek, C.: In the Land of a Thousand Gods (A History of Asia Minor in the Ancient World) (Princeton, 2016)
Marinatos, S.: »The Volcanic Destruction of Minoan Crete«, Antiquity XIII (1939)
Marinatos, S.: »Numerous Years of Joyful Life«, Annual of the British School at Athens 46 (1951)
Marinatos, S. and Hirmer, M.: Crete and Mycenae (New York, 1960)
Marinatos, S.: Excavations at Thera VII (Athens, 1976)
Markoe, G. E.: Phoenicians (Los Angeles, 2000)
Mark, S.: From Egypt to Mesopotamia (London, 1997)
Martin, L. H.: Hellenistic Religions (NY, 1987)
Martin, T. R.: Ancient Greece From Prehistoric to Hellenistic Times (London, 1996)
Matyszak, P.: Hercules The First Superhero (Canada, 2015)
Matz, F.: The Art of Crete and Early Greece (tr. by A. E. Keep) (New York, 1962)
Maxwell-Kyslop, K. P.: Western Asiatic Jewelry, ca. 3000-612 B.C. (London, 1971)
Mazzarino, S.: Fra Oriente e Occidente (Florence, 1947)
McDonald, W. A.: Progress into the Past (New York, 1967)
McDonald, J. K.: House of Eternity; The Tomb of Nefertari (Los Angeles, 1996)
McFadden, G. H. and Sjöqvist, E.: »A Late Cypriot III Tomb from Kourion Kaloriziki No. 40«, American Journal of Archaeology 58 (1954)
McNeill, W. H.: The Rise of the West (Chicago, 1963)
Megaw, A. H. S.: »Archaeology in Greece, 1964-65«, Archaeological Reports 1964-65
Meissner, B. in Orientalistische Literaturzeitung (1917)
Mellersh, H.E.L.: The Destruction of Knossos (London, 1970)
Mellink, M. J.: »Mita, Mushki, and the Phrygians«, Anadolu Arastirmalari (Istanbul, 1955)
Mellink, M. J.: »Archaeology in Asia Minor«, Journal of American Archaeology vol 63, no. 1 (January, 1959)
Mellink, M. J.: »Postscript on Nomadic Art« in Dark Ages and Nomads c. 1000 B.C.; Studies in Iranian and Anatolian Archaeology (ed. M. J. Mellink) (Leiden, 1964)
Mellink, M. J.: »Phrygian«, The Dictionary of Art 24 (ed. Jane Turner) (NY, 1996)
Mentz, A.: »Die Urgeschichte des Alphabets«, Rheinisches Museum für Philologie 85 (1936)
Messerschmidt in Keilschrifttexte aus Assur historischen Inhalts vol. I, Nr. 75
Meyer, E.: Geschichte des Alterthums I (Stuttgart, 1884)
Michalowski, K.: Art of Ancient Egypt (NY, 1968)
Michaud, J. P.: »Chronique des Fouilles en 1973«, Bulletin de correspondance hellénique 98 (1974)
Mieroop, Marc Van De: A History of Ancient Egypt (2004)
Mieroop, Marc Van De: A History of Ancient Egypt (2nd ed., 2021)
Miles, R.: Carthage Must Be Destroyed (NY, 2010)
Miller, M.: The Sicilian Colony Dates: Studies in Chronography I (SUNY Press, Albany, 1972)
Miller, S. G.: Ancient Greek Athletics (New Haven, 2004)

Miller, S. G.: »The Date of Olympic Festivals«, *Mitteilungen des Deutschen Archäologischen Instituts: Athenische Abteilung* 90 (1975)
Milojcic, V.: »Die dorische Wanderung im Lichte der vorgeschichtlichen Funde«, *Arch. Anz.* (1948-1949)
Minns, E. H.: *Scythian and Greeks* (Cambridge, 1913)
Mireaux, Emile: *Les poèmes homériques et l'histoire grecque* (Paris, 1948-49)
Mitten, D. G. and Doeringer, S. F.: *Master Bronzes from the Classical World* (Los Angeles, 1968)
Modona, A. N.: *A Guide to Etruscan Antiquities* (Florence, 1954)
Moller, A.: *Naukratis* (NY, 2001)
Monumentality in Etruscan and Early Roman Architecture (eds. M. L. Thomas and G. E. Meyers) (2012)
Moortgat, A.: »Mesopotamia«, *Encyclopedia of World Art* IX (NY, 1964)
Morgan II, C. H.: »The Terracotta Figurines from the North Slope of the Acropolis«, *Hesperia* 4 (1935)
Morris, S. P.: *Daidalos and the Origins of Greek Art* (Princeton, 1992)
Moscati, S.: *The World of the Phoenicians* (tr. A. Hamilton) (London, 1968)
Moscati, S.: *The World of the Phoenicians* (NY, 1970)
Moscati, S. et al.: *The Phoenicians* (NY, 1999)
Moser, M. E.: »The Origins of the Etruscans: New Evidence for an Old Question« in *Etruscan Italy* (ed. J. F. Hall) (1996)
Mosso, A.: *The Dawn of Mediterranean Civilization* (New York, 1911)
Müller, K.: *Tiryns III Die Architektur der Burg und des Palastes* (Augsburg, 1930)
Müller, V.: »The Beginnings of Monumental Sculpture in Greece«, *Metropolitan Museum Studies*, 5(2) (1936)
Muller, H. W.: »Egyptian Art«, *Encyclopedia of World Art*, IV (NY, 1961)
Murphie, D. F.: »Another Velikovsky Affray«, *Chronology & Catastrophism Review* 1991:1
Murphie, D. F.: »Testing Rohl's Test of Time«, *Aeon* V:l (Nov. 1997)
Murphie, D. F.: »After 200 Years It's Time to Get Serious About Dynasty XVIII and Tuthmose III«, *Aeon* V:3 (Dec. 1998)
Murray, A. S.: *Handbook of Greek Archaeology* (New York, 1892)
Murray, A. S., Smith, A. H., Walters, H. B.: *Excavations in Cyprus* (London, 1900)
Murray, O.: *Early Greece*, 2nd ed. (Cambridge, MA, 1993)
Mustili in *Annuario della R. Scuola Archeologica di Atene* XV-XVI (1932-33)
Mycenaean Studies (ed. E.L. Bennet, Jr.) (University of Wisconsin Press, 1964)
Myers, J. V. and Greenberg, L. M.: »Theomachy in the Theater: On the Fringes of the Collective Amnesia«, *Kronos* I:2 (June, 1975)
Mylonas, G. (ed.): *Studies Presented to P. M. Robinson* I (St. Louis, 1951)
Mylonas, G.: »The Cemeteries of Eleusis and Mycenae«, *Proceedings of the American Philosophical Society* 99 (1955)
Mylonas, G.: *Ancient Mycenae* (Princeton, 1957)
Mylonas, G.: *Aghios Kosmas* (Princeton, 1959)
Mylonas, G.: *Eleusis and the Eleusian Mysteries* (Princeton, 1961)
Mylonas, G.: »Priam's Troy and the Date of its Fall«, *Hesperia* 33 (1964)

Mylonas, G.: *Mycenae and the Mycenaean Age* (Princeton, 1966)
Mylonas, G.: »The Cult Center of Mycenae«, (English summary), *Pragmateiai tes Akademias Athenon*, 33 (1972)
Mylonas, G.: *Ho Taphikos Kyklos B ton Mykenon* (Athens, 1973)
Myres, J. L.: *Handbook of the Cesnola Collection of Antiquities from Cyprus* (New York, 1914)
Myres, J. L.: »Homer and the Monuments: A Review«, *Antiquity* 25 (1951)
Mysteries of the Ancient World (ed. J. Flanders) (London, 1998)
Naster, P.: *L'Asie mineure et l'Assyrie* (Louvain, 1938)
Neer, R. T.: *Greek Art and Archaeology* (NY, 2012)
Negev, A.: *Archaeological Encyclopaedia of the Holy Land* (New York,1972)
New Perspectives in Early Greek Art, ed. D. Buitron-Oliver (London, 1991)
Newgrosh, B.: *Chronology at the Crossroads* (2007)
Newton, Isaac: *The Chronologyes of Ancient Kingdoms Amended* (London, 1728)
Nicholls, R. V.: »Greek Votive Statuettes and Religious Continuity, ca. 1200-700 BC« in *Auckland Classical Essays Presented to E.M. Blaiklock* (ed. B. Harris) (New Zealand, 1970)
Nicolson, A.: *The Mighty Dead Why Homer Matters* (London, 2014)
Niese, B.: *Die Entwicklung der homerischen Poesie* (Berlin, 1882)
Nilsson, M. P.: *The Minoan-Mycenaean Religion and Its Survival in Greek Religion* (Lund, 1927)
Nilsson, M. P.: *Homer and Mycenae* (London, 1933)
Ninkovich, D. and Heezen, B.: »Santorin Tephra«, *Colston Papers*, Vol. 17 (1965)
»Notes on Art and Archaeology«, *The Academy*, vol. 42, No. 1069 (29 Oct., 1892)
Notopoulos, J. A.: »Homer, Hesiod and the Achaean Heritage of Oral Poetry«, *Hesperia* 29 (1960)
Nylander, C.: »The Fall of Troy«, *Antiquity* 37 (1963)
Oakeshott, N. R.: »Horned-head Vase Handles«, *Journal of Hellenic Studies* 86 (1966)
Ohnefalsch-Richter, M.: *Kypros, the Bible and Homer* (tr. S. Hermann) (London, 1893)
Olympia, Die Ergebnisse der von dem deutschen Reich veranstalteten Ausgrabungen (eds. E. Curtius and F. Adler), 10 vols. (Berlin, 1890-97)
»On Sothic Dating: A Special Supplement«, *Kronos* VI:1 (Fall-1980), Greenberg, Parker, Rose, Mage, Sammer, Velikovsky, Dayton, Gammon and James
Orrieux, C. and Pantel, P. S.: *A History of Ancient Greece* (transl. by J. Lloyd, 1999)
Osborne, R.: *Greece in the Making 1200-479 BC* (NY, 1996)
Osborne, R.: Archaic and Classical Greek Art (NY, 1998)
Ovid: *Fasti*, transl. by J. Frazer
Ovid: *Metamorphoses*
Padgug, R. A.: »Eleusis and the Union of Attica«, *Greek, Roman and Byzantine Studies* 13 (1972)
Page, D.: *History and the Homeric Iliad* (Berkeley, Ca., 1959)
Page, D.: »The Historical Sack of Troy«, *Antiquity*, Vol. XXXIII (1959)
Page, D.: *The Santorini Volcano and the Desolation of Minoan Crete* (London, 1970)
Pallottino, M.: *L'Origine degli Etruschi* (Rome, 1947)

Pallottino, M.: *Etruscan Painting* (tr. M. Stanley & S. Gilbert) (Geneva, 1952)
Pallottino, M.: »Etrusco-Italic Art« in the *Encyclopedia of World Art* V (NY, 1961)
Papachadzis, N. D.: »Religion in the Archaic Period« in *The Archaic Period* (eds. G. Christopoulos and J. Bastias; tr. P. Sherrard) (London, 1975)
Pallottino, M.: *The Etruscans* (London, 1975)
Palmer, L.: *Minos*, vol. IV
Palmer, L.: *Mycenaeans and Minoans* (London, 1962)
Palmer, L.: *The Interpretation of Mycenaean Greek Texts* (Oxford, 1963)
Palmerance, L.: »The Final Collapse of Santorini (Thera) 1400 B.C. or 1200 B.C.?« *Studies in Mediterranean Archaeology* 26 (Goteborg, 1970)
Papaioannou, K.: *The Art of Greece* (NY, 1989)
Parker, V.: *A History of Greece 1300-30 BC* (Chichester, 2014)
Parrot, A.: *The Arts of Assyria* (NY, 1961)
Pausanias: *Description of Greece*
Payne, H.: *Necrocorinthia* (Oxford, 1931)
Pedley, J. G.: *Greek Art and Archaeology*, 2nd ed. (London, 1998)
Pelling, C.: »The Augustan Empire, 43 B.C. – A.D. 69«, *Cambridge Ancient History* X, 2nd ed. (Cambridge, 2004)
Pendlebury, J. D. S.: *Aegyptiaca* (Cambridge, 1930)
Pendlebury, J. D. S.: *The Archaeology of Crete* (London, 1939)
Perrot, G. and Chipiez, C.: *History of Art in Phrygia, Lydia, Caria and Lycia* (NY, 1892)
Perrot, G. and Chipiez, C.: *History of Art in Primitive Greece* II (London, 1894)
Peruzzi, E.: *Mycenaeans In Early Latium* (Rome, 1980)
Phillips, J.: *Oxford Handbook of the Bronze Age Aegean* (Oxford, 2012)
Picard, C.: »Installations culturelles retrouvées au Tophet de Salambo«, *Rivista degli Studi Orientali* 42 (1967)
Picard, G. C. and C.: *The Life and Death of Carthage* (tr. by D. Collon) (London, 1968)
Picard, G. C.: *La vie quotidienne à Carthage au temps d'Hannibal* (Paris, 1958)
Pierides, A.: *Jewelry in the Cyprus Museum* (Nicosia, 1971)
Pindar: *Olympian Odes*
Pindar: »Seventh Olympian Ode«, transl. by J. E. Sandys (*Loeb Classical Library*, 1919)
Pirkei Rabbi Elieser
Plantzos, D.: *Greek Art and Archaeology c. 1200-30 BC* (Atlanta, 2016)
Plato: *Kritias*
Plato: *Laws*
Plato: *The Statesman*
Plato: *Timaeus*
Platon, N.: »Cretan-Mycenaean Art«, *Encyclopaedia of World Art* IV (New York, 1958)
Pliny: *Natural History*, transl. by J. Bostock and H.T. Riley (London, 1853)
Plommer, H.: »Shadowy Megara«, *Journal of Hellenic Studies* 97 (1977)
Pollini, J.: *From Republic to Empire* (Norman, OK, 2013)
Pomerance, L.: »The Final Collapse of Santorini (Thera)«, *Studies in Mediterranean Archaeology* vol. XXVI (Göteborg, 1970)

Pomerance, L.: *The Final Collapse of Santorini* (Thera) (Göteborg, 1971)
Pomeroy, S. B. et al.: *Ancient Greece: A Political, Social, and Cultural History* (NY, 1999)
Popham, M. R. and Sackett, L. H.: *Excavations at Lefkandi, Euboea 1964-66* (London, 1968)
Porada, E.: »Notes on the Sarcophagus of Ahiram«, *Journal of the Ancient Near Eastern Society of Columbia University*, 5 (1973)
Porter, R. M.: »Shishak-Ramesses II or Ramesses III?«, *Chronology and Catastrophism Review* XVI (1994)
Pottier, E.: »Observations sur la céramique mycénienne«, *Revue Archéologique* 28 (1896)
Pottier, E.: »Documents céramiques du Musee du Louvre«, *Bulletin de correspondance hellénique* 31 (1907)
Poulsen, F.: *Der Orient und die frühgriechische Kunst* (Berlin, 1912)
Prayon, F.: »Tomb Architecture« in *The Etruscans* (ed. M. Torelli) (2001)
Preziosi, D. and Hitchcock, L. A.: *Aegean Art and Architecture* (NY, 1999)
Pritchard, J. B.: *Ancient Near Eastern Texts Relating to the Old Testament* (Princeton, 1955)
Pritchard, J. B.: *Gibeon* (Princeton, 1962)
Pursat, J.-Cl.: *Les Ivoires Mycéniens, etc.* (Paris, 1977)
Putnam, M. C. J.: *VIRGIL'S AENEID (Interpretation And Influence)* (London, 1995)
Ramsay, W. M.: »Studies in Asia Minor«, *Journal of Hellenic Studies* 3 (1882)
Ramsay, W. M.: »Sepulchral Customs in Ancient Phrygia«, *Journal of Hellenic Studies* 5 (1884)
Ramsay, W. M.: »A Study of Phrygian Art«, *Journal of Hellenic Studies* 9 (1888)
Ramsay, W. M.: »A Study of Phrygian Art (Part II)«, *Journal of Hellenic Studies* 10 (1889)
Rason, J.: »La Cadmée, Knossos et le lineaire B«, *Revue archéologique* (1977)
Rayevsky, D. S.: »Animal Style«, *The Dictionary of Art* 2 (1996)
Reade, M. G.: »Shishak, the Kings of Judah and Some Synchronisms«, *Chronology and Catastrophism Review* 1997:2
Reade, M. G.: »Necho = Ramesses II?«, *Chronology and Catastrophism Review* 2000:2
Rehak, P.: »Aeneas or Numa? Rethinking the Meaning of the Ara Pacis Augustae«, *The Art Bulletin*, Vol 83, No. 2 (June, 2001)
Reichel, W.: *Homerische Waffen* 2nd ed. (Vienna, 1901)
Reinach, S.: »La représentation du galop dans l'art ancient et moderne« in *Revue archéologique*, 3e série, tome XXXVIII (1901)
Rice, M.: *Egypt's Making* (1991)
Rice, T. T.: *The Scythians* (London, 1975)
Richardson Jr., L.: *A New Topographical Dictionary of Ancient Rome* (London, 1992)
Richter, G.: *Kouroi* (London, 1960)
Richter, G.: *The Archaic Gravestones of Attica* (London, 1961)
Richter, G.: *The Sculpture and Sculptors of the Greeks*, rev. ed. (New Haven, 1962)
Richter, G.: *Engraved Gems of the Greeks and the Etruscans* (New York, 1968)

Richter, G.: Korai (London, 1968)
Richter, G.: *A Handbook of Greek Art* (New York, 1969)
Ridgway, B.S.: *The Archaic Style in Greek Sculpture*, 2nd ed. (Chicago, 1993)
Ridington, W. R.: *The Minoan-Mycenaean Background of Greek Athletics* (Philadelphia, 1935)
Rieu, E. V.: *The Iliad* (London, 1953)
Rix, Z.: »The Great Fear«, *Kronos* I:1 (April, 1975)
Robertson, D. S.: *Greek and Roman Architecture* (Cambridge University Press, 1969)
Robertson, M.: *A History of Greek Art* I (New York. 1975)
Robinson, D. M.: »Haus« in *Pauly-Wissowa's Real-Encylopädie*, Supp. 7 (1940)
Robinson, H.: »Excavations at Corinth: Temple Hill, 1968-1972«, *Hesperia* 45 (1976)
Rodenwaldt, G.: »Zur Entstehung der Monumentalen Architektur in Griechenland«, *Ath. Mitt.* 44 (1919)
Rodenwaldt, G.: »Mykenische Studien I«, *Jahrbuch des deutschen archäologischen Instituts* 34 (1919)
Rohl, D. M.: *Pharaohs and Kings (aka A Test of Time)* (NY, 1995)
Rolley, C.: »Les trépieds à cuve cluée«, *Fouilles des Delphes* 5.3, (Paris, 1977)
Roscher, W. H.: *Ausführliches Lexikon der griechischen und römischen Mythologie (1884-1937)*
Rose, L. E.: *Sun, Moon, and Sothis* (Deerfield Beach, 1999)
Rose, L. E. and Vaughan, R.C.: »Velikovsky and the Sequence of Planetary Orbits«, *Pensée* IVR VIII (Summer, 1974)
Rossini, O.: *ARA PACIS* (Rome, 2009)
Rostovzeff, M.: *Iranians and Greeks in South Russia* (Oxford, 1922)
Rudolph, W.: »Tiryns 1968« in *Tiryns* V (ed. U. Janzen) (Mainz, 1971)
Rudolph, W.: »Tiryns: Unterburg 1968 etc.« in *Tiryns* VIII (ed. U. Jantzen) (Mainz, 1975)
Ruggiero, P. de: *Mark Antony: A Plain Blunt Man* (Barnsley, 2013)
Runnels, C. and Murray, P. M.: *Greece Before History* (Stanford, 2001)
Rupke, J.: *Pantheon* (Princeton, 2016)
Samuel, A.: *The Mycenaeans in History* (Englewood Cliffs, 1966)
Sandars, N.K.: »A Minoan Cemetery on Upper Gypsades: The Bronzes«, *Annual of the British School at Athens* 53-54 (1958-9)
Sandars, N.K.: The Sea Peoples (London, 1978)
Sandys, J.: *The Odes of Pindar* (New York, 1924)
Sansone, D.: *Greek Athletics and the Genesis of Sport* (LA, 1988)
Santerre, H. Gallet de: *Délos primitive et archaïque* (Paris, 1958)
Sayce, A. H.: »The Inscriptions Found at Hissarlik« in H. Schliemann: *Ilios: the City and Country of the Trojans* (New York, 1881)
Schachermeyr, F.: *Poseidon und die Entstehung des griechischen Götterglauben* (Wien, 1950)
Schachermeyr, F. in *Minoica: Festschrift zum 80. Geburtstag von Johannes Sundwall* (ed. Grumach, Ernst) (Berlin, Boston, 1958)
Schachermeyr, F.: *Die ägäische Frühzeit*, Bd. 2, *Die mykenische Zeit und die Gesittung von Thera* (Wien, 1976)

Schäfer, H.: Ägyptische Goldschmiedearbeiten (Berlin, 1910)
Schäfer, J.: Studien zu den griechischen Reliefpithoi des 8.-6. Jahrhunderts v. Chr. aus Kreta, Rhodos, Tenos und Boiotien (Kalmünz, 1957)
Schaeffer, C. F. A.: Stratigraphie comparée et chronologie de l'Asie occidentale (IIIe et IIe millenaires) (Oxford University Press, 1948)
Schaeffer, C. F. A.: »Nouvelles découvertes à Enkomi (Chypre)«, in Comptes rendus, Académie des Inscriptions et Belles Lettres (Paris, 1949)
Schaeffer, C. F. A.: Ugaritica II (Paris, 1949)
Schaeffer, C. F. A.: Alasia I (Paris, 1971)
Schiering, W.: »Masken am Hals Kretisch-mykenischer und früh-geometrischer Tongefässe«, Jahrbuch des deutschen archäologischen Instituts 79 (1964)
Schliemann: Troy and Its Remains (London, 1875)
Schliemann, H.: Mycenae (New York, 1880)
Schliemann, H.: Ilios: the City and Country of the Trojans (New York, 1881)
Schliemann, H.: Tiryns (New York, 1885)
Schmidt, H.: »Die Keramik der verschiedenen Schichten« in Dörpfeld: Troja und Ilion (Athens, 1902)
Schmitt-Brandt, R.: »Die Oka-Tafeln in neuer Sicht«, Studi Micenei ed Egeo-Anatolici 7 (Incunabula Graeca 28) (1968)
Schnabel, P.: »Die babylonische Chronologie in Berossos Babyloniaca«, Mitteilungen, Vorderasiatisch-ägyptische Gesellschaft (1908)
Schöbel, H.: The Ancient Olympic Games (Princeton, 1966)
Schofield, J. N.: »Megiddo« in Archaeology and Old Testament Study (ed. D. W. Thomas) (New York, 1967)
Schofield, L.: »Lefkandi«, The Dictionary of Art 19 (ed. J. Turner) (NY, 1996)
Schuchhardt, C.: Schliemann's Excavations (tr. E. Sellers) (New York, 1891)
Schuchhardt, C.: Schliemann's Discoveries of the Ancient World (NY, 1891/1979)
Schuchhardt, W.-H.: Greek Art (NY, 1972)
Schulten, A.: Tartessos, second ed. (Madrid, 1945)
Schweitzer, B.: Greek Geometric Art (tr. P. & C. Usborne) (New York, 1971)
Scranton, R.: Aesthetic Aspects of Ancient Art (Chicago, 1964)
Scully, S.: Homer and the Sacred City (Cornell, 1994)
Searls, H. E. and Dinsmoor, W. B.: »The Date of the Olympia Heraeum«, American Journal of Archaeology 49 (1945)
Seeher, Jürgen in The Oxford Handbook of Ancient Anatolia (eds. S. R. Steadman and G. McMahon) (NY, 2011)
Sellar, W. E.: Roman Poets of the Augustan Age (Oxford, 1897)
Sernander, R.: »Klimaverschlechterung, Postglaziale« in Reallexikon der Vorgeschichte (ed. Max Ebert) VII (1926)
Servius: ad Aeneidem
Seward, Desmond: Napoleon and Hitler: A Comparative Biography (London, 1988)
Sheppard, S.: Troy Last War of the Heroic Age (Oxford, 2014)
Shipley, G.: »Archaic Into Classical«, Greek Civilization (ed. B. A. Sparkes) (Oxford, 1998)
*Shipley, L.: The Etruscans Lost Civilizations (2017)

Shuckburgh, E. S.: *Augustus Caesar* (NY, 1995 reprint)
Sicily from Aeneas to Augustus (eds. C. Smith and J. Serrati) (Edinburgh, 2000)
Siliotti, A.: *Egypt: Splendors of an Ancient Civilization* (NY, 1998)
Siliotti, A.: *Egypt Lost and Found* (NY, 1999)
Simpson, R. Hope and Lazenby, J. F.: *The Catalogue of the Ships in Homer's Iliad* (Oxford, 1970)
Simpson, W. K.: »The Vessels with engraved designs and the Repoussé Bowl from the Tell Basta Treasure«, *Journal of Near Eastern Studies* 24 (1965)
Sinos, S.: *Die vorklassischen Hausformen in der Ägäis* (Mainz, 1971)
Sjöqvist, E.: »Enkomi« in E. Gjerstad et al.: *The Swedish Cyprus Expedition* I (Stockholm, 1934)
Sjöqvist, E.: review of Catling's *Cypriot Bronzework in the Mycenaean World*, *Gnomon* 39 (1965)
Sjöqvist, E.: *Sicily and the Greeks* (Chicago University Press, 1973)
Skeat, T. C.: *The Dorians in Archaeology* (London, 1939)
Smith, C. in »Egypt and Mycenaean Antiquities«, *The Classical Review* 6 (1892)
Smith, S.: *Alalakh and Chronology* (London, 1940)
Smith, W. S.: *The Art and Architecture of Ancient Egypt* (Baltimore, 1958)
Smith, W. S.: *Interconnections in the Ancient Near East* (London, 1965)
Smith, W. S.: *The Art and Architecture of Ancient Egypt*, rev. by W. K. Simpson, 3rd ed. (London, 1998)
Smithson, E. L.: »The Tomb of a Rich Athenian Lady, ca. 850 B.C.«, *Hesperia* 37 (1909)
Snodgrass, A. M.: *Early Greek Armour and Weapons* (Edinburgh, 1964)
Snodgrass, A. M.: *Arms and Armour of the Greeks* (Ithaca, New York, 1967)
Snodgrass, A. M.: *The Dark Age of Greece* (Edinburgh, 1971)
Snodgrass, A. M.: »Late Burials from Mycenae«, *Annual of the British School at Athens* 68 (1973)
Snodgrass, A. M.: »An Historical Homeric Society?« *Journal of Hellenic Studies* 94 (1974)
Snodgrass, A. M.: review of Greenhalgh's *Early Greek Warfare* in *Journal of Hellenic Studies* 94 (1974)
Snodgrass, A. M.: review of Hammond's *A History of Macedonia*, *Journal of Hellenic Studies* 94 (1974)
Snodgrass, A. M.: Archaeology and the Rise of the Greek State (Cambridge, 1977)
Snodgrass, A. M.: *Archaic Greece: The Age of Experiment* (Los Angeles, 1980)
Soren, D. et al.: Carthage: *Uncovering the Mysteries and Splendors of Ancient Tunisia* (NY, 1990)
Sourvinou-Inwood, Ch.: »Movements of Populations in Attica at the End of the Mycenaean Period« in *Bronze Age Migrations in the Aegean* (1974)
Southern, P.: *Mark Antony* (Stroud, 1998)
Southern, P.: *Mark Antony A Life* (Stroud, 2010)
Spaeth, B. S.: *The Roman Goddess Ceres* (Austin, 1996)
Spivey, N.: *Greek Art* (London, 1997)

Sprenger, M. and Bartoloni, C.: *The Etruscans Their History, Art, and Architecture* (NY, 1983)
Stafford, E.: *Herakles* (NY, 2012)
Stanford, W. B.: The Odyssey of Homer II (New York, 1967)
Stansbury-O'Donnell, M. D.: *A History of Greek Art* (Chichester, 2015)
Starr, C. G.: *The Origins of Greek Civilization* (New York, 1961)
Stecchini, Livio C.: »The Origin of the Alphabet«, *The American Behavioral Scientist* IV.6 (February, 1961)
Stewart, A.: *Greek Sculpture: An Exploration*, Vol. I (New Haven, 1990)
*Stoddart, S. K. F.: *Historical Dictionary of the Etruscans* (2009), »Chronology«, xx-xxii
Strabo: *Geography*, transl. by H. L. Jones, Loeb Classical Library (1917)
Strommenger, E.: *5000 Years of the Art of Mesopotamia* (NY, 1964)
Strong, A.: *The Phoenicians in History and Legend* (2002)
Strong, D. E.: *Greek and Roman Gold and Silver Plate* (Glasgow, 1966)
Strong, P.: *The Classical World* (NY, 1965)
Stubbings, F. H.: »The Rise of Mycenaean Civilization« *The Cambridge Ancient History* II, part 1 (Cambridge, 1973)
Stubbings, F. H.: »The Recession of Mycenaean Civilization«, *The Cambridge Ancient History* II, 3rd ed., part 2 (Cambridge, 2000)
Stubbings, F.: *Mycenaean Pottery from the Levant* (Cambridge, 1951)
Stubbings, F.: »Arms and Armour« in Wace and Stubbings: *A Companion to Homer* (London, 1962)
Stubbings, F.: »Crafts and industries« in Wace and Stubbings: *A Companion to Homer* (London, 1962)
Studniczka, F.: »Der Rennwagen in Syrisch-phoinikischen Gebiet«, *Jahrbuch des deutschen archäologischen Instituts* 22 (1907)
Studniczka, F.: »Die Fibula des Odysseus« in E. Bathe: *Homer 11.2 Odyssey* (Leipzig, 1929)
Stuttard, D. and Moorhead, S. (among others): *Antony, Cleopatra and the Fall of Egypt* (London, 2012)
Styrenius, C. G.: *Submycenaean Studies* (Lund, 1967)
Swaddling, J.: *The Ancient Olympic Games* (Austin, 1980)
Sweeney, E.: »Were the Hittites Lydians?«, The Velikovskian V: 1 (2000)
Sweeney, E.: »Ramessides, Medes and Persians«, *The Velikovskian* V:2 (2000)
Sweeney, E.: *Egypt's Ramesside Pharaohs and the Persians* (2021)
Sweeney, N. M.: *Troy – Myth, City, Icon* (London, 2018)
Täckholm, U. in *Opuscula romana* 5 (1965)
Tanner, M.: *The Last Descendant of AENEAS* (New Haven, 1993)
Taylor, J. Du Plat: »Late Cypriot III in the Light of Recent Excavations, etc.«, *Palestine Exploration Fund Quarterly* 88 (1956)
Taylor, T.: »Scythian & Sarmatian Art«, *The Dictionary of Art*, 28 (1996)
Taylor, T.: »Thracian and Dacian Art«, *The Dictionary of Art* 30 (1996)
Taylour, W. D.: *Mycenaean Pottery Italy and Adjacent Areas* (Cambridge, 1958)

Taylour, W. D.: *The Mycenaeans* (NY, 1964)

Taylour, W. D.: »Mycenae, 1968«, *Antiquity* 43 (1969)

Taylour, W. D.: »New Light on Mycenaean Religion«, *Antiquity* 44 (1970)

Taylour, W. D.: »A Note on the Recent Excavations at Mycenae, etc.«, *Annual of the British School at Athens* 68 (1973)

Tegyey, Imre: »Messenia and the catastrophe at the end of Late Helladic III B« in Bronze Age Migrations In the Aegean (ed. R. Crossland and A. Birchall) (London, 1973)

Teixidor, J. in *The Oxford Encyclopaedia of Archaeology in the Near East*, 1 (ed. E.M. Meyers) (NY, 1997)

Terra, Helmut de: *Man and Mammoth in Mexico* (London, 1957)

The Aegean and the Near East (ed. S. Weinberg) (Locust Valley, New York, 1956)

The Ages of Homer – A Tribute To Emily Townsend Vermeule (ed. by Jane B. Carter and Sarah P. Morris) (Austin, 1995)

The Archaic Period (eds. G. Christopoulos and J. Bastias; tr. P. Sherrard) (London, 1975)

The Cambridge Companion to the Aegean Bronze Age (ed. C. W. Shelmerdine) (Cambridge, 2008)

The Cambridge Illustrated History of Ancient Greece (ed. P. Cartledge) (Cambridge, 1998)

The Dictionary of Art (ed. Jane Turner) (NY, 1998)

The Etruscans (ed. M. Torelli) (NY, 2000)

The Etruscan World (ed. J. M. Turfa) (NY, 2013)

The Greek World (ed. H. L. Jones) (Baltimore, 1965)

The Greek World (ed. Anton Powell) (London, 1995)

The Legacy of Mesopotamia (eds. S. Dalley et al.) (NY, 1998)

The Oxford Encyclopedia of Ancient Egypt (ed. in chief Donald B. Redford) (2001)

The Oxford Handbook of Ancient Anatolia (eds. S.R. Steadman and G. McMahon) (NY, 2011)

The Oxford Handbook of the Archaeology of the Levant c. 8000-332 BCE (eds. M. L. Steiner and A. E. Killebrew) (Oxford, 2014)

The Oxford Handbook of the Bronze Age Aegean (ed. E. H. Cline) (Oxford, 2010)

The Oxford Handbook of the Phoenician and Punic Mediterranean (eds. C. Lopez-Ruiz and B. R. Doak) (NY, 2019)

The Oxford History of Ancient Egypt (ed. Ian Shaw) (2002)

The Oxford History of the Ancient Near East, V. II (eds. K. Radner et al.) (NY, 2022)

The Oxford History of the Classical World (eds. J. Boardman et al.) (Oxford, 1987)

The Pantheon: From Antiquity to the Present (eds. T. A. Marder and M. W. Jones) (NY, 2015)

The Phoenicians (ed. Sabatino Moscati) (NY, 1997)

The Trojan War. The Chronicles of Dictys of Crete and Dares the Phrygian (Translated by R. M. Frazer (Jr.)) (Indiana University Press. 1966)

Thomas, C.: »Found: The Dorians«, *Expedition* 20 (1978)

Thomas, C. G. and Conant, C.: *Citadel to City-State* (Bloomington, 1999)
Thomas, C. G. and Conant, C.: *The Trojan War* (London, 2005)
Thompson, D. P.: *The Trojan War* (London, 2004)
Thompson, H. A.: »Activity in the Athenian Agora: 1966-1967«, *Hesperia* 37 (1968)
Thompson, H. A.: »The Tomb of Clytemnestra Revisited«, *University Museum*, Philadelphia (May 1975)
Thucydides: *The Peloponnesian War*
Tiryns (ed. U. Jantzen) (Mainz, 1971)
Tomlinson, R. A.: *Greek Sanctuaries* (London, 1976)
Torelli, M.: *Typology and Structure of Roman Historical Reliefs* (Ann Arbor, 1982)
Torr, C.: *Memphis and Mycenae* (Cambridge, 1896)
Tovar, A.: »On the Position of the Linear B Dialect«, *Mycenaean Studies* (ed. E. L. Bennet, Jr.) (University of Wisconsin Press, 1964)
Toynbee, J.M.C.: *The Ara Pacis Reconsidered And Historical Art In Roman Italy* (1953)
Toynbee, J.M.C.: »The Ara Pacis Augustae«, *Journal of Roman Studies* 51 (1961)
Tractate Sanhedrin
Traill, D. A.: *Schliemann of Troy* (NY, 1995)
Travlos, J.: *Pictorial Dictionary of Ancient Athens* (London, 1971)
Tritsch, F. J.: »The Women of Pylos« in *Minoica* (ed. E. Grumach) (1958)
Troja und Ilion. Ergebnisse der Ausgrabungen in den vorhistorischen Schichten von Ilion 1870-1894 (ed. W. Dörpfeld) (Athens, 1902)
TROY, City, Homer, Turkey (Istanbul, 2012)
Troy From Homer's Iliad to Hollywood Epic (ed. Martin M. Winkler) (Singapore, 2007)
Trump, David H.: *Central and Southern Italy Before Rome* (NY, 1965)
Tsountas, C. and Manatt, J. I.: *The Mycenaean Age* (New York, 1897)
Tyldesley, J.: *Ramesses: Egypt's Greatest Pharaoh* (Penguin, NY, 2000)
Ullman, B.: »How Old is the Greek Alphabet?«, *American Journal of Archaeology* 38 (1934)
Ussishkin, D.: »The Necropolis from the Time of the Kingdom of Judah at Silwan, Jerusalem«, *The Biblical Archaeologist* 33 (1970)
Vacano, O. W. von: *The Etruscans in the Ancient World* (transl. by S. Ogilvie) (Bloomington, 1965)
Vandier, J.: *La famine dans l'Egypte ancienne* (1936)
Vaughan, Agnes Carr: *The Etruscans* (1995 reprint)
Veen, Peter van der: »The Name Shishak - Peter van der Veen replies to Carl Jansen-Winkeln«, *Journal of the Ancient Chronology Forum*, 8 (1999)
Velikovsky, I.: »Theses for the Reconstruction of Ancient History«, *Scripta Academica Hierosolymitana* (1945/46)
Velikovsky, I.: *Worlds in Collision* (NY, 1950)
Velikovsky, I.: *Ages in Chaos* I (Garden City, N.Y., 1952)
Velikovsky, I.: *Earth in Upheaval* (New York, 1955)
Velikovsky, I.: »Astronomy and Chronology«, *Pensée* IV (Spring-Summer, 1973)

Velikovsky, I.: »The Scandal of Enkomi«, *Pensée* IVR X (Winter, 1974-75)
Velikovsky, I.: »Olympia«, *Kronos* I:4 (April 1976)
Velikovsky, I.: *Peoples of the Sea* (Garden City, N.Y., 1977)
Velikovsky, I.: »Astronomy and Chronology«, *Peoples of the Sea* (NY, 1977)
Velikovsky, I.: *Ramses II and His Time* (New York, 1978)
Velleius Paterculus
Ventris, M. and Chadwick J.: *Documents in Mycenaean Greek*, second ed. (Cambridge University Press, 1973)
Verbrugghe, G. P. and Wickersham, J. M.: *BEROSSOS and MANETHO, Introduced and Translated* (Ann Arbor, 1996)
Verdelis, N.: »Anaskaphe Tirynthos«, *Archalocrikon Deltion* 18 (1963)
Verdelis, N.: »Neue geometrische Gräber in Tiryns«, *Ath, Mitt.*, 78 (1963)
Vermeule, E.: »The Mycenaeans in Achaia«, *American Journal of Archaeology* 64 (1960)
Vermeule, E.: »The Fall of the Mycenaean Empire«, *Archaeology* 13 (1960)
Vermeule, E.: *Greece in the Bronze Age* (Chicago, 1964)
Vermeule, E.: »The Decline and End of Minoan and Mycenaean Culture« in *A Land Called Crete* (Northampton, Mass., 1967)
Vermeule, E.: *Greece in the Bronze Age* (Chicago, 1972)
Vermeule, E.: *The Art of the Shaft Graves at Mycenae* (Norman, OK, 1975)
Verzone, P.: *The Art of Europe: The Dark Ages* (New York, 1967)
Vickers, M. and Reynolds, J. M.: »Cyrenaica, 1962-72«, *Archaeological Reports* 1971-2
Vieyra, M.: *Hittite Art 2300-750 B.C.* (London, 1955)
Vinci, F.: »Homer in the Baltic«, *Aeon* VI:2 (Dec. 2001)
Vinci, F.: *The Baltic Origins of Homer's Epic Tales* (Rochester, VT, 2006)
Virgil: *Aeneid*
Vitruvius: *De Architectura*
Voigtländer, W.: *Tiryns* (Athens, 1972)
Vries, K. de: review of Benson's *Horse, Bird & Man*, *American Journal of Archaeology* 76 (1972)
Wace, A. J. B.: »The Palace«, *Annual of the British School at Athens* 25 (1921-3)
Wace, A. J. B.: »The Lion Gate and Grave Circle Area«, *Annual of the British School at Athens* 25 (1921-23)
Wace, A. J. B.: *Mycenae: An Archaeological History and Guide* (Princeton, 1949)
Wace, A. J. B.: »The Last Days of Mycenae«, in *The Aegean and Near East* (ed. S. Weinberg) (Locust Valley, NY, 1956)
Wace, A. J. B. and Stubbings, F.: *A Companion to Homer* (London, 1962)
Wace, H. P. and A. J. B.: »Dress« in Wace-Stubbings: *A Companion to Homer* (London, 1962)
Wace, H. et. al.: *Mycenae Guide* (Meriden, Conn., 1971)
Walters, H. B.: »On Some Antiquities of the Mycenaean Age Recently Acquired by the British Museum«, *Journal of Hellenic Studies* 17 (1897)

Walters, H. B.: *History of Ancient Pottery* I (New York, 1905)
Wardle, K. A.: »A Group of Late Helladic III B Pottery, etc.«, *Annual of the British School at Athens* 68 (1973)
Warmington, B. H.: *Carthage: A History* (NY, 1969)
Warren, P. M.: »Absolute Dating of the Aegean Late Bronze Age«, *Archaeometry* 29, 2 (1987)
Waswo, R.: *The Founding Legend of Western Civilization* (From Virgil to Vietnam) (Hanover, NH, 1997)
Webber, C.: *The Gods of Battle* (Barnsley, 2011)
Webster, T. B. L.: *From Mycenae to Homer* (New York, 1958)
Webster, T. B. L.: »Polity and Society« in Wace-Stubbings: *A Companion to Homer* (London, 1962)
Webster, T. B. L.: *From Mycenae to Homer* (New York, 1964)
Weinstock, S.: »Pax and the 'Ara Pacis'«, *Journal of Roman Studies* 50 (1960)
Welter, G.: *Aigina* (Berlin, 1938)
Westholm, A.: »Amathus« in Gjerstad, E.: *The Swedish Cyprus Expedition* II (Stockholm, 1935)
Westholm, A.: »Built Tombs in Cyprus«, *Opuscula Archaeologica* II (1941)
Wheeler, M.: *Walls of Jericho* (London, 1958)
Whitley, J.: *The Archaeology of Ancient Greece* (NY, 2001)
Whitman, C. H.: *Homer and the Heroic Tradition* (Cambridge, Mass, 1958)
Who Was Who in the Greek World (ed. Diana Bowder) (Oxford, 1982)
Wide, S.: »Aphidna in Nordattika«, *Athenische Mittheilungen*, 21 (1896)
Wiesner, J.: *Fahren und Reiten* (*Archaeologia Homerica*, I F) (Göttingen, 1968)
Wilamowitz-Moellendorf, U. v.: »Oropos und die Graer«, *Hermes* XXI (1886)
Wilkens, Iman: *Where Troy Once Stood* (NY, 1990)
Wilkinson, T.: *The Rise and Fall of Ancient Egypt* (2010)
Wilkinson, T.: *Ramesses The Great* (London, 2023)
Wilson, C.: *The Occult* (NY, 1971)
Wilson, J. in Pritchard, J. B. (ed.) *Ancient Near Eastern Texts*, etc. 2 (Princeton, 1955)
Winter, I. J.: »Phoenician and North Syrian Ivory Carving in Historical Context, Questions of Style and Distribution«, *Iraq* 38 Issue 1 (1976)
Witt, R. E.: *Isis in the Ancient World* (London, 1971)
Wood, F. and K.: *Homer's Secret Iliad: The Epic of the Night Skies Decoded* (1999)
Woodhead, A. G.: *The Greeks in the West* (London, 1962)
Woolf, G.: *The Life and Death of Ancient Cities* (NY, 2020)
Woolley, L.: *Alalakh* (Oxford, 1955)
Woolley, L.: *A Forgotten Kingdom* (London, 1959)
Woolley, L.: *Mesopotamia and the Middle East* (London, 1961)
Woolley, L.: *The Art of the Middle East* (NY, 1961)
Wright, G. E.: »Epic of Conquest«, *Biblical Archaeologist* III No. 3 (1940)
Wright, H. E.: »Climatic Change in Mycenaean Greece«, *Antiquity* 42 (1968)
Wright, J. W. in *American Journal of Archaeology* 84 (1980)

Yadin, Y.: *Hazor* (New York, 1975)

Yakar, Jak: »Anatolian Chronology and Terminology«, *The Oxford Handbook of Ancient Anatolia* (eds. S. R. Steadman and G. McMahon (NY, 2011)

Young, A. M.: *Troy and Her Legend* (Pittsburgh, 1948)

Young, R. S.: *Late Geometric Graves and a Seventh Century Well in the Agora* (Athens, 1939)

Young, R. S.: »The excavations at Yassihuyuk-Gordion, 1950« in *Archaeology* 3 (1950)

Young, R. S.: »Gordion: A Preliminary Report, 1953« in *American Journal of Archaeology* 59 (1955)

Young, R. S.: »Gordion 1956: Preliminary Report« in *American Journal of Archaeology* 61 (1957)

Young, R. S.: »The Royal Tomb at Gordion«, *Archaeology* 10 (1957)

Young, R. S.: »The Nomadic Impact: Gordion« in *Dark Ages and Nomads c. 1000 B. C.* (Leiden, 1964)

Zanker, P.: *The Power of Images in the Age of Augustus* (Ann Arbor, 1990)

Zeuner, F. E.: *The Pleistocene Period* (London, 1945)

Ziolkowski, T.: *Virgil and the Moderns* (Princeton, 1993)

Illustration Credits

Front Cover	Own work using a photo by Orlovic – Own work, CC BY-SA 4.0, https://commons.wikimedia.org/w/index.php?curid=3534971
p. 57, Fig. 1	By Orlovic – Own work (reformatted to grayscale), CC BY-SA 4.0, https://commons.wikimedia.org/w/index.php?curid=3534971
p. 57, Fig. 2	By Ali Hakan Ilban – Own work (reformatted to grayscale, cropped and enhanced), CC BY-SA 4.0, https://commons.wikimedia.org/w/index.php?curid=91068933
p. 170, Fig. 1	From A. J. B. Wace: *Mycenae: an Archaeological History and Guide*, Princeton University Press, 1949. Reprinted by permission of Princeton University Press
p. 196, Fig. 2	By Sharon Mollerus – Large Krater with Armored Men Departing for Battle, Mycenae acropolis, 12th century BC (reformatted to grayscale), CC BY 2.0, https://commons.wikimedia.org/w/index.php?curid=70213372
p. 196, Fig. 3	By Rabax63 – own work (reformatted to grayscale), CC BY-SA 4.0, https://commons.wikimedia.org/w/index.php?curid=64161911
p. 197, Fig. 4A	From N. R. Oakeshott: »Horned-head Vase Handles«, *JHS*, 86 (1966), Plate V, Courtesy of The National Museum of Athens (1426)
p. 197, Fig. 4B	From N. R. Oakeshott: »Horned-head Vase Handles«, *JHS*, 86 (1966), Plate VI, Courtesy of The Trustees of the British Museum (C736)
p. 200, Fig. 5	By Carole Raddato from FRANKFURT, Germany – This file has been extracted from another file and reformatted to grayscale, CC BY-SA 2.0, https://commons.wikimedia.org/w/index.php?curid=74703004
p. 264, Fig. 6	From G. Mylonas: *Mycenae and the Mycenaean Age*, Princeton University Press, 1966. Reprinted by permission of Princeton University Press

p. 266, Fig. 7	From A. J. B. Wace: *Mycenae: an Archaeological History and Guide*, Princeton University Press, 1949. Reprinted by permission of Princeton University Press
p. 339, Fig. 1	By Unknown author – Deutsches Archäologisches Institut Athen Neg. Nr. DAI-Athen-Mykene 63 (D-DAI-ATH-Mykene-0063), Public Domain, https://commons.wikimedia.org/w/index.php?curid=2062281
p. 343, Fig. 2a	From Montet, Pierre: *Byblos et l'Egypte Quatre Campagnes de Fouilles à Gebeil 1921-1922-1923-1924 Atlas* (Paris, 1929)
p. 343, Fig. 2b	From Montet, Pierre: *Byblos et l'Egypte Quatre Campagnes de Fouilles à Gebeil 1921-1922-1923-1924 Atlas* (Paris, 1929)
p. 347, Fig. 3	By Ali Hakan Ilban – Own work (reformatted to grayscale, cropped and enhanced), CC BY-SA 4.0, https://commons.wikimedia.org/w/index.php?curid=91068933
p. 353, Fig. 4	By Carole Raddato from FRANKFURT, Germany : Exhibition: I am Ashurbanipal king of the world, king of Assyria, British Museum (reformatted to grayscale), CC BY-SA 2.0, https://commons.wikimedia.org/w/index.php?curid=74760602
p. 354, Fig. 5	By Bernard Gagnon – Own work (reformatted to grayscale), CC BY-SA 3.0, https://commons.wikimedia.org/w/index.php?curid=37792370
p. 356, Fig. 6	By Dosseman – Own work (reformatted to grayscale, cropped and enhanced), CC BY-SA 4.0, https://commons.wikimedia.org/w/index.php?curid=96214853
p. 357, Fig. 7	By Johnbod – Own work (reformatted to grayscale, cropped and enhanced), CC BY-SA 4.0, https://commons.wikimedia.org/w/index.php?curid=38264265
p. 358, Fig. 8 left	By Rama – Own work (reformatted to grayscale, cropped and enhanced), CC BY-SA 3.0 fr, https://commons.wikimedia.org/w/index.php?curid=296609
p. 358, Fig. 8 right	By Rama – Own work (reformatted to grayscale, cropped and enhanced), CC BY-SA 3.0 fr, https://commons.wikimedia.org/w/index.php?curid=2966273
p. 365, Fig. 9	By Orlovic – Own work (reformatted to grayscale), CC BY-SA 4.0, https://commons.wikimedia.org/w/index.php?curid=3534971
p. 369, Fig. 1	By Jean-Pierre Dalbéra from Paris, France – Le musée égyptien (Turin) (reformatted to grayscale and cropped), CC BY 2.0, https://commons.wikimedia.org/w/index.php?curid=24673197

p. 369, Fig. 2	By Zde – Own work (reformatted to grayscale, cropped and enhanced), CC BY-SA 4.0, https://commons.wikimedia.org/w/index.php?curid=83841966
p. 371, Fig. 3	By Djehouty – Own work (reformatted to grayscale, cropped and enhanced), CC BY-SA 4.0, https://commons.wikimedia.org/w/index.php?curid=87642878
p. 371, Fig. 4	By Archermos – Marsyas, 07.04.2007 (reformatted to grayscale, cropped and enhanced), CC BY-SA 2.5, https://commons.wikimedia.org/w/index.php?curid=1907846
p. 372, Fig. 5	By Leo Wehrli – This image is from the collection of the ETH-Bibliothek and has been published on Wikimedia Commons as part of a cooperation with Wikimedia CH (reformatted to grayscale, cropped and enhanced),. Corrections and additional information are welcome, CC BY-SA 4.0, https://commons.wikimedia.org/w/index.php?curid=68565545
p. 373, Fig. 6	By Panegyrics of Granovetter – Own work (reformatted to grayscale, cropped and enhanced), CC BY-SA 2.0, https://www.flickr.com/photos/sarah_c_murray/4081376031/sizes/o/
p. 411, Fig. 1	By Amphipolis – Ara Pacis Aeneas/Numa (reformatted to grayscale), CC BY-SA 2.0, https://commons.wikimedia.org/w/index.php?curid=52683620
p. 423, Fig. 2	By CenozoicEra – Own work (reformatted to grayscale, cropped), CenozoicEra: "I took this photo in 1995 and I release it into the public domain", Public Domain, https://commons.wikimedia.org/w/index.php?curid=61470298
p. 423, Fig. 3	By Jean-Pierre Dalbéra from Paris, France – Bas-relief de l'Ara Pacis (villa Médicis, Rome) (reformatted to grayscale, cropped), CC BY 2.0, https://commons.wikimedia.org/w/index.php?curid=75035172
p. 426, Fig. 4	By Chris Nas. Sculpture by unknown Roman artist – Photo taken by Chris Nas (reformatted to grayscale, cropped), CC BY-SA 4.0, https://commons.wikimedia.org/w/index.php?curid=4454641
p. 434, Fig. 5	By Giovanni Dall'Orto – Own work, Attribution (reformatted to grayscale), https://commons.wikimedia.org/w/index.php?curid=5487155

Around the Subject

The Contributors

Immanuel Velikovsky

Immanuel Velikovsky was born in Vitebsk in White Russia in 1895. He studied medicine, science and other subjects, e.g. philosophy, ancient history and law at the Universities of Montpellier (France), Edinburgh (Great Britain), Moscow (Russia) and Kharkiv (Ukraine) in difficult circumstances caused by the discrimination and persecution of the Jews as well as the political and war-related chaos of the time. After getting his M.D. in Moscow in 1921 he emigrated to Germany, where he founded the scientific journal Scripta Universitatis in Berlin. In this project he came into contact with Albert Einstein, who was editor of the mathematical-physical section. This project, furthermore, laid the foundation for the Hebrew University of Jerusalem, the presidency of which was offered to Immanuel Velikovsky.

After getting married in 1923 Velikovsky settled in Palestine and started to practice as a physician. At the same time he studied psychoanalysis with Wilhelm Stekel, the first disciple of Freud, published several scientific papers about the subject and opened the first psychoanalytical practice in Palestine.

Doing research for a planned book project about Freud's dream interpretation and about a new view of Freud's heroes Oedipus and Akhnaton, Velikovsky needed access to numerous literary sources. For this reason in 1939 he travelled to New York together with his family. Shortly afterwards World War II began and he had to extend his stay for an indefinite period, finally staying in the US for good due to his unexpected discoveries.

The next 10 years he spent with intensive research about the geological and historical facts he had discovered, and presented them to the public in 1950 in his book *Worlds in Collision*. By its contents, as well as by the scandalous reaction of the representatives of the scientific establishment, this book initiated such a far-reaching and revolutionary development in many areas of science and society that until today its actuality and importance have even increased.

Velikovsky himself, however, even after the publication of four more books, was confronted with a heavy up and down of overwhelming acceptance and devastating – unfortunately mostly very unserious – rejection, resulting in a grave psychological burden for him.

After moving to Princeton in the fifties he had a close and friendly relationship with Albert Einstein, discussing his theories with him. After Einstein's death Velikovsky's *Worlds in Collision* was found open on his desk.

Inspite of more and more recent research in geology and planetology supporting his theories, Velikovsky remained the victim of a discrediting campaign until his death, which is neither in proportion with his exact scientific methodology nor with the contents and importance of his works.

He died in Princeton in 1979.

Lewis M. Greenberg

Lewis M. Greenberg completed his graduate work at the University of Pennsylvania where he received his MA and ABD certificate in art history. Specializing in the art of Greece, Rome, India, and China, he also spent extensive years of post graduate independent study involving Ancient Egyptian and Islamic art. He is currently professor emeritus of Ancient & Oriental Art History and Culture, Moore College of Art & Design. Author of *The Reign of the Swastika* (1997) and co-author of *An Introduction to Ancient Art and Architecture* (Villanova Univ. Press, 1966). Professor Greenberg was co-founder and Editor-in-Chief of the journal *KRONOS* (1975-88) and has published more than 50 scholarly articles in *Pensée, KRONOS, Chiron, AEON, Chronology & Catastrophism REVIEW* (formerly the *SIS REVIEW*), *BAR, Science, Astronomy*, and *The Velikovskian*. He has also helped to edit a part of the Greystone Press's multi-volume *Encyclopedia of Art*, and served on the editorial staffs of *Pensée, AEON, C&C REVIEW*, and *The Velikovskian*.

Jan Sammer
Jan Sammer (b. Plzen, Czechoslovakia, 1953) was an assistant to Immanuel Velikovsky (1976-1979), an archivist and editor for the Velikovsky Estate (1980-1983). He has a Bachelor of Arts from SGWU, Montreal, 1975, and a Master of International Affairs, Columbia University, NYC, 1986. He has also made contributions to *Kronos* and *Aeon* journals.

Edwin M. Schorr
Edwin M. Schorr, formerly a graduate student of the ancient Eastern Mediterranean and Near East, and a doctoral candidate in Pre-classical Aegean archaeology, also served as a research assistant to Immanuel Velikovsky for a number of years.

He also contributed articles on archaeology to *Kronos* and *Pensée*, sometimes under his nom de plume, Israel M. Isaacson in order to protect his identity from his professors.

Julian West
For more than thirty years, Julian West has been an avid follower of Velikovsky's writings as well as those of various comparative mythologists. His pursuit of the missing pieces of history in such regards has enabled him to amass a large library of appropriate literature and considerable knowledge of the subjects at hand. He is the author of several relevant published essays and lectures, and also regularly leads an online forum on catastrophism as it pertains to history and myth. Additionally, West's help as a volunteer copy editor is unparalleled – particularly his ability to retrieve obscure online source material. This, along with his technical computer skills, makes him a most valuable asset.

Books by Immanuel Velikovsky:

- *Worlds in Collision (1950)*
- *Earth in Upheaval (1955)*
- *Ages in Chaos: From the Exodus to King Akhnaton (1952)*
- *Peoples of the Sea (1977)*
- *Ramses II and his Time (1978)*
- *Oedipus and Akhnaton: Myth and History (1960)*
- *Mankind in Amnesia (1982)*
- *Stargazers and Gravediggers: Memoirs to Worlds in Collision (1983)*
- *In the Beginning (2020)*
- *The Dark Age of Greece (2023)*

Further Reading:

- de Grazia, Alfred: *The Velikovsky Affair* (1966)
- Velikovsky Sharon, Ruth: *Aba – The Glory and the Torment* (1995)
- Velikovsky Sharon, Ruth: *Immanuel Velikovsky – The Truth behind the Torment* (2003)
- Internet: www.varchive.org
- Internet: www.velikovsky.info

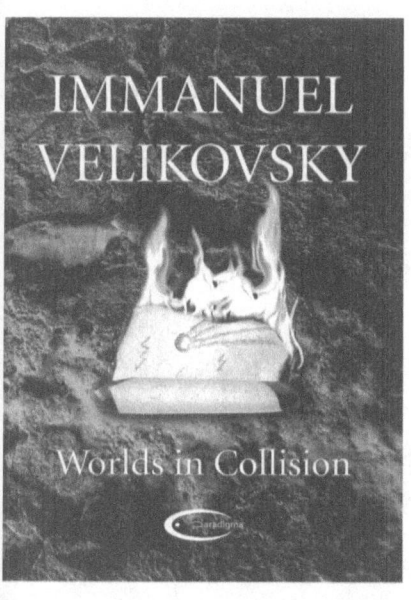

Worlds in Collision

Immanuel Velikovsky

436 pages
Paradigma Ltd.

ISBN 978-1-906833-11-4
(Softcover)
978-1-906833-51-0
(Hardcover)

With this book Immanuel Velikovsky first presented the revolutionary results of his 10-year-long interdisciplinary research to the public – and caused an uproar that is still going on today.

Worlds in Collision – written in a brilliant, easily understandable and entertaining style and full to the brim with precise information – can be considered one of the most important and most challenging books in the history of science. Not without reason was this book found open on Einstein's desk after his death.

For all those who have ever wondered about the evolution of the earth, the history of mankind, traditions, religions, mythology or just the world as it is today, *Worlds in Collision* is an absolute MUST-READ!

Stargazers and Gravediggers

Immanuel Velikovsky

344 pages
Paradigma Ltd.

ISBN 978-1-906833-17-6
(Softcover)
978-1-906833-57-2
(Hardcover)

Worlds in Collision triggered heretofore unprecedented uproar, both in society and in the scientific world. The reaction by representatives of the established sciences however was – and still is – anything but scientific and led to the term "Velikovsky Affair".

In this book, Immanuel Velikovsky, in his unmistakably clear and unique style, relates both the writing of and the reaction to the publication of his epochal work *Worlds in Collision*. Through authentic letters, we experience at first hand the beginning and unfolding of the Velikovsky Affair – from the boycotting of his publisher by leading American scientists and universities to the emotional and highly unscientific campaign to discredit the author and his work. We also get to read Velikovsky's rebuttals to the attacks and accusations, which were mostly denied publication by relevant journals and magazines.

Especially today, with the power and societal influence of science at an all-time high, this book is of fundamental importance for our understanding of science and its practitioners.

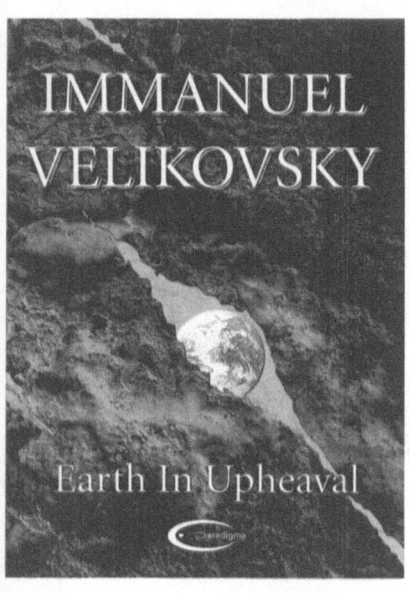

Earth in Upheaval

Immanuel Velikovsky

276 pages
Paradigma Ltd.

ISBN 978-1-906833-12-1
(Softcover)
978-1-906833-52-7
(Hardcover)

After the publication of *Worlds in Collision* Immanuel Velikovsky was confronted with the argument that in the shape of the earth and in the flora and fauna there are no traces of the natural catastrophes he had described.

Therefore a few years later he published *Earth in Upheaval* which not only supports the historical documents by very impressive geological and paleontological material, but even arrives at the same conclusions just based on the testimony of stones and bones.

Earth in Upheaval – a very exactly investigated and easily understandable book – contains material that completely revolutionizes our view of the history of the earth.

For all those who have ever wondered about the evolution of the earth, the formation of mountains and oceans, the origin of coal or fossils, the question of the ice ages and the history of animal and plant species, *Earth in Upheaval* is a MUST-READ!

In the Beginning

Immanuel Velikovsky

234 pages
Paradigma Ltd.

ISBN 978-1-906833-10-7
(Softcover)
978-1-906833-50-3
(Hardcover)

In his main work *Worlds in Collision* Immanuel Velikovsky gave a detailed reconstruction of two global natural catastrophes based on information handed down by our ancestors.

He mentions there that, as part of his intensive research, he found numerous indications of even more catastrophes that took place earlier in the history of mankind.

In *In the Beginning* the material collected by Velikovksy about this topic is presented to the public for the first time. His findings show just how turbulent the history of Earth and our planetary system was during the time of mankind and how little we actually know of all that today.

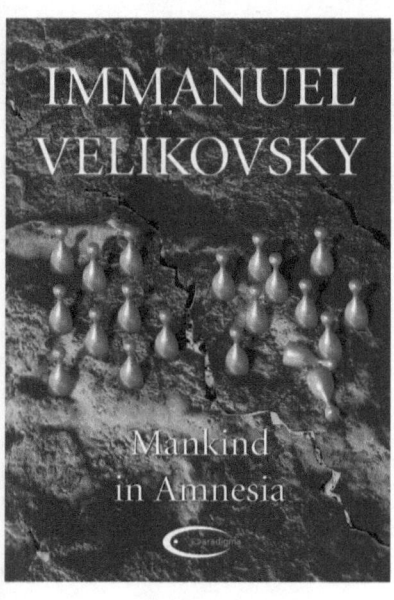

Mankind in Amnesia

Immanuel Velikovsky

196 pages
Paradigma Ltd.

ISBN 978-1-906833-16-9
(Softcover)
978-1-906833-56-5
(Hardcover)

Immanuel Velikovsky called this book the "fulfillment of his oath of Hippocrates – to serve humanity." In this book he returns to his roots as a psychologist and psychoanalytical therapist, yet not with a single person as his patient but with humanity as a whole.

After an extremely revealing overview of the foundations of the various psychoanalytical systems he makes the step into crowd psychology and reopens the case of *Worlds in Collision* from a totally different point of view: as a psychoanalytical case study. This way he shows that the blatant reactions to his theories (which are still going on today) have not been surprising but actually inevitable from a psychological perspective – which equally holds for those who have defined our view of the world. At the same time he is able to reclassify the theories of Siegmund Freud and of C. G. Jung by finding a common basis for them.

A journey through history, religion, mythology and art shows the overall range of the collective trauma and gives us – the patients – a message of extraordinary urgency and importance for the future.

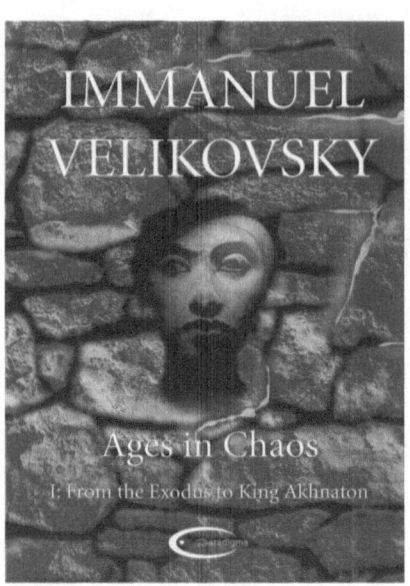 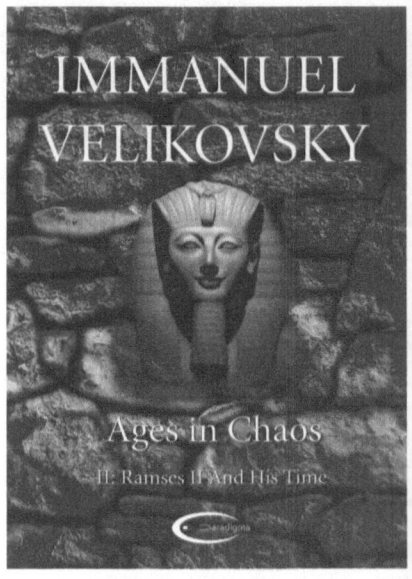

I: From the Exodus to King Akhnaton
ISBN 978-1-906833-13-8
978-1-906833-53-4

II: Ramses II and His Time
ISBN 978-1-906833-14-5
978-1-906833-54-1

In his series *Ages in Chaos*, Immanuel Velikovsky undertakes a reconstruction of the history of antiquity.

With utmost precision and the exciting style of presentation typical for him he shows beyond any doubt what nobody would consider possible: in the conventional history of Egypt – and therefore also of many neighboring cultures – a span of more than 600 years is described which has never happened! This assertion is as unbelievable and outrageous as the assertions in *Worlds in Collision* or *Earth in Upheaval*. But Velikovsky takes us on a detailed and highly interesting journey through the – corrected – history and makes us witness, how many question marks disappear, doubts vanish and corresponding facts from the entire Near East furnish a picture of overall conformity and correctness. In the end you not only wonder how conventional historiography has come into existence, but why it is still taught and published.

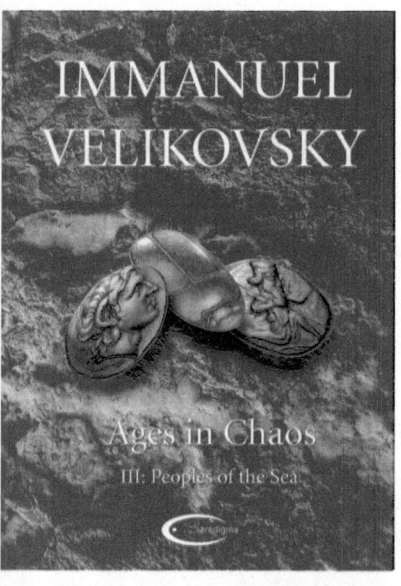

Ages in Chaos

Immanuel Velikovsky

III: Peoples of the Sea

ISBN 978-1-906833-15-2
      978-1-906833-55-8

In an extensive supplement to *Peoples of the Sea* Velikovsky delves into the fundamental question of how such a dramatic shift in chronology could have come about. Analyzing the main pillars of Egyptian chronology, he points out where the most dramatic mistakes were made and addresses the misunderstanding underlying the "astronomical chronology".

In a further supplement he discusses the very interesting conclusions that can be drawn from radiocarbon testing on Egyptian archeological finds.

Just as Velikovsky became the father of "neo-catastrophism" by *Worlds in Collision*, he became the father of "new chronology" by *Ages in Chaos*.

Oedipus and Akhnaton

Immanuel Velikovsky

216 pages
Paradigma Ltd.

ISBN 978-1-906833-18-3
(Softcover)
978-1-906833-58-9
(Hardcover)

Who hasn't heard of him – Oedipus, the tragic figure from Greek mythology whose shocking fate has moved so many generations, inspired so many writers and even found his way into modern psychology through Sigmund Freud?

Is it conceivable that this figure and his fate was not a creation of human fancy at all but the conversion of real historical happenings?

This question is posed by Immanuel Velikovsky in the present book. Like a detective, he takes the reader on a unique investigation full of suspense, breathtaking surprises and insights while meticulously searching for traces of a finding that seems to be even more incredible than the original myth itself.

The most popular pharaonic family of all – Akhnaton along with his wife Nefertiti and his son Tutankhamen – are exposed as the real protagonists of the Oedipus saga.

ABA – The Glory and the Torment

Ruth Velikovsky Sharon, Ph. D.

ISBN 978-1-906833-20-6

In this book you get to know Immanuel Velikovsky as a person. His daughter Ruth describes his childhood, his family environment and his eventful life.

Using plenty of background information, numerous anecdotes and many photographs she makes us familiar with her father, but also shows the personal dimension of the devastating campaign he encountered in the last decades of his life.

The Truth Behind the Torment

Ruth Velikovsky Sharon, Ph. D.

ISBN 978-1-906833-21-3
(Softcover)
978-1-906833-61-9
(Hardcover)

In this supplement to her father's biography, Ruth Velikovsky Sharon, PhD. depicts the true facts about the campaign against him.

She publishes informative letters in full length, that show the true nature of the undeserving, unscientific treatment of Velikovsky by the scientific establishment, a treatment that appears rather medieval than enlightened.

Ruth Velikovsky Sharon, PhD.

Immanuel Velikovsky's daughter was a psychotherapist herself, and had an extended professional consulting experience.

She has written some interesting books to present her insights to the public:

Shame on You – You Were in My Dream

Ruth Velikovsky Sharon, Ph. D.

ISBN 978-1-906833-01-5

Finally a new and easy guide to the understanding of dreams, which really makes sense! Ruth Velikovsky Sharon, PhD has developed a completely new understanding of the nature of dreams, which is fascinating because of its simplicity and its practical orientation.
This theory is presented in this book and makes it a valuable guide for parents.

The More You Explain ... The Less They Understand

Ruth Velikovsky Sharon, Ph. D.
and John Cathro Seed, M. D.

ISBN 978-1-906833-00-8

In this, perhaps the most encompassing of her works, Dr. Ruth Velikovsky Sharon brilliantly lifts the veil that shrouds the mystery of psychoanalysis, revealing intrinsic truths that can forever assist us in our journey to self-discovery and growth.

Harvard Medical School trained, Dr. John C. Seed's contribution of the Physical Health chapter will enlighten the medical community as well as the average reader, and if abided by, will help prolong life.

Insights
of a Psychoanalyst

Ruth Velikovsky Sharon, Ph. D.

ISBN 978-1-906833-04-6

In this booklet, Dr. Velikovsky Sharon, a renowned psychoanalyst, lets us partake in her rich professional experience.

Using short, clear statements she gives practical assistance for the questions of life every one of us is confronted with – even addressing points which many haven't been aware of so far in their busy everyday lives.

Imagine Art

Works of Art by
Ruth Velikovsky Sharon, Ph. D.
and Elisheva Velikovsky

ISBN 978-1-906833-02-2

The name of Velikovsky is mainly known from the scientific and historical discoveries of Immanuel Velikovsky.

Far less known is the artistic dimension in the Velikovsky family, mainly expressed by Elisheva (or "Elis") Velikovsky and Ruth Velikovsky Sharon, PhD., the wife and daughter of Immanuel Velikovsky. For everyone interested in and fond of visual and plastic arts this booklet will give an exhaustive overview of the remarkable range of the works of these two artists.

www.ingramcontent.com/pod-product-compliance
Lightning Source LLC
Chambersburg PA
CBHW021132230426
43667CB00005B/86